The Craft of
Economic Modeling

Third, Enlarged Edition

Clopper Almon
Department of Economics
University of Maryland

2017

Contents

PREFACE

This is the book I wanted to read when I began to study economics back in the 1950s. I liked science, especially physics, astronomy and mathematics, but I felt economic problems were more important. I wanted an understanding of the economy which was quantitative and testable, not just unquantified and untested theories though perhaps expressed in abstract mathematical form. But of course no such book existed then. Computers had to be developed, software written and data organized. Only then did it become possible to write the book I had wanted to read. This book is my attempt to do so.

It was mostly written in the decade 1995 – 2005 but sums up at least four decades of experience in building and using economic models both macroeconomic and multisectoral. It has been available on the Internet since about 2005 in much the present form and there have been two previous printed editions in English of Part I, a Chinese edition and a Japanese edition of that portion, and a complete Russian edition. Now that print-on-demand has made hard-copy publishing feasible for books with limited sales potential, it seemed time to bring out a printed version of the whole.

Earlier versions of Part I minus Chapter 7 were used as a text for an undergraduate course in economic modeling at the University of Maryland. The course began back in the 1960's as a conventional "business cycles" course, but evolved gradually as software and computing technology permitted into the form given here. The term project was for each student to build his or her own model of the U.S. economy, to apply it to a policy question and to make a forecast. Though the course was quite successful as taught by me or my former students, the book had little market potential, for it is a rare instructor who will use a textbook full of material he does not already know.

Chapter 7 applies the techniques developed in the earlier chapters to build a macroeconomic model of the U.S. economy. The version of the model presented here was estimated by Douglas Meade with data through 2008. The chapters of Part II that illustrate the use of a model were written before this version was estimated.

Parts II and III were written as text material for graduate courses in econometrics and empirical modeling. While the econometrics course taken by most graduate students at Maryland was almost entirely theoretical, I offered a more demanding version which also included a lot of empirical work on a time-shared computer before the days of the microcomputer.

All of the software used in these courses or in this book was written by me or my graduate students. I had started computer programming when that meant wiring a plug board. As a graduate assistant to Wassily Leontief I was delighted to move on to machine language programming of the Univac I, the first commercial computer. But once I saw Fortran, I converted quickly. It was clear to me that it would be an essential tool for building the models of the economy I hoped to construct. Somewhat to my surprise, few other young economists were learning programming. I believe that during the years that I was on the Harvard economics faculty, 1961 – 1966, no one else on that faculty was fluent in Fortran.

In 1978-79, my associate Douglas Nyhus and I had the privilege of working at the International Institute for Applied Systems Analysis in Laxenburg, Austria, near Vienna. This year was important both for establishing contacts with researchers with similar interests in other countries and for introducing me to the C programming language. It allowed programs to be written with much clearer structure than was possible with the Fortran of that time. When 16-bit microcomputers and the DeSmet C compiler became available in the early 1980s, I began writing the software which is at the base of that used in this book. When C++ and Borland Builder came along making graphical user interface programming feasible and inexpensive for the non-professional programmer, I put them to work. This book is written with that software, known as G7 and available from the Inforum website.

Unfortunately, Borland is out of business and Builder works only on Windows. Somewhere around 2010, disgusted with Windows, I decided to give Linux a try and went with the Ubuntu version. It was so much superior to Windows that I soon became a convert. But I still had to boot Windows to run G7. So I set out to rewrite G7 with free, open-source, cross-platform tools. The windowing tools I am using are called wxWidgets, so I called the new program Gwx. A user of G7 will find it very easy to switch. At present, summer of 2017, it will estimate the equations of basic macromodels. It can also read in and display in a grid an input-output table. Thus, conceptually, it is certain that the project can be accomplished. The writing of Gwx has been described in a series of tutorials, *The Gwx Story,* available from amazon.com.

Some of the material in the present book reflects the facts that it was being used as a text in an econometrics course and the software was being written at the same time. There was a parallel standard course that made little use of computers to give the students experience with estimation and model building. To be sure that my students learned also the material in the standard course, I used a standard econometrics text. Therefore I knew that they would be reading about things like the Jarque-Bera test, so I programmed some such things into the software though I am ambivalent about their importance.

Perhaps I should also add that I did not spend money on advertising the software. Therefore I could afford to put it on the Internet for free download and use. Developers of some other programs chose to advertise and charge. The advertising seems to have been successful, and at least one of them is much more widely used than G7 although lacking a number of the G7 features, especially for building multisectoral models. Thus, don't suppose that because your teacher did not use G7 that it is inferior to some expensive proprietary program. It is quite likely just as good or much better. And free.

I hope you will enjoy working through this book and building your own models. It is very different from other books and just maybe it is the one you are looking for.

Clopper Almon
Department of Economics
University of Maryland
College Park, Maryland 20742
September 2017

ACKNOWLEDGEMENTS

This book has been in the writing for thirty years or so, but the activity was particularly lively in the period 1990 – 2010. The material has been used by a score or so of instructors and by several thousand students. I am grateful to all of them for their patience with its shortcomings and suggestions for improvements. The software which accompanies the book, *G7*, was written primarily by the author but with many contributions and corrections by students and associates. In particular, I mention with gratitude those who have helped in the development of the programs. This group includes David Robison, Jane-Marie Mulvey, Pamela Megna, Douglas Meade, Kang Chen, Jeffrey Werling, Qiang Ma, Qisheng Yu and Ronald Horst. Teaching associates John Sabelhaus, Peter Taylor, William Stephens, Craig Hiemstra, Lesley Cameron, Lorraine Sullivan Monaco, and Maureen Sevigny have made many useful suggestions. Douglas Meade and Daniel Marcin have helped to port the newest version to Open Office 3.4 and update the text. Many, many others too numerous to mention have made valuable suggestions.

Special thanks go to Wang Yinchu and a team at the Economic Information Agency of Jiangsu province, who produced a Chinese translation of the second edition published by the University of Nanjing Press. Similar thanks go to Paul Salmon of the University of Rennes who translated the second edition into French and produced a French-speaking version of the programs. Likewise, Alberto Ruiz-Moncayo and Luis Sangines have produced a Spanish-speaking version of the programs while the first edition of the text was translated into Spanish under the direction of Javier Lantero at Fundacion Tomillo in Madrid. Maurizio Grassini has been active in making the programs known in Italy. His work led ISTAT to become the first central statistical office to use G data banks for official dissemination of statistics, a purpose for which they are well suited. I am indebted to Wladislaw Welfe of the University of Lodz in Poland and Maurizio Ciaschini of the University of Urbino in Italy for the opportunity to conduct in their institutions week-long intensive seminars on the use of G. Yasuhiko Sasai has produced a Japanese translation with an application to Japanese data. Georgy Serebryakov and his staff produced a hardcover Russian edition in 2012, and in the process corrected many small errors in the English.

Finally, I am grateful to all my colleagues at INFORUM who have both encouraged the work on this project and liberated me to pursue it.

INTRODUCTION

This is a book about how to build models of a business, an industry, or the whole economy. It explains techniques used both in simple, single-equation models for forecasting the sales of a single product of a single company and also in complex, many-equation models of an entire economy or of the world. The principal example in the first two parts of the book is a macroeconomic model of the USA. The title, *The Craft of Economic Modeling*, emphasizes that the book does not stop with the theory or even with a few examples. Rather, it leads the reader directly into practice, for it is accompanied by computer software and data that enable the user to apply to practical problems every technique described. Though some of the exercises are just drills in the techniques, many call for originality and creativity in handling real-life problems. Of course, as in any craft, a book can only help, not replace, a living teacher.

The computer software, the *G* regression package, version 7.3, (referred to as *G7*) and the *Build* model builder, are comprehensive, easy-to-use programs that run under Windows XP and Windows 7 or 8. They are designed for work with time-series data. Public domain versions accompany the book or are available via Internet (www.inforum.umd.edu), where thousands of economic time series are also available as data banks for *G7*. Assembling equations into a model requires the use of the Borland C++ compiler, which is also available for free download from

http://www.embarcadero.com/products/cbuilder/free-compiler.

Simply put, an economic model is a set of equations which describe how the economy or some part of it functions. In my view, a model should incorporate and test our understanding of how the economy works. Its equations should make sense. And it should be possible to test how adequate our understanding is by running it over the past and seeing how well it can reproduce history. By changing some of its assumptions and rerunning history with the changed assumptions, it is possible to analyze the effects of policies. Finally, it should be useful not only for policy analysis but also for forecasting. By studying the errors of the forecast, the builder of the model may hope to improve his or her understanding of the economy.

I must warn the reader that these simple views are by no means shared by all -- or even by most -- practitioners of model building. The vector-autoregression (VAR) school gives little or no weight to the equations expressing any sort of understanding of the economy; ability to reproduce the past, however, is of great importance. The computable general equilibrium (CGE) school gives great weight to the equations making sense but has little interest in testing the dynamic properties (if any) of its models or in the equations fitting more than one point. In my view, each of these schools is right in what it values but remiss in what it neglects. The fad current in the early 21st century, the "dynamic, stochastic, general equilibrium" or DSGE school makes the astounding assumption that the economy we live in is managed by great being who is maximizing its utility function but is constantly being hit by random shocks. The "real business cycle" (RBC) school sees the source of fluctuations in the economy in random shocks to the aggregate production function – we wake up some days and don't know how to produce as well as we did the day before.

This book is not about any of these approaches – neither VAR nor CGE nor DSGE nor RBC, which all appear to me to be some sort of anti-reality modeling. Rather its roots reach into common-sense based econometric macroeconomic models combined with multisectoral input-output models. Both of these types of models go back to the 1930s but made major progress in the 1960s as computers made possible the calculations required by large-scale versions.

Some of the equations in our models have constants which describe the behavior of firms, consumers, or other economic agents. These constants, often called "parameters", must somehow be estimated. The most frequently used way is by choosing them so that the equation describes accurately the behavior of those agents in the past. Thus, estimating the parameters is just a way to sum up the lessons of the past to forecast the future or examine how the past itself might have been different had different decisions been made. A large part of this book is about how to do that summing up. But it is just as important to choose judiciously the variables to be included in the model. Unfortunately, there is little theory about how this choice should be made. I hope that the discussion in this book will at least help to make the choice a conscious one.

Model building is a serious business because models are playthings. If that sounds paradoxical, consider that we can, fundamentally, learn in three ways: from our own real-life experiences, by hearing or reading about the experiences of others, and by play. Indeed, zoologists have observed that one of the distinguishing characteristics of human beings is the adult's retention of the ability to play. Therefore, even adults can learn. In economic policy, no one has enough personal experience to be of much value; and evaluating the experiences of others is difficult because many influences were at work in producing the actual historical outcome. That leaves play. But in the past it has been impossible to "play economy" without playing with the real economy. Models and micro computers, the super playthings of adults, open up the possibility of learning about how the economy works through play. Personally, I readily admit that nearly everything I think I know about how the economy works I have learned through play with models. When I read books or papers about the economy written by people who have not played in this way, I am often struck by how one-sided their knowledge is. Yes, I think that play with models is the best way to raise the level of public understanding of how the economy works, and that the quality of the economic policy we actually adopt depends on that public understanding. The attempts to develop that understanding by exposing college students to clearly written texts and objective multiple-choice examinations have failed. Maybe play can succeed.

When computers first made economic modeling feasible, the mystique of the machine raised expectations that models built with it would prove as infallible as the machine's arithmetic. In fact, the record of forecasters using models looks very human. That is, of course, exactly what one should expect. But expectations are seldom rational, and when it became clear that models were not the panacea that would cure all the ills of a business, some disillusion set in. Many bad models have been built, some of them by large commercial firms in the modeling business. Sometimes the salesman got the better of the scientist in the claims their builders made for them. However, I believe that those who know how sensitive a model can be to the judgmental decisions made in building it have not been disappointed in models, for they have not expected what could not be delivered. Working through this book will offer the first-hand experience with models that enables one to judge what can and what cannot be expected of them.

I should perhaps advise you that a large fraction of the economics profession regards such modeling as we will do here as *passé*. This widespread opinion is based on a misreading – or non-reading – of a well-known article by Robert Lucas which *seemed* to imply that models such as those we will be building "can, in principle, provide *no* useful information as to the actual consequences of alternative economic policies."[1] In fact, Lucas analyzed three particular models in use at that time (1975), each as applied to a particular policy question. (Each model was applied to a different question.) He actually went on to suggest how each model could be modified to give what he considered correct answers to these policy questions. His real point was not that models are useless for policy analysis but simply that the fact that a particular model has a good "track record"

---

1   Robert E. Lucas, "Econometric Policy Evaluation: A Critique" in The Phillips Curve and Labor Markets, Karl Brunner and Allan H. Meltzer, editors, Amsterdam, North Holland, 1975.

in forecasting does not mean that it will give correct answers to questions involving policy changes that invalidate some of its equations. That point is surely accepted by all model builders and users, both then and now. It by no means invalidates the use of models; in fact, quite to the contrary, it shows that models are necessary so that the effects of changes in policy can be explicitly described.

Any policy analysis requires a model, for it requires that we compare how the world would be with and without the change of policy. The only question is whether the model by which we make that comparison is explicit, subject to scrutiny and testing, or implicit, vague, held somewhere in our head and subject to change as our mood changes. Historical facts never replace a model for policy analysis, for history gives us results only with or without the policy, never both with nothing else changed.

I can hardly imagine how any systematic progress can be made in economic understanding, forecasting or policy analysis without use of quantitative models. I hope that this book can contribute to lifting the level of applied modeling and to a recognition of the judgment and skill needed to build and use them well.

Over forty years of experience as an applied model builder have affected my choice of material for this book and its presentation. As it is usually taught, econometrics is a series of exercises in applied probability theory. I made a significant investment in learning this material in the expectation that it would prove useful in building meaningful models. That expectation has been largely but not quite totally disappointed. Nor am I alone in this experience; most applied model builders with whom I have dared to discuss the matter have heartily agreed. Such a statement is a plain declaration that "the emperor has no clothes" and is not likely to persuade teachers of econometrics to adopt this book as a text, unless, of course, they want the students to know the truth.

This book emphasizes the simple, direct techniques and the common-sense analysis that I have come to trust. These and only these are presented in Part 1 of the text. As a teacher, I have found that it is fairly trivial to get a student to learn and apply some "sophisticated" technique; it is a major accomplishment to get him or her to *think* about whether the equation and the estimated parameters make sense. I have tried to coach the reader in such thinking.

The principal value of the probabilistic theory has been to show how, in certain situations, the methods of Part 1 may lead to deceptive results. Understanding those possibilities is important, so in Part 2 we look at the probabilistic theory and present some of the widely-used techniques, such as generalized least squares and two-stage least squares, which are based on the probabilistic assumptions. Through applications of these techniques to actual

14

problems with actual data, the student can form his own opinion of their value.

Part 3 turns to multisectoral models, models that distinguish different industries, such as chemicals or textiles. All of the techniques developed in Parts I and II remain useful, but must be supplemented by ways of handling the relations among industries.

A Guide to the Book

Before plunging into a theoretical discussion of any subject, one should begin with acute and sensitive observation of the phenomena it concerns. In the case of macroeconomic modeling, that means looking at the time series of economic data such as the National Income and Product Accounts (NIPA), employment, interest rates, money supply, exchange rates, and prices. The "nipashow" file, which comes with the software for this book, provides a good opportunity to practice such observations. Once the *G7* program is running, it is only necessary to say "add nipashow" to begin this display of economic data. At first, nipashow asks questions about the graphs it shows, then it simply shows other graphs and asks what the viewer sees interesting in them. Finally, it leaves both the drawing and the asking of questions up to the user. After the experience of viewing these graphs, one may well ask, How can the movement of these variables be explained? And that is where the book proper begins.

Chapter 1 illustrates the idea of a model and shows how a simple model of the economy can generate business cycles. It first uses a hypothetical model for which the reader can easily compute the solution. It then introduces a series of five models of increasing usefulness. This series illustrates identity-centered modeling, modeling that puts definitions and simple "behavioral ratios" in center stage. Model 1 incorporates only the definitional equations of the NIPA and affords a good review of the concepts in these accounts. Models 2 through 4 demonstrate the use of behavioral ratios to make the models richer and more useful. Model 5 introduces a few equations with parameters estimated with regression analysis from data on the American economy. Model 5 illustrates a fundamental point: it is not enough to have explanations of all of the parts of an economy to have an explanation of the whole. The dynamic interaction of individually sensible parts can generate quite surprising -- indeed, totally nonsensical -- results. Building a good model is far more than putting together equations which individually satisfactorily explain each component of the economy. The first section of chapter 1 does not require the use of computers. It can be discussed in class during the same week in which the "nipashow" plots are being studied.

Chapter 2 explains least-squares computations and the display of results shown by *G7*. Chapter 3 concerns how to use *G7* and particularly, how to estimate the parameters of model equations by regression. Chapter 4 shows how to combine the equations into a model and has you do some experiments and a forecast. It also explains how to use the numerous diagnostic techniques made available by the software for spotting errors in your model. The experiments reveal some weaknesses of the model, and Chapter 5 discusses ways to eliminate them. It closes with a number of suggestions on how you can use the techniques now at your disposal to make significant improvements to the model of Chapter 1. Chapter 6 gives some simple-minded maxims for getting reliable, trustworthy regression equations. Most of these maxims are too simple to be mentioned in a self-respecting textbook of econometrics. But they are the result of commenting on the work of hundreds of students over the years. I found myself saying the same thing over and over until I finally put pride aside and wrote down what I had been saying. Probably you will say to yourself as you read it, "That is obvious; I don't need to be told that." Fine, but it is terribly easy to let these errors slip in. Some very distinguished members of the economics profession have done so. I urge you to measure every equation of your model against these simple criteria.

Chapter 7 gives explains the basic mathematical theory of linear models. Its role is to help understand some of the properties that the student may find appearing in his models, particularly their tendency to generate cycles.

Part 2 begins with a fairly comprehensive quarterly aggregate model of the United States. In building it, I have, I believe, learned a lot about how the economy works. I have even come to the slightly arrogant opinion that no one should trust his understanding of how the economy works who has not put that understanding to the test of building a model. In this model, I have endeavored to get at structure and avoid reliance on lagged values of dependent variables. Thus, the model is called the Quarterly Econometric Structural model, or *QUEST*. Actually, *QUEST* connotes more than it abbreviates. Because all of the files for estimating and building *QUEST* are given, you may use it as the starting point for your own quest to build a model of the economy. Many people have felt that they learned to understand the human face or figure by modeling it. I have found the same to be true of modeling the economy. I hope that in working with *QUEST* you will also feel that you have joined in the search for a better understanding of the economy. *QUEST* also provides good examples of equations to work with in the rest of Part 2.

Part 2 continues with an explanation of optimization in models in Chapter 9. This optimization may be used either to improve the fit of the model in the historical period or to design optimal economic policy. The important technique of nonlinear regression is explained and illustrated in Chapter 10. Chapter 11 outlines some of the relations between probability theory and least-squares regression. This relationship of rather modest importance to the applied model builder has been magnified by the academic establishment to formidable proportions. The Datamaker fable, by which this subject is here introduced, is one of the best-loved sections of the book by many readers to whom this material has been presented with a straight face as if it ought to be believed. Basically, this fable says that if we are in an ideal case, the least squares we have used in Part I is, in fact, the best way to estimate equations. The rest of the chapter offers some methods, based on probability ideas, that can be tried when the ideal conditions are clearly not met. These techniques include the Hildreth-Lu procedure for dealing with auto-correlated residuals and "seemingly unrelated" regression and stacked regression with constraints across equations. Methods of estimating equations with moving-average errors are explained. The old subject of simultaneous equation bias and the new subjects vector autoregression, cointegration, and unit roots get just enough attention to show how they relate to the modeling approach used here.

Chapter 12 explains how to run a model many times with artificially introduced random errors. It helps to answer the question of how much confidence we can have in a particular model.

Part 3 extends our scope to multisectoral models. It first explains basic input-output analysis in the ideal case and then some of the practical problems arising in actual application. Special techniques for modeling consumer behavior, investment, and imports are then considered. The *Interdyme* software for building multisectoral models is then explained and illustrated.

Part 1: Classical Macroeconomic Models

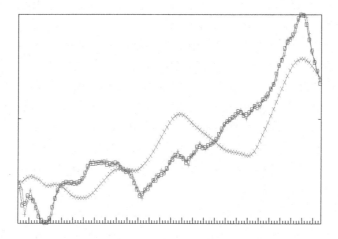

CHAPTER 1. WHAT IS AN ECONOMIC MODEL AND WHY MAKE ONE?

The tax cuts and high defense spending of the Bush administration, combined with relatively slow economic growth led to growing federal deficits from 2001 to 2007. Over the same period, US exports shrank and imports ballooned, spelling hard times for many manufacturing industries. Was there a connection between these two developments? Specifically, did the tax cuts cause manufacturing's problems? Or were they caused by a loss of competitive ability or drive?

The argument that the federal deficit was responsible for the difficulties of industry is simply that the deficit led to high real interest rates, which led to a rise in the dollar, which made American goods expensive abroad and foreign goods cheap here, and consequently stifled exports and promoted imports.

Such reasoning points to theoretical possibilities. Whether or not these possibilities have been historically important is another question, one that theory cannot decide. To answer it, one must *quantify*, in the first case,

- the effect of the federal deficit on interest rates
- the effect of interest rates on exchange rates
- the effect of exchange rates on exports and imports
- the effect of interest rates on investment, personal income, and saving.

Moreover, though the tax cuts may have had a negative effect on industry through these effects, they increased after-tax income of households, who undoubtedly spent it in part on products of industry. When all of these effects are quantified and combined into a system of equations, one has a model.

That model -- that is, those equations -- can then be solved under alternative assumptions about the tax rates. First, one may use the actual tax rates and solve the model. The result is called a historical simulation. It will not give exactly the historical values of the variables in the model, for the equations which describe the behavior of people will not be exact. However, if the historical simulation is not a pretty good approximation of reality, we had better take our model back to the drawing board before going further. Assuming that it passes the historical simulation test, we then change assumptions about the tax rates -- maybe this time we leave them unchanged from the 1990s levels -- and again solve the model. This time we get what might be called a counter-historical simulation. Comparison of the historical simulation and the counter-historical simulation will answer the question; "Did the tax cuts stifle manufacturing?"

In economics, it is, in general, impossible to answer such questions of cause and effect without some kind of model. The natural sciences allow for controlled experiment, a luxury we economists can seldom afford. Building and running models under various assumptions is our version of the controlled experiment. It must be emphasized that history alone can never answer a question of cause and effect, for history gives us only one "run" of the economy. To speak of cause and effect in economics, one must have in mind some kind of model. It may be an entirely subconscious model, or a model spelled out in theory but never quantified or tested, or an explicit, quantified model that has been subjected to careful testing and scrutiny. I need hardly say in which sort I have the greatest confidence.

In Part II, we will build a fairly comprehensive aggregate model of the US economy and will apply it to such questions as we have been discussing. But the model will also have much wider uses. In particular, it will be useful for forecasting and for analyzing the effects of policies in advance. In 2001, for example, we could have studied whether the controversial Bush tax cuts were likely to stimulate the economy or choke off recovery just as it was getting started. We could ask: "Given expected future real federal spending, what level of taxation is necessary to balance the federal budget on average over the next five years?" We can examine the effects of tight money or easy money; we can see what happens if productivity is retarded or accelerated; we can look at the effects of stronger or weaker exports. We can ask what effects the stock market has on the economy, and vice versa. In short, we can examine most of the major questions of macroeconomics.

If you, like me, find these questions both fascinating and important, then come along on the path that leads to a way to answer them.

1. An Accelerator-Multiplier Interaction Model of an Imaginary Economy

To illustrate what is meant by a model, let us begin with one so simple that we can easily calculate it by hand. To keep the numbers simple, we will just make up the constants in the equations, textbook style, out of thin air with a cursory glance at the American economy in the early 2000's. To describe even this simple model, it will be necessary to use two rather long words of Greek origin. Namely, we must distinguish between the exogenous variables and the endogenous variables. The exogenous variables are used by the model but are not determined by it; the endogenous variables are both used in the model and are determined by it. (The Greek root gen means "birth" or "born". The exogenous variables are "born" outside the model; the endogenous, within it.) Population and government spending are exogenous variables in many models; income and investment are typical endogenous variables in macroeconomic models. A system of equations which relates this quarter's values of the endogenous variables to the current values of the exogenous variables and previous values of the endogenous variables is, in economic terms, a model as we shall use that word. In more precise mathematical terms, it is a system of difference equations. By calculating the simple model we present below with a pocket calculator for a few quarters, you should get a good idea of how a system of difference equations can generate a time path of the endogenous variables that looks at least reminiscent of the actual course of the economy. You will also discover the remarkable fact that the endogenous variables may show a pronounced cyclical behavior even though there is no trace of a cycle in the exogenous variables.

Consumption in this simple economy can be described by the equation

(1) $C = .6*Y[1] + .35*Y[2]$

where C is consumption, Y is disposable income, and Y[1] is disposable income one period earlier, read as "Y lagged once."

Fixed investment follows the "accelerator" theory of investment which makes investment for expansion depend on past growth in peak output. Thus, to continue our simple economy,

(2) $I = R + 1.0*\Delta PQ[1] + 1.0*\Delta PQ[2] + .1\Delta Q[1],$

where I is gross investment, Δ indicates a first difference ($\Delta Q = Q - Q[1]$), R is replacement investment, and PQ is the current or previous peak output, thus,

(3) $PQ = Q$ if $Q > PQ[1]$ or

$PQ = PQ[1]$ otherwise.

The first term of equation 2 represents, as already said, replacement investment. The next two terms represent expansion of fixed capital when output rises above its previous peak, the output level for which we already have adequate capital. The final term in equation 2 represents inventory investment. Expansion investment -- from the way peak output is defined -- cannot be negative; inventory investment, on the other hand, can be either positive or negative.

Imports, M, are given by

(4) $M = -380 + .2(C + I + X)$

where X is exports, which are exogenous.

The output variable, Q, is

(5) Q = C + I + G + X - M

where G is government spending. Finally, disposable income is roughly Q less taxes, which we take as 28 percent of Q, so

(6) Y = .72*Q.

The exogenous variables in this simple model are:

G   government spending

X   exports

R   replacement investment.

All others are endogenous. If in some period the exogenous variables and the required lagged values of the variables Y, PQ, and Q are known, then equations (1) - (6) can be applied, one after the other in the order given, to get the values of all the endogenous variables for that period. Then one can go on to the next period, and the next, as long as the exogenous variables are known. Thus, given starting values and exogenous variables, the equations can be used to calculate the course of the economy over time. This simple fact is so fundamental that it is a good idea to impress it upon yourself by seeing it happen in your hands, rather than inside a somewhat mysterious computer.

Table 1.1 therefore provides a work-sheet for calculation of this simple model. At this point, you should get out your pocket calculator and compute at least a few lines. Since you need three lagged values of PQ to get started, the first line that you can calculate is line 4. All values, however, are shown for lines 4, 5 and 6, so you can check that you have understood the formulas. (Do not worry if your calculated values are different after the decimal from those shown in the table. The table was calculated by a computer carrying more decimal places than shown here, and the numbers were then truncated in printing.) By line 6, this economy is in recession, as you can see from the Q column. In line 7, some values are missing and need to be computed by you, but the total output, Q, is left as a check. By line 8, you are entirely on your own except for the exogenous variables. Their values, by the way, are straight-line approximations of their values from 1979 to 1992 in the American economy. Places for you to put calculated values are marked by a decimal point.

I urge you as strongly as possible to calculate a few periods of Table 1.1. until the next peak is reached and the economy turns down. Endeavor to explain why the economy turned up and why it turned down. If you understand how this simple model works, you will have no great difficulty with the more complicated models which follow. If you miss the point here, trouble lies ahead.

The economy is in recession when you begin. As you calculate, you will see it grow modestly until it passes its previous peak. Then the accelerator terms in the investment equation will drive the economy up steeply. Then growth slows; but as soon as it slows down, investment drops, and slow growth is turned into decline. This model will thus show a significant cycle. Figure 1.1 shows the course of Q which it generates. Notice, however, that there is no cycle in any of the exogenous variables. They all grow along perfectly straight lines, as you can see by noting that they rise by the same amount each period.

We have thus discovered the important fact mentioned above: the equations of economic behavior can generate cycles where there are none in the exogenous variables. From Figure 1.1, you will have noticed that the cycle is persistent and of about a constant amplitude. This is a characteristic of a non-linear model. Equations (1) - (2) and (4) - (6) are linear, that is, the dependent variable on the left is just a sum of terms each of which is just one of the other variables possibly multiplied by a constant. Equation (3) for peak output, PQ, is, however, a horse of another color and not at all linear. If all equations of a model are linear, the model itself is said to be linear, but so much as one non-linear equation and the model becomes nonlinear. This distinction is important because it may be shown mathematically that in a linear model any cycle will, in all probability, either fade away or grow explosively. Only a most particular constellation of values of the constants in the equations can give the sort of steady, persistent cycling behavior shown in Figure 1.1. Thus, in the construction of models, we should pay particular attention to the non-linearities.

Fig 1.1: Q in Simple Model

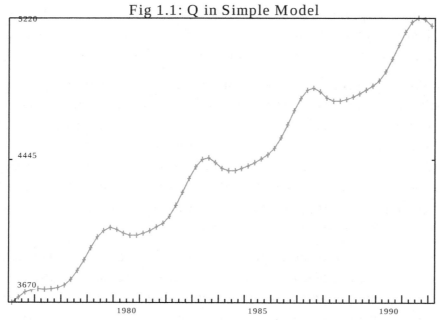

You should not conclude from this example that all such examples will necessarily show this sort of cyclical behavior. In models with strong accelerator investment equations, however, cycles are not unlikely.

Exercise

1.1.(a) Calculate the course of the imaginary economy until Q turns down again. (b) Explain why this economy turns down when it has been growing, and why it begins to grow after a few periods of decline. Remember that everything there is to know about this economy is contained in the equations. Do not bring into your explanation factors like interest rates or inflation which play no role in this economy.

Table 1.1: Worksheet for Hand-calculated Examples

Line	X	G	C	R	I	M	Q	PQ	Y
1	303.9	714.9	2653.6	518.7	631.9	337.9	3966.6	3966.6	2855.9
2	308.8	718.5	2696.7	522.5	653.6	351.8	4026.0	4026.0	2898.7
3	313.8	722.2	2738.8	526.2	648.2	361.8	4061.2	4061.2	2924.0
4	318.7	725.9	2769.0	530.0	628.1	363.1	4078.6	4078.6	2936.6
5	323.6	729.5	2785.3	533.7	588.0	359.4	4067.2	4078.6	2928.4
6	328.5	733.2	2784.8	537.5	553.7	353.4	4047.0	4078.6	2913.8
7	333.5	736.9	.	541.2	.	.	4033.7	4078.6	2904.2
8	338.4	740.5	.	545.0	.	.	.	.	.
9	343.3	744.2	.	548.7	.	.	.	.	.
10	348.3	747.8	.	552.5	.	.	.	.	.
11	353.2	751.5	.	556.2	.	.	.	.	.
12	358.1	755.2	.	560.0	.	.	.	.	.
13	363.0	758.8	.	563.7	.	.	.	.	.
14	368.0	762.5	.	567.5	.	.	.	.	.
15	372.9	766.1	.	571.2	.	.	.	.	.
16	377.8	769.8	.	575.0	.	.	.	.	.
17	382.8	773.5	.	578.7	.	.	.	.	.
18	387.7	777.1	.	582.5	.	.	.	.	.
19	392.6	780.8	.	586.2	.	.	.	.	.
20	397.6	784.5	.	590.0	.	.	.	.	.
21	402.5	788.1	.	593.7	.	.	.	.	.
22	407.4	791.8	.	597.5	.	.	.	.	.
23	412.3	795.4	.	601.2	.	.	.	.	.
24	417.3	799.1	.	605.0	.	.	.	.	.

2. An Introduction to Identity-Centered Modeling

As we move from a simple imaginary economy to a real economy, we immediately encounter two complications:

1. The accounting system becomes much more complicated with many more variables and identities relating them.

2. The behavioral relations are no longer simply made up but must be deduced from an interaction of our imagination with historical data provided by the national accounts and other sources.

In the rest of this chapter, we will go through a sequence of five models of increasing usefulness, each built from the previous one.

The first four models are very similar to those that have found wide use in business in the form of spreadsheet calculations such as those performed by Excel, Lotus and similar programs. Today, nearly anyone planning a conference, a school budget, or a complex business deal wants to see a spreadsheet to judge how the finances will come out. These spreadsheets are what may well be called *tautological* models. *Given their assumptions,* they are sure to be correct. They express their assumptions usually as simple ratios and employ simple addition or subtraction to total up the revenues and the costs and arrive at the bottom line with utmost clarity. Our first four models are patterned on these spreadsheet models, and their great virtue is their simplicity and ease of understanding. They stress, however, the part of model which is most certainly correct, the accounting identities. For this reason, I speak of this approach as *identity-centered* modeling.

The fifth model goes beyond what it is easy to do in the spreadsheets, namely, it introduces behavioral equations estimated by linear regression, that is, by fitting a mathematical equation to historical data. Relations found in this way can express much more complicated economic behavior than can the simple ratios used in previous models. Through them we can hope to find, for example, the way that investment is related to numerous factors such as growth in output, wear out of capacity, and costs of labor and capital. Models that use these equations can give a much richer description of economic behavior than can the tautological models. But the behavioral equations will not fit perfectly, so -- unlike the tautological models -- these models do not perfectly reproduce the past. How well they can reproduce it, therefore, can become a criterion in judging them.

Model 1 just sets out the variables and identities that are central to the system of national accounts used in the United States. We may call it a pure-accounting model because it makes connections among variables based only on accounting definitions, not on economic behavior. It is just a skeleton and would give strange results if we tried to make it walk. Moreover, it has many, many exogenous variables so that it would be awkward to use in practice.

Model 2 introduces a single, obvious but centrally important *behavioral* relation into the model, namely, a relation between Personal disposable income and Personal consumption expenditure. The relation which we introduce is extremely simple, namely a ratio, fixed in any one period but variable over time, between consumption and income. Because such a ratio expresses economic behavior, it is natural to call it a *behavioral ratio*. This ratio then becomes an exogenous variable while the quantity in its numerator becomes an endogenous variable. The introduction of a behavioral ratio does not reduce the number of exogenous variables. Rather it *replaces* one exogenous variable by another which is likely to be more constant, perhaps without a trend, and easier to forecast. For example, if you ask me what Personal consumption expenditure will be in 2050, off hand I would have no idea. But if you ask me what the ratio of Personal consumption expenditure to Personal disposable income will be, I could answer with some assurance, "Oh, about what it is now, somewhere between .9 and 1.0." Model 2 will also allow us to make a meaningful multiplier calculation, that is, to answer a question like, If government spending goes up by 10 billion, how much will GDP go up? The Model 1 answer would be 10 billion; Model 2 has something more interesting to say.

Model 3 carries further the process of *exogenous variable replacement* by means of behavioral ratios. It also shows how certain exogenous variables can be lumped together to reduce the total number.

Model 4 introduces another useful method of exogenous variable replacement, namely to make the variable exogenous in constant prices. Models 1, 2, and 3 worked only in current prices; model 4 introduces *deflators* so that we can also talk about both the rate of inflation and variables measured in real, constant-price terms. Forecasting of exogenous variables is often easier in real rather than in nominal (current-price) terms. For example, Social Security benefits can be calculated in real terms from the age structure of the population and the payment schedule. The dollar value of the payments, however, will depend on the increases in the Consumer Price Index (CPI) between now and the time they are actually paid. That increase is something the model should eventually forecast endogenously. Thus it makes good sense to break down the forecasting of these payments into two steps, first the constant-price or real value and then the current-price or nominal value.

Every equation in Models 1 through 4 is an identity, so our approach has earned its label as *identity-centered* modeling. Essentially, we have tried to use identities to replace variables that are hard to think about by others that are easier to grasp intuitively. Good use of identities is essential for good modeling. This recognition of the central role of identities in modeling is in stark contrast to the way that they are usually dismissed in econometric texts with the comment that an identity can be used to eliminate a variable. Of course it can, and then one is left with a variable that is hard to think about without the handle — the identity — that gives us an easy way to think about it.

Model 5, as already noted, introduces an extremely useful method of reducing the number of exogenous variables by finding behavioral relations through regression analysis. Application of this technique will occupy us through much of this book.

Model 1: The Pure Accounting Model

Table 1.2 shows the outline of the U.S. system of National Income and Product Accounts (NIPA) as a sequence of equations. The first column (op) shows the operation required to form each identity. The second column (code) shows the code name for the variable in the Quip data bank. The third column gives the verbal description of the data series, as shown in the NIPA. Finally, the value for the variable for a recent quarter is shown, in billions of dollars.

The first equation defines Gross domestic product as

$$gdp = c + v + x - m + g$$

where the variables have the meanings shown in the table. The variable names shown in the *code* column are the ones used in the Quarterly Income and Product (Quip) data bank which goes with the G software which we use in this book. Each equation after the first starts from the bottom line of the preceding one and adds or subtracts (as shown in the *op*eration column) the indicated items down to the = sign, where the result is recorded and named. Thus, the second equation is

$$gnp = gdp + irrow - iprow$$

We will refer to the first equation as the the "product side" of the accounts. The remaining equations form the "income side" and may be less familiar. They show the transition from Gross domestic product to Personal disposable income and Personal saving. (I follow the NIPA practice of capitalizing only the first letter of the first word of each line in the accounts.)

Since these accounts will form the framework for much of our modeling, it is important that we understand what they represent. The product-side equation for GDP defines it as total *final* product of the economy. The word *final* here means that products used in making other products are not counted. Thus, one farmer may grow corn and sell it to another, who feeds it to pigs, which he sells to a packer, who sells the pork to a grocer, who sells it to the final consumer. Only the value of the pork sold by the grocer goes into GDP. The word "Gross", however, means that there has been no subtraction for the wear out of capital.

We now need to follow carefully through the transition from GDP to Personal disposable income. The first step, as already noted, is to convert from Gross domestic product to Gross national product. The basic idea is that dividends or interest paid by a U.S. company to a foreign resident are part of the *domestic* product of the U.S. but of the *national* product of the other country. More completely, Income receipts from the rest of the world consist of receipts by U.S. residents of foreign interest and dividends, of reinvested earnings of foreign affiliates of U.S. corporations, and of compensation paid to U.S. residents by foreigners. Income payments to the rest of the world consist of payments to foreign residents of U.S. interest and dividends, of reinvested earnings of U.S. affiliates of foreign corporations, and of compensation paid to foreigners by U.S. residents.

Table 1.2: U.S. National Accounts in Outline

op	code	Description	2013.3
+	c	Personal consumption expenditures	11522.8
+	v	Gross private domestic investment	2732.6
+	x	Exports of goods and services	2265.9
-	m	Imports or goods and services	2767.8
+	g	Government consumption expenditures and gross investment	3137.4
=	gdp	Gross domestic product	**16890.8**
+	irrow	Income receipts from the rest of the world	822.7
-	iprow	Income payments from the rest of the world	558.6
=	gnp	Gross national product	**17154.9**
-	ncca	Consumption of fixed capital	2655.7
=	nnp	Net national product	**14499.2**
-	nbctpn	Business current transfer payments (net)	120.1
+	pibtp	Business current transfer payments to persons	44.9
-	niprf	Corporate profits with capital consumption and inventory valuation adjustments	2125.7
+	pidiv	Personal dividend income	795.9
-	netintm	Net interest and miscellaneous payments on assets	462.7
+	piint	Personal interest income	1234.4
-	nsd	Statistical discrepancy	-97.5
=	pibg	Personal income before government action	**13963.4**
+	pigsb	Personal current transfer receipts from government	2421.1
-	nisurp	Current surplus of government enterprises	-41.5
+	nisub	Subsidies (net)	59.1
-	nitpi	Taxes on production and imports	1142.7
-	nconsi	Contributions for government social insurance	1109.1
=	pi	Personal income	**14233.3**
-	piptax	Personal current taxes	1664.6
=	pidis	Disposable personal income	**12568.7**
-	c	Personal consumption expenditure	11522.8
-	piipcb	Personal interest payments	253.6
-	piptt	Personal current transfer payments	163.3
=	pisav	Personal savings	**629.1**

Thus, to get GNP from GDP, we add U.S. rest of world income receipts and subtract U.S. income payments.

The next step is to subtract from GNP an estimate of capital consumption to get Net national product. This estimate of Consumption of fixed capital is not depreciation as reported by firms in their accounts and tax returns, for that depreciation is in historical prices, prices of the years in which the assets were purchased. If prices have been increasing,

29

the resulting number understates the current cost of replacing what is wearing out. The Bureau of Economic Analysis (BEA) which makes the NIPA therefore constructs a series of capital consumption in comparable prices by putting investment in various physical assets into constant prices, say those of 2009, then applying depreciation at rates appropriate to the different kinds of assets, then summing over assets invested in various years, then summing over the various assets, and finally converting back to current year prices.

In case you got lost in those words and really want to know what I was trying to say, here is the same thing in a formula:

$$C(t) = \sum_{i=1}^{n} p_i(t) \sum_{\tau=-\infty}^{t} w_i(t-\tau) v_i(\tau) / p_i(\tau)$$

where $C(t)$ is Consumption of fixed capital in year t, n is the number of different types of physical assets (buildings, trucks, machine tools, and so on), $p_i(t)$ is the price index of product i in year t, $v_i(\tau)$ is the investment in assets of type i in year τ, and $w_i(k)$ is the fraction of the initial value of an asset of type i that depreciates in year k after it was bought. The difference between $C(t)$ and the depreciation reported for accounting purposes is called the Capital consumption adjustment (CCAdj). If this difference is positive, as it usually is, then profits have been overstated in conventional accounting, but they are corrected in the NIPA. The point of all this calculation is to provide figures for Net national product and Corporate profits that are not improperly influenced by past inflation or by modifying depreciation rules in the tax code.

Now we come to a big step, the conversion of Net national product to Personal income. We will take it in two smaller steps. In the first, everything relates to the private economy, while in the second everything is a government action. In the private-sector step, there are three smaller stages. The first is:

- nbctpn   Business current transfer payments (net)

+ pibtb   Business current transfer payments to persons

Business current transfer payments (net) include legal settlements and theft losses. We first subtract the entire amount and then add back in the portion which went to persons. The stolen case of Bourbon is counted as income to the thief and, by the way, appears in Personal consumption expenditure and thus in GDP.

The second stage is

- niprf   Corporate profits with capital consumption adjustment and inventory valuation adjustment

+ pidiv   Dividend payments to persons

Corporate profits, as such, do not go to Personal income; Dividends, however, do.

Notice that the profits here have been adjusted by the same capital consumption adjustment that was used in the Capital consumption allowance. The net effect of this adjustment on Personal income is therefore exactly zero. The inventory valuation adjustment is an adjustment for the change in the values of inventory due to price changes. If a store is using "first in first out" inventory accounting and prices have been increasing, then the store has been charging itself for inventory at less than the replacement costs of the goods sold and thus exaggerating profits. This adjustment removes this effect. Since the adjustment is also made to the amount of inventory change included in investment on the product side of the accounts, the net effect of this adjustment on personal income is also exactly zero.

Finally comes the puzzling pair

- netintm Net interest and miscellaneous payments on assets

+ piint   Personal interest income.

Net interest is all interest paid by business less interest received by business. It is also all the interest that is included in GDP. Interest paid by consumers on credit cards, automobile loans, or installment credit is not counted as part of Personal consumption expenditure and therefore is not part of GDP. (Do you think it should be?) Similarly, interest on the national debt is not part of Government purchases of goods and services. (Should it be?) Interest paid by business -- and thus included in the price of goods -- is, however, included in GDP. In particular, interest on home mortgages is included because home owners have been converted into a fictional business in the NIPA; they rent their homes to themselves and the imputed space rental value of these homes, including the interest costs, is part of Personal consumption expenditure. This pair of lines, therefore, removes all interest that is in GDP and adds back all the interest received by persons. The net effect is positive because of the large interest payments of the government to persons.

If we may, for the moment, skip the Statistical discrepancy, which should be zero conceptually, we have reached Personal income before government action. This item is not in the official accounts, but I find it a convenient point of reference. All of the transition from GDP to Personal disposable income down to this point has been the result of events in the private economy; the rest of the way is dominated by the government.

The first of the government actions, a huge one, is to add in Personal current transfer receipts from government. These include Social Security and other government retirement programs, Medicare and Medicaid payments, unemployment insurance, and all welfare programs. A small item, Current surplus of government enterprises, is subtracted. These are part of net national product, but do not go to persons. Then the Subsidies, such as those to farmers, are added in. Then the indirect taxes (Taxes on production and imports) are removed. These are taxes such as property taxes on business property or business franchise taxes or licenses. These charges are included in the prices of the products which compose GDP, but they go to governments, not persons, so they must be removed before we can get Personal income.

This would seem to me to be the logical place to draw a line and call the result Personal income. The official definitions, however, remove one more item, Contributions for government social insurance. These include Social Security contributions from both the employer and employee and other similar programs. To me, they seem more akin to personal taxes than to the other previously deducted items. In any event, once they are deducted we reach the official Personal income.

From it, deduction of Personal current taxes (mainly income and property taxes but also estate taxes and nontaxes such as fines or admission to parks) leaves Disposable personal income. (I find it peculiar that the nontaxes are not part of Personal consumption.) To reach Personal savings, we must deduct not only Personal consumption expenditures but also Personal current transfer payments, which include transfers to foreigners (mainly American residents sending money to family in the Old Country) and transfers to government. We also must remove personal interest payments, which are mostly interest paid by consumers to business. Here at last we have the interest on credit cards and consumer loans which, as mentioned above, are not counted into Personal consumption expenditure. But of course they are real outlays, so they must be removed before reaching Personal saving by the last of the identities.

We have still not explained, however, the strange little item called Statistical discrepancy. It arises because there are two different ways of measuring GDP. One is by measuring what is produced; the other measures the income generated by producing it. The first, the product measure, is given by $gdp = c + v + x - m + g$. The second, the income definition, begins with National income defined conceptually as earned income and statistically as the sum

+	nice	Compensation of employees
+	niprop	Proprietors income with CCadj and IVA
+	niren	Rental income with CCadj
+	niprf	Corporate profits with CCAdj and IVA
+	netintm	Net interest and miscellaneous payments on assets
+	nitpi	Taxes on production and imports
+	nisurp	Current surplus of government enterprises
-	nisub	Subsidies
+	nbctpn	Business current transfer payments (net)
=	ni	National income.

To get from National income to Gross domestic product, we just need to add or subtract:

+	ncca	Consumption of fixed capital
+	nsd	Statistical discrepancy
=	gnp	Gross national product

+	iprow	Income payments to rest of world
-	irrow	Income receipts to rest of world
=	gdp	Gross domestic product.

Now notice that this second, income-based route to GDP does not require estimating Personal consumption expenditure, nor Gross private domestic investment, nor anything else in the product-side definition of GDP. Conceptually, the two approaches should give exactly the same answer. Will they in practice? You can bet they won't. Many of the items in the accounts must be deduced indirectly from other data. Consider just the problem of figuring out personal consumption of gasoline. Suppose that you have reliable data on retail sales of gasoline, but how much goes to vehicles being driven for business, and therefore not part of Personal consumption, and therefore not part of GDP? There is certainly ample room for error in such estimates. The income side is no less subject to error; just think of the incentives to avoid reporting proprietor income.

The difference between the two estimates of GDP is known as the Statistical discrepancy. The statisticians making the accounts strive to keep it as close to zero as possible. The American accountants, however, claim that they will not distort one of the components from what they believe is their best estimate of it just to get a low Statistical discrepancy. In most other countries, the accountants adjust the components until the discrepancy is eliminated. In the U.S. NIPA, National income and Personal income are based on the income measurement, while Gross domestic product is based on the product measurement. The Statistical discrepancy slips between the two so that the tables balance.

I must confess to you that I find the working out of the concepts of the NIPA and the devising of ways to estimate all the components the most impressive and important contribution that economics has made to understanding the world in which we live. Today, we take these accounts more or less for granted, but it is well to remember that in 1930 they did not exist.

We can now summarize this first model in the following *master* file which shows the actual commands to the software we use to compute this model.

```
# Master File for Model 1
# 31 variables, 8 identities, 23 exogenous variables
# Gross domestic product
f gdp = c + v + x - m + g
# Gross national product
f gnp = gdp + irrow - iprow
# Net national product
f nnp = gnp - ncca
# Personal income before government action
f pibg = nnp - nbctpn + pibtp - niprf + pidiv - netintm + piint - nsd
# Personal income
f pi = pibg + pigsb - nisurp + nisub - nitpi - nconsi
# Personal disposable income
f pidis = pi - piptax
# Personal savings
f pisav = pidis - c - piipcb - piptt
```

```
# Addendum: National income
f ni = nnp - nsd
end

# Graphical checks of the identities
ti GDP
gr gdp a.gdp
ti Personal income
gr pi a.pi
ti Personal savings
gr pisav a.pisav
ti National income
gr ni a.ni
```

Lines that begin with a # are just comments for the benefit of the human reader and are ignored by the computer. Lines that begin with an "f" form the variable on the left by the expression on the right. The "end" command signals the end of the master file for the model building program. Lines below it do not go into the model but have another function.

The lines below the "end" command provide graphical checks of the correctness of the identities. If you start *G7* and on the main menu click Model | Master, you will see this master file in the green edit window to the right. Normally, you do not "run" a master file, but with this model of only identities it makes sense to do so precisely to check the identities. Click the Run button on the main menu of the green editor, and all the commands will be executed by the *G7* program. The variables on the left of the "f" commands will be *formed* and placed in a *workspace* bank. When *G7* needs a variable, it looks first in this workspace; if it finds no variable of the required name, it looks in the assigned bank "a". When *G7* has been started in the \ami directory, the bank assigned as "a" is Quip, the Quarterly Income and Product bank. Thus, when this file has been run through *G7*, the variables created by the "f" commands will be in the workspace bank. If the identities are correct, variables like *gdp, gnp, pi, pisav,* and *ni* should have the same values in both banks. To check that they do – that is, that we have made no mistake in writing down the identities – we can graph what should be the same series from the two banks. We can force *G7* to go to assigned bank "a" for a variable by putting an *a.* in front of the variable name. Thus, the command

```
gr gdp a.gdp
```

will graph *gdp* from the workspace in the first (red) line and *gdp* from the assigned bank "a" with the second (blue) line. If our identities are correct, the two lines will coincide. In the present case, passing this check is relatively simple. To see how the test works, however, you may want to deliberately mess up one of the identities, "run" the false Master file, and note how the graphs reveal that something is wrong. Be sure to return the Master file to its correct state and run it again.

There is absolutely nothing in this model to object to. It will reproduce the historical data exactly. And yet it is a rather strange model. If we increase government purchases, *g*, by $100 billion, Personal income will increase by $100 billion, Personal consumption will be unchanged, and Personal savings will increase by $100 billion. That is surely an implausible result. Are consumers utterly indifferent to their income in deciding how much to consume? Certainly not. That observation leads us to Model 2. Because we can completely analyze Model 1 so easily, we will not actually build and run it. That we will do first with Model 2.

Before moving to it, however, I should add that if perhaps you feel these NIPA accounts are somewhat complicated, you should see those used by nearly all other countries. They use a structure known as the System of National Accounts (SNA) developed by the United Nations and other international organizations. In the SNA, the basic pure-identity model requires nearly four times as many variables and three times as many identities as does our model above. In models based on the SNA, the identity checks are very important. I have on several occasions spent several days getting identities correct in models based on these accounts.

Model 2. A Behavioral Ratio for Personal Consumption

We have noted the peculiarity in Model 1 that consumption is independent of Personal disposable income. Let us introduce a ratio between them, a ratio that will be constant in any one period but which may vary over time. Because it expresses the behavior of consumers, it is natural to call it a *behavioral ratio*. The command in our software for forming this exogenous ratio is

```
fex cBR = c/pidis
```

The "fex" stands for "*f*orm the *ex*ogenous variable". It is important to realize that the "fex" command forms the variable on the left and puts it into the model's data bank, but it *does not put the equation into the model*. In this respect, it differs fundamentally from the "f" command which not only forms the variable but also puts the equation into the model.

Once we have formed the behavioral ratio, we use it in the equation

```
f c = cBR*pidis
```

The Master file is changed at the end. As far down as the definition of Personal disposable income, it is unchanged. Starting from that point, the *end* of the new master file for Model 2 is:

```
# Personal disposable income
f pidis = pi - piptax
# Personal consumption expenditure
fex cBR = c/pidis
f c = cBR*pidis
# Personal savings
f pisav = pidis - c - piipcb - piptt
# Addendum: National income
f ni = nnp - nsd
check c .2
end
```

This procedure of introducing *cBR* at first looks entirely circular. You probably wonder, what is the purpose of introducing *cBR* if we only use it to derive *c*? *c* was used to derive *cBR* in the first place! However, it is important to remember that this new variable, *cBR*, is exogenous to the model, and allows us further insight into the workings of our model economy. We can determine *cBR* for all years for which we already have economic data. For any future years, we will have to supply it, which you will see should not be very hard. Having *cBR* as an exogenous variable allows us to run counter-historical simulations which ask the question: "What if the consumption ratio had been 5% higher in all years than it was observed to be?"

(From here on, we omit the commands to check the identities.) The key new commands, lines 4 and 5 and the next to last, have been set in boldface type. Notice that Personal consumption expenditure, c, has now become an *endogenous* variable and that we have introduced a new exogenous variable, *cBR*, so the number of exogenous variables has not been changed. Furthermore, the model remains tautological in the sense that -- given the historical values of the exogenous variables -- it will reproduce exactly the historical values of the endogenous variables.

If, however, we do a *counter-historical simulation* by running the model over the historical period but with one (or more) of the exogenous variables changed from the historical values, then we get a big difference from Model 1. For example, we can increase the value of Government purchases, *g*, by 20 in all periods. The ratio of the increase in *gdp* to this increase in *g* is called the "*gdp* multiplier of *g*" or just the "GDP/G multiplier". For Model 1, that ratio was exactly 1.0 for all periods. The figure below shows its values for Model 2.

The Government Multiplier in Model 2

The key to understanding the big difference between Model 2 and Model 1 is the next to last line of the master file, the *check c .2*. Note that a value of *c* was assumed at the top of the master file for the calculation of *gdp*. At the end, just above the "check" command, the value of *c* implied by all the equations is calculated. Will it be the same as the value used at the top? If all of the other variables are at their historical values, then the answer is Yes. But if one of them, say *g*, has been changed to some other value, then the answer on the first try is No. Our "check" command checks to see if the difference between the initial and the implied value is less than .2. If so, it allows the model to go on to the next period; if not, it sends the calculations back to the top of the master file, but this time with the value of *c* implied on the previous pass as the value assumed at the top. This method of solving the equations of the model, which is known as Seidel iteration, is not certain to converge. In practice, however, it almost always does so in a well formulated model.

Clearly the economic properties of Model 2 are widely different from those of Model 1. We now have, almost certainly, too much multiplier, for we have taken no account of the fact that taxes should also go up as income rises. That and other matters will be handled in Model 3.

Before leaving Model 2, however, we should perhaps ask why there has been such a rise over time in the multiplier. You may perhaps recall from a macroeconomic course that the multiplier should be one over the savings rate. In our terms that would be $1/(1 - cBR)$. In fact, calculating the multiplier by this formula gives exactly the same graph as that shown above. Thus, the cause of the rise in the multiplier is the decline in the savings ratio, or more properly, the rise in the ratio of consumption to income.

Exercise

1.2. Build and run Model 2. Run it first with all exogenous variables at their historical values. Then run it again with one or more of them changed. Compare the results graphically. Compute and graph the multiplier. Here are the steps:

1. Start the *G7* program by double-clicking its icon. If working on your own machine, you will first need to install the software which accompanies this book, including the Borland C++ free compiler. Follow the directions in the readme.txt file. If you are working on a network for a course, your instructor will explain how to find it. G immediately asks you to select the folder and configuration file. You want to "look in" c:\ami and the file you want to "open" is g.cfg.

2. Prepare the Master file. On the main menu bar, click Model | Edit Master File. (The use of the | symbol will be our shorthand way to say: click Model and then on the drop-down menu, click Edit Master File.) An editor window opens in the upper right corner of your screen and displays the Master file of Model 1. Do "File | Save as .." to save it as Master1 in case you need it again. Edit the file to transform it into the Master file of Model 2. The editor works pretty much the way that any Windows-based word processor works. Again click "File | Save as .." on the Editor's menu and save the file as Master (*not* Master2).

3. Build the model. On the main menu of the blue window to the left, click Model | Build Macro Model. This simple step calls a console application program to build an executable model from the current version of the Master file. If all goes well, all you have to do is tap a key at the end of the operation to return to *G7*. This step, it must be emphasized, works from the file presently called Master – not Master2 , or Master3, or anything else.

4. Run a historical simulation. On the main menu, click Model | Run Macro Model (F7). A window will request the starting date, ending date, results file name, and fix file name. To say that you want the model to run from the first quarter of 2000 to the third quarter of 2013, enter the dates as follows: 2000.1 and 2013.3 . (Run your model up to the most recent period for which you have data. It may be more recent that the example I have used.) Let us call the results file "histsim2" (for "historical simulation of model 2") and use "rhoadj" for the fix file. Exactly what that strange name means we will explain soon. Then click OK. You should

get a black screen informing you that you are running the *AMI* model and giving you a]
prompt. Respond with "ti xxx" where xxx is up to 80 characters giving your <u>ti</u>tle for this run
of the model. Take the time to give a meaningful title such as "Historical Simulation of
Model 2." You then get the] command again; reply with "run". The model runs, some
printout goes by too fast to read, and the program stops with the message "Tap any key to
continue." This pause allows you to see error messages. With good luck, there will be none.

5.   Graph the results of the historical simulation. First you must adapt the hist.shw file to the
      current model. Open it in the green editor window. Commands at the top of the file open the
      banks from which the data will be taken. In the present case, we should make them

```
bank histsim2  b
bank bws  c
```

6.   On the editor's main menu, click File | Save as ... and save the file as hist2.shw. Then click Run
      on the editor's menu. A graph and a run control panel should appear. Click the "continue"
      button on this panel, or tap the letter 'c', to view all the graphs, one after another. Since the
      model is tautological, all the graphs should show only one line, though if you look closely
      you will see that there are red crosses inside the blue squares. On the control panel, you can
      click the "Max" button to maximize the size of the graph. Click the"Normal" button to return
      the graph to its size before hitting the "Max" button.

7.   Now to make a run with government purchases of goods and services, *g*, increased by $100
      billion, repeat step 4 but call the results "highgov2" and at the] prompt give a title like "ti
      Government increased by $100 billion." Then, still at the] prompt, do
```
type g
update g +100
type g
```
      You should see that the values of *g* have all been increased by 100. Then give the "run"
      command. You are doing a *counter-historical simulation*.

8.   Now make graphs comparing the historical simulation, which is in the bank *histsim2,* with the
      counter-historical simulation, which is in the bank *highgov2.* Edit the file *comp.shw.* You can
      do "ed comp.shw" in the white command box, or you can click Editor on the main menu and
      the Open on the Editor's menu and open comp.shw Window's style. Make it begin with the
      commands

```
bank highgov2 b
bank histsim2 c
```

At the end of this file, you should put the commands to compute the multiplier and graph it.
Here they are:

```
f  mult = (b.gdp - c.gdp)/(b.g - c.g)
ti The Government Multiplier in Model 2
gname mult
gdates 1980.2 2013.3
gr mult
gdates 1980.1 2013.3
```

The "gdates" commands control the dates for the beginning and end of the graphs. The

38

mult variable will be zero in the base year of the model run, for the model is not computed for that base period. Hence, in order to graph only the non-zero values of the multiplier, we begin the graphs in the second period of the run. Adapt the second date in these commands to the most recent data in your data bank. After this use, the second "gdates" command restores the dates to their normal values. Click the File | Save as ... on the main menu of the green editor window. Save the file as *comp2.shw*, that is, as a file adapted to making the comparisons for Model 2. You may then "run" the file by clicking "Run" on the main menu of the green editor window.That will save the file and execute the commands in it in G. You should see the graphs go by as you click the Continue button on the left of control panel which appears along with the graphs.

9.   Now we want to save the graphs created in step 7 so that they can be imported into a word processor. Look again at the file *comp2.shw* in the editor.You will see triplets of lines like this:

```
ti gdp — Gross Domestic Product
gname gdp
gr b.gdp c.gdp
```

The second line is what interests us here. It gives the filename of the file into which the graph will be saved if you click the "Save" button on the run control panel. To make the graphs again, you can either repeat the command "add comp2.shw" or, since you already have *comp2.shw* in the editor, you can click "Run" on the Editor menu. On several of the graphs, click the "Save" button on the run control panel. Let us say that you saved the gdp graph. Actually, you created a file named gdp.wmf, the "wmf" standing for Windows Metafile. Start your word processor and bring in this file. In WordPerfect the command is Insert | File. In Word and Open Office it is Insert | Picture.Drag the little square handles on the graph to size as you like.

Model 3. More Behavioral Ratios and Shortcutting Exogenous Variables

In the preface, I said that models are "serious business" because they are playthings. A good plaything should be simple enough to make playing with it fun. Model 2, while clearly a step in the right direction, still has an ungainly number of exogenous variables that have to be set whenever we want to run it. Furthermore, it still ignores a number of important behavioral relations. Model 3 helps with both those problems. It puts in several more important behavioral relations and eliminates a number of exogenous variables of secondary interest. In particular, there are no less than eleven exogenous variables between *gdp* and *pibg*. If we are prepared for the moment to ignore the distinctions among them, then we can make the entire transition in one step by introducing an exogenous behavioral relation *pibg* and *gdp*. Model 3 also adds a behavioral relation between Indirect taxes and GDP. It drops the distinction between "contributions for social security" and "personal taxes" and specifies the sum of the two as a behavioral ratio to a *pibg* less the Indirect taxes. At the same time, it adds important behavioral ratios between:

Imports and private demand
Personal savings and Personal disposable income

39

Interest paid by consumers to business and Personal disposable income
Personal transfers to foreigners and Personal disposable income.

The last three replace the single ratio between Personal disposable income and Personal consumption expenditure which was introduced in Model 3. Here is the new master file:

```
# Master 3
# 21 variables, 11 exogenous (not counting time)
# 7 behavioral ratios for m, pibg, nitpils, ptax, piipcb, piptt, pisav
# v, x, g, npctr remain exogenous
checkdup y
fex time = time
# Behavioral ratio for imports
fex mBR = m/(c+v+x)
f m = mBR*(c+v+x)

# Gross domestic product
f gdp = c + v + x - m + g

# Shortcut to Personal income before government action
fex pibgBR = (gdp + irrow - iprow - ncca - nbctpn - nsd - niprf +
          pidiv - netintm + piint + pibtp)/gdp
f pibg = pibgBR*gdp

# Calculate personal tax base
fex nitpilsBR = (nitpi - nisub + nisurp)/gdp
f nitpils = nitpilsBR*gdp
# ptaxbase: Personal tax base
f ptaxbase = pibg - nitpils

# ptaxBR is personal tax rate including Social Security
fex ptaxBR = (piptax + nconsi)/ptaxbase
f ptax = ptaxBR*ptaxbase

# Personal disposable income
f pidis = pibg + pigsb - nitpils - ptax

# Behavioral ratios for piipcb, piptt, and pisav
fex piipcbBR = piipcb/pidis
f piipcb = piipcbBR*pidis
fex pipttBR = piptt/pidis
f piptt = pipttBR*pidis
fex pisavBR = pisav/pidis
f pisav = pisavBR*pidis

# Implied consumption
f c = pidis - piipcb - piptt - pisav

check c .2
end
```

In Model 3, only 4 of the original 23 exogenous variables remain, namely *v*, *x*, *g*, and *pigsb*. Seven behavioral ratios, however, have been added, and one may well wonder how stable or how hard to forecast they are. On the next page are graphs of them that should help answer that question.

40

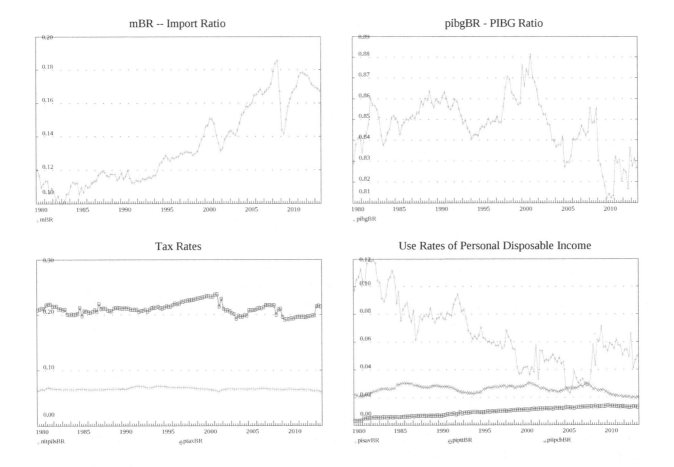

The scales have been chosen so that the variations in the variables can be seen. The PIBG ratio has remained surprisingly stable between .81 and .88; the import ratio is more volatile between .10 and .18 with a distinct tendency to rise, although it had a huge decline in 2009. The indirect tax rate (*nitpilsBR*) has remained stable throughout the period shown. The personal tax shows more variation. The Reagan tax cuts produced the slight dip in the personal tax rate between 1981 and 1984; after 1984, they began to crawl back up. The rise since 1995 reflect various "revenue enhancements" by the Clinton administration. Finally, the lower tax rate starting in 2001 reflects the Bush tax cuts, and a weakening economy. Clearly the most dramatic movement is in the Personal savings rate. The collapse and subsequent rise of personal savings is a matter into which we must look closely as we develop the model of the economy. With the exception of the savings rate, it would seem possible to make pretty good guesses about the future values of these ratios for a few years ahead.

The first game to play with a model, of course, is to calculate its GDP/G multiplier. The result is shown in the graph below.

41

The Government Multiplier in Model 3

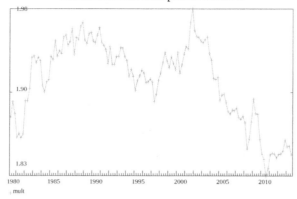

The values range between 1.8 and 2, a value typical for a purely Keynesian model with no supply constraints, such as we have here. When we account for inflation and monetary effects, the value should come down further.

Exercise

1.3. Bring your Master file up to the level of model 3. Build and run the model in both historical and counter-historical simulation. How does it respond to the increase of $100 billion in government purchases?Proceed as in the previous exercise; be sure to include a graph of the multiplier. You do not have a file that automatically makes the graphs shown above, but with what you now know, you should have no trouble making them. Remember that, after building a model, all variables in the model are in the bank called *bws*.

Model 4. Seeing Past Inflation

So far, all of our variables expressed in dollars have been in *nominal* terms, that is, in terms of the dollars actually spent. We have made no attempt to account for inflation. But anyone old enough to remember can tell you that forty years ago (1967) a dollar would buy a meal that today costs six or more. Consequently, these nominal or *current dollar* measures greatly overstate the growth that has occurred in the economy. The makers of the NIPA have, therefore, produced another set of figures for the product side of the accounts by expressing each item -- consumption, investment, exports, imports, and government purchases -- in the prices of one particular, base year. Presently (2014), that base year is 2009, but the base year is shifted forward every five years. These accounts are said to be in *constant dollars*, or *constant prices*, or *real* terms. These are all equivalent expressions.

As long as one is dealing with products which are in common use over the period studied, there is no great conceptual problem in how to measure the change in an item's price. For example, there is no great problem in putting the 1982 consumption of milk or

42

jeans into 2009 prices. But what about the 2009 price of a 1982 computer which was no longer made by 2009?

In fact, this very question of the pricing of computers has far-reaching effects in the U.S. NIPA. In the mid 1980's, BEA adopted a method known as "Hedonic" price indexes for computers, which it has extended to some other high-tech items. It looked at a variety of computers in, say, both 2012 and 2013 and recorded price and physical characteristics such as speed, RAM size, and hard disk size. By doing a regression (by methods we shall study closely in chapter 2) of price on the physical characteristics of the 2012 machines, an equation for the 2012 price as a function of physical characteristics could be determined. Coming then to the 2013 models, this function could be applied to say what their 2012 price would have been. By comparison with the actual 2013 prices, a price index between the two years can be deduced. The figure on the left below shows the resulting price index for computers and that for all other equipment. The figure on the right shows the annual percent change in computer prices -- note that the numbers are all negative.

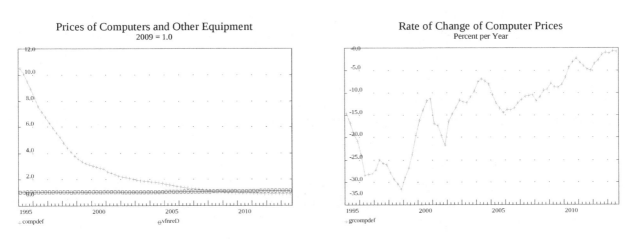

The contrast between the treatment of high-tech items and everything else is stunning and, I believe, problematic. This method of evaluating computers is not the only possibility. For example, one might evaluate the marginal product of a computer by assuming that various factors of production are paid their marginal product. When I first began programming computers in 1959, the computer cost $60 per hour and my wage was about $2.00 per hour, so the marginal product of that computer was about 30 times my marginal product. The machine on which I am typing these words is at least a thousand times more powerful than that machine, but it costs less than one percent of what I cost per hour. If I generously suppose that my marginal product has not declined over the intervening years, that *Univac-1* in 1959 must have had a marginal product about 3000 times that of the machine in front of me now — not a thousandth of it!Thus, there seems to me to be no compelling reason to use the BEA method of deflation; and, indeed, considerable reason to doubt that it is even of the right order of magnitude. Consider another example. In the 1970's, many universities and companies were usually equipped with one mainframe computer. It usually took up the space of an entire room, and surely its power is dwarfed by today's personal machines. However, these mainframes still computed an enormous amount of data and information for whomever would line up to use them. The BEA deflator takes these extremely important machines and writes off them and their contributions to GDP as nearly nothing.

Theuse of the BEA computer and other high-tech deflators affect substantially the rate of growth of real GDP. To prevent these effects from turning the accounts into nonsense, the BEA has offset the effects of the Hedonic indexes by also adopting a non-linear procedure known as "chain weighting."For each pair of adjacent years, say 2012 and 2013, the real growth ratio of each component of GDP is computed in two ways. In the first, all items are priced with the prices of the first year; in the second, all items are priced with the prices of the second. We may call the first index A and the second B. The geometric mean of the two, $\sqrt{(AB)}$ is then taken as the real growth ratio of that component between those two adjacent years. If the growth between non-adjacent years is needed, it is taken as the product of all the year-to-year growth ratios between the two years, that is, the year-to-year ratios are *chained*. To get GDP or a component in prices of a base year, say 2009, one just moves the 2009 nominal GDP forward or backward by these year-to-year growth rates.

The official constant-price series are found in the QUIP data bank with names derived from the name of the current dollar series by adding a $. Thus, the official series for real GDP is gdp$.

The use of chaining means that it is never necessary to evaluate the output of computers (or other goods) in prices more than one year distant from the year in which they were made. That is certainly an advantage, but chaining also has a major disadvantage. Namely, total real GDP, say for 2012 in prices of 2009, is not the sum of the components of real GDP. The same is true with the components. For example, the official 1970 value of fixed investment (vf$) in 2009 prices is 27 percent smaller than the sum of its three major components: residential construction (vfr$), non-residential construction (vfnrs$), and non-residential equipment (vfnre$). It will clearly be a nuisance in modeling if a total is not the sum of its parts.

Because I have serious reservations, as already explained, about the computer and other high-tech deflators and do not wish to be plagued with totals that are not the sum of their parts, I am going to adopt a radical simplification for our modeling. I am going to use the deflator for personal consumption expenditures on food as the deflator for all series in the national accounts. I choose food because it is important and I tend to trust the methods of making indexes for food prices. I also notice that when I need a subjective price index to put some dollar amount from twenty or thirty years ago into current prices, I tend to try to recall food prices. Remarkably, the trend of food prices and that of the GDP deflator computed with Hedonic indexes and chain weighting are very similar, as seen below. The food prices have, however, been somewhat more volatile, as shown in the right graph. In both graphs, the heavier, smoother line is the official GDP deflator. GDP and GDP product-side components deflated by the GDP deflator have names in the QUIP databank derived by adding R (for "Real") to the variables name in current prices.

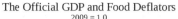

| The Official GDP and Food Deflators | Inflation in the Official GDP and Food Deflators |
| 2009 = 1.0 | Annual Growth Rate |

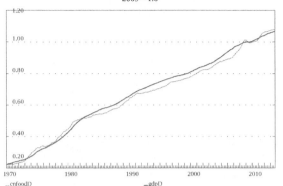
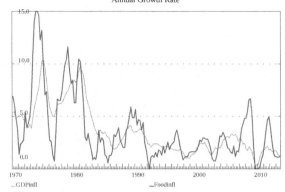

With the question of the computer deflator settled, we can turn to the proper subject of Model 4, the accounts in real terms. There are many reasons for wanting accounts in real terms. If we want to use GDP or Personal consumption expenditure as an indicator of welfare, it is certainly the measure in real terms that is relevant. If we want to relate employment to the NIPA, we clearly need measures in real terms. If we want to tie investment to growth in output, it is only real growth which is relevant. Also, forecasting exogenous variables in real terms is generally easier than in nominal terms. The model should make the conversion from real to nominal for us.

In the official accounts, each item on the real side has its own deflator, and there are no deflators on the income side except for an addendum item which gives Personal disposable income deflated by the Personal consumption expenditure deflator. Since we are using accounts in constant "GDP deflator dollars," all items have the same deflator. We will make the GDP deflator an exogenous behavioral ratio, and set the consumption deflator relative to it. All the exogenous dollar amounts will be exogenous in real terms. Here is the master file of Model 4.

```
# Master 4: Product side in real terms
# 13 exogenous (not counting time)
# 7 behavioral ratios for m, pibg, nitpils, ptax, piipcb, piptt, and pisav.
# gdpD exogenous
# vR, xR, gR, npctrR exogenous in constant dollars

checkdup y
fex time = time
# Behavioral ratio for imports
fex mBR = mR/(cR+vR+xR)
f mR = mBR*(cR+vR+xR)

# Real Gross domestic product
f gdpR = cR + vR + xR - mR + gR

# Current price values
f m = mR*gdpD
f v = vR*gdpD

# Nominal GDP
```

```
f gdp = gdpR*gdpD

# Shortcut to Personal income before government action
fex pibgBR = (gdp + irrow - iprow - ncca - nbctpn - nsd - niprf +
          pidiv - netintm + piint + pibtp)/gdp
f pibg = pibgBR*gdp

# Calculate personal tax base
fex nitpilsBR = (nitpi - nisub + nisurp)/gdp
f nitpils = nitpilsBR*gdp
# ptaxbase: Personal tax base
f ptaxbase = pibg - nitpils

# ptaxBR is personal tax rate including Social Security
fex ptaxBR = (piptax + nconsi)/ptaxbase
f ptax = ptaxBR*ptaxbase

# Government transfer payments to persons, exogenous in real terms
fex npctrR = npctr/gdpD
f npctr = npctrR*gdpD

# Personal disposable income
f pidis = pibg + pigsb - nitpils - ptax

# Behavioral ratios for piipcb, piptt, and pisav
fex piipcbBR = piipcb/pidis
f piipcb = piipcbBR*pidis
fex pipttBR = piptt/pidis
f piptt = pipttBR*pidis
fex pisavBR = pisav/pidis
f pisav = pisavBR*pidis

# Implied consumption
f c = pidis - piipcb - piptt - pisav
# convert to real terms
f cR = c/gdpD
check cR .2
end
```

It is natural to be asking at this point, "Very well, as long as we know all the exogenous variables and behavioral ratios exactly, these models enable us to calculate GDP exactly. But if we are forecasting, we don't know them. How good are the models if we must make rough guesses for the exogenous variables?" A partial answer may be had by seeing how well the models would have done in the past had we used constant values for all the behavioral ratios. I looked over the values of each behavioral ratio and picked the following typical values: *pibgBR* = .847, *mBR* = .134, *nitpilsBR* = .067; *ptaxBR* = .211, *piipcbBR* = .025; *pipttBR* = .010, *pisavBR* = .066. When the model was run with these values from 1980.1 to 2013.3, it produced the simulation shown by the line marked with a + in the graph below.

The model (red line, +'s) did quite well up through 2000 but by 2006 it went racing off beyond the economy's actual course (blue line, squares). In fact, exports were rising considerably, but the rising exports went with a rising share of imports. The neglect of this rise (we kept *mBR* constant) is responsible for the runaway growth in the simulation. My fundamental impression from this graph, however, is that it is possible to model the real growth of the economy surprisingly well given just investment, exports, government purchases and transfers. Of course, explaining the movements in the major behavioral ratios would improve the simulation. A method for doing so is introduced in Model 5.

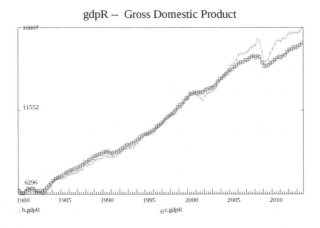

gdpR -- Gross Domestic Product

Exercise

1.4. Bring your model up to the level of Model 4. Run the counter-historical simulation with *gR* increased by 100. Using *comp.shw*, make graphs of the effects on the new, real-terms variables such as *gdpR*, *cR*, and so on. Graph the multiplier.

Model 5. Modeling Behavior with Regression

So far, we have been able to replace one exogenous variable with another which is easier to comprehend or forecast. But we have not reduced the number of exogenous variables. With Model 5, we will strike investment from the list of exogenous variables but keep it in the model, now as an endogenous variable. We will do so by fitting two equations by the method of least squares, one for *vfR*, fixed investment, and one for *viR*, inventory investment. We will also replace the rather volatile behavioral ratio for imports, *mR*, with an estimated equation. We will, in the process, reduce the number of exogenous variables by two.

The fixed investment equation explains *vfR* as a linear function of estimated replacement and lagged values of changes in real GDP. The commands to the computer, using the *G7* software, are put into a file, called *vfR.reg* in this case, and this file is then executed by *G7*. The contents of *vfR.reg* are just

```
# vfR.reg - Regression to explain fixed investment
catch vfR.cat
save vfR.sav
lim 1975.1 2013.3 2013.3
ti Gross Private Domestic Fixed Investment
f gppR = gdpR - gR
f d = gppR - gppR[1]
f replace = .05*@cum(stockf,vfR[4],.05)
con 100000 1.0 = a2
```

47

```
r vfR = replace,  d[1],  d[2],d[3],d[4],d[5],
   d[6],d[7],d[8],d[9],d[10],d[11],d[12]
save off
gr *
catch off
```

The results of the regression are a graph showing how well the equation fits and two files with the results. One of these files, created because of the command in the first line, is called the *catch* file and is intended to be looked at by humans and included in books and papers. The other, created because of the command in the second line and called the *save* file, is intended to be read by the computer in making a model. The first two commands in the *vfR.reg* file just name the catch and save files. The third, with the *lim command,* specifies the period over which the equation is to be fit; the fourth supplies a title for the graph and the catch file. Next we define gross private product gppR as gdpR less government gR. Then comes the definition of the variable *d* as the difference between one period's value of gppR and the previous period's value. (The [] notation in *G7* is to indicate lags of variables.)The next line defines the stock of fixed capital, stockf, by cumulating investment with a depreciation rate of 5 percent per quarter and the sets replacement (called replace) equal to 5 percent of the stock. We will explain the *@cum* function further in a later chapter; suffice it to say here that it does just what an accountant using declining balance depreciation does. Next is a "con" command, which will constrain the first coefficient in the regression. (The topic of constraints will be covered more fully as we go into the investment equation in more detail later.)Finally, we come to the command that we have been leading up to, the one that fits a linear function of the variables listed on the right side of the = sign to the variable on the left. This fitting is often called linear *regression*; hence the *r* as the name of the command. We will look carefully at how this fitting is done in the next chapter. The remaining commands just draw the graph of the fit and close the save and catch files. Here is the graph for our equation.

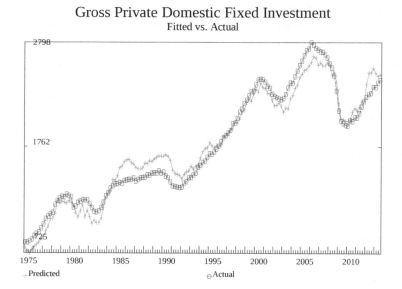

Gross Private Domestic Fixed Investment
Fitted vs. Actual

The fit is clearly quite close, almost uncomfortably close if you consider how simple the

48

equation is. Notice that it does not use the interest rate or any other financial or monetary variable. In producing a fit this close without such a variable, the computer seems not to have realized that the whole of macroeconomics pivots on the interest rate in the IS curve. Such a heretical computer should probably be burned at the stake.

The results in the "catch" file are:

```
save vfR.sav
lim 1975.1 2013.3 2013.3
ti Gross Private Domestic Fixed Investment
subti Fitted vs. Actual
f gppR = gdpR - gR
f d = gppR - gppR[1]
f replace = .05*@cum(stockf,vfR[4],.05)

con 100000 1=a2
r vfR = replace, d[1], d[2],d[3],d[4],d[5],
   d[6],d[7],d[8],d[9],d[10],d[11],d[12]
:               Gross Private Domestic Fixed Investment
  SEE   =      124.53 RSQ  = 0.9469 RHO =   0.94 Obser =   155 from 1975.100
  SEE+1 =       41.74 RBSQ = 0.9420 DW  =   0.11 DoFree =  141 to   2013.300
  MAPE  =        6.43
     Variable name       Reg-Coef Mexval  Elas   NorRes    Mean   Beta
  0 vfR                 - - - - - - - - - - - - - -    1770.99 - - -
  1 intercept           145.14515    7.2  0.08    23.61    1.00
  2 replace               0.89514  354.7  0.77     2.98 1521.91  0.922
  3 d[1]                  0.46773    2.3  0.01     2.73   55.36  0.063
  4 d[2]                  0.42834    1.7  0.01     2.51   54.31  0.058
  5 d[3]                  0.38159    1.3  0.01     2.28   53.77  0.052
  6 d[4]                  0.56294    3.1  0.02     2.05   52.86  0.078
  7 d[5]                  0.48996    2.4  0.01     1.83   52.64  0.068
  8 d[6]                  0.37098    1.4  0.01     1.66   52.23  0.051
  9 d[7]                  0.38208    1.5  0.01     1.51   51.69  0.053
 10 d[8]                  0.34284    1.2  0.01     1.36   51.10  0.047
 11 d[9]                  0.43155    1.8  0.01     1.22   51.08  0.059
 12 d[10]                 0.35102    1.1  0.01     1.12   50.80  0.048
 13 d[11]                 0.30109    0.8  0.01     1.06   51.48  0.041
 14 d[12]                 0.51476    2.7  0.01     1.00   51.03  0.070

save off
gr *
catch off
```

The column headed "Reg Coef" shows the regression coefficients, that is, the values of the parameters in the equations. The equation which will enter the model is

```
vfR = 145.1451 + 0.895139*replace + 0.467734*d[1] + 0.428344*d[2] +
        0.381594*d[3] + 0.562940*d[4] + 0.489958*d[5] + 0.370981*d[6] +
        0.382080*d[7] + 0.342839*d[8] + 0.431552*d[9] + 0.351016*d[10] +
        0.301090*d[11] + 0.514760*d[12]
```

The terms used in these numerical displays will be explained in detail in the next chapter; but, in case you have already studied statistics and regression, here is a brief explanation of the terms for reference. (Do not worry if some or all of them are unfamiliar to you; all will be made clear in due course.)

In the top panel:

Statistic Name	Description
SEE	Standard error of estimate, or the square root of the average of the squares of the misses or "residuals" of the equation. (Not adjusted for degrees of freedom.)
RSQ	(pronounced r-square) = Coefficient of multiple determination.
RHO	(Greek rho) = Autocorrelation coefficient of the residuals.
Obser	Number of observations.
SEE+1	The SEE for forecasts one period ahead using rho adjustment.
RBSQ	(pronounced r-bar-square) = Coefficient of multiple determination adjusted for degrees of freedom.
DW	Durbin-Watson statistic; contains same information as does RHO.
DoFree	Degrees of freedom = Obser minus number of independent variables.
from	Starting date of the regression
to	Ending date of the regression.
MAPE	Mean absolute percentage error.

Across the lower columns, for each variable:

Statistic Name	Description
Reg-coef	Regression coefficients for the variable.
Mexval	Marginal explanatory value: the percentage increase in SEE if the variable were left out.
Elas	Elasticity at mean.
NorRes	The "normalized" sum of squared residuals (SSR) using this and all preceding variables, that is the SSR using this and preceding variables divided by the SSR using all variables.
Mean	Mean of the variable.
Beta	What the regression coefficient would be if both dependent and independent variables were in units which made their standard deviations equal to 1.0.

It is always important to ask whether the regression coefficients are of the correct sign and reasonable magnitude. In this equation, the coefficient on *replace*, 0.83073, seems reasonably close to its theoretical value of 1.0; the coefficients on *d* are all positive. One might expect them to fade away to zero more rapidly than they do.

The *save* file for this regression is meant for reading by the computer, but is legible by humans. In case you are curious, here is what it looks like for this regression.

```
ti Gross Private Domestic Fixed Investment
f gppR = gdpR - gR
f d = gppR - gppR[1]
f replace = .05*@cum(stockf,vfR[4],.05)
r vfR =    145.145148*intercept +
             0.895139*replace +
             0.467734*d[1] +
             0.428344*d[2] +
             0.381594*d[3] +
             0.562940*d[4] +
             0.489958*d[5] +
             0.370981*d[6] +
             0.382080*d[7] +
             0.342839*d[8] +
             0.431552*d[9] +
             0.351016*d[10] +
             0.301090*d[11] +
             0.514760*d[12]
   d
```

As you see, it contains the commands to form the variables and the coefficients of the equation found by the regression. It omits other data intended to help in thinking about the results of the regression.

The equation for inventory investment is estimated by executing the following file, called viR.reg:

```
# viR.reg - Regression file for inventory investment
catch viR.cat
save viR.sav
lim 1975.1 2013.3
title viR Change in Inventory
# fs stands for "final sales"
f fsR = cR + vfR + xR + gR
f dfsR = fsR - fsR[1]
r viR = ! dfsR[1], dfsR[2], dfsR[3],dfsR[4]
save off
gname viR
gr *
catch off
```

The ! after the = sign in the *r* command means to leave out the intercept or constant term. Here are the results:

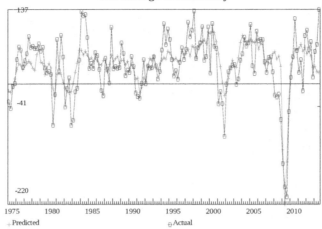

viR Change in Inventory

```
save viR.sav
fdates 1972.1 2013.3
lim 1975.1 2013.3
title viR Change in Inventory
# fs stands for "final sales"
f fsR = cR + vfR + xR + gR
f dfsR = fsR - fsR[1]
r viR = ! dfsR[1], dfsR[2], dfsR[3],dfsR[4]
:                         viR Change in Inventory
  SEE   =       35.77 RSQ  = 0.5674 RHO =   0.46 Obser  =  155 from 1975.100
  SEE+1 =       32.03 RBSQ = 0.5588 DW  =   1.07 DoFree =  151 to   2013.300
  MAPE  =      193.98
    Variable name             Reg-Coef Mexval  Elas   NorRes     Mean    Beta
  0 viR                       - - - - - - - - - - - - - - -     34.65   - - -
  1 dfsR[1]                    0.17059    8.9   0.39    1.49     80.01
  2 dfsR[2]                    0.20293    8.2   0.46    1.06     79.35   0.394
  3 dfsR[3]                    0.04296    0.4   0.10    1.02     79.71   0.083
  4 dfsR[4]                    0.05006    0.8   0.11    1.00     79.38   0.097

save off
gname viR
gr *
catch off
```

The fit here leaves room for improvement; but given the extreme volatility and small size of this variable, this equation should be usable.

Finally, the import equation is estimated by the commands in the mR.reg file

```
# mR.reg - Regression file for imports
lim 1975.1 2013.3
catch mR.cat
save mR.sav
ti mR Imports
subti  Model 5
con 100000 0.5 = a2
con 100000 0.36 = a3
r mR = xR, vR, cR
```

```
save off
gname mRreg
gr *
save off
catch off
```

The results are:

```
save mR.sav
ti mR Imports
subti  Model 5
con 100000 0.5 = a2
con 100000 0.36 = a3
r mR = xR, vR, cR
:                                          mR Imports
   SEE   =       102.43 RSQ   = 0.9790 RHO =   0.95 Obser  =    155 from 1975.100
   SEE+1 =        34.70 RBSQ  = 0.9786 DW  =   0.11 DoFree =    151 to    2013.300
   MAPE  =         7.92
      Variable name          Reg-Coef  Mexval  Elas   NorRes     Mean   Beta
   0 mR                      - - - - - - - - - - - - - - -    1331.43 - - -
   1 intercept              -590.68985    99.7  -0.44    48.91      1.00
   2 xR                        0.54276   102.7   0.43     8.50   1051.09  0.379
   3 vR                        0.30206    48.8   0.41     2.47   1805.65  0.234
   4 cR                        0.11893    57.3   0.61     1.00   6779.25  0.403

save off
gname mRreg
gr *
catch off
```

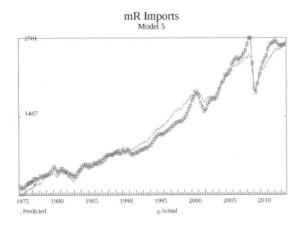

mR Imports
Model 5

The fit is close enough, but the high coefficient on exports is suspicious. It can hardly mean that 54 percent of the value of exports is imported. Rather, it would seem to be a sort of proxy variable for the openness of the economy. I am not happy with this equation, but at this introductory stage, let us accept it.

The Master File

The master file for Model 5 follows.

```
# Master 5:  Regression equations for investment and imports
# 11 exogenous (not counting time)
# 6  behavioral ratios for pibg, nitpils, ptax, piipcb, piptt, pisav
```

```
# 3 regression equations for mR, vfR, and viR
#  xR, gR, npctrR exogenous in constant dollars

checkdup y
fex time = time

# Investment
add vfR.sav
add viR.sav

f vR = vfR+viR
# Imports
add mR.sav
# Gross domestic product
f gdpR = cR + vR + xR - mR + gR
```

... and so on exactly as in Model 4.

Note the "add" commands which bring into the model the results of the regressions recorded in the .sav files.

So, how well does our masterpiece simulate the economy if it is given the historical values of all the exogenous variables? The graph below shows the answer.

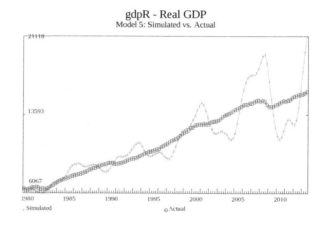

gdpR - Real GDP
Model 5: Simulated vs. Actual

The model reproduced the general trend of the economy allright, but with a powerful cycle unlike anything in the real economy. In fact, it is reminiscent of the simple model of section 1 of this chapter. Thus we see that it is very easy to produce a model which has cycles. All we need is a multiplier and an investment function based on the "accelerator" theory of investment. Indeed, our graph should make it fairly clear why our investment equation is called an accelerator; whenever the economy turns up, it accelerates that upturn. In fact, this feature of Model 5 is so prominent that we will name Model 5 the Accelerator-Multiplier Interaction model, or *AMI* for short.

The problem we now face is to find out what stabilizes the economy. We shall return to that question after two intervening chapters to explain the theory of regression and some more of the mechanics of model building. You will then be able to estimate the equations, build, and run this model yourself and go on to work on improving it.

CHAPTER 2. BASIC CONCEPTS OF LEAST SQUARES REGRESSION

In this chapter, we will be concerned with how to sum up the lessons of the past about how one variable, say the sales of automobiles, depends upon others, such as price and income. We will see how to fit to historical data equations which express this dependence. Here we will concentrate on the mechanics of this curve-fitting process and say relatively little about the examination and interpretation of the results. That will come in due course in later chapters.

1. What is the Method of Least Squares and Why Use It?

Let us begin directly with a practical problem. Suppose that you need to make forecasts of automobile sales for the next four quarters. Your first question is naturally, "What factors affect the sales of automobiles and how strongly does each of them work?"

A good bet for an important factor is certainly disposable income. It also happens to be a convenient variable because a recent issue of a business magazine shows the forecasts of it made by a dozen different forecasting firms. Let us presume that you have ten years of quarterly data on both auto sales and disposable income. How do you find the relation between the two?

The simplest way to answer that question is to plot auto purchases against income as shown on Figure 2.1 and then draw a line down the middle of the points.

You may use the edge of a transparent ruler or a tightly stretched black string to help you get a line which seems to fit. Then, given a forecast of income A, we see that automobile purchases of B would be right "on line" with that income. Mathematically, what we have done is to determine b_1 and b_2 of the following equation:

$$(1) \quad y_t = b_1 + b_2 x_t$$

where

y_t	=	automobile purchases in quarter t
x_t	=	disposable income in quarter t
b_1, b_2	=	constants, often called parameters, to be determined so that the line fits the past experience.

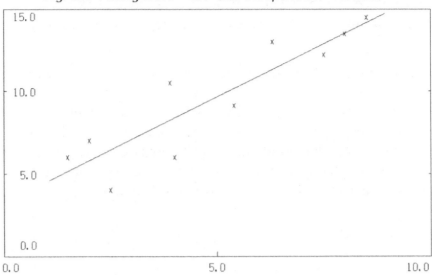

Fig. 2.1: Fitting Data with One Independent Variable

This method of "eyeing in" the line has important advantages over other methods. It allows us to see what we are doing. It is quick, easy, clear, and makes it easy to spot outliers in the data and to avoid putting a heavy weight on them. It is, however, seldom used. Theorists don't like it because no elegant theorems can be proved about it. Practitioners shun it because it is easy to see that it is subjective; more sophisticated methods allow them to cloak their subjectivity in a more opaque garment.

The real problem with the method, however, arises when we realize that automobile sales depend on more than just income. Suppose that we want to take into account the change in income, $dx_t = x_t - x_{t-1}$; then we should have to estimate

(2) $\quad y = b_1 + b_2 x + b_3 dx$

(The b_1 and b_2 of (2) may, of course, be different from those of (1).)To estimate these b's by eye in this equation, we need a three-dimensional construction to suspend the points in space. Then perhaps we might use a plane of light to find the plane which fits best. But what was simple for one variable becomes something of an engineering feat for two. But now, of course, we realize that automobile purchases should also depend on existing stocks, s, of autos, thus:

(3) $\quad y = b_1 + b_2 x + b_3 dx + b_4 s$

Now we need a four-dimensional structure of some sort; and when you have constructed it, be prepared to tackle a five-dimensional device, for automobile purchases also certainly depend on the price of automobiles, p, so that we should be estimating:

(4) $\quad y = b_1 + b_2 x + b_3 dx + b_4 s + b_5 p$

Here we seem to be pretty much past hope of making a physical picture to aid us in fitting the equation to the data. If we ever want to estimate an equation with that many parameters -- and for all practical purposes, with any more than two parameters -- we must find some way to replace vision by calculation. That switch can be dangerous, and we shall frequently find that we must check to be sure that the blind calculations have not lost their way.

To find a way to calculate the parameters, let us return to the simplest case, equation (1) and Figure 2.1, and let us agree to choose b_1 and b_2 so as to minimize the sum of the squares of the errors. Figure 2.2 shows these squares graphically. We twist and push the line through these points until the sum of the areas of the squares is the smallest. You may ask "Why the squares? Why not just get the smallest sum of absolute values of error?"Strangely, it is easy to compute the b's to minimize the sum of squares, but quite difficult to minimize the sum of absolute errors, and it is really this ease that is responsible for our preference for the squares.

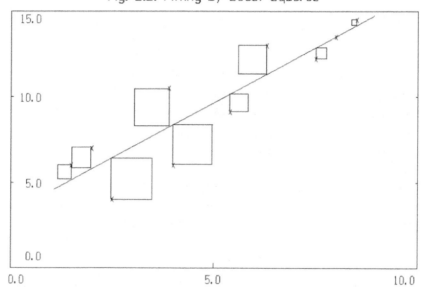

Fig. 2.2: Fitting by Least Squares

2. How to Calculate the Least Squares Regression Coefficients

To find the "least squares" values of the b's, we just minimize with respect to b_1 and b_2 the following summation:

$$(5) \quad S = \sum_{t=1}^{T} \left(y_t - (b_1\, x_{t1} + b_2\, x_{t2}) \right)^2$$

where T is the number of observations which we have, $x_{t1} = 1$ for all t and x_{t2} = income in period t. The sigma, Σ, of course, indicates summation, and the t=1 below it indicates that the summation begins with that value of t and extends to t = T, shown above the sigma. Now if S is to be minimal with respect to both b_1 and b_2, then it must be minimal with respect to b_1 with b_2 held constant. The reader who has not studied calculus must now accept on faith that the solution to equations (8) below

58

will minimize this S. But anyone who knows that the derivative of x^2 is $2x$ can follow the derivation. First, the derivative of S with respect to b_1 (with b_2 held constant) must be zero:

(6) $\quad \dfrac{\partial S}{\partial b_1} = \sum\limits_{t=1}^{T} 2\left(y_t - (b_1\,x_{t1} + b_2\,x_{t2})\right)(-x_{t1}) = 0$

Likewise, S must be minimal with respect to b_2, so

(7) $\quad \dfrac{\partial S}{\partial b_2} = \sum\limits_{t=1}^{T} 2\left(y_t - (b_1\,x_{t1} + b_2\,x_{t2})\right)(-x_{t2}) = 0$

We may see the implications of (6) and (7) more clearly if we will divide through by 2, move the terms not involving b_1 and b_2 to the right hand side, and factor out b_1 and b_2 from the sums involving them. Upon so doing, (6) and (7) become

(8)
$$b_1\, \Sigma\, x_{t1}x_{t1} + b_2\, \Sigma\, x_{t1}x_{t2} = \Sigma\, x_{t1}\,y_t$$

$$b_1\, \Sigma\, x_{t2}x_{t1} + b_2\, \Sigma\, x_{t2}x_{t2} = \Sigma\, x_{t2}\,y_t\,.$$

Here we have dropped the limits on the summation simply because they are always the same. Now bear clearly in mind that the x's and y's are known, historically observed values. Hence, all the sums are known numbers. The unknowns are b_1 and b_2. So we see that we have two linear equations in two unknowns. You solved equations like that in high school; if perhaps you have forgotten how, I shall remind you in a moment. Given that we know how to solve linear equations, we can consider our problem of how to find the b's to be solved.

So far, you may say, we have only dealt with the two-variable case, handled satisfactorily graphically. What about more variables? Well, we might as well go for the general case and consider n independent variables $x_1, \dots, x_n$, and the equation

$$y_t = b_1 x_{t1} + \dots + b_n x_{tn}.$$

Then let

$$S = \sum\limits_{t=1}^{T} \left(y_t - (b_1\,x_{t1} + \dots + b_n\,x_{tn})\right)^2$$

Differentiating with respect to $b_1, b_2, \dots, b_n$ gives

(9)
$$\frac{\partial S}{\partial b_1} = \sum\limits_{t=1}^{T} 2\left(y_t - (b_1\,x_{t1} + \dots + b_n\,x_{tn})\right)(-x_{t1}) = 0$$

$$\frac{\partial S}{\partial b_n} = \sum\limits_{t=1}^{T} 2\left(y_t - (b_1\,x_{t1} + \dots + b_n\,x_{tn})\right)(-x_{tn}) = 0$$

These may be rewritten as

$$b_1 \Sigma\, x_{t1} x_{t1} + b_2 \Sigma\, x_{t1} x_{t2} + \ldots + b_n \Sigma\, x_{t1} x_{tn} = \Sigma\, x_{t1} y_t$$

$$b_1 \Sigma\, x_{t2} x_{t1} + b_2 \Sigma\, x_{t2} x_{t2} + \ldots + b_n \Sigma\, x_{t2} x_{tn} = \Sigma\, x_{t2} y_t$$

(10) ....

$$b_1 \Sigma\, x_{tn} x_{t1} + b_2 \Sigma\, x_{tn} x_{t2} + \ldots + b_n \Sigma\, x_{tn} x_{tn} = \Sigma\, x_{tn} y_t \,.$$

Do you see the system? In the first equation, the first factor in every product is x_{t1}, in the second equation, x_{t2}, and so on. In the ith column, the second factor in each sum is x_{ti}.

Let us take a simple example with T = 5.

	t	x_{t1}	x_{t2}	x_{t3}	y_t
	1	1	10	5	17
	2	1	5	1	10
(11)	3	1	0	6	12
	4	1	10	3	16
	5	1	0	10	20

You should now verify that the equations (10) are

$$5b_1 + 25b_2 + 25b_3 = 75$$
$$25b_1 + 225b_2 + 85b_3 = 380$$
$$25b_1 + 85b_2 + 171b_3 = 415$$

Table 2.1 shows how to solve them systematically. The first three lines (L1, L2, L3) show the original equations. (The line across the top shows what the numbers in each column would be multiplied by before adding together to give the equations.)The next three show the results of eliminating b_1 from the second and third equations. To obtain them, first get the coefficient of b_1 in the first equation to be 1.0 by dividing the equation by b_1's coefficient, namely 5. The divisor is called the pivot element and is underlined in the table. The result is L4. Now to eliminate b_1 from equation 2, multiply L4 by b_1's coefficient in L2 and subtract from L2 to get L5. L6 is similarly calculated. We have now completed one pivot operation and eliminated b_1 from all equations except the first. In the next three lines, L7, L8, and L9, we similarly get 0 for the coefficient on b_2 in all but the second equation. Finally, in L10 - L12, we get zero coefficients on b_3 in all but the third equation. From these last three lines, we read the answer

$$b_1 = 4.95 \qquad b_2 = .61 \qquad b_3 = 1.40$$

60

Line	b_1	b_2	b_3 =	1	Derivation
L1	5.	25.	25.	75.	
L2	25.	225.	85.	380.	Original Equations
L3	25.	85.	171.	415.	
-----	-----	-----	-----	-----	-----
L4#	1.	5.	5.	15.	L1/5
L5	0.	100.	-40.	5.	L2 -25*L4
L6	0.	-40.	46.	40.	L3 - 25*L4
-----	-----	-----	-----	-----	-----
L7	1.	0.	7.	14.75	L4 - 5*L8
L8#	0.	1.	-0.4	.05	L5/100
L9	0.	0.	30.	42.	L6 -(-40)*L8
-----	-----	-----	-----	-----	-----
L10	1.	0.	0.	4.95	L7 -7*L12
L11	0.	1.	0.	.61	L8-(-.4)*L12
L12#	0.	0.	1.	1.40	L9/30

A # after a line number marks the line computed first in each panel of three lines.

Table 2.1: Least Squares Computations

The process we have been engaged in is known as linear regression and the b's we have found are the regression coefficients. The particular method of solution of the equations is known as Gauss-Jordan reduction. The idea of fitting the equation by minimizing the sum of squared misses first appears in Adrien Marie Legendre's *Nouvelles méthodes pour la détermination des orbites des comètes* in 1805. In 1809, Carl Friedrich Gauss published a small volume in Latin on the orbits of planets in which he not only used the method but claimed to have been using it since 1795. Given Gauss's many achievements in mathematics, there is no particular reason to doubt his claim, but he might have forgotten to describe it had Legendre not done so first. The term *regression* came from studies of human heights by Francis Galton in the late 19th century. He plotted the heights of children on the vertical axis against the average heights of their parents on the horizontal. The line he fit to this scatter of points had a slope of less than 45⁰, so he referred to it as the line of "regression towards mediocrity." The word "regression" stuck.

Exercise

2.1 Calculate the regression equation for the following data.

x1	x2	x3	y
1	5	2	14
1	4	3	13
1	6	3	17
1	7	5	20
1	6	7	19

3. Some Measures of How Well the Equation Fits

Now that we have computed the regression coefficients, we may well ask, How well does the equation fit the data? To answer, we first need to compute the values of the dependent variable "predicted" by the equation. These predicted values are denoted by $\hat{y}_t$ thus

$$\hat{y}_t = \sum_{i=1}^{n} b_i \, x_{t\,i}$$

They are shown in the third column of Table 2.2, where the actual values are shown in the second column. The misses, or "residuals",

$$r_t = \hat{y}_t - y_t \ ,$$

are shown in the fourth column. Note that the sum of the residuals is zero; it will always be zero if there is a constant term in the equation. Since we were trying to minimize the sum of squares of these residuals, this quantity is naturally of interest:

$$S = \sum_{t=1}^{T} r_t^2$$

Actually, the Standard Error of Estimate,

$$SEE = \sqrt{S/T}$$

is easier to interpret for it has the same units as the dependent variable. Indeed, we could describe it as sort of average error. (Many texts define SEE with $T-n$ instead of T in the denominator. The G7 program uses the above definition as a descriptive statistic in its own right, not an estimate -- under rather strong assumptions -- of some unobservable population parameter.)

t	y		r	r²	d	d²	f	f²	%
1	17.	18.05	1.05	1.1025	2.0	4.	-1.65	2.7225	6.18
2	10.	9.40	-0.60	0.3600	-5.0	25.	1.95	3.8025	6.00
3	12.	13.35	1.35	1.8225	-3.0	9.	-2.10	4.4100	11.25
4	16.	15.25	-0.75	0.5625	1.0	1.	-0.30	0.0900	4.69
5	20.	18.95	-1.05	1.1025	5.0	25.	0.00	0.0000	5.25
			-----	------	---	---		------	----
			0.00	4.9500	0.0	64.		11.0250	33.37

$$SEE = \sqrt{4.95/5} = .995 \qquad MAPE = 33.37/5 = 6.67$$

```
R² = 1 - (4.95/64) = .9227 RBARSQ = 1 -(4.95/2)/(64/4) = .8453

DW = 11.025/4.95 = 2.2272 RHO = (2 - 2.2272)/2 = -.1136
```

Table 2.2: The Fit of the Equation

Another measure of closeness of fit is the ratio of S, the sum of squared residuals, to D, the sum of the squared deviations from the mean of the dependent variable, $\bar{y}$. These deviations are shown in the column labeled "d" in Table 2.2. This D is, to be explicit,

$$D = \sum_{t=1}^{T} (y_t - \bar{y}_t)^2$$

The ratio S/D would be zero for a perfect fit and 1.0 in the worst possible case (provided there is a constant term in the equation.)Since it seems a bit strange to have zero as the perfect score, the S/D ratio is subtracted from 1.0 to form what is called the "coefficient of multiple determination" or "R square" or RSQ for short,

$$R^2 = 1 - S/D$$

A "corrected" R^2, written with a bar over the R, and pronounced "R bar square" is often used to allow for the fact that as more and more independent variables are added to a regression, S goes to zero. In fact, if there are as many independent variables as there are observations, the fit will normally be perfect. For the corrected R^2, therefore, S is divided by $T - n$, the number of observations less the number of independent variables. The formula is

$$\bar{R}^2 = 1 - \frac{S/(T-n)}{D/(T-1)}$$

where n is the number of independent variables, counting the constant term. Where it is not convenient to use superscripts, we call this measure $RBARSQ$. The number $T - n$ is called the number of "degrees of freedom" in the regression.

An alternative measure of closeness of fit is the mean absolute percentage error, or $MAPE$, defined by

$$MAPE = \frac{100 * \sum_{t=1}^{T} \left| \dfrac{r_t}{y_t} \right|}{T}$$

Its calculation is illustrated in the last column of Table 2.2.

Although RSQ, $RBARSQ$, and $MAPE$ are all dimensionless pure numbers, there is no

63

absolute standard of "how good is good" for them. Generally, any equation whose dependent variable has a strong trend will have a high *RSQ* while equations with volatile, untrended dependent variables will have low *RSQ*. These measures are really useful only for comparing the fit of one equation for a particular variable with another equation for the same variable.

The columns of Table 2 labeled f and f^2 are explained in the next section.

Exercise

2.2   For the data in exercise 2.1, calculate also the *SEE*, *RSQ*, *RBARSQ*, and *MAPE*.

4. Measures of Autocorrelation and their Uses.

In addition to asking how well the equation fits, it is also usual to ask, To what extent does this equation tend to "go on making the same mistake"?That is, if it erred on the high side in one period is it likely to err on the high side in the next period?If so, the residuals are said to be autocorrelated. The Durbin-Watson statistic, DW, and RHO are both measures of autocorrelation of the residuals

$$r_t = \hat{y}_t - y_t$$

The Durbin-Watson statistic is

$$DW = \sum_{t=1}^{T-1} (r_{t+1} - r_t)^2 / S$$

and

$$RHO = (2 - DW)/2$$

is the autocorrelation coefficient, ρ. *RHO* is approximately the regression coefficient, ρ', of the equation

$$r_{t+1} = \rho' r_t$$

The formula for this regression coefficient is

$$\rho' = \frac{\sum_{t=1}^{T-1} r_{t+1} r_t}{\sum_{t=1}^{T-1} r_t r_t}$$

and

64

$$DW = \sum r_{t+1}^2 + \sum r_t^2 - 2 \sum r_{t+1} r_t$$

where all of the summations go from 1 to T - 1. For large values of T, the first two summations on the right and the summation in the denominator of ρ' differ insignificantly from S, so that -- as a close approximation --

$$DW = 2 - 2\rho' \quad \text{or} \quad \rho' = (2 - DW)/2.$$

The computation of DW and RHO for the example is shown in Table 2.2 in the columns labeled f and f^2 and at the bottom of the table. Here $f_t = r_{t+1} - r_t$. The ideal values are 2.0 for DW and 0.0 for RHO; but, as before, what is a good value of RHO depends on the variables in the equations. For some variables, it is easy to get RHO under .1, while for others a RHO of .5 may be quite an accomplishment. Some ailments caused by high values of RHO and some possible treatments for them are discussed in Chapter 9 in the section on the Hildreth-Lu technique. The definition of the Durbin-Watson statistic is included here because the statistic is reported by the $G7$ regression program. $G7$ includes it as a concession to the mores of the econometric profession. It is used for testing the hypothesis that there is no autocorrelation. The tests rest on assumptions that are rarely valid in building economic models and need not detain us here.

Knowing the value of RHO can be quite helpful when forecasting with an equation. Suppose, for instance, that we have data through the last quarter of 2006 and want to forecast the first quarter of 2007. We know, moreover, that RHO is .75 and that the equation predicted a value of 326 for 2006 fourth quarter, when the actual value was only 310. The residual was, therefore, 16. Now, for the first quarter of 2007, the equation is predicting a value of 340. You can accept the prediction at face value, or you can say to yourself, "I know this equation; if it has predicted too high in one period, it is likely to predict too high in the next. In fact, the best guess for that error is RHO times the last previous error. So I am going to assume that it is now missing on the high side by .75*16 = 12, and my forecast is going to be 340 - 12 = 328. And if I had to forecast the second quarter of 2007, I would subtract . 75*12 = 9 from whatever the equation predicts, and so on into the future." Forecasts which incorporate such adjustments are called "RHO-adjusted" forecasts. We will denote the standard error of estimate of such forecasts for one period ahead by "SEE+1".

Exercise

2.3 For the data of exercise 2.1, calculate also DW and RHO. Suppose that you know the independent variables for two periods further into the future, namely:

x1	x2	x3
1	9	7
1	10	9

Calculate forecasts for these two periods with and without the RHO adjustment.

5. Statistics for Each Independent Variable

We have now covered the overall characteristics of a regression equation which are normally displayed by *G7*, the regression program which goes with this book. You have seen three of these displays in connection with Model 5 in Chapter 1.

For each individual variable, however, you will see that there are displayed six items labeled: Reg-Coef, Mexval, Elas, NorRes, Mean, and Beta. The "Reg-coef" is, of course, just the regression coefficient, the *b* for each variable, which we have just learned to compute. The "Mean" is just the mean of the variable over the sample period. The "Elas" is the elasticity calculated at the means. This elasticity, the percentage by which the dependent variable will change if an independent variable changes by one percent, is often very useful for examining the economic content of the regression coefficients. In general, the elasticity of y with respect to x is

$$elas = (\delta y/y)/(\delta x/x) = (\delta y/\delta x)(x/y),$$

where δ indicates "change in". In a linear equation, such as

$$y = a + bx,$$

$(\delta y/\delta x) = b$, so elas $= b(x/y)$ depends upon the values of x and y at which it is evaluated. It is customary to evaluate at the means. In the numeric example we worked above, the elasticity of y with respect to x_2 is $.61*5/15 = .203$. What is the elasticity of y with respect to x_3?

The Mexval, or marginal explanatory value, of each variable is simply the percentage by which the SEE of the equation would increase if the variable were omitted from the equation and the coefficients of the remaining variables were adjusted to give the best possible fit without that variable. It helps us to see how important each variable is for the fit of the whole equation. Its calculation will be explained in section 8 of this chapter.

The Beta coefficient shows what the regression coefficient would be if the units of both the dependent and independent variables were changed so that the variance of each variable was 1.0. (The variance is the sum of squares of the deviations from the mean divided by the number of observations.) It is useful for judging the sensitivity of the dependent variable with respect to each independent variable. For example, in the equation for fixed investment in Chapter 1, the beta coefficient for the "replace" variable was .781, a coefficient which represents substantial sensitivity. If "replace" moves by one of its standard deviations, investment will move by about .8 of its standard deviations.

Many regression programs automatically give Student's *t*-statistics for each variable. It is intended for evaluating the "statistical significance" of the dependent variable for the equation. However, the estimate of the standard deviation involves several highly questionable assumptions, and the application of the Student t test to the variable requires even further dubious assumptions. For ordinary, everyday use, the simple, descriptive Mexval is, in my view, far preferable to the T-stat whose meaning depends on many dubious assumptions. If, however, you wish to see the t-values, give the command "showt yes". To return *G7* to its normal output display, the command is "showt no". Like Mexval, the calculation of T-Stat will be explained in the final section of this chapter. Activation of the "show t" option in this way also causes F statistics to be printed for each variable. These F values would be used for testing the combined statistical significance of that variable and all the following variables in the regression.

The NorRes column shows how the sum of squared residuals was gradually reduced as variables were added to the regression. The entry on row k shows the sum of squared residuals when the first k variables had been introduced divided by the corresponding sum when all variables had been introduced.

Exercise

2.4 . With the data of exercise 2.1, compute the elasticity of the dependent variable with respect to x2 and x3 at the means of all variables.

6. Matrix Notation for Regression

The calculations described in the previous section can all be expressed very neatly by a shorthand known as matrix notation. Without it, some of the things to be covered in this book just cannot be explained. Since it is easy to learn, and will smooth the way for the discussion in the third section of this chapter, we may as well take a moment to introduce it right here. Perhaps you are already acquainted with it; if so, just glance at equation (10m) and then skip to the last paragraph of the section.

To introduce matrices, let us consider again the equations we just solved. They were

$$
\begin{aligned}
5b_1 + 25b_2 + 25b_3 &= 75 \\
25b_1 + 225b_2 + 85b_3 &= 380 \\
25b_1 + 85b_2 + 171b_3 &= 415 .
\end{aligned}
$$

We could economize on b's and + signs if we would write them instead as

$$
\begin{pmatrix} 5 & 25 & 25 \\ 25 & 225 & 85 \\ 25 & 85 & 171 \end{pmatrix} \begin{pmatrix} b_1 \\ b_2 \\ b_3 \end{pmatrix} = \begin{pmatrix} 75 \\ 380 \\ 415 \end{pmatrix}
$$

We have changed nothing by this rewriting; we have just introduced a shorthand. Now let us

67

think of the array of numbers on the left as a single entity and call it **A**. This **A** is a matrix. In fact, any rectangular array of numbers is a matrix. The column of numbers on the right side is then also a matrix, but since it has only one column it may also be called a "vector". Because it is a vector, we will denote it with a lower case letter and call it **c**. The column of the unknown b's is also a vector, and we may as well call it **b**. Then the whole equation can be written as just

Ab = c.

In this equation, we say that the matrix **A** is "post multiplied" by the column **b**. What that means is fully explained by looking back at the original equations. Here are a couple of examples to check your understanding of multiplying a matrix by a vector:

$$\begin{pmatrix} 3 & 7 \\ 5 & 2 \\ 6 & 1 \end{pmatrix} \cdot \begin{pmatrix} 3 \\ 2 \end{pmatrix} = \begin{pmatrix} 23 \\ 19 \\ 20 \end{pmatrix} \qquad \begin{pmatrix} 3 & 1 & 2 \\ 2 & 0 & 8 \\ 3 & 6 & 4 \\ 4 & 1 & 0 \end{pmatrix} \cdot \begin{pmatrix} 2 \\ 1 \\ 5 \end{pmatrix} = \begin{pmatrix} 17 \\ 44 \\ 32 \\ 9 \end{pmatrix}$$

Note that in order to post multiply the matrix **A** by the column vector **b**, **b** must have the same number of rows that A has columns. The result will be a column with as many rows as **A** has rows. The number of rows and columns of a matrix are called its dimensions. The matrix on the left in the first example above is said to be "3 by 2", that is it has 3 rows and 2 columns. In general, we write "**A** is (m,n)" when we mean that A has m rows and n columns.

Now suppose that we have two matrices, A and B. If they are of the same dimensions, we can define their sum, A + B, as the matrix composed of the sums of the corresponding elements in the two matrices. For example,

$$\begin{pmatrix} 3 & 5 \\ 4 & 3 \end{pmatrix} + \begin{pmatrix} 2 & 1 \\ 3 & 5 \end{pmatrix} = \begin{pmatrix} 5 & 6 \\ 7 & 8 \end{pmatrix}$$

When it comes to the product of two matrices **AB**, however, we do not define it as the matrix composed of the products of corresponding elements. Rather we define it as the matrix whose first column is the product of **A** post-multiplied by the first column of **B**, and whose second column is the product of **A** post-multiplied by the second column of **B**, and so on. Here are two examples:

$$\begin{pmatrix} 3 & 5 \\ 4 & 3 \end{pmatrix} \cdot \begin{pmatrix} 2 & 1 \\ 3 & 5 \end{pmatrix} = \begin{pmatrix} 21 & 28 \\ 17 & 19 \end{pmatrix}$$

$$\begin{pmatrix} 3 & 2 & 1 \\ 2 & 5 & 3 \end{pmatrix} \cdot \begin{pmatrix} 5 & 2 \\ 1 & 3 \\ 2 & 1 \end{pmatrix} = \begin{pmatrix} 19 & 13 \\ 21 & 22 \end{pmatrix}$$

In order for the product **AB** to be defined, **B** must have as many rows as **A** has columns. The product will have as many rows as does **A** and as many columns as does **B**. In general **AB** will not be the same as **BA**, although there are important special cases in which they are the same.

It is easy to verify that **(A + B) + C = A + (B + C)** --the order in which we add matrices makes no difference -- and that **(AB)C = A(BC)** -- the order in which we multiply makes no difference. Also, as with ordinary numbers, multiplication is distributive over addition: **A(B + C) = AB + AC.**

To express our least-squares problem in terms of matrices, we need just one more concept, the transpose of a matrix. The transpose of **A**, denoted by **A'**, is the matrix whose first column is the first row of **A**, whose second column is the second row of **A,** and so on. For example, if **A** is the matrix given by

$$A \; = \; \begin{pmatrix} 5 & 2 \\ 1 & 3 \\ 2 & 1 \end{pmatrix}$$

then the transpose is

$$A' \; = \; \begin{pmatrix} 5 & 1 & 2 \\ 2 & 3 & 1 \end{pmatrix}$$

If **A = A'**, then the matrix must be square and is said to be symmetric. You can, with a little thought, see that **(AB)' = B'A'**.

Now let us use matrix notation to write in compact form the equations of section 2 of this chapter. We will denote by **X** the matrix of observations on the independent variables and by **y** the vector of observations on the dependent variable in our previous regression example. Thus,

$$X \; = \; \begin{pmatrix} 1 & 10 & 5 \\ 1 & 5 & 1 \\ 1 & 0 & 6 \\ 1 & 10 & 3 \\ 1 & 0 & 10 \end{pmatrix} , \qquad y \; = \; \begin{pmatrix} 17 \\ 10 \\ 12 \\ 16 \\ 20 \end{pmatrix}$$

Finally let **b** denote the vector of regression coefficients. We want to choose **b** to minimize S, the sum of squared residuals. In matrix notation, S is

(9m)   **S = (y - Xb)' (y - Xb).**

This equation has been numbered (9m) because it is the matrix way of writing equation (9) of section 2. The minimizing **b** vector is given by the equation

(10m)   **(X'X)b = X'y .**

It may take a moment to see that this equation (10m) is the same as the previous equation 10. But just write out **X'** and **X** and start forming the product **X'X**, and you will soon realize that you are

69

forming the matrix **A** with which we began this section. Note that **X'X** is symmetric.

How can we show the process of solution of linear equations in matrix notation? To do so we first need a special notation for any square matrix that has 1's on the diagonal running from top left to bottom right and is otherwise zero. Such a matrix is called an "identity" matrix and is therefore denoted by **I**. Note that for any matrix **M**, **IM** = **M** and **MI** = **M**, where **I** is an identity matrix of appropriate dimension. Suppose now that we have the matrix equations **Ax** = **c**, where **A** is a square matrix and **x** and **c** are vectors. If we can find some matrix **B** such that **AB** = **I**, then **A(Bc)** = **(AB)c** = **Ic** = **c**, so **x** = **Bc** is the solution of the equations **Ax** = **c**.

But how do we find the matrix **B**? Since $AB_1 = I_1$, $AB_2 = I_2$, and $AB_3 = I_3$, where the subscript denotes a column of **B** or **I**, we could just solve these equations one-by-one for the columns of B. There is, however, an easier way; we can solve them all at once. Table 2.3 shows how. In the first three rows and first four columns of each panel you will recognize the corresponding panel of Table 2.1. In the fifth column we have written the right-hand side of the equations $AB_1 = I_1$.

5.	25.	25.	75.	1.	0.	0.
25.	225.	85.	380.	0.	1.	0.
25.	85.	171.	415.	0.	0.	1.
75.	380.	415.	1189.	0.	0.	0.
1.	5.	5.	15.	0.2	0.	0.
0.	100.	-40.	5.	-5.	1.	0.
0.	-40.	46.	40.	-5.	0.	1.
0.	5.	40.	64.	-15.	0.	0.
1.	0.	7.	14.75	0.45	-0.05	0.
0.	1.	-0.4	0.05	-0.05	0.01	0.
0.	0.	30.	42.	-7.0	0.4	1.
0.	0.	42.	63.75	-14.75	-0.05	0.
1.	0.	0.	4.95	2.083	-0.143	-0.233
0.	1.	0.	0.61	-0.143	0.015	0.013
0.	0.	1.	1.4	-0.233	0.013	0.033
0.	0.	0.	4.95	-4.950	-0.610	-1.400

Table 2.3: Regression with Matrix Inversion

Now notice that if we carry the pivot operations through this column as well as the first four we will have in it in the fourth panel the solution of the equation $AB_1 = I_1$. Note that appending this extra column had absolutely no effect on the previous four columns. Nor did the fourth column, the original right-hand side of the equations, have any effect on what happened in the fifth column. We can, therefore, append the other columns of **I** as the last two columns of the first panel in Table 2.3, carry through the pivoting on them, and get in the top three rows of the last panel the matrix **B**. We have gotten the solution for three sets of equations for considerably less than three times the work required for one.

70

The matrix **B** which we have found in this way is called the "inverse" of **A** and is denoted by **A⁻¹**. xxxFrom its construction, we know that $AA^{-1} = I$. It is also true that $A^{-1}A = I$, for if we start from the last panel of Table 2.3 and think of it as representing the equations $A^{-1}C = I$ where A^{-1} is known and **C** is unknown, we can solve these equations for **C** by retracing our steps one-by-one back up Table 2.3 and discover that $C = A$. So $A^{-1}A = I$. Thus, every right inverse is also a left inverse.

We will also often use the fact that the inverse of a symmetric matrix is itself symmetric. If A = A', then

$$I = (AA^{-1})' = (A^{-1})'A' = (A^{-1})'A$$

and post multiplying both sides of this equation by A^{-1} gives

$$A^{-1} = (A^{-1})' ,$$

which is to say, A^{-1} is symmetric.

We can now summarize our discussion so far in one equation: the regression coefficients are given by the equation

(12) $b = (X'X)^{-1}X'y.$

For future reference, we need one more concept, the trace of a square matrix. The trace is simply the sum of the diagonal elements. Thus, if **C** is (m,m), then the trace of **C**, *tr* **C**, is just

$$tr\, C = \sum_{t=1}^{m} c_{ii}$$

If **A** is (m,n) and **B** is (n,m) then **AB** and **BA** are both defined but are not generally equal to one another or even of the same dimension. But both are square so that *tr(AB)* and *tr(BA)* are both defined. Now it is a remarkable and useful theorem that *tr(AB) = tr(BA)*. To see why this is true, just note that any element of **A**, say a_{13}, will enter into the sum that forms *tr(AB)* exactly once and that one time it will be multiplied by the symmetrically placed element of **B**, b_{31}. Now notice that the element also enters *tr(BA)* exactly once and is again multiplied by the same element of **B**. Thus the sums that form *tr(AB)* and *tr(BA)* consist of exactly the same elements and must therefore be equal to one another. Working a small example will make this proof plain.

Exercise

2.5 For the data of exercise 2.1, compute $(X'X)^{-1}$, then $X'y$, and then, by matrix multiplication, $b = (X'X)^{-1}X'y$.

7. A Shortcut to the Sum of Squared Residuals

The last row of each panel of Table 2.3 provides a short-cut to the calculation of S, the sum of squared residuals. We have not yet explained this row. In the top panel, it contains the row vector $(y'X, y'y)$, which is the transpose of the fourth column, so the first four rows and columns form a symmetric matrix. As we generate the successive panels, we carry through the pivot operations on the last row just as on the other rows.

Now let me point out a surprising "coincidence". In the fourth panel of Table 2.3 we find, in the position where $y'y$ was originally, the number 4.95. This is exactly the value that we got for S by a totally different procedure in Table 2.2. Can it be that we can find the sum of squares by pivoting instead of by calculating all of the residuals, squaring them and summing? Yes, that is true. And it is useful in many ways. Let us see why it is so.

By the time we reach the last panel in Table 2.3, we will have subtracted from the original last row some combination of the rows above it and gotten, in the first three positions, zeroes. What combination of the rows above it did we subtract? Since we originally had in those positions $y'X$ and, after subtracting we have 0, we must have subtracted a combination, given by the row vector c, such that $c(X'X) = y'X$. In fact, this c is really just b', the transpose of the vector of regression coefficients, for

$$(X'X)b = X'y$$

so

$$b'(X'X)' = y'X$$

and

$$b'(X'X) = y'X$$

since $(X'X)' = X'X$. Therefore what has been subtracted from the final position of this last row is $b'X'y$. What was originally in it was $y'y$, so what is left is $y'y - b'(X'y)$. The direct approach to calculating S first calculates

$$r = y - Xb = y - X(X'X)^{-1}X'y$$

and then forms

$$
\begin{aligned}
S \quad &= r'r \\
&= y'y - y'X(X'X)^{-1}X'y - y'X(X'X)^{-1}X'y + \\
&\quad y'X(X'X)^{-1}X'X(X'X)^{-1}X'y \\
\\
&= y'y - y'X(X'X)^{-1}X'y = y'y - b'X'y,
\end{aligned}
$$

which is exactly what the pivoting gave.

Now suppose for a moment that we had set out to regress x_2 on x_1. We would have formed exactly the same 2-by-2 matrix that we see in the upper left corner of panel 1 of Table 2.3 and the final result would have been the 2-by-2 in the upper left corner of panel 2. The value of S for this problem would have been 100 and the regression coefficient would have been 5. Similarly, if x_3 had

72

been regressed on x_1, the value of S would have been 46 and regression coefficient 5. (Because x_1 is the constant 1, the regression coefficients are the means, and the values of S are the sum of squared deviations from the means.) *In general, we see that in panel i+1, after i pivot operations, we can see the regression coefficients and values of S for the regression on the first i variables of each of the remaining variables.* Thus, the regression panels show a great deal about the relations among the variables. Can you give an interpretation for the element in the third row and fourth column of the third panel (the number is 42)?

For computing the NorRes (Normalized sum of squared Residuals) coefficients shown in the standard *G7* display of results, it is necessary only to store away the value of S, the value in the lower right corner of the array, at each iteration. These values are then all divided by the last of them to produce the NorRes display.

Please note that each pivot element was the S value for the variable about to be introduced when regressed on all the previous values. If a pivot element is zero, the regression cannot continue; but a zero pivot can occur only if the variable about to be introduced was perfectly explained by the previous variables. If this happens when, say the third variable is about to be introduced, the *G7* program will give the message "Variable 3 is a linear combination of preceding variables," and will abort that particular regression.

A moment's study of Table 2.3 shows that in each panel three of the columns are the columns of the identity matrix. In working with a computer, these identity columns just waste space, and it is usual to store only the non-identity columns of the matrix, as shown below in Table 2.4. I will refer to this sort of table as regression with compact inversion.

Exercise

2.6   Extend your previous computation with the data of exercise 2.1 to include the "dependent variable" row in each computation. What is S when only x1 is used as an explanatory variable? When only x1 and x2 are used? When all three are used? What are the regression coefficients for x3 regressed on x1 and x2?

8. Mexvals and Derivatives -- Measures of the Importance of Each Variable

So far, we have not developed a way to say anything about how important any particular variable is to the whole equation. One measure designed to help in answering this question is the "mexval" of a variable. A variable's mexval, or marginal explanatory value, is defined as the percentage that *SEE* will increase if the variable is omitted from the regression and not replaced by any other, though the coefficients on the remaining variables are adjusted to do as well as possible without their departed comrade.

5	25	25	75
25	225	85	380
25	85	171	415
75	380	415	1189
0.2	5	5	15
-5.0	100	-40	5
-5.0	-40	46	40
-15.0	5	40	64
0.45	-0.05	7.0	14.75
-0.05	0.01	-0.4	0.05
-7.0	0.4	30.0	42.0
-14.75	-0.05	42.0	63.75
2.083	-0.143	-0.233	4.95
-0.143	0.015	0.013	0.61
-0.233	0.013	0.033	1.40
-4.950	-0.610	-1.400	4.95

Figure 2.4: Regression with Compact Inversion

Mexval is easily calculated in the process of regression with compact inversion. With n independent variables, this form of regression leads to a final panel like this:

a_{11} ... a_{1n} a_{1m}

... ...

a_{n1} ... a_{nn} a_{nm}

a_{m1} ... a_{mn} a_{mm}

where $m = n + 1$. Remember that the lower right element is the sum of squared residuals. Note also that the values of the a's do not depend upon the order in which the row reduction was done, that is, in regression terms, they do not depend on the order of introduction of the variables. Let us suppose that variable i was the last to be introduced and let us denote the elements of the panel before its introduction with a'. Then we have the following relation between the a and a':

$a_{ii} = 1/a'_{ii}$ and $a'_{ii} = 1/a_{ii}$

$a_{im} = a'_{im}/a'_{ii}$ and $a'_{im} = a_{im}/a_{ii}$

$a_{mm} = a'_{mm} - a'_{im}a'_{im}/a'_{ii}$ and $a'_{mm} = a_{mm} + a_{im}a_{im}/a_{ii}$

Thus, the drop in the sum of squares of the residuals as variable i was introduced -- and the increase in that sum of squares if it is now excluded from the equation -- is a_{im}^2/a_{ii}.

The standard error of estimate of the equation would therefore rise from

74

to

$$SEE = \text{sqrt } (a_{mm}/T)$$

$$SEE' = \text{sqrt } ((a_{mm} + a_{im}^2/a_{ii})/T).$$

where T is the number of observations. Therefore,

$$\text{mexval}_i \quad = 100*((SEE'/SEE)-1)$$
$$= 100*(\text{sqrt}(1+(a_{im}^2/a_{ii}a_{mm}))-1).$$

For the example of the text, we find

$$\text{mexval}_1 = 100*(\text{sqrt}(1 + (4.95^2/(2.083*4.95)))\ -1) = 83.74$$
$$\text{mexval}_2 = 100*(\text{sqrt}(1 + (\ .61^2/(0.015*4.95)))\ -1) = 143.0$$
$$\text{mexval}_3 = 100*(\text{sqrt}(1 + (1.40^2/(0.033*4.95)))\ -1) = 258.9\ .$$

(The numbers at the right are calculated from a more precise inverse than that shown above.)

The insights of this section and the last can be combined to calculate the derivatives of regression coefficients with respect to one another. Suppose that we were to decide that we did not trust the value provided by regression for the coefficient of some variable and that we wanted to fix the value of that coefficient. What effect would that fixing have on the other coefficients? More precisely, what would be the derivatives of the other coefficients with respect to that coefficient, if the others are determined to minimize the sum of squared errors, given the value of the fixed coefficient? Suppose the original equation was written $y = Xb + Zc + r$, where Z is a T-by-1 vector and c is a scalar. We are asking, What is the derivative of the least-squares value of b with respect to c? The least squares estimate of b, given c, is $b = (X'X)^{-1}(X'y - X'Zc)$, from which it is clear that the derivative of the vector b with respect to the scalar c is

$$db/dc = - (X'X)^{-1}(X'Z),$$

which is just the negative of the regression coefficients of Z on all the other variables. Now think of Z as one more independent variable. This negative of the regression coefficients of Z on the columns of X is just the negative of what would have been in Z's column before it was pivoted on. To get it back, we just unpivot. In the notation developed in this section, if we want to think of Z as column i, we want a'_{ji}. From the pivot operation, we have $a_{ji} = 0 - a'_{ji}/a'_{ii}$ and $a_{ii} = 1/a'_{ii}$. These may be solved for $-a'_{ji} = a_{ji}/a_{ii}$. In other words, to get the derivatives of all of the regression coefficients with respect to coefficient i, we just divide the ith column of $(X'X)^{-1}$ by its diagonal element. These derivatives are very useful for seeing the sensitivity of one coefficient with respect to another. I have often seen it happen that an equation has several coefficients with nonsensical values, but by fixing one of the coefficients to a sensible value, the others also became sensible. The derivatives are useful for spotting such situations.

2.7   Compute the mexvals for x1, x2, and x3 with the data of exercise 2.1. Compute the derivative of b_1 and b_3 with respect to b_2.

9. Leverage, a Measure of the Influence of Individual Observations

We mentioned in discussing the fitting of simple regressions by eye that one of the advantages of that method was that it made clear which observations were outliers -- observations which, if included, would have a lot of influence on the regression coefficients. Spotting outliers can be important because the data at the outlier point may be erroneous. One simple indicator of outlier observations is the "leverage" variable, defined, for observation t, simply as the derivative of the predicted value at t, $\hat{y}_t$ with respect to the observed value at t, y_t. If this derivative is very high for a particular observation, that observation must have a strong influence on one or more of the regression coefficients. Such observations should be checked for the accuracy of the data; if the data is accurate, however, the observation should not be discarded, for it is precisely the observation which, by standing out from the others, reveals what the equation really is.

The leverage variable is easily calculated. The vector of predicted values is

$$\hat{y}_t \ = \ Xb \ = \ X\,(X\,{}'\,X\,)^{-1}X\,{}'\,y$$

so the derivative of the predicted value at t, $\hat{y}_t$, with respect to the observed value at t, y_t, is simply the tth diagonal element of the matrix $X(X'X)^{-1}X'$. Obviously, if we want only the diagonals of this matrix, we do not have to compute the whole matrix to find them. Rather, we could pre-multiply the first column of X' by $(X'X)^{-1}$ and then pre-multiply this column by the first row of X to get the first element of the leverage vector.

Note that leverage uses only values of X, not of y, and that observations other than the first entered the calculation of the leverage on the first observation only through the $(X'X)^{-1}$ matrix.

The leverage variable is automatically computed and placed in the workspace bank with the name *lever* after each regression in *G7*. It may be graphed or displayed like any other variable.

CHAPTER 3. INTRODUCTION TO G 7.3

From Chapter 1, you are already somewhat familiar with *G7*, the regression and modeling program we will be using throughout this book. It is part of a closely integrated package of programs that can both estimate a single equation or build a multisectoral model involving hundreds of equations. In Chapter 1, I tried to tell you as little about *G7* as I could; I wanted to concentrate on the logical succession of models. Here we will proceed more systematically through the basic functions of *G7*. Please pardon some occasional repetition of what you already know.

1. Tutorial of the Basics

Double click on the *G7* icon to start the program. You will be immediately given a choice of folder (formerly called directory) in which to start *G7*. This step is necessary because *G7* looks for a g.cfg file in the folder from which it starts, and this file determines the characteristics of the workspace which G creates and the initial assigned data bank. For this tutorial, you should select the c:\ami folder. To do so, you should click "Browse" on the screen that appears when you start the program until the c:\ami folder comes into view and then *double* click the ami folder or (b) single click the ami folder and tap the 'Enter' key, or (c) enter c:\ami\g.cfg in the edit box at the bottom of the window. Whatever route you choose, you should see "c:\ami" in this box. Then click the OK button, or tap Alt-O. The folder selection form disappears. Click OK again to proceed.

You then see the *G7* main form. It has a menu at the top, a few speed buttons, a white, one-line *command box,* and a large blue *results* area. Click on the Bank menu and select Look. You will see a list of the assigned banks. Select one of them and click OK. A window opens in the upper right of the screen. It has a list of the data series in the assigned bank. Run the cursor down the list until you find one that interests you. Tap 'Enter'. Below you will see a graph and to the left, in the results area, the numerical values of the series. (The first number in each line is the date of the first observation in that line; then follow the data for four successive quarterly observations.) The cursor will have gone back to the command box, but if you wish to see another series, click on the "look" window again and continue looking. If you tap a letter key, the cursor will move to the next entry beginning with that letter. To find a word or phrase, like "Personal income", click on Find in the menu and fill in the box. Note that you can search up or down from where you are in the file.

Now let us suppose that you would like to run a regression of real Gross private fixed investment on past changes in real GDP and an estimate of the investment required to replacement capital that is wearing out. If the cursor is not already in the command box, click there. We first set the limits for the regression, the starting and ending dates. To make the regression go from 1975 first quarter to 2013 third quarter, type

    lim 1975.1 2013.3

and tap 'Enter'. (If your data bank has data more recent than the third quarter of 2013, by all means use it.) You should see your command echoed in the results area. Then give a title to the regression with something like

```
ti Gross Private Domestic Fixed Investment
```

Next, you must form *d*, the first difference of real GDP by

```
f   d = gdpR - gdpR[1]
```

The remaining variable we need is requirements for replacement, which you may calculate by

```
f   replace = .05*@cum(stockf,vfR[4],.05)
```

It is not necessary for the regression, but you may be interested to see how this replacement compares with investment spending. To draw a graph with the two, type

```
gr replace vfR
```

Now you are ready for the regression itself. Just type

```
r vfR = replace, d[1], d[2], d[3], d[4], d[5], d[6], d[7], d[8], d[9], d[10], d[11]
```

There should now appear in the results area the numeric display similar to what you saw for Model 5 in Chapter 1. The font in the results area is set small so that you see most of the regression output. Many people, however, find that it is uncomfortably small. If you want a larger font click File | Auto Font Size, so as to remove the check mark by this item. Then click File | Font and set the size. Personally, I often pick the font called Fixedsys, which cannot be sized but the one available size works nicely. You should, however, stick to a monotype font, that is, one in which all letters are the same width. You may also set the font color and "script" or character set. If you are using titles and comments in a language such as Greek, Russian, Turkish, or Polish with characters that do not appear in the Western European languages, be sure to select the proper character set for the results window. It will be automatically carried over to the editor, the look command, and other displays. By clicking File | Background color, you can select the background color of the results window. Your choice of font (typeface, size, color, and character set) and your choice of background color will be remembered when you next start *G7*. (This generally pleasant feature can be confusing if you are using *G7* on a public machine in a computer lab; you will start off with the settings of the previous user.)

To obtain the graph of the regression just done, give the command

```
gr *
```

To see the graph better, it may be maximized by clicking the maximize button, the middle button in the upper right corner of the graph. Click again the button in the same place to get the graph back to its original size. If you would like to save the graph for comparison with later graphs, select Graph | Shift1 from the main menu. The graph shifts to a smaller window in the upper right of the screen. You can also use Graph | Shift2. Thus, you can view three different graphs at once.

In order to save your work, you should put the commands necessary to do regressions into files and then execute (or *add*) those files. To put them in a file, open the *G7* editor. Click Editor on the main menu and a simple editor opens in the upper right screen. Type into it

```
lim 1975.1 2013.3
ti  Gross Private Domestic Fixed Investment
f    d = gdpR - gdpR[1]
f    replace = .05*@cum(stockf,vfR[4],.05)
r    vfR = replace, d[1], d[2], d[3], d[4], d[5], d[6], d[7], d[8], d[9], d[10], d[11]
gr   *
```

On the Editor's menu, select File | Save as, and save the file with the name vfR.reg. Then to execute it, simply click Run in the editor menu. (Clicking Run also saves the file to your disk.) Alternatively, if the file you want to run is not already in the editor, you can do File | Execute and in the window which then opens, you may either click the name of the file and then OK, or type in the name and tap 'Enter'. Either way, you should now see the results and be faced with a "dialog" box demanding to know what you want done with the graph. For the moment, click the Continue button.

A third way to execute your vfR.reg file is to enter the command


```
add vfR.reg
```

in the white command box. The results are exactly the same.

Your command file, vfR.reg, is fine so far, but it does not save the results in a way which can be put into a paper or included into a model. Click back on the editor window and modify the file there so that it is

```
addprint y
catch vfR.cat
save vfR.sav
gdates 1975.1 2013.3
lim 1975.1 2013.3
ti Gross Private Domestic Fixed Investment
f d = gdpR - gdpR[1]
f replace = .05*@cum(stockf,vfR[4],.05)
r vfR = replace, d[1], d[2],d[3],d[4],d[5],
    d[6],d[7],d[8],d[9],d[10],d[11]
gr *
save off
gname vfR
gr *
catch off
```

The new material is in bold. Save this file and "run" it again. (You will find that the command box remembers your previous commands. You can get them back either with the down and up arrow keys or by clicking on the arrow at the right end of the command box.)

When the program stops and demands to know what to do with the graph, click the Save button.

You will have made three new files:

vfR.sav	The results to be used later by the computer in building a model. This file was made by the "save vfR.sav ... save off" pair of commands.
vfR.cat	The results to be brought into a word processor. This file was made by the "catch vfR.cat ... catch off" pair of commands.
vfR.wmf	The graph in a form to be brought into a word processor. This file was made when you clicked "Save" on the "Continue add file" dialog box.

You can look at vfR.sav with *G7*'s editor. If the aqua green editor window is showing, click on the Open item on its menu and open vfR.sav file. Otherwise, first click Editor on the main menu to create an editor window. You will see that the vfR.sav file contains the commands to create the variables and the regression results written as an equation.

To appreciate the uses of the other two files, you should open your word processor. You may first minimize *G7* by clicking on the little square in the upper right with the _ in it. Then open your word processor and import vfR.cat into it. In WordPerfect or Word, use the command Insert | File. In OpenOffice Writer, you need to open the file in one window, and then copy and paste it into your document. When you do so, you are apt to find that the columns look wavy. To correct that problem, put the imported text into a monotype font such as Courier or Line printer. To do so, select the text whose font you want to change, click on the button whose caption shows your present font, and select from the list. If you are using fonts that contain a number of different character sets, such as Cyrillic, Greek, West European, East European, you should be sure to select also the "script" (= character set) you desire.

When you clicked "Save" on the "Continue add file" dialog box, you caused the graph to be saved as a Windows metafile, a file which has the instructions for redrawing the file on any device supported by Windows. This file has the name vfR.wmf. It may be imported into a word processing program such as WordPerfect, Word or OpenOffice. In WordPerfect, the command is the same as to import text -- Insert | File. Word needs more help from you; the command is Insert | Picture. When it is first imported, the graph may be small; but it can be stretched by dragging with the mouse. Getting graphs to go where you want them when you have a number of graphs on a page is a problem with all present word processors. In WordPerfect, you have a choice of attaching the graph to a page, paragraph, or character. Probably character is your best choice.

You should now close the word processor and return to *G7*.

Let us explore the other options on the "Continue add file" dialog box. To do so, give the command "add vfR.reg" again. (By using the up and down arrow keys you can find this command among those already executed and just execute it again.) The program will stop, as before, with the "Continue add file" dialog box demanding to know what to do with the graph. The simplest answer is to click the "Cont." button to continue the add file, throwing away the graph. Next to it on the right is the "Stop" button, which exits from the command file. Further to the right are the "Max" and "Normal" buttons which blow up the graph to fill the full screen and restore it to its normal size, respectively. Then comes the "Save" button, which, as we know, saves the graph as a Windows metafile with the filename specified by a previous gname command. The "Print" button sends the graph directly to the printer. The "Shift1" and "Shift2" buttons move the graph to storage areas 1 and 2 where the graph remains visible as the add file moves on to subsequent commands. A graph in these storage areas can also be resized.

In working with multisectoral models, it is common to have add-files which draw graphs for many sectors. Especially for use with them, "gname" can be started with a name and number, for example:

```
gname out 1
```

The name of the save file for the first graph drawn will then be out1.wmf, for the second out2.wmf, and so on. Note that the numbers increase with each graph drawn whether or not it is saved.

If you have a graph showing and would like to save it but are not in an add file and do not have an appropriate name already assigned for the file, use Graph | Save from the main menu. You will be prompted for a file name.

The next step is to use add-files within add-files. Look at the runall.reg with the editor. You will find

```
fdates 1960.1 2013.3
lim 1975.1 2013.3
add vfR.reg
add viR.reg
add mR.reg
```

The "fdates" command sets the range of dates over which the "f" commands work. (The default fdates are the same as the default regression limits in specified in the g.cfg file.) Adding or executing this one file will cause three other files to be executed. Try it. After the first graph has been drawn, you will find that the program stops and demands that you tell it what to do with the graph. The simplest answer is to click the "Cont." button to continue the add file, throwing away the graph.

At this point, your first results on the blue screen will have scrolled out of sight. But you can use the scroll bars on the blue results window to bring them back into view. You can, by the way, use standard Windows cut-and-paste techniques to move material from this window to a word processor. The result may be somewhat disconcerting at first, for the color of the text (yellow) will move with the text but not the color of the background. If your word processor document has a white background, you will then have yellow text on a white background. In WordPerfect, the reveal codes key allows you to find the color change command and delete it, revealing the text in the normal text color. In Word or OpenOffice, commands in the Format menu control these colors.

As you work, the results window may become so full that tiny movements of the scroll bar produce big changes in what text is shown. You can clear the results window at any time by clicking File | Clear results or by giving the "clear" command in the command box or in an "add" file. The results area is large but not infinite. If you come close to filling it up, the oldest part at the top is automatically deleted.

You will notice also the item File | Auto font size. By clicking it, you can toggle a check mark next to it. If the check mark is visible, then widening or narrowing the results window by dragging its right border with the mouse will cause the size of the font to change so that the basic regression display fills the screen. If you do not want this automatic change in the size of the font, click this item so that the check mark disappears. This feature has no effect if using the FixedSys font, which gives type of pleasant size and clarity.

All of the commands under the Edit item on the main menu apply to the results window.

The Help menu explains the commands available from the command line in G. See especially the help reference section.

2. Digression on Graphs in G

While it is very simple to get a quick graph in *G7*, it is also possible to refine the graph. In order to produce nice looking reports, it is worth digressing from model building for a moment to learn what sorts of graphs you can make.

The dates over which series are graphed is controlled by the "gdates" command. This command may be followed by two or three dates, for example:

```
gdates 1980.1 2013.3
gdates 1980.1 2013.3 2017.4
```

Graphs drawn following the first of these commands will cover the period 1980.1 — 2013.3. Graphs drawn following the second cover the same period but have a vertical line following 2013.3. This vertical line is useful, for example, to divide history from forecast or the period over which a regression was fit from the period over which it was tested. Exception: graphs drawn with the "gr *" command use dates set by the "limits" command for the previous regression.

For greater variety in your graphs, choose Graph | Settings on the main menu. You will get a window for setting the characteristics of up to seven lines on the graphs. You can select the color, width (in pixels), style (solid, dotted, dashed, dash dot, and dash dot dot -- these work only for lines 1 pixel wide), mark, fill, and left and right parameters. The last three apply only if the type "bar" is chosen for the mark. The fill has to do with what sort of hatching appears in bars. The left and right parameters, numbers between 0 and 1, show where, within the space allocated for the bar, the left and right edges of the bar go. For example, with left = .1 and right = .9, the bar will be in the center of the allowed space, and the bars will be four times as wide (.8 units) as the space between them (.2 units). To eliminate the line connecting points marked by bars, set its width to zero. Experiment with what you can do with these options. If you wish to save your graph settings for a future run of G, click the "Save to file" button at the bottom of the screen. You will be asked for a filename. Any valid file name is acceptable, but let us suppose you say "graphs.set". Then the next time you start G you can give the command "add graphs.set" and have your settings back. You can even add at the bottom of the g.cfg file the line

```
Initial command; add graphs.set
```

and you will automatically have back your settings.

Normally, *G7* automatically adjusts the vertical scale to include all points on any series being graphed, but only the top, bottom and middle of the vertical scale are labeled. You can, however, control the vertical range of the graph with the "vrange" or "vr" command. For example:

```
vr 0 500 1000 1500 2000
```

will cause graphs to be drawn with a range from 0 to 2000 and horizontal lines at 0, 500, 1000, 1500, and 2000. These lines will be labeled. The default is to put the labels inside the box of the graph, but you can put them outside by first giving the vertical axis label command, "vaxl". It can be

```
vaxl out
```

to put them outside the frame of the graph or

```
vaxl in
```

to put them inside the frame. The "vr" command continues in force until another *vr* command is given. To simply turn it off and go back to the default, use

```
vr off
```

One particularly useful form of the "vr" command is

```
vr 0
```

which sets the lower boundary of the following graphs to be 0, while the top is picked by the program to fit in the highest point in any series. Try graphing gdpR with careful vertical axis labeling done with the "vr" and "vaxl" commands.

In addition to the "title" command, which we have used frequently, there is the "subtitle" command, which can be abbreviated to "subti", which provides a subtitle for the graph. The title and subtitle remain until replaced by another title or subtitle. To remove either of them altogether, just give the command immediately followed by a carriage return. The "legend" command controls whether or not the legend normally at the bottom of the graph is included or not. The format is "legend yes" or "legend no". Try using the "subtitle" and "legend" commands.

In working with multisectoral models, it is common to have add files which draw graphs for many sectors. Especially for use with them, "gname" can the started with a name and number, thus

```
gname out 1
```

The name of the save file for the first graph drawn will then be out1.wmf, for the second out2.wmf, and so on. Note that the numbers increase with each graph drawn whether or not it is saved.

Besides the ordinary "gr" command, there are three other variants of it. The "mgr" or "multi graph" command chooses a separate scale for each series graphed. For example, you may want to put the Treasury bill rate, *rtb*, and Residential construction, *vfrR*, on the same graph. But they have totally different scales. The answer is to make the graph with "mgr", for example, "mgr rtb vfrR". Try it.

Semi-logarithmic graphs are popular because series growing at a constant percent per year appear as straight lines. It is, however, often desirable to label the vertical axis in the original units. This is done by the "lgr" command. For example, to graph the Standard and Poor's composite index of 500 stocks from 1980.1 to 2011.3, we could do

```
f lsp500 = @log(sp500)
vr 100 200 400 800 1600 3200 4800
gdates 1980.1 2011.3
lgr lsp500
```

Do it and note the straightness of the line and the labeling of the vertical axis in the original units.

Finally, for graphs in which the horizontal axis is not time but some other variable, use the "sgr"or "scatter graph" command. For details, see the help file.

3. Building a Model

From Chapter 1, we are already familiar with building and running models that do not include regression equations. The last model, Model 5, involved regression, but we did not build or run it. Here we add the inclusion of regression equations and review all the steps.

Four of the six steps in building a model appear under the Model menu item. The first step is to **create a master file** which specifies the regression result files — the .sav files — which will be used in the model and other identities necessary for the model. Selecting Model | Master will show the current contents of the master file in the editor. Note that each regression equation is brought into the model with a command of the form "add xxx.sav" , where xxx is the usually the name of the dependent variable in the regression. This must be the same name that appeared on the "save" line in the .reg file by which the equation was estimated. When you are adding an equation to the model, the first thing you should do is to modify the master file to include the new equation. Generally, it is not crucially important where the "add" command appears, but it is natural to place it after the determination of the explanatory (right-hand-side) variables which it uses.

At the bottom of the master file there should be one or more "check" commands. Model 5, for example, has the command

```
check cR   .2
```

The check commands control the iterative solution of simultaneous models as explained relative to Model 5 in Chapter 1.

Note carefully that you conclude the editing of a Master file by clicking Save on the editor menu — **not** by clicking Run. You want to use the Master file as input into the Build program, not the G program. Clicking Run will accomplish nothing useful and may consume a good bit of time as you respond to various "bad command" messages.

The second step is to **estimate all the equations** and save the results in .sav files. This step is not mentioned under the Model menu items, because it is involves all the other capabilities of G. We have already seen several examples and the following chapters have many more.

The third step is to **build the model**. This step is accomplished by selecting Model | Build. For it to work completely, the C compiler must have been installed. This step runs the Build program, which reads the master file and all the .sav files, writes a C++ program, heart.cpp, to execute the model, and compiles and links this program to produce an executable file, run.exe, which is the model in the form of a program ready to run. This step also creates:

bws	A data bank containing all the variables used in the model.
run.gr	A command file for G to graph all the variables in the model.
run.err	A record of all the diagnostic information provided by the Build program. Be sure to check it by looking at it with the editor. If you have included the command "addtype y" in your Master file, this file will also contain everything in the Master file and in the files which are "added." If you include at the top of the Master file the command "checkdup y", Build will check every "f" or "fex" command to see if it is calculating a variable which has been calculated before and, if so, whether the values are identical. This check is a powerful way to spot a source of frequent errors in building models. Check your run.err file often.
exogall.reg	A command file for *G7* to create mechanical projections of all exogenous variables in the model by regressing them on time. Look at exogall.reg to see what it does. The projections will be put into files with the variable name as the name of the file and "xog" as the extension.
run.xog	A file to use all the .xog files made by running exogall.reg.
skipall.fix	A file to "skip" the calculation of all the variables calculated by regression equations. When all the regression equations are skipped, these variables become essentially exogenous and the model becomes tautological. Hence, its historical simulation should completely reproduce history. If it fails to do so, there is something wrong with the identities. Since it is *very* easy to make mistakes in the identities, it is always important to run a model with all regressions skipped. This file makes it easy to do so.
run.nam	A file with the names of all variables in the model and their numbers necessary to read the

	heart.cpp program should you have to do so. With luck, you won't need to ever look at heart.cpp or run.nam.
heart.dat, heart.dim, run.lag, run.map	These files are internal to the system. You should not need to ever look at them.

The fourth step is to **run the model**. It is accomplished by selecting Model | Run. You will be asked to fill in a form with the starting and stopping dates, the name of the output bank, and the name of the "fix" file. For the quarterly demonstration model, use the most recent twenty years for which you have data. The first simulation can be a historical one with actual values for all of the exogenous variables. Hence we may name the output bank "histsim". The "fix" files are where we specify various alternative scenarios or assumptions for forecasts. For the moment, we want a fix file with only rho adjustment values. This file is called rhoadj.fix, but we leave off the .fix in entering its name in the dialog box. When you click the OK button, you get a] prompt. Give a full title to your run, something like

```
ti Historical Simulation of Model 4
```

You get the] prompt again, and you type "run", and the model runs.

The fifth step is to **look at the results graphically**. To do so for a historical simulation, we need to assign in one bank the actual data in the bws bank and in another the alternative for comparison — here histsim. We do so with the commands

```
bank histsim b
bank bws   c
```

Then we have a number of "title", "gname", and "graph" commands to make the graphs. We can put all of these in an add file, such as hist.shw, when we execute the file by

```
add hist.shw
```

A simple hist.shw file is may look like this:

```
bank histsim b
bank bws c
gdates 1980.1 2013.3
title GDPR -- REAL GROSS DOMESTIC PRODUCT
gname gdpR
gr b.gdpR c.gdpR

title cR -- CONSUMPTION
gname gcR
gr b.cR c.cR

title vfR -- GROSS PRIVATE FIXED INVESTMENT
gname vfR
gr b.vfR c.vfR
```

and so on for as many series as we want to graph. In the "gr" lines, the "b." and "c." tell *G7* to look for these series in and only in bank b or bank c, respectively. The effect of this command, therefore, is to graph the gdpR series from histsim as the first line, the red line, and then to graph the gdpR series from bws as the second, the blue line. The result is a graph with the actual historical course of gdpR shown in blue (true is blue) and the model's calculated gdpR shown in red.

The sixth step is to **make tables**. Table-making is found on the Model | Tables menu item. Selecting this item brings up a form for preparing input data to the *Compare* program, which will actually make the tables. At the top of the form, you are asked for the name of the "stub" file. The stub file fundamentally gives the names of the series to be put into the table and the dates to be listed. It may contain, however, many commands to the *Compare* program which are described in the *G7* help files. An appropriate initial stub for the *AMI* model is in the file ami.stb, so put "ami" in the stub file edit window. We will come back to the contents of the stub file in a moment.

At the top right of the form is space for the name of the "output file," the text file which will be produced as the output of the comparison. An acceptable entry would be "histsim.out".

Next, you must specify how you want to show the alternative bank. The base bank, the first, will always be shown in actual values. The others, however, may be shown as deviations from the base, as percentage deviations from the base, or as actual values. Usually — but not always — the best choice is deviations, so that is the default value.

Then we must enter the types and names of the banks we want to compare. The types are easy: throughout Parts 1 and 2 of this book, the type is always *workspace*. Since we are making a comparison of a the histsim bank against the bws bank, put "bws" in the name field for the first bank and "histsim" in the name field for the second bank. Then click OK.

Compare is a console application program; it will run in a window. Normally, there is nothing to do except tap any key when the program has finished. However, if *Compare* finds fault with your commands, it will let you know in this window, so look for messages before blithely tapping a key.

When *Compare* has finished and the window has closed, look at the output file, histsim.out, in our example, with the editor. Be sure that the editor is using a monospaced font, such as Courier, Line Printer, or Fixedsys; otherwise, the columns of numbers may not line up vertically.

Now let us look at that ami.stb file. Here it is.

```
\dates 1990 1995 2000 2008 2009 2010 2011 2012 2013
\under =
\7 1 65 2 2 45
;
&
gdpR           ;Real Gross domestic product
cR             ;  Personal consumption
vR             ;  Gross private domestic investment
vfR            ;    Fixed investment
viR            ;    Inventory change
xR             ;  Exports
mR             ;  Imports
gR             ;  Government purchaes
;
```

```
gdpD          ;GDP Deflator
gdp           ;Gross domestic product
pibg          ;  Personal Income before gov
nitpils       ;  - Taxes on production & imports
ptax          ;  - Personal taxes
npctr         ;  + Gov transfers to persons
pidis         ;  = Personal disposable income
piipcb        ;  - Interest paid by consumers
piptt         ;  - Transfers to foreigners
c             ;  - Personal consumption expenditure
pisav         ;  = Personal saving
```

The commands beginning with a \ are commands to *Compare*. The first one, and the one you may well wish to change, sets the dates for the data to be shown. A date like 2000 is an annual date, and *Compare* will take an annual average of the quarterly data in our model. We could also give a quarterly date like 2010.2. If we include intervals in the dates, like 2005-2010, *Compare* will show the growth rate over that period. The growth rates will be calculated with continuous compounding. (Other compounding specifications are available, but are generally inferior to the default.) The \under command just sets the character which will be used for underling in the table.

The \ command by itself, as in the third line, sets the following parameters:

fw   field width of the numbers in the table
dp   decimal places to be shown in the table
pl   page length, in lines
tm   top margin, in lines
bm   bottom margin, in lines
tw   width of the titles on the left side of the page.

An & at the beginning of a line causes the dates to be written across the page and underlined with the underline character. A line with a * in the first position forces a new page. The other lines, that is to say, most lines, have variable or expression on the left followed by a " ; " followed by a title. The title will appear at the left of the page and the value of the expression will be shown in the columns under the appropriate dates.

There are many other *Compare* commands. You may also wish to look at Compare.pdf which is in the pdg directory.

You are now in a position to begin trying to use the software by doing the exercise at the end of the chapter.

4. Using Help

As is usual in Windows programs, the last item on the menu is Help. When you click on it, you should get a window with two books, one labeled Tutorial and the other labeled Command reference. If you click on either of them, it will open and show you the topics in it. To go to one of these topics, double click on it or put the cursor on it and tap the 'Enter' key. The text for the topic will appear in a box at the right of the screen. You may need to enlarge the window to read it easily. The tutorial is similar to what you have just read in this chapter. You can move forward or backward through it by using the "browse" buttons at the top, marked by >> and <<. After the tutorial, you will find the command reference for *G7*. These commands are those which you give in the white command box or include in a command file to be "added." If you click on "contents" at the top, you get back to the window with the books. If you click "index" you get references to keywords which the help author identified in the text. When you pick one of these, you get in the lower window a list of topics where the keyword occurred. If you still do not find what you want, you can do a full text search of the help material by clicking on the "Find" tab and waiting — at least the first time — while the computer makes a listing of every word that occurs at any point in the help text.

In the Command reference section, you should first read the first three topics. After that, each topic should be self-contained. It is my own experience in using help files for Windows programs that they are often clipped, circular, and unclear. They try to substitute hypertext links for old-fashioned clarity. In contrast, I hope that you will find the *G7* help text clear and with what you need to know all in one place. Examples are plentiful.

Exercises

3.1.   Create and run .reg files for all of the regressions used in Model 5 of Chapter 1. Modify the Master file as shown in Chapter 1 to make the model include these regression equations. Build and run the model in historical simulation. Make graphs and tables. In doing this exercise, you should read over the section on Model 5 in Chapter 1 and then try to do the whole exercise without looking again at Chapter 1. Only if you get hopelessly stuck should you look back before finishing. Then you might want to compare the way you did the exercise with the way I did it.

3.2.   Develop an equation relating employment (*emp*) to real GDP, *gdpR*, include it in your model, build and run the model in historical simulation. You should:
       Modify the master file to use the new equation
       Create a file with the editor to estimate the equation
       Run that file so as to get the results in a .sav and a .cat file.
       Choose Model | Build from the main menu
       Choose Model | Run to run the new model
       Edit your .shw file to put in a graph for employment
       Execute this file and save the employment graph
       Edit ami.stb to put in a line for employment
       Choose Model | Tables to make the numerical listing of the results.

When all the computing work has been done, go into your word processor and bring in your new master file, your emp.reg file, the resulting .cat file, the graph of the fit of the equation, the graph of employment in the historical simulation of the model, and the table comparing the historical simulation with actual values. You will find that to show the text files correctly with numbers in nice straight columns, you need to use a monotype font such as Courier or Line Printer.

CHAPTER 4. FORECASTS AND EXPERIMENTS

Let us take stock of where we are, what we have done, and where we have to go. In Chapter 1, we saw what a model was, but we learned little about how to actually make one. In Chapter 2, we looked carefully at theoretical aspects of fitting equations to data. In Chapter 3, we first saw how this curve fitting was done in practice with the *G7* program and how the equations can be combined into a model, and how that model can be run in historical simulation, that is, with historical values of all the exogenous variables. In this chapter, we will see how to run counter-historical simulations or "experiments with the past" by changing the values of one or another of the model's exogenous variables from what they actually were to what they might have been. The model will then spell out the effects of these changes on all the endogenous variables in the model. In this way, it gives us a sort of controlled experiment by means of the model. We will also see how to use the model to make forecasts. We have but to forecast the exogenous variables and then use the model to calculate the endogenous variables. Indeed, we can make not just one forecast but a number of them, with different projections of the exogenous variables. Usually a number of the exogenous variables represent policy variables such as government spending, tax rates, or money supply. Thus, comparison of the outcomes of the simulations with different projections for these variables enables us to evaluate the wisdom of pursuing various policies. This use of models is perhaps their most important application.

Unfortunately, I have found no way to prevent users of the *G7* software from occasionally making egregious errors that cause their models to explode or collapse or, more rarely, hang. There are, however, several tools for finding these errors, and they are described at the end of this chapter in the section on debugging of models.

Some of the deficiencies of *AMI* are already visible and more will become apparent in this chapter. In the next chapter, Chapter 5, we will look at some techniques for developing equations which can, to some extent, remove those deficiencies. That chapter ends with a list of problems which outline a research program for turning *AMI* into a fully respectable macroeconomic model. You can, at that point, set to work on making your own model. The final chapter, Chapter 6, reviews a number of qualitative factors in judging an equation. Fundamentally, an equation should make sense. It should, at a minimum, be conceivable that such a relation as you are estimating should exist in the economy over a number of years. It is surprisingly easy to write down equations that fit fairly well but make no sense. Chapter 6 develops a checklist of pitfalls to look out for.

Your work through the rest of this book will be an iterative application of the material in the last four chapters. To improve the simulation or forecasting properties of your model, as found using the techniques of this chapter, you will look for new relations using, perhaps, the techniques described in Chapter 5. Then you pass your new equation in review before the checklist of Chapter 6. When it passes, you return to the techniques of Chapter 3 to include it in the model, and build and run the model in historical simulation. Then you come back to the methods of this chapter to test the model in counter-historical simulation and forecasting. When you are satisfied with those results, you are ready to tell the world -- or at least your class -- about your model.

1. Counter-historical Simulation

You might well suppose that a good performance in historical simulation would be a quite adequate test of a model. Indeed, it is a necessary condition for a model to be useful. But it is by no means sufficient. For it is easy to build a model that does quite well in a historical simulation, especially over the period for which it was fit. The trick is simply to make some key variables exogenous or derived *by identity* from exogenous variables.

For example, the equation for fixed investment in *AMI,* (in the vfR.reg file) contains the lines

```
f   d = gdpR - gdpR[1]
```

Now if we change from defining d in terms of gdpR to defining it in terms of gnp$, thus

```
f   d = gnp$ - gnp$[1]
```

we will see no appreciable change in the fit of the equation but a big improvement in the historical simulation of the model. Try it for yourself. It works like magic, stage magic, that is, for the improvement is only in the appearances, not in the essence. Indeed, the essence of the model is much damaged by the change. Why does the change work such wonders on the historical simulation? Just because gnp$ is not otherwise in the model. Formally, it is exogenous although logically it should be endogenous. But because it is exogenous, when the historical simulation is run, fixed investment will be calculated from actual, historical real GNP, not that calculated by the model itself. Thus, the simulated value of vfR will be almost exactly the predicted value found in fitting the equation. That fit, you will recall, was much closer than that of the historical simulation where the simulated value, not the historical value of gdpR, had to be used in calculating d.

We will call this sort of deceptive exogeneity *false exogeneity*. It usually occurs by accident, unthinkingly. But the possibility of this occurrence is enough to make us leery of judging a model by its historical simulation alone. And so we are led to try some counter historical simulations.

A counter-historical simulation is just a simulation over the historical period with one (or possibly more) of the exogenous variables set at values different from what they actually were historically. The simplest way to do this is to start the run of the model (with Model | Run) just as you would for a historical simulation except that in the bottom box where you have previously given "histsim" you give a name (of eight or less letters and no spaces) for the data bank to be created by this run. For example, if you are going to increase government purchases of goods and services by \$20 billion, you might call the bank "gRup20". When you click OK and get the] prompt, give a title something like

```
ti Counter-historical simulation with gR increased by $20 billion.
```

You then get the] prompt again. Give the command

```
type gR
```

and you will get the historical values of gR displayed on the screen and the] prompt again. This time give the command

```
update gR +20
```

and then again

```
type gR
```

By comparing what you now get with what you got from the first "type gR", you should see that each and every value of gR has been increased by 20. You can abbreviate "update" to "up" . To subtract \$20 billion, the command would be

```
up gR -20
```

or to increase each value by 20 percent,

```
up gR *1.20
```

To specify the complete course of gR to see, for example, the effects of a major reduction in gR beginning in 1995 and falling from 1684 at the beginning of the year down to 1500 by 1997.1 and remaining there for the year and then rising steadily to 2200 by 2013.3, you can use the following:

```
up gR
1995.1 1684 0 0 0   0 0 0 0
1997.1 1500 0 0 1500    0 0 0 0
1999.1 0 0 0 0    0 0 0 0    0 0 0 0    0 0 0 0    0 0 0 0    0 0 0 0
2005.1 0 0 0 0    0 0 0 0    0 0 0 0    0 0 0 0    0 0 0 0
2010.1 0 0 0 0    0 0 0 0    0 0 0 0    0 0 2200
```

Here we have made use of the capacity of the program to replace a zero by a linearly interpolated value. In effect, the program draws a straight line from the 1684 in 1995.1 to the 1500 in 1997.1, and then another straight line from the 1500 at 1997.4 to the 2200 at 2013.3. Remember that the first number on each line is the date of the *first* observation on the line. There is no effective limit on how many numbers can be on the line. As you can see, you have the capacity to run a wide variety of counter historical simulations by altering the exogenous variables.

You can also modify the values produced by the equations of the model. You could ask, for example, how would the economy have behaved if investment had always been 20 percent above what the equation predicted. Such modifications of the predicted values are referred to as "fixes" There are four types of fixes available to you:

| cta | Constant term adjustment (also called "adds"). Add a specified amount to the value calculated by the equation. The amount added can be different in different periods. |

mul	Multiplicative fix. Multiply the value calculated from the equation by a specified factor, which may be different in different periods.
ovr	Over-ride the equation. Discard the value calculated and use the one specified.
rho	Add a rho-adjustment to the variable
skip	Ignores the value predicted by the equation and uses the historical value in its place.

The format for the first three is similar:

fixtype <variable_name>
data lines

For example

```
cta cpcR
1998.3 -20 -20    -25 -30 -30 -25   -15 -12 -10 -8   -4   -2 ;
```

The format for the rho-adjustment fix is

rho <variable_name> <rho_value>
for example

```
rho vfR .9
```

The format for skip is just

skip <variable_name>

for example

```
skip cpcR
```

These fixes work only when applied to variables which are the dependent variable in a regression. When applied to other variables, the forecasting program does not reject them; it just never uses them. Furthermore, *only one can be applied to any one variable*. If more than one is applied, only the last takes effect. For example, if somewhere in the fix file after the above "cta cpcR" there should appear "rho cpcR .9", the cta will be completely forgotten by the program without any warning.

Constant term adjustments are useful but easily abused. If, for example, construction of a major new oil pipeline had recently been announced, it might be fair to assume that the equation in the model doesn't know about the announcement and would forecast better with the help of a constant term adjustment. On the other hand, the worst abuse is to piece out the imperfections of the model in running a scenario. For example, if the scenario is an increase in money supply, and the model fails to show an increase in investment, it is an abuse of the cta to use one to pump up investment and to claim that the rise was a result of the increase in money supply, something "we know has to happen even though the model refuses to show it." This abuse, unfortunately, is not unknown in the commercial model building industry. In my own forecasting, I make extensive use of rho adjustments, which are a sort of automatic cta, but I seldom use a cta directly.

The values of *rho* in the various regressions can be conveniently captured for use in a .fix file by *G7*'s "rhosave" command. The format is

> rhosave <filename>

for example,

```
rhosave    rho.fix
```

After giving this command, estimate all the equations by doing "add runall.reg" — a good reason for keeping your runall.reg file up to date as you add more regressions to the model. Then give the command

```
rhosave off
```

and the file in which the values of rho are being saved will be closed and available for importing into the rhoadj.fix file or any other .fix file.

When making tables from a counter-historical run, the base of comparison is nearly always the historical simulation and *never* the actual historical values. Why? If we compare with the historical simulation, we know that the differences we are looking at are the result of the changes we made in the exogenous variables or in the equations by the fixes. Whereas if we compared the counter-historical simulation with the actual historical values, the differences would be a combination of errors in model and the effects of the changes we made in the exogenous variables. The whole value of having the model is to isolate the effects of the changes you made, so be sure to use histsim as the base against which to compare your counter-historical simulation.

Exercise

4.1   Do the suggested counter historical simulation with gR increased by $50. Then try $100 and $200. (The table maker will let you have up to eight alternatives.) Does there appear to be any limit on how big gdpR can be made by increasing government expenditure? Is anything bad happening as a result of increasing gR? Do you believe that what you have found to be properties of the *AMI* model are in fact properties of the U.S. economy? If not, you have used counter-historical simulation to reveal defects of a model. How do you think *AMI* might be improved?

2. Forecasting

A forecast is made, of course, by running the model over a future period. Like any other run, it is made by clicking Model | Run and filling in the blanks. But, unlike historical and counter historical simulations, a forecast will not have sensible values of exogenous variables unless you provide them. You do so via the .fix file.

The work of forecasting therefore centers on preparing this fix file. It must contain projections of all the exogenous variables and may contain also instructions for modifying the results of the regression equations by cta, mul, ovr, and rho fixes.

I suggest that you make a file called fore.fix to hold this information. To make it, start *G7*'s editor (File | Editor) with a blank screen. (If the editor already has something in it, use the Editor's File | New command to clear the screen.) Then use the Editor's File | Insert command to insert the file rhoadj.fix. The top line of the file gives a title which you should be sure to change for your forecast. With the cursor just below this line -- that is, at the beginning of the second line -- select File | Insert, and insert the file run.xog. This file was created when you did Model | Build. Here is what it contains for the basic *AMI* model.

```
add time.xog
add gdpD.xog
add xR.xog
add gR.xog
add pibgBR.xog
add nitpilsBR.xog
add ptaxBR.xog
add npctrR.xog
add piipcbBR.xog
add pipttBR.xog
add pisavBR.xog
```

As you see, it is a series of "add" commands to include in the data for your forecast the values of each exogenous variable in the model. You must create the .xog files with the future values of each exogenous variable. (In the *AMI* model, the first is for "time"; future values for it are already in the model's historical bank, and you should delete the line for it in the fore.fix file.) You should now save this file. You are perfectly free to save it with any legal file name provided that you remember what it is, but I will assume that you used fore.fix.

Now you must get to work creating the .xog files that have the future values of the exogenous variables. The format of these files is familiar. Future values are specified by "update" commands exactly like the update (or up) commands used in the counter historical simulation but with future dates. (Of course, update commands like "update xxx +20" will not work because there is nothing to which to add the 20.) When forecasting, you can use linear interpolation to automatically fill in zero values in the exogenous variables. (Actual values of zero for an exogenous variable should be replaced by very small values.)

For exports, xR, we could express its forecast in either of two possible ways in the xR.xog file. We could have

```
update xR
   2011.4      1856.269     1852.852     1850.222     1848.333
   2012.4      1847.142     1846.607     1846.690     1847.354
   2013.4      1848.566     1850.293     1852.505     1855.173
   2014.4      1858.271     1861.774     1865.657     1869.899
   2015.4      1874.478
```

or

```
update xR
2011.4    1856.269    1852.852    1850.222    1848.333
2012.4  0 0 0 0  0 0 0 0   0 0 0 0
2015.4    1874.478
```

The second makes use of the interpolation abilities of the update command, whereas the first provides a value for every period. Because this projection is very close to a straight line, there is little practical difference between the two.

The first of these updates was prepared in a very mechanical way by regressing xR on time and using the predicted value of the forecast using the rho adjustment. The historical values followed by this forecast are in the variable called *depvar* created by *G7* when the "mode f" has been given. (The f in "mode f" is for "forecast".) The *G7* commands to create this file were

```
bank bws b
mode f
tdates 2013.4 2017.4
limits 1980.1 2013.3 2017.4
ti xR
r b.xR = time
gr *
f xR = depvar
save xR.xog
sty xR
save off
```

This command file first assigns the data bank "bws". This bank is the one created when the model was built. It has all the variables in the model and no others. Most of the variables in the model are in the Quip data bank which is automatically assigned when *G7* is started, but some, such as *taxrate* and the various behavioral ratios, are made up in the process of building the model. By assigning the bws bank as bank b by

```
bank bws b
```

these variables become available by putting a "b." in front of their name. In this command file, the *limits* command caused the equation to be fit from 1980.1 to 2013.3 and then forecasted to 2017.4. The forecast worked because the only independent variable is time, one of only two variables with future values in the Quip bank. After the forecast is completed, the *depvar* variable (depvar = dependent variable) contains the actual values of the dependent variable for the historical period and the forecasted values with rho adjustment for the future period. The command

```
f   xR = depvar
```

gives xR not only the correct historical values but also the forecast. After opening the xR.xog file for saving, the command

```
sty xR
```

causes the past and forecasted values of xR to be written to xR.xog. (sty is short for "silent type" — "silent" because the values are not written to the screen.) This command wrote into the xR.xog file the first of the "update xR" displays shown above. In the regression, we could have used, besides

```
     r xR = time
```
also
```
     r xR = xR[1]
```
or even
```
     r xR = time, xR[1], xR[2]
```
for lagged values of the dependent variable are available for forecasting. The resulting forecasts are, of course, somewhat different.

The fore.fix file may contain either the command "add xR.xog" or the contents of the xR.xog file can be brought into fore.fix and the line "add xR.xog" deleted. I myself generally prefer this second way of working, because it puts all of the projections in one place where they are easily seen by the user.

The sort of mechanical projection illustrated here for exports makes sense for a few variables like population and possibly exports. It does not make sense to use it for tax rates, defense expenditures, and other policy variables. Projections of such variables should be thought about carefully in the light not only of their recent trends but also of current political developments. Mechanical forecasts can also be made for these variables, but *only as a starting point for thinking about them.*

If you discover any surprise exogenous variables in run.xog, ask where they came from. Did you really mean for them to be exogenous or are they just sort of accidental exogenous variables? If the latter, you have false exogeneity and should modify the model to eliminate it. If you find yourself making exogenous projections for variables that are clearly not independent of the endogenous variables in the model, revise the model to eliminate them. Typical examples are to find that gdp (current dollar GDP) is exogenous while gdpR is endogenous. Or that the consumer price index (cpi) is exogenous while the gdp deflator, gdpD, is endogenous. If you find yourself making exogenous projections of variables that are *not* largely external to the economy in the short run (such as population and labor force) or that do not represent policy (such as money supply, tax rates, or government spending), **stop!** Your model has in it one of those tricks that both make the historical simulation look good and render the model useless. Get rid of the false exogeneity by either adding an equation for the variable or use a variable that is already endogenous in place of the offender.

After this exhortation to think about your projections of the exogenous variables, I must now confess that the *Build* program automatically made a file for making these mechanical projections of all of the exogenous variables. It is called *exogall.reg*. To use it, you must first edit the second and third lines to specify the dates over which you want the regression run and the projections printed. (If your forecasts fail to go as far into the future as you intend, you probably need to add an "fdates" command to specify the range over which "f" commands work, for example:

```
     fdates 1960.1 2020.4
```

That done, just execute the file, and you will get *.xog* files for all the exogenous variables. Look at one or two of them such as xR.xog or gR.xog. The fore.fix file can then be made to use all these exogenous projections inserting into it (File | Insert) the run.xog file.

I repeat, use these mechanical projections *only* as starting points for thinking about economically justifiable projections. When you have thought about a particular exogenous projection and edited the .xog file that contains it, I suggest that you save your edited version with the extension *.xg* instead of *.xog*. Edit *fore.fix* to use the *.xg* file. The reason for this suggestion is to avoid accidental destruction of your carefully edited files by doing "*add exogall.reg*" again, perhaps because changes in the model have added some new exogenous variables.

Inclusion of the rho adjustment factors is particularly important for a good short-term forecast, for they avoid abrupt changes in variables as the model "jumps onto" the equation. Use the *rhosave* command described above to get all the rho fixes together in a convenient way.

You can, of course, use the cta, mul, and ovr fix types as well. If you have used a "cta", "mul", or "ovr" adjustment on any variable, say x, you can check the values of that adjustment by doing "ty x:f" at the] prompt.

Experiments with the model can be very useful both in testing it and, once you are satisfied with it, in learning about the economy.

Exercise

4.2   Make a forecast with *AMI* over the next five years. You will have to make independent forecasts of all exogenous variables. Put them, as described above into a file that you may call "fore.fix". When your "fore.fix" file is ready, make the forecast with something like the following on the form obtained by Model | Run

   Start date 2013.4
   Stop date 2017.4
   Fix file   fore
   Output bank my4cast

You should, of course replace the dates by dates appropriate to the time at which you are working. The Start date must be a period for which full data are available. The name "my4cast" is just an example. Be sure that the fore.fix file has in it rho fixes for all the regression equations.

Use *G7* to graph the forecasts. You will probably want to create a "fore.shw" file which will make graphs with nice titles. Make tables showing your forecast. To do so, you will need to edit the \dates line at the top of the ami.stb file to show the periods you are interested in. To get growth rates, put the dates between which you want the growth rate with a hyphen between them in place of a date in this line. You may find it convenient to keep a copy of the stub file with these dates as fore.stb.

4.3.   Make other forecasts with *AMI* with different values of the exogenous variables. Compare the results both graphically (with the gr command) and numerically (with Model | Tables).

3. Debugging Models

You may be so lucky as to never have a model that behaves so badly that you know it must have a serious error in it. Chances are, however, that sooner than you would like you will encounter a serious error. The model may not converge, it may produce values of NAN (Not A Number) for some variable, may take the logarithm of a negative number, divide by zero, produce utterly ridiculous values for one or more series, or otherwise complain that it is sick and needs your care. The *G7* software gives you various diagnostic tools for finding the problem.

Even if the model shows no evident problem, you should check the correctness of its identities by running a historical simulation and, at the] prompt, give the command

```
add skipall.fix
```
This skipall.fix is a file created by Build which applies a "skip" command to every regression equation. Consequently, this historical simulation should precisely reproduce the data, that is the bank it creates should be identical to the bws bank. To find out if they are identical, assign one as bank b, the other as bank c, and add run.gr, thus

```
bank histsim  b
bank bws  c
add run.gr
```
All the graphs should show the two lines on top of one another so that they look like one line. If you see two lines on any graph, you know you have an error in the identities.

The most common problem is that you have given two different variables the same name. This error is virtually certain to cause trouble if lagged values of either variable are used. *G7* has a special check for this problem. Be sure that the master file begins with the command "checkdup y"; this command will cause Build to check for duplicate names. If it finds such a problem, it will record it in the file run.err. If you also have "addprint y" somewhere before the spot where the trouble occurs, you can pinpoint exactly which statement is changing the value. You should look at the run.err file with the *G7* editor and search for the word "Error". If you find such a change of definition, you should correct it.

Another debugging tool is the use of the "maxit" command when running the model. You will recall that in each period the *AMI* model goes through a cycle of computations to go from the assumed value of disposable income to the implied value, and then repeats this cycle with the implied value of the first round as the assumed value of the second round. An error in the model will normally make the implied value from the first round nonsense and then everything in the second round nonsense. To spot where the error is, it can be helpful to limit the number of iterations to one. Then the variables calculated in the first period are sensible down to the point where the error occurs; but from that point on, one or more of them is nonsense. Here are the steps in this process. We shall suppose that the historical simulation which is giving trouble starts in 1980.1.

1. Run a historical simulation from 1990.1 to, say, 2000.4, but when you get the] prompt where you would normally type "run", type first

    maxit 1

and then run. The program will then perform one iteration, report that it has not converged, and ask what you want to do. Answer g   for go to next period. Let us say that the bank you produced in this way was called histsim.

2 In *G7*, do
```
bank bws c
bank histsim b
gdates 1990.1 2000.4 2013.3
add run.gr
```

The red and the blue lines should be identical before (to the left of) the vertical line and should be close to one another to the right of it. If you find a difference before the vertical line, there is an error in an identity or "f" statement. If there is a big difference to the right (but no difference to the left), there is an error in the regression equation. With this sort of pinpointing of the error, you should be able to spot it.

If neither of these methods shows up the error, take the model back to its simplest form by removing all the regression equations. To do so, just put a # in from of each line of the form "add xxx.sav" in the master file. If there are no errors in the identities, that should certainly produce a model which runs. Then put the equations back in one by one (by removing the #'s), each time running the model. When the equation you have just put back causes the model to malfunction, you know that the trouble is in the interaction between that .sav file and what is already in the model. That process should certainly identify which .sav file is making trouble and enable you to see the problem.

If you already know how to use the Borland C++ debugger and wish to use that knowledge to debug your model, you need to know that the model itself is in the file hearta.cpp and run.nam gives the correspondence between the names of the variables and their position in the vp array in the program. It is beyond the scope of this book, however, to explain the use of the debugger. I very seldom find it necessary or helpful for these models.

Exercise 4.4. Check the identities of the *AMI* model.

CHAPTER 5. TECHNIQUES FOR IMPROVING A MODEL

The exercise at the end of the previous chapter pointed to a major problem with *AMI*. As you increased government spending, real GDP and just about everything good got better and better. It would seem that all problems could be solved by the government's just buying more goods and services. Many of the early econometric models from the 1950's and 1960's had this sort of simplistic Keynesian character. Today almost no one would argue that they were adequate representations of economic reality. Making a model show the adverse effects of liberal fiscal (and monetary) policy will take us through some of the major problems of macroeconomics of the last thirty years. It will also require us to introduce some new tools for working with regression.

What happens if the government tries to achieve very high levels of employment by increasing spending? Any student of elementary macroeconomics knows, or believes he knows, that inflation will accelerate, perhaps in a never ending spiral. (If your macro is a bit rusty, look up in your macro book the Phillips curve with the acceleration modification.) According to this theory, it is not the absolute level of inflation which depends on unemployment, but the deviation of inflation from its expected value. This expected value, in turn, is usually thought to be a weighted average of past values of inflation. While the theory says nothing about the distribution of weights in the weighted average, a common assumption is that the weights decline exponentially. Such a variable can be easily created with *G7*'s @cum() function.

1. Working with the @cum Function

The "cum" in @cum is short for "cumulate". The function creates a variable, y, from a given variable, x, by the following formula:

$$y_t = (1-s)y_{t-1} + x_t$$

where *s* is a number between 0 and 1. In *G7*, we would create *y* from *x* by this equation with the formula

```
f y = @cum(y,x,s) .
```

(The @cum function is slightly strange in that the series which is the result of the cumulation -- which I shall call the *cumulate* and is here indicated by *y* -- must be given to the function as an argument. That is because, when the model is running, the @cum function must know the previous value of *y* as well as the current value of *x* in order to calculate the current value of *y*.) We can write the formula for y_t as a function of the preceding values of *x* as

$$y_t = \sum_{\tau=0}^{t-1} (1-s)^\tau x_{t-\tau}$$

For example, if $s = .1$, then by the time we get to $t = 100$, we would have

$$y_{100} = 1.0x_{100} + .9\,x_{99} + .81\,x_{98} + .72\,x_{97} + .656\,x_{96} + \ldots$$

The weights form a geometric series with sum equal $1/s$ if we take infinitely many terms -- and very, very close to $1/s$ if we stop when the individual terms become less than, say, .01 . In many applications, such as the present one, we would like to have the sum of weights equal to 1.0. We can achieve that in either of two, not quite equivalent, ways. The first is to multiply s, since that is equivalent to dividing by $1/s$. For example, if s is .1, we can define y by

```
f y = 0.1*@cum(cx, x, 0.1)
```

This y will have the same dimensions as x. Note that we had to introduce a different variable, cx, which is the pure, unmultiplied cumulate of x as the first argument in the @cum function.

The @cum() command has an approximate physical analogy in the filling of a leaky bucket from a water pipe. The rate of inflow is x, the level of the water is y; the outflow through the leak is proportional to the level of water in the bucket. Thus the outflow equals sy and s is called the spill rate.

The problem with this way of making the weights sum to 1.0 is that it does not work exactly, especially not near the beginning of the data bank when we have only a few observations. The second way solves this problem by dividing by exactly the sum of weights of the terms so far included. To get this sum, we just compute the cumulate of the series which is 1.0 from the beginning of the data bank. Following the analogy mentioned above to a bucket with a leak in it, these cumulates of 1.0 are called "unit buckets." Here is the formula for calculating the ten-percent unit bucket, which we may as well call ub10:

```
f  ub10 = @cum(ub10, 1.0, 0.10)       .
```

Let us now apply these ideas to computing expected inflation.

2. Rates of Change with Continuous Compounding

The measure of the price level which we shall use is the GDP deflator, for that is the one we shall need to compute GDP in current prices, which we shall soon need. This variable appears in the Quip data bank with the name gdpD. It measures the level of prices in any quarter relative to the average in the base year, currently 2009. It is thus not directly a measure of inflation. Rather, the corresponding measure of inflation is the percentage rate of change of gdpD. How do we compute this percentage rate of change? One possibility would be

```
f infl = 400.*(gdpD - gdpD[1])/gdpD[1]
```

Why the 400 on the right instead of the 100 you perhaps expected? Because we are working with quarterly data so the change observed is only over a quarter of a year, but inflation — like interest rates with which they are often compared — are conventionally stated in percent per year, not per quarter. Please compute this variable and graph it. You will find a very jagged series. To get a smoother series which we have a better chance of explaining, we will take inflation over the last year. It can be calculated in *G7* by

```
f infl = 100.*(gdpD - gdpD[4])/gdpD[4]
```

An alternative definition is to take the natural logarithm of *gdpD* and the to take the difference of the logarithm, like this:

```
f    lgdpD = 100.*@log(gdpD)
f    infl = lgdpD  - lgdpD[4]
```

The first definition corresponds to the idea of annual compounding of growth rates, while the logarithmic definition corresponds to continuous compounding. For natural growth processes, continuous compounding is the only natural way to measure the rate of growth. All others introduce an extraneous element — the period of compounding — into describing the process. Further, continuous compounding is the only way to get the same growth rates both up and down. If, for example, a series goes from 100 in year 1 to 120 in year 2 and back to 100 in year 3, annual compounding says it went up by 20 percent and then fell by 16.67 percent to get back to where it had been. Thus the rises seems to have been bigger than the fall! The continuous, logarithmic definition says it rose by 18.23 percent in the first year and fell by 18.23 percent in the second, so that the two changes are recognized as being of the same magnitude but in opposite directions.

3. Inflation I — The Wolf in Sheep's Clothing

Now with inflation defined, we can undertake to define expected inflation with the @cum function. We would have

```
f    lgdpD = 100.*@log(gdpD)
f    infl = lgdpD  - lgdpD[4]
f    ub10 = @cum(ub10, 1.0, .10)
# call expected inflation "inflex"
f    inflex = @cum(cinfl, infl[1], .10)/ub10
```

Put these commands into *G7* and graph the series you have created. Since the price deflator data in the Quip data bank begins in 1969, you might want to begin some of the graphs back near that date to watch how the @cum function works.

Before we can try an equation for inflation, we need to define unemployment in terms of the employment variable for which you already have an equation. Besides *emp*, the Quip data bank also contains a variable for the civilian labor force, *lfc*. To compute the unemployment percentage we need

```
f   u = 100.*(lfc - emp)/ lfc
```

You can now put all the preceding ideas together and formulate a regression as follows:

```
r infl = inflex, u, u[1], u[2], u[3]
```

The fit, shown below, over the period 1977.1 to 2013.3 is surprisingly good considering that only the unemployment rate has been used as an explanatory variable. However, it does predict extremely low inflation in the last several quarters, due to the high unemployment rate.

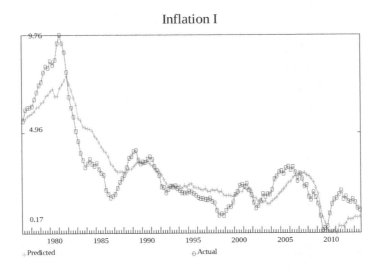

Inflation I

Now put the equation in the model and run it. Because we are interested here in testing how well this equation simulates when it has to use (in the definition of *inflex*) the prior values of *infl* which it itself generated, I have isolated this equation from the rest of the model. Namely, I have used actual unemployment, not that generated by the model. This change required simply replacing the line defining u, given previously by

```
    f   u = 100.*(lfc  -  emp)/ lfc
```
by
```
    fex   u = 100.*(lfc  -  emp)/ lfc
```

You will recall that a "fex" is used for forming exogenous variables. It puts the variable on the left into the model, but not the equation. When we go to actually use the model, we certainly want u to be endogenous. For the moment, however, so that we can concentrate on the interaction of the inflation equation with itself, the "fex" definition is desirable. Subsequent simulations of the inflation equation in this chapter are all done with the equation isolated in this way.

Once the model has been run in historical simulation, plot *infl* from the bws and histsim banks. The result, shown below diverges quickly, and is much too high in the rest of the simulation. Remember that the fitted equation (see above) was not bad. Although the forecast roughly follows the pattern of actual inflation. It is well above the actual level throughout the rest of the forecast period.

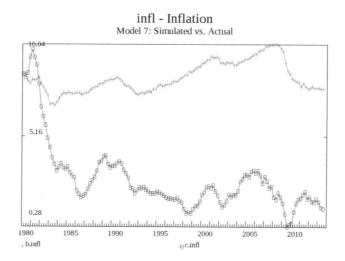

infl - Inflation
Model 7: Simulated vs. Actual

The beginning of that divergence warns us that we should look carefully at the equation for explosive tendencies. One way to check for them is to run the model with constant values of unemployment. Since we have left unemployment exogenous, we can easily set its values when we run the model. The lines marked by + signs in the graph below shows the results of running it from 1982.1 to 2013.3 with three different constant values of unemployment, namely 4, 5 and 6 percent, to produce the top, middle, and bottom lines, respectively. Here, the dangerously explosive nature of this equation becomes apparent. It is hard to believe that at an unemployment rate of 4 percent, prices would go into an upward spiral reaching 18 percent per year after 30 years! Indeed, this equation turns out to be a wolf ready to eat alive an unsuspecting modeler.

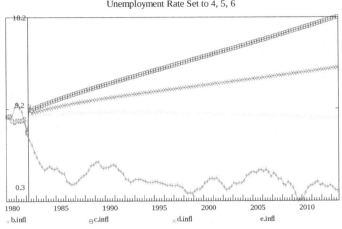

Inflation 1 Equation in Historical Simulation
Unemployment Rate Set to 4, 5, 6

This example shows the value of a historical simulation, for while we have seen that a good historical simulation is no guarantee of a good model, a bad one, such as we have here, is surely an indication of an unusable model.

Since the equation is misbehaving badly, we had best have a close look at it. Its numerical output is shown below.

```
:                              Inflation I
  SEE   =       0.90 RSQ  = 0.8128 RHO =   0.95 Obser  =  147 from 1977.100
  SEE+1 =       0.28 RBSQ = 0.8062 DW  =   0.10 DoFree =  141 to   2013.300
  MAPE  =      29.45
     Variable name          Reg-Coef Mexval Elas   NorRes     Mean   Beta
  0 infl                    - - - - - - - - - - - - - - -     3.17  - - -
  1 intercept               1.59921    7.7   0.51    5.34     1.00
  2 inflex                  1.04040  126.8   1.14    1.28     3.48   0.963
  3 u                       0.15231    0.1   0.31    1.02     6.45   0.117
  4 u[1]                   -0.57609    0.3  -1.17    1.00     6.45  -0.441
  5 u[2]                    0.12615    0.0   0.26    1.00     6.45   0.097
  6 u[3]                   -0.02141    0.0  -0.04    1.00     6.45  -0.016
```

Look at the coefficient on inflex: 1.04. That means that if expected inflation rises by one percentage point, inflation itself will rise by 1.04 percentage points. Notice in the graph of the fit that there were positive errors in 1997 for several consecutive quarters. When these quarters were hit in the simulation, expected inflation rose well above actual inflation and the 1.04 "perpetuation factor" took hold and generated this runaway inflation. It could very well happen, by the way, that a few consecutive quarters of misses on the low side could start a plunge of inflation down into negative values.

A more reasonable value for the coefficient of *inflex* would be 1.0 or perhaps something a bit below 1.0. Values above 1 for this coefficient are almost certain to make for an unstable model. Of course, *G7* did not realize that our *inflex* was expected inflation. It had

107

no idea of what was a reasonable value for its coefficient. It just picked one to minimize the sum of squared errors. How can we tell *G7* what would be a reasonable value? That question brings us to the matter of soft constraints.

4. Soft Constraints

Suppose that we want to suggest to *G7* that a value for b_2 of .9 would be appropriate. How can we do so? We can simply manufacture some new, artificial observations. In these observations, the value of x_2, inflex in the present case, is 1.0, the value of *infl*, the dependent variable, is .9, and the values of other variables are 0 (including x_1, the variable which is multiplied by the intercept). Thus, we have an observation that looks something like this

$$x_1 \quad x_2 \quad x_3 \ldots x_n \quad y$$
$$0 \quad 1 \quad 0 \ldots 0 \quad .9$$

The residual from this observation will be .9 - $1b_2$. Pretty clearly the value of b_2 which minimizes the square of this one residual is .9. Of course, there are other residuals whose squares go into the sum of squared residuals which is being minimized, so including one such observation won't result in a b_2 which is exactly .9 . But as more and more such observations are added, the value of b_2 will certainly move towards .9. Thus, we can say that by the addition of such observations we are *softly constraining* the estimated regression coefficients.

The command in *G7* for adding one such artificial observation for each natural observation is just

```
con 1 .9 = a2
```

and to add 10 such observations per natural observation is

```
con 10 .9 = a2
```

The general form of the constraint or con command is

    con <count> <left> = <right>

where

count	is the number of artificial observations per natural observation.
left	is a number, the left side of the equation which expresses the constraint.
right	is any linear expression in the coefficients of the equation.

Some examples of con commands illustrating the "right" element are

```
con 3    .9 = a2
con 200   0 = a2 - 2a3 + a4
con 1000  1 =  a3 + a4 + a5 + a6    .
```

(The letter a is used here to denote the regression coefficients instead of the b which we have used in the text because *G7* is able to estimate several regression equations at once with constraints across the equations. In such tasks, a is used for the coefficients of the first equation, b for coefficients of the second, and so on. We will come to such problems in Part 2.)

The natural question at this point is: "How do I know how many of the artificial observations to use?" Is it really conceivable that, as the third example seems to imply, I would ever want to use 1000 artificial observations per natural observation? The only general rule about how many to use is "As many as it takes to accomplish what you want done." And yes, it is quite common to take large numbers of artificial observations, because their impact depends on the dimensions of the variables. Suppose, as in the third example above, that we are trying to constraint the sum of four coefficients, all of them between 0 and 1, to be 1.0. The discrepancy is likely to be .2 or .4 at worst. Now if the dimension of the dependent variable is such that the *SEE* for the equation is 1200, then it is going to take a lot of observations with an error of .2 to make the least-squares algorithm "listen" to the constraint. Indeed, it is going to take a thousand, or maybe ten thousand. Experiment to find out what it takes for your particular equation.

5. Inflation II — A Rough-hewn Timber

Let us return now to estimating the equation for inflation and add to the previous commands just this one:

```
con 20 .9 = a2
```

The resulting equation is:

```
                                    Inflation 2
  SEE   =          0.93 RSQ   = 0.8022 RHO =    0.95 Obser   =   147 from 1977.100
  SEE+1 =          0.29 RBSQ  = 0.7952 DW  =    0.10 DoFree  =   141 to    2013.300
  MAPE  =         29.96
     Variable name                 Reg-Coef  Mexval   Elas   NorRes      Mean   Beta
  0 infl                           - - - - - - - - - - - - - - - -       3.17 - - -
  1 intercept                      1.61892      7.4   0.51    23.68      1.00
  2 inflex                         0.91894    384.7   1.01     1.21      3.48  0.851
  3 u                              0.28450      0.2   0.58     1.02      6.45  0.218
  4 u[1]                          -0.66438      0.4  -1.35     1.00      6.45 -0.509
  5 u[2]                           0.06496      0.0   0.13     1.00      6.45  0.050
  6 u[3]                           0.05850      0.0   0.12     1.00      6.45  0.045
```

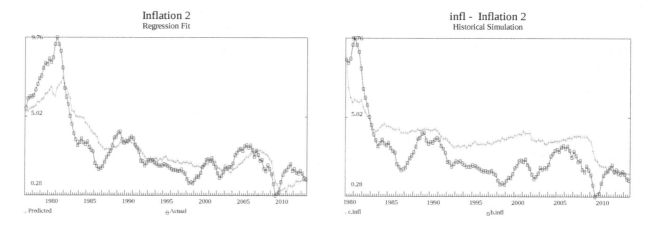

The constraint did the job required of it and got b_2 down just barely under 1.0 (.92). The fit is worse, as you can see from the increase in *SEE* or by comparing the graph on the left below with the earlier graph of the fit. But the simulation results, as you can see on the right, are improved. We have an equation which we could conceivably use, but it lacks finesse, as we shall see.

How does this equation hold up under testing with constant values for unemployment? The graph below shows runs with constant unemployment at 4, 5, and 6 percent. These results are certainly more plausible than the results with the first version of the equation, though still not acceptable

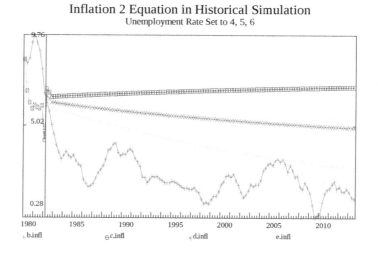

It is often difficult to get newcomers to model building to apply soft constraints because they tend to have some sort of feeling that "the computer knows best" or that it isn't "scientific" to provide information and understanding that is not in the database. The considerable improvement in the simulation in this case should provide some assurance that thinking about equations and imposing requirements based on those thoughts can make our models more capable of imitating economic reality.

6. Inflation III — Accounting for External Shocks

If we look closely at the fit of this last inflation equation, we see that the biggest problems arise in the 1976 to 1980 period, the time of the second "oil shock." At the time, journalists and "the man in the street" were blaming the whole of inflation on the oil shock. We have seen that we can explain the broad outlines of inflation without mention of oil prices, but it is at least worth an experiment to see if we "imported" the high inflation of those years by a faster rise in the price of imported goods than in the price of comparable domestic goods. For "comparable" domestic goods, we will use U.S. exports. While we obviously do not export the same goods that we import, both aggregates involve tradable goods and services. The measure of the relative prices we will use is calculated by the line

```
fex  relpri = 100.*@log((m/m$)/(x/x$))
```

and its rate of inflation, which we can call imflimp for "inflation imported" is

```
f inflimp = relpri - relpri[4]
```

We have used the official deflated values of imports and exports, because their deflators reflect the specific prices of the goods traded, whereas our xR and mR are both deflated by the same deflator. We will define *relpri* by a "fex" rather than by an "f" because we want to think of this variable as exogenous. A littler experimentation with the lags led to the equation

```
r infl = inflex, u, u[1], u[2], u[3], inflimp[2], inflimp[3]
```

The graph of the fit, on the left, looks very good; there are only two or three periods of noticeable errors. The *inflimp* variable helped explain the drop in the inflation rate in 1997, and the rise in inflation in 2001. Though on the low side, the historical simulation on the right shows a further improvement in the last several years.

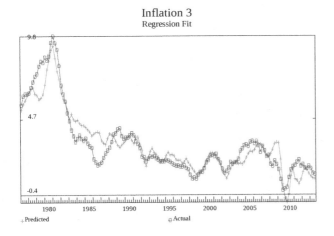

Inflation 3
Regression Fit

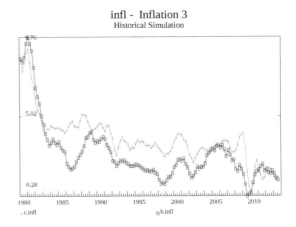

infl - Inflation 3
Historical Simulation

```
                          Inflation 3
 SEE    =        0.74 RSQ   = 0.8731 RHO =    0.90 Obser   =  147 from 1977.100
 SEE+1 =         0.33 RBSQ  = 0.8667 DW  =    0.20 DoFree  =  139 to    2013.300
 MAPE  =       24.57
    Variable name            Reg-Coef  Mexval  Elas   NorRes     Mean     Beta
 0 infl                      - - - - - - - - - - - - - - - -     3.17  - - -
 1 intercept                  1.19644     6.2   0.38    37.11    1.00
 2 inflex                     0.90842   493.0   1.00     1.90    3.48   0.841
 3 u                          0.09651     0.0   0.20     1.60    6.45   0.074
 4 u[1]                      -0.55774     0.4  -1.14     1.57    6.45  -0.427
 5 u[2]                       0.22366     0.1   0.46     1.57    6.45   0.171
 6 u[3]                       0.03875     0.0   0.08     1.57    6.45   0.030
 7 inflimp[2]                 0.06240     1.6   0.01     1.09    0.52   0.109
 8 inflimp[3]                 0.10449     4.4   0.02     1.00    0.52   0.182
```

There is, however, an anomaly in the numerical results of all of the equations we have used so far. We turn now to correcting it.

7. Inflation IV: Using Distributed Lags

Look at the coefficients for the *u* variables in the last regression. The first is positive, the opposite one would expect; the second is *negative*; the third is positive again; and the fourth is again negative. That is certainly not what I had in mind when I put in several lagged values of unemployment. I just thought it might take some time for prices to respond to unemployment. I had no expectation that the direction of causality should reverse in the middle and must confess that I would be very uncomfortable forecasting or simulating the economy with such an equation. As with the coefficient on *inflex*, I expect that the plausibility of the results of our model would be much enhanced by smoothing out those three coefficients. By "smoothing out" I mean making them lie more nearly on a straight line. If they lay exactly on a straight line then we would have

$$a3 - a4 = a4 - a5$$

or

$$0 = a3 - 2a4 + a5$$

If a6 is also on that line, then

$$0 = a4 - 2a5 + a6.$$

And if that line passes through zero one period further out, then

$$a6 = .5a5$$

or

$$0 = a5 - 2a6$$

We can impose these constraints with the "con" command previously introduced, thus

    con 2 0 = a3 - 2a4 + a5
    con 2 0 = a4 - 2a5 + a6
    con 2 0 = a5 - 2a6

112

This use of the "con" command in this way to impose a smooth pattern on coefficients is quite common. But it frequently happens that we have a number of lagged values of some variable, perhaps five or ten, and we want to impose smoothness over all their estimated coefficients. For example, in Chapter 1, the first regression we looked at (with *vfR* as dependent variable) had 12 lagged values of *d*, with coefficients a3 through a14. If you look closely at these coefficients, you will see some implausible jumps from one to another. If we wish to smooth them out, we could impose constraints like the following:

```
con 100   0   = a3 - 2a4 + a5
con 100   0   = a4 - 2a5 + a6
con 100   0   = a5 - 2a6 + a7
con 100   0   = a6 - 2a7 + a8
con 100   0   = a7 - 2a8 + a9
con 100   0   = a8 - 2a9 + a10
con 100   0   = a9 - 2a10 + a11
con 100   0   = a10 - 2a11 + a12
con 100   0   = a11 - 2a12 + a13
con 100   0   = a12 - 2a13 + a14
con 100   0   = a13 - 2a14
```

where it is assumed that a15 is zero.

Now it is a bit tiresome to type all of these lines, so *G7* provides a shorthand, the "sma" command:

```
sma 100 a3 a14   1
```

This one command is the exact equivalent of the eleven "con" commands. The 100 serves the same purpose as the 100, the "count" parameter, in the "con" commands. The a3 and a14 are the first and last coefficients in the sequence of "con" commands. The "con" commands are imposing the constraint that the coefficients lie on a straight line, which is a polynomial of degree 1; the one 1 at the end of the *sma* command indicates that it also should impose softly a straight line. If the 1 were replaced by a 2, 3, or 4, etc., the "sma" would impose softly a polynomial of degree 2, 3, or 4, respectively.

The "sma" command as given above includes the presumption that a15 is zero, so that a13, a14, and a15 = 0 should lie on a straight line; or, as in the last of the "con" commands, 0 = a13 - 2a14, or a14 = .5a13. If this constraint is *not* desired, then the command should end with an "f" , thus

```
sma 100 a3 a14 1 f
```

The "f" is for "free" or "floating", not tied down to zero at the end.

Why the name "sma"? The "sma" is a "soft" version (suggested by Robert Shiller) of the lag estimation system introduced by Shirley M. Almon, my late wife, and generally known as the Almon lag. By picking sufficiently large values of the "count" parameter, one can use the "sma" command to produce the original Almon lag, though I think it is seldom desirable to do so. Several regression packages have a function called "Almon" which implements this lag. Since I wished to be clear that this was Shirley's work, not mine, I have used her initials as the name of the command.

Applied to the present equation for inflation, the *sma* command equivalent to the three *con* commands given above is

```
sma 20 a3  a6 1
```

The numerical results are quite satisfactory:

```
:                                 Inflation 4
  SEE    =        0.75 RSQ   = 0.8715 RHO =    0.90 Obser   =  147 from 1977.100
  SEE+1 =         0.33 RBSQ  = 0.8650 DW  =    0.20 DoFree =  139 to    2013.300
  MAPE  =       25.12
     Variable name         Reg-Coef  Mexval  Elas   NorRes      Mean    Beta
  0 infl                   - - - - - - - - - - - - - - -        3.17  - - -
  1 intercept              1.26823     7.5    0.40   36.63       1.00
  2 inflex                 0.90874   490.0    1.00    1.87       3.48   0.841
  3 u                     -0.08666     4.9   -0.18    1.84       6.45  -0.066
  4 u[1]                  -0.06330     7.6   -0.13    1.71       6.45  -0.048
  5 u[2]                  -0.04059     3.7   -0.08    1.61       6.45  -0.031
  6 u[3]                  -0.01946     1.2   -0.04    1.56       6.45  -0.015
  7 inflimp[2]             0.06540     1.7    0.01    1.08       0.52   0.114
  8 inflimp[3]             0.09965     4.0    0.02    1.00       0.52   0.173
```

The coefficients on u are now quite sensible and the cost in terms of a worse fit is quite small; *SEE* remains at 0.73, so there was little loss in explanatory power. The graph of the fit is virtually indistinguishable from that of the Inflation III equation. The graph on the right below shows the historical simulation.

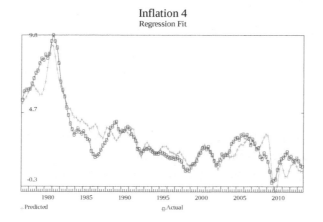

Inflation 4
Regression Fit

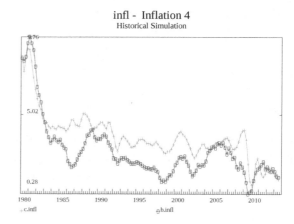

infl - Inflation 4
Historical Simulation

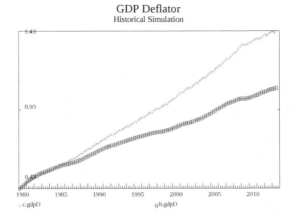

GDP Deflator
Historical Simulation

The model needs at various points the price level, *gdpD*, as well as the inflation rate. We work back from the inflation rate to the price level by the equations

```
f lgdpD = lgdpD[4] + infl
f gdpD = @exp(.01*lgdpD)
```

The historical simulation for *gdpD* is shown in the third graph of the group just above. In the present case, this simulation is acceptable only until about 1987, after which point inflation is too high, and gdpD drifts upward above the actual deflator value. It should be obvious that the procedure we have used thus far can produce results for the historically simulated *gdpD* which deviate steadily more and more from the historical value.

This deflator is as important to us as is the rate of inflation, indeed, perhaps more so. For it is what we shall use to convert *gdpR* to *gdp*. And it is the ratio of *gdp* (in current prices) to some measures of the money supply which will indicate credit conditions. Thus, a systematic error in *gdpD* is a cause of considerable concern.

8. Inflation V: Working in Levels instead of Rates of Change

How can we get the equation to work well for *gdpD*? Well, the obvious answer is to estimate the equation for *gdpD* (or *lgdpD* — its logarithm) instead of for *infl*. How can we do that? First just note that inflation by the logarithmic definition is the first difference of *lgdpD*, so *lgdpD* is just the cumulate of inflation. That being the case, we can convert our equation to work in levels by just cumulating with 0 spill rate all the variables which appear on the right side. Because these inflation rates are expressed as annual rates while the cumulation is done quarterly, the annual rates have been multiplied by 0.25 before cumulation. The *G7* commands to do so are just

```
f cinflex = @cum(cinflex,0.25*inflex,0.)
f cu = @cum(cu, 0.25*u, 0)
f cinflimp = @cum(cinflimp,0.25*inflimp,0)
```

115

and the cumulate of the constant term is just a time trend. Thus, the regression command in *G7* is

```
r   lgdpD = cinflex, cu,cu[1],cu[2],cu[3],cu[4], cinflimp[2],
      cinflimp[3], time
```

and the commands to compute from *lgdpD* the deflator and inflation (which should immediately follow the below the *r* command) are

```
f gdpD  =  @exp(.01*lgdpD)
f infl  =  lgdpD - lgdpD[4]
```

As before, a constraint was put on the coefficient for *cinflex*, and the "sma" command was used to smooth the coefficients on *cu*. After some experimentation I decided to use the 2nd and 3rd lags of the cinflimp variable. The numerical results are

```
:                              Inflation 5
   SEE    =      1.26 RSQ   = 0.9986 RHO =    0.95 Obser  =   155 from 1975.100
   SEE+1  =      0.42 RBSQ  = 0.9985 DW  =    0.10 DoFree =   145 to    2013.300
   MAPE   =     86.65
       Variable name         Reg-Coef  Mexval   Elas   NorRes     Mean    Beta
   0 lgdpD                   - - - - - - - - - - - - - - -      -38.53  - - -
   1 intercept              -147.72339   392.0   3.83   748.82     1.00
   2 cinflex                   0.80903   592.0  -1.86     3.93    88.68   0.925
   3 cu                       -0.02992     1.1   0.46     3.69   586.74  -0.246
   4 cu[1]                    -0.01498     0.7   0.23     3.69   580.21  -0.123
   5 cu[2]                    -0.00385     0.0   0.06     3.68   573.68  -0.032
   6 cu[3]                     0.00071     0.0  -0.01     3.60   567.17   0.006
   7 cu[4]                    -0.00068     0.0   0.01     3.46   560.67  -0.006
   8 cinflimp[2]               0.30611     2.4  -0.24     1.55    30.16   0.048
   9 cinflimp[3]               0.21771     1.2  -0.17     1.55    30.00   0.035
  10 time                      1.26894    24.4  -1.30     1.00    39.50   0.423
```

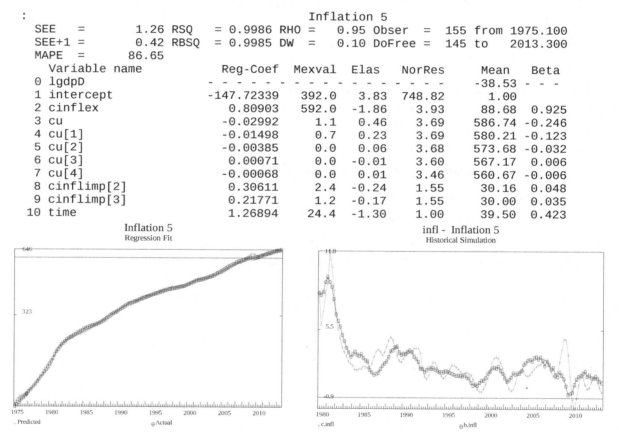

116

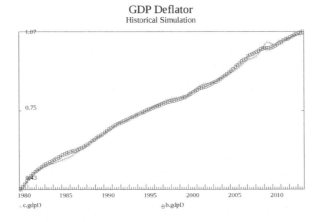

GDP Deflator
Historical Simulation

The historical simulation results are shown above. The historical simulation of the inflation variable *infl* is a bit too cyclical, but manages to track the level of inflation correctly. The historical simulation of the deflator, *gdpD* is now quite good and this forecast is clearly superior to the previous ones. This last lesson is an important one. It matters whether we work in levels or differences. In general, my experience is that it is best to work at the level of the most "integrated" concept that we want to use, in our case, the levels of prices, not the rate of inflation. The trouble with working at the "differenced" level, inflation in our case, is that if we miss on, say, the low side a few times, then the cumulated function gets on the low side and many periods may go by before it catches up.

Exercise

5.1. Include in your current version of the *AMI* model an equation for the price level. First test the equation by itself by defining unemployment with a "fex" command. Then replace the "fex" with just "f" so that unemployment becomes endogenous. Then rerun your experiments with increasing *gR* and watch what happens to inflation.

9. Ways to Improve *AMI*

Addition of the inflation equation to *AMI* began a process of making the model more comprehensive. You can now carry that process further in many directions. Here are some possibilities.

Improve the Investment Equations.

The graphs of the historical simulations of *AMI* showed large errors in the simulation of total fixed investment. The effects of these errors on the rest of the model can be seen by running a historical simulation with the statement "skip vfR" in the .fix file. This statement will cause the model to use the actual value of *vfR* rather than the equation's value. The improvement in the model's performance is striking. The first step in improving the fixed investment equation is certainly to make use of the distinction which the national accounts offer among three different types of fixed investment: (1) Residential investment (2) Nonresidential structures and (3) Producers' durable equipment. Residential investment should depend heavily on personal disposable income, interest rates, and the stock of housing created by a bucket. Do not be surprised if this stock of housing has a negative sign. The negative coefficient would simply mean that if we have housing, we don't need to build it. Equipment investment can follow very much the pattern of the equation we used in *AMI* for all investment, but with the stock formed from only equipment investment and with a faster spill rate than was used for total investment.. Nonresidential structures are apt to be quite a problem, probably because of their great diversity, from electric power plants and oil pipelines to churches and swimming pools.

Improve the Savings Function.

AMI uses exogenous behavioral ratios for Personal savings, Interest paid by persons to business, and Personal transfers to foreigners. That approach implies that these ratios are unaffected by, say, the interest rate, a most unlikely result. Now is a good time to replace the exogenous ratios by economically meaningful relations.

The identity relating income, consumption, interest payments, and savings points out that an increase in interest payments relative to income can come out of either consumption or savings. Thus, the best place to begin work may be on these interest payments. Interest rates, automobile and other durable purchases would be good candidates for explanatory variables, but clearly you do not expect an additive relationship nor one involving just current values of interest rates and durable purchases. With interest payments explained, the savings ratio would be the next in line. Here also interest rates might be expected to play a role, along with the ratio of *piipcb* to *pidis*. It has also been suggested that the ratio of the contributions to social insurance (Social Security) to disposable income might play a role. You may also find that automobile purchases in the current quarter help explain savings, for the accounts consider that you totally consume the car the moment you buy it. Thus, a quarter of unusually high automobile expenditures might well prove to be one of low savings. But if you use automobile purchases (*cdmvR*), you will need to add an equation to explain it.

The remaining variable in the income-consumption-savings identity, personal transfers to foreigners (*pipttf*), is small and could be left as an exogenous ratio.

Expand the financial sector.

So far, money supply has played no role in the model and interest rates, if used, have remained exogenous. The monetary policy variable, however, is not interest rates — which are strongly influenced by inflation — but some measure of the money supply. The Quip data bank has several measures of money supply including M1 and M2. They are natural exogenous variables for the model, though exact modeling of them from the variable the Federal Reserve's open market operations control directly, the unborrowed reserves, is itself a tricky matter. Begin your study here by graphing the ratios of each of these measures of money supply to GDP. With the results of those graphs clearly in mind, develop an equation for the rate on 90-day Treasury bills, *rtb*. Remember that expected inflation plays a big role in determining interest rates.

Expand the Government Sector

The government sector in *AMI* is both highly aggregated and incomplete. Section 3 of the NIPA give the accounts of Federal and of State and local governments separately. Include these accounts in the model so that it can calculate the deficit of the Federal government and the surplus or deficit of the State and local governments. You will probably want to leave many of the expenditures exogenous in constant prices; interest payments will certainly depend upon accumulated deficits and interest rates. Likewise, unemployment insurance costs depend on the level of economic activity. On the revenue side, you may want to make tax rates exogenous while the tax bases are endogenous. *AMI*'s one *taxrate* variable is an example, but you should have a number of rates for different taxes.

Improve the Foreign Sector

You can add an equation for exports as a function of foreign demand, *fgndem* in Quip. This variable is constructed as a weighted average of total real imports of our trading partners. By looking at our exports relative to it, we can judge whether we are gaining or losing shares in world markets. You will find that the change has been considerable. Can you explain it by changes in relative prices? You have in Quip exports in current and constant prices (*x* and *xR*) and the same for imports (*m* and *mR*). You may wish to exclude petroleum from the price index for imports, and you have the necessary material for doing so in Quip. You may also wish to revisit the import equation and put in variables for relative prices. And, of course, if you find these relative price variables valuable, you may want to develop equations for them also.

CHAPTER 6. GOOD ADVICE AND BAD EXAMPLES

1. Good Advice

How can you tell a good equation from a bad one? If there were any single rule, it would not be necessary for *G7* to print out its many statistics and graphs. It could just report the coefficients and give some numerical grade to the equation. Students who themselves are going to receive a silly numerical or alphabetical grade on their equation want to know what is expected. Unfortunately, there are absolutely no absolute answers to that question. Judging an equation requires thought. What *G7* offers is food for thought but is no substitute for thought itself. In this chapter, we shall discuss some ways of thinking about equations.

Since R^2 is used to measure the closeness of fit, a beginner often assumes that R^2 is also the measure of his success in developing an equation. "How high should my R^2 be?" is frequently asked, but there can be no general answer. For some items, say inventory change, .50 may be quite satisfactory; for others, say consumption of food, anything below .98 would be embarrassing. If R^2 alone, then, is inadequate as a guide, what else should be considered in judging the quality of an equation? Here are some things a good equation should do.

1. **Account for important influences.** If the equation is for food consumption, it should certainly account for the influences of income and the price of food relative to other commodities. On the other hand, if it fails to include the percentage of women in the labor force, or the stock of home appliances, or the stock of housing, or the price of electricity and gas, it can hardly be seriously faulted. In fact, if one of these other factors turned out to be crucial, one should be suspicious.

2. **Economize on variables.** In forecasting, every independent variable must either be produced in the model or must be exogenously forecasted. Be sparing, therefore, in the use of special-purpose variables. Especially avoid variables whose forecasting is tantamount to forecasting the dependent variable. For example, the Federal Reserve discount rate would prove a very good variable for explaining the Treasury bill rate in the *QUEST* model. Since the model does not, however, otherwise explain the discount rate, an exogenous forecast of it would be required, and making an exogenous forecast of the discount is just about the same thing as forecasting the T-bill rate. Do not clutter up the equation with numerous variables of small marginal explanatory value (mexval), for each unnecessary variable reduces the efficiency with which the coefficients on the others are estimated. Remember Occam's razor, and prefer a simple equation to a complicated one. On the other hand, if there are strong reasons for believing that a variable should enter the equation and if in fact it does so and with a plausible coefficient, do not throw it out just because its mexval is low or its t-statistic is less than 2.0 in absolute value.

3. **Avoid false exogeneity.** You can very easily eliminate the excessive cycles in *AMI* by making investment depend on changes in real National income instead of changes in real Gross private product. Why? Because real National income is not otherwise in the model, so it is technically an

exogenous variable in the model. Consequently, when the model is run in historical simulation it will always have exactly the historical values of National income, and the predicted values for investment will be those found when the equation was fit. But National income is closely related to GDP and cannot rightfully be considered exogenous. If you run an experiment by increasing, say, exports, you will get no impact on investment because the exogenous National income is not affected although GDP is affected. In the logic of the national accounts, National income should also be affected, but because you have left it exogenous, it is not. When it comes to forecasting, you will have to produce an exogenous forecast of National income. If this forecast turns out to be out of line with the GDP forecast, you will have a problem. All these problems arise because of what I call the false exogeneity of National income. Avoid all such false exogeneity. Limit the exogenous variables to policy variables, such as tax rates or government expenditures, or variables truly unaffected by short-run economic fluctuations, such as population.

4. **Use appropriate dimensions.** If the dependent variable is, say, food expenditure per capita, then it would be inappropriate to use total disposable income to explain it. Total income might grow because total population was growing but without any change in income per capita to increase food purchases per capita. Similarly, one would not use the total population aged 16-25 in this equation, though the fraction of the population in that age range might be quite appropriate. Or again, the index of food prices would be inappropriate -- because food is not the only thing whose price has gone up -- but the ratio of food prices to an overall price index could be used. Failure to get appropriate dimensions is a common problem with student regressions.

5. **Mix trend and stationary variables only with utmost caution.** Roughly speaking, a trend variable is one which, you know without plotting, would, if plotted, go from the lower left to the upper right of the screen. GDP, population, the consumer price index, and the quantity of money are familiar examples. A stationary series, again roughly speaking, is one where you cannot count on such a trend. The growth rate of GDP or quantity of money, an interest rate, the price of imports relative to domestic goods, the price of gasoline relative to the price of shoes, or rainfall or mean temperature for the year are typical examples. If a stationary variable, say the interest rate, is used to explain a trended variable, say the level of aggregate investment, then one has built into the very form of the equation a declining relative importance for the interest rate as the economy -- and with it, aggregate investment -- grows. Conversely, if one tries to explain a stationary variable, say an interest rate, with a trended variable, say the quantity of money, one is clearly looking for a relation which cannot exist. This simple fact is the valid point behind the recent vogue for studying "cointegration".

6. **Avoid "umbrella" variables.** Once I was criticizing the equation of a student who had used residential construction to explain interest rates. High levels of residential construction seemed to cause interest rates to fall. When the student finally understood my objections, he exclaimed, "Oh, I see. It is as if I had used the number of people carrying umbrellas to explain rainfall." Exactly. The independent variables should "cause" the dependent variable, not vice-versa. While the question of what "cause" means in economics is not always clear, a little common sense applied to eliminating such "umbrella" variables will pay good dividends.

7. **Allow for lags as necessary.** Any relevant variable may act with a lag or a distributed lag.

Those lags should be looked for, and if found, the lag distribution should be encouraged, via buckets or soft constraints, to take on a sensible shape. On the other hand, lagged values of the dependent variable should not be used to express lags, since their use will generally distort the parameters on other variables and lead to excessively long lags.

8. **Have plausible parameter values.** Try your best to interpret every parameter in intuitive terms. Of every regression coefficient (except perhaps the intercept) one should ask "Does that value for this coefficient make sense?" If the answer is "no," there may be a case for using soft constraints. For some equations, it is the elasticities which should make sense. To continue the food example, one would expect the income elasticity to be positive but definitely less than 1.0, while the price elasticity should be negative and probably less than 1.0 in absolute value. (In other equations -- and especially for variables with means close to zero -- the elasticities have no intuitive value.)

9. **Fit adequately.** Look at the plot of the regression. Has the equation explained the trend and the major variations from the trend? An equation that misses by a wide margin on the same side for years at a time is missing something important. Try to think what might be the cause and to find a variable to express that cause. Note that this point comes near the end of the list, not at the top.

10. **Show stability of the coefficients when the sample period is changed.** One way to check for this stability is to try the equation with a test period of two or three years at the end of the fit period. Another is through the use of the "recur" command in *G7*. If the coefficients change significantly when the period of fit is changed, then they probably do not reflect a true structure but just an accident of the period you are looking at. Both of these techniques are illustrated in the next section. The *lever* variable should also be checked mainly to spot spurious observations.

Note that the first six points can be and should be taken care of before you ever try to estimate the equation. They are the most important for the functioning of the model.

Until these criteria become second nature, you should use them as a checklist for each equation in your model.

2. Bad Examples

Since the *QUEST* model contains numerous examples of more or less good equations, we will take the opposite approach here and show some examples of equations that are definitely bad. Except for the last, we should not immortalize these bad examples with beautiful graphs, so I will just show the setup of the equations and the numerical results.

Consumption depends on population, so we could do the following:

```
title Consumption and Population
r c = pop
```

with these results:

```
:                             Consumption and Population
  SEE    =      368.97 RSQ   = 0.9847 RHO =    0.99 Obser   =   135 from 1980.100
  SEE+1 =       64.27 RBSQ  = 0.9846 DW  =    0.02 DoFree =   133 to    2013.300
  MAPE  =        6.96
     Variable name              Reg-Coef  Mexval  Elas   NorRes     Mean   Beta
  0 c                           - - - - - - - - - - - - - - - - - 5958.40 - - -
  1 intercept               -23073.93146   541.7  -3.87    65.27    1.00
  2 pop                     107141.63968   707.9   4.87     1.00    0.27  0.992
```

The *RSQ* is terrific, although the *MAPE* leaves room for improvement. But look at the elasticity of population. A one percent increase in population seems to cause a nearly five percent increase in consumption. How can that be? One problem is certainly that we have used current dollar consumption so that we are, in effect, using population to explain inflation. We have, in my terms, inappropriate dimensions. The next equation reduces that problem by using consumption in constant prices, like this:

```
title Real Consumption and Population
r c$ = pop
```

with these results:

```
:                           Real Consumption and Population
  SEE    =      219.91 RSQ   = 0.9897 RHO =    0.98 Obser   =   135 from 1980.100
  SEE+1 =       46.58 RBSQ  = 0.9897 DW  =    0.03 DoFree =   133 to    2013.300
  MAPE  =        2.68
     Variable name              Reg-Coef  Mexval  Elas   NorRes     Mean   Beta
  0 c$                          - - - - - - - - - - - - - - - - - 7213.87 - - -
  1 intercept               -13984.42528   552.3  -1.94    97.45    1.00
  2 pop                      78230.71829   887.2   2.94     1.00    0.27  0.995
```

The *MAPE* is better and the *SEE* is lower, and the *RSQ* is slightly better. The elasticity of consumption with respect to population is lower but still unreasonably high. The problem is that we have not accounted for some important influences, notably increasing income. So we could throw in real disposable income like this.

```
title Real Consumption, Population and Income
r c$ = pop, pidis$
:                         Real Consumption, Population and Income
  SEE    =       87.76 RSQ   = 0.9984 RHO =    0.70 Obser   =   135 from 1980.100
  SEE+1 =       63.22 RBSQ  = 0.9983 DW  =    0.61 DoFree =   132 to    2013.300
  MAPE  =        0.91
     Variable name              Reg-Coef  Mexval  Elas   NorRes     Mean   Beta
  0 c$                          - - - - - - - - - - - - - - - - - 7213.87 - - -
  1 intercept                 -250.68900     0.1  -0.03   611.85    1.00
  2 pop                       -956.04426     0.0  -0.04     6.28    0.27 -0.012
  3 pidis$                       0.96695   150.6   1.07     1.00 7987.62  1.011
```

Now the elasticity on population is deceptive, and strange. It seems to say that if population increases by one percent, consumption will *decrease* by .04 percent. But that calculation assumes that income remains constant. If income also goes up by one percent, so that per capita income stays constant, then consumption goes up by -.04 + 1.07 = 1.03

percent. That is certainly better than the previous equations. But what we would probably really like to see is an equation which makes consumption go up exactly one percent when population goes up one percent and per capita income is unchanged. We can impose that requirement by working with *per capita* income. Does this equation do the trick?

```
title Consumption and Income per Capita
f ypc$ = pidis$/pop
r c$ = ypc$
:                               Consumption and Income per Capita
   SEE   =      151.92 RSQ  = 0.9951 RHO =    0.81 Obser  =   135 from 1980.100
   SEE+1 =       93.15 RBSQ = 0.9951 DW  =    0.39 DoFree =   133 to    2013.300
   MAPE  =        1.98
     Variable name            Reg-Coef  Mexval  Elas   NorRes     Mean    Beta
   0 c$                       - - - - - - - - - - - - - - -     7213.87 - - -
   1 intercept            -4325.19359    434.6  -0.60   204.20      1.00
   2 ypc$                      0.39887   1329.0   1.60     1.00  28929.12  0.998
```

No, it does not. It has violated the "appropriate dimensions" maxim again because it is relating *total* consumption to *per capita* income. Here is the equation we should have estimated.

```
title Consumption per Capita and Income per Capita
f cpc$ = c$/pop
r cpc$ = ypc$

:                        Consumption per Capita and Income per Capita
   SEE   =      306.22 RSQ  = 0.9967 RHO =    0.69 Obser  =   135 from 1980.100
   SEE+1 =      223.43 RBSQ = 0.9967 DW  =    0.63 DoFree =   133 to    2013.300
   MAPE  =        0.91
     Variable name            Reg-Coef  Mexval  Elas   NorRes     Mean    Beta
   0 cpc$                     - - - - - - - - - - - - - - -    26081.09 - - -
   1 intercept            -2486.40441     80.1  -0.10   307.52      1.00
   2 ypc$                      0.98750   1653.6   1.10     1.00  28929.12  0.998
```

The elasticity of consumption with respect to population -- with per capita income constant -- is 1.0 by definition with this equation. The elasticity of consumption per capita with respect to income per capita turns out to be somewhat greater than 1.0. That is because the equation mistakenly attributes the secular decline in the savings rate in the United States to increasing income. The decline had other causes, which we will discuss in connection with the *QUEST* model in Part 2.

Although this last equation passes the maxims of this chapter fairly well, it probably suffers from more subtle problems. If, for some reason, consumption is higher in a particular quarter than it "should" have been according to the equation, then -- because consumption influences income -- income is probably unusually high in that quarter. Thus, the error term in this equation is probably correlated with the independent variable. This problem is referred to as "simultaneous equation bias" or sometimes (less accurately) as "least squares bias." What to do about it is dealt with in Part 2.

Here is an example adapted only slightly from a recent major work of a major economist. It begins from the idea that consumption expenditures per capita on automobiles depends on income per capita and the price of automobiles. The price of automobiles is expressed by taking the ratio of automobile purchases in current prices to the same thing in constant prices. The example goes as follows:

```
f pauto = cdmv/cdmv$ # price of automobiles
f cdmvpc$ = cdmv$/pop
f ypc$ = pidis$/pop
r cdmvpc$ = ypc$, pauto
```

```
:                         Consumption per Capita of Automobiles
  SEE   =     120.29 RSQ   = 0.7030 RHO =    0.90 Obser   =   135 from 1980.100
  SEE+1 =      53.52 RBSQ  = 0.6985 DW  =    0.21 DoFree  =   132 to   2013.300
  MAPE  =      10.28
    Variable name           Reg-Coef  Mexval  Elas   NorRes    Mean    Beta
  0 cdmvpc$                - - - - - - - - - - - - - - -     1029.50 - - -
  1 intercept              -95.80447     0.6  -0.09    3.37     1.00
  2 ypc$                     0.02334    12.6   0.66    1.07 28929.12   0.574
  3 pauto                  478.52469     3.3   0.44    1.00     0.94   0.289
```

Both variables turn out to be highly significant and the income elasticity is 0.66, a reasonable value. However, the elasticity on *pauto* comes out to positive 0.44, which is the wrong sign. How can that be? Do you see what the problem is without reading further?

The problem lies, of course, with the *pauto* variable. As calculated, it is an index of automobile prices, not the price of automobiles relative to other competing goods. The variable which should have been used was

```
f pauto = (cdmv/cdmv$)/(c/c$)
```

Try the regression with this variable. You should be quite unhappy with the results, for they actually show an even larger positive price elasticity. There are many other things to consider with regard to automobile consumption. I'll not pursue this equation further here since a full treatment is given later with the *QUEST* model in Part 2. Suffice it here to emphasize the importance of thinking about the whole structure of the equation and considering the plausibility of the magnitudes of each coefficient, rather than just looking at the correctness of the signs on the coefficients.

There are a number of ways of fooling yourself into thinking that you have a good equation when, in fact, what you have is trash. Here is one way. We need an equation for construction of non-residential structures, *vfnrsR*, and we suppose that it might be proportional to the difference between need for such structures, which we take to be proportional to real GDP, *gdpR*, and the stock of such structures. So we make up an equation like this:

```
ti vfnrsR - Non-residential Structures
lim 1980.1 2013.3
f ub01 = @cum(ub01,1.,.01)
# Make up stock of structures
f StockSt = @cum(cumSt,vfnrsR,.01)/ub01
r vfnrsR = gdpR,StockSt
```

It doesn't work very well, so let's try lagging the stock of structures one quarter with this regression command:

```
r vfnrsR = gdpR,StockSt,StockSt[1]
```

Now we get the following wonderful results:

```
:                              vfnrsR - Non-residential Structures
  SEE   =       14.70 RSQ   = 0.9578 RHO =    0.96 Obser  =   135 from 1980.100
  SEE+1 =        5.02 RBSQ  = 0.9568 DW  =    0.08 DoFree =   131 to    2013.300
  MAPE  =        3.20
    Variable name              Reg-Coef  Mexval  Elas   NorRes      Mean    Beta
  0 vfnrsR                     - - - - - - - - - - - - - - -      343.34  - - -
  1 intercept               -104.18180     8.4  -0.30    23.68      1.00
  2 gdpR                       0.00504      6.5   0.16    13.07  11006.94   0.212
  3 StockSt                   56.45992    261.1  46.78    13.05    284.49  24.621
  4 StockSt[1]               -55.27296    261.3 -45.64     1.00    283.51 -24.196
```

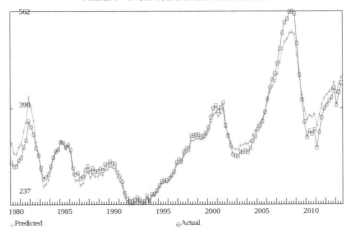

vfnrsR - Non-residential Structures

The fit is fantastic; the mexval's are enormous; what could be wrong? First of all, we used the current value of the dependent variable in making up the *StockSt* variable; that will cause problems in forecasting. Now, without the unit bucket adjustment, the current value of the stock is just the dependent variable plus 99 percent of the lagged value of the stock. So the regression can just turn that identity around to compute the dependent variable from the current and lagged values of the stock. The use of the unit bucket adjustment blurs the identity just enough that we may not recognize immediately what a silly thing we have done. Certainly, the equation is utterly worthless for forecasting or counter-historical simulation.

If we define the stock using the lagged value of the dependent variable, as with the command

```
f StockSt = @cum(cumSt,vfnrsR[1],.01)
```

then the regression can reconstruct this lagged value from *StockSt* and *StockSt[1]*. That

127

lagged value of the dependent variable, as we will see in the next section, is one of the most deceptive, destructive, and dangerous variables you can put into an equation with which you hope to capture structure.

In teaching the uses of regression, the first problem is to get students to think of possible variables that could be used to explain a given variable. Then, the second problem is to bring them under control. It is not unusual to encounter regressions like this one:

```
save vfnrsR.sav
ti vfnrsR - Non-residential Structures
f d = gdpR - gdpR[1]
f ub01 = @cum(ub01,1.,.01)
f StockSt = 100.*@cum(cumSt,0.25*vfnrsR[1],.01)/ub01
f m1R = m1/gdpD
f niprfR = niprf/gdpD
r vfnrsR = gdpR[1],d[1],d[2],d[3],d[4],d[5],d[6],d[7],
   d[8],d[9],d[10],StockSt[1],m1R, m1R[1],rtb,rtb[1], niprfR, niprfR[1]
```

```
:                         vfnrsR - Non-residential Structures
  SEE    =      26.91 RSQ   = 0.8586 RHO =    0.77 Obser   =  135 from 1980.100
  SEE+1 =       17.23 RBSQ  = 0.8367 DW  =    0.45 DoFree  =  116 to    2013.300
  MAPE   =       5.89
```

	Variable name	Reg-Coef	Mexval	Elas	NorRes	Mean	Beta
0	vfnrsR	- - - - - - - - - - - - - - - -				343.34	- - -
1	intercept	-282.70519	5.2	-0.82	7.07	1.00	
2	gdpR[1]	0.02274	11.0	0.72	3.83	10937.61	0.955
3	d[1]	-0.12546	4.0	-0.02	3.41	68.28	-0.134
4	d[2]	-0.05108	0.6	-0.01	3.38	67.98	-0.055
5	d[3]	-0.00140	0.0	-0.00	3.38	67.63	-0.002
6	d[4]	0.02310	0.1	0.00	3.35	67.58	0.025
7	d[5]	0.01326	0.0	0.00	3.30	67.51	0.014
8	d[6]	0.03124	0.3	0.01	3.28	67.58	0.033
9	d[7]	0.03773	0.4	0.01	3.25	68.26	0.041
10	d[8]	0.05076	0.7	0.01	3.21	66.99	0.055
11	d[9]	0.07218	1.4	0.01	3.19	66.81	0.078
12	d[10]	0.04295	0.5	0.01	3.15	66.66	0.046
13	StockSt[1]	0.05900	8.2	1.21	3.09	7048.02	0.652
14	m1R	0.42069	3.2	1.69	2.21	1378.49	1.885
15	m1R[1]	-0.54130	5.2	-2.16	2.18	1367.42	-2.351
16	rtb	5.15165	0.9	0.07	1.20	4.86	0.252
17	rtb[1]	11.68761	4.3	0.17	1.05	4.95	0.575
18	niprfR	-0.09716	1.5	-0.29	1.05	1019.62	-0.614
19	niprfR[1]	0.13069	2.4	0.38	1.00	1009.15	0.815

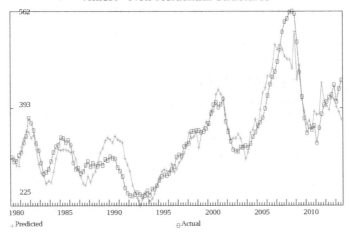

vfnrsR - Non-residential Structures

The fit is undeniably excellent. The negative sign on M1 lagged and the positive signs on the interest rate should give one pause. But I have often been more or less told by the ingenious and proud creators of such equations, "How do you know what those signs ought to be? Look at this fit!"

Well, one way that often shows that warnings of theoretically wrong signs should have been heeded is to fit the equation over only part of the period and to use the end of the data to test how the equation performs outside the period over which it was fit. Let's try this with the above equation. We change only the "limits" line to

```
lim 1980.1 1997.4 2013.3
```

The fit over the shorter period is actually slightly better:

```
:                    vfnrsR - Non-residential Structures
  SEE   =      11.60 RSQ  = 0.8680 RHO =    0.73 Obser  =    72 from 1980.100
  SEE+1 =       8.16 RBSQ = 0.8232 DW  =    0.54 DoFree =    53 to   1997.400
  MAPE  =       3.35 Test period:  SEE   95.09 MAPE   17.92 end  2013.300
    Variable name        Reg-Coef Mexval  Elas   NorRes    Mean    Beta
  0 vfnrsR               - - - - - - - - - - - - - - -    295.92  - - -
  1 intercept           120.87993    2.2   0.41    7.58      1.00
  2 gdpR[1]              -0.00864    0.8  -0.25    5.73   8414.33 -0.374
  3 d[1]                 -0.05298    1.8  -0.01    5.73     64.37 -0.100
  4 d[2]                 -0.00328    0.0  -0.00    5.63     63.06 -0.006
  5 d[3]                  0.04009    1.3   0.01    5.35     61.22  0.074
  6 d[4]                  0.06749    3.7   0.01    4.99     60.03  0.125
  7 d[5]                  0.08636    5.2   0.02    4.65     59.58  0.159
  8 d[6]                  0.01830    0.3   0.00    4.53     59.28  0.034
  9 d[7]                  0.00447    0.0   0.00    4.51     59.95  0.008
 10 d[8]                  0.03291    1.0   0.01    4.48     59.11  0.063
 11 d[9]                  0.03533    1.2   0.01    4.45     58.49  0.067
 12 d[10]                 0.01090    0.1   0.00    4.44     58.54  0.021
 13 StockSt[1]            0.03075    5.5   0.67    3.74   6475.56  0.416
 14 m1R                   0.11393    0.4   0.46    1.50   1200.24  0.799
```

129

```
15 m1R[1]                    -0.21881     1.8  -0.88     1.41   1193.91 -1.546
16 rtb                        1.71196     0.6   0.04     1.29      7.07  0.159
17 rtb[1]                     6.50303     7.2   0.16     1.20      7.17  0.611
18 niprfR                     0.04511     0.4   0.10     1.02    681.03  0.254
19 niprfR[1]                  0.10336     1.2   0.24     1.00    673.56  0.558
```

but the forecast into the test period is not as good, as you can see from the SEE and MAPE in the test period in the table above or even more dramatically in the graph below.

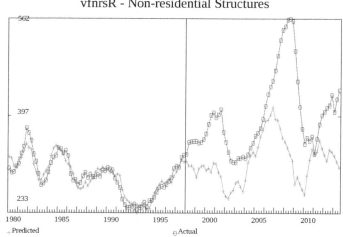

vfnrsR - Non-residential Structures

Another way to check the reliability of a regression is through the use of *recursive regression* by *G7*'s "recur" command. This amounts to running the same regression a number of times with progressively longer periods of fit and observing what happens to the values of the estimated regression coefficients. In *G7*, we need make only two minor changes is the commands to do recursive regression. Just change

```
lim 1980.1 2013.3
...
r vfnrsR = gdpR[1],d[1],d[2],d[3],d[4],d[5],d[6],d[7],
```

to

```
lim 1980.1 1997.4 2013.3
...
recur vfnrsR = gdpR[1],d[1],d[2],d[3],d[4],d[5],d[6],d[7],
```

The first regression will be over the period 1997.4 to 2013.3, the next over 1997.3 to 2013.3, and so on until the last is over 1980.1 2013.3. The results will pour out on the blue screen, but to make it easier to see what is happening, *G7* enters the values of each coefficient as time series in its workspace bank. These series are named *b1, b2, b3*, etc., up to the number of variables in the regression. The value of a particular *b* in a particular period is the value of that regression coefficient in the regression beginning in that period. Thus, *b1* for 1997.4 is the value of the intercept in the regression from 1997.4 to 2013.3. Also entered into the workspace are the standard deviations of the coefficients, *s1, s2, s3,* etc., as computed by the standard formulas.

The results are best viewed by graphing each coefficient and two standard deviations on either side. Here is a *G7* command file which will do the job for the present example.

```
do {f lb = b%1 -2*s%1;
    f ub = b%1 +2*s%1;
    ti Regression Coefficient %1;
    gname coef%1;
    gr lb b%1 ub} (1-19)
```

This command file uses the *do* command of *G7* to repeat the same commands with substitution of text; it is fully described in the *G7* help files and need not detain us here.

What one would hope to find in these graphs is something not worse than the graph on the left below for coefficient 19. Nearly all of the estimated values, the middle line, are within two standard deviations of any other value on that line, by standard deviations calculated for any period. If all of the coefficients had graphs like that of number 19 (the coefficient for *niprfR[1]*), we could say that the recursive regression examination had been passed satisfactorily.

Regression Coefficient 19;   Regression Coefficient 13;

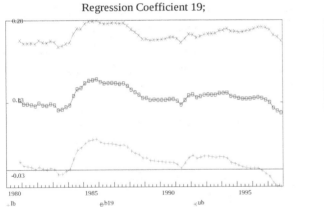
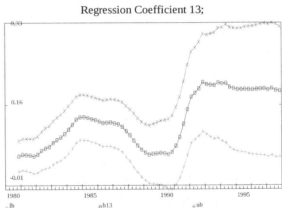

Unfortunately, that is by no means the case. A much more typical result is that for Coefficient 13 for the stock of structures. Estimation beginning in 1981.1 gives a very low coefficient; estimation beginning a few quarters sooner or later gives a much larger coefficient. "How can that be?" you may well ask. The answer can only be that there was no stable structure of the kind posited by this regression. Thus, this equation fails examination by recursive regression and thereby illustrates how the method can perhaps save us from using equations which would make embarrassing forecasts.

Next, let us look at a problem of mixing trended and stationary variables. We can see it in the problem of relating imports to domestic demand and exchange rates. Here is one approach using a "terms of trade" (tot) variable defined as the ratio of the prices of imported goods relative to the prices of domestically produced goods.

```
ti m$ -- Imports
" Define Domestic Demand
f dd$ = c$ + v$ + g$ + x$
" define terms of trade as ratio of foreign to domestic prices.
f tot = (m/m$)/(gnp/gnp$)
r m$ = dd$, tot
```

Over a long period, Domestic Demand (dd$) and Imports ($m$$) both grow substantially. The terms of trade variable (tot), however, is essentially a relative price. It is unlikely to have a long-term, secular trend. Consider a future year when dd$ will have doubled, and, let us say, $m$$ has tripled, but tot is about the same then as now. Will a change of, say .1, change $m$$ by the same dollar amount then as now? The form of the equation requires an answer of "yes", but I think you will agree that the correct answer should be "No, the effect will be larger." The problem is that we have mixed stationary and trend variables.

One approach to the problem just posed is to regress the logarithm of $m$$ on those of dd$ and tot. Then the elasticity of imports with respect to terms of trade will be constant. But we will have only shifted the problem. If the elasticity of imports with respect to domestic demand is greater than 1.0 -- which is likely -- then with sufficient growth in domestic demand, imports will exceed domestic demand and domestic production will have become negative. Here we have a case of what I call *asymptotic idiocy*. One detects it by asking what happens to the equation as the variables move far along the trends they are likely to follow. Actually, trend-stationary problems are just a special case of it.

My long involvement in long-term forecasting has perhaps made me overly sensitive to the asymptotic idiocy problem. It is certainly defensible to use for a short forecast an equation which is asymptotically idiotic, but it does seem to me that one should be aware of the problem. Unfortunately, avoiding asymptotically idiotic equations often requires non-linear equations with coefficients which are laborious to estimate. We will see a method for doing so in Part 2.

If you are working on the improvement of *AMI* along the lines suggested at then end of Chapter 4, you already have a number of equations to which to apply the ten-point check list of this chapter.

3. The Worst Example

A lagged value of the dependent variable is frequently used as an independent variable not just by greenhorn students of modeling but also by serious professionals who should know better. Such equations are, for reasons I will explain, exercises in self deception. They are, however, frequently excused with a comment to the effect that they allow for a distributed lag. Now allowing for a distributed lag is, as we have seen, frequently a good thing to do. We therefore need to see first why the lagged value of the dependent variable might possibly be a way to include a distributed lag and then why it usually does something quite different.

Let us suppose, then, that y depends upon infinitely many prior values of x with exponentially decreasing weights. The true equation relating y and x is then supposed to be

$$(1) \qquad y_t = a + b \sum_{i=0}^{\infty} \lambda^i x_{t-i} + \epsilon_t$$

where $0 < \lambda < 1$. At first glance, this equation seems to call for a regression of y on an infinity of prior values of x. But the assumption of exponentially declining weights allows us to perform a trick with the equation. First we lag the equation once and then multiply both sides by λ to get

$$(2) \qquad \lambda y_{t-1} = \lambda a + b \sum_{i=1}^{\infty} \lambda^i x_{t-i} + \lambda \epsilon_t$$

Notice that the infinite summation on the right side of the two equations is the same except that the summation in equation (2) lacks the first term of the summation in equation (1). Subtracting (2) from (1) therefore gives

$$(3) \qquad y_t - \lambda y_{t-1} = a(1-\lambda) + bx_t + \epsilon_t - \lambda \epsilon_{t-1}$$

which we rewrite in a form to be estimated as

$$(4) \qquad y_t = b_1 + b_2 x_t + b_3 y_{t-1} + \epsilon_t - \lambda \epsilon_{t-1}$$

We can now estimate equation (4) without the slightest concern about an infinite number of independent variables. The estimate of b_3 is the estimate of λ. More flexible forms of lags can be obtained by including more than one lagged value of the dependent variable. One should note, of course, that if the error terms in equation (1) are independent, then the ones in equation (4) are autocorrelated and correlated with one of the independent variables, namely y_{t-1}.

Now this transformation is indeed a clever trick and has mesmerized many model builders into a rather indiscriminate use of lagged values of the dependent variable to account for lags. The problem is that the equation with the lagged dependent variable may fit very well for reasons totally unrelated to the supposed distributed lag on one particular variable. Namely, the dependent variable may well depend upon many factors which change slowly relative to the period of observation. The lagged value of the dependent variable sums up perfectly the effects of all these factors for one period earlier. But, since the factors change slowly, that summary is still an excellent representation of their values in the present period. Thus, the lagged value of the dependent variable will explain most of the variation in the dependent variable and leave only a little noise to identify the coefficients of the other variables in the regression.

Now equations with lagged values of the dependent variable offer an alternative way of calculating the predicted value. Namely, instead of using the actual lagged value of the dependent variable in computing the predicted value, we can use the value predicted for the first period to calculate the prediction for the second period, and then use the predicted value for the second period to calculate the prediction for the third, and so on. We will call the variable computed in this way *BasePred*, because it uses the actual lagged value only in the base period. If G detects the lagged value of the dependent variable, it automatically computes this *BasePred* and graphs it as a third line when the "*gr* *" command is given. If the above analysis is applicable to your equation, the fit of the ordinary predicted value should be very close, while that of *BasePred* may be anywhere from so-so to dreadful. Let us look at two examples.

In the first, we regress inflation on its own lagged value and the unemployment rate. The results are shown below.[2]

---

2   If the lagged value of the dependent variable is included among the independent variables, the Durbin-Watson statistic is invalid in the best of circumstances. Durbin devised another statistic for this situation known as the Durbin H. If the error terms are uncorrelated, the distribution of H approaches the normal with mean zero and unit standard deviation as the sample size grows. When G detects the presence of the lagged value of the dependent variable among the independent variables, it automatically replaces the Durbin Watson with the Durbin H.

```
:                                     Inflation
   SEE    =        0.29 RSQ   = 0.9754 RHO =    0.48 Obser   =  135 from 1980.100
   SEE+1  =        0.25 RBSQ  = 0.9750 DurH =   5.61 DoFree  =  132 to   2013.300
   MAPE   =       11.03
      Variable name           Reg-Coef  Mexval   Elas   NorRes     Mean    Beta
   0 infl                     - - - - - - - - - - - - - - - - -    2.83  - - -
   1 intercept                 0.31715     3.6   0.11    40.68     1.00
   2 u                        -0.04320     2.9  -0.10    39.16     6.46  -0.039
   3 infl[1]                   0.96914   525.7   0.99     1.00     2.88   0.996
```

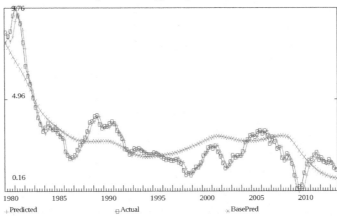

Inflation
Equation with Lagged Dependent Variable

As you can see, the fit of the equation as normally calculated is fantastic; the fit of the *BasePred* line, however, shows that the equation is worthless for forecasting beyond a few periods. It has failed to identify the connection between unemployment and changes in inflation which our earlier equations identified fairly well.

Another example is given by regressing Residential Construction on the real interest rate and two lagged values of the dependent variable. The R^2 is even better than before, and the performance on the *BasePred* test is even more miserable. It doesn't even do well right at the beginning.

```
:                               Residential Construction
   SEE    =       13.71 RSQ   = 0.9939 RHO =   -0.13 Obser   =  135 from 1980.100
   SEE+1  =       13.58 RBSQ  = 0.9938 DurH =   -2.05 DoFree  =  131 to   2013.300
   MAPE   =        2.38
      Variable name           Reg-Coef  Mexval   Elas   NorRes     Mean    Beta
   0 vfrR                     - - - - - - - - - - - - - - - - -  478.46  - - -
   1 intercept                11.55952     2.7   0.02   164.60     1.00
   2 rtbR                     -1.12629     1.5  -0.00   138.15     2.03  -0.015
   3 vfrR[1]                   1.72175   178.1   1.72     2.25   477.37   1.725
   4 vfrR[2]                  -0.74026    50.0  -0.74     1.00   476.49  -0.743
```

135

Residential Construction
Equation with Lagged Dependent Variable

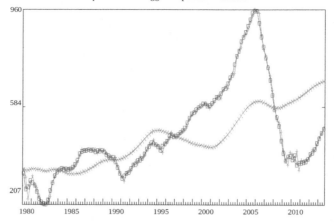

Just because you get a close fit when using a lagged value of the dependent variable, do not suppose that you have arrived at any kind of structural relation between the dependent and independent variables. Possibly you have found such a relation, but much more probably you have simply found that the determinants of the dependent variable change slowly from period to period. Those determinants may or may not have anything to do with the independent variable you have specified. If the dependent variable has a trend, *BasePred* will generally follow that trend, but that following is no evidence of having found a structural relation.

When distributed lags are estimated by direct regression by putting a variable into a "bucket" (as we did in creating *inflex* in the inflation examples of Chapter 5), and the independent variables fail to explain the dependent, we immediately recognize that fact by poor fit. When the lagged value of the dependent variable is slipped into the equation, we no longer have that warning. We can get excellent fits without having found any causal relation between the independent and dependent variables. I, therefore, find the lagged value of the dependent variable deceptive and avoid it. Self-deception, however, is always popular, and the use of the lagged value of the dependent variable has reached epidemic proportions. This use, I believe, is responsible for much poor forecasting and bad policy analysis which has done nothing to engender respect for the economic forecasting profession on the part of the general public.

CHAPTER 7. *QUEST* - A QUARTERLY ECONOMIC STRUCTURAL MODEL

In previous chapters, we have developed a very simple model and suggested some directions in which it could be expanded. Now we will follow some of the suggestions while trying to heed the good advice of the last Chapter 6. In particular, our model will

refine the consumption and employment functions presented previously.

divide fixed investment into three major components, equipment, residences, and other structures, and develop appropriate equations for each.

develop an equation for imports.

complete the income side of the model with equations for capital consumption, profits, dividends, interest rates, interest payments and income, employee compensation and proprietor income.

calculate revenues from various taxes, government expenditures in current prices (from variables exogenous in constant prices), interest payments, and budgetary deficits or surpluses for the federal government and, separately, for the combination of state and local governments.

The word "structural" in the name of the Quest model is noteworthy. Quest is a model intended to embody and test an understanding of how the economy works. It is concerned with how aggregate demand affects employment, how employment affects unemployment, how unemployment affects prices, how prices and money supply affect interest rates and incomes, and how incomes, interest rates, and prices affect investment, consumption, imports, and exports, which make up aggregate. demand. The model embodies a view of how each link in this closed-loop chain works. Satisfactory performance is not to judged by how well it works forecasting a few quarters ahead, but by how well it holds up over a much longer period. Can it keep employment within a few percent of the labor force over decades? Can it keep inflation in line with the increase in money supply though it does not use money supply in the inflation equation? Can it right itself if thrown off course for a few quarters? We will test it in 28-year historical simulation, time enough for it to go seriously astray if it is inclined to do so.

In this respect, Quest is quite different from most quarterly models of my acquaintance. They are usually aimed at short-term forecasting, usually of not more than eight quarters. They can therefore make extensive use of lagged values of dependent variables in the regression equations. The use of these lagged dependent variables gives close fits but leaves little variability for identifying the parameters of the underlying structural equations, which are often rather weak in such models. Our interest centers in the structural equations. In estimating the equations of Quest, therefore, we have avoided lagged values of dependent variables in the regression equations. When used for short-term forecasting, Quest uses the rho-adjustment method of error correction described in Chapter 2.

Models often have a special purpose, a special question they are designed to answer. Quest is basically a general-purpose marcoeconomic model, but it would be less than fair to the reader not to mention that there was a particular question on my mind as I worked on it in the summer of 1999. As in the summer of 1929, exactly seventy years earlier, the economy was growing strongly and the stock market was at unprecedented — and, quite possibly, unjustified — highs. The run-up in the stock market was generally attributed to the influx of footloose capital from Asian markets. At the first sign of a drop, this capital could leave as suddenly as it came. The stock market would then fall. But how would that fall affect employment and output in the real economy? As I revised the model in the summer of 2001, the stock market had declined significantly, and economic growth had slowed sharply. How far the fall would go and how sharp the recession would be was still unclear. A further revision came in the spring of 2009, after the calamitous events of 2008. Would the economy recover? How long would it take? The version of the model presented here is that estimated by Douglas S. Meade at that time.

The stock market plays no role in the National Income and Product accounts, but its performance can make people feel wealthy or poor and thus influence how they spend or save. It determines how much equity in a firm must be diluted in order to raise a given amount of capital by issuing stock. In this way, it affects the cost of capital as perceived by the owners of companies, and thus may affect investment. We will enter the Standard & Poor index of the prices of 500 stocks as an explanatory variable in a number of behavioral equations, and finally we will try to explain this variable by corporate profits and interest rates and some *ad hoc* dummy variables to represent the dotcom bubble and the subprime mortgage boom and collapse, events which clearly cannot be explained by basic macroeconomics. The stock market variable proves very helpful in a number of the equations.

1. The Behavioral Equations

Investment

Investment is the most volatile part of GDP but also the part that depends least on other developments in the same quarter. Construction must be planned and financing arranged before work is begun, and once begun, proceeds independently of current developments in the economy. Much the same is true of investment in Producer durable equipment. These are therefore good places to begin the iterative calculation of for each quarter. Gross private domestic investment in Quest is treated in the four major parts available in even the aggregated version of the NIPA: Producers' durable equipment, Non-residential construction, Residential construction, and Change in business inventories.

The first and largest is investment in **Producers' durable equipment**. Four variables are used to explain it: (1) replacement, calculated from past investment with a wear-out rate of 5 percent per quarter, (2) the first difference in the previous peak gross private product, to represent the need for expansion investment, (3) the stock market and (4) unemployment. Each requires a comment.

Replacement is calculated by assuming that 5 percent of the equipment stock wears out each quarter. The function @cum(stockEq,vfnreR[4],.05) cumulates investment (*vfnreR*) with the the 5 percent per quarter wear-out rate to create the stock of equipment series, *stockEq*. Multiplying this series by .05 – or dividing by 20 -- gives the quarterly wearout or replacement required to maintain the stock of capital. There is a slight problem, however, because our data begins only in 1955 and in the early years of the fitting process, some of the capital may have been invested before 1955. We can make a rough adjustment for this problem by dividing, not by 20, but by the variable *ub05* calculated by @cum(ub05,1.0,.05). It cumulates a series of 1's, so it goes 0, 1.00, 1.95, 2.85, ... and approaches 20 asymptotically. Thus, the two commands

    f ub05 = @cum(ub05,1.0,.05)

    f repEq = @cum(stockEq,vfnreR[4],.05)/ub05

produce a series, *repEq*, which should approximate the investment necessary to replace the equipment which is wearing out each quarter. We should expect it to have a regression coefficient of about 1.0 in the equation to explain investment. The figure below shows this replacement as the light line in comparison to gross investment, the line marked by squares. We see that replacement has usually been a floor under gross investment, the only exceptions being in the financial panic of the last two quarters of 2008.

The second basic reason for investment, after replacement, is to provide capital for expansion. One might suppose that future expansion would determine present investment, but much experience shows that it is past expansion which determines present investment. Firms like to maintain some excess capacity so that they can respond to opportunities to expand sales. But *after* an expansion of sales, more capacity is needed to be ready for further expansion. We use Gross private product as the indicator of the need for capital and its first difference as the need for expansion capital. Before taking its first difference, however, we put it through the @peak function. The @peak function is the highest value which the variable has ever had up to and including the present. The use of the @peak function makes little difference in estimating the equation, but it makes the model more stable, since the first difference terms cannot go negative in a downturn. Some of the investment response to an increase in output comes almost immediately; some requires a much longer time, over two years, so we estimate a distributed lag over 7 quarters. If we just put in all 7 lagged values into the regression without any constraint on their regression coefficients, we get very erratic, implausible coefficients. So we softly constrain the coefficients, after the first two, to lie on a straight line. This is the function of the command

    sma 5000 a5 a9 1

There are several reasons why the stock market affects investment. High stock prices mean that capital can be raised with little dilution of equity of existing stock holders. A rising stock market also promotes business optimism. It is also indicative of good profits, which can be used to finance investment.

Finally, unemployment leads to pessimism about future growth and suppresses investment.

Macroeconomic textbooks stress the importance of interest rates in determining investment. High interest rates should suppress investment. Diligent search has failed to find a consistent negative relation between real interest rates and investment in equipment. Probably the effect is small and is outweighed by the contrary effect that strong investment demand means strong demand for funds, which causes interest rates to rise. We will find negative effects of interest rates in the equation for residential construction, but not here in the larger equipment investment series. The IS-LM analysis that occupies a prominent place in many macroeconomic textbooks rests on the sensitivity of investment to interest rates. The fact that this sensitivity is so slight that it is difficult to detect certainly suggests that the IS-LM interaction is of minor importance in macroeconomic equilibrium and that some other mechanism is responsible for the ability of the economy to provide most or less full employment for any given labor force.

We first give the commands to the G regression program to create the variable, then give the results.

```
ti Equipment Investment
f gppR = (gdp - gdpg)/deflate
f pgppR = @peak(pgppR,gppR,.0)
f d = pgppR - pgppR[1]
# Equipment replacement, used also in Labor Productivity
f ub05 = @cum(ub05,1.0,.05)
f repEq = @cum(stockEq,vfnreR[4],.05)/ub05
spr stockEq

fex sp500R = sp500/deflate
f dsp500R = sp500R - sp500R[1]
f ue = lfc -emp
con 10000 1 = a2
sma 5000 a5 a9 1
sma 100 a12 a17 1

r vfnreR = repEq, d[1], d[2],d[3],d[4],d[5], d[6],d[7], sp500R[1],
    dsp500R[1],dsp500R[2],dsp500R[3], dsp500R[4], dsp500R[5], dsp500R[6],dsp500R[7],
ue[1]
```

Equipment Investment

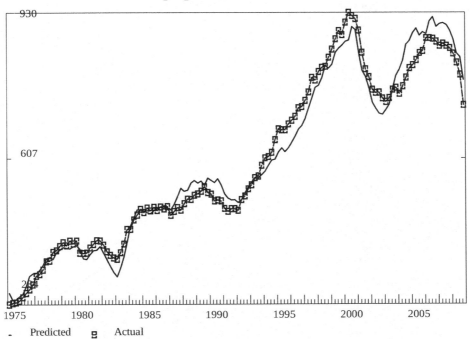

- Predicted   ▫   Actual

```
:                        Equipment Investment
  SEE    =       30.88 RSQ  = 0.9724 RHO =   0.91 Obser  =  136 from 1975.100
  SEE+1  =       13.16 RBSQ = 0.9684 DW  =   0.18 DoFree =  118 to   2008.400
  MAPE   =        4.21
     Variable name          Reg-Coef  Mexval  Elas  NorRes     Mean   Beta
  0  vfnreR               - - - - - - - - - - - - - - - -     597.95 - - -
  1  intercept            202.81619    27.6   0.34   43.71      1.00
  2  repEq                  0.92477   234.7   0.79    4.06    508.01   0.851
  3  d[1]                   0.14959     1.4   0.01    3.56     47.04   0.035
  4  d[2]                   0.17950     1.9   0.01    3.15     47.04   0.042
  5  d[3]                   0.12455     1.7   0.01    3.08     47.04   0.029
  6  d[4]                   0.11557     3.7   0.01    2.82     47.04   0.027
  7  d[5]                   0.10604     3.8   0.01    2.57     47.04   0.025
  8  d[6]                   0.08591     2.5   0.01    2.38     46.75   0.020
  9  d[7]                   0.05066     1.4   0.00    2.15     46.43   0.012
 10  sp500R[1]              0.02204     1.0   0.02    1.81    614.83   0.047
 11  dsp500R[1]             0.16286     1.7   0.00    1.73      5.70   0.036
 12  dsp500R[2]             0.17721     2.0   0.00    1.67      6.20   0.038
 13  dsp500R[3]             0.14910     1.8   0.00    1.59      6.05   0.032
 14  dsp500R[4]             0.09311     0.7   0.00    1.54      6.79   0.019
 15  dsp500R[5]             0.15977     2.1   0.00    1.46      6.75   0.033
 16  dsp500R[6]             0.18737     2.9   0.00    1.39      6.71   0.038
 17  dsp500R[7]             0.17799     2.5   0.00    1.32      6.08   0.036
 18  ue[1]                 -0.01739    15.1  -0.22    1.00   7666.19  -0.117

id vfnre = vfnreR*deflate
```

In the regression results shown above, equipment replacement, which theoretically should have a coefficient of 1.00 had, in fact a coefficient of .92, close enough for the interpretation to seem justified. The *d* has coefficients which first rise and then fall,

141

indicating that it does, indeed, take time for investment to react to changes in output. The graph below shows this response.

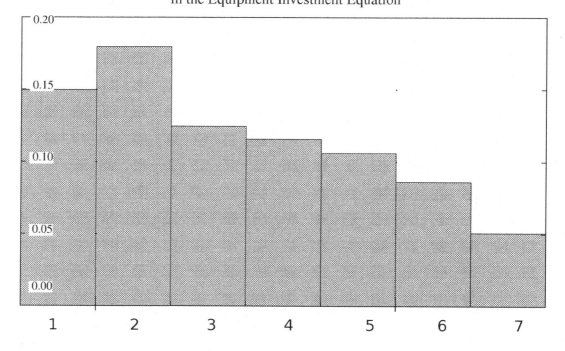

Distributed Lag on Changes in Output
in the Equipment Investment Equation

(The graphing of regression coefficients in G is possible because after the regression is estimated, the regression coefficients, along with some of the other regression results, are stored like a time series in the variable *rcoef,* beginning at the beginning of the data bank. The simplest way to see what is where is to do "type rcoef" with the dates at the beginning of the workspace bank, 1955.1 in the case of the Quest model.)

Investment in **Non-residential construction** — stores, office buildings, industrial plants, pipelines, churches, hospitals, airports, parking lots, and so on — is one of the hardest series to explain. Even the booming economy of the late 1990's barely brought it back to the levels it reached in the recession years of the early 1980's. Our equation is motivated by the idea that investment is proportional to the difference between the desired stock and the actual stock of structures, and that the desired stock is a linear function of the real Gross private product, gppR. Thus, the basic idea is that

$$vfnrsR = \lambda(a + b * gppR - StockSt)$$

where *vfnrsR* is real investment in non-residential construction, and *StockSt* is the stock of those structures. Several depreciation rates have been tried for calculating the stock of structures without much effect on the fit of the equation. One percent per quarter was chosen. By introducing lagged values of the first difference of *gppR*, the desired level of the stock is allowed to rise gradually following an increase in *gppR*.

The natural variable to add next is some sort of interest rate. These all had positive — wrong — signs with lags of three years or less. This strong, *positive* relation with interest rates suggested using interest income, which, indeed proved somewhat helpful. The reasoning is that persons with significant amounts of interest income might be likely to investment in real estates.

The rates of change of the stock market value variable — but not its level — also proved somewhat helpful. This variable may be measuring optimism about the future of the economy.

Finally, two special dummy variables were introduced. The first, called *taxacts*, is a series of 1's for the period between 1981 and the 1986. The 1981 act allowed passive partners in real estate development (as well as active partners) to count paper depreciation at double declining balance rates against their ordinary income. Investors looking for tax shelters poured billions of dollars into non-residential construction. The 1986 act repealed this provision for non-residential construction. It did not even "grandfather" in the buildings that had been built while the 1981 act was in force. Thus, many investors who had bought tax shelters found themselves with more or less worthless holdings. Though the 1986 act was not passed until the middle of the year, its passage was anticipated, and investment was cut back at the beginning of the year.

The second dummy, called *subnrs* (for *sub*prime effects on *n*on-*r*esidential *s*tructures) represents the effects of the subprime mortgage crisis on non-residential construction. These effects were, perhaps surprisingly, *positive*. There has long been noted a negative relationship between residential and non-residential construction. Residential has been more volatile, but the two draw on the same labor market and to some extent the same materials. Thus, times of a slump in residential construction have often been times of low costs and consequent booms in non-residential construction. Our *subnrs* dummy therefore begins at 1 in 2006.1 – the beginning of the subprime mortgage crisis -- and rises by 1 each quarter up to 2008.1, remains at that peak level for three quarters and then descends back down by 1 per quarter until reaching 0.

Here are the commands:

```
ti vfnrsR - Non-residential Structures
fex gppR = (gdp - gdpg)/deflate
f pgppR = @peak(pgppR,gppR,.0)
f dpgppR = pgppR - pgppR[1]
f ub01 = @cum(ub01,1.,.01)
f StockSt = 100.* @cum(cumSt,0.25*vfnrsR[4],.01)/ub01
fex subnrs = 0.
update subnrs
2006.1  1 2 3 4  5 6 7 8  9 9 9 8  7 6 5 4  3 2 1;
fex taxacts = 0
update taxacts
```

```
1982.1  1 1 1 1  1 1 1 1  1 1 1 1  1 1 1 1;
fex sp500R = sp500/deflate
fdup dsp500R = sp500R - sp500R[1]

r vfnrsR = gppR[4],StockSt[1], taxacts, dsp500R[4],dsp500R[5],dsp500R[6],
npiniR[1], subnrs
```

And here are the results:

vfnrsR - Non-residential Structures

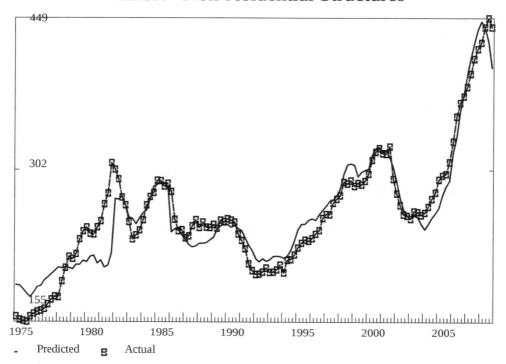

- Predicted   ⊟ Actual

```
                   vfnrsR - Non-residential Structures
   SEE    =      19.61 RSQ  = 0.8902 RHO =   0.87 Obser  = 136 from 1975.100
   SEE+1 =      10.08 RBSQ = 0.8833 DW   =   0.26 DoFree = 127 to   2008.400
   MAPE  =       6.16
     Variable name           Reg-Coef  Mexval  Elas   NorRes     Mean    Beta
   0 vfnrsR                   - - - - - - - - - - - - - -     260.28 - - -
   1 intercept               335.57545   57.6   1.29    9.11     1.00
   2 gppR[4]                   0.04989   41.5   1.26    4.29  6574.08   1.684
   3 StockSt[1]               -0.12955   27.5  -2.31    4.10  4647.57  -1.839
   4 taxacts                  46.45902   20.4   0.02    2.93     0.12   0.253
   5 dsp500R[4]                0.01540    0.0   0.00    2.84     6.79   0.010
   6 dsp500R[5]                0.02471    0.1   0.00    2.75     6.75   0.016
   7 dsp500R[6]                0.04371    0.3   0.00    2.64     6.71   0.028
   8 npiniR[1]                 0.23807   24.9   0.71    2.16   779.49   0.837
   9 subnrs                   13.76815   47.1   0.03    1.00     0.52   0.434
   id vfnrs = vfnrsR*deflate
```

Investment in **Residential constuction**, quite in contrast to non-residential
construction, proves to be quite sensitive in the proper, negative, way to interest rates.

144

Otherwise, the approach to the equation is similar except that a combination of disposable income and the stock market value is presumed to determine the desired stock.

The subprime mortgage boom and crash has had profound affects on this sector. The subprime mortgage business – making mortgage loans to people who could not qualify for loans that could be guaranteed by the government Sponsored Enterprises (Fannie Mae, Freddie Mac) – barely existed in 2002. By 2005, it accounted for about a quarter of mortgage originations. These mortgages were arranged by brokers who passed the mortgages on to Wall Street firms, such as Bear Stearns and Lehman Brothers, who packaged many together and sold off *tranches* of the income from them. Some tranches were safe and some risky, by design. The Wall Street firms were more successful at selling safe tranches than risky ones, so they ended up holding the risky ones themselves. From the beginning, serious delinquency rates ran at about 6 percent; but at the end of 2006 they began to rise, reaching 14 percent by the end of the next year and 22 percent by the end of 2008. The two Wall Street firms just mentioned failed and others were in serious trouble. By the end of 2008, the subprime mortgage originations had all but ceased.

These developments had, of course, a huge impact on the demand for housing and thus, for residential construction. There is no use even pretending to explain them with broad economic variables such as interest rates or personal income. We have had recourse to another dummy variable, *subprime*, defined as shown below. With it, we get a good fit and sensible coefficients on other variables.

```
ti Residential Construction
lim 1980.1 2008.4

fex ldeflate = 100.*@log(deflate)
fex infl = ldeflate - ldeflate[4]
fex ub10 = @cum(ub10,1.0,.10)
freq ub10  4
# inflex is expected inflation
fex inflex = @cum(cinfl,infl[1],.10)/ub10
# rtbex is the real interest rate
fex rtbex = rtb - inflex

f ub01 = @cum(ub01,1.,.01)
f StockHouse = 100.*@cum(cvfrR,0.25*vfrR[2],.01)/ub01

f pidisaR = pidisa/deflate
f dpidisaR = pidisaR - pidisaR[1]
fex sp500R = sp500/deflate
fex subprime = 0.
update subprime
2003.1  1  2  3  4    5  6  7  8    9 10 11 12
2006.1 12 12 12 12   11 10  9  8    5  4  3  2  1;

sma 100 a7 a11 1

r vfrR = pidisaR[5], dpidisaR[5], dpidisaR[6], sp500R[3], StockHouse,
rtbex[4],rtbex[5],rtbex[6],rtbex[7], rtbex[8], subprime
```

Residential Construction

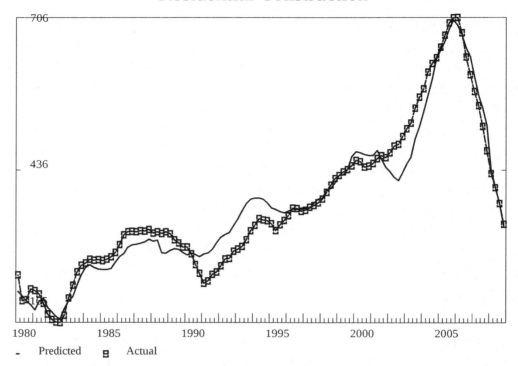

```
:                            Residential Construction
  SEE    =       29.33 RSQ  = 0.9503 RHO =    0.93 Obser  =  116 from 1980.100
  SEE+1  =       10.87 RBSQ = 0.9451 DW  =    0.13 DoFree =  104 to   2008.400
  MAPE   =        6.85
     Variable name          Reg-Coef  Mexval  Elas   NorRes     Mean    Beta
   0 vfrR                  - - - - - - - - - - - - - - - - -   372.75 - - -
   1 intercept             567.68447    69.6   1.52    20.12     1.00
   2 pidisaR[5]              0.14612    43.9   2.28     4.90  5814.88   1.639
   3 dpidisaR[5]            -0.06726     0.5  -0.01     4.86    43.67  -0.024
   4 dpidisaR[6]            -0.01477     0.0  -0.00     4.82    43.62  -0.005
   5 sp500R[3]               0.13370    20.8   0.24     4.81   668.34   0.398
   6 StockHouse             -0.18007    45.9  -3.07     4.81  6354.04  -1.742
   7 rtbex[4]               -4.47634    10.9  -0.03     4.79     2.32  -0.062
   8 rtbex[5]               -3.51276    13.0  -0.02     4.62     2.33  -0.048
   9 rtbex[6]               -2.56761    11.3  -0.02     4.21     2.32  -0.036
  10 rtbex[7]               -1.66146     7.2  -0.01     3.81     2.30  -0.023
  11 rtbex[8]               -0.80808     3.9  -0.00     3.34     2.28  -0.011
  12 subprime               28.69757    82.8   0.12     1.00     1.53   0.750
```

```
id vfr = vfrR*deflate
```

Finally, investment in **Change in business inventories** is unchanged from the AMI model but is repeated here for completeness.

```
title viR Change in Inventory

# fs stands for "final sales"
f fsR = cR + vfR + xR + gR
f dfsR = fsR - fsR[1]
sma 1000 a1 a4 1
```

```
r viR = ! dfsR[1], dfsR[2], dfsR[3],dfsR[4]
```

viR Change in Inventory

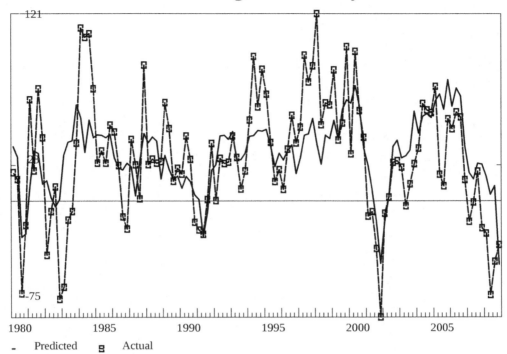

```
:                            viR Change in Inventory
  SEE    =     29.63 RSQ   = 0.4300 RHO =    0.49 Obser  =  116 from 1980.100
  SEE+1 =      25.81 RBSQ  = 0.4147 DW  =    1.01 DoFree = 112 to   2008.400
  MAPE   =    213.43
   Variable name           Reg-Coef  Mexval  Elas   NorRes      Mean   Beta
  0 viR                    - - - - - - - - - - - - - - -       27.97  - - -
  1 dfsR[1]                 0.26295    15.5   0.64    1.27      68.58
  2 dfsR[2]                 0.14638    10.7   0.37    1.01      71.18  0.223
  3 dfsR[3]                 0.02699     0.4   0.07    1.00      71.05  0.041
  4 dfsR[4]                -0.00477     0.0  -0.01    1.00      70.60 -0.007
id vi = viR*deflate
```

Imports

The equation for imports uses shares of investment and exports in private demand to explain the ratio imports to private final demand. (Various other variables have been used in the past. For example, a strong market attracts foreign investors, who buy dollars to buy American stocks, thereby pushing up the dollar and making imports attractive to Americans. In the last four years, however, this variable largely lost its usefulness and its sign changed, so it has been discarded). A time trend plays an important role. It is given its own name, *imptime,* so that in forecasting we can slow down or accelerate the growth of this trend without affecting other time trends.

```
save mR.sav
```

```
ti Import Ratio to Private Demand
add lim80
add lim80
lim 1980.1 2008.4
# Compute real interest rates
#fex ldeflate = 100.*@log(deflate)
#fex infl = ldeflate - ldeflate[4]
#f rtbReal = rtb - infl
fex sp500 = sp500/deflate
# pgdp = private demand for gdp
f pgdp = x + vf + c
f pgdpR = pgdp/deflate
f imprat = 100.*m/pgdp
f xrat = 100.*x/pgdp
f vfrat = 100.*vf/pgdp
f sprat = 100.*sp500R/pgdpR
fex imptime = time
#con 100 .10 = a5
r imprat = xrat, vfrat, imptime
```

Import Ratio to Private Demand

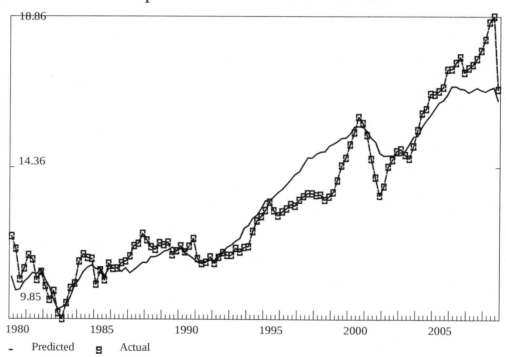

- Predicted   ▣   Actual

```
:                           Import Ratio to Private Demand
  SEE   =        0.67 RSQ  = 0.9069 RHO =    0.89 Obser  =  116 from 1980.100
  SEE+1 =        0.33 RBSQ = 0.9044 DW  =    0.23 DoFree =  112 to    2008.400
  MAPE  =        3.66
     Variable name          Reg-Coef  Mexval  Elas   NorRes    Mean    Beta
  0 imprat              - - - - - - - - - - - - - - - - -   13.33  - - -
  1 intercept              -9.22347    15.2  -0.69    10.74    1.00
  2 xrat                    0.28376     8.4   0.23     6.93   10.62   0.165
  3 vfrat                   0.52122    28.1   0.67     6.80   17.01   0.330
  4 imptime                 0.26921   160.8   0.80     1.00   39.62   1.031
```

```
id m = imprat*pgdp/100.
id mR = m/deflate
```

148

Personal consumption expenditures, the largest single component of GDP, is derived indirectly. We first assume a value for it – either the value in the previous quarter in the first iteration on a quarter or the value found in the previous iteration on subsequent iterations – and then compute real domestic demand from the real investment calculated from the equations already described plus the assumed real Person consumption plus exogenous real Exports and exogenous real Government purchases of goods and services. From this real domestic demand, we can compute imports and subtract them from the domestic demand to get real GDP. From the real GDP, we calculate employment, unemployment, inflation, and then nominal GDP. From these variables and a number of tax rates and behavioral ratios, we calculate Personal disposable income. Persons can "dispose" of their disposable income in four ways: (1) they can pay interest on their debts with it, (2) they can save it, (3) they can remit it to foreigners, or (4) they can spend it on consumption. Many simplified expositions of national accounts found in economics textbooks fail to mention the interest payments and transfers, but as can be seen from the graph below, these payments have been of as important as savings in the U.S. over the last ten years. The transfers, which have been a steady trend, we take as a proportion of Personal disposable income. We will develop equations for the interest payments and for savings. Consumption will then be defined by identity. The national income accountants treat savings as the residual, which is why it bounces about so much. Interest payments depend heavily on automobile purchases, so we will first develop an equation for that. (Remember that interest on home mortgages is *not* part of Interest paid by consumers to business, because home ownership is considered a business in the NIPA.)

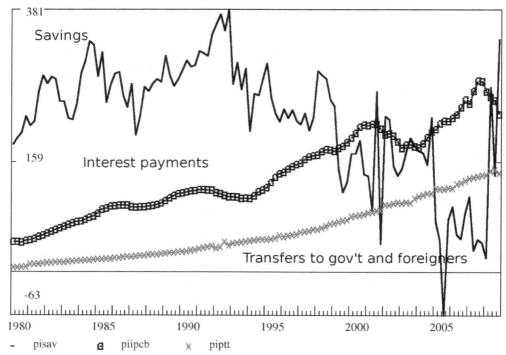

Saving, Interest Payments, and Transfers of Persons

| - | pisav | ₿ | piipcb | X | piptt |

Our equation for personal consumption expenditures on **motor vehicles** uses real disposable income accrued per capita, yRpc, lagged values of its first difference, dyRpc, the Treasury bill rate, rtb, multiplied by yRpc as an indicator of credit conditions, and an estimate of the wear-out of motor vehicles, mvWear.

Disposable income accrued is in most quarters exactly the same as disposable income. In a few quarters, however, billions of dollars of bonuses that should normally have been paid in the fourth quarter of one year were, for tax reasons, paid in the first quarter of the next. Consumers definitely based their consumption on the accrued rather than the disbursed income. We will therefore almost always use Personal disposable income accrued, *pidisa*, not Personal disposable income, *pidis*, but we will call it simply "disposable income."

The increments in this real disposable income per capita are crucial variables in this equation. The the sum of their coefficients is 1.56. Since we are dealing with quarterly flows at annual rates, this 1.56 implies that a rise in annual income of $1 leads to an increase in the stock of motor vehicles of $.39 (= 1.56 x ⎕ .25). The pattern of this distributed lag is shown below. The smoothness of the pattern is due to the *sma* command which "softly" required that the coefficients after the first lie on a straight line.

The deviation of the interest rate, rtb, from a typical value, here taken as 5 percent, is multiplied by yRpc so that the amplitude of its swings will grow at approximately the same rate as the growth in the dependent variable.

The replacement variable, calculated with a wear-out rate of 10 percent per quarter, came out with a coefficient very close to the expected 1.0. On the other hand, the income variable, yRpc, had a small negative coefficient. That does not mean that motor vehicle expenditures do not depend on income, but rather that the dependence comes about entirely by expansion of the stock in response to an increase in income and then replacement of that stock. The unemployment variable is has the expected sign. An increase in the unemployment rate from 4 percent to 5 percent would produce a 4 to 5 percent reduction in motor vehicle sales. Surprisingly, the "subprime" variable came out with a negative sign. Perhaps people taking out subprime mortgages to buy houses did not buy new automobiles.

```
ti Motor Vehicles
subti Personal Consumption Expenditure Per Capita in 2000 $
# cdmvRpc is per capita consumption of motor vehicles in constant dollars
fex cdmvRpc  = cdmvR/pop
#Disposable Income per Capita
fex pidisaR = pidisa/deflate
f yRpc = pidisaR/pop
f dyRpc = yRpc - yRpc[1]
# Interest rate X ypcR to represent credit conditions
f rtbXypc = .01*(rtb -4.)*yRpc
f u = 100.*(lfc - emp)/lfc
# (Real rate was tried, but was much less effective.)
# Create wearout of automobiles assuming 8% per quarter wearout rate
f spilla = .10*@exp(-.02*(time -15.))
f mvWearpc = spilla*@cum(mvSt,cdmvR[1],spilla)/pop
spr mvSt
sma 10000 a4 a15 1
con 10000 .98 = a2
r cdmvRpc = mvWearpc, yRpc,dyRpc,dyRpc[1],dyRpc[2],dyRpc[3],dyRpc[4],
dyRpc[5],dyRpc[6],dyRpc[7],dyRpc[8],dyRpc[9], dyRpc[10],dyRpc[11],
dyRpc[12], rtbXypc[1],u,subprime
```

Motor Vehicles
Personal Consumption Expenditure Per Capita in 2000 $

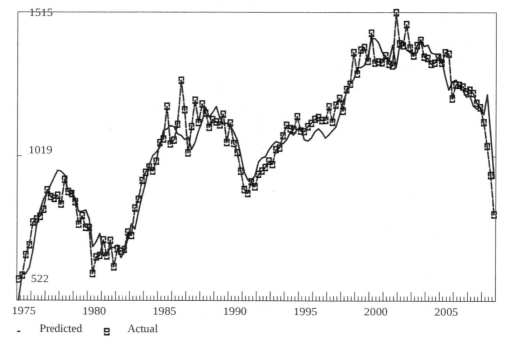

- Predicted   ☐ Actual

```
:                              Motor Vehicles
   SEE   =      64.72 RSQ  = 0.9193 RHO =   0.48 Obser  =  136 from 1975.100
   SEE+1 =      57.50 RBSQ = 0.9069 DW  =   1.04 DoFree =  117 to    2008.400
   MAPE  =       4.73
      Variable name          Reg-Coef Mexval  Elas  NorRes      Mean   Beta
    0 cdmvRpc                 - - - - - - - - - - - - - - -   1073.94  - - -
    1 intercept              349.03289    6.1  0.33   14.56      1.00
    2 mvWearpc                 1.00624   90.1  0.86    3.53    921.43  0.731
    3 yRpc                    -0.00592    1.3 -0.12    3.41  21387.02 -0.111
    4 dyRpc                    0.15853   13.3  0.01    3.28     97.69  0.150
    5 dyRpc[1]                 0.18463   22.2  0.02    3.07    100.33  0.170
    6 dyRpc[2]                 0.17474   17.8  0.02    2.95    107.39  0.146
    7 dyRpc[3]                 0.16155   15.9  0.02    2.82    102.82  0.133
    8 dyRpc[4]                 0.15382   15.0  0.01    2.71    101.37  0.129
    9 dyRpc[5]                 0.16318   17.1  0.02    2.53    100.89  0.137
   10 dyRpc[6]                 0.14933   14.9  0.01    2.37     99.17  0.127
   11 dyRpc[7]                 0.13923   13.2  0.01    2.23     98.55  0.119
   12 dyRpc[8]                 0.11600    9.4  0.01    2.11     97.27  0.099
   13 dyRpc[9]                 0.07908    4.6  0.01    2.04     99.48  0.069
   14 dyRpc[10]                0.04909    1.8  0.00    2.01    100.54  0.043
   15 dyRpc[11]                0.02714    0.6  0.00    2.01     99.94  0.024
   16 dyRpc[12]                0.05467    1.3  0.01    1.99     98.35  0.048
   17 rtbXypc[1]              -0.10872   19.5 -0.03    1.60    305.87 -0.266
   18 u                      -29.76042    9.5 -0.17    1.33      6.22 -0.186
   19 subprime               -14.70883   15.5 -0.02    1.00      1.31 -0.208
id cdmvR = cdmvRpc*pop
id cdmv = cdmvR*deflate
```

For **Interest paid by consumers to business**, the dependent variable is expressed as a percent of disposable income. The most important explanatory variable tries to capture the interest payments on past automobile purchases. It is assumed that the loans are paid off at the rate of about 9 percent per quarter, so that about 35 percent is paid off in the first year. The outstanding amount, if all automobiles are bought with loans, is called *autfi* (automotive financing.) The interest on this amount at the Treasury bill rate (*rtb*) is called *autfir*. If the interest rate charged is *rtb+a,* then the payments should be *a*autfi + autfir*. If all automobiles and nothing else were financed, the coefficient on *autfir* should be 1.0. In the equation as estimated, both these variables are expressed as percent of disposable income, *autfin* and *autfis*, respectively. The coefficient on *autfis* comes out close to the expected 1.0, while the value of *a,* the coefficient of *autfin*, emerges as .01478, so the financing rate appears to be less about 1.5 above the Treasury bill rate, less than I would have expected. Notice the large values of Beta for *autfis*; the dependent variable is quite sensitive to it.

The other important variable is the exponentially-weighted average — created with the @cum function — of recent values of the savings rate. Its justification is that one way that people can save is by paying off debt on which they are paying interest. It should also be pointed out that interest payments on debt other than automotive, in so far as they are a constant fraction of disposable income, are absorbed into the intercept of the equation. The last variable, the rate of change of the money supply, was intended to indicate the ease of getting loans. It did not prove successful.

```
title piipcb - Interest Paid by Consumers to Business
#  shipcb is share of interest in disposable income less savings and transfers
fex shipcb =  100.*piipcb/pidisa
# autfi is a consumption of motor vehicles bucket with a spill of 0.09
f autfi  =  @cum(autfi ,.25*cdmv,.09)
spr autfi
f autfin = 100.*autfi/pidisa
f autfir = @cum(autfir,.0025*rtb*cdmv,.09)
spr autfir
f autfis = 100.*autfir/pidisa
fex intshare = 100.*piipcb/pidisa
#  b1sr is a savings rate bucket with a spill rate of 0.12
f b1sr   = @cum(b1sr,rpisav,.12)
f dm1    = (m1 - m1[1])/m1[1]
r intshare = autfin,autfis,b1sr, dm1, dm1[1]
```

```
:                   piipcb - Interest Paid by Consumers to Business
  SEE   =        0.17 RSQ   = 0.6889 RHO =    0.95 Obser  =   136 from 1975.100
  SEE+1 =        0.05 RBSQ  = 0.6770 DW  =    0.10 DoFree =   130 to    2008.400
  MAPE  =        5.55
     Variable name        Reg-Coef  Mexval   Elas   NorRes      Mean    Beta
  0 intshare              - - - - - - - - - - - - - -         2.45  - - -
  1 intercept              1.22020    7.5    0.50     3.21     1.00
  2 autfin                 0.06235    3.4    0.31     3.01    12.08   0.171
  3 autfis                 1.85108   71.7    0.54     2.55     0.71   1.457
  4 b1sr                  -0.01540   52.7   -0.34     1.01    53.57  -1.332
  5 dm1                   -0.59378    0.1   -0.00     1.00     0.01  -0.028
  6 dm1[1]                -0.72812    0.1   -0.00     1.00     0.01  -0.031
```

```
f piipcb = .01*intshare*pidisa
```

piipcb - Interest Paid by Consumers to Business

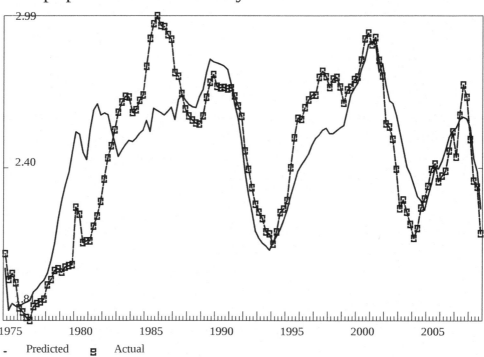

- Predicted   □ Actual

Textbooks of macroeconomics usually make the **savings rate** depend on the interest rate. Our equation uses the Treasury bill rate. I have experimented with various versions of the real rate of interested but the nominal rate works as well or better than any of them. The variable of greatest value in explaining the last thirty years of experience, however, is the ratio of the stock market index, *sp500*, to GDP. When the stock market has soared, the savings rate has plummeted. The logical connection between this variable and the savings rate is clear. When stocks go up, stock holders feel wealth and spend more. They are also able to borrow against their stock. Stock prices probably also reflect home prices and the possibility of borrowing on home equity loans. The first difference of the stock price variable shows that the full effect of a change is not felt immediately. Similarly, the rate of change in per capita disposable income shows that there is a lag in the adjustment of consumption to changes in income. The most important variable for the stability of the model, however, is the unemployment rate. Unemployed people are clearly not likely to be savers – though their plight might induce others to save. If unemployment does, in fact, reduce the savings rate, this fact could prove a stabilizing influence and enable the economy to provide employment for those who want work.

In fact, the problem of just how the economy is able to track the labor force, providing employment for most of it most of the time, is one of the major questions of economics. The

154

classical economists argued, that unemployment would cause wages to fall, making it profitable to employ the excess workers. Building such a mechanism into a macroeconomic model, however, will do little for stability, for the fall in the wage rate will reduce labor income, which will reduce personal income, which will reduce consumption, and create more unemployment, not less. The IS-LM analysis relies on the sensitivity of investment to interest rates to control the level of unemployment. But we have seen that there is very little such sensitivity. That lack of sensitivity has led to the feeling that fiscal policy is the only way to achieve stability. But many governments are unable to engage in large deficit spending, but somehow the economies of their countries manage to provide a high level of employment for qualified workers. How do they do it? A direct influence of unemployment on the savings rate could be the explanation.

In the United States, the fluctuations in unemployment have not been large enough to see this effect so clearly that the regression equation picks it up. To get a stable model, however, it has been *forced* into the equation with G's *con* command. Once we get a reasonably stable model, we can then subject it to systemic optimization of the fit, with these parameters among those varied in the optimization.

```
ti Personal Saving Rate
fex rpisav = pisav*100./pidisa
fex sp500R = sp500/deflate
f sp500Rpc = sp500R/pop
# Original idea, but variable may be trended
f sp500Rpclag = (sp500Rpc[3] + sp500Rpc[4] + sp500Rpc[5])/3.
f dsp500Rpc = sp500Rpc - sp500Rpc[1]

# Non-trended variable with less good fit
f sp500ratio = sp500R/gdpR
f dsp500ratio = sp500ratio - sp500ratio[1]

f unempr = 100.*(lfc - emp)/lfc
f pidisR = pidis/deflate
f pidisRpc = pidisR/pop
f dpidisRpc = 100.*(pidisRpc - pidisRpc[4])/pidisRpc[4]

con 50 -.25 = a3
con 50 -.20 = a4
con 50 -.15 = a5
r rpisav = rtb,unempr,unempr[1],unempr[2],sp500ratio, dsp500ratio, dpidisRpc
```

```
:                              Personal Saving Rate
  SEE   =        1.64 RSQ   = 0.7701 RHO =    0.87 Obser   =  136 from 1975.100
  SEE+1 =        0.87 RBSQ  = 0.7576 DW  =    0.26 DoFree  =  128 to    2008.400
  MAPE  =       70.34
    Variable name          Reg-Coef Mexval  Elas  NorRes       Mean     Beta
  0 rpisav               - - - - - - - - - - - - - - -        5.96  - - -
  1 intercept             13.81580   86.0   2.32    6.57       1.00
  2 rtb                    0.28935    8.3   0.28    4.35       5.79    0.255
  3 unempr                -0.23093   41.0  -0.24    3.62       6.22   -0.096
  4 unempr[1]             -0.18321   27.3  -0.19    3.24       6.22   -0.076
  5 unempr[2]             -0.13710   16.1  -0.14    3.08       6.22   -0.057
  6 sp500ratio           -94.54581   70.3  -1.17    1.26       0.07   -0.837
  7 dsp500ratio           62.05516    1.5   0.00    1.21       0.00    0.087
  8 dpidisRpc              0.39754    9.9   0.14    1.00       2.08    0.233
```

```
cc if(time > 54.0 && rpisav < 2.0) rpisav = 2.0;
id pisav = 0.01*rpisav*pidisa
```

Personal Saving Rate

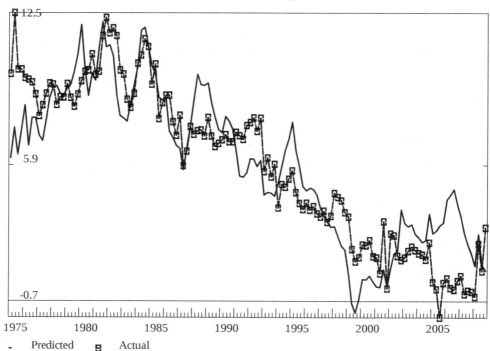

- Predicted   ⊟ Actual

There has almost certainly been a regime change in consumer lending. I doubt that we will see any time soon a resumption of the casual attitude toward credit worthiness on the part of lenders which characterized the subprime mortgage spree and brought the savings rate so low. In other words, I don't trust this equation if it says we are going back to savings rates below 2 percent. Consequently, for forecasting, I have built into the model a floor of 2 percent for future savings rates. Unfortunately, this floor may also remove the stabilizing effect of the equation.

In a conventional textbook on econometric methods, there is sure to be a chapter on simultaneous equation methods, methods for estimation when the dependent variable of an equation may influence one of the dependent variables. The essence of the problem is that, even if we know exactly the structure of the equations that describe the economy but they have random errors which we cannot observe, we may not get unbiased or even consistent estimates of the coefficients by applying least squares to the data. That is, even if we had an infinite number of observations, our estimates of the coefficients would not be right. The problem arises because, through another equation in the simultaneous system, an explanatory variable may be correlated with the error term in the equation in which it is an

156

independent variable. The prime example is precisely income in the consumption equation, for if there is a large positive "disturbance" to the equation – a consumption spree – income will go up. This "backdoor" relationship between consumption and income would make the estimate of the coefficient on income tend to be too large, just as we experienced in our equation. This problem, known as *simultaneous equation bias,* or less correctly as *least squares bias,* was a major theoretical concern in the early days of econometric theory, and various ways were devised to avoid it. Some of these were known as *full-information maximum likelihood, limited-information maximum likelihood, two-stage least squares,* and instrumental variables.

In our model, the equation most likely to be affected is the savings equation. A positive error in this equation will reduce consumption and income, increase unemployment and hold down the stock market. So we may well ask, How can this bias be avoided?

If we are concerned, for example with our variable *dpidisRpc,* one way to control this bias -- the instrumental variable approach -- is to regress disposable income, *pidisa,* on other variables not dependent on *pisav* in the same period, and then to use the predicted value from this regression instead of the actual *pidisa* in estimating the equation. I regressed *pidisa* on itself lagged once and on current values of *v, g,* and *x.* The coefficient on dpidisRpc was increased from .37517 to .38294. The difference is in the expected regression but hardly worth worrying about.

Productivity, Employment, and Unemployment

First of all, we need to note that our employment variable, *emp,* is civilian employment and does not count members of the military. As far as I can see, people in the military do not exist for the Bureau of Labor Statistics (BLS). All of the familiar data on labor force, employment, and unemployment statistics are for civilians only. I have been unable to find a BLS series on military employment. The right way to handle this problem would be to construct a quarterly series on military employment and use it to convert all of the BLS series to a total labor force basis. The difficulty of maintaining this series, however, and the loss of comparability with familiar BLS statistics has led me to go into the other direction, namely, to deduct real compensation of the military – which is readily available in the NIPA – from *gdpR* to get *gdpcR,* real civilian GDP and to use it to explain civilian employment.

Our dependent variable will therefore be the logarithm of civilian labor productivity, real civilian GDP divided by civilian employment. Regressed simply on *time,* over the period 1975.1 – 2008.4, the coefficient on *time* is 0.0155, that is, 1.55 percent per year. Besides time, however, there are at least two other factors readily available which should be tried. From the investment equation, we have available the stock of equipment from which we can make up a capital-output ratio. This ratio was more volatile than the dependent variable, so it was smoothed. To avoid spurious correlation from having real GDP in the denominator of both variables, we have used only lagged values in this variable, *capouts*.

Another factor is real GDP itself. It could influence productivity by economies of scale and by the opportunities which growth gives to eliminate inefficiencies without the painful process of laying off workers. There is, however, a problem with this variable, for it occurs in the numerator of the dependent variable. Thus, any random fluctuation in it will show up automatically as a similar fluctuation in productivity. Thus, if we are really looking for long-term relations, the *gdpR* variable may get too high a coefficient relative to the *time* variable. To control for this situation, the equation was run with gdpR[1] as the most recent value of this variable. The coefficient on *time* came to only 0.00687. We then constrained the coefficient at that value, restored the use of the current value of *gdpR*, and re-estimated the equation.

Fluctuations in productivity are explained largely by the lagged values of the percentage change in real GDP, here calculated as the first difference of the logarithm. Notice the big surge in productivity which follows an increase in real GDP. It is initially produced by existing employees simply working harder and longer and perhaps by some postponable work simply being postponed. Gradually, however, employment is brought up to the levels appropriate for the level of output. For every 1 percent increase in real GDP, we find an increase of 0.32 percent in productivity.

```
ti Labor Productivity
# Military compensation in real terms
fex gfdccemR = gfdccem/deflate
# Create Civilian GDP
f gdpcR = gdpR - gfdccemR
fex lLabProd = @log(gdpcR/emp)
f lgdpcR = @log(gdpcR)
f pcGdpcR = lgdpcR - lgdpcR[1]
fdup repEq = @cum(stockEq,vfnreR[4],.05)/ub05
f pgdpcR=@peak(pgdpcR,gdpcR,.0)
f capout = repEq/pgdpcR
f lcapouts = @log(.5*capout[1]+.3*capout[2]+.2*capout[3])

sma .001 a4 a11 1

r lLabProd = time,lgdpcR[1],pcGdpcR, pcGdpcR[1],pcGdpcR[2],pcGdpcR[3],
pcGdpcR[4],pcGdpcR[5],pcGdpcR[6],pcGdpcR[7], lcapouts
```

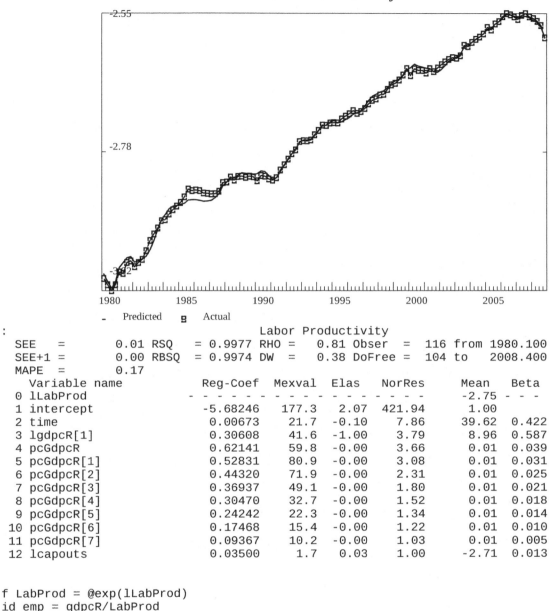

Labor Productivity

	Labor Productivity						
SEE =	0.01 RSQ	= 0.9977	RHO =	0.81	Obser =	116 from	1980.100
SEE+1 =	0.00 RBSQ	= 0.9974	DW =	0.38	DoFree =	104 to	2008.400
MAPE =	0.17						

	Variable name	Reg-Coef	Mexval	Elas	NorRes	Mean	Beta
0	lLabProd	- - - - -	- - -	- - -	- - - -	-2.75	- - -
1	intercept	-5.68246	177.3	2.07	421.94	1.00	
2	time	0.00673	21.7	-0.10	7.86	39.62	0.422
3	lgdpcR[1]	0.30608	41.6	-1.00	3.79	8.96	0.587
4	pcGdpcR	0.62141	59.8	-0.00	3.66	0.01	0.039
5	pcGdpcR[1]	0.52831	80.9	-0.00	3.08	0.01	0.031
6	pcGdpcR[2]	0.44320	71.9	-0.00	2.31	0.01	0.025
7	pcGdpcR[3]	0.36937	49.1	-0.00	1.80	0.01	0.021
8	pcGdpcR[4]	0.30470	32.7	-0.00	1.52	0.01	0.018
9	pcGdpcR[5]	0.24242	22.3	-0.00	1.34	0.01	0.014
10	pcGdpcR[6]	0.17468	15.4	-0.00	1.22	0.01	0.010
11	pcGdpcR[7]	0.09367	10.2	-0.00	1.03	0.01	0.005
12	lcapouts	0.03500	1.7	0.03	1.00	-2.71	0.013

```
f LabProd = @exp(lLabProd)
id emp = gdpcR/LabProd
cc if(emp > lfc) emp = lfc;
```

With labor productivity known, **employment** is just computed by dividing real GDP by it; **unemployment** is computed by subtracting employment from the labor force.

Interest rates

The key to obtaining a somewhat satisfactory explanation of the interest rate was to use as the dependent variable the "expected" or "perceived" real interest rate — the nominal rate on 90-day Treasury bills minus the expected rate of inflation. The main explanatory variable is the M2 velocity and its past changes. The M1 velocity was also tried, but only its first difference proved useful.

```
ti Real Treasury Bill Rate

fdup ldeflate = 100.*@log(deflate)
fdup infl = ldeflate - ldeflate[4]

fex ub10 = @cum(ub10,1.0,.10)
freq ub10  4

# inflex is expected inflation
#fdup inflex = @cum(cinfl,infl[1],.10)/ub10
fex rtbex = rtb - inflex
f v1 = gdp/m1
f v2 = gdp/m2
f dv1 = v1 - v1[1]
f dv2 = v2 - v2[1]
f empr = emp/lfc

sma .1 a4 a14 2
r rtbex = v2,dv1,dv2,dv2[1],dv2[2],dv2[3],
dv2[4],dv2[5],dv2[6],dv2[7],dv2[8],dv2[9],dv2[10],empr[1],empr[2]
```

Real Treasury Bill Rate

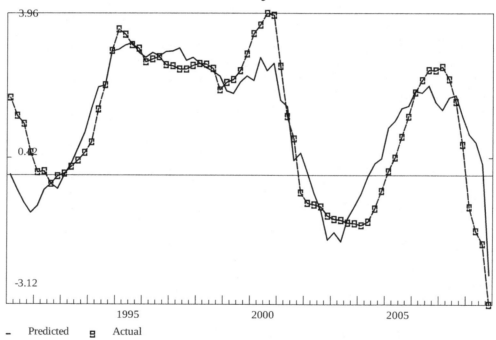

_ Predicted   ◘ Actual

```
:                           Real Treasury Bill Rate
  SEE   =        0.80 RSQ   = 0.7708 RHO =    0.85 Obser  =   72 from 1991.100
  SEE+1 =        0.48 RBSQ  = 0.7094 DW  =    0.31 DoFree =   56 to   2008.400
  MAPE  =      106.76
    Variable name        Reg-Coef  Mexval  Elas   NorRes    Mean    Beta
  0 rtbex               - - - - - - - - - - - - - - - - -   1.26  - - -
  1 intercept            -76.69637   13.3  -60.95    4.36   1.00
  2 v2                     6.92467   15.1   10.76    1.65   1.96   0.420
  3 dv1                    1.67016    2.3    0.04    1.47   0.03   0.155
  4 dv2                    6.53795    1.0   -0.00    1.47  -0.00   0.076
```

```
 5 dv2[1]                      7.30537     2.5   0.01   1.47    0.00  0.071
 6 dv2[2]                      7.80311     5.9   0.01   1.47    0.00  0.076
 7 dv2[3]                      8.03167    11.1   0.01   1.47    0.00  0.078
 8 dv2[4]                      7.99188    15.1   0.01   1.46    0.00  0.077
 9 dv2[5]                      7.68765    15.0   0.01   1.46    0.00  0.074
10 dv2[6]                      7.12301    12.2   0.01   1.45    0.00  0.069
11 dv2[7]                      6.29591     9.0   0.01   1.43    0.00  0.061
12 dv2[8]                      5.19246     6.4   0.01   1.39    0.00  0.051
13 dv2[9]                      3.78964     4.6   0.01   1.32    0.00  0.037
14 dv2[10]                     2.06360     3.3   0.00   1.19    0.00  0.020
15 empr[1]                   -45.30459     0.4 -34.04   1.04    0.95 -0.261
16 empr[2]                   113.26786     1.9  85.12   1.00    0.95  0.651
```

```
id rtb = rtbex + inflex
cc if(rtb< 0.5) rtb = 0.5;
```

The Income Side of the Accounts

To understand the connections and relevance of the remaining equations, one needs to recall the basic identities of the income side of the NIPA. In the following quick review, the items for which regression equations have been developed are shown in bold. All other items are either determined either by identities or by behavioral ratios or are left exogenous.

```
#gnp — gross national product
#    + gdp      Gross domestic product
#    + irrow    Income receipts from the rest of the world
#    - iprow    Income payments to the rest of the world
#    = gnp      Gross national product

id gnp = gdp + irrow - iprow

# Net National Product

#    + gnp      Gross national product
#    - ncca     Capital consumption allowances with IVA and CCAdj
#    = nnp      Net national product

id nnp = gnp - ncca

# ni  -- National income  — from the product side
#    + nnp      Net national product
#    - nsd      Statistical discrepancy
#    = ni       National income

id ni = nnp - nsd

# The alternative, income-side definition of national income.

#    + niceprop Compensation of employees and Proprietor income
#    + niren    Rental income
#    + niprf    Corporate profits
#    + netint   Net interest
#    + nmiscpay Misc. payments (rents & royalties)
#    + nitpi    Taxes on production and imports
#    - nisub    Less: Subsidies
#    + nbctpn   Business current transfer payments
#    + nisurp   Current surplus of government enterprises
```

161

```
#      = ni          National income


# pi — Personal Income
#     + ni           National income
#     - niprf        Corporate profits with IVA and CCA
#     + pidiv        Personal dividend income
#     - netint       Net interest
#     + piint        Personal interest income
#     - nconsi       Contributions for social insurance
#     + ngtpp        Government transfer payments to persons
#     - nbctpn       Business current transfer payments (net)
#     + nibctpnp     Business current transfer payments to persons
#     - nsurp        Surplus of government enterprises
#     - nwald        Wage accruals less disbursements
#     - nitpils      Taxes on production and imports less subsidies
#     + pigsb        Government social benefits to persons
#     = pi           Personal income

# npini — Personal interest income
# npini = + netint    Net interest
#         + gfenip    Net interest paid by the Federal government
#         + gsenip    Net interest paid by state and local governments
#         + piipcb    Interest paid by consumers to business
```

Notice that we have two different definitions of National income, one derived from GDP and one from adding up the five types of factor income which compose it. We will compute it both ways but scale the positive components of the income definition to match the product definition. (These statisticians who make up the accountants also create national income both ways. The difference is the statistical discrepancy. The statisticians work over their estimates to reduce this discrepancy but, at least in the U.S. accounts, it is not totally eliminated.)

In all, there are eight different items to be determined by regression: Capital consumption allowances, four components of National income, Personal dividend income, and two Net interest payments by government. One other item, Interest paid by consumers to business, has already been discussed.

Capital consumption allowances

The computation of capital consumption allowances was explained in Chapter 1. Here we are seeking just a rough approximation of this process. We divide investment into two types: equipment and structures. For each, we set up a two-bucket wear-out system. For equipment, both buckets have a spill rate of 5 percent per quarter; for structures, both buckets have a spill rate of 1 percent per quarter. The weights on the spill streams from the two equipment buckets are softly constrained to add to 1.0, as are the weigts on the spill streams from the two structures buckets. Finally, a variable called *disaster* allows for the exceptional capital consumption by hurricane Andrew and by the Los Angeles earthquake of 1994. The fit was extremely close.

```
save ncca.sav
ti ncca -- capital consumption allowance
add lim75
add lim75
lim 1975.1 2008.4

dfreq 4
# Wearout of Equipment
f ub05 = @cum(ub05,1.,.05)
spr ub05
f repEq1R = @cum(c1vfnreR,vfnreR,.05)/ub05
f repEq2R = @cum(c2vfnreR,repEq1R,.05)/ub05
spr c1vfnreR
spr c2vfnreR

# Equipment wearout in current prices
f repEq2 = repEq2R*deflate
f repEq1 = repEq1R*deflate

# Wearout of Structures
f ub01 = @cum(ub01,1.,.01)
spr ub01
f vfsR = vfrR + vfnrsR
f repSt1R = @cum(c1vfsR,vfsR,.01)/ub01
f repSt2R = @cum(c2vfsR,repSt1R,.01)/ub01
spr c1vfsR
spr c2vfsR

# Structure wearout in current prices
f repSt1 = repSt1R*deflate
f repSt2 = repSt2R*deflate

fex disaster = 0
# disaster 92.3 = Hurricane Andrew;   94.1 = L.A. earthquake
# 01.3 World Trade Center attack
# 05.3 Hurricane Katrina
update disaster
1992.3 1 0 0 0 0  1;
update disaster
2001.3 1;
update disaster
2004.1 0 0 1 0  0 0 5 0  0 0 0 0  0 0 0 0  0 0 1 0;

spr disaster
con 500 1 = a2 + a3
con 500 1 = a4 + a5
r ncca = repEq1, repEq2, repSt1, repSt2,disaster
```

ncca -- capital consumption allowance

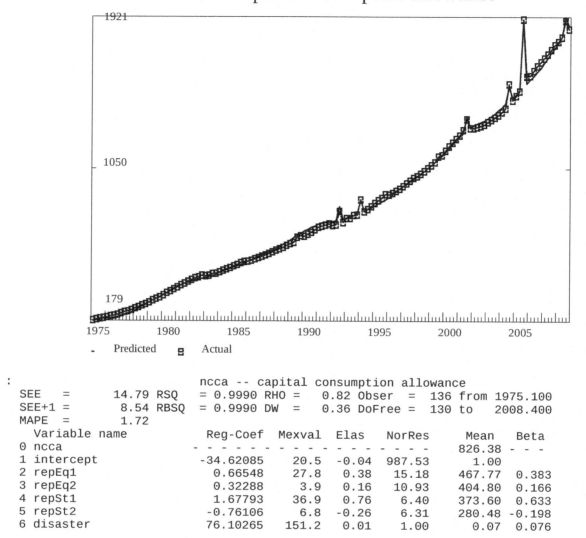

- Predicted ⊟ Actual

```
:                              ncca -- capital consumption allowance
  SEE    =      14.79 RSQ   = 0.9990 RHO =    0.82 Obser  =  136 from 1975.100
  SEE+1  =       8.54 RBSQ  = 0.9990 DW  =    0.36 DoFree =  130 to   2008.400
  MAPE   =       1.72
     Variable name            Reg-Coef  Mexval   Elas    NorRes     Mean    Beta
  0 ncca                      - - - - - - - - - - - - - - -   826.38  - - -
  1 intercept                 -34.62085    20.5  -0.04   987.53     1.00
  2 repEq1                      0.66548    27.8   0.38    15.18    467.77   0.383
  3 repEq2                      0.32288     3.9   0.16    10.93    404.80   0.166
  4 repSt1                      1.67793    36.9   0.76     6.40    373.60   0.633
  5 repSt2                     -0.76106     6.8  -0.26     6.31    280.48  -0.198
  6 disaster                   76.10265   151.2   0.01     1.00      0.07   0.076
```

Components of national income

Compensation of employees and **Proprietor income** are modeled together since our employment variable does not separate employees from proprietors. The ratio of the combination to total employment gives earnings per employed person, which, when put into real terms, is regressed on labor productivity and the unemployment rate. Since employment appears in the denominator of both the dependent and independent variables, I checked for spurious correlation by using only lagged values of labor productivity. The coefficient on labor productivity actually rose slightly, so there is little reason to suspect spurious correlation. The use of the unemployment variable in this equation is a mild infraction of the rule against using a stationary variable to explain a trended one, but percentage-wise the growth in the dependent variable has not been great in recent years.

Both the dependent variable and labor productivity are in logarithmic terms, so the regression coefficient is an elasticity. This elasticity turns out to be slightly less than 1.0. Note that while the mexvals on the two lagged values of the unemployment rate are both very small, the combined effect, as seen in the NorRes column, is substantial.

```
save nice.sav
ti Real Earnings per Employed Person
add lim75
add lim75
lim 1975.1 2008.4
fex wageR = (nice+niprop)/(emp*deflate)
fex lwageR = @log(wageR)
r lwageR = lLabProd,lLabProd[1],u[3],u[4]
```

Real Earnings per Employed Person

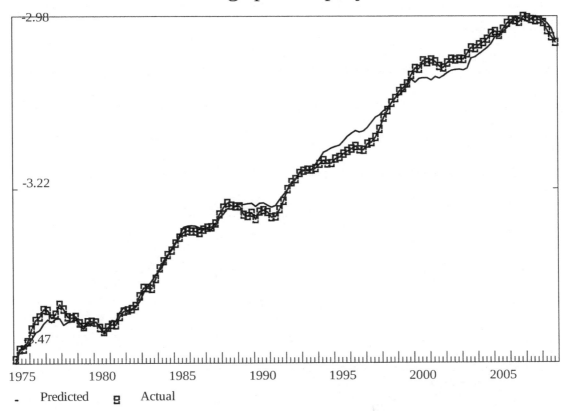

- Predicted   ▣ Actual

```
:                       Real Earnings per Employed Person
  SEE   =      0.01 RSQ  = 0.9936 RHO =   0.91 Obser  =  136 from 1975.100
  SEE+1 =      0.00 RBSQ = 0.9934 DW  =   0.17 DoFree =  131 to   2008.400
  MAPE  =      0.30
```

Variable name	Reg-Coef	Mexval	Elas	NorRes	Mean	Beta
0 lwageR	- - - - - - - - - - - - - -				-3.21	- - -
1 intercept	-0.55273	143.6	0.17	155.21	1.00	
2 lLabProd	0.71899	8.3	0.62	1.29	-2.79	0.735
3 lLabProd[1]	0.22312	0.8	0.19	1.23	-2.79	0.230
4 u[3]	-0.00169	0.1	0.00	1.01	6.22	-0.016
5 u[4]	-0.00360	0.5	0.01	1.00	6.22	-0.034

```
f wageR = @exp(lwageR)
f nicepro = wageR*emp*deflate
```

Rental income is the smallest component of national income. It is the income of persons (not corporations) from renting out a house, a room or two in a house, or a commercial property. In particular, it includes the net rental income imputed to owner-occupants of houses, that is, the imputed space rental value less mortgage interest, taxes, and upkeep expenses. In view of this content, it is not surprising that the stock of houses should be one of the explanatory variables. It is not, however, able to explain why rental income, after decades of virtual constancy, began to rise rapidly in 1994. The only variable at our disposal to explain this takeoff is the stock market value variable. Perhaps the rise in the stock market was accompanied by a parallel rise in the value of commercial real estate, which shows up in the rental income. Destruction of property by natural disasters counts as negative rental income, so hurricane Katrina required a special dummy variable.

```
save niren.sav
ti Rental Income, Real
fex sp500R = sp500/deflate
f nirenR = niren/deflate
# StockHouse defined in vfrR.reg
#fex StockHouse = 100.*@cum(cvfrR,0.25*vfrR[2],.01)/ub01

# Outliers/Disasters
#05.1 Hurricane Katrina
fex Katrina = 0;
update Katrina
2005.3 1;

r nirenR = StockHouse[8],disaster,sp500R
```

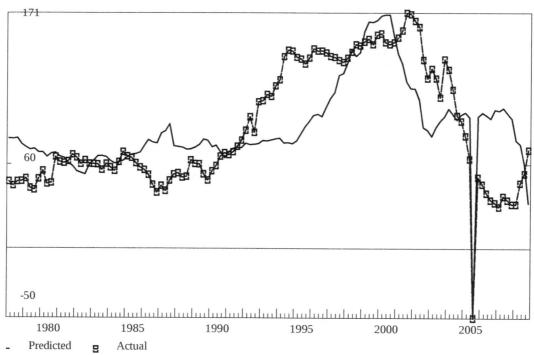

Rental Income, Real

```
:                                Rental Income, Real
   SEE   =       31.55 RSQ   = 0.4855 RHO =    0.94 Obser  =  124 from 1978.100
   SEE+1 =       10.97 RBSQ  = 0.4726 DW  =    0.12 DoFree =  120 to   2008.400
   MAPE  =       37.41
      Variable name          Reg-Coef  Mexval  Elas   NorRes     Mean  Beta
   0 nirenR                   - - - - - - - - - - - - - - -     86.89  - - -
   1 intercept                 77.04555   10.1   0.89     1.94     1.00
   2 StockHouse[8]             -0.01266    5.2  -0.84     1.85  5735.05 -0.338
   3 Katrina                 -146.57228    8.1  -0.01     1.66     0.01 -0.298
   4 sp500R                     0.11819   28.8   0.96     1.00   707.55  0.835

f niren = nirenR*deflate
```

The **Corporate profits** modeled here are the "economic" profits of the NIPA, not the "book" profits that appear in the financial reports of the corporations. The difference lies in the two factors: Inventory valuation adjustment (IVA) and Capital consumption adjustment (CCA) which eliminate from profits distortions caused by inflation. The equation is quite simple. It uses only real Gross private product and changes in its peak value. When real GDP rises by $1, profits rise permanently by $0.11, but in the same quarter with the rise in GDP, they go up by a stunning $0.60. Sixty percent of the increase goes into profits. Thus, profits are much more volatile than GDP. Now does this volatility amplify or dampen business cycles? Because profits are *subtracted* from GDP in the course of calculating Personal income, the volatility in profits actually makes Personal income more stable and contributes to overall economic stability.

```
save niprf.sav
title niprfR -- Corporate Profits with IVA and CCAdj
#f gppR = (gdp - gdpg)/deflate
#f pgppR = @peak(pgppR,gppR,.0)
#f d = pgppR - pgppR[1]
f niprfR = niprf/deflate
sma 1000 a3 a6 1
r niprfR =  gppR, d, d[1], d[2], d[3], subprime
```

niprfR -- Corporate Profits with IVA and CCAdj

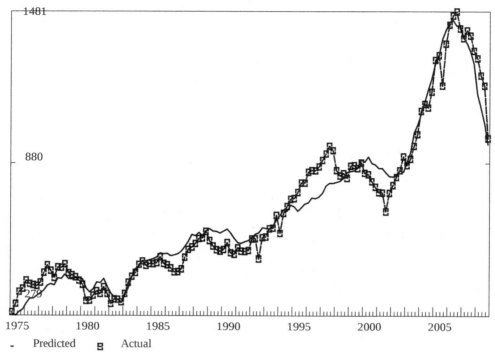

- Predicted   B Actual

```
:                     niprfR -- Corporate Profits with IVA and CCAdj
  SEE   =      64.16 RSQ   = 0.9553 RHO =    0.83 Obser  =   136 from 1975.100
  SEE+1 =      35.75 RBSQ  = 0.9532 DW  =    0.34 DoFree =   129 to    2008.400
  MAPE  =       8.71
     Variable name        Reg-Coef  Mexval  Elas   NorRes      Mean   Beta
  0 niprfR              - - - - - - - - - - - - - - -       694.46 - - -
  1 intercept            -81.23702     4.4  -0.12    22.37      1.00
  2 gppR                   0.10497   169.6   1.02     2.82   6762.26  0.695
  3 d                      0.14134     0.5   0.01     2.79     47.04  0.020
  4 d[1]                   0.14347     1.3   0.01     2.74     47.04  0.020
  5 d[2]                   0.11719     0.7   0.01     2.71     47.04  0.017
  6 d[3]                   0.06413     0.2   0.00     2.69     47.04  0.009
  7 subprime              33.56382    63.9   0.06     1.00      1.31  0.356
```

```
id niprf = niprfR*deflate
```

Net interest is all interest paid by business less interest received by business. It is modeled by estimating the debt of business and multiplying it by the interest rate. Business debt is taken to be its initial amount at the beginning of the estimation period, D_0, plus accumulated external financing since then, bdebt. This need for external financing is investment minus internal sources of funds — profits and capital consumption allowances less profits taxes and dividends paid (which are equal to dividends received plus dividends paid abroad minus dividends received from abroad). The external financing can be accomplished either by borrowing or by issuing equities. We will derive the net interest equation as if all of the funding was by debt; we can then recognize that part of it will be financed by issuing stock. Not all debt is refinanced ever quarter, so we smooth the

Treasury bill rate, producing *srtb*. Business does not necessarily pay the Treasury rate, so we add to *srtb* a constant, *a*, to approximate the rate it does pay. Theoretically, then, we should have

$$\text{netint} = D_0*(a + \text{srtb}) + \text{bdebt}*(a + \text{srtb}).$$
$$= aD_0 + D_0*\text{srtb} + a*\text{bdebt} + \text{bdebt}*\text{srtb}$$

The fit obtained with this regression is acceptable, but the regression coefficients were not entirely consistent with expectations. The coefficient on *srtb*bdebt*, which should have been 1.0, came out when unconstrained a bit above 1.0 and was constrained down to 1.0. The coefficient on business debt, which should surely be less than .1 by the theory, came out at 0.30. But the main discrepancy is that the coefficient on *srtb*, which should be the initial debt — and therefore positive — is decidedly negative. Perhaps high interest rates induce firms to switch away from debt financing and towards equities.

```
title netint -- Net Interest
f ub100 = @cum(ub10,1.,.1)
spr ub100
f srtb = 0.01*@cum(crtb,rtb[1],.1)/ub100
spr crtb
f bdef = v - (ncca + niprf - nictax - nicdiv)
# business deficit
#Note: sodre fdates 1980.1 2008.1
#fdates 1960.1 2008.1
f bdebt = @cum(bdebt,.25*bdef,0.0)
spr bdebt
f rXbdebt = srtb*bdebt
# netint = bdebt(0)*(a +srtb) + bdebt*(a+srtb) ; and divide both sides by deflate
con 10000 1 = a4
#con 100000 .1 = a3
r netint = srtb, bdebt,rXbdebt
```

netint -- Net Interest

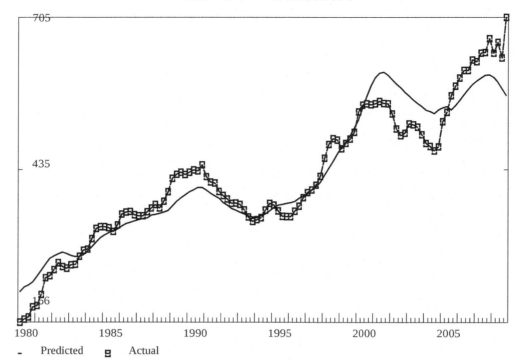

- Predicted   ⊟ Actual

```
:                              netint -- Net Interest
  SEE   =       36.26 RSQ  = 0.9076 RHO =    0.93 Obser  =  116 from 1980.100
  SEE+1 =       14.48 RBSQ = 0.9051 DW  =    0.14 DoFree =  112 to   2008.400
  MAPE  =        7.04
    Variable name          Reg-Coef  Mexval  Elas   NorRes      Mean    Beta
  0 netint                - - - - - - - - - - - - - - -      421.58 - - -
  1 intercept              88.25265     3.1   0.21   18.42      1.00
  2 srtb                  -97.52282     0.0  -0.01   11.96      0.06  -0.020
  3 bdebt                   0.13316    69.4   0.58    8.88   1834.51   0.871
  4 rXbdebt                 1.00895   197.9   0.23    1.00     94.09   0.161
```

Dividends

The most important determinant of **dividends**, not surprisingly, is profits; and most of our equation just amounts to a long distributed lag on past profits. Because appreciation of the value of stock can also substitute, in the eye of the investor, for dividends, we have also included changes in the value of the stock market, which gets the expected negative sign.

```
title Dividends
# nicatax -- Profits after tax
f nicatax = niprf - nictax
f ub10 = @cum(ub10,1.,.10)
#spr ub10 strangely causes trouble for Build
f sprf = @cum(cprf,nicatax,.10)/ub10
r nicdiv =  nicatax, nicatax[1], nicatax[2], sprf[3]
```

Dividends

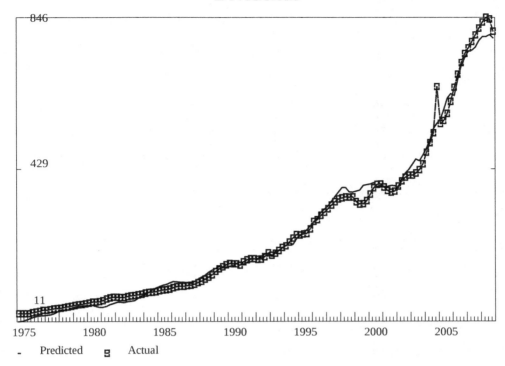

- Predicted   ▣   Actual

```
:                                    Dividends
  SEE    =      19.04 RSQ   = 0.9923 RHO =    0.66 Obser  =  136 from 1975.100
  SEE+1  =      14.48 RBSQ  = 0.9921 DW  =    0.69 DoFree =  131 to   2008.400
  MAPE   =      10.09
     Variable name          Reg-Coef  Mexval  Elas  NorRes     Mean    Beta
  0 nicdiv                   - - - - - - - - - - - - - -      258.28  - - -
  1 intercept               -36.29296   49.2  -0.14  130.11     1.00
  2 nicatax                  -0.00460    0.0  -0.01    4.13   445.63  -0.007
  3 nicatax[1]                0.06295    0.2   0.11    2.75   438.70   0.094
  4 nicatax[2]                0.25228    5.6   0.42    1.95   430.87   0.374
  5 sprf[3]                   0.44868   39.6   0.62    1.00   357.30   0.539
```

Government budget

The basic accounting of federal government expenditures in the NIPA may be summarized in the following table. The state and local account is similar except that the grants-in-aid item, *gfegia*, is a receipt rather than an expenditure.

```
+ gfr    Current receipts
    + gfrt        Current tax receipts
     gfrtp   Personal tax receipts
     gfrti   Taxes on production and imports (Excises, duties, licenses)
     gfrtc   Corporate income taxes
     gfrtr   Taxes from rest of the world
    + grfcsi       Contributions for social insurance
    + gfra         Income receipts on assets
```

171

```
  gfraint      Interest receipts
  gfraroy      Rents and royalties
+ gfrct          Current transfer receipts
  gfrctb       From business
  gfrctp     From persons
+ gfrsurp       Current surplus of government enterprises

- gfe     Current expenditures
    + gfece         Consumption expenditures
    + gfet      Transfer payments
    gfetsbp       Government social benefits to persons
    gfetsbr       Government social benefits to rest of the world
    gfetogia      Grants-in-aid to State and local governments
    gfetorow      Other current transfer payments to the rest of the world
    + gfeint        Interest payments
    gfeintp       To persons and business
    gfeintr       To the rest of the world
    + gfesub        Subsidies
    - gfewald Less: Wage accruals less disbursements

= gfsav Net Federal Government Saving

+ gfct       Capital transfer receipts (Estate and gift taxes)
- gfctp Captial transfer payments
- gfv        Gross government investment
- gfnpnpa    Net purchases of non-produced assets
+ gfconfc   Consumption of fixed capital

= gfnet Federal net lending (+) or borrowing (-)
```

In Quest, the **Personal tax receipts** are calculated by behavioral ratios (*gfrtpBR* and *gsrtpBR* for federal and state-and-local cases, respectively) relative to a specially created variable called *pTaxBase* defined as

>   + Personal income

>   + 0.5*Contributions to social insurance

>   - Government social benefits to persons

Half of Contributions to social insurance are added because, in the federal tax income tax and most state income taxes, one is taxed on income *inclusive* of the employee's half of the Social security tax, but these contributions have been subtracted from Personal income in the NIPA. We have subtracted Government transfer payments to persons on the grounds that most of these payments are either explicitly non-taxable or go to people with low incomes and are taxed at low rates.

The **Corporate profits taxes** are calculated by behavioral ratios – essentially tax rates -- (*gfrtcoBR* and *gsrtcBR*) relative to Corporate profits. The voluntary remittances of the Federal Reserve System to the Treasury are considered corporate taxes in the NIPA and are treated as exogenous in real terms (gfrtcfR). **Taxes on production and imports**, in the federal case, are mostly gasoline, diesel, alcohol and tobacco taxes and customs duties, so they are modeled by a behavioral ratio (*gfritiBR*) relative to Personal consumption expenditure. In the state-and-local case, they also include retail sales taxes and franchise and licensing taxes. This broader base led to taking GDP as the base of the behavioral ration (*gsrtiBR*). Finally, **Contributions for social insurance** are modeled by behavioral ratios (*gfrcsiBR* and *gsrcsiBR*) relative to earned income, approximated by National income less Net interest and Corporate profits.

Turning to the expenditure side, the GDP component, Government purchases of goods and services, is specified exogenously in real terms in three parts, federal defense (*gfdR*), federal non-defense (*gfnR*) and state and local (*gsR*). In addition, we specify exogenously in real terms government investment (*gfvR* and *gsvR*). **Current consumption expenditures** are then calculated by the identities

$$gfece = gfd + gfn - gfv$$
$$gsece = gs - gsv$$

Transfer payments, at the federal level, are divided among Unemployment insurance benefits, Transfers to foreigners, and Other. Unemployment insurance benefits are singled out for special treatment to get their automatic stabilizer effect. A behavioral ratio (*pigsbuBR*) makes them proportional to unemployment in real terms. The other two transfer payments are exogenous in real terms through the exogenous variables *gfetsbrR* and *gfetsbpoR*. The last is, of course, the huge one. **Grants-in-aid**, *gfetogiaR*, is also exogenous in real terms.

Both the federal government and the state and local governments both borrow and lend money. Consequently, they have both interest payments and receipts. The difference between the two levels of government, however, is profound; and the approach which works well for the federal government does not work at all for the state and local governments. For the **Net interest paid by the federal government**, which is a huge net borrower, we can calculate the overall deficit or surplus in each quarter and cumulate this amount to obtain a rough estimate of the net amount on which the government is earning or paying interest. By use of G's *fdates* command, we make the cumulation of the deficit or surplus begin at the same time that the regression begins. (The *fdates* command controls the dates over which the *f* commands work.) Because not all debt is refinanced instantly with the change in the interest rate, we use an exponentially weighted moved average of the rates, *frtb* or *srtb*, to multiply by the debt. We should then have

$$gfenip = InitialDebt*frtb + fcumdef*frtb$$

where *fcumdef* is the cumulated deficit of the federal government. The InitialDebt thus becomes a parameter in the regression equation. Notice that there is no constant term in this equation. We have therefore forced G to omit the constant term by placing a ! after the = sign in the *r* command. We have also included *rtb* as a separate variable in addition to *frtb* so that the regression can take an average of them to produce the best fit.

The same approach will not work at all for the **Net interest paid by state and local governments**, largely because these governments can borrow at low rates because the

173

interest they pay is exempt from federal income tax. Thus, the rate they pay on their debt is far below the rate they receive on their assets, so the net indebtedness is not sufficient to make even a rough guess of the interest payments.

In this situation, we have had recourse to a simpler device of relating both expenditures and receipts of interest to total purchases of goods and services, *gs*.

```
title gfenip -- Net Interest Paid by the Federal Government

f ub100 = @cum(ub100,1.,.1)
f frtb = @cum(cfrtb,.01*rtb,.1)/ub100
# Calculate federal government deficit
f fcumdef = @cum(fcumdef,-.25*gfnet,0.0)

f frXfcumdef = frtb*fcumdef[1]
f rXfcumdef = rtb*fcumdef[1]
f gfenip = gfeint - gfraint
con 300 1 = a3
r gfenip =  ! frtb, rtb, frXfcumdef, rXfcumdef
```

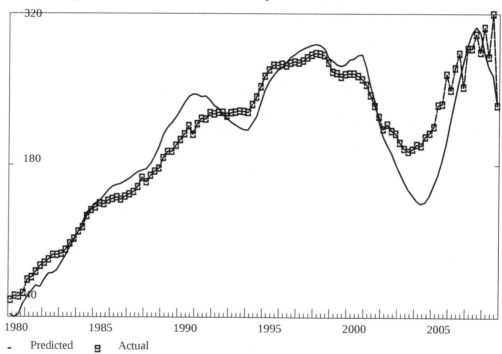

gfenip -- Net Interest Paid by the Federal Government

- Predicted   ⬚ Actual

```
:                gfenip -- Net Interest Paid by the Federal Government
  SEE   =       22.56 RSQ  = 0.8847 RHO =   0.88 Obser  =  116 from 1980.100
  SEE+1 =       10.75 RBSQ = 0.8816 DW  =   0.24 DoFree =  112 to   2008.400
  MAPE  =        9.31
     Variable name          Reg-Coef  Mexval  Elas   NorRes    Mean   Beta
  0 gfenip              - - - - - - - - - - - - - - -    206.04 - - -
  1 frtb                  -167.04688     0.3  -0.05    31.35     0.06
  2 rtb                      0.55181     0.0   0.02    30.11     5.64  0.026
  3 frXfcumdef               1.48277   112.5   0.93     1.04   128.87  0.943
```

```
4 rXfcumdef              0.00155    2.1   0.09    1.00  11675.93  0.134
```

ti Interest Paid by State and Local Governments
r gseint =   gs

Interest Paid by State and Local Governments

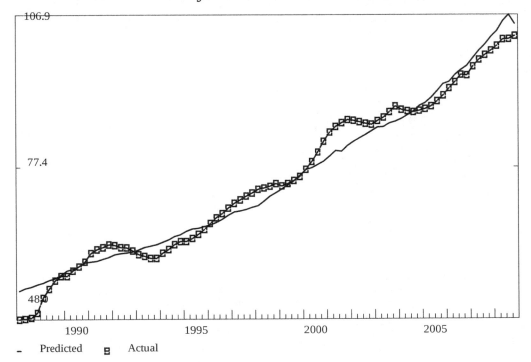

- Predicted   B   Actual

```
:                  Interest Paid by State and Local Governments
   SEE   =      2.48 RSQ   = 0.9731 RHO =    0.95 Obser   =   84 from 1988.100
   SEE+1 =      0.96 RBSQ  = 0.9728 DW  =    0.10 DoFree  =   82 to   2008.400
   MAPE  =      2.83
      Variable name         Reg-Coef  Mexval  Elas   NorRes      Mean   Beta
   0 gseint              - - - - - - - - - - - - - - -     74.79 - - -
   1 intercept            30.33833   302.0   0.41   37.22     1.00
   2 gs                    0.04142   510.1   0.59    1.00  1073.18  0.986
```

175

Interest Received by State and Local Governments

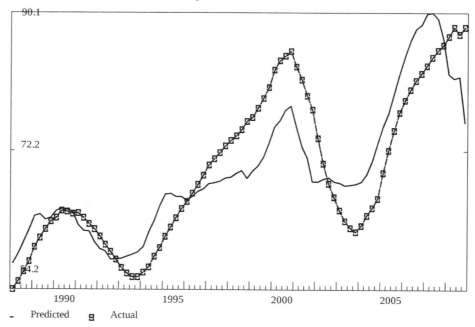

- Predicted   g   Actual

```
f gsXrtb = gs*rtb
r gsraint =   gs, gsXrtb, rtb
:                   Interest Received by State and Local Governments
  SEE   =       4.97 RSQ  = 0.7445 RHO =   0.96 Obser  =   84 from 1988.100
  SEE+1 =       1.52 RBSQ = 0.7349 DW  =   0.09 DoFree =   80 to   2008.400
  MAPE  =       5.90
    Variable name            Reg-Coef  Mexval  Elas   NorRes     Mean   Beta
  0 gsraint              - - - - - - - - - - - - - - -       69.54 - - -
  1 intercept            36.11397    29.2   0.52    3.91      1.00
  2 gs                    0.02137    18.5   0.33    1.70   1073.18  0.785
  3 gsXrtb                0.00193     3.5   0.12    1.01   4165.20  0.342
  4 rtb                   0.57518     0.3   0.04    1.00      4.29  0.115

f gsenip = gseint - gsraint
```

Subsidies less current surplus of government enterprises are small and have been taken exogenously in real terms for all levels of government. **Wage accruals less disbursements** are generally zero and have been left exogenous in nominal terms.

With these items, we are able to calculate the **Net federal government saving** and **Net state and local government saving** on the NIPA basis. To calculate **Net lending (+) or borrowing (-)**, however, we need a few more items. The most important of these is **consumption of fixed capital.**

Until fairly recently, all government purchases were considered current expenditures in the NIPA. Thus, the construction of a road entered into the GDP only in the year it was built; services from the road were not counted as part of the GDP. In the private sector, however, the consumption of fixed capital, depreciation expense, enters into the price of goods consumed. Thus, a capital expenditure in the private sector is counted in GDP twice, once as fixed investment in the year in which it is made and then again in the prices of goods and services as it is consumed in future years. (In Net Domestic Product, this second appearance has been removed.) To give government capital formation similar treatment, the NIPA have recently begun to distinguish between current expenditures and capital expenditures. The capital expenditures are then amortized to create a consumption of fixed capital expense. Our technique for estimating this consumption given previous investment is similar to what we used in the private sector. Here are the equations for the two level of governments.

```
ti Federal Investment and Consumption of Fixed Capital
gr gfv gfconfc
ti FederalConsumption of Fixed Capital
fex gfvR = gfv/deflate
f gfv = gfvR*deflate
f ub02 = @cum(ub02,1.,.02)
f gfvrep = deflate*@cum(gfvstk,gfvR,.02)/ub02
gr gfvrep gfconfc
r gfconfc = gfvrep
```

FederalConsumption of Fixed Capital

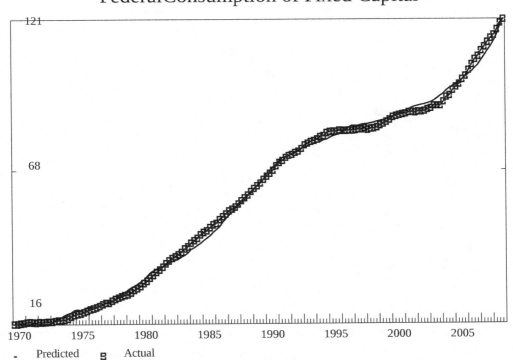

- Predicted   ⊟ Actual

```
:                        FederalConsumption of Fixed Capital
   SEE   =      1.48 RSQ  = 0.9977 RHO =   0.96 Obser  =  156 from 1970.100
   SEE+1 =      0.40 RBSQ = 0.9977 DW  =   0.08 DoFree =  154 to   2008.400
   MAPE  =      2.48
      Variable name       Reg-Coef  Mexval   Elas   NorRes    Mean    Beta
   0 gfconfc              - - - - - - - - - - - - - - - -     59.88  - - -
   1 intercept            -3.46300    42.8   -0.06   430.31    1.00
   2 gfvrep                1.05234  1974.4    1.06     1.00    60.19  0.999
```

177

```
ti State and Local Consumption of Fixed Capital
fex gsvR = gsv/deflate
f gsv = gsvR*deflate
f ub02 = @cum(ub02,1.,.02)
f gsvrep = deflate*@cum(gsvstk,gsvR,.02)/ub02
r gsconfc = gsvrep
```

State and Local Consumption of Fixed Capital

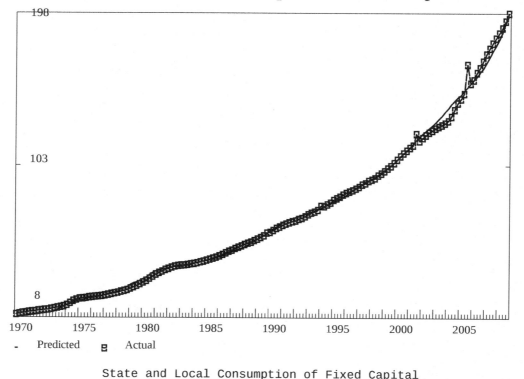

- Predicted   ᴮ   Actual

```
:                   State and Local Consumption of Fixed Capital
  SEE   =      2.40 RSQ   = 0.9976 RHO =   0.68 Obser  =   156 from 1970.100
  SEE+1 =      1.77 RBSQ  = 0.9976 DW  =   0.64 DoFree =   154 to   2008.400
  MAPE  =      3.53
     Variable name          Reg-Coef  Mexval  Elas   NorRes     Mean    Beta
  0 gsconfc             - - - - - - - - - - - - - - -    70.32   - - -
  1 intercept            -10.03940   139.1  -0.14  414.47      1.00
  2 gsvrep                 0.77085  1935.9   1.14    1.00    104.25   0.999
```

The spill rates were chosen after some experimentation to get a good fit. The replacement calculated for the federal government is fairly close to the NIPA capital consumption series; for state and local government, however, the calculated replacement is much above that used in the NIPA.

As a result of recent changes in the NIPA, **Estate and gift taxes** are no longer counted as government revenues but appear, more correctly, as **Capital transfers.** For the Federal case, they have been made exogenous in real terms (*gfctpR*) while for state and local governments, they are proportional (*gsrtrpBR*) to disposable income.

The final item in the government accounts is the **Net purchases of non-produced assets** such as land or existing buildings. These purchases cannot go into GDP, precisely because the land or the stock is not produced. On the other hand, they enter the cash "bottom line" of the governments. The federal item is taken as a behavioral ratio, *gfnpnaBR*, to total federal purchases of goods and services. The state and local is exogenous in real terms, *gsnpnaR*.

From these variables, the complete government accounts as set out at the beginning of this section can be computed.

The Stock Market Value

The **real stock market value** variable, *sp500R* – the Standard and Poor 500 index deflated by the GDP deflator – has been used in a number of equations. Now we turn to trying to explain the variable with other variables in the model. Fundamentally, the value of a stock should be the present value of the stream of future profits discounted by the rate of interest. I have tried this approach, but it does not work as well as simply relating the value of the stock market, as measured by the Standard and Poor 500 index to GDP. Both variables were deflated to be in prices of 2000 and then put in logarithms. No macroeconomic variable, however, is going to explain the run up in stock prices connected with the dot-com bubble or the crash connected with the bankruptcy of Lehman Brothers and the AIG failure, both connected with the subprime mortgage crisis. Without apology, I have included a dummy variable for both of these events. The use of this dummy expresses my belief that both were avoidable and not the necessary logic of the market. There is also a tendency of the market to accelerate whatever is happening, whether it is going up or going down. This has been expressed by the lagged first difference of the dependent variable. This tendency is likely the result of widespread use program trading based on delta (or higher order) hedging derived from the Black-Scholes formula for option pricing.

```
ti Real S&P 500 Index
fex Lehman = 0
update Lehman
2008.2 1 2 5   5   4   3   2    1;
fex sp500R = sp500/deflate
f lsp500R = @log(sp500R)
f dellsp500R = lsp500R - (lsp500R[3]+lsp500R[4] + lsp500R[5])/3.
f lgdpR = @log(gdpR)
r lsp500R = lgdpR,dotcom, dellsp500R[1], Lehman
```

Real S&P 500 Index

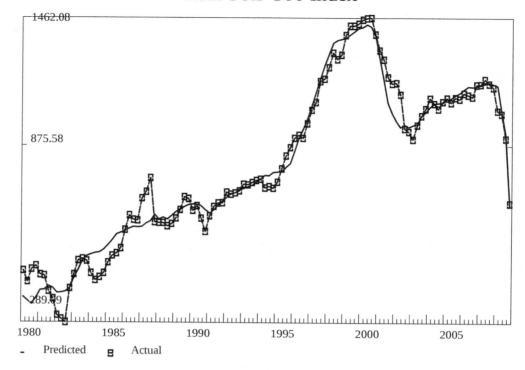

- Predicted   ⊟ Actual

```
:                                   Real S&P 500 Index
   SEE   =        0.08 RSQ  = 0.9853 RHO =    0.73 Obser  =  116 from 1980.100
   SEE+1 =        0.05 RBSQ = 0.9847 DW  =    0.54 DoFree =  111 to   2008.400
   MAPE  =        0.96
     Variable name          Reg-Coef  Mexval  Elas   NorRes     Mean   Beta
   0 lsp500R                - - - - - - - - - - - - - - - -      6.35  - - -
   1 intercept             -13.74202   377.2  -2.16   67.81      1.00
   2 lgdpR                   2.22881   585.0   3.15    5.99      8.98   0.893
   3 dotcom                  0.04990   112.8   0.01    1.36      1.48   0.255
   4 dellsp500R[1]           0.12655     2.1   0.00    1.26      0.06   0.027
   5 Lehman                 -0.08090    12.2  -0.00    1.00      0.07  -0.065
```

```
f sp500R = @exp(lsp500R)
f sp500 = sp500R*deflate
```

2. Historical Simulation

The model was given a mild optimization as described in the next chapter with only the constant terms of the three fixed investment being subject to change. It was then run in a historical simulation from 1980.1 to 2008.4. That is to say, the exogenous variables were given their actual, historical values and the endogenous variables were calculated. The exogenous variables included government expenditures and exports in real terms, the labor force, various tax rates, and the dummy variables for hurricanes, earthquakes, the dot-com bubble, the subprime crisis, and the Lehman Brothers failure and its fallout on financial markets. The results were then compared graphically with the historical series for the endogenous variables. Some of these comparisons are shown on the following pages. The historical values are marked by squares, and model predictions are shown by the lines without marking of the points.

The most pronounced deviation between the historical simulation and the historical values themselves was that the model produced a substantial recession in 2001 while the real economy showed only a brief slackening of growth.   In 2002, growth resumed in both the model and in the real economy, but the model did not catch up until the 2008 downturn. In trying to find the cause of this miss by using the "skip" command on various regression equations, the main culprits turned out to be the stock market variable (*sp500R*), the capital consumption allowance (*ncca*), and the expected real Treasury Bill rate (*rtbex*). Surpressing the equations for these endogenous variables gave the two graphs below.

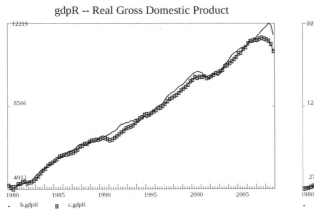

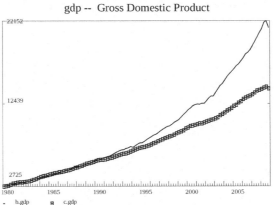

Using historical values for these equations gives a real GDP simulation that is very close to, but sometimes slightly above, the historical values. The values slightly above historical values set off inflation that pushes nominal GDP far above its actual values.

This situation brings out a major problem in modeling the U.S. economy over these last three decades. In theory, the quantity of money should provide a sort of anchor for the nominal value of GDP while employment and labor productivity provide the anchor for real GDP. We have looked for every opportunity to make unemployment push up demand, for example, by reducing the savings rate. We are aided in this effort by the relative constancy of the significance of a given rate of unemployment. An unemployment rate of 8 percent is "high unemployment" in any year in the period, and a 4 percent rate is "low unemployment" in any year. On the monetary side, however, there is no such constancy of significance.

181

gdpR -- Real Gross Domestic Product

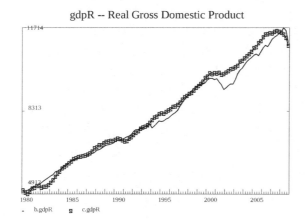

gdp -- Gross Domestic Product

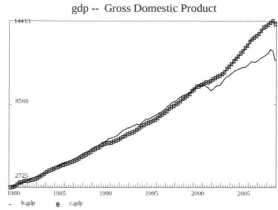

vfnrsR -- Non-residential Structures

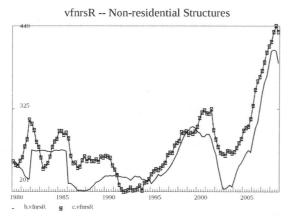

vfnreR -- Equipment Investment

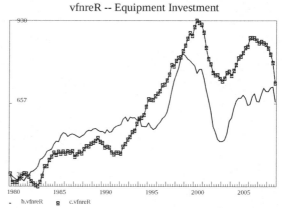

vfrR -- Residential Construction

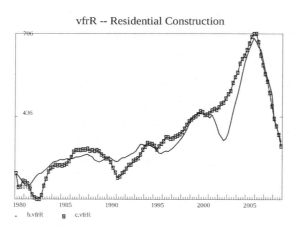

Exports and Imports

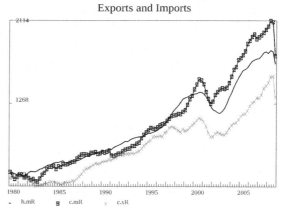

182

cR -- Personal Consumption Expenditure

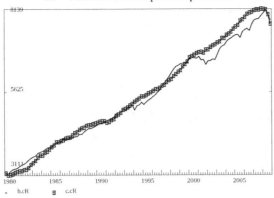

b.cR   c.cR

rpisav -- Personal Savings Ratio

b.rpisav   c.rpisav

rtb -- Rate on New 90-day Treasury Bills

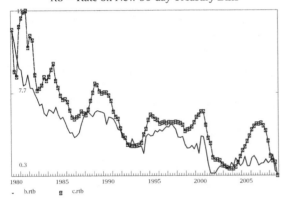

b.rtb   c.rtb

u -- Unemployment

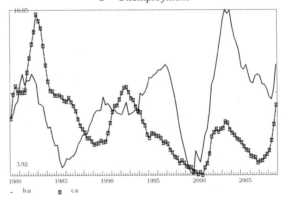

b.u   c.u

sp500ratio -- sp500R/gdpR

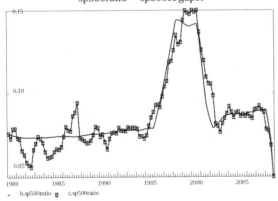

b.sp500ratio   c.sp500ratio

sp500R -- S&P 500 Stock Market Index, Real

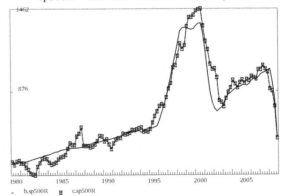

b.sp500R   c.sp500R

PART II: ADVENTURES WITH MACROMODELS

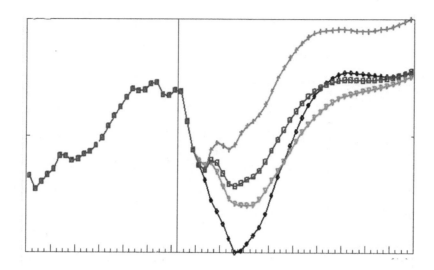

CHAPTER 8. ALTERNATIVE FORECASTS

Having built our model in Chapter 7, we can now begin to play with it. I must mention, however, that the model we will play with is not precisely the one estimated in Chapter 7. All of the experiments reported here in Part II were performed with a very similar version of Quest but estimated only through 2000. I wanted to show in Chapter 7 how the model was able to deal with the crash of 2008. The chapters of Part II, however, were written in or before 2000. Since their point is to illustrate techniques not to make claims for a particular model, it did not seem worthwhile to rewrite the chapters with presumably minor changes in the results. In this chapter, we look at alternative forecasts made in 2000.

1. The Exogenous Variables

For reference to help you design your own experiments, here is a list of the exogenous variables:

lfc	Civilian labor force
pop	Population
xR	Exports
gm1	Growth rate of M1
relpri	Prices of imports relative to prices of exports, used in inflation equation
Lehman	dummy variable in the stock market equation
nbtrpBR	Behavioral ratio for business transfer payments
nbtrppBR	Behavioral ratio for business transfer payments to persons
nsd	Statistical discrepancy
nwald	Wage accruals less disbursements

In the government sector, there are usually parallel variables for federal (in the first column below) and state-and-local governments (in the second column). All variables ending in R are in constant prices. Those ending in BR are ratios to some other variable as explained in the government section in Chapter 7.

Federal	S&L	Description
gfdR		Purchases of goods and services for defense
gfnR	gsR	Purchases of goods and services, non-defense
gfvR	gsvR	Capital investment
pituibBR		Unemployment insurance benefit rate
gfetpfR		Transfer payments to foreigners
ogfetpR	gsetpR	Other transfer payments
gfeifBR		Interest payments to foreigners
pitfBR	pitsBR	Personal tax rates
gfribtBR	gsribtBR	Indirect business tax rate
gfrprfBR	gsrprfBR	Profit tax rates
gfrcsiBR	gsrcsiBR	Social security tax rates

gfctrBR	gsctrBR	Estate and gift tax rates
gfpnaBR	gspnaBR	Ratio for purchases of non-produced assets
gfeslsR	gseslsR	Subsidies less surplus of government enterprises
gfetpfR		Transfer payments to foreigners
gfegiaR		Federal grants in aid to state and local government
gfeald	gseald	Wage accruals less disbursements

2. A Stock-Market Experiment

To study the effect of the stock market on the cyclical evolution of the American economy, we have formulated four alternative projections. They differ only in the projection of the real value of the stock market index, *sp500R*. All four alternative projections are made by adding a factor to the endogenous equation for *sp500R*. In naming the alternatives, we expand on the custom of distinguishing between "bulls" and "bears". The alternatives are:

Name	Mark	Description
Bull	+ plus	The add factor reaches a minimum in 2001.3, climbs back to its highest historical value by 2002.4, and continues to grow at the same rate at which it grew from 1996 to the peak in 2000. (Red, if you are reading on a screen.)
Sheep	□ square	The add factor stays where it was in 2001.3. (Blue)
Bear	Δ triangle	The add factor is generated automatically by the rho-adjustment process. (Purple)
Wolf	◆ diamond	The add factor, which was 400 in 2001.1 hits 100 by 2001.4 and drops on down to -100 by 2001.4, where it stays for a year before moving up to -10 by the end of 2005. (Black)

All of the alternatives reflect the Bush tax cut of 2001 and otherwise use middle-of-the-road projections of exogenous variables. Here are the comparison graphs.

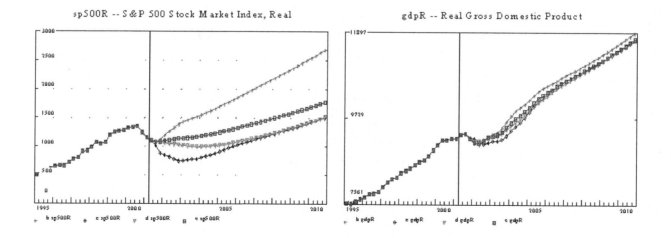

186

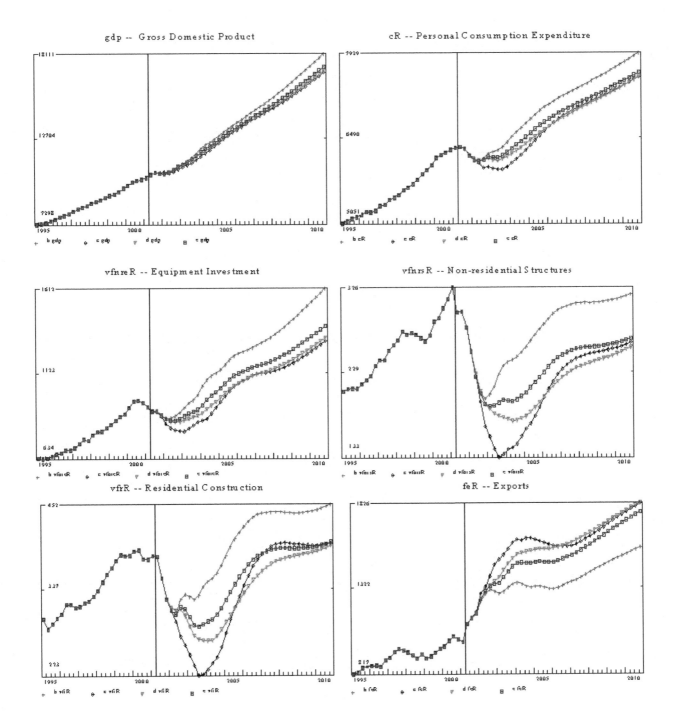

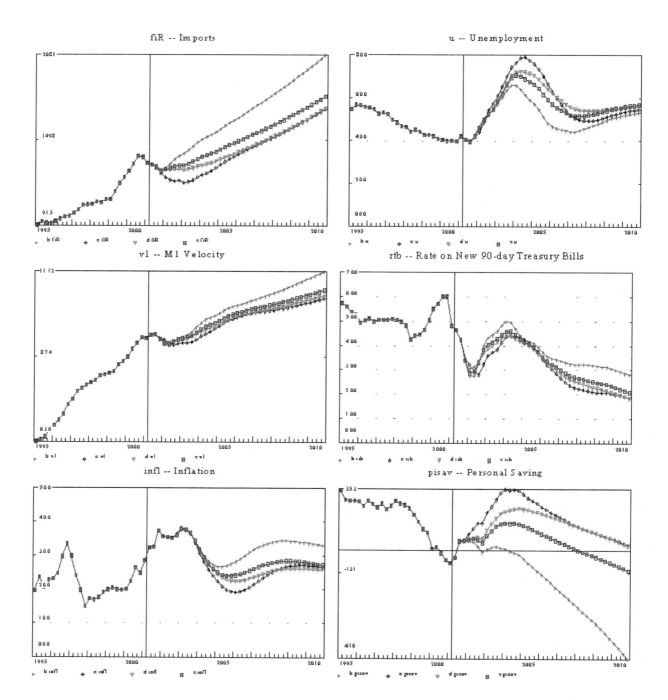

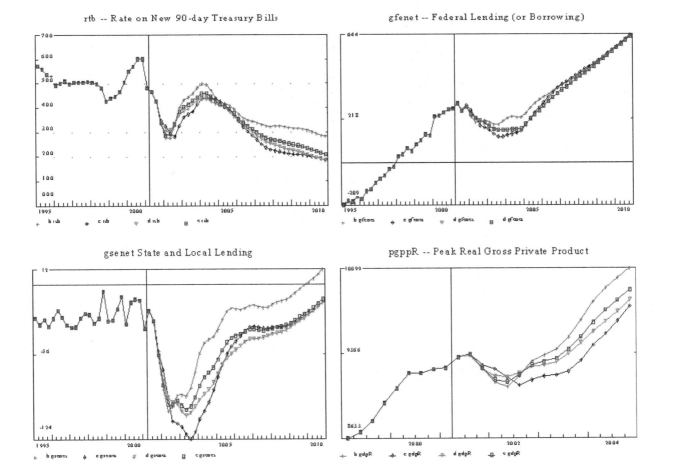

All the alternatives agree that we were in for a considerable recession beginning in the last quarter of 2001. For comparison, it is useful to remember that the recession beginning in 1990 lasted three quarters and saw a drop of 1.7 percent in real GDP. The one predicted here should also last three quarters (or four for the Wolf scenario) but the drop in real GDP may be on the order of 2 or 3 percent. Looking over the graphs above show much greater drops in consumption and investment. Exports and imports, however, act as very strong stabilizers, and -- in this model -- respond very quickly to changes in the stock market. The response is so fast that Bull, which activates the export-import stabilizers least of the four, turns out to have the sharpest and deepest recession, at 3 percent in three quarters. Wolf, which activates them most, has a 2.9 percent drop over four quarters, while Sheep loses 2.6 percent over three quarters and Bear drops only 2.0 percent over three quarters. .

Once the recovery is underway, the alternatives assume the expected order according to speed of Bull, Sheep, Bear, and Wolf. The maximum GDP difference between Wolf and Bull is 4.2 percent.

The combination of the tax cuts and the recession wipe out half of the Federal budget surplus. The model does not distinguish between the social insurance trust funds and the general budget, but it is clear that the general budget will be in deficit during the recession. The State and Local deficit is sharply increased by the recession, and one can expect cut backs in expenditures to avoid these deficits.

189

After the recession, unemployment stabilizes at about 5.5 percent and inflation at about 2.5 percent. Personal savings, after rising during the recession, shows a disturbing tendency to diminish.

3. Conclusions

The conclusions I draw from the results are:
> The stock market is quite important to the economy, moreso than I would have thought.
> Given the stock market behavior, the model can predict the rest of the economy, especially its real variables, fairly well.
> The boom in the stock market which began in 1995 is responsible for the strong economy of the period 1996 - 2000.
> The causes of this boom in the market lay outside the U. S. economy.

These external causes are not hard to find. Beginning in 1996, weakness in Asian and other economies led to an influx of foreign investment into the U.S. stock market. Without the externally driven rise in the stock market, the years 1996 - 2000 would have shown weak but positive growth. The exceptional prosperity of the period was the result of the bull market superimposed on a fundamentally stable but not especially dynamic economy.

All in all, it appears that the model is capable not only of generating a substantial cycle but also, when the exogenous variable are stable, of producing stable growth at plausible levels of unemployment and inflation.

CHAPTER 9. OPTIMIZATION IN MODELS

Up to this point, we have estimated equations in isolation and then combined them into a model and observed how the model worked. Occasionally, we have revised the estimate of some regression coefficient to improve the functioning of the model. In this chapter, we will see how to modify coefficients in a comprehensive way to improve the performance of the model in historical simulation. The same techniques, with a different objective function and different parameters, can then be used to design policies. Let us begin, however, with improving the performance of the model in historical simulation.

1. Improving the historical simulation

Creating an Objective Function

The first step in optimizing must be to create an objective function. This objective function must be built into our model. Our software uses the convention that it **minimizes** the value in the last period of the simulation of some specified variable. (How we tell the program which variable it should minimize will be shown in the next section.). For example, to optimize the performance of the Quest model in historical simulation, we would probably initially want to concentrate on real GDP (*gdpR*) and the GDP deflator (*gdpD*). Let us say that we want to minimize the sum of the squares of their relative, fractional differences from their historical values. We then need to record the historical values in variables which will not be changed in the model, so we create two exogenous variables, *gdpRX* and *gdpDX* for that purpose by the equations:

> fex gdpRX = gdpR
> fex gdpDX = gdpD

The relative difference between the model's real GDP in any period and the historical value for that period would be (gdpR-gdpRX)/gdpRX and for the GDP deflator it would be (gdpD-gdpDX)/gdpDX. The contribution to the objective function from these discrepancies in any one period would be

> f miss = @sq((gdpR-gdpRX)/gdpRX)+@sq((gdpD-gdpDX)/gdpDX)

where *@sq( )* is the squaring function. Finally, the objective function itself, the sum over all periods of these period-by-period contributions, would be the value in the last period of the simulation of the variable *misses* defined by

> f misses = @cum(misses, miss, 0.)

These statements can be conveniently placed at the end of the Master file of the model just before the "check" commands.

Selecting parameters to vary

With the objective function in place, the next step is to select from all the regression coefficients s in the model those which will be varied in looking for an optimum. One might ask, "Why not vary all of them?" Our objective function, however, is quite a complicated function of all these coefficients, so the only feasible optimization techniques are those that involve some sort of trial-and-error search with the whole model being run to evaluate the objective function for each proposed point, that is, for each set of regression coefficient values. The number of points that has to be searched increases with the dimension of the point. We will see, however, that optimizing with respect to a relatively small number of coefficients – a dozen or so – can produce a substantial improvement in the Quest model.

The optimization method we will use is known as the simplex method. A *simplex* in n-dimensional space is a set of n+1 points in that space. For example, a triangle is a simplex in 2-dimensional space and a tetrahedron is a simplex in 3-dimensional space. The method requires that we specify an initial simplex of points; it will then take over, generate a new point, and, if that point is better than the old worst point in the simplex, drop the worst point and add the new point to the simplex. It has four different ways of generating new points. First it *reflects* the worst point through the midpoint of the other points. If that works, it tries to *expand* by taking another step of the same size in the same direction. If the expansion gives a better point than did the reflection, that point is added to the simplex and the worst point is dropped. If the reflection gave a point better than the worst point but the expansion did not improve on it, the reflected point is added to the simplex and the worst point dropped. If the reflection failed to give a point better than the worst point, the algorithm *contracts*, that is, it tries a point halfway between the worst point and the midpoint of the other points. If this point is better than the worst point, it is added to the simplex and that worst point dropped. Finally, if all of these trials have failed to yield a point better than the worst point, the algorithm *shrinks* the simplex towards the best point by moving all the other points halfway towards it. When the value of the objective function is practically the same at all the points and the points are close together, it stops.

Our task is to supply the initial simplex. One obvious point for inclusion is the values of the coefficients estimated by the original regressions. We specify the other points by varying each coefficient, one-by-one, from this base. For each coefficient, we will specify a "step size" for this variation. The initial points of the simplex are then the original values of the parameters that may be varied and then, for each parameter, a point with that parameter increased by its "step size" and all the other parameters at their original values. Note that with n parameters, this method will give n+1 points, a simplex in n-dimensional space.

Mechanically, how do we specify the parameters to be varied and their step sizes? An example for Quest will be helpful. We will optimize on parameters from the consumption function, that is, the equation for *cRpc,* and the most important of the investment equations, that for *vfnreR.* For ease of reference, here are excepts from the regression results of the consumption equation.

```
:                        Personal Consumption per capita
    Variable name        Reg-Coef  Mexval  Elas   NorRes    Mean     Beta
  0 cRpc                 - - - - - - - - - - - - - - -    17419.94   - - -
  1 intercept           785.42866    1.1    0.05  792.49      1.00
  2 yRpc                   0.77579   31.8    0.86    9.50  19284.28   0.711
  3 dyRpc                 -0.39068    8.5   -0.00    9.25    104.29  -0.018
 ....
 13 piipcbRpc            -0.24243    0.1   -0.01    1.29    507.34  -0.008
 14 intsavRpc            -0.48752   10.1   -0.03    1.09   1151.80  -0.044
 15 rtbexXdi             -0.00161    1.5   -0.01    1.03  55178.74  -0.015
 16 ur                 -1417.2942    1.3   -0.01    1.00      0.17  -0.020
```

Examination of the historical simulations shown in the previous chapter shows that the equipment investment equation is a major generator of the boom in the mid 1980's that was much stronger in the historical simulation than in reality. Could inclusion of an unemployment variable in this equation help stabilize the model? One could argue that, in times of tight employment, capacity constraints may result in orders for capital goods may not be filled promptly so that actual investment may be less than would be desired on the basis of other factors. The number of persons unemployed, *ue*, was put in with the following results:

```
f ue = lfc -emp
:                         Equipment Investment
    Variable name        Reg-Coef  Mexval  Elas   NorRes    Mean    Beta
  0 vfnreR               - - - - - - - - - - - - - - -     510.68   - - -
  1 intercept            36.82448    1.7    0.07  120.92     1.00
  2 repEq                 0.97140  465.9    0.77   10.00   404.92   0.629
 .....
 24 dsp500R[7]            0.02980    0.1    0.00    1.05     8.60   0.005
 25 ue                   -4.60458    2.4   -0.07    1.00     7.64  -0.036
```

The unemployment variable got a negative coefficient, which would only make the cycles worse. No doubt we have here a case of simultaneous equation bias, for booming investment will drive down unemployment. Rather than try instrumental variables or other simultaneous equations techniques, let us just make this coefficient one of the variables on which we optimize.

The specification of which parameters to use in optimization and their step sizes is now provided by the following file, which we may call Fit.opt.

```
misses
20
vfnreR
#  1  2  3  4  5  6  7  8  9 10 11 12 13 14 15 16 17 18 19 20 21 22 23 24 25
  .1  0  0  0  0  0  0  0  0  0  0  0  0  0  0  0  0  0  0  0  0  0  0  0 .1
cRpc
#  1     2  3  4  5  6  7  8  9 10 11 12 13    14 15 16
  .1 .001  0  0  0  0  0  0  0  0  0  0  0  .005  0  1
```

The first line of the file gives the name of variable whose last value is to be minimized.

The second line specifies the maximum number of parameters which will be varied in the course of the optimization. It does not hurt if it is larger than the number actually used. Here we have set the maximum at 20 but will only use 6.

The next line says that some parameters will come from the equation for *vfnreR*. The third line begins with a # which marks it as simply a comment ignored by the program. For us, however, it is very useful since it numbers the 25 regression coefficients which occur in the equation for *vfnreR*. The line below it gives the step sizes for each of these 25 coefficients. A coefficient given a step size of 0 is not involved in the optimization. Thus we see that coefficient 1, the intercept, is given a step size of .1 and that the coefficient of *ue* is also given a step size of .1.

The next triplet of lines does the same for three coefficients in the *cRpc* equation, the intercept, the coefficient of the inflationary interest that "should" be saved, and the reciprocal of the unemployment rate.

Note that in both equations, the intercept is included among the variables on which we optimize. The reason is that, unless a variable happens to have a mean of zero, changing the coefficient on it will require a change in some other variable's coefficient to keep the sum of errors in the equation zero. The intercept is a natural choice for this other variable since it seldom has an economic significance which we want to preserve.

With this file created, we are ready to optimize our objective function.

Optimizing

When the model with the objective function has been built (by clicking Model | Build in G), we can run it in optimizing mode. Click Model | Run and then in the top right corner of the screen in the panel labeled "Type of Simulation" click the radio button for "Optimizing". Fill in the dates of the simulation and the "fix" file as usual. Specify the name of the bank which will contain the optimized model run. I usually call it "Optima", but any word of 8 or less letters and numbers will do. Finally, in the window labeled "Optimization file name", give the name of the file created in the previous step. In our case, it is OptSpec.opt, which is what the program puts in that window by default. The root-name of this file (the part before the .opt) will be used to label several of the files resulting from the optimization. Then click OK. You will then get a black DOS screen with the usual] prompt. You can provide a title for the run with a "ti" command or supplement the "fix" file. When running Quest over history, I often give the "skip sp500R" here to use historical values of the S&P 500 index. When you have no further fixes to add, give the command "run" as usual.

When optimizing, the model does not print dates and the values of variables being checked. Instead, it reports for each move of the simplex whether the action was to reflect, expand, contract, or shrink. It also shows the value of the objective function at the best and worst points of the simplex.

The implementation of the simplex method used by our program is borrowed from section 10.4 of *Numerical Recipes in C* by William H. Press *et al.* (Cambridge, 1988; the code and text is available on the Internet at www.nr.com .) This code seems prone to reach local minima. Therefore, when an optimum is reported by the borrowed code, our routine takes it as a starting point and then uses the step sizes to vary it. If one of the new points is better than the supposed optimum, the algorithm is started again, with the message "Starting or restarting optimization" printed on the screen.

When no further improvement appears possible, you will get a list of the parameters with their starting values and their optimized values. This information will also be written into the file Changes.chg. When you then tap any key the model will be run with the optimized parameters and the results stored in the bank you indicated on the Run model screen.

When Quest was optimized with the objective function given above with respect to the parameters specified by the OptSpec.opt file shown above, the coefficients were changed as follows:

```
Resulting coeficients after maximization (183 runs).
Variable        Old:            New:
vfnreR
   intercept    36.8245         36.2423
   ue           -4.6046         -0.6041
cRpc
   intercept    785.4286        804.7291
   yRpc         0.7758          0.7669
   intsavRpc    -0.4875         -0.4898
   ur           -1416.2942  -1464.8260
```

One might suppose that these changes are so small that the optimization must have made little difference in the objective function. That impression, however, is quite misleading as shown in the graphs below. In them, the heavy (blue) line with no marking of points is the actual, historical line. (In the first two graphs, it lies along the horizontal axis, for of course the historical data fits itself perfectly.) The (red) line marked with + is generated by the model before optimization; the (green) line marked with x is from the optimized model. Remember that we are trying to minimize errors, so lower is better.

From the first graph, we see that the optimization achieved a 65 percent reduction in the objective function. The second graph shows that the contribution to the error fell essentially to zero over the last five years. I must confess that I was surprised by how much was achieved by such small changes in so few parameters. The second and third graphs show that the main improvement lay in the GDP deflator, while real GDP was little changed.

However, the last two graphs, especially the last, point to a problem. The simulation of equipment investment in the optimized model is terrible! In specifying our objective function, we implicitly hoped that if we had a good simulation for real GDP, we would have a good fit for its components. That hope, however, proved false. The lesson seems to be

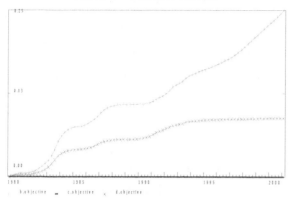

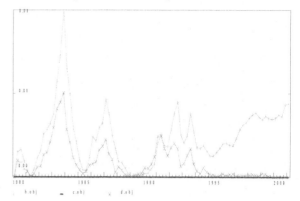

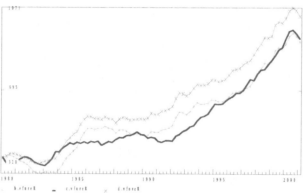

that if some parameters of the equation for a particular variable are included in the optimization, that variable needs to be in the objective function.

With that lesson in mind, we go back and respecify the objective function to include both equipment investment and personal consumption as follows:

```
fex gdpRX = gdpR
fex gdpDX = gdpD
fex vfnreRX = vfnreR
fex cRX = cR
f miss = @sq((gdpR-gdpRX)/gdpRX)+@sq((gdpD-gdpDX)/gdpDX) +
    0.1*@sq((vfnreR-vfnreRX)/vfnreRX) + 0.1*@sq((cR-cRX)/cRX)
```

With this revised objective function, the optimized coefficients in comparison to the original values were as follows

```
Resulting coeficients after optimization (108 runs).
Variable      Old:        New:
vfnreR
   intercept   36.8245     -86.2489
   ue          -4.6046       9.5125
cRpc
   intercept  785.4286     797.5327
   yRpc         0.7758       0.7600
   intsavRpc   -0.4875      -0.3995
   ur       -1416.29      -767.88
```

With this objective function, the change in the equipment investment equation is more

196

substantial, and its unemployment term takes on a stabilizing role. In the consumption equation, on the contrary, the stabilizing role of the *ur* is reduced. The coefficient on income, where we were concerned about simultaneous equation bias, is little changed from the least-squares estimate. The reduction in the coefficient on *intsavRpc* also reduces the stabilizing effect of this variable.

As before with the simpler objective function, we get a substantial reduction in the objective function, in this case, 57 percent. Again, the biggest improvement is in the GDP deflator, where we achieve essentially a perfect simulation over the last eight years. The equipment investment simulation, as hoped, is much improved, though the performance in the last few years is not quite as good as in the model before optimization. Its weight in the objective function should perhaps be increased. All in all, however, the optimization appears to have fixed the most striking problem with the original Quest, namely, the upward creep of the GDP deflator.

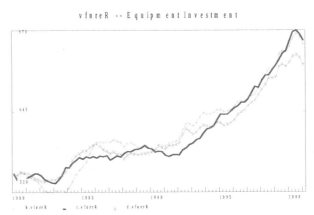

Using the optimized model

How can one use the optimized model for simulation or forecasting? Let us assume that you used Fit.opt as the name of the optimization specification file. Then the optimization created a file by the name of Fit.dat in the directory with the model. It is of exactly the format of the heart.dat file which is created to hold the coefficients for your model when you ran Build. All that you need do to run the optimized model is simply to give this file the name "heart.dat". You can simply type "dos" in the G command line box and then, in the DOS window which opens type

```
copy heart.dat  orig.dat
copy fit.dat heart.dat
exit
```
If you now do Model | Run, the model you run will be the optimized one.

A word about step sizes

The efficiency, and indeed the success, of the optimization can depend on the step sizes.

If they are taken too large, the model can be thrown into an unstable region in which it does not converge and the optimization fails. If they are chosen too small, either many iterations may be necessary to find an optimum, or, if they are really small so that there is little difference in the objective function at the different points and the points are very close together, the optimality test may be passed almost immediately and the process halted before it has really begun. As a rule of thumb, I usually have taken the step sizes at about one percent of the parameter's initial value. If the size of your coefficients make you want to use step sizes below about .01, you should probably change the units of the variables so as to get bigger coefficients. Thus, you may need to experiment with step sizes and the units of variables to get the optimization to run smoothly.

2. Finding optimal policies

Let us turn now to finding optimal policies in a model. We will, of course, need a different objective function, one based not on closeness of fit to history but on achieving desirable social goals. We must also find a way to represent the policy variable as the dependent variable in a regression. Since this second matter requires a new technical wrinkle, let us deal with it first.

Representing policy variables by regression equations

We would like to be able to approximate a policy variable such as *pitfBR,* the federal income tax rate, by a piece-wise linear function of a relatively small number of constants, which will appear as regression coefficients and can be varied by our optimization process. Such a function is shown in the graph on the top right of this page.

To generate the approximation by regression, we need a series of what I shall call linear interpolation functions. Each of these begins at 0 and remains 0 until its particular time interval comes; then it rises by 1 each period until the end of its interval, whereafter it remains constant at whatever value it has reached. For representing the federal personal tax rate, I took the beginning of the intervals to be the third quarter of the first year of each presidential term. Thus, except for the first which represented the tail end of the Carter policies, each of the variables rises from 0 to 16, the number of quarters in a four-year term. A graph of these variables is on the right. I have called these functions tax1, tax2, ..., tax6. Once we have them, we can obtain the piecewise linear approximation by a simple regression:

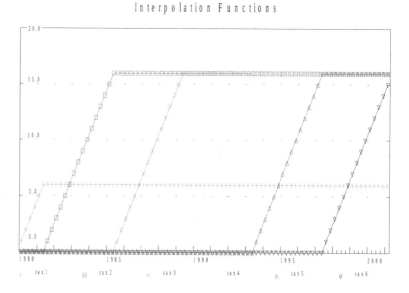

Interpolation Functions

```
r pitfBR = tax1, tax2, tax3,
tax4, tax5, tax6
```

The regression coefficients in this equation are the precisely the parameters with respect to which we optimize to find the optimal tax policy.

We could, of course, create these interpolation variables by hand and introduce them via *fex* and *update* commands into the model. G, however, offers a simpler way of generating them automatically by the *intvar* command. The command necessary to generate our six variable is

```
intvar tax 1980.1 1981.3 1985.3 1989.3 1993.3 1997.3
```

The word after the command, "tax" in this example, provides the root of the variable names which will be created by appending 1, 2, 3, etc. to this root. The dates which follow then mark the beginning of each variable's activity.

The complete regression file to compute the representation of *pitfBR* follows:

```
catch pitfBR.cat
add lim80
#  pitfBR -- Federal Personal Tax Rate

fex pTaxBase = pi - ngtpp + 0.5*nconsi + nibtax
fex pitfBR = 100.*gfrptx/pTaxBase
save pitfBR.sav
intvar tax 1980.1 1981.3 1985.3 1989.3 1993.3 1997.3
ti pitfBR -- Federal Personal Tax Rate
subti Actual and Piecewise Linear Interpolation
r pitfBR = tax1,tax2,tax3,tax4,tax5, tax6
save off
gname pitfBR
gr *
catch off
```

(The two *fex* commands above the *save* command are so placed because they are provided in the Master file.) The results of the regression are

```
:                   pitfBR -- Federal Personal Tax Rate
  SEE   =      0.27 RSQ   = 0.9250 RHO =   0.37 Obser   =   85 from 1980.100
  SEE+1 =      0.25 RBSQ  = 0.9192 DW  =   1.26 DoFree  =   78 to   2001.100
  MAPE  =      1.95
    Variable name          Reg-Coef Mexval  Elas   NorRes      Mean    Beta
  0 pitfBR               - - - - - - - - - - - - - - -         10.02 - - -
  1 intercept             10.35670   407.2   1.03    13.33      1.00
  2 tax1                   0.11258     3.4   0.07    13.07      5.82   0.091
  3 tax2                  -0.12431    67.4  -0.17    12.47     13.46  -0.655
  4 tax3                   0.04077    11.9   0.04    10.75     10.45   0.297
  5 tax4                  -0.05790    23.3  -0.04     9.32      7.44  -0.445
  6 tax5                   0.11661    73.5   0.05     2.24      4.42   0.790
  7 tax6                   0.11938    49.8   0.02     1.00      1.41   0.436
```

Because of the progressivity of the income tax, growth in real income increases this average tax rate. This steady upward movement during the Carter and Clinton administrations is evident in the coefficients of *tax1, tax5,* and *tax6*; the sharp cuts of the first Reagan administration shows up in the negative coefficient on *tax2*. The administration of George Bush, contrary to the impression of many, cut taxes substantially, as seen in the coefficient of *tax4*.

Once this regression has been performed, it is introduced into the Master file just as any other regression with the lines

```
#  pitax -- personal taxes and non-tax payments
f pTaxBase = pi - ngtpp + 0.5*nconsi + nibtax
fex pitfBR = 100.*gfrptx/pTaxBase
# add regression for tax rate to allow optimization
add pitfBR.sav
id   gfrptx = .01*pitfBR*pTaxBase
```

(There is a reason for the factor of 100 in the definition of pitfBR; originally it was not there, and all the regression coefficients were 1/100 of the values shown above. The appropriate step size in the optimization therefore seemed to be about .00001. With this step size, the optimization stopped very quickly at a point very close to the initial point. In other words, it failed to optimize. Evidently, the small step size allowed the termination test to be passed long before it should have been. From this experience came the advice given above that the step sizes should not be too small.)

Putting in this additional regression meant that the optima.dat file from the optimization of the previous model no longer matched the heart.dat file for this new model. Consequently, before putting in a new objective function, I reoptimized this model with the historical fit objective function to get an Optima.dat file which could later be copied to Heart.dat so that the tax optimization should be done with the model optimized for fit. In this step, I gave at the] prompt not only the "skip sp500R" command but also "skip pitfBR" command to use precise historical tax rates in optimizing for fit.

In the next section we will develop a "socially deplorable" objective function to which we give the name *misery*. This objective function we then minimize with respect to the federal personal income tax. The specification of parameters to be varied to minimize the last value of this "misery" function are given by the following FedTax.opt file:

```
misery
20
#Optimize tax rate
pitfBR
#   1    2    3    4    5    6    7
    1  .01  .01  .01  .01  .01  .01
```

The first line of the file gives the name of variable whose last value is to be minimized. The second line specifies the maximum number of parameters which will be varied in the course of the optimization. It does not hurt if it is larger than the number actually used. Here we have set the maximum at 20 but will only use 7. The next line says that some parameters (in the present case, all parameters) will come from the equation for pitfBR. The next line begins with a # which marks it as simply a comment ignored by the program. For us, however, it is very useful since it numbers the regression coefficients which occur in the equation for *pitfBR*. The line below it gives the step sizes for each of the coefficients.

A Social Objective Function

Specifying a socially desirable objective function, or its negative to be minimized, is not necessarily easy. I began with minimizing what has been called the "misery index," the sum of the inflation rate and the unemployment rate. The optimization quickly drove unemployment negative so that $1/u$ in the consumption function became a huge negative number and the model simply broke down with attempts to take logarithms of giant or negative numbers. I then went over to the sum of the *squares* of these two misery indicators. That worked better, but took no account of the budget deficit. Paying interest on the federal debt imposes an efficiency loss in collecting the taxes with which to pay it, so I added a third misery indicator, the ratio of interest on the federal debt to GDP. Finally, to give about equal weight to all three, I took 2 percent unemployment as ideal, rather than 0 percent. The resulting objective function was then expressed by these lines in the Master file:

```
# For optimal tax
fex obj1 = 0
fex obj2 = 0
fex obj3 = 0
f obj1 = @sq(u - 2.)
f obj2 = @sq(infl)
f obj3 = @sq(100.*gfenip/gdp)
f obj = obj1+obj2+obj3
fex misery = 0
f misery = @cum(misery, obj, 0.)
```

Note that both objective functions, *misery* and *misses* and perhaps others, can be included in the model. To optimize policy in a model that has already been optimized for fit, I copied the Optima.dat file (created in optimizing for fit) to Heart.dat with the G command

dos copy optima.dat heart.dat

and then did Model | Run again to minimize *misery* using the FedTax.opt file shown in the preceeding section.

The Misery-minimizing Tax Rate

The old and new coefficients are shown below.

Changes in Federal Taxation

Variable	Historical:	Optimal
Intercept	10.3567	10.1689
Carter	0.1126	0.2090
Reagan I	-0.1243	-0.0450
Reagan II	0.0408	0.0807

201

Bush	-0.0579	-0.2317
Clinton I	0.1166	-0.0622
Clinton II	0.1294	0.2347

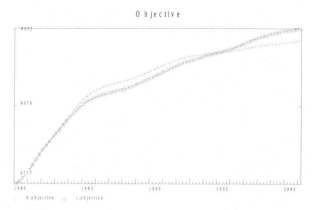

The new tax rates resulting from the optimization are shown by the (red) line marked with + in the graph on the right. The optimal policy would have been higher taxes in the Reagan years, a rapid drop in the Bush administration, continued low rates in the first Clinton administration, followed by a sharp rise in the second. The second graph shows that, quite unlike the objective in the optimization for fit, in this policy optimization the historical policy would have been better than the optimal one up to 1995. We seem to have a clear case of the usual macroeconomic dilemma: what is pleasant in the short run is painful in the long run and vice-versa.

The next three graphs show the effects of the tax change on the three components of the misery index we are minimizing. All three are plotted on the same scale to facilitate comparison of the contribution.

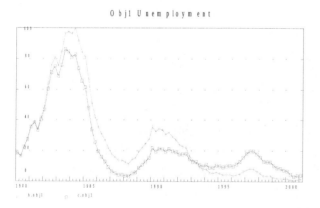

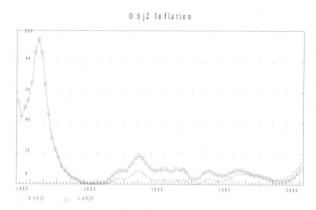

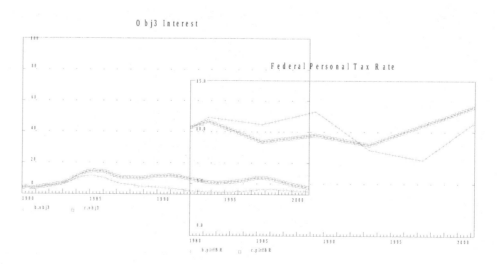

The following three graphs show the variables in the misery index in more customary units without squaring; the last graph shows real GDP.

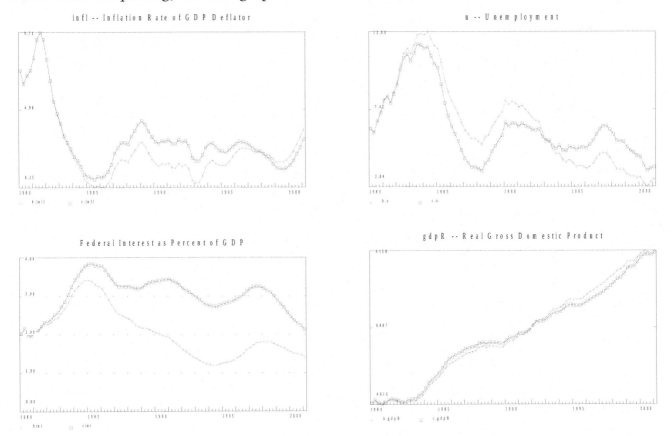

The optimal tax policy accepted a bit more unemployment and some loss in real GDP early in the simulation in order to get higher real GDP, lower unemployment, and much lower prices near the end of the period. Inflation with the optimized tax rate is lower throughout the period except for the last three years where it rises slightly. The interest component of the objective function is uniformly reduced. Though this component does not have the spike in the early 1980's that the others do, the difference between the two lines is of similar magnitude to the differences of the other two indicators.

This exercise illustrates how models can be used in designing of policies. While the changes implied by the optimal policy bear out my own beliefs that the Reagan tax cuts were utterly irresponsible, the subsequent policy changes were not, I believe, altogether obvious consequences of the assumptions.

CHAPTER 10. PROBABILITY THEORY AND REGRESSION

If you have studied regression previously, you may have been slightly shocked that I have not yet said anything about "testing of hypotheses" or the "significance" of variables. My reticence to write about these topics stems from a profound doubt of their appropriateness for use in model building. There is, to be sure, a standard method which is explained with conviction in scores of text books. In years of experience, I have found that the assumptions on which it rests have little to do with the reality in which I, as a builder of economic models, live. I have therefore emphasized other ways of working.

Were I, however, to omit all mention of this other, probabilistic approach and of the beautiful theorems which can be proved using it, then, if you already know this material, you might well conclude that I am ignorant of this wonderland. If, on the other hand, you are new to this work and, having finished this book, go out into the world and find people discoursing learnedly of unbiased, efficient, consistent, blue estimators about which you know nothing, you may feel that your education was deficient. So in this one chapter, and to some extent in the last, we need to look at what this other approach has to offer. You must allow me, however, to explain from time to time as we go along why I do not put much stock in the methods.

To avoid boring you – and to stress the metaphysical, transcendent nature of the assumptions – I will begin the account in the form of a fable.

1. The Datamaker Fable

There is, as you should know, a "true" equation of exactly the form you are estimating with coefficients β and a Great Datamaker, who knows β and has picked a matrix of explanatory variables, X, once and for all and has then generated many vectors, y, by picking vectors of random errors, e, and calculating

$$y = X\beta + e.$$

(Datamaker is called The Data Generating Process by many of his devotees.) Because y depends on random elements, it is said to be stochastic. X, by contrast, is fixed, non-stochastic. Datamaker has thrown into the universe many such y vectors, each bundled with the true X matrix. One of these struck the earth, and we have had the good fortune to come upon it. Our job is to figure out what β was. Datamaker sometimes plays a trick on us and includes in X a variable which in fact was not used in making up y – or which had a zero value in β. We must be very careful to detect any such jokers and must not include them in our estimated equation.

Everyone who has caught such a sample computes the least-squares estimate of β by

$$b = (X'X)^{-1}X'y.$$

Now there are many, many beings throughout the universe who catch the packets thrown by

Datamaker. Each one computes b, all using the same value of X but each having a different y. (There are no others on Earth, however, because on Earth the y of the bundle happens to be called something like "Consumer expenditures on automobiles in the USA, 1960 to 1995." We never see that piece of history rerun with other values of e, so we must suppose that Datamaker has sent his other bundles flying elsewhere in the universe.) The b's computed by beings all over the universe are thus random variables, since each depends upon the e used by Datamaker in making up its y. We may therefore speak of their expected values (or means), their standard errors, their variances and covariances, just as of any other random variables.

Expressing our b in terms of the true β and the random error vector, e, that happened to be used in making up the particular y vector we caught, we have

$$b = (X'X)^{-1} X'(X\beta + e) = \beta + (X'X)^{-1} X'e.$$

If we assume that the expected value of e is 0, $(E(e) = 0)$ then

$$E(b) = \beta + (X'X)^{-1}X'E(e) = \beta.$$

(The first equation follows because X is constant and non-random; the second because $E(e) = 0$.) Thus, the expected value of b is β, and we say that b is an unbiased estimate of β. That means that if the vast number of b's computed throughout the universe are all sent to Universal Central Data Processing and averaged, the average would be β. That is supposed to make us feel good about the one and only b we will ever see.

If we assume that the elements of e are independent and all have the same variance, σ^2, -- so that $E(ee') = \sigma^2 I$ -- then we can calculate the variances and covariances of the elements of b by taking the expected value of $(b - \beta)(b - \beta)'$, thus

$$E(b - \beta)(b - \beta)' = E((X'X)^{-1} X'e\, e'X(X'X)^{-1})$$

$$= (X'X)^{-1} X'\sigma^2 I X(X'X)^{-1}$$

$$= \sigma^2 (X'X)^{-1}$$

so the variances of the b's are the diagonals of this matrix; the standard deviations are their square roots. If we knew σ^2, we could calculate the standard deviations precisely. In fact, we never know σ^2 and must estimate it. The most natural estimate might be r'r/T, the variance of the residuals. This estimate would be biased, for -- as we shall show --

$$E(r'r) = (T - n)\sigma^2,$$

where T is the number of observations or rows of X and n is the number of independent variables, or columns of X. To see why this formula holds, note first that

$$r = y - Xb = X\beta + e - X(X'X)^{-1}X'(X\beta + e)$$

$$= e - Me$$

205

where $M = X(X'X)^{-1}X'$. This M is a remarkable matrix. Note that $M = M'$, and $M'M = MM = M$ and that

$$tr\ M = tr\ (X(X'X)^{-1})X' = tr\ X'X(X'X)^{-1} = tr\ I = n,$$

where tr indicates the *trace* of a square matrix, the sum of its diagonal elements, and I is the (n,n) identity matrix. (The second equality uses the property that $tr(AB) = tr(BA)$ if both products are defined.) Now

$$r'r = (e - Me)'(e - Me) = e'e - 2e'Me - e'M'Me = e'e - e'Me.$$

Since r'r is a scalar, r'r = tr r'r. So

$$
\begin{aligned}
E(r'r) &= E(tr\ r'r) = E(tr(e'e - e'Me)) = E(e'e) - E(tr(ee'M)) \\
&= T\ \sigma^2 - tr(E(ee'M)) \quad \text{(Since the expected value of a sum is the sum of the expected values.)} \\
&= T\sigma^2 - tr(\sigma^2 IM) \quad \text{(Where I is T by T)} \\
&= T\sigma^2 - \sigma^2(tr\ M) = (T - n)\sigma^2.
\end{aligned}
$$

Thus, if we use $s^2 = r'r/(T - n)$, we will have an unbiased estimate in the sense that $E(s^2) = \sigma^2$.

This is indeed a remarkable result, for it tells us the variance of all the b estimates flowing into Universal Central Data Processing solely on the basis of our one pathetic sample!

The *t-values* are the ratio of each regression coefficient to the estimate of its standard deviation made using this s^2.

If the e are normally distributed, and if the true value of some element of β is zero, this ratio will have a Student t distribution. (A good bit of mathematics is required to back up that simple statement; see my book *Matrix Methods in Economics* (Addison-Wesley, 1967) Chapter 6. I have used the expression "t-value" to mean something which, under some assumptions, has a Student t distribution without, however, alleging that those assumptions are in fact valid. This Student distribution depends on T-n, but for values of T - n over 30, the distribution is practically indistinguishable from the normal. So if T-n > 30, then under all of the previous assumptions -- namely the existence of a true equation of the form we are estimating, X non-stochastic, and the elements of e independent of each other but all having a normal distribution with zero mean and the same variance -- we can say, "If the true value of the regression parameter is zero, the probability that we will observe a t-value of over 2.0 in absolute value is less than .05." If we observe such a value, we are then supposed to be "95 percent *confident*" that the true value is different from zero, and we are entitled to say that our variable is "statistically significant at the 5 percent level."

You may be advised to discard variables that are not statistically significant at some specified level, often 5 percent, and then to re-estimate the equation so as to get an equation in which all variables are significant. There is, however, a serious problem in following this advice, as we shall see in the next section.

A further commonly used statistic must be mentioned, namely Fisher's F, named for Sir Ronald A. Fisher (1890 - 1960), who found the exact mathematical distribution of this and numerous other statistics and (alas!) popularized the use of significance tests in the social sciences. The F-test uses exactly the same assumptions as does the t-test but may be applied to test whether several elements of β are all zero.

If one regression has used m independent variables and produced a sum of squared residuals of SSR_m and a second regression has just added more independent variables to it to reach a total of n and produced a sum of squared residuals of SSR_n, then the F statistic for testing the significance of the extra variables is

$$F = \frac{(SSR_m - SSR_n)/(n - m)}{SSR_n/(T - n)} .$$

This F is said to have n - m degrees of freedom in the numerator and T - n in the denominator. Tables of values of F for various levels of significance may be found in most statistics textbooks. The derivation of the distribution of the F statistic is fully derived in my book cited above.

If you want G to show you the t- and F-values, give it the command

```
showt y
```

To turn off the showing of these values, use

```
showt n
```

The t-value that appears for each variable is for testing whether its β coefficient is zero. The F-value for each variable is for testing whether *its and all following* β coefficients are zero.

If you are seriously interested in testing, you should also ask whether the error terms in your equation are normal. The usual procedure is to examine moments of the residuals, μ, μ_2, μ_3, and μ_4. The β_1 test statistic for symmetry and the β_2 test statistic for peakedness or kurtosis are then

$$\beta_1 = \frac{\mu_3^2}{\mu_2^2} \quad \text{and} \quad \beta_2 = \frac{\mu_4}{\mu_2^2}$$

For the normal distribution, $\beta_1 = 0$ and $\beta_2 = 3$. If one is willing to make the assumption that the distribution of the error term belongs to the rather large class of distributions known as the Pearson family (which includes the normal), then a convenient test statistic is offered by the Jarque-Bera statistic

$$J = T\left(\frac{\beta_1}{6} + \frac{(\beta_2 - 3)^2}{24}\right)$$

which, under the hypothesis that $\beta_1 = 0$ and $\beta_2 = 3$, has a chi-square distribution with two degrees of freedom. J will be less than 5.99 95 percent of the time and less than 9.21, 99 percent.[3] To get these statistics in G, use the command

normality <y | n | f>

The command

normality y

turns on the printing of the Jarque-Bera test, which will be labeled "JarqBer". The command

normality n

turns off this printing. The command can be abbreviated to just *norm*. If the option 'f' (for full) is chosen, then before the regression results are shown, a table appears with moments and measures of symmetry and peakedness, as well as the Jarque-Bera statistic. If a "catch" file is active, this table will go into it.

A final question is the relation of the t-values to the mexvals presented by G. In the notation of Part 1, Chapter 2, Seciton 8, we have seen that

$$\text{mexval}_i = 100 * (\text{sqrt}(1 + (a^2_{im}/a_{ii}a_{mm})) - 1).$$

In this same notation, the t-value for the ith variable is

$$t_i = a_{im} / \text{sqrt}(a_{mm}a_{ii}/(T - n))$$

so in terms of t, the mexval for the same variable is

$$\text{mexval} = 100 * (\text{sqrt}(1 + t^2/(T-n)) - 1).$$

Thus, in the same equation where T - n is the same for all variables, t-values and mexvals convey the same information. The difference is in ease of interpretation, ease of explanation, and "honesty". The mexval is exactly what it claims to be; the t-value has a t-distribution only if all the Datamaker assumptions are valid.

In comparing the usefulness of variables in equations of differing values of T - n (the "degrees of freedom") there is, of course, a difference in informational content. A variable with a t-value of 3 in a regression with 10 degrees of freedom would be sorely missed if

---

3 This test is suggested in Jan Kamenta, *Elements of Econometrics*, 2nd Edition, New York, Macmillan 1986, pp. 286-287. He cites an unpublished paper by C.M. Jarque and A.K. Bera from 1981.

dropped -- mexval = 40; whereas a variable with the same t-value in an equation with 1000 degrees of freedom, while more "significant" by the t-test, could be dropped without noticeable effect on the fit -- mexval = 0.45. If you believe in Datamaker, you will like t-values; if not, mexvals may tell you exactly what you want to know in the two cases, while you will find the t-values to be tricky to compare.

2. Datamaker with a Stochastic X Matrix

In hardly any of the behavioral equations of the Quest model or other econometric model are the independent variables non-stochastic; in most of them the independent variables are current or lagged values of endogenous variables of the model. It is, of course, wholly illogical to assume that what is a stochastic variable in one equation is non-stochastic in the another. It is therefore natural to ask, Can we extend the "unbiased-estimator" result in some way to stochastic X matrix?

Although one can still do a few things with the expected value concept, it will prove much more fruitful to use the concept of a *probability limit* or *plim*. Suppose that x is a random variable and that m(t) is a function of t observations on x. (For example, m(t) might be the mean of t observations of x.) If there exists a number a such that for any $\delta > 0$ and any $\varepsilon > 0$ there exists a positive integer N such that when $T > N$,

$$\text{prob}(\,|\, m(T) - a \,|\, > \delta) < \varepsilon,$$

then a is said to be the probability limit of m(t) or plim m(t) = a.

Probability limits have an important property not shared by expected values. If $E(x) = a$ and $E(y) = b$, it is not generally true that $E(xy) = ab$. If, however, plim x = a and plim y = b, then plim xy = ab and plim x/y = a/b if b is not zero. This should be more or less obvious if you are accustomed to working with limits. Its detailed proof is more laborious than enlightening and we will skip it.

Suppose now that

$$y(t) = x(t)\beta + e(t)$$

where $x(t)$ is a row vector of the independent stochastic variables. Let us now make estimates of β using T observations, thus

$$b(T) = (X(T)'X(T))^{-1}X(T)'y(T)$$

where we have shown the familiar X and y matrices explicitly as X(T) and y(T) to emphasize that they have T rows. If now plim b(T) = β, we say that b(T) is a *consistent* estimate of β. This "consistency" concept corresponds in the case of stochastic x(t) to the "unbiased" concept for the non-stochastic X matrix.

Is the least-squares estimator consistent? If we multiply both sides of the first equation of this section by x(t)' and average over T observations, we get

$$(\beta \, x(t)'y(t))/T = ((\beta \, x(t)'x(t))/T)\beta + (\beta \, x(t)'e(t))/T.$$

Note that if we neglected the last term on the right and solved for β we would have the least-squares estimator of β. If we can argue that the plims of all three terms exist and that the plim of the last term is zero, then we can reasonably claim -- using the algebraic properties of plim mentioned above -- that our estimator is consistent. The existence of the first two plims is usually handled by assumption, namely, we assume that the sample grows, not by actually going forward in time into new, uncharted seas, but by rerunning history, by calling on the cosmic Datamaker to give us more observations from the same historical period on which we already have one. Then we don't have to worry about x variables with trends that don't have plims.

What can we say about the last term, the plim $(\beta \, x(t)'e(t))/T$? If the elements x(t), though random variables, are actually determined before t -- perhaps they are lagged values of endogenous variables -- and e(t) is not correlated with the error terms which went into determining them, then we can reasonably assert that plim ▢ x(t)'e(t)/T = 0 and that the least squares estimates are consistent.

But consider two other possibilities.

1. One of the elements of x(t) is determined in period t and depends on y(t). For example, in the AMI model of Chapter 1, consumption depends on income in the same period and this income depends, via the GDP identity, on consumption. Thus it becomes impossible to hope, much less to argue, that income is uncorrelated with the errors in the consumption function. The least squares estimator of the consumption equation is then inconsistent, and increasing the sample size will only make it home in on the wrong values. This situation, mentioned in the development of the Quest model, is known as *simultaneous equation bias* or inconsistency.

2. The elements of x(t) were all determined before period t but e(t) is autocorrelated, that is, plim e(t)e(t-1) ≠ 0. Suppose, to take the worst case, that y(t-1) is among the elements of x(t). Then e(t) is correlated with y(t-1), which is an element of x(t), so plim βx(t)'e(t) cannot be zero and the least-squares estimator is inconsistent. Even if y(t-1) is not among the elements of x(t), there could be other endogenous variables determined at time t-1 and depending on y(t-1) so that a relation between them and e(t) would creep in. Note that autocorrelation of the residuals, a sign only of inefficiency under the assumption that X is non-stochastic, becomes -- in the stochastic case -- a warning of the possibility of the more serious sin of inconsistency. Indeed, if the lagged value of the dependent variable is among the independent variables, it is as good as conviction.

Clearly, there are degrees of inconsistency. It may exist without being a serious problem if the relation between e(t) and the suspect element of x(t) is weak or if the fit of the equation is very close. But we may need ways to deal with it. Some are presented in the rest of this chapter.

3. Does the Datamaker Fable Apply to Our Work?

Clearly, Datamaker has a lot going for him. The assumption of his existence makes all this beautiful mathematics applicable to the real world. Indeed, there is much more mathematics that can be developed by elaborating on Datamaker. There is a whole profession that works on these further elaborations. To question the existence of Datamaker in much of Academe is more socially disturbing than harboring doubts about Santa Claus in kindergarten. And yet, we cannot avoid the question, Does the fable apply to our work?

What possible meaning can be given to β or to the variances and covariances of b? Can we take seriously the idea that there is a true equation of the form that we are fitting? Suppose, for example, that we are studying the demand for automobiles. In fact this demand depends upon the decisions of myriads of individuals subject to myriad influences. One person buys a new car because he has just wrecked his old one; another, who was planning to buy, postpones her purchase because the price of personal computers has dropped and she has decided to buy a computer instead of a car. Another couple is having a baby and needs a different kind of car. We formulate an equation that says that automobile purchases depend on relative prices and income. Can we take seriously the idea that there is a "true" equation of this vastly over-simplified form? Can we honestly suppose that we know exactly what variables are in the X matrix when we know that inside of five minutes we will try other independent variables? Can we even make believe that the variables in X are non-stochastic, fixed values when we know that tomorrow or next week we may be studying almost any one of them as the dependent -- and therefore stochastic -- variable in another regression?

Though my answer to all these questions is a resounding "No" for most regressions based on time series, there is a situation where speaking of β and of the standard deviation of the estimated regression coefficients seems to be to be perfectly meaningful. Indeed, this situation shows clearly why these concepts are not meaningful in most regressions based on economic time series.

This other situation may arise when regression is applied to a sample of cross section data. Suppose that y is salaries of faculty members at the University of Maryland where I teach. I draw a random sample of fifty salaries from the personnel records and compute the mean, that is, I regress the salaries on just a constant term. What is this regression coefficient an estimate of? Clearly it is an estimate of the mean of the whole population, that is, of all faculty members at the University of Maryland, and it makes perfect sense to compute its standard deviation. Now suppose I add to the independent variables dummy variables for the academic rank of the faculty members and do a regression. What now are the b's estimates of? Equally clearly, it seems to me, *they are estimates of the coefficients which would be found if the regression were done on the whole population,* that is, on all faculty at this university. Their variances and covariances are perfectly meaningful. No more than with the mean, however, are they meant to be an estimate of the true way that the university sets salaries. They are just one way of describing the salary structure at the university.

All is fine so long as we are working with a sample. But what if we now get the personnel records of all faculty and run the regression on the whole population. If only the constant term is used, its regression coefficient *is* the mean salary. It is meaningless to talk about its standard deviation, but the regression program will, nevertheless print out this meaningless standard deviation. If there are several explanatory variables, the b which we get is what a moment ago we were calling β. It is meaningless to talk about the variances and covariances of its elements. The regression program will, of course, if you let it, spit them out, but they are utterly meaningless, for β is a constant vector whose true value we have now found!

In doing this regression, we are looking for a *description* of the salary structure at this university. We are not claiming that any such equation and random mechanism is actually used in setting salaries. When we have all the possible observations, our regression gives us the description we want. Only by dragging in some far-fetched concept of all possible Universities of Maryland can one find any meaning for these variances and covariances. Notice also that if we had all but one or two of the faculty members, our b would be a much better estimate of β than would be indicated by the variances and covariances. Thus we see that as our sample size increases towards the whole population, the regression coefficients become better and better descriptive statistics while their variances and covariances become more and more meaningless.

If we return now to the time-series regression which are our main concern in this book, what can we say about the nature of β? If I estimate a regression for investment over the period 1975 - 2000, I would claim only that it is a *description* of investment behavior in the last quarter of the 20th century. I have *all* the data, the whole population, not a sample cast my way by a cosmic Datamaker. The equation may be a good description or a bad description, depending on how well it conforms to the "good advice" of Chapter 6, Part1. But it is not an *estimate* of an unknown, *true* β. If I use the equation to forecast to 2010, I would only be trying to see what will happen if my description remains valid.

Thus, if we are to be serious, we have to admit that variances and covariances of our regression coefficients and the tests based on them make little or no sense. We must admit that we are simply fitting grossly oversimplified equations to a complex reality. Instead of testing, testing, testing as advised by some, we must ask the plainer but harder questions of the "good advice" in Chapter 6. We must think, compute, and re-think to get as good a description as we can, one that would be workable in the sense that forecasts made with it are helpful and counter-historical simulations using it contribute to understanding the effects of policy.

In this way, we also avoid the "pretest" trap that plagues those who would rely on testing. Anyone with much experience in building models will admit that when we begin studying a question with regression, we don't know which variables to include among the explanatory set. So we generally include a lot of variables that prove to have little or no explanatory value as shown by t-tests. So we throw them out and present the final equation with nice, "significant" coefficients on all the variables. What is wrong with that? Well, when we threw a variable out, we may have been making a mistake. Maybe it really did have a non-zero coefficient in β. We really have no idea how likely it was that we made such a mistake. We know that, if we were using a 5 percent t-test, that there was a .05 probability that we would not throw it out even though we should have, but the probability of the other mistake – often called a type II error -- is unknown. But this other mistake can kill us, for if we threw out a variable that belongs in, then we are not estimating the true equation. And if we are not estimating the true equation, all the formulas for variances and covariances are wrong and all the tests invalid.

Thus, while at first it seemed that Datamaker's habit of throwing into X some jokers that were not really used in making y was pretty innocuous, on closer inspection it turns out to be a really nasty trick that brings the application of the theory to a most embarrassing impasse. From a practical point of view, we have to experiment to find variables that work. But as soon as we do, any claim that we are making valid tests of hypotheses is untenable.

The same problem does not arise if we admit that we are just looking for plausible though much over-simplified descriptions of behavior. One who has relied on (probably invalid) t-tests may suppose that once one drops t-tests, any old equation that fits the data is acceptable. Actually, nothing could be farther from the truth. The discipline of plausibility along the lines of the "good advice" of Chapter 6 is far stricter than that of "significant" t-tests.

4. What's Better Than Least-Squares? The Gauss-Markov Theorem and GLS

One may, however, accept the idea that regression coefficients are descriptions, not estimates of some unknowable, true parameters and still ask whether there might be better descriptors. And here Datamaker's supporters have a fall-back position. They may say, "All right, we will put aside testing hypotheses. But suppose, just for the sake of argument, that the data were created more or less as described by the Datamaker story with exactly the equation you have selected by following all the rules of 'good advice.' Wouldn't you want the fitting process to come up with a good approximation of that true equation?"

If you say, "Not especially. I want nothing to do with that ridiculous Datamaker," you will be following the practice of many builders of applied models, and I'll have no objection. I myself, however, am a little more tolerant of belief in Datamaker. I don't want to be accused of blasphemy against Datamaker only to worship Ordinary Least Squares. So, if assenting to this question leads us to ways that get better descriptions, descriptions that are more plausible and hold up better over time, why not look at them? It is in that spirit that the rest of this chapter looks at some alternatives to ordinary least squares suggested by pursuing this limited Datamaker idea.

First of all, however, we need to recognize that ordinary least-squares (OLS) may have some pretty good properties. There is a remarkable proposition, known as the Gauss-Markov theorem, which establishes conditions in which OLS is hard to improve upon. This theorem states that if the data is generated by a Datamaker process but without necessarily using normal errors, then least squares will be the minimum-variance unbiased estimators that can be expressed as a linear function of the dependent variable.

More specifically, if $y = X\beta + e$, with $E(e) = 0$ and $E(ee') = \sigma^2 I$ while X is fixed and non-stochastic, then not only is the least squares estimate of β unbiased, in the sense that $E(b) = \beta$, but it is the "best linear unbiased estimate" in the sense that any other estimate of β that is a linear function of the y will have larger variances – a property summarized by saying that the estimate is "blue." A "linear" estimate in the sense of this theorem means one that can be calculated as a linear combination of the y, that is by multiplying some constant matrix times y. Note that the least-squares estimate qualifies as linear for it is obtained by premultiplying y by $(X'X)^{-1}X'$. "Best" in the sense of this theorem means having the smallest variance. An estimating method which achieves this smallest variance is said to be *efficient*.

To demonstrate this proposition, let c be another linear, unbiased estimate of β which we may without any loss of generality suppose to be given by

$$c = ((X'X)^{-1}X' + C)y$$

where C is a constant matrix depending perhaps on X but not on y or β. If this c is to be unbiased, then

$$\beta = E(c) = E((X'X)^{-1}X' + C)(X\beta + e) = \beta + CX\beta.$$

If this equation is to hold for all possible β, $CX = 0$ must hold. Now to find the variances of c, we first note that

$$c - \beta = ((X'X)^{-1}X' + C)(X\beta + e) - \beta$$

$$= ((X'X)^{-1}X' + C)e$$

since $CX = 0$. The matrix of variances and covariances of C is therefore

$$E((c - \beta)(c - \beta)') = ((X'X)^{-1}X' + C)E(ee')((X'X)^{-1}X' + C)'$$

$$= \sigma^2((X'X)^{-1}X' + C)((X'X)^{-1}X' + C)'$$

$$= \sigma^2((X'X)^{-1} + CC')$$

since $CX = 0$. Since the diagonals of CC' are the sums of squares, they must be positive and therefore the variances of c must be greater than those of b, the least squares estimate, which appear as the first term on the right in the last line.

Thus, under all of the assumptions we have made, the least-squares estimates are "blue". Note that for this theorem, we did not need to assume that the e have a normal distribution. But note also that we derived it by arguing that $CX\beta = 0$ for *all* β. If we have reason to believe that β satisfies some constraints then $CX\beta = 0$ would not have to hold for all β but only for those satisfying the constraints. In that case, therefore, more efficient estimates of β may found by imposing the constraints with, for example, G's *con* or *sma* commands.

This theorem has guided the development of methods to deal with cases in which $E(ee')$ is not $\sigma^2 I$. These methods are special cases of Aitchen's Generalized Least Squares (GLS). We will explain the general idea here and two special cases in the following sections.

Let us suppose that the Datamaker assumptions hold except that $E(ee') = \Omega \neq \sigma^2 I$. The least squares estimates will then still be unbiased and consistent. They may not, however, be efficient. Can we find efficient estimates? If we know Ω, the answer is Yes, by use of what is called *generalized least squares (GLS)*, which we will now explain. To be a variance-covariance matrix, Ω must be positive semidefinite. The principal axes theorem (see my *Matrix Methods in Economics,* page 117) then guarantees the existence of a matrix V such that $V'V = VV' = I$ and $V'\Omega V = D$, where D is a non-negative diagonal matrix. We can then define another diagonal matrix R with diagonal elements $r_{ii} = 1/\sqrt{d_{ii}}$ where d_{ii} is the ith diagonal element of D, so that $R'DR = I$. Let $B = VR$. If we now multiply

$$y = X\beta + e$$

on the left by B', we have

$$B'y = B'X\beta + B'e$$

and

$$E(B'ee'B) = B'\Omega B = R'V'\Omega VR = R'DR = I .$$

Thus, the OLS regression of the transformed y, $B'y$, on the transformed X variables, $B'X$, satisfies the conditions of the Gauss-Markov theorem and produces *efficient* estimates of β. The result of that regression will be

$$b^{GLS} = (X'BB'X)^{-1}X'BB'y = (X'\Omega^{-1}X)^{-1}X'\Omega^{-1}y .$$

The simplification given by the second of the = signs follows from the fact that

$$BB' = \Omega^{-1}$$

which comes from

$$V'\Omega V = D$$

by inverting both sides to get

$$V^{-1} \Omega^{-1} V'^{-1} = D^{-1} = RR'$$

and then multiplying both sides on the left by V and on the right by V' to yield

$$\Omega^{-1} = VRR'V' = B'B.$$

Consequently, in computing we never need to apply the principal axes theorem and associated algorithms to find V. We just need the conceptually simpler Ω^{-1}.

The only problem with this panacea is that Ω is really never known. If the method is to be of any use, we have to make some assumptions that allow us to estimate it. In the next two sections, we will look at two such assumptions that may offer useful alternatives to ordinary least squares. The first relates to the case of a time series regression in which the error of one period is correlated with the error of the next. The second relates to systems of equations in which errors in different equations may be related.

Here we should note that the simplest such assumption is to suppose that Ω is diagonal with diagonals that vary in some way that can be estimated from the residuals of the regression. For example, with time series data, their square roots might be a linear function of time that can be estimated by regressing their absolute values on time. In such a case, the GLS estimate is found by simply dividing the dependent and independent variables of each observation by the standard deviation of the error term for that observation and then applying OLS to the resulting observations. In G, such a procedure is given by this series of commands for regression of y on x:

```
r y = x
f srrs = @sqrt(@sq(resid))
r srrs = time
f scale = predic
f yScaled = y/scale
f xScaled = x/scale
r yScaled = xScaled
```

You may ask for an example where this method has made estimates more plausible, and I will have to confess that I could not find one among the equations of QUEST or any other equation I could make up with the time series data that accompany this book. Generally, the procedure made no difference because there was little or no trend in the residuals. I believe that this version of GLS may be more applicable with cross-section data where the differences in size of observation may be much larger than they usually are with economic time series.

5. The Hildreth-Lu Technique for Autocorrelation of Residuals

If the value of RHO on G's regression display indicates that the "true" errors may be autocorrelated, then, as we have just seen, the least-squares estimates are not "efficient." Worse still, if the lagged value of the dependent variable is among the independent variables, then autocorrelation in the error terms means that the errors are correlated with at least one variable in the X matrix, so the least squares are not consistent. The Hildreth-Lu technique may be helpful in the face of such evidence of autocorrelation.

This technique begins from the assumption that the errors are autocorrelated by the first-order autocorrelation scheme

$$e(t) = \rho e(t-1) + u(t)$$

where the u(t) are not autocorrelated. If we know ρ, there is a simple remedy. Let us write

$$y(t) \quad = \quad ßx(t) + e(t)$$

$$y(t-1) \quad = \quad ßx(t-1) + e(t-1).$$

and then multiply the second equation by ρ and subtract from the first to get

$$y(t) - \rho y(t-1) \quad = \quad ß(x(t) - \rho x(t-1)) + e(t) - \rho e(t-1)$$

$$= \quad ß(x(t) - \rho x(t-1)) + u(t).$$

Notice now that the error term is not autocorrelated, so OLS gives us efficient estimates of this equation.

Of course, we do not know ρ. The Cochrane-Orcutt suggestion was to use the ρ estimated from the OLS estimate. It may happen, however, that the very problems we are trying to circumvent cause the OLS estimate of ρ to be poor; then the method may be even worse than OLS. A better procedure was suggested by Hildreth and Lu: try a range of values of ρ and pick the "best" one. This is the method included in G. The general form of the Hildreth-Lu command is

    hl <rho1> <rho2> <incr> <y> = <x1>, [x2,] [x3,] ...[xn]

Here rho1 is the starting guess of ρ, incr is the amount by which it is incremented on each iteration and rho2 is an upper limit on the guess. The y and x1, ..., xn are as in the r command. For example,

    hl 0 1. .1 cR = gR, vR, feR, -fiR

will regress c\$ - ▯c\$[1] on g\$ - ▯g\$[1] and v\$ - ▯v\$, first with ▯ = 0, then with ▯ = .1, and so on up to ▯ = .9. A maximum of ten values of ▯ will be tried on any invocation of the command. The results of each regression are displayed, and the assumed value of ▯ is shown as RHO-HL on each display. Once an approximate range of interest for ▯ has been identified, the equation can be rerun with a smaller value of incr. No more than 20 variables in all are presently permitted in the hl command in G.

At the end of the process, you will get a table with this heading:

    RHO-HL   SEE 1-AHEAD   RHO-EST   SEE LONG-RUN

The RHO-HL shows the assumed ▯, the SEE 1-AHEAD shows the standard error of estimate (SEE) of the estimated equation (without using any further rho adjustment of the forecast), the RHO-EST shows the rho of the estimated equation, and SEE LONG-RUN shows the standard error of using the fitted equation on the original, undifferenced data, without a knowledge of the true lagged value of the dependent variable, as must be done in forecasts of more than one period ahead.

If the "save" command is on for model building, all of the estimated equations will be placed in the ".sav" file as undifferenced equations suitable for going into a model. You must choose which one you want.

The above example, estimated by ordinary least squares, gives the following results

```
:                         Multiplier Estimates
  SEE    =      68.19 RSQ   = 0.9980 RHO =    0.78 Obser  =  105 from 1975.100
  SEE+1  =      42.31 RBSQ  = 0.9979 DW  =    0.43 DoFree =  100 to    2001.100
  MAPE   =       0.97
     Variable name          Reg-Coef Mexval  Elas   NorRes      Mean   Beta
  0 gdpR                   - - - - - - - - - - - - - - -    6237.65  - - -
  1 intercept             -457.82310   11.5  -0.07   501.59      1.00
  2 vR                        1.40468   50.9   0.23    67.95   1026.15  0.250
  3 gR                        3.34416  300.2   0.65     7.79   1220.11  0.510
  4 feR                       2.35637   88.3   0.23     1.02    595.92  0.339
  5 -fiR                      0.33296    0.9  -0.04     1.00   -691.98  0.059
```

The hl command in the example gave the output summary table:

HL rho	SEE 1 ahead	Est. rho	SEE long
0.000000	68.185463	0.784687	68.185455
0.100000	62.975750	0.740949	68.189636
0.200000	58.092529	0.682434	68.208275
0.300000	53.619797	0.605829	68.257622
0.400000	49.660053	0.508860	68.372414
0.500000	46.329838	0.392330	68.634872
0.600000	43.744110	0.262790	69.280540
0.700000	41.972450	0.134028	71.159630
0.800000	40.928905	0.024735	78.298286
0.900000	39.859150	-0.023783	129.082184

In choosing which ρ to use, we need to look at everything in this summary table and at the regression coefficients. The first column in the table is simply the assumed value of ρ. Let us look first at the Rho-Est column. If the transformation did not eliminate autocorrelation in the transformed equation -- and sometimes it does not -- then the transformation was based on a false assumption about the structure of the error and may have made matters worse. The value of HL Rho which gives the Rho-Est closest to zero is of special interest; let us call it ρ^*. In our case, it lies in the interval [.8 , .9], and we can pin it down more closely with the command hl .8 .9 .01 gdpR = gR, vR, feR, -fiR

with the following results:

HL rho	SEE 1 ahead	Est. rho	SEE long
0.800000	40.928894	0.024736	78.298286
0.810000	40.849819	0.015745	79.840630
0.820000	40.771847	0.007264	81.688118
0.830000	40.693424	-0.000630	83.922455
0.840000	40.612625	-0.007836	86.654854
0.850000	40.526974	-0.014209	90.039986
0.860000	40.433220	-0.019560	94.297501
0.870000	40.326958	-0.023624	99.743355
0.880000	40.202152	-0.026041	106.840851
0.890000	40.050323	-0.026317	116.276627

From these results, we can, with sufficient accuracy, say that ρ^* is .83. As a first guess, it is the $\square$ we want.

Next, however, we should look at "SEE 1 ahead", the standard error of the transformed equation. If this "SEE 1 ahead" reaches a minimum for ρ below ρ^*, we might prefer that lower ρ. In our example, however, "SEE 1 ahead" goes right on declining past ρ^*.

But it is important to look also at "SEE long-run". It will generally be rising as HL rho is increased. If it rises sharply for values of Rho-HL lower than ρ^*, as it seems to me to be doing in the example, you may want to pick a value before the sharp rise. Otherwise, you would be making a substantial sacrifice of the equation's ability to fit the data when it does not have the actual lagged value of the dependent variable to fall back on.

The usual advice is simply to pick ρ^* as the value of the HL ρ, re-estimate the equation, and be done with it.

Following this advice, we would pick $\rho = .83$. I, however, would be reluctant to see the long-term performance of the equation so much worsened, with the SEE long rising from 68.2 to 83.9. I would be more interested in a value of perhaps $\rho = .6$, which would give some improvement in the one-period-ahead forecast, with a drop from 68.18 to 43.74 in the "SEE 1 ahead" and a rise of the "SEE long run" only from 68.18 to 69.28.

But how much better off would I really be in forecasting one period ahead? The one-period ahead forecast of the OLS equation with the usual, automatic rho-adjustment is 42.31 (not visible in the summary table but shown on the full printout). This is only very slightly worse than the 42.28 found for the rho-adjusted forecast of the equation estimated with a Hildreth-Lu $\square$ of .6 and not much worse than the 40.69 with the usually chosen Hildreth-Lu ρ of .83. Thus, the short-term forecasting ability of the equation has not been noticeably helped by the Hildreth-Lu procedure, while the long-term forecasting ability has been impaired, a little for $\rho = .6$, a lot for $\rho = .83$.

Next, we should look at the regression coefficients and ask if the coefficients have become any more sensible. The usual multiplier analysis gives equal weight to a dollar of any one of these demands. So, theoretically, all of the regression coefficients should be the same. Let us look at them for three values of the Hildreth-Lu ρ. We find:

HL-rho	0	.6	.83
1 intercept	-457.82310	-159.45291	-64.98312
2 vR	1.40468	1.26041	1.17343
3 gR	3.34416	3.37155	3.54343
4 feR	2.35637	2.24681	2.09337
5 -fiR	0.33296	0.15618	0.20951

The largest coefficient was made steadily larger; the three smallest all were even smaller with the Hildreth-Lu estimate. Thus, the coefficients do not become more reasonable with the use of the Hildreth-Lu procedure.

Finally, two plots should be made and studied before deciding to accept a Hildreth-Lu estimate in place of the OLS estimate. One plot shows the errors of the one-period-ahead forecast from both equations with the rho-adjustment technique of Part 1 Chapter 2 applied to the least-squares equation. The second plot shows the errors of the OLS prediction and the prediction with the Hildreth-Lu values of the parameters but without the lagged value of the dependent variable. This comparison shows how the two equations will do in historical simulation or long-term forecasting when the last actual lagged value of the dependent variable has faded into the remote past. The line marked by the + signs shows the OLS errors in both graphs. Here they are for our example, with the Hildreth-Lu lines computed with $\rho = .83$.

The least-squares fit is always better in the second graph; the question is by how wide a margin. If the margin is wide, and it sometimes is, I lose interest in the Hildreth-Lu estimates. In the present case, I find little difference.

The example is pretty typical of my own experience with the Hildreth-Lu technique. When one goes beyond the usual textbook advice, I have seldom found that I want to use it. My impression is that about ninety percent of the time, it makes little difference; you use it if you believe the Datamake fable and skip it if you don't. It is capable, however, of sometime seriously degrading the long-term forecasting ability of the equation and producing nonsensical regression coefficients. My advice is to never use the technique without examining the results carefully in the way shown in this section. Indiscriminate use is dangerous.

For reference, here is the file used to make all the calculations discussed in this section.

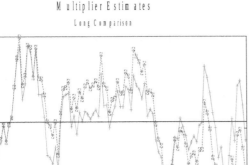

```
title Multiplier Estimates
add lim75
gdates 1975.1 2001.1
r gdpR = vR,gR,feR,-fiR
hl 0 1. .1 gdpR = vR,gR,feR,-fiR
hl .8 .9 .01 gdpR = vR,gR,feR,-fiR
hl .83 .83 .01 gdpR = vR,gR,feR,-fiR
gname hlshort
subti Short Comparison
f OLSshort = predp1 - depvar
f HLshort = hlshort - depvar
gr OLSshort HLshort
gname hllong
subti Long Comparison
f OLSlong = predic - depvar
f HLlong = hllong - depvar
gr OLSlong HLlong
```

EXERCISES

1. Re-estimate all of the equations of the model in Chapter 8 with the Hildreth-Lu
   technique. Be sure to examine carefully the two plots for each equation. Which
   equations, if any, were definitely improved by the method? Were there any where you
   would definitely prefer the ordinary least squares?

2. Rebuild and simulate the AMI model with the Hildreth-Lu estimates developed in
   exercise 1. (If there are some HL estimates that you really do not like, stick to the OLS
   estimate for them.) Is the performance of the model improved? Run some policy
   experiments and make some forecasts with the two models. What differences do you
   note?

6. Stacked and Seemingly Unrelated Regression

Stacked regression allows us to impose constraints on regression coefficients across two or more related regressions. We can take as an example the estimation of the demand for food and the demand for gasoline, each as a function of its own price, the price of the other, and a "demand curve shifter" which is disposable income per capita in the case of food and an estimate of the stock of cars per capita in the case of gasoline. A theorem of microeconomics suggests that the price of food should have the same coefficient in the equation for the demand for gasoline that the price of gasoline has in the equation for the demand for food. We can set up the estimation as follows:

```
f lim 1970.1 2001.1
f ypc$ = pidis$/pop
f food = cfood$/pop
f gasoline= cgaso$/pop
f dc = c/c$
f pfood = (cfood/cfood$)/dc
f pgasoline = (cgaso/cgaso$)/dc
f ub = @cum(ub,1.,.08)
f cars1 = @cum(cars1,cdmv$,.08)/ub
f cars2 = @cum(cars2,cars1,.08)/ub
f carspc = (cars1+cars2)/pop
title Demand for Food
r food = ypc$, pfood, pgasoline
title Demand for Gasoline and Oil
r gasoline= carspc, pfood, pgasoline
```

The results are:

```
:                              Demand for Food
  SEE    =       37.03 RSQ   = 0.9718 RHO =    0.88 Obser   =   125 from 1970.100
  SEE+1 =        18.41 RBSQ = 0.9711 DW  =    0.25 DoFree =   121 to    2001.100
  MAPE  =         1.09
     Variable name              Reg-Coef Mexval  Elas   NorRes      Mean   Beta
  0 food                        - - - - - - - - - - - - - -     2719.34  - - -
  1 intercept              1964.62501      59.4   0.72    35.52      1.00
  2 ypc$                      0.06547     318.0   0.43     1.19  18058.19  0.923
  3 pfood                  -374.85603       3.4  -0.14     1.02      1.04 -0.070
  4 pgasoline               -27.93018       1.2  -0.01     1.00      1.29 -0.033

:                          Demand for Gasoline and Oil
  SEE    =       12.13 RSQ   = 0.7194 RHO =    0.84 Obser   =   125 from 1970.100
  SEE+1 =         6.78 RBSQ = 0.7124 DW  =    0.33 DoFree =   121 to    2001.100
  MAPE  =         2.15
     Variable name              Reg-Coef Mexval  Elas   NorRes      Mean   Beta
  0 gasoline                    - - - - - - - - - - - - - -      447.25  - - -
  1 intercept               140.15273       4.0   0.31     3.56      1.00
  2 carspc                    0.06003      58.2   0.20     1.60   1483.05  0.861
  3 pfood                   262.63407      15.4   0.61     1.56      1.04  0.475
  4 pgasoline               -43.56514      24.7  -0.13     1.00      1.29 -0.502
```

Stacked Regression

Clearly, the coefficient on the price of gasoline in the food equation, -27.93, is by no means equal to the coefficient of the price of food in the gasoline equation, 282.63. If we want to *impose* that equality, we "stack" the regressions as follows:

```
stack
  r food = ypc$, pfood, pgasoline
  r gasoline= carspc, pfood, pgasoline
  con 1  0 = a4 - b3
do
```

In the constraint command, an *a* refers to a coefficient in the first equation, a *b* refers to a coefficient in the second equation, and so on up to the number of equations in the stack. In the example, we are softly constraining the fourth coefficient in the first equation to be equal to the third coefficient in the second equation. Note that the constraint command must follow all of the "r" commands under the "stack" command. In effect, the "stack" command combines the regressions under it into one big regression and applies the constraint in this combined regression. The combined regression may be thought of as looking something like this:

$$\begin{pmatrix} y1 \\ y2 \end{pmatrix} = \begin{pmatrix} X1 & 0 \\ 0 & X2 \end{pmatrix} \begin{pmatrix} a \\ b \end{pmatrix} + \begin{pmatrix} r1 \\ r2 \end{pmatrix}$$

We have, in effect, "stacked" one regression on top of the other. Now the errors of the first equation may well have a different variance than those of the second. In the present example, the variance of the r1 is about four times as large as the variance of the r2. If the two were combined without taking account of that difference, most of the adjusting to accommodate the restraint would be done by the second equation. We can, however, easily get the variances to be of similar size by first estimating the individual equations separately, calculating the SEE of each equation separately, and then dividing both the independent and dependent variables of each equation by the SEE of that equation. If a regression is then done on these "normalized" variables, the SEE will be 1.0 for both equations.

This is exactly what the "stack" command does. It first reports the individual equations, which are the same as shown above, and then reports the variances of each equation as the diagonal elements of a "Sigma Matrix", like this in our example:

The Sigma Matrix
1371.33198   0.00000
    0.00000 147.16666

The Sigma Inverse Matrix
0.0007 0.0000
0.0000 0.0068

```
                    Demand for Gasoline and Oil
Regression number 1, food
  SEE   =      37.89 RSQ   = 0.9705 RHO =   0.89 Obser  =   250 from 1970.100
  SEE+1 =      18.12 RBSQ  = 0.9698 DW  =   0.22 DoFree =   242 to   2001.100
  MAPE  =       1.13 SEESUR = 1.08
    Variable name           Reg-Coef  Mexval   Elas   NorRes     Mean     Beta
  0 food                  - - - - - - - - - - - - - - - -      2719.34  - - -
  1 intercept            2088.13832    32.4    0.77    1.03       1.00
  2 ypc$                    0.06526   182.2    0.43    1.00   18058.19   0.920
  3 pfood                -537.15829     3.1   -0.21    1.00       1.04  -0.101
  4 pgasoline              10.66789     0.1    0.01    1.00       1.29   0.013


  :                   Demand for Gasoline and Oil
Regression number 2, gasoline
  SEE   =      13.86 RSQ   = 0.6337 RHO =   0.88 Obser  =   250 from 1970.100
  SEE+1 =       6.92 RBSQ  = 0.6247 DW  =   0.24 DoFree =   242 to   2001.100
  MAPE  =       2.53 SEESUR = 1.08
    Variable name           Reg-Coef  Mexval   Elas   NorRes     Mean     Beta
  5 gasoline               - - - - - - - - - - - - - - - -       447.25  - - -
  1 intercept             404.65497    64.1    0.90    1.95       1.00
  2 carspc                  0.04439    22.2    0.15    1.12    1483.05   0.637
  3 pfood                  10.66910     0.1    0.02    1.12       1.04   0.019
  4 pgasoline             -26.65290     5.6   -0.08    1.00       1.29  -0.307
```

We can now see that the equality of a4 and b3 has been assured with little cost to SEE of either equation. Do the magnitudes of the price and "demand shifters" seem reasonable to you? The "SEESUR" measure which appears on these displays is the SEE of the combined, stacked regression. Without the constraint, it would be 1.00 because of the normalization.

Seemingly Unrelated Regression (SUR)

If we now think of the errors in the stacked regression, we realize that -- although the equations are "seemingly unrelated" -- there is one obvious possibility for correlation among the error terms. Namely the error in period t in one equation may be correlated with the error in period t in the other equation. Perhaps, whenever we spend more on gasoline than we "should" according to the equation, simultaneously spend less on food. If that is so, then the least squares estimates of the stacked system is not the "best", that is, it does not have minimum variance. It is, therefore, a candidate for being improved by application of generalized least squares.

To estimate Ω , we assume that all the off-diagonal elements are zero except that $E(e_{it}e_{jt}) = \sigma_{ij}$, where e_{it} and e_{jt} are the errors in the ith and jth equations of the stacked system, that is, that contemporaneous cross correlations are not necessarily zero. The matrix of these contemporaneous cross correlations we will call Σ. From its inverse we can easily construct Ω^{-1} and compute the GLS estimate. Because many elements of $\square$ are zero, there are shortcuts to making the calculations.

In G, the setup for applying GLS to this "seemingly unrelated regression" or SUR problem is as simple as the stack command. Here are the commands to estimate our previous example by SUR.

```
sur
  r food = ypc$, pfood, pgasoline
  r gasoline= carspc, pfood, pgasoline
do
```

G first estimates the equations independently, then prints out the estimate of the Σ matrix and its inverse based on the residuals from the separate regressions, like this:

```
The Sigma Matrix
  0 1371.33198    65.65089
  1   65.65089   147.16666

The Sigma Inverse Matrix
  0  0.0007 -0.0003
  1 -0.0003  0.0069

   Seemingly Unrelated Regression of Demand for Food and Gasoline
Regression number 1, food
   SEE   =      37.04 RSQ   = 0.9718 RHO =    0.88 Obser  =   250 from 1970.100
   SEE+1 =      18.34 RBSQ  = 0.9711 DW  =    0.24 DoFree =   242 to    2001.100
   MAPE  =       1.09 SEESUR =      1.00
      Variable name         Reg-Coef  Mexval  Elas   NorRes    Mean    Beta
   0 food                  - - - - - - - - - - - - - - - - -  2719.34 - - -
   1 intercept            1988.32281    33.8   0.73    1.02    1.00
   2 ypc$                    0.06514   202.8   0.43    1.00  18058.19  0.918
   3 pfood                -392.19094     1.9  -0.15    1.00    1.04  -0.074
   4 pgasoline             -27.71240     0.6  -0.01    1.00    1.29  -0.033

Regression number 2, gasoline
   SEE   =      12.13 RSQ   = 0.7194 RHO =    0.84 Obser  =   250 from 1970.100
   SEE+1 =       6.78 RBSQ  = 0.7124 DW  =    0.33 DoFree =   242 to    2001.100
   MAPE  =       2.15 SEESUR =      1.00
      Variable name         Reg-Coef  Mexval  Elas   NorRes    Mean    Beta
   5 gasoline              - - - - - - - - - - - - - - - -   447.25 - - -
   1 intercept             141.83479     2.1   0.32    2.28    1.00
   2 carspc                  0.05979    32.2   0.20    1.30  1483.05  0.858
   3 pfood                 261.34901     7.9   0.61    1.28    1.04   0.472
   4 pgasoline             -43.55446    13.0  -0.13    1.00    1.29  -0.502
```

Comparing these regression coefficients with the original ones shows that the effects of SUR are trifling. This outcome is fairly typical of my experience. In fact, if the independent variables are exactly the same in the two regressions, SUR has no effect. The real reason for using "carspc" instead of "ypc$" in the Gasoline equation was to show at least some slight effect of SUR.

Of course, we can now add the constraint to SUR like this

```
title SUR for Food and Gasoline-- with cross-equation constraint
sur
  r food = ypc$, pfood, pgasoline
  r gasoline= carspc, pfood, pgasoline
  con 1  0 = a4 - b3
do
```

with these results:

```
:          Seemingly Unrelated Regression of Demand for Food and Gasoline
Regression number 1, food
   SEE    =       38.25 RSQ    = 0.9700 RHO =    0.89 Obser  =   250 from 1970.100
   SEE+1  =       17.88 RBSQ   = 0.9692 DW  =    0.22 DoFree =   242 to    2001.100
   MAPE   =        1.14 SEESUR =        1.08
      Variable name          Reg-Coef  Mexval  Elas   NorRes     Mean   Beta
   0 food                    - - - - - - - - - - - - - - -    2719.34  - - -
   1 intercept            2220.35697    38.0   0.82    1.02       1.00
   2 ypc$                    0.06425   180.7   0.43    1.00   18058.19  0.906
   3 pfood                -653.05646     4.9  -0.25    1.00       1.04 -0.122
   4 pgasoline              16.05632     0.2   0.01    1.00       1.29  0.019

:          Seemingly Unrelated Regression of Demand for Food and Gasoline
Regression number 2, gasoline
   SEE    =       13.79 RSQ    = 0.6372 RHO =    0.88 Obser  =   250 from 1970.100
   SEE+1  =        6.92 RBSQ   = 0.6282 DW  =    0.24 DoFree =   242 to    2001.100
   MAPE   =        2.53 SEESUR =        1.08
      Variable name          Reg-Coef  Mexval  Elas   NorRes     Mean   Beta
   5 gasoline                - - - - - - - - - - - - - - -     447.25  - - -
   1 intercept             397.14551    60.7   0.89    1.95       1.00
   2 carspc                  0.04495    22.5   0.15    1.12    1483.05  0.645
   3 pfood                  16.05747     0.2   0.04    1.12       1.04  0.029
   4 pgasoline             -25.83077     5.7  -0.07    1.00       1.29 -0.298
```

The results for some of the coefficients are noticeably different from the stacked without SUR. The price interaction, in particular, is stronger. Which is more plausible is hard to say.
G will accommodate up to ten regressions under a "stack" or "sur" command.

We notice that the essential idea for practical application of GLS was some notion of the structure of Ω. The assumption that the errors have the sort of autocorrelation for which we applied the Hildreth-Lu method leads to a structure for Ω; and in this case GLS can be shown to be almost exactly the same as Hildreth-Lu.

SUR should be used only if you are a firm believer in the fable about a true equation. Otherwise, it may give you parameters which will suit your purposes far less well than do the parameters given by ordinary least squares. Let me try to explain why that is so. Any generalized least squares method amounts to minimizing not r'r but $r'\Omega^{-1} r$, where r is the vector of residuals. Let us consider a system of two stacked equations. Let us suppose that

$$\Sigma = (1/3)\begin{pmatrix} 2 & 1 \\ 1 & 2 \end{pmatrix} \quad \text{and} \quad \Sigma^{-1} = \begin{pmatrix} 2 & -1 \\ -1 & 2 \end{pmatrix}$$

Then, for three observations on each equation, the Ω^{-1} matrix is shown in the first six columns of the panel below.

```
        Ω⁻¹                    A    B    C
|  2  0  0 -1  0  0 |   2    2   1.2 |
|  0  2  0  0 -1  0 |  -1   -1  -0.6 |
|  0  0  2  0  0 -1 |  -1   -1  -0.6 |
| -1  0  0  2  0  0 |   2   -2  -1.2 |
|  0 -1  0  0  2  0 |  -1    1   0.6 |
|  0  0 -1  0  0  2 |  -1    1   0.6 |
```

Consider now three alternative estimates of the parameters. Estimate A gives the residuals shown in the column labeled A, while estimates B and C give the residuals shown in the columns labeled B and C. The value of $r' \Omega^{-1} r$ for estimate A is 12; for estimate B, 36; and for estimate C, 12.96. The SUR criterion will pick estimate A. Are you sure you want that estimate? Estimate C gives residuals which are forty percent lower in absolute value for every observation. Furthermore, the residuals in estimates B and C cancel out in each period; in the first period, for example, the first equation has a miss of +1.2 while the second equation has a miss of -1.2. SUR likes estimate A because the residuals follow the expected pattern of a positive correlation between the errors of the two equations. OLS is indifferent between A and B but strongly prefers C to either of them.

In most examples I can think of, I also would prefer estimate C. Suppose, for example, that the two equations are for (1) investment in equipment and (2) investment in structures. Suppose that I make a forecast using estimate A; and, sure enough, it turns out that both equations overestimate by 2, so that total investment is over-predicted by 4. Am I going to be happier than if one had been over-predicted by 1.2 while the other was under-predicted by 1.2, so that the errors exactly canceled out? Am I going to be consoled by the thought that these equations always tend to make errors that compound rather than cancel? Not I. How about you?

Of course, if you really believe the fable about there being a true equation of exactly the form you are estimating, then you will believe that SUR gives you more efficient estimates of the true parameters. But if you recognize that all you are trying to do is to get an equation which gives you a crude approximation of the way the economy works, then you may very well want to avoid SUR and all GLS procedures.

7. Comment on Maximum Likelihood Methods

Generalized least squares is a special case of a family of methods known as "maximum likelihood" methods. These methods all amount to expressing, as a function of the parameters of the equation, the probability that the sample should have occurred and then choosing the parameters to maximize that probability. What the method really amounts to depends on the assumption about the form of the probability function, and that often amounts chiefly to assumptions about the Ω matrix. If one assumes that $\Omega = \sigma^2 I$, then the ordinary least squares estimates are maximum likelihood estimates. But if one allows more and more elements of Ω to be unknown and determined by the maximizing process, the results can be very like choosing alternative A in the above example. In practice, that amounts to tolerating habitual mistakes while avoiding unusual ones. Mathematical statisticians assure us that under fairly general assumptions maximum likelihood estimates have desirable large sample properties, namely, they are both consistent and asymptotically efficient. These assurances, however, are only as good as the Datamaker assumption. As soon as we admit that we know perfectly well that we are not estimating the true model and that we don't even know all the relevant variables and are just looking for reasonable, workable approximations, the comfort from these theorems vanishes.

Some people say that they find maximum likelihood "an intuitively appealing" method. I expect this appeal is because we find it difficult to think about joint probabilities. Our thinking gravitates to the case of independent, identically distributed errors, and there maximum likelihood is the same as ordinary least squares. When one holds clearly in mind what maximum likelihood does when there are significant dependencies among the errors of the equations, the method becomes very unappealing, at least to me. A further comment on Full Information Maximum Likelihood is on page 241.

8. Equations with Moving Average Error Terms

Autocorrelation of the residuals may be caused by other structures than the one used for the Hildreth-Lu technique. For example, we could imagine that the error term is a *moving average* of independent error terms, thus

(1) $e(t) = u(t) + h_1 u(t\text{-}1) + h_2 u(t\text{-}1),$

where the u's are independent random variables. Notice that in this case the errors are autocorrelated but not in the way assumed by the Hildreth-Lu procedure. Applying Hildreth-Lu is likely to make the situation worse. This assumption about the error term is fundamental to a technique that was popularized by G. E. P. Box and G. M. Jenkins.[4] In this line of literature, the independent variables are often simply the lagged values of the dependent variable, so the method is often referred to as ARMA (AutoRegressive Moving Average) or ARIMA (AutoRegressive Integrated Moving Average) if differencing has been used to produce a stationary series. The application of the technique to economic data has been nicely discussed in the textbook by Pindyck and Rubinfeld.[5] The general form of the equation used in ARMA analysis is

---

4 G. E. P. Box and G. M. Jenkins in *Time Series Analysis* (San Francisco, Holden-Day, 1970)

5 Robert S. Pindyck and Daniel L. Rubinfeld , *Econometric Models and Economic Forecasts*, New York, McGraw-Hill, 1976, 1981,1991.

(2) $y(t) = b_1x_1(t) + b_2x_2(t) + \ldots + b_px_p(t) + u(t) + h_1u(t-1) + \ldots + h_qu(t-q)$

where the:

   $x(t)$ are observable variables which may or may not be lagged values of the dependent
      variable
   b are matching constants to be estimated.
   $u(t)$ is an unobservable random variable with an unchanging distribution, often assumed to be
      normal, with each observation independent of all previous ones.
   $h_1, \ldots, h_q$ are constants to be estimated.

If q = 0, the b can be estimated by ordinary least squares.   The special problem arises if q > 0, for the $u(t)$ are unobservable. We will see how that inconvenience is overcome.

The technique became enormously popular in the 1970's and 1980's because almost any time series could be forecasted one or two periods ahead with some accuracy and almost no work by using only lagged values of the dependent variable as x variables. Thousands of papers were written and probably millions of forecasts made with the technique. Conferences on forecasting were completely dominated by its practitioners. The main questions were how to decide how many lagged values of the dependent variable should be used and how many lags of $u(t)$ were needed. Needless to say, answers to these questions added little to our understanding of how the economy works.

Nonetheless, these techniques have a place in the toolkit of a structural model builder. In the first place, in any forecast with a structural model the errors of the equations must also be forecast, either explicitly or implicitly. If nothing is done about them, the implicit forecast is that they are zero. The use of rho adjustment in models built with G makes a simple autoregressive forecast of the errors. But the question naturally arises as to whether better forecasts of the errors could be made if more care were devoted to them. This is a natural problem for ARMA techniques.

Another use arises in updating data. In the U.S. National Income and Product Accounts, the first release for each new quarter has no data for corporate profits or other series dependent on them. Yet QUEST must have data on all these series in order to start from the new quarter. Making up these one-quarter-ahead forecasts is a possible application of ARMA techniques. Annual models with industry detail are often used in November or December for forecasting the year ahead. At that season, perhaps nine months of data has been accumulated on the current year. To get the annual number for the current year in such a series, we need a forecast of just the next three months. ARMA methods can be usefully applied to this problem.

Because of these ancillary uses with structural models, as well as to understand what is in the snake oil bottles sold by many forecasters, you need ARMA in your bag of tricks. We will explain how the estimation is done in G and, of course, the commands for using it.

As already observed, if $q = 0$, the b can be estimated by ordinary least squares. The special problem arises if $q > 0$, for the $u(t)$ are unobservable. If we make a guess of the b and h vectors, and assume that the u(t) were zero before the beginning of the period of fitting, then we can recursively *calculate* the $u(t)$. The idea of the fitting process is then to choose the b and h vectors to minimize the sum of squares of these calculated $u(t)$. The problem in doing so, however, is that these $u(t)$ are highly non-linear functions of the h and b vectors. Many books about time series leave the matter there with the comment that the programs take care of the minor detail of how the equation is estimated.

As with least squares, however, I want you to understand what the computer is doing when using G, so that you realize how utterly mechanical the process is and do not suppose that any special trust should be placed in the results. In the case of moving average errors, different programs may give different results, so it may be important to know the limits of the method used.

The process used in G is iterative. It begins by assuming that the h vector is zero and uses ordinary least squares to compute an initial estimate of the b vector. Then it computes approximate values of the partial derivatives of the predicted values with respect to each element of b and h and regresses the current estimate of $u(t)$ on these partial derivatives. (We'll see how these partials are computed in a moment; therein lies the trick.) The resulting regression coefficients are added to the current estimates of b and h and, if all goes well, the process is repeated until convergence. "If all goes well" is said for good reason. There is no guarantee that the process will converge or even that each step will reduce the sum of squared errors. In G, however, if the full step does not reduce the sum of squared errors, a step of half that size is tried, and if that does not work, a step of one quarter the size is tried, and so on down to one 64th. If even that tiny step does not help, the process stops and prints the message "Iterations XX. Cornered." where XX is the number of iterations completed, counting the one that could not be completed. If, on the other hand, the convergence criterion (that no element of h should change by more than .001) is met, the message is "Iterations XX. Converged."

This process cannot be guaranteed to produce the global minimum sum of squares, but it produces a value that is no worse than the initial estimate and sometimes much better. Also, without elaborate checking, it avoids explosive equations.

It remains to explain how to approximate the partial derivatives of the predicted values with respect to each element of b and h. To motivate the method, it is convenient to use the lag operator, L, defined by the equation

$$Lz(t) = z(t-1)$$

for any time-series variable, z(t). Powers of L work as expected:

$$L^2z(t) = L(Lz(t)) = L(z(t-1)) = z(t-2)$$

and so on for higher powers. In this notation, the general form of the equation we are trying to estimate is

(3) $y(t) = b_1 x_1(t) + \ldots + b_p x_p(t) + (1 + h_1 L + h_2 L^2 + \ldots + h_q L^q)\, u(t)$

Since $u(t) = y(t) - p(t)$, where $p(t)$ is the predicted value, the partial derivatives of the predicted values are the *negatives* of the partial derivatives of u(t) with respect to b and h. We can write $u(t)$ as

(4) $u(t) = (1 + h_1 L + h_2 L^2 + \ldots + h_q L^q)^{-1}(y(t) - (b_1 x_1(t) + \ldots + b_p x_p(t)))$.

The negative of the partial derivative of $u(t)$ with respect to b_j is then

(5) $z_j(t) = (1 + h_1 L + h_2 L^2 + \ldots + h_q L^q)^{-1} x_j(t)$

and the negative of the partial of u(t) with respect to h_j

(6) $z_{q+j}(t) = (1 + h_1 L + h_2 L^2 + \ldots + h_q L^q)^{-2}\, L^{\,j}\, (y(t) - (b_1 x_1(t) + \ldots + b_p x_p(t))$.

To solve (5) for $z_j(t)$, we rewrite it as

(7) $(1 + h_1 L + h_2 L^2 + \ldots + h_q L^q) z_j(t) = x_j(t)$

or

(8) $z_j(t) = -\, h_1\, z_j(t-1) - h_2\, z_j(t-2) - \ldots - h_q\, z_j(t-q) + x_j(t)$

We start off with the approximation that $z_j(t) = 0$ for $t < 0$. Then we can recursively compute the values for all the more recent values of t. Similarly, for the partials with respect to the h's,

(9) $(1 + h_1 L + h_2 L^2 + \ldots + h_q L^q)^2\, z_{q+j}(t) = L^{\,j}\, (y(t) - (b_1 x_1(t) + \ldots + b_p x_p(t)))$.

Let us define the elements of a vector g by

(10) $(1 + h_1 L + h_2 L^2 + \ldots + h_q L^q)^2 = 1 + g_1 L + g_2 L^2 + \ldots + g_{2q} L^{2q}$

Then (9) can be written as

(11) $z_{q+j}(t) = -\, g_1\, z_{q+j}(t-1) - g_2\, z_{q+j}(t-2) - \ldots - g_{2q}\, z_j(t-2q) + e(t-j)$,

where $e(t)$ is the residual using only the x variables with the current values of the b parameters. If we begin with the approximation that the values of all variables in equation (11) are zero before $t = 0$, we can then solve the equation recursively for the values of $z_{q+j}(t)$.

   Such is the theory of the estimation. The practice is much easier. The command is just

        bj <q> <y> = <x1>, [x2,] ..., [xn]

where q is the order of the moving average error. For example,

```
bj 3 d = d[1],d[2],d[3]
```

The ! to suppress the intercept also works, thus

```
bj 3 d = ! d[1],d[2],d[3]
```

The command takes its name from Box and Jenkins, authors of the book cited above. Here is an almost classical example applied to annualized quarter-to-quarter rates of growth of U.S. real GDP. Because the method is so frequently used with lagged values of the dependent variable as the only independent variable, we will take first such an example. The G commands to set up the problem are just

```
ti BJ Demo: Real GDP Growth
lim 1970.1 2001.3 2005.4
mode f
f lgdpR = @log(gdpR)
f d = 400.*(lgdpR - lgdpR[1])
bj 3 d = d[1],d[2],d[3]
vr -12 -8 -4 0 4 8 12 16
gname bj1
gr *
```

And here are the results.

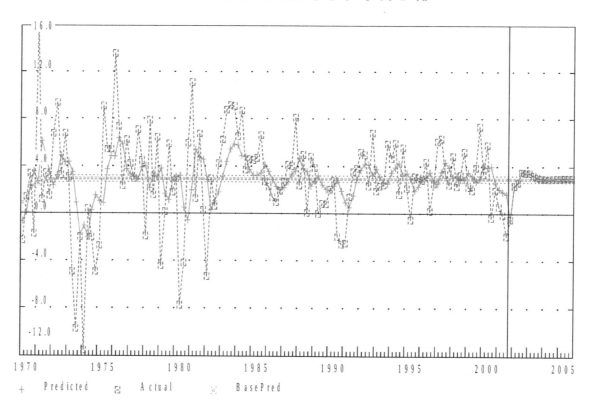

232

```
                              BJ Demo: Real GDP Growth
 SEE    =        3.83 RSQ   = 0.1266 RHO =   -0.00 Obser   =  127 from 1970.100
 SEE+1  =        3.83 RBSQ  = 0.1053 DurH = 999.00 DoFree  =  123 to   2001.300
 MAPE   =     1930.84
    Variable name         Reg-Coef  Mexval  Elas   NorRes      Mean    Beta
 0 d                      - - - - - - - - - - - - - -          2.92  - - -
 1 intercept              1.62239     4.5    0.56    1.14       1.00
 2 d[1]                   0.25565     3.2    0.25    1.03       2.91   0.256
 3 d[2]                   0.16613     1.3    0.17    1.00       2.92   0.167
 4 d[3]                   0.02402     0.0    0.02    1.00       2.91   0.024

Iterations 3. Cornered.

 :                            BJ Demo: Real GDP Growth
  SEE   =        3.80 RSQ   = 0.1896 RHO =   -0.00 Obser   =  127 from 1970.100
  SEE+1 =        0.00 RBSQ  = 0.1491 DurH = 999.00 DoFree  =  120 to   2001.300
  MAPE  =      153.64
    Variable name         Reg-Coef  Mexval  Elas   NorRes      Mean    Beta
 0 d                      - - - - - - - - - - - - - -          3.93  - - -
 1 intercept              1.38956     0.5    0.47    1.24       1.34
 2 d[1]                   0.66263     0.6    0.66    1.10       3.89   0.809
 3 d[2]                   0.10811     0.0    0.11    1.09       3.90   0.132
 4 d[3]                  -0.23370     0.2   -0.23    1.08       3.90  -0.285
 5 d_mu[1]               -0.41293     0.3    0.00    1.02      -0.03  -0.548
 6 d_mu[2]               -0.03871     0.0   -0.00    1.01       0.00  -0.051
 7 d_mu[3]                0.20081     0.1    0.00    1.00       0.05   0.264
```

The first table shows the regression without the moving average errors. The second shows the results with them. The calculated $u(t)$ variable is given the name of the dependent variable plus the suffix _mu. It is entered into the G workspace bank with this name, and the h parameters are shown as the regression coefficients of its lagged values in the second table, while the estimates of the b are shown as the regression coefficients of the usual independent variables in this second table. Other statistics for particular variables in the second table are derived from the last regression and may not have much meaning. In the graph, G detects as usual the presence of lagged dependent variables and calculates a third line, BasePred, the predictions the equation would have made using as lagged values of the dependent variable the equation's own prediction.

These results are fairly typical of my experience with the method. The SEE dropped ever so slightly from 3.83 to 3.80. The regression coefficients jumped around gaily; BasePred very quickly goes to the average value; the forecast also very quickly converges to the historical average.

Here is another example with errors from the equipment investment equation in QUEST. For a comparison, we take the automatic rho-adjustment forecast. The commands used were

```
add vfnreR.reg
f e = resid
ti Error from Gross Equipment Investment
lim 1980.1 2001.3 2005.4
```

233

```
mode f
bj 2 e = ! e[1],e[2],e[3]
f  fancy = depvar

# For comparison
r e = ! e[1]
f  plain = predic
ti Error Forecasts for Equipment Investment
vr -10 -5 0
gr plain fancy 2001.4 2005.4
```

The original investment regression began in 1975, so the error series begins in that year. To have historical data on lagged values of e, the regression period was then shortened. Here are the results for the bj command and the comparison of the forecasts.

```
:                    Error from Gross Equipment Investment
   SEE    =       9.70 RSQ    = 0.6496 RHO =    0.01 Obser  =   87 from 1980.100
   SEE+1  =       9.71 RBSQ   = 0.6413 DurH = 999.0 DoFree =   84 to   2001.300
   MAPE   =     181.74
      Variable name           Reg-Coef  Mexval  Elas   NorRes    Mean    Beta
   0 e                      - - - - - - - - - - - - - - - -     -1.31  - - -
   1 e[1]                      0.64455    18.8   0.49    1.05    -0.99
   2 e[2]                      0.25956     2.5   0.13    1.01    -0.68   0.264
   3 e[3]                     -0.08432     0.4  -0.04    1.00    -0.63  -0.086

Iterations = 3. Cornered.

:                    Error from Gross Equipment Investment
   SEE    =       9.70 RSQ    = 0.7247 RHO =    0.01 Obser  =   87 from 1980.100
   SEE+1  =       0.00 RBSQ   = 0.7113 DurH = 999.0 DoFree =   82 to   2001.300
   MAPE   =     326.63
      Variable name           Reg-Coef  Mexval  Elas   NorRes    Mean    Beta
   0 e                      - - - - - - - - - - - - - - - -     -1.49  - - -
   1 e[1]                      0.78320     0.0   0.66    1.05    -1.26
   2 e[2]                      0.22574     0.0   0.14    1.01    -0.90   0.245
   3 e[3]                     -0.15725     0.0  -0.09    1.01    -0.84  -0.171
   4 e_mu[1]                  -0.13894     0.0  -0.06    1.01    -0.65  -0.076
   5 e_mu[2]                  -0.06913     0.0  -0.03    1.00    -0.55  -0.038

:                  Gross Equipment Investment and Replacement
   SEE    =       9.96 RSQ    = 0.6311 RHO =   -0.15 Obser  =   87 from 1980.100
   SEE+1  =       9.83 RBSQ   = 0.6311 DurH =  -1.74 DoFree =   86 to   2001.300
   MAPE   =     194.89
      Variable name           Reg-Coef  Mexval  Elas   NorRes    Mean    Beta
   0 e                      - - - - - - - - - - - - - - - -     -1.31  - - -
   1 e[1]                      0.79307    65.2   0.60    1.00    -0.99
```

When tested on real data, it is always possible, of course, that a lack-luster performance of the method is due simply to the fact that it is inappropriate for the problem at hand. It is therefore interesting to fabricate an example where we know that the model is appropriate and see if the estimating method gets the right answer. Here is such a test.

```
ti Fabricated MA
lim 1970.1 2001.3
f one = 1
f ep = @normal()
f ep2 = ep + 2.*ep[1] + ep[2]
f dep = rtb + ep2
bj 2 dep = ! rtb
gr *
```

The @normal() function returns a random normal deviate with mean 0 and variance 1. Given the way the dependent variable is made, one would hope for $h_1 = 2$ and $h_2 = 1$. Of course, every time you run this command file, you get a different answer because of the random nature of the *ep* variable.

```
:               Fabricated MA Residual and Original Error
  SEE    =        2.50 RSQ   = 0.5971 RHO =    0.61 Obser  =   127 from 1970.100
  SEE+1  =        2.00 RBSQ  = 0.5971 DW  =    0.78 DoFree =   126 to   2001.300
  MAPE   =       83.99
    Variable name              Reg-Coef  Mexval  Elas   NorRes     Mean    Beta
  0 dep                        - - - - - - - - - - - - - - - -     6.54  - - -
  1 rtb                          1.02251  205.4  1.03    1.00      6.56

Interations = 51. Converged.
```

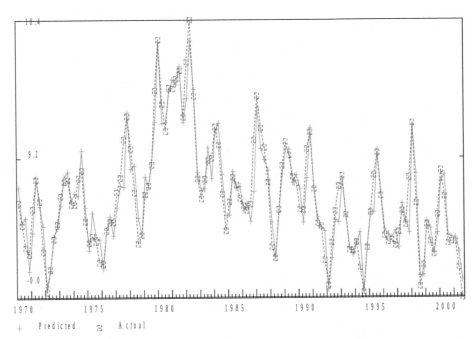

```
:                    Fabricated MA Residual and Original Error
 SEE    =       1.18 RSQ   = 1.0000 RHO =    0.61 Obser  =   127 from 1970.100
 SEE+1  =       0.00 RBSQ  = 1.0000 DW  =    2.14 DoFree =   124 to    2001.300
 MAPE   =      27.66
   Variable name          Reg-Coef  Mexval   Elas   NorRes      Mean  Beta
 0 dep                  - - - - - - - - - - - - - - -         -1.90 - - -
 1 rtb                   1.06490    398.1  -0.96 9999.99        1.71
 2 dep_mu[1]             1.91765  20063.6   2.97 9999.99       -2.94 1.922
 3 dep_mu[2]             0.94776   9875.5  -1.08    1.00        2.17 0.947
```

The method ran to convergence, the estimates of the h are in the right general neighborhood but are both a little low, while the SEE is a little high. In repeated runs of this test, each time with different random errors, the coefficient on rtb fluctuates a little around the "true" value of 1.0; but the estimates of h are consistently below their "true" values of 2 and 1. In this special, fabricated example, the reduction in the SEE is quite substantial. Moreover, as shown in the graph below of the original errors, ep, and the computed $u(t)$, the process has been fairly successful in figuring out what the ep were. In repeated runs of this example, it always runs to convergence and the estimates of the elements of h are *always* low. Though I am convinced that the method is working as intended, the estimates of the h appear to me to be biased a bit towards zero. Tightening the convergence test reduced this problem, so it may have something to do with starting from $h = 0$.

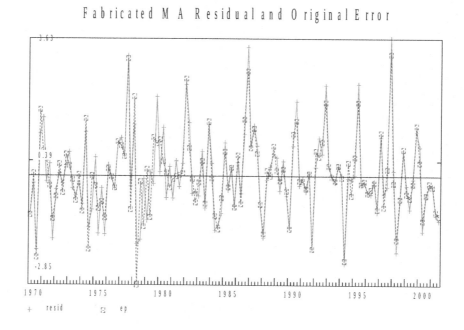

Fabricated M A Residual and Original Error

The Autocorrelation Function

Regression with moving average error terms is in its element when the independent variables are all lagged values of the dependent variable. The sources cited above give

236

much attention to how to choose *p* and *q* in this case. A key tool in this connection is the autocorrelation function, which simply shows the correlation between the current and earlier values of a stationary variable. Once it has been computed, it is easy to compute, via relations known as the Yule-Walker equations, the approximations of the regression coefficients when regressing the current value on one lagged value, on two lagged values, on three lagged values, and so on. In G the command is

>   ac <series> [n]

where n is the number of correlations to be computed. The computation is done on the series between the first and second dates on the last *limits* command. The default value of n is 11. For example:

>   ac viR 12

gives these results:

```
Autocorrelation function
 1.0000  0.5250  0.3137  0.2170 -0.0048 -0.0909 -0.0375 -0.0911 -0.1610 -0.0329  0.0138  0.0055
Partial Autocorrelation
 0.525
 0.497  0.053
 0.495  0.030  0.046
 0.504  0.036  0.146 -0.202
 0.494  0.043  0.148 -0.176 -0.052
 0.498  0.058  0.136 -0.180 -0.093  0.084
 0.503  0.052  0.125 -0.171 -0.090  0.115 -0.062
 0.495  0.067  0.113 -0.193 -0.074  0.121  0.002 -0.127
 0.510  0.067  0.099 -0.184 -0.051  0.108 -0.006 -0.185  0.118
 0.504  0.077  0.099 -0.190 -0.048  0.118 -0.011 -0.189  0.089  0.056
 0.505  0.078  0.097 -0.191 -0.047  0.118 -0.013 -0.188  0.090  0.062 -0.012
 0.503  0.084  0.106 -0.210 -0.048  0.130 -0.018 -0.208  0.100  0.070  0.041 -0.104
```

The "triangle" shows the regression coefficients as calculated from the autocorrelation function via the Yule-Walker equations. The first line shows (approximately) the regression coefficients on one lagged value; the second, on two; and so on. (Actually doing the regressions will give slightly different results because, in any finite series, the correlation between, say, x(t-3) and x(t-4) -- calculated by the regression program -- will be slightly different from that between x(t) and x(t-1) -- which is used in its place by the Yule-Walker equations.)

The numbers down the diagonal of the triangle are know as the partial autocorrelation function. The command also puts the autocorrelation function into the work space with a name given by the variable with _ac suffixed. It can then be graphed. Since dates have no meaning for it, the absolute positions in the series (indicated by numbers following a colon) are used to specify the range to be graphed. In our case, the command would be:

>   gr viR_ac : 1 11

If a process is a pure autoregression, with no moving average terms, the autocorrelation function is a declining exponential. If, on the other hand, it is a pure moving average process of order q, its autocorrelation function will fall to zero after q terms. In real data, of course, either of these extreme outcomes is very rare. In practice, you will probably just try a number of alternative specifications. You can easily write a G command file with an argument (the variable name) which will compute a handful of equations for you; you have only to pick the best. Some programs will do even that for you, but it seems to me important to look over the candidates.

9. The Classical Econometrics of Simultaneous Equations

Identification

In the early days of econometrics, before the computer made computation of regressions with more than two or three independent variables feasible, models were small; but a lot of thought went into theoretical problems of estimation. One of these was *identification*, a problem most simply illustrated by estimating the supply and demand curves for a product. The quantity demanded is a function of price, so we might suppose that if we estimated

(1) $q_t = a_1 + a_2 \, p_t$

we would have a demand function. But the quantity supplied is also a function of the price, so maybe what we got when we estimated (1) was the supply curve! In fact, what we estimate might be any combination of the demand and supply curve. If we wish to *identify* which curve we are estimating, to find the economic structure, we need more information. For example, if we know that the supply of the product we are studying is a function of rainfall, r_t, so that the quantity supplied is

(2) $q_t = b_1 + b_2 \, p_t + b_3 \, r_t$

then we have a chance of identifying a demand curve of the form of equation (1). Graphically, we can imagine the demand curve fixed and stable while the supply curve jumps about depending on rainfall. The observed price-quantity combinations thus all fall on the stable demand curve, which becomes identified.

Note that the identification was possible because of the *exclusion* of the rainfall variable from the demand equation. Careful analysis of this situation led to the result that an equation in a system of N equations is identified if it excludes N-1 or more of the variables in the system. [6] If exactly N-1 variables are excluded, the equation is said to be *exactly identified*; if more than N-1 are excluded, the equation is said to be *over identified*. In these

---

6 See G. S. Maddala, *Econometrics* (McGraw-Hill, New York, 1977) pp. 471 - 477. It is indicative of the decline in the importance of the topic that this clearly written appendix was dropped from the second edition of the book.

counts, N is the number of regression equations; each lagged value of an endogenous variable and all exogenous variables count as exogenous. Since most of these variables are excluded from any one regression, current models of the economy such as Quest and other models you are likely to build are vastly over-identified. Furthermore, a known value of a parameter in a regression equation is as good as an exclusion for the counts. The subject has therefore become one of more pedagogical and historical interest than of practical importance.

Estimation

We have already noted that if one of the independent variables in a regression actually depends, through other equations on the dependent one, least squares estimates may be inconsistent. For example, if in one equation consumption depends upon income but via another equation income is consumption plus investment and government expenditures, then there is danger of inconsistency, which may be called *simultaneous equation bias*. In the early days of econometrics, the 1940's and 1950's, this problem was considered central, and a number of techniques were developed. All of them are, in my opinion, vastly inferior to the dynamic optimization which we have already studied and which solves simultaneous equation bias as a sort of minor side benefit. Nevertheless, a few words about these older techniques are perhaps in order just so you will know what they are.

In estimating QUEST, we used an *instrumental variable* approach to this problem for estimating the consumption function. We wanted consumption to depend on disposable income, but disposable income depends, via the accounting identities, on consumption. So we regressed disposable income on its own lagged values and used the predicted value as current period disposable income in the consumption function.

Following this approach to its logical conclusion leads to the method of two-stage least squares, 2SLS for short. In the first stage, each endogenous independent variable is regressed on all of the exogenous variables in the model. The predicted values are then used as the simultaneous values for all endogenous variables in a second "stage" regression. The predicted values, depending only on exogenous variables, certainly do not depend on the error in the equation being estimated. Hence, the cause of simultaneous equation bias has been removed.

This method can be applied in G. If the variable only occurs without lag or if you want to use the first stage also for lagged values, the procedure is simple. Recall that after each regression the predicted values are in the workspace under the name "predic". After each first-stage regression, use an f command to copy this "predic" to a variable having the name of the dependent variable of the preceding regression. Thus if "yRpc" were the dependent variable in the first stage regression, then we should follow the equation with

    f yRpc = predic

We then just re-estimate the equation.

If, however, we have both yRpc and yRpc[1] in the equation and we want to use the first stage estimate for the first but the actual value in the lagged position, then we have to go to a little more trouble. When all of these first stage regressions have been done, we copy the workspace to a new bank and then assign this bank as B. The commands are

```
dos copy ws.* first.*
bank first B
zap
```

The *zap* gives us a clean workspace. Then in the regression commands where we want to use the first stage estimate, we prefix a "b." to the name of variable. (The b. will not appear in the .sav file, so it will work right in building a model.)

There are several problems with this procedure. The first is that in models of any size there are enough exogenous variables to give an almost perfect fit in the first stage so that the second stage differs insignificantly from the OLS estimate. It is not unusual for the number of exogenous variables to equal or exceed the number of observations used in fitting the equations. The first stage fit is then perfect and the second stage is identical to OLS. Various arbitrary rules are used to cut off the number of regressors in the first stage to get some difference between OLS and 2SLS, but these differences are then just as arbitrary as the cutoff rules.

A second problem with textbook 2SLS is that it assumes linearity in the model. Without linearity, it is not correct to suppose that the endogenous variables are linear functions of the exogenous ones. The suggestion is then sometimes made to use squares and cross products of all of the exogenous variables. This procedure, however, will exacerbate the first problem of too many exogenous variables. It also does not insure that the right kind of non-linear functional relation has been approximated.

Three-stage least squares (3SLS) amounts to applying SUR to the second stage equations. Like SUR, GLS, and maximum likelihood methods in general, it rests upon the assumption that errors that recur in certain patterns are more palatable than "erratic" errors of the same size. Given that rather strange assumption, it is hardly surprising that its use has not, so far as I am aware, improved the performance of any model.

The combination of G and Build makes possible another approach to the problem of simultaneous equation bias which avoids both of the difficulties with 2SLS. It may be called Systemic Two-stage Least Squares, S2SLS, for it makes use of the whole model or system of which the equation is a part. It was my brainchild and I had high hopes for it; but I have to tell you at the outset that it sounds good in theory but does not work well. It goes as follows.

1. Use OLS to estimate the equations of the model.

2. Put the model together and run it in historical simulation. This can be a "static" simulation which uses the historical values for all lagged values. (Just give the command *static* at the] prompt before giving the command *run*.)

3. Use the predicted values from the model as the values of the simultaneous independent variables and re-estimate the equations.

It is clear that the estimates from the third step will not suffer from simultaneous equation inconsistency, for the independent variables are computed without any knowledge of the errors in the equations. There is also no particular problem about nonlinearities; the nonlinearities in the model are fully incorporated in the calculation of the historical simulation values. Nor is there any problem about perfect fit on the first stage, unless, of course, the model is perfect -- a situation we need not worry about.

After step 2, change the names of original .sav files and of the bws and histsim banks by these G commands

```
dos ren    *.sav    *.sv1
dos ren    histsim.*    histsim1.*
dos ren    bws.*    bws1.*
```

Then, in preparation for step 3, edit the .reg files where you want to apply the technique and put a "b." in front of each variable for which you want the program to use the value from the first step. Save the file with a different name; for example, save the changed cR.reg as cR2.reg. Do *not*, however, change the name of file saved in the *save* commands.

Then do

bank histsim1   b

and *add* the newly edited files which do the regressions. Build and run the model as usual.

My experience with the method has been no better than with the others, which is to say, not good. You may certainly try it, but it has never given results that I wanted to use.

If you have studied econometrics, you have perhaps learned that the supposedly ultimate method in the area of estimation of simultaneous equation models is something known as Full Information Maximum Likelihood or just FIML. Its theoretical statistical properties are about the same as those of 3SLS, so there is little reason to prefer it.

Does G offer FIML? No, but I am glad you asked, for this very FIML offers one the clearest examples of the way that maximum likelihood estimates prefer large, systematic errors to small erratic ones. To explain the example requires the notion of a *recursive* system. A simultaneous system is recursive if it is possible to write the equations in an order so that the first variable depends only on predetermined variables (exogenous and lagged values of endogenous), the second variable depends only on the first and predetermined variables, the third depends only on the first two and predetermined variables, and so on.

When applied to a recursive system, FIML leads -- via a long derivation which need not detain us [7] – to minimizing the determinant of the matrix of sums of squares and cross

---

7 See G.S. Maddala *Econometrics* (1977, McGraw-Hill) page 487, the formula between C-50 and C-51. For a recursive system $|\mathbf{B}| = 1$ in Maddala's notation. This useful appendix was omitted from the

products of the residuals. To be specific, let us suppose that we have a system of two equations and the dependent variable of equation 2 does not appear in equation 1 – the condition that makes the system recursive. Let the misses from the first equation form the first column of a matrix R while the misses of the second equation form the second column. FIML then minimizes the determinant of R'R. Consider two estimates of the parameters. One gives the R'R matrix on the left below; the other gives the R'R on the right. Which estimate would you prefer:

$$R'R = \begin{pmatrix} 4 & 0 \\ 0 & 4 \end{pmatrix} \quad \text{or} \quad R'R = \begin{pmatrix} 8 & 7 \\ 7 & 8 \end{pmatrix} \quad ?$$

I have no hesitancy in saying that, other things equal, I would prefer the one on the left. The criterion used in FIML, however, chooses the estimate on the right, for its determinant is 15 while the determinant of the matrix on the left is 16. In this example, it is clear how maximum likelihood methods tolerate large errors in one place if they are correlated with large errors in another, but are strongly averse to erratic errors. If I, however, have one equation for residential construction and another for non-residential, and the first over-predicted last quarter, I am not at all consoled to discover that the other also over-predicted, even if they have often done that before. To use FIML without being fully aware of this tendency is naive, more naive than using plain OLS with full consciousness of its problems.

10. Vector Autoregression

Following the discussion of autoregression is a natural place to say a few necessary words about vector autoregression (VAR), which has been a "hot" topic in recent years. The idea is simplicity itself. Let us consider a system described by the equations

$$(1) \qquad x_t = A_0 x_t + A_1 x_{t-1} + \ldots + A_p x_{t-p} + f(t) + \epsilon_t$$

where x is a vector of stationary variables, the A's are constant matrices, f(t) is a vector of exogenous variables, and ϵ_t is a vector of random, exogenous variables. The classical school of econometrics investigated the conditions under which the A matrices, especially A_0, could be identified. These conditions involved some sort of prior knowledge, usually that some of the elements of A_0 were zero. The VAR school [See Sims 1980] rejected the notion of prior knowledge and also of the division of the variables between endogenous and exogenous. They therefore dropped the *f(t)* term of (1), used only stationary variables, and moved the first term to the left, so that (1) became

$$(2) \qquad (I - A_0) x_t = A_1 x_{t-1} + \ldots + A_p x_{t-p} + \epsilon_t \qquad .$$

On pre-multiplying both sides of (2) by $(I - A_0)^{-1}$ we get an equation of the form

_____

second edition of the book.

242

(3) $x_t = B_1 x_{t-1} + \ldots + B_p x_{t-p} + \eta_t$

where

(4) $B_i = (I - A_0)^{-1} A_i$

Clearly nothing can be said about the B_i matrices, except that if A_i is all zero, so is B_i.

Christopher Sims's initial experiments with the VAR approach simply regressed each variable on the lagged values of all the others, and made a model out of the results. By careful selection of the variables – and thus a lot of implicit theorizing – he was able to get two simple models that made the approach look promising.

Soon, however, it turned out that successful unconstrained VAR models were uncommon. Soft constraints were then introduced to softly require that the diagonal elements of B_1 should be 1.0 and that all other elements of the B's should be zero. In other words, it was assumed that each equation consisted principally of regression on the lagged value of the dependent variable. The regressions with soft constraints were referred to as *Bayesian* regression because of the thought processes used in picking the strength of the constraints. The result was therefore referred to as Bayesian vector autoregression, or BVAR.

The BVAR's have proven much more useful than the VAR's. One should not miss the irony in this outcome. The VAR school began with total agnosticism; it denied all *a-priori* knowledge of the values of parameters. It then proceeded to assume *a-priori* values for all parameters!

I believe that you can see why one who hopes, as I do, to use models to express and test our understanding of the economy will not be very interested in the a-theoretic VAR or BVAR approach. It seems to have rejected propositions like "Personal consumption expenditure is more likely to depend on after-tax income than before-tax income," as unfounded assumptions and then to have embraced the assumption that all variables are determined mainly by their lagged values. Such an apotheosis of the lagged value of the dependent variable is not likely to appeal to one who has seen the dangers of the lagged values of the dependent variable, as shown in Chapter 6.

On the other hand, as a purely mechanical, mindless way to forecast several variables one or possibly two periods ahead, the BVAR method is reported to be moderately successful.

11. Cointegration, Unit Roots

In section 7, we looked at the estimation of equations with moving average errors. If, in equation (2) of that section, all the x variables are just lagged values of the dependent variable, the equation become the autoregressive moving average (ARMA) equation

(1) $\qquad y_t = b_0 + b_1 y_{t-1} + b_2 y_{t-2} \ldots + b_p y_{t-p} + \epsilon_t + h_1 \epsilon_{t-1} \ldots + h_q \epsilon_{t-q}$

where ϵ_t is white noise. We will find it useful to write (1) with the lag operator L, thus:

(2) $\qquad (1 - b_0 - b_1 L - b_2 L^2 \ldots - b_p L^p) y_t = (1 + h_1 L \ldots + h_q L^q) \epsilon_t$

or, for short,

(3) $\quad B(L) y_t = H(L) \epsilon_t$

where *B(L)* and *H(L)* are polynomials in *L*.

In these equations, y_t is white noise transformed by an ARMA process. We have previously viewed (1) as a rough-and-ready way to forecast a variable for which we can think of no better explanation. Beginning around 1970, however, this sort of equation came to be used in ever wider circles to *define* what was meant by the expression *time series*. The term *time series analysis* is now, sadly, often used to refer exclusively to the study of these things which might better be called "ARMA-ed random variables" or ARVs for short.

Now I must say plainly that I do not think that any of the series in the national accounts of the United States or any other country, or any other major economic series is an ARV. Their changes over time are profoundly influenced by tax rates, government spending, money supply and many other variables that are the product of thoughtful human decisions. History matters, not just random variables transformed by a constant ARMA process. To limit the term "time series" to mean "ARV" is therefore a pretty strange use of words, since most time series in the broad and natural sense of the words cannot be "time series" in the narrow sense. Consequently, I will call an ARV an ARV.

In the limited world of ARV's, however, it is possible to give precise meaning to some terms we have used in broader senses. "Stationary" is a good example. If *y(t)* is an ARV and $E(y(t)) = \mu$ for all t and $E(y(t) - \mu)(y(t-j) - \mu) = \gamma_j$ for all t and any j, then *y(t)* is said to be *covariance stationary* or *weakly stationary*. Although there is a concept of *strictly stationary*, it is a common practice that I will follow to use simply "stationary" to mean "covariance stationary".

ARV's are, of course, special cases of the solutions of systems of linear difference equations studied in Chapter 7, namely, the special case in which the input function is a weighted average of q values of a white noise variable. An ARV can be stationary only if all the roots of the homogeneous linear difference equation – that is, of the polynomial *B(L)* – are inside the unit circle in the complex plane. Otherwise, it will, as we have seen, be explosive and not have a constant mean, as required by the definition of stationarity.

Clearly, economic series characterized by growth cannot even seem to be a stationary ARV. Consequently, one may want to investigate a class of ARV's whose first differences are stationary ARV's. If y_t is stationary, we can write

(4) $\quad y_t = \dfrac{H(L)}{B(L)} \epsilon_t$,

and if x_t is a variable whose first difference is equal to y_t , that is, $(1 - L) x_t = y_t$, then

(5) $\quad (1 - L) x_t = \dfrac{H(L)}{B(L)} \epsilon_t$

or

(6) $\quad (1 - L) B(L) x_t = H(L) \epsilon_t$.

Thus, it is clear that the characteristic polynomial of x_t has the same roots as does that of y_t plus one more real root equal to exactly 1, that is to say, a *unit root*. Because x_t is created by summing successive values of y_t , a process that would correspond to integration if we were working with continuous time, is said to be *integrated of order 1* or *I(1)* for short. A stationary ARV is correspondingly said to *integrated of order 0*, or *I(0)* for short.

We can now at last say what is meant by *cointegration* [8]. If x_t and y_t are two I(1) ARV's and if there exits a number β such that $y_t - \beta x_t$ is I(0), that is, stationary, then x_t and y_t are said to be *cointegrated.*

Intuitively, if x_t and y_t are cointegrated, it makes sense to regress one on the other; the residual will not grow ever larger and larger. There is thus a sort of equilibrium relation between and x_t and y_t . On the other hand, if they are not cointegrated, they may drift apart over time without any persistent relation between them.

Cointegration is definitely a good thing to have in your regression. For one thing, it can be shown that the ordinary least squares estimate is "superconsistent" in the sense that it converges to the true values at a rate of T instead of $\sqrt{T}$. Moreover, cointegration sometimes can resolve identification in simultaneous equation systems that are not identified by the classical rules. For example, if we regress the price (p) on the quantity demanded (q) with data from a market described by the following two equations,

$$\text{demand curve:} \quad p_t + 1\, q_t = u_{d\,t} \quad\quad u_{d\,t} = u_{d\,t-1} + \epsilon_{d\,t}$$
$$\text{supply curve:} \quad p_t - 1\, q_t = u_{s\,t} \quad\quad u_{s\,t} = \rho\, u_{s\,t-1} + \epsilon_{s\,t} \quad |\rho| < 1$$

we will get a consistent estimate of the supply curve! Why? Note that u_d is I(1), so p and q , which are both linear combinations of u_d and u_s , is also I(1). Moreover, the supply is a cointegrating relation between them. Ordinary least squares will pick it out because it will

---

8 The classic reference from which the concept of cointegration caught on in the economics profession is R.F. Engle and C.W.J. Granger, "Cointegration and Error Correction: Representation, Estimation and Testing," *Econometrica*, Vol 55, No. 2, 1987, pp 251-276.

have a finite variance, while the variance in the demand curve goes to infinity as T does. You can see this phenomenon by running a number of times this regression file:

```
fdates 1960.1 2010.4
f ed = @normal()
f es = @normal()
f ud = @cum(ud,ed,0)
f us = @cum(us,es,.8)
f p = .5*ud + .5*us
f q = +.5*ud - .5*us
lim 1965.1 2010.4
r p = ! q
```

You will almost certainly get a coefficient on q close to 1.0, that is to say, an estimate of the supply curve. (How to know in any real situation which curve has I(0) residuals is, of course, another matter.

Clearly, if you are trying to explain by regression an I(1) ARV, y_t, you want to have a cointegrated x_t among the independent variables. The regression on only this variable, however, may not be very good. The residuals may be an ARV with a rich structure which could be exploited for better fit and forecast. This ARV might be a linear combination of various stationary ARV's that you can observe. The original Engle and Granger article suggested estimating first the cointegrating equation and then estimating another, the so-called error correction equation, for dynamic adjustment in the equation. Other studies by random simulation experiments[9] found that it was better to put the dynamic adjustment into the initial estimation. Another result of the theory is that if y_t and x_t and are cointegrated, the regression should be done between them, not their first differences, as was previously frequently advised.

Right from the beginning of this book, we have followed methods that seem to be suggested by the theory of cointegration. In the investment equation for the AMI model, the dependent variable clearly has a trend, as does the replacement variable. The first differences in output, on the other hand, might or might not be I(1); yet they clearly add an important element to the regression. If they are I(1), then they become part of the cointegrating vector; if not, they contribute to explaining the residuals; we don't have to decide which they do. But now suppose that we want to add the real interest rate as an explanatory variable. It is clearly not I(1), so let us suppose it is I(0). Then, as far as the theory of cointegration offers a guide, we could add it into the equation. But here is where this theory is an insufficient guide. If, over time, the effect on investment (measured in constant dollars per year) of a one percentage point change in the interest rate has increased because of the increase in the size of the economy, then the variable we need is not the

---

9A. Banerjee, J. Dolado, D.F. Hendry, and G. Smith, "Exploring Equilibrium Relationships in Econometrics through Static Models: Some Monte Carlo Evidence," *Oxford Bulleting of Economics and Statistics*, Vol. 48, 1986, pp. 253-277.

interest rate itself but its deviation from mean *multiplied* by some measure of the size of the economy. This procedure, of course, has already been advocated. Finally, the cointegration literature advises analyzing the error term and adding a projection of it to the equation in forecasting. That is exactly what our rho adjustment does automatically.

If cointegration is so nice, perhaps you would like *prove* that your equation has it. My advice is "Forget it!". You need to prove that your residuals do *not* have a unit root. You might think that all that you need do is to regress the residual of your regression on its lagged value and test whether or not the regression coefficient could be 1.0. Stochastic experiments (often called Monte Carlo experiments after the famous gambling casino) with made up data have shown that if you used the ordinary t or normal tables, you would far too often conclude that you had found cointegration. Tables for this test based on these experiments and published D. A. Dickey and W. A. Fuller should be used for such testing.[10] Using these tables, it is usually impossible to reject the hypothesis that there is a unit root -- and therefore no cointegration.

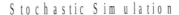

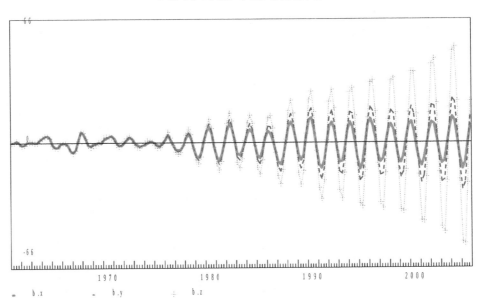

Why it is so hard to reject the unit root hypothesis is clear if we recall the graph from the stochastic simulation of three models from Chapter 7 and reproduced here for ease of reference. The inner of the three lines we know, from the way it was generated, to be I(0), while the middle one we know to be I(1). There is clearly not much difference between the two. If one were given the inner series, it would be hard to prove without an enormous amount of data that it was not I(1). The usual result, therefore, is that the hypothesis of a unit root in the residuals cannot be absolutely ruled out, although they very well may not have one. So we come back to common sense: if the equation makes sense and the value is

---

10 They are reprinted in James D. Hamilton, *Time Series Analysis*, Princeton, 1994, Appendix D.

ρ is modest, use it. I can only agree with Maddala's summary of the situation, "In a way, in the case of both unit roots and cointegration, there is too much emphasis on testing and too little on estimation."[11] .

I find cointegration a useful concept to bear in mind in formulating a regression. It also, almost incidentally, gives us one more reason for wanting the value of ρ, the autocorrelation coefficient of the residuals, to be well below 1.0. On the other hand, complicated testing of whether the residuals actually are stationary is so apt to prove indecisive that it is hardly worth bothering with. Economic understanding of the situation we are modeling is much more helpful than mechanistic analysis based, ultimately, on the assumptions that the series involved are ARV's, when they almost certainly are not.

---

11 G.S. Maddala, *Introduction to Econometrics*, 2nd Edition, New York, Macmillan, 1992, p.601.

CHAPTER 11. NONLINEAR REGRESSION

Occasionally, it is necessary to estimate a function which is not linear in its parameters. Suppose, for example, that we wanted to estimate by least squares a function of the form

(1) $y = (1 - (1-x)^{a0})^{a1}$.

There is no way to make this function linear in the parameters a0 and a1, and estimate them by ordinary least squares. We will have to resort to some variety of non-linear technique. There are many of these, and each has its merits and its problems. None is guaranteed to work on all problems. The one built into G has worked on most problems I have tried it on, but if you find a case where it does not work, please let me know.

Generally, nonlinear methods need to be given starting values of the parameters. The method then varies the parameters to "feel around" in the nearby space to see if it can find a better point. If a better point is found, it then becomes the home base for further "feeling around." The methods differ in the ways they "feel around." While some methods use only the starting values, the one adopted here allows the user to specify also the initial variations. These variations are then also used in terminating the search.

1. Lorenz curves

We will illustrate the method with an example of fitting a Lorenz curve to data on earned income from a sample of 2500 individuals from the 1990 *U. S. Census of Population and Housing*. A Lorenz curve, $y = L(x)$, shows, on the y axis, the fraction of income total received by those persons whose income was in the lowest 100x percent. Thus the point (.50, .21) would indicate that the lowest 50 percent of the population gets 21 percent of the total income. Notice that any Lorenz curve, $L(x)$, must have the properties that $L(0) = 0$, $L(1) = 1$, $L'(x) > 0$, and $L''(x) \geq 0$ for $0 \leq x \leq 1$. Any function with these properties we may call a Lorenz function. If $L_1(x)$ and $L_2(x)$ are both Lorenz functions, then

$\lambda L_1(x) + (1 - \lambda)L_2(x)$ with $0 \leq \lambda \leq 1$

is also a Lorenz function, as is $L_2(L_1(x))$ – in words, convex combinations of Lorenz functions are Lorenz functions and Lorenz functions of Lorenz functions are Lorenz functions. Here are two examples of Lorenz functions, as may be quickly verified.

$L_1(x) = x^{\beta}$ with $\beta \geq 1$ and $L_2(x) = 1 - (1-x)^{\alpha}$ with $0 \leq \alpha \leq 1$.

Then, using the fact that Lorenz functions of Lorenz functions are Lorenz functions, we see that equation (1) above is in fact a Lorenz function for $a1 \geq 1$ and $0 \leq a0 \leq 1$. It is this form that we shall fit to our data. (The first use seems to be in R.H. Rasche *et al.*, "Functional forms for estimating the Lorenz Curve," *Econometrica*, vol. 48, no. 4, [1980], pp 1061-1062.)

Because, unlike nearly all other examples so far in this book, this data is not time series, G should be started in a special directory with a G.cfg file including the lines:

```
Default regression limits; 0 20 20
Default base year of workspace file; 0
First month covered; 1
Default maximum number of observations per series in workspace; 30
```

You can then introduce the data without the artificiality of using dates for observation numbers that, in fact, do not refer to dates. The part of the command file to read in the data is then

```
ti Lorenz curve for Average Income within Families
fdates 0 30
matdat 0
       x          y
 0.000000   0.000000
 0.050512   0.004259
 0.100082   0.013013
 0.150477   0.025874
 0.200518   0.042053
 0.250206   0.062013
 0.300012   0.085112
 0.350053   0.111390
 0.400212   0.140735
 0.450018   0.173396
 0.500059   0.209550
 0.550453   0.249876
 0.600377   0.294181
 0.650183   0.342411
 0.700224   0.395880
 0.750265   0.455556
 0.800071   0.523243
 0.850230   0.600566
 0.900035   0.690201
 0.950194   0.804458
 1.000000   1.000000;
gdates 0 20
gr x y
lim 1 20
```

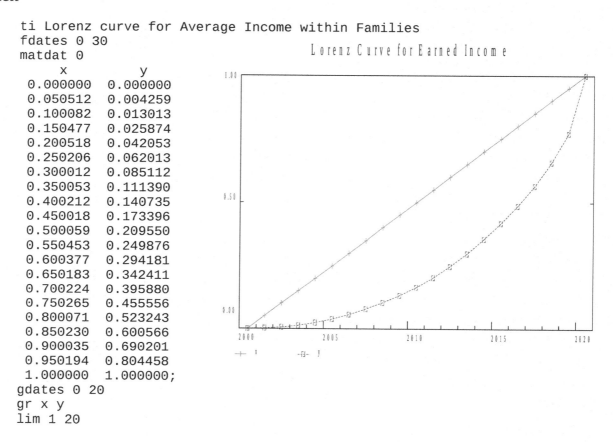

The *matdat* command reads in matrix data, that is, data in which values for different variables in a given period or unit of observation appear across a line. The number following the *matdat* command is the date, or in our case, the observation number of the first observation which follows. (If it is not given, then the date or observation number should appear at the beginning of each line.) Note the *;* at the end of the data. The *gdates* and *gr* commands are for visual checking of the data by the graph shown to the right. The *lim* commands sets the limits -- or range of observations -- for the nonlinear regression command that lies ahead.

The general form for doing nonlinear regression in G is the following:

nl [-] <y> = <non-linear function involving n parameters, a0, a1, ...an-1>

<n, the number of parameters>
<starting values of the parameters>
<initial variations>

The optional - following the *nl* will cause printing of intermediate results. Normally it is not necessary. The commands to do the nonlinear regression are then,

```
nl y = @exp(a1*@log(1.-@exp(a0*@log(1.-x))))
2
0.5  2.5
0.05 0.1
gr *
```

The results are:

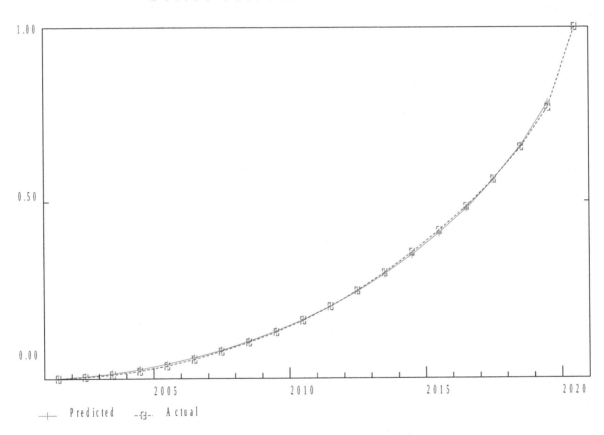

Lorenz Curve for Earned Income

```
Lorenz curve for Earned Income
     SEE = 0.223659
     Param        Coef     T-value      StdDev
       a0       0.698208     1.81      0.386664
       a1       1.863359     1.53      1.215625


     The Variance-Covariance Matrix
```

```
1.4951e-01    4.4554e-01
4.4554e-01    1.4777e+00
```

A word must be said about t-values and standard deviations in non-linear regression. They are computed by G in a standard way by linearizing the function around the optimal point. Consequently, they are only good for movements within the range of approximate validity of these linearizations. In the present case, it might appear from the standard deviations that a1 could easily be less than 1 and a0 could easily be more than 1. But for such values of a0 and a1, the function is not a Lorenz curve! Thus, utmost caution should be used in interpreting or relying on these statistics.

Now it may appear from the above graph that this form of the Lorenz curve fits this data extremely well. But one of the uses of a Lorenz curve is to calculate the amount of income within various brackets. We can look at the percentage error in the income for each of the 20 "ventile" brackets of the data by the commands:

```
update predic
0  0.
20 1.000
fdates 1 20
f difp = predic - predic[1]
f difa = y - y[1]
f difrel = 100.*(difp - difa)/difa
```

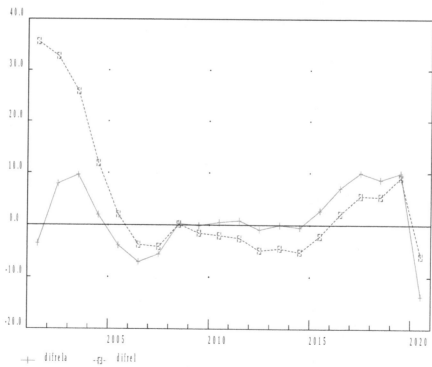

Alternate Fit Relative Error in Income

The result is shown by the line marked with squares in the graph above. The errors of over 30 percent in the two lowest brackets are quite likely unacceptably high. Thus, far from fitting virtually perfectly, as one might gather from the first graph, the fit leaves a lot to be desired.

The first step towards a better fit is to fit so as to minimize the sum squares of these percentage errors. That can be done by the following commands.

```
gdates 1 20
fdates 0 20
f ze = 0
f difrela = 0
f z = 0
fdates 1 19
ti Alternate Fit Relative Error in Income
nl f z = @exp(a1*@log(1.-@exp(a0*@log(1.-x)))) ;
   f difp = z - z[1];
   f difrela = (difp - difa)/difa;
   ze = difrela
2
0.5 2.5
0.01 0.01

# Put the 0 and 1 in z at the beginning and end
update z
0  0
20 1.
fdates 1 20

f difrela = 100.*(z - z[1] - difa)/difa
vr -20 -10 0 10 20 30 40
gr difrela difrel
vr off
```

Here we have employed the capacity of G to use a number of statements in the course of defining the predicted value. The first of these, on the same line with the *nl* command, calculates a variable called *z* from the formula for the Lorenz curve. The second line computes *difp*, the fraction of income in each bracket (except the last). The third line then calculates *difrela*, the percentage errors in these income fractions. Notice that each of these intermediate lines ends with a *;* . The final line, which does *not* end in a *;* , has the desired value on the left (in this case, zero) and the predicted value on the right. The remaining lines calculate the values of the difference for the whole range of the function, including the uppermost bracket and produce the graph shown above. The new fit is shown by the curve marked with + signs.

The fit is generally improved but is poor enough to invite us to try a different form of Lorenz curve. As already observed, the product of any two Lorenz curves is also a Lorenz curve, so we could take a product of the Rasche curve we have estimated so far with a simple exponential. The commands for estimating this function are

```
nl f z = @exp(a2*@log(x))*@exp(a1*@log(1.-@exp(a0*@log(1.-x)))) ;
   f difp = z - z[1];
   difrelpa = (difp - difa)/difa;
   ze = difrelpa
3
0.15 .17  2.
0.01  0.01 .01
```

The numerical results are

253

Param	Coef	T-value	StdDev
a0	0.405709	5.52	0.073498
a1	0.523675	3.93	0.133357
a2	1.536559	10.38	0.147986

The relative errors are shown in the graph below by the line marked by squares. Comparison with the relative errors of the simple Rasche suggested that a linear combination of the two types of curves might be tried. In the full function, there would have been six parameters to estimate. G's algorithm kept pushing the Rasche parameters that have to be between 0 and 1 out of that range, so they were fixed at values found previously. The first line of the estimation was

```
nl - f z = a0*@exp(a1*@log(x))*@exp(a3*@log(1.-@exp(.15366*@log(1.-x)))) +
           (1-a0)*@exp(a2*@log(1.-@exp(.6982*@log(1.-x))));
```

And starting values were:
```
4
0.5 2.0451  1.8633 .17024
0.01 .01     .01     .01
```

The resulting relative errors are shown by the line marked with + signs in the graph below. The fit is considerably improved for the first four brackets and is about the same for the rest of the curve.

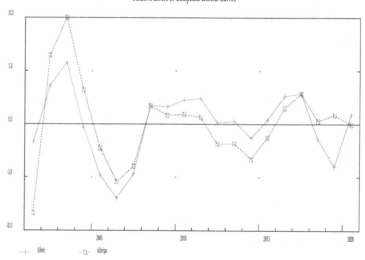

Relative Errors of Composite Lorenz Curves

In this function note the - after the *nl* command; it turns on debugging dumping of the value of the objective function and of the parameters every time an improved solution is reached.

2. The downhill simplex method, Powell's direction set method, and details

We have spoken above rather vaguely of "feeling around" by the nonlinear algorithm. Now we need to describe a bit more precisely what is happening.

Initially, S, the sum of squared errors, is calculated at the initial value of each parameter. Then, one-by-one, the parameters are changed by adding the initial variations, and S is recalculated at each point, thus yielding values at n+1 points (a simplex). Points in the simplex are then replaced by better points generated by the "reflection, expansion, or contraction" operations to be described in a moment or the simplex is shrunk towards its best point. The process continues until no point differs from the best point by more than one-tenth of the initial variation in any parameter.

New points for the simplex are generated and selected in a way best described in a sort of "program in words" as follows:

Reflect old worst point, W, through mid-point of other points to R(eflected).
If R is better than the old best, B {
    expand to E by taking another step in the same direction.
    if E is better than R, replace W by E in the simplex.
    else replace W by R.
    }
Else{
    contract W half way to mid-point of other points, to C(ontracted)
    if C is better than W, replace W by C.
    Else Shrink all points except B half way towards B.
    }

As applied in G, once the algorithm converges, steps of the initial size are made in each direction around the presumed optimum. If any better point is found, the program prints "Fresh start" and starts the process again. It is not unusual to see several "Fresh start" notices.

Though, like all non-linear algorithms, this one is not guaranteed to work on all problems, it has certain advantages. It is easily understood, no derivatives are required, the programming is easy, the process never forgets the best point it has found so far, and the process either converges or goes on improving forever. While by no means the most "sophisticated" of algorithms, it has a reputation for robustness.

The principal problem that I have with the algorithm is that it sometimes tries to evaluate the function at points that lead to arithmetic errors. For example, it may try to evaluate the logarithm of a negative number. My advice in such cases is to use the debugging dump option, the - after the *nl* command. You will often see what parameter is causing the trouble. Use the information from the dump to get a better starting point and use a rather small initial step size.

The recovery of G in cases of arithmetic error leaves something to be desired. You will get the message that the error has occurred and you click "Cancel" in order not to see the error many more times. Unfortunately that click which stopped the execution of the command file did not close that file. Attempts to save the command file from the editor will be refused. Instead, use File | Save as .. and save with some other name, like "temp." Exit G, restart it, bring "temp" into the editor and use File | Save as .. to save it with its proper name.

Soft constraints on the parameters can be built into the objective function. For example,

$$\text{nl zero} = @sq(y - (a0 + a1x1 + a2x2)) + 100*@sq(@pos(-a2))$$

will "softly" require a2 to be positive in the otherwise linear regression of y on x1 and x2. The word "zero" on the left side causes G to minimize the sum of the expression on the right rather than the sum of the squares of the differences between it and the left side. The word "last" on the left causes G to minimize the value of the expression in the last observation of the fit period. This feature can be used in conjunction with the @sum() function -- which puts the sum of its argument from the first to last observation of the fit period into the last observation.

Following the *nl* command, there can be f commands, r commands, and con commands before the non-linear equation itself. These may contain the parameters a1, a2, etc.; they should each be terminated by ';'. The non-linear search then includes the execution of these lines. E.g.:

```
nl x1 = @cum(s,v,a0);
y = a1 + a2*x1
```

These special features allow G's non-linear command to handle a wide variety of non-linear problems such as logit analysis, varying parameter estimates, and errors-in-variables techniques. It is beyond our scope here to explain all these possibilities.

Finally, the *save* command creates a file with the nonlinear equation with the estimated parameters substituted for a0, a1, etc. And the *catch* command captures the output to the screen to the named file as usual.

Besides the downhill simplex method, G also has available nonlinear regression by *Powell's direction set method*. The format for using it is almost exactly the same except that the command is *nlp*. The line of "step sizes," however, is used only as a convergence criterion. As in the *nl* command, when one iteration of the algorithm does not change any parameter by more than one tenth of its "step size," the process is declared to have converged.

Powell's method uses a sequence of one-dimensional minimizations. For a problem with *n* parameters, the method has at any time a set of *n* directions in which it minimizes. It starts simply with the unit vectors in n-dimensions. It does a one-dimensional minimization first in the first direction, then from the point found in that direction, it does another one-dimensional minimization in the second direction, and so on. When a minimization has been done in each of the *n* directions, the net step, the vector difference between the final point and initial point, usually enters the set of directions in place of the direction in which minimization produced the largest drop. Another step equal to the net step is then tried. The process is then repeated. In some situations, however, it is not desirable to change the set of directions. The exact criterion and details of the algorithm are given in William H. Press, et al. *Numerical Methods in C* (Cambridge University Press, 1986.))

Which method is better? Powell is supposed to be a more "sophisticated" use of the information; and in very limited comparative tests, it has reduced the objective function faster in terms of the number of evaluations of the function. This sort of comparison can be made by running both methods on the same problem and using the ' - ' following the command to show the progress of the algorithm. However, you may find problems on which the downhill simplex works best. In any event, neither algorithm is perfect, so it is good to have a second in case one fails to work.

3. Logistic functions

Besides Lorenz curves, another common application of nonlinear regression in economics is to the estimation of *logistic* functions. These functions, sometimes called growth curves, often describe fairly well the path of some variable that starts slowly, accelerates, and then slows down as it approaches an asymptotic value. They can also describe a declining process. The general form is

$$y(t) \; = \; a_0 \; + \; \frac{a_1}{1 \; + \; a_2 \, e^{a_3 t}} \quad .$$

Two examples are shown below. The rising curve has a negative a3 parameter; the falling curve has a positive. Otherwise, the parameters are the same so that the curves look like mirror images of one another around the point where t = 0, chosen for this example in 1981. (This origin of time is not another parameter, for any change in it can be compensated by a change in the a2 parameter.)

Growing and Declining Logistic Curves

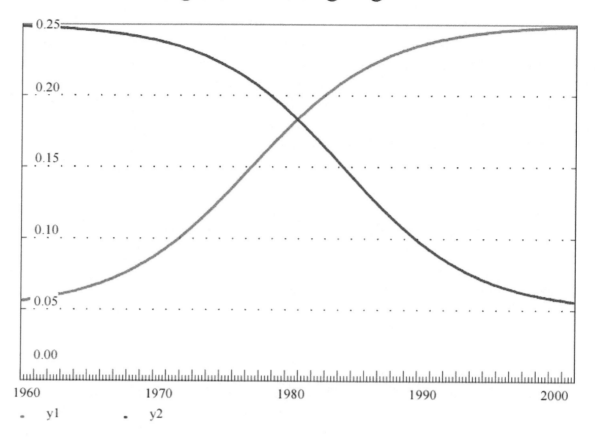

The commands were:

```
f tm21 = time - 21
# the rising curve
f y1 = .05+ .2/(1 + .5*@exp(-.2*tm21))

# the falling curve
f y2 = .05+ .2/(1 + .5*@exp(.2*tm21))
```

As an application of this family of curves, we may take the ratio of imports to GDP in the US in the period 1960.1 to 2001.4. The historical course of this ratio is shown by the irregular line in the graph below. The logistic fit to it is shown by the smooth line.

258

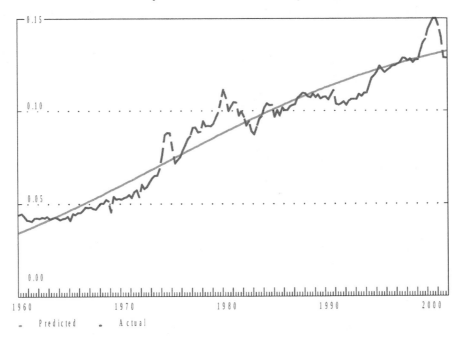

The G command for fitting this line are

```
ti Logistic Curve for Imports
f tm25 = time - 25.
lim 1960.1 2001.4
nlp firat = a0 +a1/(1. + a2*@exp(a3*tm25))
  4
  .04  .20   .02  -.01
  .001 .001  .001  .001
```

The numerical results were:

```
  Logistic Curve for Imports
SEE = 0.007542
Param        Coef     T-value      StdDev
   a0     -0.009051    -0.34      0.026917
   a1      0.160953     4.25      0.037894
   a2      0.468872     7.85      0.059702
   a3     -0.070660    -3.81      0.018550
```

Around the basic framework of the logistic, one can add variations. The asymptotes can be affected by replacing the simple constant a_0 by a linear expression in explanatory variables. The same can be done with the other constants. Indeed, the t variable need not be time but can be a function of other variables. Thus, the form gives rise to a large family of functions; they all require nonlinear estimation.

A final word of warning, however. Many logistic curves have been fit to rising series.

259

Unless the curve has nearly reached its upper asymptote, the estimate of that asymptote has often proven unreliable. The first application of the curve was to automobile ownership in the United States. In about 1920, the researchers predicted that the market would be effectively saturated by 1923. Moreover, the rising logistic provides no information about when the decline will begin.

CHAPTER 12. STOCHASTIC SIMULATION

When we estimate the mean household income of a city of 10,000 households on the basis of a random sample of 100 households, we can convey to the users of the estimate some idea of the accuracy of the number by stating also its standard deviation. Can we in some similar way give users of a model an idea of its reliability?

Yes and no. The comparison of the historical simulation of the model with the actual history is already conveys some idea of the accuracy of the model. In this chapter, we will show how to go further and recognize that we know that the regression equations are inexact and that they will almost certainly err in the future just as they have erred in the past. We will make up random additive errors for the equations that have the same standard errors and autocorrelation coefficients as were found for the residuals. We can then run the model with these random errors added to the equations. In fact, we can easily run it a number of times – 50, 100, or more – each time with a different set of random additive errors and calculate the mean and standard errors of each variable in the model.

We can go further and recognize that the regression coefficients are not known with certainty. We can generate random variations in them which have the same variance-covariance matrix as was found in the course of the regression calculation. While these calculations are most easily justified by invoking the Datamaker hypothesis, we can also say that we are interested in the model forecasts that would be generated by random variations in the coefficients that would not reduce the fit of equations by more than a certain amount.

In this chapter, we will see how to make such calculations. But we should be aware of the limits of these calculations. They do not tell us how much error may be introduced into the forecasts by errors in the forecasts of the exogenous variables. If we are willing to specify the extent of those errors, they too can be accounted for. But it is also possible that in the future one or more relation which has held quite dependably in the past may cease to hold. Or, following the line of the Lucas critique, we may by a change in some policy variable push the model into territory in which we have no experience and in which one or more of the equations ceases to work. The techniques explained here cannot be expected to warn us of such problems.

We will first explain simulation with random additive errors and then add the random coefficients as well.

1. Random additive errors

Of the residuals in each equation we know from the regression results the standard error, σ, and the autocorrelation coefficient, ρ. We need to make up random additive errors to the equation which have that same σ and ρ. From *Numerical Recipes in C* (pages 204-217), we borrow a (quite clever) pseudo random number generator that produces "random" independent normal deviates with mean 0 and variance 1. Let us multiply it by a constant, a, to get a variable ϵ, with mean zero and variance a^2. From it, we can make up the variable ζ by the equation

(1) $\qquad \zeta_t = \rho\,\zeta_{t-1} + \epsilon_t$

Now since the mean of ϵ, is 0, so is the mean of ζ, while the variance of ζ will be given by

(2) $\qquad \sigma_\zeta^2 = E(\zeta_t \zeta_t) = E((\rho\zeta_{t-1} + \epsilon_t)(\rho\zeta_{t-1} + \epsilon_t)) = \rho^2 \sigma_\zeta^2 + \sigma_\epsilon^2$

since ϵ_t is independent of ζ_{t-1} by construction. So

(3) $\qquad \sigma_\zeta^2 = \sigma_\epsilon^2/(1 - \rho^2) = a^2/(1 - \rho^2).$

If we now set σ_ζ^2 equal to the variance of the residuals from the regression, and ρ equal to the autocorrelation coefficient from the regression, we can solve this last equation for a, the factor by which the unit random normal deviates must be multiplied so that equation (1) will give a series of random additive error terms, ζ_t, with the required properties.

The application of stochastic simulation in G is extremely simple. First, the necessary information from the regressions must be saved in the .sav files. To do so, just give G the commands

> stochastic yes
> add runall.reg

in the white command box. The first turns on the saving of the necessary information for stochastic simulation; the second -- if you have kept your runall.reg up to date -- just re-computes the equations with the extra information being saved. Then build the model as usual with Model | Build. When you do Model | Run, however, click the "stochastic" radio button on the right as shown to the right. When

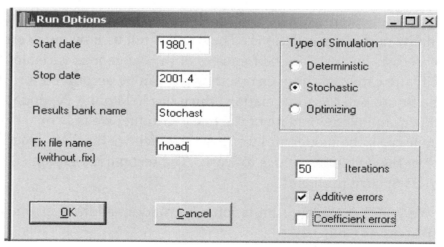

you do so, the extra stochastic options box appears in the lower right, and you can specify the number of simulations you want to make and whether you want just the additive error terms, as shown here, or also random error in the regression coefficients. As shown here, the program will run 50 complete runs of the model with only additive errors.

When a model is run in stochastic simulation, it produces *two* output banks. One is named, as usual, in the "results bank" field on the "Run Options" form. It will contain the average value for each variable in the model from the simulations. The other is always called "sigma" and gives the standard deviation of each variable as found from the simulations.

How these two banks can be used in making graphs is illustrated in the "show file" snippet below.

```
bank stochast d
bank sigma c
bank histsim b
bank bws e
gdates 1981.1  2001.4
#Use special graphics settings
add stoch.set

ti gdpD -- GDP Deflator
gname gdpD
f   upper = b.gdpD +1.*c.gdpD
f   lower = b.gdpD -1.*c.gdpD
gr  b.gdpD  upper lower d.gdpD e.gdpD

ti gdpR -- Real Gross Domestic Product
gname gdpR
f   upper = b.gdpR+2.*c.gdpR
f   lower = b.gdpR-2.*c.gdpR
gr b.gdpR upper lower d.gdpR e.gdpR
```

These two graphs for the optimized Quest model are shown below. In each case, there are *three* lines in the channel or cone marked out by the lines on either side. One of these central lines (marked by + signs) is the average of the simulations, a second (marked by x) shows the deterministic simulation done with all the error terms zero. Theoretically, in a nonlinear model the deterministic simulation is not necessarily the expected value of the stochastic simulations. In the case of these – and virtually all – variables is Quest, there is very little difference between them. The lines at the top and bottom of the cone are one standard deviation above and below the average. The line marked by Δ signs is the actual, historical course of the variable. It appears that the historical course generally stayed within the one sigma bounds.

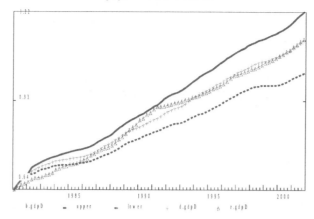
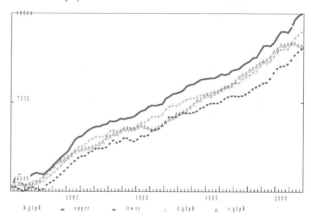

2. Random regression coefficients

In Chapter 9, section 1, we saw that we can, under the Datamaker assumptions, compute the variances and covariances of the regression coefficients by the formula

(1) $V = E(b - \beta)(b - \beta)' = E((X'X)^{-1} X'e \, e'X(X'X)^{-1})$

$$= (X'X)^{-1} \sigma^2 I X(X'X)^{-1}$$

$$= \sigma^2 (X'X)^{-1}$$

We will see how to generate random error terms in the regression coefficients which will have this same V matrix of variances and covariances. These errors can then be added to the regression coefficients and the model run with the altered coefficients.

To generate random errors with the required variance-covariance matrix, we must compute the characteristic vectors and values (or eigenvectors and eigenvalues) of the V matrix. Since V is symmetric and positive definite, it is known by the principal axes theorem that there exists a matrix, P, of the characteristic vectors such that

(2) $P'P = I$

(3) $D = P'VP$

where D is a diagonal matrix with positive elements (the characteristic values of V) on the diagonal.

Equation (2) implies that $P' = P^{-1}$, but a left inverse is also a right inverse, so $PP' = I$. Multiplying (3) on the left by P and on the right by P' therefore gives

(4) $PDP' = PP'VPP' = V$

If we let R be the diagonal matrix which has on its diagonal the square roots of the diagonal elements of D, then $RR' = D$ and from (4) we have

264

(5) $PRR'P' = PP'VPP' = V$.

If $\boldsymbol{\varepsilon}$ is a vector of independent random normal variables with zero mean and unit variance, then,

(6) $\boldsymbol{\eta} = \boldsymbol{PR\varepsilon}$

is a vector of random variables that have $\boldsymbol{V}$ as their variance-covariance matrix, for

(7) $\mathrm{E}(\eta\eta') = \mathrm{E}(\boldsymbol{PR\varepsilon\varepsilon'R'P'}) = \boldsymbol{PR}\mathrm{E}(\boldsymbol{\varepsilon\varepsilon'})\boldsymbol{R'P'} = \boldsymbol{PRIR'P'} = \boldsymbol{PRR'P'} = \boldsymbol{V}$

where the last equality follows from (5).

Computing the $\boldsymbol{PR}$ is a bit of work, so it is not done by G when the regression is estimated. Instead, when a regression is done by G after a "stochastic yes" command, the variance-covariance matrix of the regression coefficients is put into the .sav file. When the model is built, the $\boldsymbol{PR}$ matrix, called the *principal component matrix,* is computed and put into the heart.dat file. When the model is run in stochastic simulation with the "random coefficients" box checked, the $\boldsymbol{\eta}$ vector is computed and added to the point estimate of the regression coefficients. The coefficients thus generated are constant through any one run of the model, but many runs of the model may be made, each with different coefficients.

Computing of $\boldsymbol{PR}$ is done with algorithms from *Numerical Recipes in C*; Householder's method is used to get a tridiagonal matrix, and the QL algorithm is used to finish the job.

The two graphs below show the results of fifty stochastic simulations of Quest with *only* random coefficients – no additive error terms. It is readily seen by comparison with the graphs of the additive errors that random coefficients are much less important, at least in Quest, than are the additive errors. It is also clear that the one-sigma range was not large enough to hold the historical series.

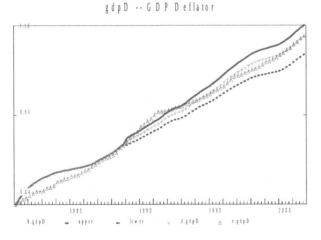

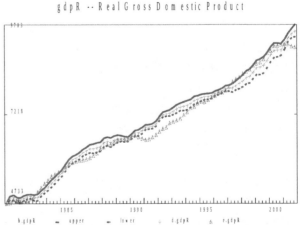

CHAPTER 13. WORKING WITH THE SNA INSTITUTIONAL ACCOUNTS

In previous chapters of this book, we have worked with the system of accounts used in the United States. The layout of these accounts is different from that advocated by the United Nations and other international organizations and used by most other countries. The U.S. system is older and, in my opinion, much easier to understand. The international system, known as the System of National Accounts (SNA), has an elegance which appeals to accounting specialists, but is hard for the casual user to penetrate. The builder of a macromodel for these countries, however, must master the SNA system, so in this chapter you will find a guide to the SNA maze.

The simplest presentation of the SNA system which I have met is for China. For 1992 and following years, China's National Bureau of Statistics (NBS) has prepared and published in its yearbooks a table entitled "Flow of Funds Accounts (Physical Transactions)." In the SNA, these accounts are more commonly called the "institutional accounts" to avoid confusion with the accounts NBS calls "Flow of Funds (Financial Transactions)," which are usually called simply the "Flow of Funds Accounts."

These institutional accounts provide a complete picture of payments among (1) enterprises, (2) financial institutions, (3) governments, (4) households, and (5) the rest of the world – the five "institutions" referred to in the name.   They thus provide a good framework for economic modeling. We first explain the accounts – for the brief comments usually published with them are inadequate for understanding how they work – and then illustrate how they can be used as a modeling framework.

1. How the Institutional Accounts Work

Basically, the intstitutional accounts begin from the value added by each institution and then show how – by payments of wages, social security contributions, taxes, dividends, interest, and transfers – that value-added changes hands and becomes the income of households and governments. They also show the consumption expenditures of households and governments and the investment of all four domestic institutions. In the final line, they show each intitution's savings or need for external financing.

Consistency between payments and receipts is maintained for each type of transaction. For example, the sum of wages paid is equal to the sum of wages received; the sum of interest payments is equal to the sum of interest receipts, and so on. Payments by an institution are referred to as its "Use" of funds while receipts are a "Source" of funds.

The Institutional accounts unfold through a sequence of five subaccounts, as shown in Table 1, the accounts for 2000. Do not worry if you cannot read the numbers clearly. It is the structure of the table that matters for us.

Table 3-21 Flow of Funds Institutional Transactions Accounts, 2000

Transaction
Units: 100 million yuan.

# Transaction	Non-financial Enterprises Use	Source	Financial Institutions Use	Source	Governments Use	Source	Households Use	Source	Total Domestic Use	Source	Rest of World Use	Source	Total Use	Source
# Account 1: Production														
1. Net Exports	0.00	0.00	0.00	0.00	0.00	0.00	0.00	0.00	0.00	0.00	2240.30	0.00	2240.30	0.00
2. Value Added	0.00	50666.93	0.00	2133.19	0.00	8605.38	0.00	20068.60	0.00	83281.10	0.00	0.00	0.00	83281.10
3. Compensation of Laborers	18156.53	0.00	778.46	0.00	8180.98	0.00	28195.40	5324.88	53021.37	5324.88	16.89	56.18	53038.06	5329.06
(1) Wages and Related Income	18804.28	0.00	609.12	0.00	8180.98	0.00	28195.40	50750.29	50789.78	50750.29	16.89	56.18	50806.47	50806.47
(2) Employer's Contribution for Social Security	2322.26	0.00	169.34	0.00	0.00	0.00	1374.49	2491.59	2491.59	2491.59	0.00	0.00	2491.59	2491.59
4. Taxes on Production, Net	12198.00	0.00	987.59	0.00	173.60	14701.68	39.89	3148.07	14187.40	14701.68	952.18	0.00	14701.68	14701.68
5. Income from Properties	6334.50	2034.61	5358.54	5645.50	454.47	239.23	39.89	2978.88	10341.94	1683.99	973.88	483.63	13175.94	13175.94
(1) Interest	4527.50	1999.98	5300.08	5613.80	454.47	239.23	0.00	2978.88	10341.94	1683.99	18.50	1848.50	11315.62	11315.62
(2) Dividend	1807.00	18.48	0.00	31.70	0.00	0.00	0.00	126.78	1807.00	176.96	0.00	1848.50	1625.50	1625.46
(3) Rent on Land Use	0.00	0.00	0.00	0.00	0.00	0.00	0.00	0.00	0.00	0.00	0.00	0.00	0.00	0.00
(4) Others	0.00	16.15	38.46	0.00	0.00	0.00	0.00	22.31	38.46	38.46	0.00	0.00	38.46	38.46
A. Total Primary = Lines 1+2+3+4+5	38857.03	52697.54	7094.59	7778.69	8809.05	23546.29	27809.78	84436.55	80170.45	16845.07	3249.17	218.31	83419.62	170647.38
B. Source - Use in line A by institution	16040.51	16040.51	709.59	684.10	8809.05	14737.24	27809.78	58626.77	80170.45	82828.62	3249.17	-1060.86	87227.76	87227.76
# Account 2: Taxes and transfers														
6. Total Income from Primary Distribution	0.00	16040.51	0.00	684.10	0.00	14737.24	0.00	58626.77	0.00	82828.62	0.00	0.00	0.00	82828.62
7. Current Transfer	2842.21	169.99	508.86	352.00	2583.46	5199.08	3382.92	4110.86	9317.45	9839.93	567.97	45.49	9885.42	9885.42
(1) Taxes on Income	1068.82	0.00	156.86	0.00	671.60	2686.28	671.60	0.00	2686.28	2686.28	0.00	0.00	2686.28	2686.28
(2) Payment to Social Security	0.00	0.00	0.00	0.00	2347.09	2491.59	2491.59	2347.09	4838.68	4838.68	0.00	0.00	4838.68	4838.68
(3) Allowances	30.00	0.00	0.00	0.00	0.00	0.00	0.00	308.60	308.60	308.60	0.00	0.00	308.60	308.60
(4) Others	899.39	169.99	352.00	352.00	7.77	12.21	219.73	1463.17	1474.89	1937.37	567.97	45.49	2042.86	2042.86
C. Lines 6+7	2842.21	16210.50	508.86	1036.10	2583.46	19936.32	3382.92	60941.63	9317.45	9814.55	567.97	45.49	9885.42	9817.404
D. Sources - Uses in line C, by institution		13388.29		527.24		17352.86		57962.71		82828.62		-52.44		82828.62
# Account 3: Disposable income and consumption														
8. Total Disposable Income	0.00	13388.29	0.00	527.24	0.00	17352.86	0.00	57962.71	0.00	88811.10	0.00	0.00	0.00	88811.10
9. Final Consumption Expenditure	0.00	0.00	0.00	0.00	11705.26	0.00	42911.40	0.00	54616.66	0.00	0.00	0.00	54616.66	0.00
(1) Household Consumption	0.00	0.00	0.00	0.00	0.00	0.00	42911.40	0.00	42911.40	0.00	0.00	0.00	42911.40	0.00
(2) Government Consumption	0.00	0.00	0.00	0.00	11705.26	0.00	0.00	0.00	11705.26	0.00	0.00	0.00	11705.26	0.00
E. Lines 8+9	0.00	13388.29	0.00	527.24	11705.26	17352.86	42911.40	57962.71	54616.66	88811.10	0.00	0.00	54616.66	88811.10
F. Sources - Uses in line E, by institution		13388.29		527.24		5647.60		14651.31		34194.44		0.00		34194.44
# Account 4: Savings and Investment														
10. Savings	0.00	13388.29	0.00	527.24	0.00	5647.60	0.00	14651.31	0.00	34194.44	0.00	-1635.63	0.00	3255.492
11. Capital Transfer	0.00	4557.42	0.00	1.00	4558.42	0.00	4903.36	0.00	4558.42	4558.42	3.89	3.89	4562.31	4562.31
12. Gross Capital Formation	24316.77	0.00	116.89	0.00	3161.32	0.00	4709.36	0.00	32499.84	0.00	0.00	0.00	32499.84	0.00
(1) Gross Fixed Capital Formation	24633.77	0.00	116.89	0.00	3161.32	0.00	4709.36	0.00	32623.84	0.00	0.00	0.00	32623.84	0.00
(2) Changes in Inventories	-318.00	0.00	0.00	0.00	0.00	0.00	194.00	0.00	-124.00	0.00	0.00	0.00	-124.00	0.00
13. Minus Items from Other Non-financial Capital	0.00	0.00	0.00	0.00	0.00	0.00	0.00	0.00	0.00	0.00	0.00	0.00	0.00	0.00
G. Lines 10+11+12	24316.77	17925.71	116.89	528.24	7722.24	5647.80	4907.25	14651.31	37062.15	3075.86	0.00	-1635.63	37062.15	3711.723
H. Sources - Uses in line G, by institution	-6390.06	-6390.06	411.35	411.35	-2074.84	-2074.84	9744.06	9744.06	1690.71	1690.71	-1635.63	-1635.63	55.08	55.08
# Account 5: Financing														
14. Net Financial Investment	-6390.06	0.00	411.35	0.00	-2074.84	0.00	9744.06	0.00	1690.71	0.00	-1635.63	0.00	55.08	0.00
15. Statistical Discrepancy	1120.76	0.00	-344.49	0.00	1074.78	0.00	-1846.01	0.00	5.02	0.00	-60.10	0.00	-55.08	0.00
16. Financial Investment Net	-5269.30	0.00	66.86	0.00	-999.88	0.00	7898.05	0.00	1695.73	0.00	-1695.73	0.00	0.00	0.00

The first of these is the Production account. Its first line shows Net Exports as a use of funds by the Rest of the world. The usefulness of this line appears when we come to the modeling, otherwise, it is rather peripheral to the main concern of the accounts. (Curiously, NBS calls the item "Net exports" but shows the negative of net exports as a source of funds for the rest of the world. This "double negative" is not an error but seems highly unnatural. In Table 1, we have changed the presentation to follow the more natural practice of showing Net exports as a positive number for use of funds by the Rest of the world.)

The main work of the accounts begins from line 2, where we find the Value added by each of the four domestic institutions. The sum of these four items is precisely Gross domestic product (GDP) as measured by the production approach, which the NBS takes as the definitive GDP. It differs from GDP measured by the expenditure approach by a statistical discrepancy.

The units of the table are in *yi* yuan, where one *yi* is ten thousand ten thousands, or 100 million. (To get numbers in billions, move the decimal point one place to the left.) We will abbreviate "*yi* yuan" to yy. We also abbreviate, not quite accurately, "non-financial enterprises" to "firms", "financial enterprises" to "banks", and "Rest of the World" to "RoW".

Other than these first two (and the last two) lines, all lines in the table are of two types: distribution lines and balance lines. The characteristic of a distribution line is that the sum of the sources equals the sum of the uses. Lines 3, 4, and 5 are typical distribution lines. Line 6 is the first balance line. We will explain how balance lines are derived when we reach it.

Line 3 begins the movement of value added from the sectors where it was created to those where it is consumed or saved. This line shows payment of Compensation of laborers as a *use* of funds by all four domestic institutions. The recipients are mainly households, where the payments appear as a *source* of income. A small amount, 56.18 yy, of wages are also paid to persons resident abroad and an even smaller amount, 16.69 yy, are paid by firms outside China to residents of China. The fact that Households pay Compensation of laborers (in the amount of 26195.4 yy) as well as receive it (in the amount of 53241.88 yy) emphasizes the fact that "Households" include family businesses as well as wage-earner families. Indeed, about half of all wages are paid by Households. The next two lines, 3.1 and 3.2, just divide this compensation between Wages and Employers' contribution to social security. The latter is considered a payment to Households (a source) in this line; but, to jump ahead, in Line 7.2 exactly the same amount, 2491.59 yy, is shown as a payment by Households (as a use) to Governments (as a source). (This division of Line 3 began only in 1999, so we will not use it in our model.)

Line 4, Taxes on production, shows an uncomplicated illustration of the uses = sources principle. All four domestic institutions pay these taxes; that is, they all have *use* entries. Only one, Governments, receives these payments, so its *source* entry is equal to the sum of the four *use* entries.

Line 5, Income from properties, is as complicated as Line 4 was simple. This type of income includes Interest, Dividends, Rent on land, and Other property income (such as rents and royalties.) All institutions both pay and receive this type of income. The table shows the transactions separately for Interest (which all institutions both pay and receive), Dividends (which only firms and RoW pay and Governments do not receive), Rent of land (which supposedly no one pays and no one receives), and Others (paid by Banks and received by Firms and Households). There is no explanatory note on this last item, but one may suspect that it is the imputed financial services rendered without payment by financial institutions, the mysterious FISIM (Financial Services Indirectly Measured) of national income accountants worldwide.

At this point, the first subaccount, called the Production account, is complete. It has shown primarily payments for services rendered, either by labor or capital. The Taxes on production, Line 4, are a bit of an exception to this idea, but they are at least payments for permissions, licenses, use of land, use of capital, or sales, not taxes on the net income of businesses. At this point, the accounts take a balance. In Line A, all the *uses* and all the *sources* of each institution are summed up, and the difference, *sources* minus *uses*, is shown in Line B as *sources*. Line B is a typical balance line showing the *sources* minus *uses* in a subaccount. Neither Line A nor Line B as a balance is shown in the official tables. Instead, Line B appears as Line 6, Total income from primary distribution, with no word of explanation about where it comes from. In fact, it is both the balance line of the Production subaccount and the beginning of the second subaccount, Taxes and transfers. The other balance lines, Lines 8, 10, and 14, will be derived in a similar way and function as the balance line of one subaccount and the beginning of the next. Nothing of this process is explained in the official presentation of these accounts in the yearbooks, so it seems safe to assume that no one has understood them without bringing a knowledge of how they work from some other country.

The second subaccount, Taxes and transfers, shows, in the same *sources* = *uses* format, the distribution lines for Taxes on income, Social security transactions, Allowances, and Other current transfers. The Social security transactions line (Line 7.2) contains two quite different types of transactions: the payments of Social security taxes by households to the government (Use by Households = Source for Governments) and the payments of social security benefits by governments to the elderly (Use by Governments = Source for Households). "Allowances" seems to mean "housing allowances" or "food allowances" which are essentially supplements to wages to compensate employees for unusual living expenses. They are *uses* of funds by firms and governments and *sources* for households. Line C shows the sums of *uses* and *sources* for this subaccount, and Line D is the subaccount's balance line, the *sources* minus the *uses* in line C for each institution. This balance line has a particularly important name: Disposable income.

As always, the next account – here, Disposable income and consumption – begins from the balance line of the previous account, in this case, Disposable income, Line 8. This account shows Final consumption expenditures of Households in Line 9.1 and of Governments in Line 9.2. The balance line for the account shows Savings by each by each of the four domestic institutions. Government consumption in this table, by the way, is identical to Government consumption in the "expenditure-approach" GDP tables. The difference in Household consumption is of the order of 0.01 percent, that is, the numbers are essentially the same.

This balance line of this subaccount, Line 10 Savings, is then the first line of the next – the fourth – subaccount, Savings and investment. The next line, Line 11 Capital transfers, includes primarily grants from Governments (as a *use*) to Firms (as a *source*) for the purpose of capital investment. Gross fixed capital formation, a *use* of funds, is then shown for each domestic institution in Line 12.1, and Inventory investment appears in Line 12.2 as a *use* of funds.

Investment, like consumption, is the same as in the GDP accounts by the expenditure approach, as are Net exports. Thus, the statistical discrepancy in the Institutional accounts between GDP as the sum of value added and GDP as consumption plus investment plus net exports is very nearly the same as the statistical discrepancy between GDP by the expenditure approach and GDP by the production approach.

The balance line of the fourth account shows the need for net financial investment required by each institution. This line appears as Line 14, Net financial investment. The sum of the line should be zero but will differ from zero by exactly the statistical discrepancy just mentioned. Finally, Line 16 shows Net financial investment as derived from the Flow of Funds Table (Financial Transactions). Lines 14 and 16 should be the same, but they are not, so between is placed Line 15 of statistical discrepancy, institution by institution.

2. Institutional Accounts as a Framework for Macroeconomic Modeling, CTM

These accounts can provide an excellent accounting basis for a macroeconomic model of China. We will illustrate their use in a simple, "tautological" model we call CTM, for Chinese Tautologcial Model. A "tautology" is a statement true by the definitions of its words, and our model will be hold exactly for the historical data by the definition of its variables and equations. Put slightly differently, when run with historical values of exogenous variables, it reproduces exactly the historical values of the endogenous variables. As we shall see, however, a tautological model is not totally uninteresting or without economic properties. More importantly, however, it provides an accounting structure for more developed models.

To use the institutional accounts for the construction of a model, we had to convert the tables for the years 1992 - 2000 into a databank of individual time series. The first step was to get the tables for each year into worksheets in an Excel workbook. This was relatively easy for 1992 - 1999, where the data came in spreadsheets on the CD which accompanied the yearbooks. The table for 2000, however, from the 2003 yearbook, was available only as a PDF file. Worse still, zero entries appeared as blanks. Now when cutting and pasting text from a PDF, any number of blanks are copied as one blank. Hence, every line of the resulting table had be carefully edited by hand to get the numbers into the right cells. It is to be hoped that the NBS will take mercy on the users of its tables and go back to the former method of publication, or at least put a 0 where there is an empty cell in the table.

From this point, the process was fairly easy because of the G modeling software's ability to create VAM files with time series of vectors and matrices. It is also easy to extract a time series of the values of in a particular cell of the matrix. In this way was created a time-series data bank, Zhongguo, containing these series and a number of other series from the yearbooks.

To make this bank, and to use these accounts as a basis for a model, we need names for the time series of each cell. We have made up such names using five letters. The first three letters indicate the transaction type and are shown in the first column of Table 1. The fourth letter indicates the institution:

    e Non-financial Enterprises
    b Banks and other financial institutions
    g Governments
    h Households
    d Total domestic
    r Rest of World
    t Total

The final letter is
    u for Use or
    s for Source.

Our model will go only as far as Line 14, the balance line for the fourth account. Thus we will have four balance lines, each involving four or five identities – one for each domestic institution plus one for total domestic if we need it. In some cases, such as Line 7 Property income, we need to sum up several detailed lines to get the total. The identities for Subaccount 1 are as shown in the box on the next page.

Just from the production subaccount, we have 19 identities. From the remaining subaccounts down through Line, there are another 27 identites, for a total of 46. The number of non-zero cells, however, is about 121. We could make a model with just these 46 identities and some 75 (= 121 - 46) exogenous variables. There would be absolutely nothing wrong in this model, but it would be very misleading. In it, for example, an increase in government consumption expenditure would affect only governments' saving and need for external financing. It would have no effect on value added in Line 2, not to mention, no effect on consumption or tax collections. Clearly, we need more relations to create a meaningful model.

At this point, the traditional macroeconomic model builder turns to regression analysis to fill in behavioral relations between the various variables to reduce the number of exogenous variables. We have no objection to that approach, save to say that the task of developing something close to 75 regression equations is a big job. We will employ a simpler approach of establishing *behavioral ratios* between closely related variables. These ratios are established using G's *fex* command. To review from the AMI and QUEST models, if *tax* and *taxbase* are two variables in the databank, the command

fex taxrate = tax/taxbase

will put the variable *taxrate* into the data bank of the model which is being built, but will *not* put the equation into the model. This last fact makes the command very useful for forming exogenous variables, such as *taxrate* in this example. In fact, *fex* stands for "form an exogenous variable." The *fex* command can then be followed by an *f* command, such as

f tax = taxrate*taxbase

This command calculates the tax, an endogenous variable, as a product of the exogenous *taxrate* and the (probably) endogenous *taxbase*. The variable *taxrate* is a good example of a "behavioral ratio," a ratio between two variables which describes very simply the relation between two variables which are closely connected by the economic behavior of firms, banks, governments, or households or by the workings institutions such as tax laws. The behavioral ratios are not constant over time; they are time series variables like any other variable, but we may hope that, if judiciously selected, they may be more nearly constant and easier to predict than the variables they connect.

There is an important difference between the accounting identities and behavioral ratios. The identities are either right or wrong. The behavioral ratio, however, is neither. It can only be said to be somewhere between sensible and crazy. For example, a behavioral ratio between the consumption expenditures of households and their disposable income would be reasonably sensible; one between their consumption and interest receipts of firms would be, we would suppose, crazy. Neither would be either right or wrong.

It is generally easier to make exogenous projection in constant prices than in current prices. The *fex* command provides a convenient way to do so. Suppose we want to make government consumption expenditure (gcegu) exogenous in real, constant-price, terms but endogenous in current prices. If *gdpD* is the GDP deflator, the following two commands will do the trick:

fex gceguR = gcegu/gdpD
f gcegu = gceguR*gdpD

Identities of the Production Subaccount

```
# Compensation of labor received by households = payments by other institutions minus #
payments to persons resident abroad.
f colhs = coleu+colbu+colgu+colhu+colru - colrs
# Taxes on production received by governments = taxes paid by other institutions
f tpngs = tpneu+tpnbu+tpngu+tpnhu
# Interest received  by RoW from China = interest paid in or to China less interest
#       received in China
f intrs =  inteu+intbu+intgu+inthu+intru - (intes+intbs+intgs+inths)
# Dividends  received by RoW from China = dividends paid in or to China less dividends
#       received in China
f   divrs = diveu+divru - (dives+divbs+divgs+divhs)
# Other property income.  Banks are the only payers; firms and households, the only
# recipients
f   opihs = opibu - opies

# Sum up property income sources and uses by each institution
f inpeu = inteu+diveu
f inpes = intes+dives+opies
f inpbu = intbu+opibu
f inpbs = intbs+divbs
f inpgu = intgu
f inpgs = intgs
f inphu = inthu
f inphs = inths+divhs+opihs
f inpru = intru+divru
f inprs = intrs+divrs

# Primary income balance line identities
f pries = vades+inpes-coleu-tpneu-inpeu
f pribs = vadbs+inpbs-colbu-tpnbu-inpbu
f prigs = vadgs+tpngs+inpgs-colgu-tpngu-inpgu
f prihs = vadhs+colhs+inphs-colhu-tpnhu-inphu
```

Now let us apply some of these ideas to turning the Institutional accounts into a simple model based on behavioral ratios. The first thing we need to do is to establish a connection between GDP as the sum of the Value-added row in Line 2 and GDP as the sum of consumption + investment + net exports. Before we can establish that connection, however, we must recognize that there is a statistical discrepancy, so our model begins by defining it as an exogenous variable with this equation:

fex StatDisc = vades+vadbs+vadgs+vadhs - (hcehu+ gcegu+cffdu+cfidu-nexrs)

273

Now, from starting values – or values of the preceeding interation of the model – we compute GDP:

$$f \ GDP = hcehu + gcegu + cffdu + cfidu - nexrs + StatDisc$$

Next, using behavioral ratios, we allocate this GDP as value-added to the four domestic institutions. Value added by governments is mainly the wages of government employees, who are necessary to the administration of government programs, so it seems appropriate to take government value added, vadgs, as a behavioral ratio to government final demand:

```
fex vadgsBR = vadgs/gcegu
f  vadgs = vadgsBR*gcegu
```

Family businesses often sell to consumers, so it is natural to take their value added as a ratio to household consumption:
```
fex vadhsBR = vadhs/hcehu
f vadhs = vadhsBR*hcehu
```

We then split the rest of GDP rest between firms and banks, with firms as the residual:

```
fex vadbsBR = vadbs/(GDP-vadgs - vadhs)
f vadbs = vadbsBR*(GDP-vadgs - vadhs)
f vades = GDP - vadbs - vadgs - vadhs
```
The next line, Line 3, is Compensation of labor. It is natural enough to take the *uses* as behavioral ratios to value added for the four domestic institutions, leave the tiny RoW entries exogenous, and give the balance to households as a *source* of income.

```
ti Labor Compensation by Institution
# Enterprises
fex coleuBR = coleu/vades
f   coleu = coleuBR*vades
# Banks
fex colbuBR = colbu/vadbs
f  colbu = colbuBR*vadbs
# Governments
fex colguBR = colgu/vadgs
f  colgu = colguBR*vadgs
# Households
fex colhuBR = colhu/vadhs
f  colhu = colhuBR*vadhs
# Leave Rest of World items exogenous and  give the balance to households
f colhs = coleu+colbu+colgu+colhu+colru - colrs
```

We continue in this way down through Line 12 of the Institutional accounts. The details are shown in the Master file in the Appendix. When we have reached the computation of household consumption expenditure as a function of household disposable income, it is time to check whether the computed GDP is close to the value that was used in computing Value added by the various institutions at the beginning. If the difference is more than 1 yy, the model starts the cycle of computations over with the personal consumption implied in the first round assumed at the beginning of the second round. This cycle is repeated until convergence is obtained. This behavior is induced by the command

        check GDP 1.0

just before the end of the master file in the appendix.

3. Structural Changes in China as Seen in the Behavioral Ratios

We have alleged that well-chosen behavioral ratios are likely to be more stable and easier to predict than absolute levels of variables. Large changes in them may also indicate policy changes. Let us look quickly at some of the important behavioral ratios in CTM. We can start with the taxrates of the taxes on production and taxes on income for each of the three private domestic intstiutions. The figures below show these six tax rates plotted on the same scale.

Tax on Production Behavioral Ratios

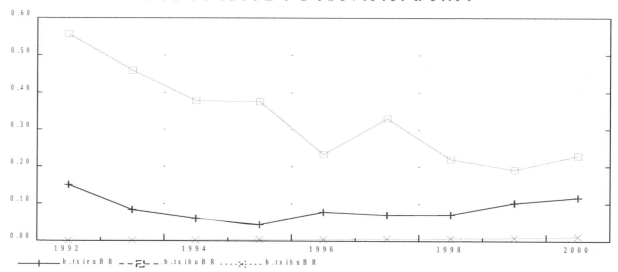

For firms and households, the rates have been fairly constant with a slow rise, while for financial institutions, the taxes on production have risen sharply while those on income have declined. A striking development is the rise in the dividend payout ratio of enterprises. In the 1992-1994, almost no dividends were paid; the payments rose sharply in 1995 and have recently run between 6 and 8 percent of disposable income. The personal savings rate, over 30 percent up through 1998, dropped to about 25 percent in 2000. Both of these ratios still depict an economy with very high savings that are absorbed by rapid investment.

4. Properties of the Chinese Tautological Model, CTM

We noted above that a tautological model is not necessarily uninteresting or without economic properties, for we can study its responses to changes in historical values of the exogenous variables. We have run CTM with several such changes. The first graph below shows the multiplier effect of an increase in government spending on Real GDP. This multiplier has run between 1.9 and 2.4, a range surprisingly similar to that of the multiplier for a similar tautological model of the USA, where the range was 1.9 - 2.0.

Such multipliers must be interpreted with extreme caution. They assume that the economy can have real growth to match any increase in demand. Neither capital nor labor supply pose any constraint on growth. When these constraints are taken into account, demand pushing against their limits turns into inflation and the real GDP multiplier becomes close to zero; but modeling such effects is well beyond the scope of CTM.

We noted above that the household saving rate fell significantly in 1999 and 2000. We can use CTM to ask how much of the growth in GDP in these years was to be attributed to the rise in the multiplier caused by this drop in the saving rate. The second graph below shows, in the heavy line marked by +'s, how real GDP growth would have been affected had the spending ratio of households (hcehuBR) remained constant at its 1992 level. The line marked by x's shows how this same variable would have been affected had government consumption expenditure remained constant at it 1992 level. The line marked by squares is the historical data.

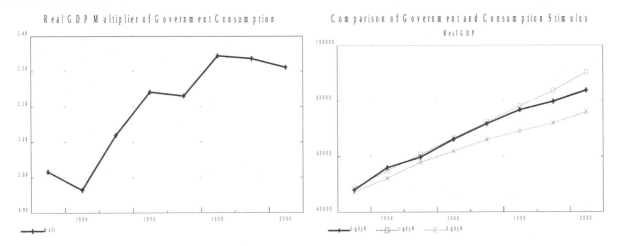

The comparison shows that, between 1998 and 2000, about half of the growth could be attributed to the rise in the household spending ratio. Over the whole period, about one third of the growth would have disappeared had government spending remained constant. Most of the growth is to be attributed to the stimulus of the rapid rise in investment.

The real importance of CTM lies, however, not in what it can do by itself but in how it can be used as a framework for a fully modern econometric model with regression equations for investment, employment, inflation, interest rates, imports, profits, dividends, household consumption and other variables. Developing such a model is altogether feasible, but lies beyond the scope of this book.

Finally, we hope that on seeing how valuable these accounts can be, the NBS will be stimulated to present them in a more readily understandable way, to prepare them on a more timely basis – the equivalent accounts are available a few months after the close of the reference year in some countries – and to distribute them in an easy-to-use format such as a spreadsheet.

Include exogenous exports and imports for use later #when we use CTM as a driver for the
input-output table.
These exports and imports are from Customs and
are not equivalent to the (not released)
exports and imports in the national accounts.

fex exportsR = exports/gdpD
fex importsR = imports/gdpD
f exports = exportsR*gdpD
f imports = importsR*gdpD

Include the GDP deflator as an exogenous variable
fex gdpD = gdp/gdpR

First we find the statistical discrepancy between the # sum of value added and GDP by the
expenditure approach. (Net exports appears here
with a minus sign because in the
Chinese Institutional accounts Net imports are
strangely called Net Exports.)

fex StatDisc = vades+vadbs+vadgs+vadhs - (hcehu+ gcegu+cffdu+cfidu-nexrs)

f GDP = hcehu+gcegu+cffdu+cfidu - nexrs + StatDisc
Allocate GDP to sectors
Take government value added as a function of
government final demand
fex vadgsBR = vadgs/gcegu
f vadgs = vadgsBR*gcegu
Take household value added as a function of
household consumption
fex vadhsBR = vadhs/hcehu
f vadhs = vadhsBR*hcehu
Split the rest between firms and banks
fex vadbsBR = vadbs/(GDP-vadgs - vadhs)
f vadbs = vadbsBR*(GDP-vadgs - vadhs)
f vades = GDP - vadbs - vadgs - vadhs

ti Labor Compensation by Institution
Use proportions to value added
fex coleuBR = coleu/vades
f   coleu = coleuBR*vades
fex colbuBR = colbu/vadbs
f   colbu = colbuBR*vadbs
fex colguBR = colgu/vadgs
f   colgu = colguBR*vadgs
fex colhuBR = colhu/vadhs

f   colhu = colhuBR*vadhs
Leave Rest of World items exogenous and
give the balance to households
f colhs = coleu+colbu+colgu+colhu+colru - colrs

ti Taxes on production

```
fex tpneuBR = tpneu/vades
f   tpneu = tpneuBR*vades
fex tpnbuBR = tpnbu/vadbs
f   tpnbu = tpnbuBR*vadbs
fex tpnguBR = tpngu/vadgs
f   tpngu = tpnguBR*vadgs
fex tpnhuBR = tpnhu/vadhs
f   tpnhu = tpnhuBR*vadhs
#i Balance to Government as Source
f tpngs = tpneu+tpnbu+tpngu+tpnhu


# Interest
# First get all interest paid by Non-financial
# institutions
fex inteuBR = inteu/vades
f   inteu  = inteuBR*vades
fex intguBR = intgu/vadgs
f   intgu  = intguBR*vadgs
fex inthuBR = inthu/vadhs
f   inthu  = inthuBR*vadhs
# Relate interest received by financial institutions to
# this total
fex intbsBR = intbs/(inteu+intgu+inthu)
f   intbs  = intbsBR*(inteu+intgu+inthu)
# Relate interest paid by financial institutions to the
# interest they receive
fex intbuBR = intbu/intbs
f   intbu  = intbuBR*intbs
# Relate interest paid to Non-finanacial Institutions to
# total domestic payments
fex intrsBR = intrs/(inteu+intbu+intgu+inthu)
f   intrs  = intrsBR*(inteu+intbu+intgu+inthu)
fex intesBR = intes/(inteu+intbu+intgu+inthu)
f   intes  = intesBR*(inteu+intbu+intgu+inthu)
fex intgsBR = intgs/(inteu+intbu+intgu+inthu)
f   intgs  = intgsBR*(inteu+intbu+intgu+inthu)
fex inthsBR = inths/(inteu+intbu+intgu+inthu)
f   inths  = inthsBR*(inteu+intbu+intgu+inthu)
# Determine interest from RoW as a balancing entry
f intrs =  inteu+intbu+intgu+inthu+intru - (intes+intbs+intgs+inths)


# Dividends
# Calculate dividends paid by firms
fex diveuBR = diveu/(vades-coleu-inteu)
f   diveu = diveuBR*(vades-coleu-inteu)
# Add these to dividends received from RoW and
# distribute
fex divesBR = dives/(diveu+divru)
f   dives = divesBR*(diveu+divru)
fex divbsBR = divbs/(diveu+divru)
f   divbs = divbsBR*(diveu+divru)
fex divgsBR = divgs/(diveu+divru)
f   divgs = divgsBR*(diveu+divru)
fex divhsBR = divhs/(diveu+divru)
f   divhs = divhsBR*(diveu+divru)
# Put the balance in RoW
```

```
f   divrs = diveu+divru - (dives+divbs+divgs+divhs)

#  Other property income
#  Financial institutions are the only payers
fex opibuBR = opibu/vadbs
f   opibu  = opibuBR*vadbs
fex opiesBR = opies/opibu
f   opies = opiesBR*opibu
f   opihs = opibu - opies

#  Sum up property income
f inpeu = inteu+diveu
f inpes = intes+dives+opies
f inpbu = intbu+opibu
f inpbs = intbs+divbs
f inpgu = intgu
f inpgs = intgs
f inphu = inthu
f inphs = inths+divhs+opihs
f inpru = intru+divru
f inprs = intrs+divrs

#Primary income balance line identies
f pries = vades+inpes-coleu-tpneu-inpeu
f pribs = vadbs+inpbs-colbu-tpnbu-inpbu
f prigs = vadgs+tpngs+inpgs-colgu-tpngu-inpgu
f prihs = vadhs+colhs+inphs-colhu-tpnhu-inphu

#  Taxes on income
fex txieuBR = txieu/pries
f   txieu  = txieuBR*pries
fex txibuBR = txibu/pribs
f   txibu  = txibuBR*pribs
fex txihuBR = txihu/prihs
f   txihu  = txihuBR*prihs
f txigs = txieu+txibu+txihu

#  Payment to social security
fex txshuBR = txshu/colhs
f txshu = txshuBR*colhs
f txsgs = txshu
# Payments by the government to Social Security
# recipients
# (txshs= txsgu) are left exogenous in real terms.
fex txsguR = txsgu/gdpD
f   txsgu = txsguR*gdpD
f txshs = txsgu

#  Current transfer allowances
fex ctaeuBR = ctaeu/vades
f   ctaeu  = ctaeuBR*vades
fex ctabuBR = ctabu/vadbs
f   ctabu  = ctabuBR*vadbs
fex ctaguBR = ctagu/vadgs
f   ctagu  = ctaguBR*vadgs
f ctahs = ctaeu+ctabu+ctagu
```

```
# Other current transfers
# Financial institutions are a special case, for their
# Use and Source entries are always identical.
fex ctobuBR = ctobu/pribs
f  ctobu  = ctobuBR*pribs
f  ctobs = ctobu
fex ctoeuBR = ctoeu/pries
f  ctoeu = ctoeuBR*pries
fex ctoguBR = ctogu/prigs
f  ctogu = ctoguBR*prigs

fex ctohuBR = ctohu/prihs
f  ctohu = ctohuBR*prihs
# Add up total uses and allocate as sources,  with
# households as the balancing item.
fex ctoesBR = ctoes/(ctoeu+ctogu+ctohu+ctoru)
f   ctoes = ctoesBR*(ctoeu+ctogu+ctohu+ctoru)
fex ctogsBR = ctogs/(ctoeu+ctogu+ctohu+ctoru)
f   ctogs = ctogsBR*(ctoeu+ctogu+ctohu+ctoru)
fex ctorsBR = ctors/(ctoeu+ctogu+ctohu+ctoru)
f   ctors = ctorsBR*(ctoeu+ctogu+ctohu+ctoru)
f ctohs = ctoeu+ctogu+ctohu+ctoru-ctoes-ctogs-ctors

# Line 8:  Disposable income balance line
f dines = pries+ctoes-txieu-ctaeu-ctoeu
f dinbs = pribs+ctobs-txibu-ctabu-ctobu
f dings = prigs+txigs+txsgs+ctogs-txsgu-ctagu-ctogu
f dinhs = prihs+txshs+ctahs+ctohs-txihu-txshu-ctohu

# hcehu ; Household consumption expenditure
fex hcehuBR = hcehu/dinhs
f hcehu = hcehuBR*dinhs
f hcehuR = hcehu/gdpD
# gcedu ; Government consumption expenditure, exogenous in real terms
fex gceguR = gcegu/gdpD
f   gcegu = gceguR*gdpD

ti Gross fixed investment, exogenous in real terms
# Business = firms + banks
fex cffbusR = (cffeu+cffbu)/gdpR
fex cffguR = cffgu/gdpD
fex cffhuR = cffhu/gdpD
f cffbus = cffbusR*gdpD
f cffgu  = cffguR*gdpD
f cffhu  = cffhuR*gdpD
f cffdu = cffbus + cffgu +cffhu
f cffduR = cffdu/gdpD
# Inventory investment
fex cfiduR = (cfieu +cfibu + cfigu + cfihu)/gdpD
f cfidu = cfiduR*gdpD
f GDP = hcehu+gcegu+cffdu+cfidu - nexrs + StatDisc

check GDP 1.0

end
```

CHAPTER 14. WHY LINEAR SYSTENS TEND TO OSCILLATE

1. The General Solution of a System of Linear Difference Equations

In Chapter 1, we found that the *AMI* model had a pronounced tendency to cycle. Observers of the economy have often thought they discerned cycles. Indeed, the term "business cycle" has become part of the language. In modeling, our descriptions of the economy do not seem to have anything to do with cycles. Where, then, do the cycles come from? In this short chapter, we shall try to answer that question.

In this first section, we will seek the general solution of a system of difference equations such as can, with some approximation, represent many of our models. It will be an abstract and analytical section. In the following sections, that general solution will enable us see some interesting features of models and, perhaps, of economies. I must emphasize, however, that this chapter is aimed at *understanding qualitatively* the results of models, not at calculations you would ever be likely to want to make. We will find, for example, the *form* of the general solution of a linear model. You generally want, however, a particular solution, and it, as you already know, is calculated directly, without any reference to that general form. We will show how one could, in principal, calculate analytically a frequency response function for a linear model. In practice, in models of any size, it is easier to calculate it from simulations of the model, as is suggested by the exercise at the end of the chapter.

Many of the equations of our models take a form somewhat like the following:

(1) $\qquad y_{t+1} = Ay_t + f_t$

where y_t is a vector of endogenous variables, f_t is a vector of exogenous variables, and A is a matrix. If some variable, say u, appears on the right with values lagged further back than t, we can easily introduce v defined by

(2) $\qquad v_{t+1} = u_t$

so that

(3) $\qquad v_t = u_{t-1}$

and use v_t in place of u_{t-1} while including (2) among the equations. Among the exogenous values, a lagged variable, say $x[4]$, can be simply regarded as the value in period t of x four periods earlier. Thus, the presence of variables with more than one lag does not prevent us from *thinking* of the model as though it were described by the equation (1).

Nonlinearities, however, such as $gdp = gdpR*gdpD$, cannot be described exactly in system (1). They can, however, be represented approximately by the first terms of the Taylor series approximation. Thus, equation (1) comes close enough to describing many models to be worth studying.

Equation (1) is called a system of *linear, first order difference equations*. The term *first order* refers to the fact that at most only one lagged value of any variable appears. In the form (1), the differences are not evident, but if we subtract y_t from both sides, it becomes

$$(4) \quad y_{t+1} - y_t = (A - I)y_t + f_t$$

and the differences on the left side are apparent. (Systems described in continuous time would have the form $\dfrac{dy(t)}{dt} = Ay(t) + f(t)$, which is a system of linear *differential* equations. The mathematical theories of differential and difference equations are closely parallel, except that for difference equations there is no problem of the existence of a solution, since the equations tell us precisely how to calculate it.)

We will now show that any one of the variables in a system of n first-order equations, such as equation (1), follows an nth - order difference equation not involving the other variables in the system. That is, the value for period $t+n$ can be expressed as a linear function of the values of the same variable in n previous periods and the exogenous variables. This fact will allow us to apply some well-known results about the roots of polynomials to characterize the solutions of the difference equations.

We will at first concentrate on the *homogeneous* part of the system, that is to say, the part of the system obtained by dropping the exogenous variables. Let us begin by writing this homogeneous part of the system (1) out in more explicit form:

$$(5) \quad \begin{vmatrix} y_{1,t+1} \\ y_{2,t+1} \\ y_{3,t+1} \\ \cdots \\ y_{n,t+1} \end{vmatrix} = \begin{vmatrix} a_{11} & a_{12} & a_{13} & \cdots & a_{1n} \\ a_{21} & a_{22} & a_{23} & \cdots & a_{2n} \\ a_{31} & a_{32} & a_{33} & \cdots & a_{3n} \\ \cdots & \cdots & \cdots & \cdots & \cdots \\ a_{n1} & a_{n2} & a_{n3} & \cdots & a_{nn} \end{vmatrix} \begin{vmatrix} y_{1t} \\ y_{2t} \\ y_{3t} \\ \cdots \\ y_{nt} \end{vmatrix}$$

From this system, we want to derive a single equation for y_t of the form

$$(6) \quad y_{1,t+1} + c_{n-1} y_{1,t+n-1} + \ldots + c_0 y_{1t} = 0 \quad .$$

First, we now solve the second of these equations for y_{2t} and substitute in all the equations, thus:

$$
(7) \quad
\begin{vmatrix} y_{1,t+1} \\ y_{2,t+1} \\ y_{3,t+1} \\ \cdots \\ y_{n,t+1} \end{vmatrix}
=
\begin{vmatrix}
0 & 1 & 0 & \cdots & 0 \\
a_{21}-\dfrac{a_{22}a_{11}}{a_{12}} & \dfrac{a_{22}}{a_{12}} & a_{23}-\dfrac{a_{22}a_{13}}{a_{12}} & \cdots & a_{2n}-\dfrac{a_{22}a_{1n}}{a_{12}} \\
a_{31}-\dfrac{a_{32}a_{11}}{a_{12}} & \dfrac{a_{32}}{a_{12}} & a_{33}-\dfrac{a_{32}a_{13}}{a_{12}} & \cdots & a_{3n}-\dfrac{a_{32}a_{1n}}{a_{12}} \\
\cdots & \cdots & \cdots & \cdots & \cdots \\
a_{n1}-\dfrac{a_{n2}a_{11}}{a_{12}} & \dfrac{a_{n2}}{a_{12}} & a_{n3}-\dfrac{a_{n2}a_{13}}{a_{12}} & \cdots & a_{nn}-\dfrac{a_{n2}a_{1n}}{a_{12}}
\end{vmatrix}
\begin{vmatrix} y_{1t} \\ y_{1,t+1} \\ y_{3t} \\ \cdots \\ y_{nt} \end{vmatrix}
$$

The matrix on the right of (7) we shall call B_2. It may be obtained from the matrix A on the right of (5) by post-multiplication of A by

$$
(8) \quad M_2 =
\begin{vmatrix}
1 & 0 & 0 & \cdots & 0 \\
\dfrac{-a_{11}}{a_{12}} & \dfrac{1}{a_{12}} & \dfrac{-a_{11}}{a_{12}} & \cdots & \dfrac{-a_{11}}{a_{12}} \\
0 & 0 & 1 & \cdots & 0 \\
\cdots & \cdots & \cdots & \cdots & \cdots \\
0 & 0 & 0 & \cdots & 1
\end{vmatrix}
$$

Thus,

$$
B_2 = AM_2
$$

Notice that while we have now eliminated y_2 on the right of (7), it still appears on the left. To continue the process of eliminating y_2, we use the first equation of (5) advanced by one period (so that it is an equation for $y_{1,t+2}$) to write $y_{1,t+2}$ as a linear combination of the equations (7). The resulting equation for $y_{1,t+2}$ does not contain any reference to y_2. If we put this equation in place of the second equation in (7), the system will have the form

$$
(9) \quad
\begin{vmatrix} y_{1,t+1} \\ y_{2,t+1} \\ y_{3,t+1} \\ \cdots \\ y_{n,t+1} \end{vmatrix}
=
\begin{vmatrix}
0 & 1 & 0 & \cdots & 0 \\
d_{21} & d_{22} & d_{23} & \cdots & d_{2n} \\
d_{31} & d_{32} & d_{33} & \cdots & d_{3n} \\
\cdots & \cdots & \cdots & \cdots & \cdots \\
d_{n1} & d_{n2} & d_{n3} & \cdots & d_{nn}
\end{vmatrix}
\begin{vmatrix} y_{1t} \\ y_{1,t+1} \\ y_{3t} \\ \cdots \\ y_{nt} \end{vmatrix}
$$

where the matrix D_2 on the right is derived by premultiplying B_2 by N_2 given by

$$
(10) \quad N_2 =
\begin{vmatrix}
1 & 0 & 0 & \cdots & 0 \\
a_{11} & a_{12} & a_{13} & \cdots & a_{11} \\
0 & 0 & 1 & \cdots & 0 \\
0 & 0 & 0 & \cdots & 1
\end{vmatrix}
$$

thus,

(11) $D_2 = N_2 A M_2$.

Note that

(12) $N_2 M_2 = I$;

in other words, N_2 and M_2 are inverses of one another.

In (9) we have succeeded in eliminating y_2 from the system. We can now repeat this process to eliminate, one by one, all the variables other than y_1 from the system. When finished, we will have a system of the form

(13)
$$
\begin{vmatrix}
y_{1,t+1} \\
y_{1,t+2} \\
y_{1,t+3} \\
\dots \\
y_{1,t+n}
\end{vmatrix}
=
\begin{vmatrix}
0 & 1 & 0 & \dots & 0 \\
0 & 0 & 1 & \dots & 0 \\
\dots & \dots & \dots & \dots & \dots \\
0 & 0 & 0 & \dots & 1 \\
-c_0 & -c_1 & -c_2 & \dots & -c_{n-1}
\end{vmatrix}
\begin{vmatrix}
y_{1,t} \\
y_{1,t+1} \\
y_{1,t+2} \\
\dots \\
y_{1,t+n-1}
\end{vmatrix}
$$

A matrix of the form shown on the right of (13) is called a *Frobenius* matrix, and the method we have just explained for deriving a Frobenius matrix from a given matrix A is called the Danilevsky process. The Frobenius matrix is also called the *companion* matrix.

From the last equation of (13), we read, after bringing all the right-hand side to the left side of the equation,

(14) $y_{1,t+n} + c_{n-1} y_{1,t+n-1} + c_{n-2} y_{1,t+n-2} + \dots + c_0 y_{1\,t} = 0$

If we now try a solution of (14) of the form

(15) $y_{1t} = \lambda^t$

where λ is just a (possibly complex) number and the superscript t denotes raising to a power, then we see (after dividing both sides of the resulting equation by λ^t) that there will be such a solution if and only if λ is a solution (or root) of the *characteristic polynomial*

(16) $\lambda^n + c_{n-1}\lambda^{n-1} + c_{n-2}\lambda^{n-2} + \dots + c_0 = 0$

One may reasonably ask at this point: Would we have gotten a different polynomial in (16) if we had chosen to convert (5) into a single equation involving only values of y_2 instead of y_1? The answer is No, but to demonstrate that fact, an alternative interpretation of the transformation process is useful. Let us return to the homogeneous part of equation (5),

(17) $y_{t+1} = A y_t$

and ask, under what condition would

(18) $y_t = v \lambda^t$

285

be a solution, where v is a constant vector? Direct substitution in (17) and cancellation of λ^t from both sides shows that the condition is that

(19) $\qquad v\lambda = Av$.

Values of λ for which (19) holds are called *characteristic* values of the matrix A and the corresponding vectors are called *characteristic* vectors. (The half-German words *eigenvalues* and *eigenvectors* are also in common use in English. One occasionally sees the older *proper* or *secular* values and vectors.) Well, how does one go about finding the characteristic polynomial? You may encounter books that tell you that for (19) to have a non-zero solution, $A - \lambda I$ must be singular, so its determinant must be zero, and its determinant is a polynomial in λ. That is true but useless information, since computing the determinant as a function of λ is an enormous and complicated job by the usual definitions of determinants when n is more than 2 or 3. Is there a simpler way?

There is, and you already know it; but to bring that knowledge into consciousness we need a simple definition and theorem. A matrix A is said to be *similar* to a matrix B if there exists a nonsingular matrix M such that $A = MBM^{-1}$. You can easily show that if A is similar to B, then B is similar to A, so we can say simply that they are similar without bothering over which is similar to which. Moreover, if A and B are similar and B and C are similar, then A and C are similar. The theorem we need is simply: *Similar matrices have the same characteristic roots.* Proof: suppose that $Bv = \lambda v$ and $A = MBM^{-1}$. Then $A(Mv) = MBM^{-1}(Mv) = MBv = M(\lambda v) = \lambda(Mv)$, so that λ is also a characteristic value of A with Mv as the associated characteristic vector.

Now recall that in the Danilevsky method, N_2 and M_2 are inverses of one another, so that D_2 in (11) is similar to A. At each further step in the Danilevsky method, similarity is maintained, so that the Frobenius matrix in (13) is similar to A. Furthermore, λ is a characteristic root of the Frobenius matrix if and only if it satisfies the polynomial equation (16), for in that case

$$(20) \qquad \lambda \begin{vmatrix} 1 \\ \lambda \\ \lambda^2 \\ \dots \\ \lambda^{n-1} \end{vmatrix} = \begin{vmatrix} 0 & 1 & 0 & \dots & 0 \\ 0 & 0 & 1 & \dots & 0 \\ \dots & \dots & \dots & \dots & \dots \\ 0 & 0 & 0 & \dots & 1 \\ -c_0 & -c_1 & -c_2 & \dots & -c_{n-1} \end{vmatrix} \begin{vmatrix} 1 \\ \lambda \\ \lambda^2 \\ \dots \\ \lambda^{n-1} \end{vmatrix}$$

No two *different* Frobenius matrices are similar to one another, for if they were similar, they would have the same roots and therefore have the same bottom row, and therefore be identical. If we had wanted an equation in y_2 instead of y_1, we would have begun the Danilevsky process by interchanging the first and second rows and then the first and second columns. You can easily verify that the matrices which accomplish these operations by pre- and post-multiplication are inverses of one another, so that the resulting matrix is similar to the original A. Thus, the final Frobenius matrix is similar to A and thus is the same as the one obtained without interchange of rows and corresponding columns.

We can now bring to bear on the solution of a system of difference equations a few well-known facts about the roots of polynomials. These are:

(a) An nth degree polynomial $P(\lambda)$ – such as (16) – has n roots $\lambda_1, \lambda_2 \ldots, \lambda_n$, and can be factored and written $P(\lambda)=(\lambda-\lambda_1)(\lambda-\lambda_2)\ldots(\lambda-\lambda_n)$. If the roots are not all distinct, tiny changes in the coefficients of the polynomial will make them distinct.

(b) Some or all of the roots may be complex, that is, they may be of the form $a + bi$, where a and b are real numbers and $i^2 = -1$. Any complex roots occur in conjugate pairs: if $a + bi$ is a root, so is $a - bi$.

We will consider only the case in which all the roots are distinct, since, for equations with empirically determined coefficients, that is almost certainly the case. If the roots of A are distinct, the corresponding characteristic vectors, V_1 , V_2 , ..., V_n, are linearly independent, for suppose that, to the contrary, one of them, say, V_{r+1}, is a linear combination of r linearly independent ones:

$$(21) \qquad V_{r+1}=\sum_{j=1}^{r} b_j V_j \quad .$$

We could then multiply both sides of (21) by A to obtain

$$(22) \qquad \lambda_{r+1} V_{r+1}=\sum_{j=1}^{r} \lambda_j b_j V_j$$

But we could also simply multiply both sides of (21) by λ_{r+1} and subtract from (22) to get

$$(23) \qquad 0=\sum_{j=1}^{r} b_j(\lambda_j-\lambda_{r+1}) V_j$$

But since all the $(\lambda_j-\lambda_{r+1})\neq 0$, equation (23) contradicts the assumption that V_1, ..., V_r are linearly independent.

We have now found n *different* solutions, $V_1\lambda_1^t, V_2\lambda_2^t, \ldots, V_n\lambda_n^t$, , to the homogenous system of difference equations (5) or (17). You can also easily see that multiplying any one of these solutions by a constant gives a solution and that the sum of several solutions is also a solution. Thus

$$(24) \qquad y_t=\sum_{j=1}^{n} b_j V_j \lambda_j^t$$

is also a solution. We may, in fact, call it the *general* solution of the homogeneous equation, for the b_j can be determined to satisfy any *initial condition*, that is, to give any required value of y_0, since for $t = 0$, (24) becomes

$$(25) \qquad y_0=\sum_{j=1}^{n} b_j V_j$$

which is just a non-singular system of linear equations to determine the b's.

Finally, let x_t be *any* solution of the non-homogeneous equation (1), which we repeat here with x as the argument:

(26) $x_{t+1} = Ax_t + f_t$

Note that this x_t may very well not satisfy the initial conditions we will need. The general solution of the system (1) is then

(27) $y_t = \sum_{j=1}^{n} b_j V_j \lambda_j^t + x_t$

That is to say, the values of the b's can be determined to match any initial condition. In the case of complex roots, the roots occur in conjugate pairs and the corresponding characteristic vectors are also complex conjugates. The b's corresponding to conjugate vectors will also be conjugate. Thus, all complex numbers occurring in the summation on the right of (27) occur in conjugate pairs, so that the complex parts cancel out. Thus, though the right side of (27) may be strewn with complex numbers, the left side, the part we actually see in the solution, has only real numbers.

2. Frequency Response

We have given much attention in the preceding section to the general solution of the homogeneous equations but said almost nothing about particular solutions to the full, non-homogeneous system

(1) $y_{t+1} = Ay_t + f_t$

or, in terms of the single, n^{th} order equation for one of the variables,

(2) $y_{1,t+n} + c_{n-1} y_{1,t+n-1} + c_{n-2} y_{1,t+n-2} + \ldots + c_0 y_{1\ t} = f(t)$

We will now employ mainly the single equation form (2) and drop the 1 subscript, since the same equation right-hand side applies to any of the variables.

In the study of dynamic systems, the function $f(t)$ is often called the *input* function, while y is the *output*, terms which correspond closely to our exogenous and endogenous variables.

There is not a lot that can be said in general about the particular solutions, but for specific $f(t)$ functions, there are easily found particular solutions. For example, if $f(t)$ is a constant, then there is a particular solution which is constant and its value is easily calculated from (2). If $f(t)$ is a polynomial in t, then there is a particular solution having the form of a polynomial of the same degree in t.

If

(3) $f(t) = \gamma^t$

where γ is some possibly complex constant, then, as you can see by substitution, there is a particular solution $y_t = b\gamma^t$ where b is a constant with value

(4) $b = \dfrac{1}{\gamma^n + c_{n-1}\gamma^{n-1} + c_{n-2}\gamma^{n-2} + \ldots + c_0}$.

This function is called the *frequency response* function for reasons we now need to explain.

As already noted, some of the λ may be complex; if so, they occur in conjugate pairs. In this context, a complex root is most revealingly thought of in its polar representation,

$$(5) \quad \lambda = r(\cos\alpha + i\sin\alpha)$$

as illustrated in Figure 7.1 to the right. The particularly attractive aspect of the polar representation is that multiplication of two complex numbers amounts to the multiplication of their absolute values, r, and *addition* of their angles, α. Thus, if

$$\lambda_1 = r(\cos\alpha + i\sin\alpha)$$
$$\lambda_2 = r(\cos\beta + i\sin\beta)$$

Figure 7.1

then

$$\lambda_1\lambda_2 = rs(\cos\alpha\cos\beta - \sin\alpha\sin\beta + i(\sin\alpha\cos\beta + \cos\alpha\sin\beta))$$
$$= rs(\cos(\alpha+\beta) + i\sin(\alpha+\beta))$$

by the formulas for the sine and cosine of the sum of two angles. With λ given by (4),

$$(6) \quad \lambda^t = r^t(\cos t\alpha + i\sin t\alpha) \ .$$

Thus, terms of the general solution coming from real roots either grow or decline exponentially, while terms stemming from complex roots oscillate, with the amplitude of the oscillations either growing or declining exponentially depending on the absolute value of the root. The frequency of the oscillation is determine by the angle α of the root; it does not change as the amplitude swells or dampens. If all of the roots of the homogeneous part are less than 1.0 in absolute value, the system is said to be *stable*.

In a stable system, a major question is how it responds to a sinusoidal input represented by (3). According to the absolute value of b in equation (4), the frequency response curve, the system may magnify the oscillations at some frequencies while dampening them at others.

To illustrate these ideas, we may consider a second order system with two complex conjugate roots given by $\lambda_1 = r(\cos\alpha + i\sin\alpha)$ and $\lambda_2 = r(\cos\alpha - i\sin\alpha)$. For this system, the polynomial (7.1.6) is given by

$$(7) \quad (\lambda - r(\cos\alpha + i\sin\alpha))(\lambda - r(\cos\alpha - i\sin\alpha)) = \lambda^2 - \lambda 2r\cos\alpha + r^2 = 0 \ .$$

Let us take three cases, all with $\alpha = \pi/4$ so that $\cos\alpha = .70711$, and with $r = .99$, 1.0, and 1.01, respectively. In the first case, the system is just inside the stable zone; in the third, it is mildly explosive; and in the second, it is exactly on the boundary. The three equations, in the form of equation (4), are

$$y_t - 1.40008\,y_{t-1} + .9801\,y_{t-2} = 0$$
$$y_t - 1.41422\,y_{t-1} + 1.0000\,y_{t-2} = 0$$
$$y_t - 1.42836\,y_{t-1} + 1.0201\,y_{t-2} = 0$$

These three equations were simulated from 1960.1 to 2007.4 with the initial condition that $y_{1960.1} = 0, y_{1960.2} = 0,$ and $y_{1960.3} = 1.0$. The result is shown in the graph labeled "Deterministic Solutions" below. All three equations show a strict periodicity of 8 periods per cycle, as could be predicted from the fact that $\alpha = \pi/4$ radians, so that it requires 8 periods to move completely around the 2π radians of the full circle. The top equation, with r = .99 diminishes steadily in amplitude; the middle one, with r = 1.00 keeps a constant amplitude; the third, with r = 1.01 gradually increases in amplitude.

Deterministic Solutions

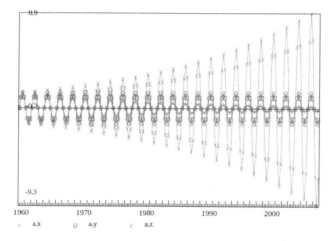

(The simulations were made by running a model made from the following Master file:

```
fex y = 0
fex z = 0
fex x = 0
r x = 1.400078*x[1] - .9801*x[2] + e1
d
r y = 1.41422*y[1] - 1.00*y[2] + e1
d
r z = 1.428362*z[1] -1.0201*z[2] + e1
d
end
```

and *e1* was given the value of 1 in 1960.3 and otherwise 0.)

These results are, of course, exactly in line with expectations from the theory. But now let us try something different.

Let us simulate the equations with random error terms, ε_t, generated by the *@normal()* function of *G7* to be a series of independent random variables each normal (0,1). One might imagine that these shocks would cancel out or that the result would be utterly chaotic. In fact, the result is quite different, as shown by the graph below labeled "Stochastic Simulation". At the beginning, the result is quite irregular and quite similar for all three equations. Then gradually a pattern emerges, namely exactly the 8-period cycle of the deterministic simulations. The equation with the root just outside the unit circle is clearly exploding, but the equation with the root just inside the unit circle is *not* converging to zero but to a sort of limit cycle. The equation with the root on the unit circle seems *labile*, equally prone to expanding or contracting.

Stochastic Simulation

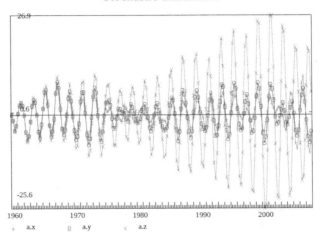

α/π	$|b|$
0.00	1.72
0.05	1.80
0.10	2.07
0.15	2.74
0.20	4.95
0.25	71.07
0.30	4.22
0.35	1.99
0.40	1.27
0.45	0.92
0.50	0.71
0.55	0.58
0.60	0.50
0.65	0.43
0.70	0.39
0.75	0.36
0.80	0.33
0.85	0.32
0.90	0.30
0.95	0.30
1.00	0.30

This tendency of the system to oscillate at a specific frequency when subject to utterly random shocks is surely both beautiful and somewhat mysterious. I will refer to it as the *emergent cycle* phenomenon. You will recognize it as reminiscent of the cycles which appeared in running the *AMI* model of Chapter 1. Our analysis, however, can now throw some light on why it happens.

Think about what equation (3) would mean if γ were a complex number lying on the unit circle in the complex plane. If we think of time as continuous, its real part would follow a cosine function while its imaginary part followed a sine curve. If time is discrete, then we observe only equally spaced points on those curves. The particular solution, $y_t = b\gamma^t$, looks much the same – also sine and cosine functions with the same frequency as the input function – but with a different amplitude given by the absolute value of b. The box to the right shows the absolute value of b calculated by equation (4) for various values of γ lying on the unit circle at values of α/π shown in the left column of the box. At a frequency of $.25\pi$, there is an enormous, 71-fold amplification of the input signal. This frequency corresponds, of course, to the root which lies just inside the unit circle at that frequency. Other frequencies are much less magnified, and the high frequencies are damped. This function is called the *frequency response function* of the system. It is closely related to the *transfer function* commonly used in engineering analysis of systems. A graph of the function for our equation is shown below.

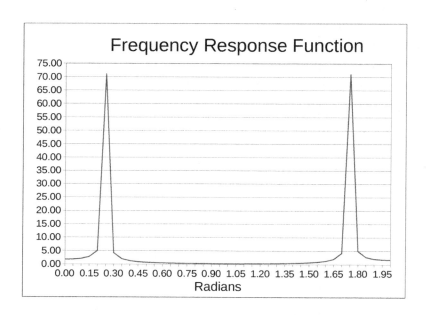

3. Explaining the Emergent Cycle Phenomenon

We can think of the input to the system, the series of random shocks, as the sum of T different functions, where T is the number of periods over which the system is run:

$$(8) \quad f(t) = f_1(t) + f_2(t) + \ldots + f_T(t)$$

where $f_j(t) = 0$ for $j \neq t$, and is equal to the value of the shock in period t for $j = t$. Because of the linearity of the system, the solution with the input $f(t)$ is the sum of the solutions for each of the separately. The solution for $f_j(t)$ is zero for $t < j$; thereafter, it follows a damped sinusoidal curve that can be thought of as $y_{j\,t} = b_j r^t \gamma^t$, where $r\gamma$ is the root, with γ lying on the unit circle. (In systems of order higher than 2, there may be other terms in the solution for y_{jt}; we assume that all but the largest complex root damp away quick and leave us concerned only with its contribution to the solution.) The complex number b_j is determined by the initial condition. By (8), therefore, the output, *y(t)*, is

$$(9) \quad y_{jt} = \left(\sum_{j=1}^{t} b_j r^{t-j} \right) \gamma^t = A_t \gamma^t \quad ,$$

where the second equation defines the complex number A_t. The γ^t on the right represents a steady sinusoidal function with a fixed frequency. Multiplication by the complex number A_t in front of it changes its amplitude and shifts its phase – that is, it adds the angle of A_t to that of y' – but it does not change its frequency. At first, as the system starts up, each period brings significant changes to A_t, and the output does not look much like a sine curve. As A_t builds up, however, as it will do if r is close to 1, the new addition to A_t, which is probably typical of the terms already in it, will bring little change to the number, so that the change in $f(t)$ over a few periods will be determined chiefly by y' and will look much like a sine curve.

An alternative way to explain the emergent cycle phenomenon is to use a different decomposition of the input function, this time as a sum of sine and cosine functions as follows. Let T+1 be the total length of the simulation with observations numbered $t = 0, 1, 2, ...$ T, and, to keep matters simple, let T be an even number and define $M = T/2$. Further, define the angles

$$(10) \qquad \omega_j = \frac{2\pi j}{T+1} \quad \text{for } j = 1, ..., M$$

and the variables

$$(11) \qquad x_j(t) = \cos\omega_j t \quad \text{and} \quad y_j(t) = \sin\omega_j t \quad \text{for } j = 1, 2, ..., M$$

Notice that as t goes from 0 to T, the cosine function $x_1(t)$ makes one complete cycle (except for the last point), $x_2(t)$ makes two complete cycles (except for the last point), and so on. The same is true for the sine functions. Now let us imagine regressing the input function, $f(t)$ on these $2M$ variables plus an intercept. Since we have T variables and T points, we will get a perfect fit and can write

$$(12) \qquad f(t) = a_0 + \sum_{j=1}^{M} a_j x_j(t) + b_j y_j(t)$$

(There is no problem about the linear independence of the various x_j and y_j variables; in fact, they are orthogonal, so the a's and b's can be computed one-by-one, but these facts need not detain us here.)

To use what we know about the frequency response function, equation (4), we just need to convert (16) into a weighted sum of powers of a complex number on the unit circle. To do so, just define

$$\gamma_j = \cos\omega_j + i\sin\omega_j$$

and denote its complex conjugate by $\bar{\gamma}_j = \cos\omega_j - i\sin\omega_j$. Then

$$(13) \qquad \gamma_j^t = \cos\omega t + i\sin\omega t \quad \text{and} \quad \bar{\gamma}_j^t = \cos\omega t - i\sin\omega t$$

and

$$(14) \qquad \frac{a_j}{2}(\gamma_j^t + \bar{\gamma}_j^t) - \frac{ib_j}{2}(\gamma_j^t - \bar{\gamma}_j^t) = a_j\cos\omega_j t + b_j\sin\omega_j t$$

or, by defining $d_j = (a_j - i b_j)/2$,

$$(15) \qquad d_j y_j^t + \bar{d}_j \bar{y}_j^t = a_j \cos \omega_j t + b_j \sin \omega_j t .$$

Equation (12) can now be written as

$$(16) \quad f(t) = a_0 + \sum_{j=1}^{M} d_j y_j^t + \bar{d}_j \bar{y}_j^t$$

as was desired.

The frequency response function of the system, the absolute value of equation (4), evaluated at each y_j will thus show how much the system amplifies or dampens the various frequencies in the input function. Naturally, it may take a while for the strongly amplified frequency to emerge, since the initial conditions and the terms from the homogeneous part may play a prominent role at first. But as they fade out, we will observe the emergent cycle phenomenon.

This second way of trying to understand the emergent cycle phenomenon is connected with the subjects of *Fourier* and *spectral* analysis of time series. The word *spectrum* indicates the origins of the subject in the physics of light, while the expression *white noise* for a series of independent, identically distributed random variables is a hybrid between the physics of light and the physics of sound. In many technical studies, ranging from vibration in airplanes to patterns in the human heart beat, it is often just as natural to think in terms of the fraction of the total variance of the series accounted for by sinusoidal curves of different frequencies as to think in terms of the original time series. For a given T, the share of the sinusoidal curves with angular frequency ω_j in the total variance is $(a_j^2 + b_j^2)/2$. If, however, we double T, there will be twice as many frequencies, and the fraction of the variance explained by any one will go down. To get a measure associated with ω_j which is potentially independent of the length of period over which it was estimated, one conventionally concentrates on the function

$$(17) \qquad s(\omega_j) = \frac{T}{8\pi}(a_j^2 + b_j^2)$$

which is called the *spectrum* of the series. The real usefulness of this way of looking at a time series is that the spectrum of the output of a linear system is the spectrum of the input multiplied by the frequency response function of the system, as we have essentially already seen.

We have seen, I believe, that the *concepts* of spectral analysis can be useful in *understanding* why models of the economy -- and even the economy itself -- can have a tendency to cycle. Is it useful to look at the spectra of economic time series? I was once hopeful that it might be. And for analysis of seasonal patterns, perhaps it is. But for the study of business fluctuations in the economy, I have been unimpressed. All the interesting historical particularities of each cycle get mushed together. For heart beats or airplane vibrations, the only thing that matters is the repetitious pattern. But we live inside business cycles; we watch them develop, we follow each with its own fascinating quirks. We have stories to tell about what caused this or that turn of a series. All that gets lost in the spectra which, to me at least, look pretty uninteresting.

Looking at the response of a model to a cycle in an exogenous variable, however, could be much more interesting. Most models, of course, are nonlinear, even if only in the value = price*quantity equations. The strict linearity assumptions about the model made in this chapter will not hold in practice. Nonetheless, you may find here some interesting possibilities for experimentation with your model, as suggested in the following exercise.

Exercise

7.1 Explore the sensitivity of your model to cycles in the exogenous variables. For example, if gR is an exogenous variable, make up this substitute for it:

f   gRalt = gR + 100.*@sin(2*3.14159*.2*time)

This *gRalt* will have a sine curve of amplitude 100 with a five year period added to the historical values of *gR*. Save it into a file, edit the file to introduce the variable with "update gR", and *add* this file at the] prompt before running the model. Compare the results of the model run with this value of government purchases with the historical simulation. Repeat the experiment with different values of the fraction before the *time* variable. Does your model, or more specifically, *gdpR* in your model, respond differently to different frequencies of variation in *gR*?

Part III. Multisectoral Models

Input-Output Flow Table

Seller \ Buyer	Agriculture	Mining	Gas & Elec	Manufac- turing	Com- merce	Trans- port	Ser- vices	Govt. Ind	Consump- tion	Govern- ment	Invest- ment	Exports	Imports	Final Demand	Row Sum
Agriculture	20	1	0	100	5	0	2	0	15	1	0	40	-20	36	164
Mining	4	3	20	15	2	1	2	0	2	1	0	10	-10	3	50
Gas&Electric	6	4	10	40	20	10	25	0	80	10	0	0	0	90	205
Mfg	20	10	4	60	25	18	20	0	400	80	200	120	-170	630	787
Commerce	2	1	1	10	2	3	6	0	350	10	6	10	0	376	401
Transport	2	1	5	17	3	2	5	0	130	20	8	5	0	163	198
Services	6	3	8	45	20	5	20	0	500	40	10	30	-20	560	667
GovInd	0	0	0	0	0	0	0	0	0	150	0	0	0	150	150
Intermediate	60	23	48	287	77	39	80	0							614
Deprec.	8	4	40	40	25	30	20	0							167
Labor	68	21	31	350	150	107	490	150							1367
Capital	20	2	56	60	40	12	59	0							259
Indirect tax	8	0	20	50	109	10	18	0							215
Value added	104	27	147	500	324	159	587	150							2008
ColSum	164	50	205	787	401	198	667	150	1477	312	224	215	-220	2008	

CHAPTER 15. INPUT-OUTPUT IN THE IDEAL CASE

15.1. Input-Output Flow Tables

Multisectoral models begin from an accounting of the flows of goods and services among various industries of the economy. Table 15.1 shows a simple interindustry accounting, or input-output flow table, for an imaginary but not unrealistic eight-sector economy which we will call *Tiny*. The simplicity is to make it easy for us to concentrate on essential concepts without being overwhelmed by big tables of data. In Table 15.1, the selling industries are listed down the left side of the table. The last industry, abbreviated as "GovInd," is "Government Industry", a fictitious industry which simply supplies the government with the services of its own employees. Below these come the classes of factor payments: Depreciation, Labor compensation, Capital income (such as interest, profits, rents, or proprietor income), and Indirect taxes (such as property taxes, sales taxes, and excise taxes as on alcohol, tobacco, and gasoline). Note the similarity of these categories of factor payments to the categories of national income. Their sum is the row named Value added. Across the top of the table the same eight industries are listed as buyers of products. Here they are followed by columns corresponding to the principal divisions of the "product side" of the national accounts:

- Con - Personal consumption expenditure

- Gov - Government purchases of goods and services

- Inv - Investment

- Exp - Exports

- Imp - Imports (as negative numbers)

In input-output terms, these are the final demand columns. The next-to-last column, labeled FD for "Final Demand," shows their sum. It is shaded to emphasized that it is derived by summing other columns. The next last column, also shaded, is the sum of all the (non-shaded) elements row.

Across each row of the table the sales of that industry to each of the industries and final demand columns are shown. Thus, the 100 in the Agriculture row and Manufacturing (Mfg) column means that Agriculture sold 100 billion dollars (bd) of products to Manufacturing in the year covered by this table. Typical sales here are grains to milling, live animals to meat packing, or fruits and vegetables to plants which can or freeze them. The 15 in the Personal consumption (Con) column of the same row means that Agriculture sold 15 bd of products directly to households during the year. These sales are primarily fresh fruits and vegetables and eggs. In the table shown here, which is in producer prices, agricultural products are recorded at the price the farmer received for them. These products are not necessarily bought at the farm gate. Going through wholesale and retail trade channels does not change the industry of origin of a product; going through a manufacturing process does. Thus, an orange sold as an orange to she who eats it appears as a sale from Agriculture to Personal consumption, despite the fact that it was purchased in a store. Another orange that was turned into frozen orange juice appears first as a sale from Agriculture to Manufacturing at the price received by the farmer. It then reappears as a sale from Manufacturing to Personal consumption at the manufacturer's price. Yet the price paid by the ultimate consumer is neither the price received by farmer in the first case nor by the manufacturer in the second. Where is the difference, the commercial margin? In this table, it is in the sales of Commerce to Personal consumption expenditure. Transportation margins are handled similarly. Tables made with this pricing convention are said to be "in producer prices". We shall look at other ways of handling the problem of margins in Chapter 16.

As we look down the column for an industry, we see all the products which it needs for making its own. In the Agriculture column, we see first of all 20 bd from Agriculture itself. These are sales primarily of feed grains to animal husbandry, but include also sales of seed, hay, manure, and other products. These sales within the industry are common and are referred to in input-output jargon as "diagonals" because they appear on the main diagonal of the table. Further down the Agriculture column we see 4 bd for Mining, primarily crushed limestone, but also some coal. The 20 bd spent on Manufacturing bought gasoline, fertilizers, and pesticides. The 2 bd spent on Commerce were trade margins on these manufactured products. The 2 bd spent on Transport included transportation margins on the products of the other industries as well as costs incurred by the farmer in getting products to market. The purchases from Services includes the services of veterinarians, lawyers, and accountants. All the purchases of the industries from each other are called "intermediate" purchases because they do not go directly to the final user but are "mediated" by other industries. The sum of the intermediate purchases by each industry are in the row labeled "Intermediate" and shaded, as before, to show that it is derived by adding other entries in the table.

Below the "Intermediate row" are the value-added rows. We find that Depreciation of

Table 15.1. Input-Output Flow Table

Seller \ Buyer	Agri	Min	Gas & Elec	Mfg	Com	Trans-port	Ser-vices	Gov Ind	Con	Gov	Inv	Exp	Imp	FD	Row Sum
Agriculture	20	1	0	100	5	0	2	0	15	1	0	40	-20	36	164
Mining	4	3	20	15	2	1	2	0	2	1	0	10	-10	3	50
Gas&Electric	6	4	10	40	20	10	25	0	80	10	0	0	0	90	205
Mfg	20	10	4	60	25	18	20	0	400	80	200	120	-170	630	787
Commerce	2	1	1	10	2	3	6	0	350	10	6	10	0	376	401
Transport	2	1	5	17	3	2	5	0	130	20	8	5	0	163	198
Services	6	3	8	45	20	5	20	0	500	40	10	30	-20	560	667
GovInd	0	0	0	0	0	0	0	0	0	150	0	0	0	150	150
Intermediate	60	23	48	287	77	39	80	0							614
Deprec.	8	4	40	40	25	30	20	0							167
Labor	68	21	31	350	150	107	490	150							1367
Capital	20	2	56	60	40	12	59	0							259
Indirect tax	8	0	20	50	109	10	18	0							215
Value added	104	27	147	500	324	159	587	150							2008

equipment came to 8 bd. Labor received 68 bd. (In our imaginary economy, we imagine that proprietor income has been divided between labor and capital income. In most actual tables, it will be shown separately or classified as capital income.) The 20 bd of capital income includes interest payments, corporate profits, and capital's portion of proprietor income. The 8 bd of Indirect taxes is mostly property taxes.

The Capital income row of value added includes both corporate profits and proprietor income. Since it is the total of sales minus the total of expenses, the column sum for each industry is equal to its row sum. For example, the row sum of Agriculture is 164 and the column sum (of the unshaded entries) is 164, and so on for all eight industries. This fact has a remarkable consequence which is the cornerstone of national accounting, namely that the sum of all the value-added entries is equal to the sum of all the final demand entries. In our table, each of these groups of entries is surrounded by a double line and each adds to 2008. Why is the total the same? Since the sum of each of the eight industry rows is equal to the sum of the corresponding column, the sum of all eight rows, 2622, say R," is equal to the sum of all eight columns, say C, which is also 2622. Thus we have R = C. But the total of the final demands, D, is R minus the total of the intermediate flows, say X, or D = R - X. Likewise, the total value added, V, is C, the sum of all the industry columns, less the sum of that part of them which is intermediate, or V = C - X. But R = C implies that R - X = C - X or D = V. Naturally, this D or V has a name, and that name is Gross Domestic Product. We have thus proved the fundamental identity of national accounting: Gross Domestic Product (GDP) is the same whether measured by the products that go to final demand or by the income which goes to factors. In our table, this identity appears in the fact that the sum of the FD column, 2008, is the sum of the Value added row, also 2008, which is the GDP of this economy. Arrayed in format of national accounts, our economy would appear as in Table 15.2.

Table 15.2 The Income and Product Account

Gross domestic produc	2008	Gross domestic produ
Personal consumptio	1477	- Depreciation
Investment	224	= Net domestic prodi
Exports	215	- Indirect taxes
Imports	-220	= National income
Government purchas	312	Labor income

Before leaving Table 15.1, we must make a fundamental point about it. With one small exception, the table makes sense in physical units. We can measure the output of Agriculture in bushels, that of Mining in tons, that of Gas and Electricity in BTU's, Transport in ton-miles, Labor in worker hours, Capital income in ounces of gold, and so on. Wassily Leontief, maker of the first input-output table, used to often insist in seminars that any calculations had to make sense in physical terms[12].

The small exception, however, is important: the column sums of a table in physical terms are utterly meaningless since all the elements are in different units. Naturally, the row totals -- which are meaningful -- do not equal the meaningless totals of the corresponding columns. This point would seem so obvious as to be not worth making were it not for the fact that it is often forgotten, precisely by the makers of input-output tables. For if a table is made in the prices of some year other than the year to which it refers, it is essentially in physical units. Thus, we can make a table for 2000 in 1980 prices, where the physical measure in each row is "one 1980 dollar's worth" of the product. In other words, the physical unit for each product is how much of it one dollar would buy in 1980. For any product for which a price index can be made, 2000 dollar amounts can be converted into 1980 dollar physical units by the price index. For value added, since there is no very natural unit, one can simply deflate all of the value-added cells by the GDP deflator. The total real value added will then be the same as total real final demand. One can have in this way a perfectly sensible, meaningful table. *But its column sums are meaningless and certainly do not equal the corresponding row sums.*

Unfortunately, some table makers have disregarded this fact and have simply forced the value added in each industry of such a table to equal the difference between the row sum of the industry and the sum of the intermediate inputs into it. The results make as much sense as saying that five squirrels minus three elephants equals two lions. The arithmetic is right but the units are crazy.

This practice is called "double deflation" because first the outputs are deflated and then the purchased inputs deflated and subtracted from the deflated output to obtain a mongrel, mixed-up-units number, possibly positive but also possibly negative, mistakenly alleged to be a measure of "constant-price value added". It is indeed what would have been left over for paying primary factors, had producers gone right on producing with the previous period's inputs after prices have changed. That is certainly no measure of "real value added," for it is not, in all probability, what producers did. The error would perhaps be easier to see if labor input, for which we have some measures of cost, were considered as an intermediate input and indirect taxes were simply subtracted in current prices from output. The double-deflation procedure should then give a measure of "real capital income." In such a table, the deflators for capital income would be different in different industries. The residuals might well be negative, especially if there were a few years between the two periods. Trying to deflate the difference between two numbers that are very close together by deflating each of the two numbers by different deflators and then taking the difference between the two deflated items is simply asking for trouble.

The difficulties due to double deflation are often masked by the taking the time periods

---

12 In fact, tables in physical terms have been developed for several countries, and are essential to the study of materials flows.

of the tables close together and "chaining" the index, so that negative values are unlikely. But the calculation still really does not make sense. Unfortunately, these procedures are sanctioned by international statistical standards, and many statistical offices engage in them. Economists have made matters worse by taking these mixed-units numbers as measures of "real" product in studies of productivity.

As far as I am aware, there is no satisfactory way of measuring real productivity at the individual industry level, precisely because industries cooperate with one another in production, and how they do so changes. In one year, for example, the "television set industry" is a collection of plants that make the cabinets, the tubes and the electronics, and assemble the sets. In a later year, the industry has become assembly plants that buy cabinets, tubes, and electronics and assemble them. Clearly, changes in sales (even in constant prices) divided by labor input in worker hours in this one industry is not an appropriate measure of productivity increase. Rather, changes in "productivity" in this case is meaningful only as applied to how much labor and capital is required by the whole economy to produce a television set. We shall see how it can be meaningfully calculated. The meaningful, correct calculation has nothing whatever to do with double deflation. But the quest to allocate the changes in whole-economy productivity for particular products to individual industries is a search for a nonexistent – and superfluous – El Dorado[13].

15.2. Input-Output Equations. The Fundamental Theorem.

An input-flow table describes an economy in a particular year. Its greatest value, however, lies in the ability it gives us to answer the question What would the outputs, value added, and intermediate flows have been had the final demands been different? To answer that question in the simplest possible way, we must assume that the ratio of each input into an industry to that industry's output remains constant when the final demands are changed. These ratios are known as the "input-output coefficients," and may be defined by

$$a_{ij} = \frac{x_{ij}}{q_j}$$

where x_{ij} is the flow from industry i to industry j in Table 14.1 and q_j is the output of industry j, that is, it is the sum of row j or column j in the same table. For example,

$$a_{1,4} = \frac{100}{787} = 0.12706$$

Table 14.3 shows the complete matrix of these input-output coefficients corresponding to Table 14.1.

Table 15.3. Input-Output Coefficients

---

13 A mythical "city of gold", searched for by Sir Walter Raleigh and many Spanish explorers.

	Agric	Mining	Gas&Elec	Mfg	Com	Trans	Serv	GovInd
Agriculture	0.1220	0.0200	0.0000	0.1271	0.0125	0.0000	0.0030	0.0000
Mining	0.0244	0.0600	0.0976	0.0191	0.0050	0.0051	0.0030	0.0000
Electricity	0.0366	0.0800	0.0488	0.0508	0.0499	0.0505	0.0375	0.0000
Manufacturing	0.1220	0.2000	0.0195	0.0762	0.0623	0.0909	0.0300	0.0000
Commerce	0.0122	0.0200	0.0049	0.0127	0.0050	0.0152	0.0090	0.0000
Transportation	0.0122	0.0200	0.0244	0.0216	0.0075	0.0101	0.0075	0.0000
Services	0.0366	0.0600	0.0390	0.0572	0.0499	0.0253	0.0300	0.0000
GovInd	0.0000	0.0000	0.0000	0.0000	0.0000	0.0000	0.0000	0.0000

If we are willing to suppose that these coefficients remain constant as the final demand vector changes, then for any vector of final demands, f, we can calculate the vector of industry outputs, q from the equation

$$q = Aq + f \qquad (15.2.1)$$

where A is the square matrix of input-output coefficients in Table 15.3. If we happen to choose as f the column vector of final demands in Table 15.1, (the first eight elements of the FD column: (36,3,90, ..., 150)'), then q should be the column vector of industry outputs of Table 15.1 (the vector of row sums of the eight industry rows: (164,50,205,...,150)'). For other values of f, of course, we will find other values of q.

One way of solving (15.2.1) is to rewrite it as

$$(I - A)q = f$$

or

$$q = (I - A)^{-1} f$$

The matrix of $(I - A)^{-1}$ on the right of this equation is known as the *Leontief inverse* of the A matrix. For our example, it is shown in Table 14.4. Its elements have a simple meaning. Element (i,j) shows how much of product i must be produced in order to produce one unit of final demand for product j. This interpretation is readily justified by taking f to be a vector of zeroes except for a 1 in row i. Then q will be the ith column of (I - A)$^{-1}$, and its jth element will show exactly how much of product j will have to be produced in order to supply exactly one unit of i to final demand. In our example, in order to supply one unit of Agricultural product to final demand, 0.1691 units of Manufacturing must be produced. Note that, in the example, all elements of the Leontief inverse are non-negative. In view of the economic interpretation, that result is hardly surprising. Later in this chapter, we will show mathematically that the Leontief inverse from an observed A matrix is always non-negative.

Table 15.4. The Leontief Inverse $(I - A)^{-1}$

	Agri.	Mining	Gas&El.	Mfg.	Comm.	Transport	Services	Govt Ind.
Agriculture	1.1647	0.0620	0.0107	0.1634	0.0263	0.0165	0.0096	0.0000
Mining	0.0405	1.0830	0.1126	0.0352	0.0144	0.0150	0.0092	0.0000
Gas & Electric	0.0617	0.1137	1.0683	0.0748	0.0623	0.0641	0.0452	0.0000
Manufacturing	0.1691	0.2530	0.0538	1.1201	0.0791	0.1091	0.0396	0.0000
Commerce	0.0184	0.0276	0.0093	0.0185	1.0077	0.0180	0.0106	0.0000
Transport	0.0210	0.0319	0.0304	0.0297	0.0120	1.0151	0.0102	0.0000
Services	0.0604	0.0911	0.0548	0.0791	0.0612	0.0379	1.0368	0.0000
Govt Industry	0.0000	0.0000	0.0000	0.0000	0.0000	0.0000	0.0000	1.0000

We may also ask how much of a primary resource, such as Labor or Capital, would be needed for the production of a given final demand. We may define the resource coefficients similarly to the input-output coefficients by

$$r_{ij} = \frac{y_{ij}}{q_j}$$

where y_{ij} is the payment to factor i by industry j. For example, from Table 15.1, $y_{2,4}$, the payment to resource 2, Labor, by industry 4, Manufacturing, is 360. If we denote by R the matrix of the r_{ij}, then the vector of total payments to each resource for an output vector q is Rq, and for a final demand vector, f, it is

$$R(I - A)^{-1} f \quad .$$

If we now think of each row of this matrix as a row vector and sum these vectors – a process which makes sense if all the rows are measured in monetary values in the prices of the year of the table – we get a row vector v of value-added per unit of output. Just as previously we asked how output q, would change if f changed while A remains constant, we can now ask how prices p would change if v changed while A remains constant. The row vector p must satisfy the equations

$$p = pA + v \qquad\qquad (14.2.2)$$

These equations state simply that the price of a unit of each product is equal to the cost of all products used in producing that unit (the first term on the right) plus value-added per unit produced. Just as the equations (15.2.1) provide the fundamental connection in multisectoral models between final demands and outputs, so these equations provide the fundamental connection between unit value added and prices. If we want to know how specific changes in productivity or in wages in one or several industries will affect prices in all industries, these equations are the key. If we calculate the prices for v vector given in the table, we should find that all prices are equal to 1.

There is, furthermore, a relation of fundamental importance between the solutions of the two sets of equations. Namely, given any A, f, and v, the q and p which satisfy $q = Aq + f$ and $p = pA + v$ also satisfy

$$vq = pf \qquad (15.2.3)$$

This equation says that the value of the final demands evaluated at the prices implied by equations (15.2.2) are equal to the payments to the resources necessary to produce those final demands by (15.2.1). Thus, if our outputs and prices satisfy the required equations, we can be certain that GDP measured by the final demands in current prices will be equal to the GDP measured by the payments to resources (or factors) in current prices. If we build these equations into our models, we can be certain that the models will satisfy the basic accounting identity in current prices. This relation may well be called the fundamental theorem of input-output analysis. Fortunately, it is as easy to prove as it is important, and you should produce your own proof. If you need help desperately, turn the book upside down and read it.

Multiply (14.2.1) on the left by p to get
(A) $pq = pAq + pf$
Multiply (14.2.2) on the right by q to get
(B) $pq = pAq + vq$
Subtract (B) from (A) to get
(C) $0 = pf - vq$ or $pf = vq$

304

15.3. Combining Input-Output and Institutional Accounts

The national accounts which we have presented so far in connection with the input-output table lack some of the concepts which we found very useful in macroeconomic modeling, such as Personal income, Personal disposable income, Personal saving, Personal income taxes, and Government transfers to persons. The basic "institutions" in national accounts are (1) Persons, (2) Businesses, (3) Governments, and (4) Rest of World. Sometimes businesses are divided between financial and non-financial businesses, but we will not make that distinction in *Tiny*. "Persons" includes non-profit corporations such as private universities. The Rest of the World, abbreviated as RoW, shows only transactions of "institutions" of other countries with the "institutions" of the country concerned.

The institutional accounts begin with the allocation of components of value added from the input-output accounts to the institutions which receive them. Labor income is allocated to Persons; Depreciation and Capital income is allocate to Business; Indirect taxes are allocated to Governments. Government transfers, such as social insurance and welfare payments, are then moved from Governments to Persons, to give Personal income. Then taxes are moved from Persons and Business to Governments, with Disposable income as the balance.

Table 14.5. TINY: NIPA-Style Presentation Year 2000	
Persons	
+ Labor income	1367
+ Interest and dividends received	220
+ Government transfers	150
= Personal income	1737
- Personal taxes	226
= Disposable income	1511
- Personal consumption expenditure	1477
= Personal saving	34
Business	
+ Depreciation	167
+ Capital income	259
- Interest and dividends payed	220
- Investment	224
= Business saving	-28
Governments	
+ Indirect taxes	215
+ Personal taxes	226
- Government purchases of goods and services	-312
- Government transfers to persons	-150
= Government saving	-21
Rest of World	
+ Imports	220
- Exports	215
= RoW saving	5

There are several ways to present these accounts. The simplest is similar to that used in the USA NIPA and should be familiar from the discussion of the AMI model in Part 1 of this book.

A consequence of the fundamental identity of the total value added and the total final demand in the input-output table is that the total saving is identically zero. You can exercise your mental arithmetic to quickly verify this identity for *Tiny*. The NIPA-style account is clear, easy to read, and easy to convert into a program for calculation. Furthermore, data for several years can be conveniently shown in parallel columns that make comparison easy. Its disadvantage is that its form does not make evident why total saving is zero or what are matching entries. For example, the form of the accounts does not show that Personal taxes paid by Persons is the same as Personal taxes received by Governments.

That shortcoming is overcome in a second way of presenting the institutional accounts, a way I will call the Balances presentation. This presentation also makes clear why total saving is zero. It is shown in the table below.

Table 15.6. Institutional Accounts for TINY: Balances Presentation

Transaction	Persons	Business	Gov	RoW	=	PCE	Gov	Inv	NetExp
Primary distribution	1367	426	215	0	=	1477	312	224	-5
Interest and dividends	220	-220			=				
Gov't transfers	150		-150		=				
Balance: Inst. Income	1737	206	65		=	1477	312	224	-5
Direct taxes	-226		226		=				0
Balance: Disposable income	1511	206	291		=	1477	312	224	-5
Personal consumption	-1477				=	-1477			
Government purchases			-312		=		-312		
Business investment		-224			=			-224	
Net imports				5	=				5
Balance: Saving	34	-18	-21	5	=	0	0	0	0

In the first line, the "Primary distribution" of Value added, labor income is given to Persons; Depreciation and Capital income, to Business; and Indirect taxes, to Governments. To the right of the = sign are the components of Final demand. The sum of the items to the left of the = sign is, of course, equal to the sum of those on the right.

Next follow two transfer lines that (1) move Interest and dividends from the Business column to the Persons column, and (2) move Government transfers to persons from the Government column to the Persons column. The next line, labeled "Balance: Institutional Income," is a balance line, the sum of the preceeding lines. In the Persons column, it gives Personal income. Below it, the Direct taxes transfer line moves personal income taxes from Persons to Government and could also move corporate profit taxes from Business to Governments. (For *Tiny*, however, we have assumed that these corporate taxes are zero.) The next balance line, the sum of the previous balance line with the intervening transfer line, gives Disposable income by institution. Then follow the lines which subtract the final demand expenditures from the institutions which make them. The final balance line then gives the savings of each institution on the left of the = sign and zeroes on the right. Of course, the sum of the items on the left of this last line equals the sum of the items on the right, namely, zero. Thus, this presentation makes it clear why total saving, including that of the Rest of the World in our country, is always zero. The major disadvantage of this layout is that it cannot show data for several years in close proximity for easier comparison.

The international System of National Accounts (SNA) uses a presentation based on the Balances Presentation, but somewhat more complicated and much less clear. Here it is for *Tiny*.

Table 14.7. Institutional Accounts for TINY: SNA-Style Presentation

Institution	Persons		Business		Governments		Rest of World	
Transaction	Sources	Uses	Sources	Uses	Sources	Uses	Sources	Uses
Primary distribution	1367		426		215		220	215
Interest and dividends	220			220				
Government transfers	150					150		
Personal tax		226			226			
Totals	1737	226	426	220	441	150	220	215
Balance:Disposable income	1511		206		291		5	
Personal consumption expenditures		1477						
Government expenditures						312		
Business investment				224				
Totals	1511	1477	206	224	291	312	5	
Balance: Saving	34		-18		-21		5	

Under each institution are two columns, one for sources of funds for the institutions and one for uses of funds. Instead of a single line for each of the balances, two lines are necessary, one to take the totals and one to show (in the Sources column) the result of subtracting total uses from total sources. I have not shown a balance line of Institutional income (of which Personal income is a highly useful instance) because this concept plays no role in the SNA, which thus fail to give a concept useful as a base for calculating personal income taxes. The SNA presentation does not make clear why total saving is zero and requires two lines for each balance instead of one. However, I have seen a number of presentations in which the total lines ares omitted, thus making it very hard for the reader to figure out what is going on. The main virtue of the SNA presentation is that it largely avoids negative numbers.

Yet a fourth presentation combines the input-output table with the institutional accounts in what is called a Social Accounting Matrix or SAM. The SAM for *Tiny* is shown in Table 14.8. In an input-output table, the row sums equal the corresponding column sums for the industries. The SAM generalizes that idea so that all accounting identities are expressed by requiring the sum of each row to equal the sum of the corresponding column in a square matrix. In the SAM for *Tiny*, the first rows are those of the input-output table, both the products and the value-added. Below these rows, we add a row for each institution, one for each final demand column, and finally a row for saving. Between the columns for industries and the final demand columns we slip columns with the same names as the value-added rows, and then a column for each institution. After the final demand columns, we append one corresponding to the Savings row. The "Primary distribution" line of the SNA-Style accounts is then represented by the total of each type of value added into the cell at the intersection of row for the institution receiving the income and the column of the type of income. At this point, the row totals equal the column totals for the industries and for value-added components. The transfers among institutions are then shown by entering the amount in the row of the receiver and the column of the payer. The totals of each final demand column are entered into the corresponding row in the column of the institution purchasing that final demand. All row totals now equal corresponding column totals except for the four institutions. Their row totals are their receipts while their column totals are their expenditures. They differ by the amount of saving by each institution. So if we now enter these savings in the Saving row at the bottom of the table, the row totals equal the column totals also for the institutions. The row sum of the Saving row is, as has been said repeatedly, zero, so to match the Saving row, we just need an all-zero Saving column.

Social Accounting Matrices have proven quite popular with economists. They are a way to combine national accounts with a consistent input-output table and institutional accounts. Their main advantage is that the form makes the consistency evident. But as the input-output table increases in detail, the SAM becomes worse as a way of actually viewing data. Consequently, we will make no further use of SAM's and will generally use the NIPA-like presentation because of the important advantage that data for several years can be shown in parallel columns.

To illustrate the use of integrated national accounts in combination with interindustry tables, we need historical series for at least the national accounts aggregates. I have made up such a data bank for *Tiny* with the values shown above for the year 2000 and with values for other years from 1978 to 2003 made up by assuming a movement similar to that of the corresponding entry in the USA NIPA. These "historical" series are in the *Tiny* data bank.

Table 14.8. A Social Accounting Matrix for TINY

	1	2	3	4	5	6	7	8	9	10	11	12	13	14	15	16	17	18	19	20	21	22	23
	Ag	Min	G&E	Mfg	Com	Trans	Serv	Gov Ind	Dep	Labor	Capital	Ind Tax	Per-sons	Bus	Gov't	RoW	PCE	Gov	Invest	Exp	Imp	Sav	Tot
1 Ag	20	1	0	100	5	0	2	0									15	1	0	40	-20		164
2 Mining	4	3	20	15	2	1	2	0									2	1	0	10	-10		50
3 G&E	6	4	10	40	20	10	25	0									80	10	0	0	0		205
4 Mfg	20	10	4	60	25	18	20	0									400	80	200	120	-170		787
5 Commerce	2	1	1	10	2	3	6	0									350	10	6	10	0		401
6 Transport	2	1	5	17	3	2	5	0									130	20	8	5	0		198
7 Services	6	3	8	45	20	5	20	0									500	40	10	30	-20		667
8 GovInd	0	0	0	0	0	0	0	0									0	150	0	0	0		150
9 Deprec.	8	4	40	40	25	30	20	0															167
10 Labor	68	21	31	350	150	107	490	150															1367
11 Capital	20	2	66	60	40	12	59	0															259
12 IndTax	8	0	20	50	109	10	18	0															215
13 Persons										1367				220	150								1737
14 Firms									167		259												426
15 Gov't												215		226									441
16 RoW																							0
17 PCE													1477										1477
18 Gov Purch															312								312
19 Invest														224									224
20 Export																215							215
21 Import																-220							-220
22 Saving													34	-18	-21	5							0
23 Col Sum	164	50	205	787	401	198	667	150	167	1367	259	215	1737	426	441	0	1477	312	224	215	-220	0	

308

15.4. A Historical Note

All of us tend to presume that the world was made the way we found it; if there were input-output tables in it when we arrived, then they must have always been there. Of course, that is not the case. In fact, they are so much connected with the work of one man, Wassily W. Leontief, that without his remarkable contribution they would probably not have been developed until decades later. Born in St. Petersburg in 1906, he was already a university student when the Bolsheviks began taking over the educational program. He joined a group protesting this process, was caught pasting up a poster, spent a while in jail and was periodically jailed and interrogated thereafter. Though deeply interested in the economy of his country and in the efforts at economic planning, he clearly had little to hope for opportunities from the Bolshevik government. Even as an undergraduate, however, his paper on "The Balance of the Economy of the USSR" describing efforts in Russia to investigate interindustry relations came to the attention of professors in Germany. When he graduated from the University of Leningrad in 1926, he was offered the possibility of graduate study in Germany, but it was already difficult to get out of the Soviet Union. By an extraordinary turn of fate, he developed a bone tumor on his jaw. It was removed, but the surgeon warned him that he would surely soon die. Armed with the surgeon's written statement, he argued to the officials that he should be allowed to leave the country since he would certainly be useless and possibly expensive to the government. The argument worked, and in 1925 he arrived in Germany with the tumor in a bottle. It was there re-examined and found ... benign! His work in Germany led, via Nanjing, to an appointment at the National Bureau of Economic Research in New York. His theoretical writings came to the attention of the Harvard faculty which offered him an instructorship. He accepted the Harvard offer on the condition that he be given a research assistant to help him build what we would now call an input-output table. The reply informed him that the entire faculty had discussed his request and had unanimously agreed that what he proposed to do was impossible and, furthermore, that even if it were done, it would be useless. Nonetheless, they were so eager to have him come that they would grant the request and hope that he would use the resources for better purposes. He didn't. In 1936, his first results were published; in 1939 a book *Structure of the American Economy* appeared. It had input-output tables for the United States for 1919 and 1929. The theoretical parts of the book had the major ideas of input-output analysis: coefficients, simultaneous solution, and price equations. During World War II, Leontief constructed, with support of the U.S. Bureau of Labor Statistics (BLS), a 96-sector table for 1939 and, by 1944 was able to study changes in employment patterns which could be expected after the end of the war. In 1947, a second edition of the book appeared with the addition of a 1939 matrix and a comparison of input-output and single-equation projections.[14] In 1973, he was awarded the Nobel prize in economics for this work. Leontief remained active until shortly before his death in 1999 at the age of 93.

In 1949, a group at the BLS began work on a 400-sector table for 1947. A 190-sector table was published in 1952, but financing – which had come through the Defense budget –

---

14   The spelling of Leontief's name in Latin letters was for German speakers; English speakers almost invariably mispronounce it, though he never corrected anyone. In *Wassily*, the *W* is pronounced V, the *a* is long as in "father," and the accent is on the *si* which is pronounced "see". In *Leontief* the accent is on *on* and the *ie* is pronounced like the ye in "yet". The final *f* is a soft v.

for the more than fifty people working on the project was discontinued early in the Eisenhower administration, so that neither the full table nor the extensive documentation of the details of its production were ever published.

In other countries, making of tables spread rapidly. They were incorporated in the United Nation's standard System of National Accounts prepared by Richard Stone. In 1950, the first international conference on input-output methods was sponsored by the United Nations; the eleventh (without U.N. support) was held in 1995.

In the late 1950's, Soviet authors, eager to make input-output acceptable in their country, put together a table for the Soviet Union in 1924 and argued that all the essential ideas had originated in the Soviet Union. The difference, however, between what they could find in the literature of that period and Leontief's comprehensive treatment only heightens an appreciation of his contribution.

Gradually, it has come to be recognized that an input-output table is not only useful for economic analysis and forecasting but is also an essential step in making reliable national accounts. The statistical offices of most major industrial countries, therefore, prepare input-output tables, often on a regular basis. Annual tables for France, the Netherlands, Norway, and Japan are prepared as a part of annual national accounting. In the USA, a comprehensive table is made every five years in the years of economic censuses (years ending in 2 and 7) and is used in revising and "benchmarking" the national accounts. Recently, annual tables are prepared.

In 1988, the International Input-Output Association was organized as a group of individuals interested in using input-output techniques. In 1989, it began publishing its own journal, *Economic Systems Research*.

The Interdyme modeling system, like the *G7* program, was developed by the Inforum group in the Department of Economics at the University of Maryland. It has been used in developing and linking dynamic input-output models of about twenty countries. Most of these models have been developed and used mainly in the country concerned.

CHAPTER 16. INPUT-OUTPUT COMPUTATIONS

16.1. Introduction to Input-Output Computing with Just *G7*

In this section, we will see how to turn the *Tiny* input-output table and data bank into a simple input-output model using only commands available in *G7*. In this model, we will move each final demand column forward and backward over the period 1995 to 2003 by the index of the corresponding GDP component in the *Tiny* data bank. Then we move all the final demand vectors except investment up by 3.0 percent per year from 2003 to 2010. Investment is moved forward by a wavy series composed of a base series growing at 3.0 percent per year plus a sinusoidal function. Input-output coefficients and the composition of the five final demand components are kept constant. Outputs by each industrial sector are then calculated for every year from 1995 to 2010. With the additional assumption that the shares of each type of income in value added by each industry remain constant, we calculate income of each type in each industry. Piecewise linear trends in the input-output coefficients, value-added coefficients, and composition of the final demand vectors could easily be introduced, but that has been left as an exercise. This model is incomplete and somewhat inconsistent with itself for many reasons, including the following:

1. It does not assure consistency of Personal consumption expenditure with the Personal income it implies;

2. It does not relate the imports of a product to the domestic use of the product;

3. Investment is not detailed by industry and related to the growth of the industry as found by the model.

Introducing such features to exploit the full potential of input-out modeling will require the Interdyme software described in the following chapter. Despite these limitations, such simple models as the one described here, though with greater industry detail and more finely divided final demands, have been widely used by groups which have a macroeconomic model and want the industry outputs consistent with the its final demand forecasts.

Working with input-output in *G7* requires the use a VAM (Vectors And Matrices) file. As the name suggests, this type of data bank holds time series of vectors and matrices. *G7* has commands which can add, subtract, multiply, and invert matrices and add and subtract vectors and multiply them by matrices. Thus, the operations discussed so far, and several others, can easily be performed in *G7*. A VAM file differs in two important respects from the G data banks we have worked with so far:

1. In the standard G bank, all elements are the same size. Specifically, a time series of a single variable begins at the base year of the data bank and extends over the number of observations in the bank, as specified by the G.CFG file. In VAM files, elements are time series of vectors or matrices of various dimensions. As in the standard G bank, all time series are the same length.

2. In standard G banks, we can create new series as we work, for example, with *f*, *fex*, or *data* commands. In VAM files, we buy the flexibility of having elements of various sizes by

specifying at the outset (in a file usually called VAM.CFG) the contents of the file, that is, the names and dimensions of each vector or matrix in the bank along with the names of the files giving the titles of the row or columns of the vector or matrix. One might suppose that it is a bit of nuisance to have to specify this structure of the VAM file at the outset. In practice, however, this need to pre-specify structure proves a useful discipline in building complex models. If, as a model evolves, it becomes necessary to revise the specification of the VAM file, it is easy to copy the contents of the old file into the new, enlarged file, or simply to remake the VAM file.

We can illustrate the use of the VAM file and some new *G7* commands for making some simple calculations with the input-output table presented in section 1 of this chapter. In this example we will assume that the IO data are for the year 2000. The box below shows the VAM.CFG file for this model, which is called *Tiny* It and all the files used in this chapter are in TINY.ZIP. I suggest that you make a folder, copy TINY.ZIP into it, and unzip it.

Figure 16.1.

VAM.CFG for the *Tiny* Model

```
1995 2010
# Vam file for Simplest Model
FM       8   8   0   sectors.ttl sectors.ttl #Input-output flow matrix
AM       8   8   0   sectors.ttl sectors.ttl #Input-output coefficient matrix
LINV     8   8   0   sectors.ttl sectors.ttl # Leontief inverse
out      8   1   3   sectors.ttl # Output
pce      8   1   0   sectors.ttl # Personal consumption expenditure
gov      8   1   0   sectors.ttl # Government spending
inv      8   1   0   sectors.ttl # Investment
ex       8   1   0   sectors.ttl # Exports
im       8   1   0   sectors.ttl # Imports
fd       8   1   0   sectors.ttl # Total final demand
dep      8   1   0   sectors.ttl # Depreciation
lab      8   1   0   sectors.ttl # Labor income
cap      8   1   0   sectors.ttl # Capital income
ind      8   1   0   sectors.ttl # Indirect taxes
depc     8   1   0   sectors.ttl # Depreciation coefficients
labc     8   1   0   sectors.ttl # Labor income coefficients
capc     8   1   0   sectors.ttl # Capital income coefficients
indc     8   1   0   sectors.ttl # Indirect taxes coefficients
pcec     8   1   0   sectors.ttl # Personal consumption shares
invc     8   1   0   sectors.ttl # Investment shares
govc     8   1   0   sectors.ttl # Gov shares
exc      8   1   0   sectors.ttl # Export shares
imc      8   1   0   sectors.ttl # Import shares
x        8   1   0   sectors.ttl # Working space
y        8   1   0   sectors.ttl # Working space
```

The first line in VAM.CFG gives the beginning and ending years for the VAM file. The next line, the one beginning with a #, is a comment to clarify the structure of the file. Comments beginning with a # can be placed anywhere in the file. Next are the lines describing the vectors and matrices. Each line shows the following:

1. The name of the vector or matrix.

312

2. Its number of rows.
3. Its number of columns.
4. The maximum number of lags with which a vector occurs in the model or a 'p' if the matrix is a "packed matrix" – a device useful in large-scale models.
5. The name of a file containing the rows titles of a vector or matrix.
6. If applicable, the name of a file containing the columns titles of a matrix.
7. A # followed by a brief description of the element.

As far as the computer is concerned, these lines are free format; all that is needed is one or more spaces between each item on a line. However, this is a file also read by humans, so putting in spaces to make the items line up in neat columns is a good idea. Figure 16.1 shows the VAM.CFG file for the *Tiny* model based on the example of section 1 of the last chapter. (The VAM.CFG file on the zip file has more vectors than shown here. The extra ones will be used in the next chapter and, in the meanwhile, will do no harm.)

To create a vam file from a vam configuration file the command in *G7* is

vamcreate <vam configuration file> <vam file>

For example, to create the vam file HIST.VAM from the configuration file VAM.CFG, the command is

vamcreate vam.cfg hist

The "vamcreate" command may be abbreviated to "vamcr", thus:

vamcr vam.cfg hist

At this point, the newly created vam file has zeroes for all its data. We will now see how to populate the bank and work with the data. The first step is to assign it as a bank. The command is

vam <filename> <letter name of bank>

For example, we could assign HIST.VAM to the 'b' position by typing:

vam hist b

Letters 'a' through 'v' may be used to designate banks. However, it is generally a good practice to leave 'a' as the G bank which was initially assigned.

In order to avoid continually entering the bank letter, most commands for working with VAM files use the default VAM file. It is specified by the "dvam" command

dvam <letter name of bank>

For example, we can set the VAM file in position 'b' as the default by typing:

dvam b

A vam file must already be assigned as a bank before it can be made the default. However, if several VAM files are assigned, the default can be switched from one to another as often as needed.

313

The usual ways to introduce data into a VAM file are with the "matin" command for matrices and the "vmatdat" command for vectors. We can illustrate them with the data for Tiny from section 15.1.

Figure 16.2

The Flows.dat File for Introducing the Input-Output Flow Matrix into the VAM File

```
matin FM 2000 1 8 1 8   15
#            Agricul Mining Elect  Mfg Commerce Transp Services Govt
Agriculture     20      1     0   100     5       0       2      0
Mining           4      3    20    15     2       1       2      0
Electricity      6      4    10    40    20      10      25      0
Manufacturing   20     10     4    60    25      18      20      0
Commerce         2      1     1    10     2       3       6      0
Transportation   2      1     5    17     3       2       5      0
Services         6      3     8    45    20       5      20      0
Government       0      0     0     0     0       0       0      0
```

The "matin" command on the first line is followed by the matrix name in VAM.CFG, then by the year to which the matrix belongs, then the number of the first row and last row in the following rectangle of data, then the number of the first column and last column in the rectangle. (In the present case, the rectangle is the whole table; but this ability to read in a table rectangle-by-rectangle is quite useful for reading tables scanned from printed pages.) The last number on the "matin" line is the skip count, which specifies the number of characters to be skipped at the beginning of each line. These characters usually give sector names or numbers. The # in the first position marks the second line as a comment. Then come the data; each line is in free format after the initial skip. (Do not use tabs in characters which are to be skipped; the tab character will be counted as just one character.)

The FD.dat file shown below in Figure 15.3 illustrates the introduction of vectors, in this case, the final demands. The "vmatdat" command is rather flexible; it can introduce a number of vectors for one year or one vector for a number of years. The vectors can be the rows or the columns in the following rectangle of data. Because of this flexibility, we have to tell the command how to interpret the rectangle of data. The command must therefore by followed by a 'c' or an 'r' to indicate whether the vectors appear as columns or rows in the following rectangle of data. Here, the vectors are clearly columns. The next number is the number of vectors in the rectangle; here 5. Next is the number of years represented in the rectangle. Here it is 1, for the columns are different vectors for the same year. (Either the number of vectors or the number of years must be 1.) The next two numbers are the first and last element numbers of the data in the rectangle, and the last is the skip count. Since this command is introducing several vectors for one year, that year is specified at the beginning of the next line, and the names of the vectors follow it. (If we were introducing data for one vector for several years, the vector name would be in the first position on this line, followed by the year numbers.)

314

Figure 16.3. The FD.DAT File for Introducting the Final Demands into the VAM File

```
vmatdata c 5 1 1 8 15
2000            pce  gov  inv    ex      im
#             PersCon  Gov Invest Exports
Imports
Agriculture      15    1    0    40     -20
Mining            2    1    0    10     -10
Electricity      80   10    0     0       0
Manufacturing   400   80  200   120    -170
Commerce        350   10    6    10       0
Transportation  130   20    8     5       0
Services        500   40   10    30     -20
Government        0  150    0     0       0
```

The value-added rows are introduced by the "vmatdat" command and data shown in the box below. In this example, vectors are read in as rows.

Figure 16.4

The VA.DAT File for Introducing the Value-added Vectors

```
vmatdata r 4 1  1 8 15
2000  dep lab cap ind
#            1     2     3     4     5     6     7     8
Depreciation 9     4    40    40    25    30    20     0
Labor       68    21    31   350   150   107   490   150
Capital     20     2    56    60    40    12    59     0
Indirect tax 8     0    20    50   109    10    18     0
```

Here, finally, are the *G7* commands to create the VAM file and load the data into it:

```
# tiny.pre – Create the VAM file for Tiny
vamcreate vam.cfg hist
vam hist b
dvam b
# Bring in the intermediate flow matrix
add flows.dat
# Bring in the final demand vectors
add fd.dat
# Bring in the value added vectors
add va.dat
```

The complete set of commands for making the calculations described in this section are in the file GMODEL.PRE, shown in figure 15.5. To fit this large file on a single page, some commands have been doubled up on a single line but separated by a semicolon – a trick which works in *G7* just as in C++.

Figure 16.5. Gmodel.pre File to Build a *Tiny* Model Using only *G7*, No Interdyme

```
      Zap; clear
      bank tiny
      vamcreate vam.cfg hist
      vam hist b; dvam b
      # Bring in the intermediate flow matrix
      add flows.dat
      show b.FM y 2000
      # Bring in the final demand vectors
      add fd.dat
      # Bring in the value added vectors
      add va.dat
      fdates 2000 2000
      # Add up the intermediate rows
      getsum FM r out
      # Add on the final demand vectors to get total output
      vc out = out+pce+gov+inv+ex+im
      show b.out
      # Copy intermediate flows to AM and convert to coefficients
      mcopy b.AM b.FM
      coef AM out
      vc depc = dep/out; vc labc = lab/out
      vc capc = cap/out; vc indc = ind/out
      # Copy the 2000 coefficient matrices to all the other years
      fdates 1995 2010
      # Copy the 2000 AM matrix into 1995 - 2010
      dfreq 1
      f one = 1.
      index 2000 one AM
      # Demonstrate that AM has been copied by showing its first
column.
      show b.AM c 1
      index 2000 one depc; index 2000 one labc
      index 2000 one capc; index 2000 one indc
      # Move the four final demand columns by their totals
      # in the historical years, 1995 - 2003
      fdates 1995 2003
      index 2000 pcetot pce; index 2000 invtot inv ; index 2000 govtot
gov
      index 2000 extot  ex; index 2000 imtot  im
      # Extend the final demands from 2003 to 2010 using a
      # 3 percent growth rate for all but inv and a wavy
      # pattern for it.
      fdates 1995 2010
      # Create a time trend
      f time = @cum(time,one,0)
      f g03 = @exp(.03*(time-9))
      ty g03
      f waves = g03 + .3*@sin(time-9)
      ty waves
      fdates 2003 2010
      index 2003 g03   pce; index 2003 waves inv; index 2003 g03
gov
      index 2003 g03   ex; index 2003 g03   im
      # Take the Leontief inverse of the A matrix
      fdates 1995 2010
      mcopy b.LINV b.AM
      linv LINV
      show b.LINV y 2000
      # Add up the final demands
      vc fd = pce+gov+inv+ex+im
      show b.fd
      # Compute total outputs
      vc out = LINV*fd
      show b.out
      # Compute Value added
      # The following are element-by-element multiplication
      vc dep = depc*out; vc lab = labc*out
      vc cap = capc*out; vc ind = indc*out
      gdates 1995 2003 2010
      fadd graphs.fad sectors.ttl
```

Now let us look at some of the data we have introduced by displaying them in a grid on the screen. The command

```
show FM   y   2000
```

will show a spreadsheet-like grid containing the flow matrix (FM) for the year 2000. To adjust the default column width and the number of decimal places in the display, click the Options menu item. Not only does this display look like a spreadsheet, it also works like one in that you can copy and paste data from one to the other.

To look at a row, say row 2, of the FM matrix for all years of the VAM file, the command is

```
show FM r 2
```

Similarly, to show column 5 for all years, the command is:

```
show FM c 5
```

Thus, in showing a matrix, we have to choose among showing the whole matrix for one year and showing one row or one column for all years. The choice is indicated by the letter – a 'y', 'r' or 'c' – following the matrix name.

Showing vectors is simpler because we do not have to make this choice; we just name the vector and get all values for all years. Here are two examples

```
show ind    # Display the indirect tax vector
show b.pce  # Display the personal consumption expenditure vector
```

The second of these examples illustrates that the "show" command allows us to specify a bank other than the default VAM file.

Now that we have added the data and displayed it to check that it was accurately read, we can begin to perform computations. To calculate the input-output coefficient matrix, we need out, the vector of outputs by industry. It was not read in, but it can be computed by summing the rows of the FM matrix and then adding to this row sum the final demand columns. Here are the two calculations and the "show" command to view the result:

```
# Add up the intermediate rows
getsum FM r out
# Add on the final demand vectors to get total output
vc out = out+pce+gov+inv+ex+im
show b.out
```

We are now ready to copy the flow matrix, stored in FM, to AM and then convert it to input-output coefficients by dividing each element of each column by the corresponding element of the out vector. We copy the matrix with the "mcopy" command. The general form of the "mcopy" command to copy matrix or vector A from bank x to element B in bank y is

```
mcopy  y.B [=] x.A
```

The = sign is optional but is useful reminder of which way the copy is going. The y. is optional if y is the default VAM file, and the same is true for the x.. Since this copy and these calculations need be done only for one year, 2000, we first set the fdates so that the "mcopy" and "coef" commands work only on the years from 2000 to 2000 (which is to say, only for 2000). Here are the commands

```
# Copy intermediate flows to AM and convert to coefficients
fdates 2000 2000
mcopy b.AM = b.FM
coef AM out
show AM y 2000
# Create value-added coefficient vectors.
vc depc = dep/out
vc labc = lab/out
vc capc = cap/out
vc indc = ind/out
# Set fdates back to the entire range of the VAM file.
fdates 1995 2010
```

With the input-output coefficients calculated, we can now go on to illustrate finding the Leontief inverse, calculating outputs from exogenous forecasts of final demands, calculating value-added components, and displaying, graphing, and making tables of the results. We will first copy the input-output coefficient matrix and the value-added coefficient vectors from 1995 to 2010. We can conveniently do this with *G7*'s "index" command. This command is used to move all elements of a vector or matrix in the default VAM file forward or backward in proportion to a guide series. Its general form is:

index <base year>   <guide series>   <matrix or vector>

It operates over the range specified by the current fdates. Since we just want to copy the coefficients to all the years, our guide series will be simply a series of 1's, which we shall call *one*. Here are the commands

```
# Copy the 2000 AM matrix into 1995 - 2010
dfreq 1
f one = 1.
index 2000 one AM
index 2000 one depc
index 2000 one labc
index 2000 one capc
index 2000 one indc
show AM c 1
```

The last command displays the first column of the AM matrix for all the years in a grid; all columns of this display should, of course, be identical. For purposes of illustration, we will let *AM* remain constant in all years.

The final demands, however, will move in a slightly more interesting way. Between

1995 and 2003, the elements of each final demand column will follow the index of the total of that column as given by the corresponding aggregate in the national accounts. Here are the *G7* commands to make that happen.

```
# Move the four final demand columns from the 2000 value by their totals
# in the historical years, 1995 - 2003
fdates 1995 2003
index 2000 pcetot pce
index 2000 invtot inv
index 2000 govtot gov
index 2000 extot  ex
index 2000 imtot  im
```

From the base of 2003, we will have all components of final demand except investment grow at a steady 3 percent per year to 2010. Investment will also have one component growing at this same rate but added to it – to make the results more interesting to view – will be a sine curve with a period of 2π years. Here are the commands for this operation.

```
fdates 1995 2010
# Create a time trend
f time = @cum(time,one,0)
f g03 = @exp(.03*(time-9))
f waves = g03 + .3*@sin(time-9)
fdates 2003 2010
index 2003 g03   pce
index 2003 waves inv
index 2003 g03   gov
index 2003 g03   ex
index 2003 g03   im
```

To add up the components of final demand to *fd*, we use the "vc" (for vector calculation) command. It can add up any number of vectors to get a total. Here are the commands.

```
# Add up the final demands
vc fd = pce+gov+inv+ex+im
show fd
```

We are now going to ignore the fact that the AM matrix is the same in all years – we could have changed it had we wanted to – and take its Leontief inverse in all years in the fdates range. The command

```
linv  <square matrix> [year]
```

converts the square matrix into its Leontief inverse. For example,

```
linv A
```

converts A into $(I-A)^{-1}$. We then multiply this inverse by the final demand vector to compute the output vector. The "linv" command works over the fdate range unless the

319

optional year argument is present.

```
# Take the Leontief inverse of the A matrix
mcopy LINV = AM
linv LINV
show LINV y 2000
# Compute total outputs
vc out = LINV*fd
show b.out
```

With the outputs known, we can compute the implied value-added of each type by each industry with the following commands. In them, the "vc" command will recognize that the dimensions of the vectors on the right are such that element-by-element multiplication makes sense and perform the calculation.

```
# Compute Value added
# The following are element-by-element multiplication
vc dep = depc*out
vc lab = labc*out
vc cap = capc*out
vc ind = indc*out
show lab
```

As we went along, we showed results in spreadsheet-like grids to check that our answers were generally reasonable. Now we need to graph the results. In doing so, we use the fact that elements of vectors in a VAM file can be referred to in *G7* simply by the name of the vector followed by a numeral. We can graph the second element of the out and pce vectors from the VAM file assigned as bank 'b' with the graph command like this:

```
gr  b.out2   b.pce2
```

If the VAM file is the default, we can omit the bank letter and period. Thus, in the instance just given, we could just use the following command:

```
gr out2  pce2
```

This way of referring to a time series of elements of a vector works also for "type" and "r" commands and for the right-hand side of "f" or "fex" commands. Similarly, we can refer to an element of a matrix in a type, graph, or regression command or the right side of an "f" command. Specifically, to retrieve an element of a matrix, type the matrix name followed by the row number, followed by a dot, followed by the column number. For example,

```
type AM3.5
```

will print to the screen the values of the element in the third row and fifth column of the AM matrix.

We can get a lot more graphs very quickly by use of *G7*'s "fadd" command. The name "fadd" is a contraction of "file-directed add command." It works with text substitution in a way that is very convenient in working with multisectoral models. The general form is

```
fadd  <command file>   <argument file>
```

In our case, the "command file" will be GRAPHS.FAD:

```
vr 0
ti %3 %5
subti Output and Final demand
gname out%3
gr b.out%3 b.fd%3
subti Depreciation,Labor income, Capital income, Indirect taxes
gname va%3
gr b.dep%3 b.lab%3 b.cap%3 b.ind%3
ti
subti
```

The argument file will be the same SECTORS.TTL file which we used for supplying row and column titles for the matrices and vectors in the VAM file, namely:

```
Agricul      ;1    e    "Agriculture"
Mining       ;2    e    "Mining and quarrying"
Elect        ;3    e    "Electricity and gas"
Mfg          ;4    e    "Manufacturing"
Commerce     ;5    e    "Commerce"
Transport    ;6    e    "Transportation"
Services     ;7    e    "Services"
Government   ;8    e    "Government"
```

Note that some of the lines in the command file – for example, the second – have a % followed by a number. These numbers refer to "arguments" from the "argument" file. For example, on the first line of the argument file, argument 1 is Agricul, argument 2 is ;, argument 3 is 1, argument 4 is e , and argument 5 is Agriculture . Normally an argument is delimited by a space or punctuation. Enclose arguments which contain spaces – such as the names of some sectors – in quotation marks. When the second line of the command file,

```
ti %3 %5
```

is executed with the arguments 3 and 5 from the first line of the argument file replacing the %3 and %5, the effect is that *G7* executes the command

```
ti 1 Agriculture
```

The effect of the "fadd" command is that the entire command file is executed first with arguments from the first line of the argument file, then with the arguments from the second line of the argument file, and so on. Thus, with the single command

```
fadd  graphs.fad  sectors.ttl
```

G7 will draw graphs like the two shown below for Agriculture for all sectors.

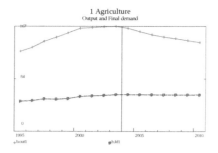

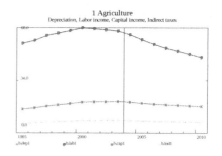

We have used some but not all of the *G7* commands for matrix arithmetic in a VAM file. For reference, here are some others.

minv A   converts A into its inverse
madd A = B + C   adds B and C and stores in A
madd A = B - C   subtracts C from B and stores result in A
mmult A = B*C   multiply B and C and store result in A
mmult A = B'C   multiplies B transpose by C and stores result in A
mmult A = B&C   does element-by-element multiplication of B and C and stores in A
mmult A = B/C   element-by-element division of B by C stored in A
mtrans A B   the transpose of B is stored in A

In all of them, the command may be followed by an optional year in which to do the calculation; absent the year, the calculation is done for all years in the *fdates* range.

For tabulating the contents of a VAM file, we use exactly the same program, *Compare*, as we have used for macro models. It has, however, some features used exclusively with vectors and matrices. First of all, when we click Model | Tables on the *G7* main menu, we need to choose "vam" as the type of the first bank, then give "hist" as its name; in the "Stub file" control, fill in "tiny", and in the "Output file name" box type "tiny.out".

Figure 15.6

The TINY.STB File

```
\dates 1995 2000 2005 2010 1995-2000 2000-2005 2005-2010
\pages off
\noformat
\title TINY G-ONLY MODEL, ILLUSTRATIVE FORECAST

; out  Output of Industries
&
out1 ;1 Agriculture
out2 ;2 Mining and quarrying
out3 ;3 Electricity and gas
out4 ;4 Manufacturing
out5 ;5 Commerce
out6 ;6 Transportation
out7 ;7 Services
out8 ;8 Government
;
\add tiny.tab pce "Personal Consumption Expenditure"
;
\add tiny.tab gov "Government Expenditures"
;
\add tiny.tab inv "Investment by Supplying Industry"
;

# The next line forces a new page
*
\matcfg Matlist.cfg
\center Matrix Listing
\row
\cutoff .001
\matlist 1-8
```

The first line with the "\dates" command is familiar from macro models. Since we want to bring the results into a word processor for printing, I have turned off the page numbering and all commands to the printer in the next two lines. The "\title" command gives a title to be printed across the top of each page of output. As with macro stub files, a line beginning with a ";" just puts the rest of the line in the output file, and a "&" command puts a line of dates across the page. The next eight lines print the output and its growth rates for the eight industries of the *Tiny* model for the dates specified.

We have not previously used *Compare's* "\add" command, which works just like *G7*'s "add" command, including a feature of the "add" command which we have yet used, namely, that it accepts arguments. The TINY.TAB file is shown in the box below. Instead of the lines in TINY.STB for printing the output of industries, we could have used the single line

\add tiny.tab out "Output of Industries"

The effect would have been exactly the same.

F

Figure 16.7

The TINY.TAB File

```
;  %1 %2
&
%11 ;1 Agriculture
%12 ;2 Mining and quarrying
%13 ;3 Electricity and gas
%14 ;4 Manufacturing
%15 ;5 Commerce
%16 ;6 Transportation
%17 ;7 Services
%18 ;8 Government
```

The TINY.TAB is a bit confusing because of the strings "%11" , "%12", and similar strings below them. To the eye, this may look like a reference to argument 11 or argument 12. But the computer knows that there can be only nine arguments and thus the third character in these strings is not part of the argument specification. It will read these as "argument 1 followed by the character 1" or "argument 1 followed by the character 2."

The results the tabulations described thus far are shown in Figure 15.8 below.

The last five lines of TINY.STB are concerned with making a matrix listing from the VAM file. A matrix listing is best explained by looking at the results, which are shown for the first three industries in the Figure 15.9 below. For each row of the input-output table, the matrix listing shows each element of the identity:

output = intermediate demand + final demand.

Indeed, each element is shown for each year specified by the "\dates" command. Growth rates of the element are shown for the periods specified by the same command. This matrix listing technique is important not only for the information it displays, but also the consistency of the forecasts which it emphasizes.

Figure 16.8

```
    TINY G-ONLY MODEL, ILLUSTRATIVE FORECAST

out  Output of Industries
                          1995    2000    2005    2010   95-00  00-05  05-10
1 Agriculture           140.7   164.0   189.6   216.7    3.1    2.9    2.7
2 Mining and quarrying   43.5    50.0    57.5    66.1    2.8    2.8    2.8
3 Electricity and gas   171.1   205.0   228.6   263.8    3.6    2.2    2.9
4 Manufacturing         663.0   787.0   908.3  1030.9    3.4    2.9    2.5
5 Commerce              331.0   401.0   439.9   510.0    3.8    1.9    3.0
6 Transportation        164.3   198.0   220.3   254.4    3.7    2.1    2.9
7 Services              555.8   667.0   738.2   854.7    3.6    2.0    2.9
8 Government            133.2   150.0   177.7   206.5    2.4    3.4    3.0

  pce Personal Consumption Expenditure
                          1995    2000    2005    2010   95-00  00-05  05-10
1 Agriculture            12.4    15.0    16.3    19.0    3.9    1.7    3.0
2 Mining and quarrying    1.6     2.0     2.2     2.5    3.9    1.7    3.0
3 Electricity and gas    65.9    80.0    87.1   101.2    3.9    1.7    3.0
4 Manufacturing         329.7   400.0   435.7   506.2    3.9    1.7    3.0
5 Commerce              288.5   350.0   381.2   442.9    3.9    1.7    3.0
6 Transportation        107.2   130.0   141.6   164.5    3.9    1.7    3.0
7 Services              412.1   500.0   544.6   632.7    3.9    1.7    3.0
8 Government              0.0     0.0     0.0     0.0    0.0    0.0    0.0

  gov Government Expenditures
                          1995    2000    2005    2010   95-00  00-05  05-10
1 Agriculture             0.9     1.0     1.2     1.4    2.4    3.4    3.0
2 Mining and quarrying    0.9     1.0     1.2     1.4    2.4    3.4    3.0
3 Electricity and gas     8.9    10.0    11.8    13.8    2.4    3.4    3.0
4 Manufacturing          71.0    80.0    94.8   110.1    2.4    3.4    3.0
5 Commerce                8.9    10.0    11.8    13.8    2.4    3.4    3.0
6 Transportation         17.8    20.0    23.7    27.5    2.4    3.4    3.0
7 Services               35.5    40.0    47.4    55.1    2.4    3.4    3.0
8 Government            133.2   150.0   177.7   206.5    2.4    3.4    3.0

  inv Investment by supplying industry
                          1995    2000    2005    2010   95-00  00-05  05-10
1 Agriculture             0.0     0.0     0.0     0.0    0.0    0.0    0.0
2 Mining and quarrying    0.0     0.0     0.0     0.0    0.0    0.0    0.0
3 Electricity and gas     0.0     0.0     0.0     0.0    0.0    0.0    0.0
4 Manufacturing         147.2   200.0   240.2   257.5    6.1    3.7    1.4
5 Commerce                4.4     6.0     7.2     7.7    6.1    3.7    1.4
6 Transportation          5.9     8.0     9.6    10.3    6.1    3.7    1.4
7 Services                7.4    10.0    12.0    12.9    6.1    3.7    1.4
8 Government              0.0     0.0     0.0     0.0    0.0    0.0    0.0
```

Figure 16.9

TINY G-ONLY MODEL, ILLUSTRATIVE FORECAST

Matrix Listing

Seller: 1 Agriculture

	1995	2000	2005	2010	95-00	00-05	05-10
Sales to Intermediate							
1 Agriculture	17.2	20.0	23.1	26.4	3.1	2.9	2.7
2 Mining and quarrying	0.9	1.0	1.2	1.3	2.8	2.8	2.8
4 Manufacturing	84.2	100.0	115.4	131.0	3.4	2.9	2.5
5 Commerce	4.1	5.0	5.5	6.4	3.8	1.9	3.0
7 Services	1.7	2.0	2.2	2.6	3.6	2.0	2.9
SUM: Intermediate	108.1	128.0	147.4	167.7	3.4	2.8	2.6
Sales to Other Final Demand							
Personal consumption expenditure	12.4	15.0	16.3	19.0	3.9	1.7	3.0
Government consumption	0.9	1.0	1.2	1.4	2.4	3.4	3.0
Exports	33.1	40.0	45.4	52.8	3.8	2.5	3.0
Imports	-13.7	-20.0	-20.8	-24.1	7.6	0.8	3.0
Output	140.7	164.0	189.6	216.7	3.1	2.9	2.7

Seller: 2 Mining and quarrying

	1995	2000	2005	2010	95-00	00-05	05-10
Sales to Intermediate							
1 Agriculture	3.4	4.0	4.6	5.3	3.1	2.9	2.7
2 Mining and quarrying	2.6	3.0	3.5	4.0	2.8	2.8	2.8
3 Electricity and gas	16.7	20.0	22.3	25.7	3.6	2.2	2.9
4 Manufacturing	12.6	15.0	17.3	19.6	3.4	2.9	2.5
5 Commerce	1.7	2.0	2.2	2.5	3.8	1.9	3.0
6 Transportation	0.8	1.0	1.1	1.3	3.7	2.1	2.9
7 Services	1.7	2.0	2.2	2.6	3.6	2.0	2.9
SUM: Intermediate	39.5	47.0	53.2	61.0	3.5	2.5	2.7
Sales to Other Final Demand							
Personal consumption expenditure	1.6	2.0	2.2	2.5	3.9	1.7	3.0
Government consumption	0.9	1.0	1.2	1.4	2.4	3.4	3.0
Exports	8.3	10.0	11.4	13.2	3.8	2.5	3.0
Imports	-6.8	-10.0	-10.4	-12.1	7.6	0.8	3.0
Output	43.5	50.0	57.5	66.1	2.8	2.8	2.8

Seller: 3 Electricity and gas

	1995	2000	2005	2010	95-00	00-05	05-10
Sales to Intermediate							
1 Agriculture	5.1	6.0	6.9	7.9	3.1	2.9	2.7
2 Mining and quarrying	3.5	4.0	4.6	5.3	2.8	2.8	2.8
3 Electricity and gas	8.3	10.0	11.1	12.9	3.6	2.2	2.9
4 Manufacturing	33.7	40.0	46.2	52.4	3.4	2.9	2.5
5 Commerce	16.5	20.0	21.9	25.4	3.8	1.9	3.0
6 Transportation	8.3	10.0	11.1	12.8	3.7	2.1	2.9
7 Services	20.8	25.0	27.7	32.0	3.6	2.0	2.9
SUM: Intermediate	96.3	115.0	129.6	148.8	3.5	2.4	2.8
Sales to Other Final Demand							
Personal consumption expenditure	65.9	80.0	87.1	101.2	3.9	1.7	3.0
Government consumption	8.9	10.0	11.8	13.8	2.4	3.4	3.0

Perhaps you are wondering how the *Compare* program knows what elements go into the identity and what are the names of the sectors and final demands. The answer was given to the program in the "matrix listing configuration file" whose name, MATLIST.CFG, was given to *Compare* in the command

\matcfg matlist.cfg

The matrix listing configuration file to produce the matrix listing shown above is in the box below.

The MATLIST.CFG File for TINY

```
Matrix listing identity;out=AM*out+pce+gov+inv+ex+im
# Title file name for the rows of out, the lefthand side vector
out; "sectors.ttl"
# Title file names for matrix columns
AM; "sectors.ttl"
# headers for each term
header for out;      "Output"
header for AM*out;   "Intermediate"
header for pce;      "Personal consumption expenditure"
header for gov;      "Government consumption"
header for inv;      "Investment"
header for ex;       "Exports"
header for im;       "Imports"
```

In the MATLIST.CFG file, any line beginning with a # is a comment and anything before the " ; " is likewise a comment. The first line gives the crucial identity on which the matrix listing is built. Recall that *Compare* has the VAM file and thus knows all the matrix and vector names and dimensions. It knows how to correctly interpret the expression "AM*out." The next line gives the file name of the sector titles for the vector on the left. The following line provides the file names for column titles of any matrices appearing in the identity. Here we have only one such matrix. Next come headers for each section of the table, where a section is a vector or a matrix-vector product.

We return now to the TINY.STB file to explain the last four lines, namely

\center Matrix Listing
\row
\cutoff .001
\matlist 1-8

The "\center" command centers text on the page. The command "\row" tells Compare to interpret the identity of the matlist configuration file as an identity in the rows. (The other possibility, "\column", would be used for showing the identity – that holds only in current prices – between the value of the output of an industry and the sum of its intermediate inputs and value-added components.) The "\cutoff" command eliminates the printing of entries which account for less than the specified fraction of the total of the row or column being listed.

Finally, the "\matlist" command instructs Compare to make the matrix listing for the group of sectors following the command. This is our first encounter with the *group* concept which is quite useful when working with multisectoral models. A group is just a collection of integers; it can be specified in a rather flexible way. Our specification, 1 - 8, means every sector from 1 to 8. An equivalent specification would be 1 2 3 4 5 6 7 8. If we want just 1 to 3 and 6 to 8, we could write any of following:

1-3 6-8
1 2 3 6 7 8
1-8 (4 5)

The numbers in the parenthesis are omitted from the list created by the ranges to the left; the parenthesis can also include ranges.

You may now want to ask, "Shouldn't we connect personal consumption expenditure to labor and capital income?" Of course we should, but to do so goes beyond what we can do in *G7* alone. It requires the Interdyme modeling system, which is similar to *Build* but for multisectoral models. Everything we have covered in this section is directly relevant to working with Interdyme, but surely you need to pause here and be sure that you have mastered the large amount of information we have already covered.

What better exercise could there be than to build your own *Tiny* model? Please complete exercise 1 and the others to explore some other ideas.

Exercises

1. Make up the input-output table for your own imaginary economy in 2005. It should have five to ten sectors, but not eight. Use different sector titles. Make forecasts to 2025. Graph the forecasts and make tables of output and other vectors. Make a matrix listing.

2. For the economy of our example, what levels of output and use of primary imputs would be required for the final demand (40, 6, 100, 600, 400, 170, 700, 148)?

3. How much of each of the four factors does one dollar of each of the final demands contain?

4. Was this economy a net exporter or importer of depreciation?

5. What would happen to the prices of each of the eight products if all indirect taxes were eliminated?

6. Greenhouse gases are emitted by the production of the various sectors of our model economy. Measured in tons per billion dollars of output, the emission coefficients for the various sectors of our economy are

    2.1 1.3 6.1 1.8 1.0 4.3 0.8 0.0

    What is the emission of greenhouse gases per billion dollars of final demand for each of the eight products? How much is attributable to a billion dollars of each of the types of final demand -- consumption, government, etc.? Was this country a net exporter or importer of greenhouse gas emissions?

7. The input-output flow table illustrated in the text was for year A. A comparable table for the same country but for a later year, year B, may be found in the files YBF.DAT, YBX.DAT and YBV.DAT in the TINY.ZIP file. (You have to fix up the correct commands to get the data into G.) Price indexes for the eight sectors from year A to B are given by the vector
    (1.01 1.10 1.06 1.07 1.15 1.24 1.18 1.20),
    while the cost of labor increased twenty percent between the two years. (The price indexes are in the file PINDEX.DAT.) What has happened between the two years to total labor requirements for producing one unit of final demand for each product?

8. Return to exercise 7 but now consider that the depreciation and capital income are produced with material inputs in the proportions given by the investment vector of the year in question. Ignore the indirect taxes and imports. The reciprocals of the labor requirements are productivity indexes for the economy in producing the various products supplied to final demand.

    Exercises 7 and 8 illustrate correct ways of studying productivity of the economy in making various final products. As we noted in section 14.1, it is impossible to know what has happened to productivity in a single *industry*, because the industry may have reduced its primary inputs while increasing its intermediate inputs; and the double-deflation method, supposed to handle this problem, is totally fallacious. The same problem does not arise in looking at total labor required, indirectly as well as directly, for the production of each unit delivered to final demand, for if the direct supplier to final demand has shifted required labor to other industries by buying more intermediate goods, that indirect labor will be automatically picked up. Thus, input-output calculations may offer a way of studying trends in productivity by product which elude methods which do not take into account indirect effects.

9. Read the *G7* help file for the "lint" command. Specify different (but consistent) values of the AM matrix, value-added coefficient vectors, and final demand vector shares for 1995 and 2010, use the "lint" command to interpolate values for other years, and repeat the calculations of the text with these time-varying coefficients. *Consistent* here means that the final-demand share columns sum to 1.0 and the sum of each column of AM plus the sum of the value-added shares in the same industry equals 1.0. Thus, these calculations are, in essence, in current prices, not constant prices.

16.2. Iterative Solutions of Input-output Equations

Before moving on to the Interdyme software, we must explain one of the mathematical techniques it uses extensively, namely the Seidel iterative solution of the input-output equations. In actual input-output computations, the Leontief inverse is seldom used, for the equations

$q = Aq + f$ or $p = pA + v$ can be solved directly from the A matrix in about the same time required to multiply $(I - A)^{-1}$ by f or v. Thus, the effort of calculating $(I - A)^{-1}$ would be pointless. Moreover, for large matrices, many cells of A are zero. This fact can be exploited to reduce the computer storage required for the matrix. But the Leontief inverse will have non-zeroes nearly everywhere, so there is no way to reduce the space required for it. Further, changes to A are easily recorded and applied, but a change of one element in A can easily change all the elements in the inverse. Thus, from the point of view of solving the equations, nothing is gained and a good deal lost by computing the inverse.

How to solve the equations without the use of the inverse is the subject of this section. We will explain two methods of successive approximation, for it is worth knowing that both work even though we mainly use the second. The first, the simple iterative method, takes as a first approximation of q, $q_0 = f$. Then, given the nth approximation, q_n , the next approximation is

$$q^{n+1} = Aq^n + f \qquad\qquad (15.2.1)$$

If the process converges so that one q is indistinguishable from the previous one, then the vector to which it has converged is clearly the solution of the equation. In economic terms, we first set the output equal to the final demands. Then we increase it to allow for the intermediate goods needed by the first approximation and then increase it again for the intermediate goods needed for the second approximation, and so on.

It is clear from equation (15.2.1) that if the matrix A is non-negative and f is non-negative, then no element of q ever becomes negative in the course of the iterations. Thus, the conditions on A that insure the convergence also insure that a non-negative f leads to a non-negative q. Thus, our inquiry, initially motivated by considerations of practical computation, also provides an answer to the theoretical question of whether an economy could exist with a given f and A, for the economic interpretation of Aq is dependent on all elements of q being non-negative.

The second method, the Seidel process, takes the same first approximation, and then, to get the second approximation, solves first the first equation for q_1, given all the other elements of q. Then, using this new value of q_1 and the old values of q_3, q_4, etc., solve the second equation for q_2, and so on. If the A matrix is triangular, that is, if all the entries above the main diagonal are zero, this method gives the right answer with one iteration. If it is not triangular, the whole process is repeated until little or no change occurs with each new iteration. While no actual input-output matrix is ever exactly triangular, the sectors can often be taken in an order which makes the matrix almost triangular, and this near triangularity speeds the convergence process.

Instead of starting this process with the final demands, it is also possible to start with any guess of q. In dynamic models, a good guess, namely the previous year's q is available. With a good starting point, four or five iterations of the Seidel process is usually sufficient to produce adequately accurate solutions. If twenty percent of the elements of A are non-zero -- a fairly typical situation -- we can make five iterations of the Seidel process in the same time which would be required to multiply f by the inverse if we had it.

If A is not an input-output matrix but just any old matrix you happen to meet on the street, there is not much chance that either of these methods will converge and give a solution. What then makes us so sure that they will converge for an input-output matrix? To discuss *convergence*, we need to be able to say how far apart two vectors are. The concept of the *norm of a vector* gives us that ability. We even need to be able to say how far a given vector is from the solution when we do not know what the solution is. The concept of the *norm of a matrix* enables us to turn that trick. We will now explain these two concepts.

We can say how far apart two vectors are if we can say how "long" a vector x is, that is, how long the line is which connects x with the origin or zero point. For if $\|x\|$ represents the length of any vector, then the length of the difference of two vectors a and b, $\|a-b\|$, serves as a measure of how far apart they are. How shall we measure the length of a vector? In two dimensions, the usual length of the vector (x_1, x_2) is $\sqrt{x_1^2 + x_2^2}$. This concept of length readily generalizes to vectors of any dimension by the definition $\|x\| = \sqrt{x'x}$. This formula, called the Euclidean length (or norm), gives one possible way of measuring length.

Why, however, do we bother to take the square root in the Euclidean norm? Because we certainly want *any* way of calculating the length of x to be such that multiplying each element of x by a scalar, λ, multiplies the length of x by the absolute value of λ:

(a) $\quad \|\lambda x\| = |\lambda| \|x\|$

Other properties which any definition of length should have are:

(b) $\quad \|0\| = 0 \quad$ and $\quad \|x\| > 0 \; if \; x \neq 0$

and

+(c) $\quad \|x + y\| \leq \|x\| + \|y\|$

Property (c) expresses the requirement that the shortest distance between any two points must be a straight line. Let us denote the points by x and $-y$. Then we must have

$$\|x - (-y)\| \leq \|x\| + \|-y\|$$

since $\|x\|$ is the distance from x to 0 (the origin of the vector space) and $\|-y\|$ is the distance for 0 to $-y$, while $\|x - (-y)\|$ is the distance directly from x to $-y$. By applying property (a) to the second term on the right, this requirement may be written more simply as (c) above.

Any way of assigning a number, $\|x\|$, to each vector, x, of the vector space in such a way that (a), (b), and (c) are satisfied is called a *norm* of the space, and $\|x\|$ is read "the norm of x". It is quite remarkable that we can often prove the convergence of a process in terms of a norm without knowing exactly which norm we are using. Besides the Euclidean norm, there are two more important examples of norms:

the l-norm: $\|x\| = \sum_{i=1}^{n} |x_i|$

the m-norm: $\|x\| = max_i |x_i|$

You may easily verify that each of these norms has the required three properties, though the values they give as the norm of a given vector may be quite different. For example, the vector (1, -3, 2) has a Euclidean norm of 3.74, while its l-norm is 6 and its m-norm is 3. (The l in l-norm refers to Henri Lebesgue, a French mathematician of the early years of the twentieth century.)

Exercise 10: Draw the unit circle for each of these three norms. (The unit circle is the locus of points with norm 1.)

With each of these three norms, if x^k, for $k = 0, 1, 2$, etc., is a sequence of vectors and x* is a vector such that

$$\lim_{k \to \infty} \|x^k - x^*\| = 0$$

then

$$\lim_{k \to \infty} x^k = x^* \ .$$

That is, convergence of a sequence of vectors in norm implies element-by-element convergence. This property is easily seen for the examples of the three norms and is a characteristic of finite dimensional vector spaces.

What we now want to show is that if q^* is a solution of the input-output equations, so that if

$$q^* = Aq^* + f \tag{15.2.2}$$

then the sequence $q^0, q^1, q^2, \ldots$ defined by

$$q^{k+1} = Aq^k + f \tag{15.2.3}$$

converges in norm to q*. Subtracting the first equation, (15.2.2), from the second, (15.2.3), gives

$$q^{k+1} - q^* = A(q^k - q^*), k = 1,2,3 \ldots \tag{15.2.4}$$

If we have computed to iteration m, then setting $k = m$ in this equation gives
$$q^{m+1} - q^* = A(q^m - q^*)$$

But setting $k = m+1$ in (15.2.4) gives

$$q^{m+2} - q^* = A(q^{m+1} - q^*)$$

Together the last two equations imply

$$q^{m+2} - q^* = A(q^{m+1} - q^*) = A^2(q^m - q^*)$$

For any positive integer, p, similar reasoning applied p times gives

$$q^{m+p} - q^* = A^p(q^m - q^*) \tag{15.2.5}$$

We would like to be able to show that the norm of the vector on the left of (15.2.5) goes to zero as p goes to infinity. T o do so, we need to extend the concept of norm to matrices. We introduce that extension by a question:

Is there a number, call it $\|A\|$, such that

$$\|Ax\| \leq \|A\| \ \|x\| \tag{15.2.6}$$

for all x?

There are indeed such numbers, and we call the least of them (for any norm of the vectors) the *norm* of A. Intuitively speaking, the norm of the matrix A is the greatest "stretch" which multiplication by A performs on any vector. For the l-norm and m-norms of the vectors, the corresponding norms of a matrix are easily computed, as we shall see in a moment. Note that the norms of matrices also have the three same basic properties of the norms of vectors:

    a) $\|A\| = 0$ if and only if $A = 0$.

    b) $\|\lambda A\| = |\lambda| \|A\|$

    c) $\|A + B\| \leq \|A\| + \|B\|$

plus a fourth, which can be easily verified from the definition

    d) $\|AB\| \leq \|A\| \|B\|$

For the l-norm and m-norms of the vectors, the corresponding norms of a matrix are easilty computed, as we shall see in a moment. First, however, note that we can apply this inequality repeatedly to equation (15.2.5). After applying it p times, we have

$$\|q^{m+p} - q^*\| = \|A\|^p \|q^m - q^*\|$$

If we can show that $\|A\| < 1$ for *some* norm, then for that norm

$$\|A\|^p \to 0 \ as \ p \to \infty$$

and therefore $q^k \to q^*$ as $k \to \infty$ and the iterative calculations converge to the solution.

The norm of the n-by-n matrix A induced by the m-norm of vectors, and therefore called the m-norm of the matrix, is the maximum row sum, namely:

$$\|A\|_m = max_i \sum_{j=1}^{n} |a_{ij}|$$

while the norm of A induced by the l-norm of vectors, and therefore called the l-norm of the matrix, is the maximum column sum, namely,

$$\|A\|_l = max_j \sum_{i=1}^n |a_{ij}|$$

We shall prove the formula for the l-norm, and leave that for the m-norm as an exercise. (The Euclidean norm of A is more complicated and not of immediate concern to us. It is the largest characteristic root of $A'A$.) For the l-norm proof, let

$$\alpha = max_j \sum_{i=1}^n |a_{ij}|$$

Then $\|A\|_l \le \alpha$ because, for any x,

$$\|Ax\|_l = \sum_{i=1}^n |\sum_{j=1}^n a_{ij} x_j| \le \sum_i \sum_j |a_{ij}||x_j| = \sum_j |x_j| \sum_i |a_{ij}| \le \sum_j |x_j| \alpha = \alpha \|x\|_l$$

On the other hand, let k be the number of the column with the largest sum of absolute values, so that

$$\alpha = \sum_{i=1}^n |a_{ik}|$$

and then choose a vector, x, with $x_k = 1$ and $x_j = 0$ for all $j \ne k$. Then $\|x\|_l = 1$ and

$$\|Ax\|_l = \sum_i |\sum_j a_{ij} x_j| = \sum_i |a_{ik}| = \alpha = \alpha \|x\|_l$$

Therefore, $\|A\|_l \ge \alpha$. But we have already shown the opposite inequality, so the only possibility is that $\|A\|_l = \alpha$.

If an input-output A matrix comes from an observed economy with a positive value-added in every industry, then the column sums of every column are less than 1 and therefore the l-norm of the matrix is less than 1. Thus, returning to the iterative solution of the input-output equations, we see that it will indeed converge if such is the source of A. Furthermore, in that case, $(I-A)^{-1}$ will be non-negative, because if we start from an f vector which is all zero except for a 1 in some position, the resulting solution will never have any opportunity to acquire any negative elements in the course of the iterative process. But the columns of $(I-A)^{-1}$ are precisely the solutions of such equations, so the whole matrix is non-negative.

The norm of the A matrix not only allows us to be sure that the iterative process converges, it also allows us to set an upper bound on how far we are from the solution at any stage. If, as before, q^k indicates approximation k, then

$$q^{k+p} - q^k = q^{k+1} - q^k + q^{k+2} - q^{k+1} + \dots + q^{k+p} - q^{k+p-1} \tag{15.2.7}$$

But since

$$q^{m+1} = Aq^m + f \quad \text{and} \quad q^m = Aq^{m-1} + f$$

for any positive integer m, subtraction of the second equation from the first gives

$$q^{m+1} - q^m = A(q^m - q^{m-1})$$

Repeatedly applying this equation gives

$$q^{k+1} - q^k = A(q^k - q^{k-1})$$
$$q^{k+2} - q^{k+1} = A^2(q^k - q^{k-1})$$
$$\dots$$
$$q^{k+p} - q^{k+p-1} = A^p(q^k - q^{k-1})$$

and substitution in the above equation (15.2.7) gives

$$q^{k+p} - q^k = (A + A^2 + A^3 + \dots + A^p)(q^k - q^{k-1})$$

Taking the norms of both sides and applying properties (c) and (d) of the norms of matrices gives

$$\|q^{k+p} - q^k\| \leq \|A + A^2 + A^3 + \dots + A^p\| \, \|q^k - q^{k-1}\|$$
$$\leq [\|A\| + \|A\|^2 + \|A\|^3 + \dots + \|A\|^p] \, \|q^k - q^{k-1}\|$$

Now as p → ∞, q^{k+p} → q^* and the sum of the geometric progression on the right goes to $\|A\|/(1 - \|A\|)$ because $\|A\| < 1$. Thus, when we have reached iteration k, we know that the distance to the true solution is less than $\|q^k - q^{k-1}\| \|A\|/(1 - \|A\|)$. In other words, when the differences of the successive approximations get small, we can be sure that we are close to the true solution.

Now suppose for a moment that A is a matrix in physical units -- with coefficients in units like kilowatt hours per pound -- so that column sums are meaningless and the l-norm perhaps much greater than 1. Further let w be an all-positive vector of the hours of labor -- the only primary input -- required per physical unit of output in each industry. Can an economy exist with this technology? In other words, if the vector f of final demands is all positive, will the vector of outputs, q, such that $q = Aq + f$ also be all positive? (Mathematically, it is quite possible for some element of q to be negative, but it is economic nonsense to run an industry at a negative level. Coal can be converted into electricity, but all the electricity in the world can't make a ton of coal.)

The answer to these questions lies in the solution of $p = pA + w$ (where p is a row vector). If p is all positive, then it can be thought of as a vector of prices (with an hour of work as the numeraire) at which each process has a positive value added. If we now change the units of measurement of output of each product to one "hour's worth," the coefficient matrix, say A^*, in these new units corresponding to A in the old units will have columns whose sums are each less than 1. Thus, in these units, the iterative procedure will converge. But the iterative procedure in the original units (with A) would give successive approximations which differ from those with A^* only in their units. Hence the process would converge in the original units as well and will be non-negative. Since the Leontief inverse is non-negative, any vector of non-negative final demands can be met by non-negative levels of output of all the industries.

16.3. The Seidel Method and Triangulation

As mentioned at the outset of the previous section, there is a variation of the iterative method, known as the Seidel method, which converges even faster. In it, one starts with f as the initial guess of the solution just as in the simple iterative method, but then solves the first equation for the first variable and puts this value into the guess, then solves the second equation for the second variable and puts that value into the guess, and so on. Formally,

$$q_i^{(k+1)} = [\sum_{j=1}^{i-1} a_{ij} x_j^{(k+1)} + \sum_{j=i+1}^{n} a_{ij} x_j^{(k)} + f_i]/(1-a_{ii})$$

In input-output work, the f vector is generally non-negative as are the elements of the A matrix. Hence, in the simple iterative method, the approximate solutions form a monotonically increasing sequence of vectors. The Seidel approximate solutions are also monotonically increasing but are always larger than the corresponding simple iterative solution. Hence, they also converge to the solution and do so faster than does the simple iterative method.

If all the non-zero elements of A are on or below the main diagonal, A is said to be triangular. If A is triangular, one pass of the Seidel process is sufficient to reach the exact solution. If A is merely almost triangular, a few iterations will suffice for a good solution. It general, input-output matrices arrive from the statistical offices more or less triangulated in exactly the wrong way. They start with Agriculture first, later Textiles, then Apparel. The right order for a fast Seidel solution is the reverse, Apparel, Textiles, Agriculture. It is not, however, necessary to physically re-arrange the rows and columns. All that is necessary is to take the rows in the Seidel operation in the order that would make the matrix nearly triangular.

For large matrices, however, it may be convenient to have a mechanical way to generate an approximately triangular order. A simple but effective is to pick as the first industry the one which has the smallest ratio of intermediate to final demand in its row. Then move into final demand all the inputs into this industry and again pick from the remaining sectors the one with the lowest ratio of intermediate to final in its row. Continue until all industries have been selected.

Solving input-output equations by the Seidel method is not only generally much faster than inverting the $I-A$ matrix by Gauss-Jordan reduction, it may even be faster than multiplying $(I-A)^{-1}$ by f when $(I-A)^{-1}$ is already known. How can that be? It is common for the A matrix to be quite sparse. A 300-by-300 matrix may have some 9,000 non-zero elements, not 90,000. It can be stored in a "packed" form in which only non-zero elements are stored, and the Seidel algorithm can be written to use this packed form, so that only as many multiplications and additions are required per iteration as there are non-zero elements. Thus, if the Seidel process requires less than ten iterations in our example, it will require less than 90,000 multiplications and additions. The Leontief inverse, however, will generally have 90,000 non-zeroes and thus multiplying it by f involves exactly 90,000 multiplications and additions. To economize on both space and solution time, large, sparse matrices are thus best stored in a packed form; and equations involving them should be solved by the Seidel process without ever inverting the matrix.

Exercises

11. Using C, C++, Fortran, Basic or any programming language you know, write a program to compute the triangular order of a matrix. Apply it to the flow matrix used as an example in this chapter. Write the results as a vector of integers, the first being the number of the equation to be taken first; the second, that of the equation to be taken second, etc.

12. Write a program to use the Seidel method to solve input-output equations, taking the equations in the order specified by the vector produced in exercise 7. Apply the program to solve exercise 1 earlier in this chapter.

CHAPTER 17. BUILDING MULTISECTORAL MODELS WITH INTERDYME

17.1. Introduction to Interdyme

In section 16.1, we became acquainted with the VAM file and saw that *G7* could do a number of calculations with the matrices and vectors in these files. By the end, however, we came up against the limits of building models in *G7* by itself. To integrate regression equations and input-output we proceed to Interdyme. Interdyme makes use of the Seidel process for solving the input-output equations, so we had to explain that before getting into Interdyme itself. Starting in this section, we will build several successive versions of the *Tiny* model in Interdyme. We will being in this section with the version called "Model 1".

Interdyme is a collection of C++ programs which make it easy to construct interindustry dynamic models involving regression equations, input-output computations with matrix algebra, and lag relationships that provide dynamics. In this section, we will introduce Interdyme by building a simple Interdyme model of *Tiny* with just one regression equation and rudimentary institutional accounts.

We are going to assume that the historical period for which we have data extends up through 2003 and that the forecast period will be 2004 – 2010. At this point, the HIST.VAM has been worked with considerably and may have things in it which would prove confusing, so we will rebuild it from scratch in *G7* by doing

> add tiny.pre

where TINY.PRE is the file shown in the box on the next page. This file will fill in all the matrices and vectors for the historical period, but in the forecast period only the coefficients are filled in, not the input-output flows. In particular, output is not calculated in the forecast period. Thus, if – after Interdyme has been run – we find data for industry output in the forecast period, we can be sure that it was calculated by Interdyme.

Regression Equations and Accounting Identities

We can conveniently begin with the most familiar part, the regression equation and the accounting identities. The regression equation is estimated in *G7* by the following command

    add invtot.reg

where invtot.reg is the following file

```
catch invtot.cat                # Open up the catch file
save invtot.sav                 # Open up the save file
ti TINY investment equation     # Title for regression or graph
dfreq 1                         # Set default frequency to 1 (annual)
f ub20 = @cum(ub20,1.,.20)      # Form a "unit bucket" for capital stocks
```

338

```
f capstk = @cum(invcum, invtot[1], .20)/ub20     # Calculate capital stock
f delGDP = gdp – gdp[1]             # First difference of GDP
con 2000 1.03 = a1                  # Soft constraint for regression
lim 1982 2003                       # limit of the regression
r invtot = ! capstk, delGDP[1], delGDP[2]   # regression with no constant term
save off                           # close the save file
```

The TINY.PRE File

```
# tiny.pre - File to create VAM file for Interdyme TINY
vamcreate vam.cfg hist
vam hist b
dvam b
# Bring in the intermediate flow matrix
add flows.dat
# Bring in the final demand vectors
add fd.dat
# Bring in the value added vectors
add va.dat
fdates 2000 2000
# Add up the intermediate rows
getsum FM r out
# Add on the final demand vectors to get total output
vc out = out+pce+gov+inv+ex+im
# Copy intermediate flows to AM and convert to coefficients
mcopy b.AM b.FM
coef AM out
# The following are element-by-element vector divisions
vc depc = dep/out; vc labc = lab/out; vc capc = cap/out; vc indc = ind/out
# Compute share vectors of final demands
vc pcec = pce/pcetot{2000}; vc invc = inv/invtot{2000}
vc govc = gov/govtot{2000}; vc exc  = ex/extot{2000}
vc imc = im/imtot{2000}
fdates 1995 2010
# Copy the 2000 AM matrix into 1995 - 2010
dfreq 1
f one = 1.0
index 2000 one AM;
# Create a time trend
f time = @cum(time,one,0)
# Move the five final demand columns by their totals in the historical
#   years, 1995-2003
fdates 1995 2003
index 2000 pcetot pce; index 2000 invtot inv;  index 2000 govtot ov
index 2000 extot ex; index 2000 imtot im
# Keep value added and final demand coefficients constant
fdates 1995 2010
f one = 1.
index 2000 one depc; index 2000 one labc
index 2000 one capc; index 2000 one indc
index 2000 one pcec; index 2000 one invc; index 2000 one govc;
index 2000 one exc;  index 2000 one imc
# The remaining calculations are done for the historical period
#   1995 - 2003 only
# Take the Leontief inverse of the A matrix
fdates 1995 2003
mcopy b.LINV b.AM
linv LINV
# Add up the final demands
vc fd = pce+gov+inv+ex+im
# Compute total outputs
vc out = LINV*fd
# Computer value-added flows
vc dep=depc*out; vc lab=labc*out; vc cap=capc*out; vc ind=indc*out
store
close b
# We should now have outputs and final demands in the historical period, but only coefficients in
the forecast period.
```

```
gr *                            # Graph of the regression fit
catch off                       # Close the catch file
```

with the following results (from the catch file)

```
:                        TINY investment equation
 SEE   =      13.51 RSQ  = 0.8360 RHO =   0.60 Obser  =   22 from 1982.000
 SEE+1 =      11.45 RBSQ = 0.8187 DW  =   0.79 DoFree =   19 to   2003.000
 MAPE  =       7.24
    Variable name          Reg-Coef  Mexval  Elas   NorRes     Mean   Beta
 0 invtot               - - - - - -  - - - - -  - - - - -    161.06 - - -
 1 capstk                 0.99562    402.8    0.89    1.52    144.50
 2 delGDP[1]              0.35900     17.0    0.11    1.00     47.67  0.231
 3 delGDP[2]              0.03007      0.1    0.01    1.00     47.06  0.020
```

The national accounts are given by the file ACCOUNT.SAV as follows:

```
# The Accountant for Tiny
# Personal interest and dividends
fex pintdivrat = pintdiv/capinc
f pintdiv = pintdivrat*capinc
# Personal income
f pi = labinc + pintdiv + pgovtran
# Personal taxes
fex ptaxrat = ptax/pi
f ptax = ptaxrat*pi
# Personal disposable income
f pdisinc = pi - ptax
# Personal saving
fex psavrat = psav/pdisinc
f psav = psavrat*pdisinc
f pcetot = pdisinc - psav
# Government income
f ginc = indtax + ptax
# Government saving
f gsav = ginc - govtot - pgovtran
# Business saving
f bsav = capinc - pintdiv - invtot
# RoW saving
f RoWsav = imtot - extot
```

All of this file should be familiar from the Master file of macromodels and the previous discussion of the Institutional accounts in this chapter.

IdBuild, the Interdyme Version of the Build Program

Both of these .SAV files will be passed through the *IdBuild* program, the Interdyme version of the *Build* program. It is much easier to run *IdBuild* than to explain what all it does. Basically, *IdBuild* converts the *G7*-estimated parts of the model into C++ code. Clicking Model | IdBuild not only runs *IdBuild* but also compiles the C++ code it has written and combines it with the other C++ modules of the Interdyme system to make an executable program. Thus, running *IdBuild* just requires two mouse clicks. Recounting what it does will take us a little longer, but some understanding of the results is necessary to play your creative role in writing MODEL.CPP that pulls together the pieces of the Interdyme system.

First, we must note that *IdBuild* is not so omniscient as *Build* and needs our help on one point. *Build* knows about all the variables and equations in the macromodel it is building. Therefore, it can arrange for getting all of them into the model, can figure out which ones are endogenous, and can write a file for making quick projections of all those which remain exogenous. Because part of an Interdyme model may be written directly in C++ without going through *IdBuild*, *IdBuild* does not necessarily know about all the variables in the model and does not know about the possible definition of some variables in the C++ code. A file called PSEUDO.SAV is used to inform *IdBuild* of the variables which are used in the C++ code or otherwise needed in the data bank produced by *IdBuild* but not used in any of the .SAV files processed by *IdBuild*. In *Tiny*, there is only one variable of this sort, *timet*, which is used in the regressions for projecting exogenous variables. The second function of the PSEUDO.SAV file is to tell *IdBuild* which variables will be defined in the C++ code and therefore do not need regressions in EXOGALL.REG to make quick, mechanical projections. In *Tiny*, there are five such variables, as we shall see below, called *gdp, deprec, labinc, capinc,* and *indtax*. Here is the PSEUDO.SAV file for *Tiny*:

```
# PSEUDO.SAV file for TINY
# Time
f timet = timet
# GDP Gross domestic product
f gdp = gdp
# Depreciation income
f deprec = deprec
# Capital income
f capinc = capinc
# Labor income
f labinc = labinc
# Indirect taxes
f indtax = indtax
```

With these files in place, we are ready to look at the MASTER file, which is just the following:

```
#  Master File for TINY
iadd invtot.sav
iadd account.sav
iadd pseudo.sav
end
```

The only commands in the Master file for *IdBuild* are comments, "iadd" commands to bring in the various .SAV files, and the end command to signal the end of the commands.

IdBuild requires a configuration file called BUILD.CFG. In it, I recommend that you make the name of the workspace bank HIST, which is the way the file is supplied.

Once these files are ready, *IdBuild* can then be run. I would suggest that, for the

341

moment, you do so from within *G7* by the command

```
dos c:\pdg\idbuild master
```

Later, when you have written the MODEL.CPP file, you can run *IdBuild* and compile and link MODEL.CPP and other parts of the Interdyme program by clicking Model | IdBuild. We will get to that point soon. Right now we should have a quick look at the output of *IdBuild*. It is reminiscent of that of *Build*. The EXOGALL.REG file, for example, begins as:

```
bank hist b
mode f
tdates <StartType> <EndType>
limits <StartReg> <EndReg> <EndForecast>
ti govtot
r b.govtot = timet
gr *
f govtot = depvar
save govtot.xog
sty govtot
save off
```

As with a macromodel, areas marked with the <...> in the third and fourth lines must be replaced by dates and the file then passed through *G7* to generate for each variable a .XOG file with exogenous forecast for each of the exogenous variables. The file RUN.XOG will contain an "add" command for each of these files. For *Tiny*, RUN.XOG is

```
dos copy hist.* base.*
wsb base
add pintdivrat.xog
add pgovtran.xog
add ptaxrat.xog
add psavrat.xot
add govtot.xog
add extot.xog
add imtot.xog
add pgovtran.xog
add pintdivrat.xog
add ptaxrat.xog
add psavrat.xog
wsb ws
[possibly also lines, not needed in TINY, to project exogenous vectors in
the vam file, like this:
vam base b
dvam b
vmatdat …
]
```

Note the effect of the first two and the last commands when executed in *G7*. As noted above, HIST is the recommended name (specified in BUILD.CFG) for the workspace bank generated by *IdBuild*. The first command above copies this G bank and VAM file to a G bank and VAM file with the name BASE. The second line makes this bank the workspace bank of *G7*. The subsequent lines add the files with the projections of all the exogenous variables.

342

These projections go into the G workspace bank, namely, into BASE. The "wsb ws" command makes WS the workspace bank of *G7* and thereby frees the BASE bank. As in the case of macromodels, you should check the mechanical exogenous projections, shape them to your preferences, and put revised versions into files with the extension .XG, and make a revised RUN.XOG, calling it something like BASE.XG. For the moment, we will let well enough alone and just use RUN.XOG with the mechanically generated projections. This would also be the appropriate place to put into BASE.VAM the forecasts of any exogenous vectors or matrices not already projected by running TINY.PRE. (In *Tiny*, there are no such vectors or matrices.) Remember, however, that if you make any changes to RUN.XOG you should change the name to RUN.XG or something more descriptive. Otherwise, the next time *IdBuild* is run, your carefully prepared RUN.XOG will be overwritten.

Like *Build*, *IdBuild* also writes RUN.GR, a command file for *G7* which will graph all timeseries variables handled through *IdBuild*.

Running *IdBuild* generates a number of other files to facilitate the writing of the C++ program to run the model. One of these is TSERIES.INC as follows:

```
GLOBAL Tseries ub20, invtot, invcum, capstk, gdp, delGDP, pintdivrat,
capinc, pintdiv, labinc, pgovtran, pi, ptaxrat, ptax, pdisinc, psavrat,
psav, pcetot, indtax, ginc, govtot, gsav, deprec, bsav,
imtot, extot, RoWsav, timet;
```

This is just a listing of all the macro variables in the model in a format suitable for use in the model.

Like *Build*, *IdBuild* also writes a file of C++ code called HEART.CPP. It is shown in the box on the next page, in somewhat abbreviated form, for *Tiny*. Wherever four dots occur, thus ...., lines have been omitted which just repeat for the other variables listed above in TSERIES.INC the same function above and below the four dots for *invtot* and *ginc*. The Master file had the two following lines:

```
iadd invtot.sav
iadd account.sav
```

Each of these resulted in a corresponding function of C++ code in the HEART.CPP file, namely *invtotf()* and *accountf()*, respectively. These are functions which can be called from MODEL.CPP, the user-written part of Interdyme system. The function name is created by adding an 'f' to the end of the name of the file. A glance at *accountf()* shows that it is just an adaptation for C++ of the G commands in ACCOUNT.SAV. The function *invtotf()* is the same for INVTOT.SAV with the extra feature that the numerical values of the regression coefficients have been stripped off and put in a separate file, HEART.DAT, which will automatically be read to supply values to the *coef* variable. The regression coefficients are treated this way so that they can potentially be varied when optimizing the fit of the model, just as was done with macromodels. *IdBuild* recognizes the special function of the line

```
iadd pseudo.sav
```

in the MASTER file and does not generate a corresponding function in HEART.CPP.

Also in the HEART.CPP file are the C++ functions *tserin()* and *uptseries()*. The first of these reads in the historical values and exogenous projections of the time series variables; it is executed at the beginning of any run of the model. The second, *uptseries()*, is called at the beginning of the calculation of the forecast for any year. It looks at the starting value of each of the time series variables and if it is -.000001, the value *G7* uses to indicate a *missing value,* then it replaces that missing value with the value of the series in the previous year. For example, in *Tiny*, no exogenous projection is made for Personal income, since it is endogenous. Thus, its starting value in 2004 would be -.000001. If the model starts with this very bad guess of Personal income, it eventually converges to the correct value, but it will converge much faster if it starts with a good guess, and the previous year's value is usually a pretty good guess. Note that exogenously projected values will not be affected, because they will not be -.000001.

```cpp
#include "dymesys.h"
#include "heart.h"
extern short t;
extern float **coef;
FILE *fmatrix;
float depend;
#include "tseries.inc"
/* end of standard prolog */
void invtotf()
{
    /*  TINY investment equation */
    ub20[t]=cum(ub20,1.,.20);
    capstk[t]=cum(invcum, invtot[t-1],.20)/ ub20[t];
    delGDP[t]= gdp[t]- gdp[t-1];
    /* invtot */ depend = coef[0][0]*capstk[t]+coef[0][1]*delGDP[t-1]+coef[0][2]*delGDP[t-2];
    invtot.modify(depend);
}
void accountf()
{
    pintdiv[t]= pintdivrat[t]* capinc[t];
    pi[t]= labinc[t]+ pintdiv[t]+ pgovtran[t];
    ptax[t]= ptaxrat[t]* pi[t];
    pdisinc[t]= pi[t]- ptax[t];
    psav[t]= psavrat[t]* pdisinc[t];
    pcetot[t]= pdisinc[t]- psav[t];
    ginc[t]= indtax[t]+ ptax[t];
    gsav[t]= ginc[t]- govtot[t]- pgovtran[t];
    bsav[t]= capinc[t]- pintdiv[t]- invtot[t];
    RoWsav[t]= imtot[t]- extot[t];
}

void tserin()
{
    timet.in("timet");
    invtot.in("invtot");
    ....
    ginc.in("ginc");
}
void uptseries()
{
    //Function to replace missing values or macro vrariable with lagged values.
    if(timet[t]< .0000009 && timet[t]> -.0000011) timet[t] = timet[t-1];
    if(invtot[t]< .0000009 && invtot[t]> -.0000011) invtot[t] = invtot[t-1];
    ....
    if(ginc[t]< .0000009 && ginc[t]> -.0000011) ginc[t] = ginc[t-1];
}
```

A final file created by *IdBuild* is CALLALL.CPP , a bit of C++ code which calls all of the functions written by *IdBuild* in the HEART.CPP file. It is used in conjunction with managing rho adjustments as will be explained below in conjunction with the MODEL.CPP file. Here is the important part of CALLALL.CPP for *Tiny*.

```cpp
void callall()
{
invtotf();
accountf();
}
```

So far, there has been a lot of similarity between building Interdyme models and building macromodels with *G7* and *Build*. Now we venture into new territory with the writing of the MODEL.CPP file. The box on the following page shows the part of this file that distinguishes *Tiny* from any other model built with Interdyme. I have more than once encountered the reaction, "C++ is hard; I don't have time to learn it, so I'll just stay with the models I can build in Excel." It is true that some of the advanced features of C++ can be rather arcane, but the objects such as Vector, Matrix and others used in Interdyme are already written, in separate files. The code that you will need to write is in no more complicated than the simplest level of Basic, Fortran, or C. But with the Interdyme infrastructure, you can easily write the code for the matrix and vector operations that are essential for working with input-output models but are tedious to program in those other languages.

The box shows the C++ code that defines *Tiny*. First of all, you need to know a few things about C++ grammar. Anything following a // on the same line is a comment, useful for humans but ignored by the computer. A comment extending over more than one line is begun with a /* and ended with a */. Every C++ statement ends with a semicolon. More than one statement can be put on one line or a single statement can be broken onto two or more lines between words. C and C++ are case sensitive: *x* is not the same as *X*. For any variable *x*, x++ means "add 1 to *x*." Before a variable name, like *Iteration* or *oldinvtot*, can be used, we must declare what kind of variable it is by statements like

```
int Iteration; // declare Iteration to be an integer
float oldinvtot; //declare oldinvtot to be a floating point, real number
```

A group of statements, indicated by enclosing the statements in curly braces like these { }, can be used anywhere a single statement could be used, notably in **for, do, while, if, else**, and **else if** constructions. The **for** loop that fills most of the box of *Tiny* code is a good illustration of this point. It looks something like this:

```
for (t = godate; t<= stopdate; t++) {
    ....
    }
```

where the .... represents many lines of code. The command means: start *t* off equal to *godate*, which is the beginning year of the run you are making, something like 1995, then do all the statements represented by the .... with that new value of *t*, then increment *t* by 1 – that's the t++ near the end of the line – and do all the statements represented by the .... with that value of *t*, and keep doing all this as long as *t* is less than or equal to *stopdate*, a number that other parts of Interdyme will have made equal to the last year of your run, something like 2010. Now the generic form of the for loop is written

for (*initialization, condition, increment*) *statement*

The Core of TINY's MODEL.CPP File

```cpp
for (t = godate; t<= stopdate; t++) {
   if (MaxFlag == 'n') printf("%d ",t);
   // Load all vectors and matrices.
   load(t);
   uptseries();
   // Start of code particular to TINY:
   Iteration = 0;
   // The loop for convergence on pcetot and invtot.
   while(Iteration < 20){
       Iteration++;
       oldinvtot = invtot[t]; oldpcetot = pcetot[t];
       if(t>= MacEqStartDate)
           invtotf();
       inv = invtot[t]*invc;      pce = pcetot[t]*pcec;
       gov = govtot[t]*govc;      im  = imtot[t]*imc;
       ex  = extot[t]*exc;
       // Add up final demand vectors
       fd = pce + gov + inv + ex + im;
       // Solve input-output equations by Seidel method
       Seidel(AM, out, fd, triang, toler);
       // Compute value-added vectors
       // The Interdyme ebemul() function does element-by-element multiplication
       dep = ebemul(depc,out);  lab = ebemul(labc,out);
       cap = ebemul(capc,out);  ind = ebemul(indc,out);
       // The Accountant for Tiny
       gdp[t] = fd.sum();
       if(t>MacEqStartDate){
           deprec[t] = dep.sum(); labinc[t] = lab.sum();
           capinc[t] = cap.sum(); indtax[t] = ind.sum();
           accountf();
           }
       // Form the convergence test
       invdif = fabs(invtot[t] - oldinvtot);
       pcedif = fabs(pcetot[t]- oldpcetot);
       printf("Iter %2d pce = %7.1f pcedif = %6.2f invdif = %6.2f\n",Iteration,
           pcetot[t],pcedif,invdif);
       if(invdif < .5 && pcedif < .5) break;
       }
   // End of code particular to TINY
   // Here when both Investment and PCE have converged
   // Standard end of the spin() function:
   if(MaxFlag == 'y')
           shiftback(t);
   else{
       // Store the values of vectors and matrices for this period.
       store(t);
       printf("\n");
       }
   }
```

It starts off one or more variables in the *initialization*, checks that the *condition* is true and, if it is, executes the *statement*, then revises the variable that was initialized as prescribed by the *increment*, checks the condition, and executes the *statement*, and so on as long as the *condition* is true. When the *condition* is no longer true, control passes to the next statement below the **for** loop. How the *initialization*, *condition*, and *increment* work in the example is clear enough, but our particular point here is that the *statement* executed is the compound statement composed of all the simple statements enclosed by the braces that open right after the closing parenthesis of the for statement. I should also mention that indentation in C and C++ is solely for the benefit of the human reader; it doesn't matter to the computer.

The construction

if (*condition*) *statement*
else if (*condition*) *statement*
else *statement*

works in an entirely similar way. Any number of **else if** lines may be used. In writing the conditions, any of the following operators may be used:

== is equal to
!= not equal
< is less than
> is greater than
>= is greater than or equal
<= is less than or equal
|| or
&& and
! not

Besides the **for** keyword, the keywords **while** and **do** can also be used to write loops. The general form of the **while** is

while(*condition*) *statement*

which executes the statement as long as the condition is true. There is an example in the *Tiny* code:

```
while(Iteration < 20){
```

For the **do** keyword, the syntax is

do *statement* **while** (*condition*);

The *statement* executes until the *condition* becomes false. Since the *condition* is tested after each pass through the loop, the loop will execute at least once. In practice, the **do** loop is seldom used.

Finally, we need to mention three statements for jumping about in the code. The most commonly used is **break**, which breaks out of the innermost loop where it is found. There will be an example in the *Tiny* code below. The **continue** statement shifts control to the end of the innermost loop, while

goto *label;*

sends control to the *label*. The *label* is a line with one word ending in a colon, like *top*: or *finish*: . In good C++ style, the **goto** is seldom used; but it is useful when breaking out of a deep nest of loops. (If you have ever used Fortran, please note that the function of the C++ **continue** statement is totally unlike that of the Fortran CONTINUE statement.)

That is about all you need to know about C++ in general to use Interdyme. We can now turn to the C++ code in the box. First of all, there are a few Interdyme-specific functions and variables you need to know about. In the second line of code, we meet the variable *MaxFlag*; it is a single letter, either 'y' or 'n' for "yes" or "no". It will be 'y' only if the user has specified that we are to do an optimization. We will assume that it is 'n'. In that case, the *printf()* function writes to the screen the year which is about to be computed. (For the full capabilities of *printf()* or the C++ alternative keyword out, you can consult the help file of your C++ compiler.)

The program then calls the Interdyme functions *load(t)* to load into the computer's random access memory (RAM) from the computer's hard disk the starting values for year *t* of all vectors and matrices in the VAM file on the hard disk. At the bottom of the for loop, the *store(t)* function stores their newly computed values back to the VAM file.

Besides the matrices and vectors handled by the VAM file, most Interdyme models will also have macro variables such as GDP, total labor force, total employment, unemployment, or an interest rate, which for any given period, have only one number – not a vector or matrix of numbers – as their value. Because such variables occur also in macroeconomic models, we refer to them as *macro variables*, even though they may be quite "small" or very specific variables, such as "children under 5 years of age". They are carried in a G bank which generally has the same root name as the corresponding VAM file. Similarly, we will refer to as *macro equations* all of the regression equations handled one-by-one, as in macro models.

The call to the function *uptseries()* at the beginning of MODEL.CPP checks all the macro variables, and where it finds a value missing in the current period, period *t*, it inserts the value of that macro variable from the previous period. As noted above, this replacement gets the iterative process of solution off to a good start. On the other hand, exogenous variables that have specified values are not affected by the call to *uptseries()*. The *uptseries()* function was written by *IdBuild* and is in the file HEART.CPP.

At this point, we begin the code that is particular to *Tiny*. Through the general Interdyme structure, the person running the model provides a value for the variable *MacEqStartDate*, the date at which the macro equations of the model begin to be computed. *Tiny* has only one macro equation, namely that for *invtot(t)*, total investment. Since we have known accounts up through 2003, we will set *MacEqStartDate* equal to 2003. (How we do so, we will see shortly.) Prior to this date, the Interdyme model for *Tiny* produces the same results as did the *G7*-only model. In 2003, only *invtot* and *gdp* may be different. Other macro variables are not affected because the national income accountant function, *accountf()*, is not called until the next year. In practice, we will normally set the rho-adjustment factor for all of the macro variable regression equations in this year (how that is done will be explained below). Those variables will not differ from historical values in this last year of historical macroeconomic data.

Once *t* has passed the *MacEqStartDate*, the final demands determine output (via the Seidel input-output calculations), but output determines value-added which in turn determines (via the institutional accounts) Personal income. This thenv determines total Personal consumption expenditure, which is one of the final demands. Just as in macro models we solve this circularity by iteration. That is, we start off with one set of final demand totals – *pcetot[t]*, *invtot[t]*, *govtot[t]*, *extot[t]*, *imtot[t]* – and compute along until will have calculated new values. We then compare the new values with the old, and if the differences exceed the tolerances we set, we go back to compute with the new values of the variables, final demands, outputs, value added, and the variables just listed. We repeat the process until convergence is reached or the iteration counter exceeds 20, whereupon we go on to the next year. Since *govtot[t]*, *extot[t]* and *imtot[t]* are exogenous, they will not vary from iteration to iteration, so only the values of *pcetot[t]* and *invtot[t]* are checked for convergence. In fact, the form of the regression equation we estimated has no dependence of *invtot[t]* on variables in period *t*, so we do not for the present model need to check *invtot[t]*, but we leave the check because in principle there could be such a dependency. The lines of code that drive the looping process are:

```
Iteration = 0;
// The loop for convergence on pcetot and invtot.
while(Iteration < 20){
   Iteration++;
   oldinvtot = invtot[t]; oldpcetot = pcetot[t];

   /*****************************************************************
      The substance of the model, which follows here, has been cut out to
      emphasize the testing of convergence. This substance computes new
      values of invtot[t] and pcetot[t].
      *****************************************************************/

   // Form the convergence test
   invdif = fabs(invtot[t] - oldinvtot);
   pcedif = fabs(pcetot[t]- oldpcetot);
   printf("Iter %2d pce = %7.1f pcedif = %6.2f invdif = %6.2f\n",Iteration,
      pcetot[t],pcedif,invdif);
   if(invdif < .5 && pcedif < .5) break;
   }
```

The first line initializes an integer, *Iteration*, to 0. The line

```
while(Iteration < 20){
```

sets up the loop that iteratively solves the circularity just explained. The first line within the loop increments *Iteration* by one, so we see immediately that this loop will not be executed more than 20 times. We then store away the starting values of *invtot[t]* and *pcetot[t]*. Then we execute the substance of the model, which results in changing these values. When that work is complete, we use the standard C++ function *fabs()* to take the absolute value of the difference between the previous and the new values of these two variables. If both of those values are less than .5, we break out of the **while** loop. More complicated models may have more complicated convergence tests, but *Tiny's* example is pretty typical.

Once convergence has been reached, the main thing to be done is to call *store(t)*, which stores back to the computer's hard disk this period's values of the vectors and matrices.

With the iterative solution of the circularity understood, we turn to the the substance of the model. It is easily followed in the code in the box below. The first thing we see is the call to *invtotf()*

350

when *t* is greater than or equal to the starting date for macro equations. The next three lines show multiplication of a vector (such as *invc*) by a scalar (such as *invtot[t]*). Then follows the addition of five vectors to form the vector *fd*. Then the function *Seidel()* is called to compute the output vector *out* implied by the final demand vector *fd*, and the input-output coefficient matrix *AM*. The the value-added vectors are computed via element-by-element multiplication of the coefficient vectors with the output vector. Then *gdp* and the value-added component totals are computed as sums of vectors. Finally, the accountant is called to make up the national accounts.

Substance of MODEL.CPP for TINY

```
if(t>=MacEqStartDate)
    invtotf();
inv = invtot[t]*invc;   pce=pcetot[t]*pcec;
gov = govtot[t]*govc;   im = imtot[t]*imc;
ex = extot[t] * exc;
fd = pce + gov + inv + ex + im
Seidel(AM, out, fd, triang, toler);
dep = ebemul(depc,out);   lab = ebemul(labc, out);
cap = ebemul(capc, out); ind = ebemul(indc, out);
// The Accountant for Tiny
gdp[t] = fd.sum();
if(t>MacEqStartDate) {
    deprec[t] = dep.sum();   labinc[t] = lab.sum();
    capinc[t] = cap.sum();   indtax[t] = ind.sum();
    accountf();
    }
```

This code has several vector and matrix operations. The Interdyme code, nestled away in other modules (.CPP files) where you do not need to bother reading it, defines what a Vector and Matrix are and instructs the computer how to read them, add or subtract them, multiply a Matrix by a Vector, sum up the elements of a Vector, and do both inner-product and element-by-element multiplication of two Vectors. Let me emphasize: Matrix and Vector are not general C++ features; it is the other modules of Interdyme working in the background that give you these handy tools for writing the code for input-output models. In fact, though we have used here only vector addition, Interdyme has a rather complete library of matrix and vector routines.

The Interdyme function *Seidel(AM, out, fd, triang, toler)* solves by the Seidel method the equation

$$out = AM*out + fd$$

using the order of equations specified by the integer vector *triang* and with the convergence tolerance specified by *toler*. The value of integer vector, or *Ivector*, is given by the file TRIANG.IV. For *Tiny*, its value is

8 7 5 6 4 3 1 2

351

The Interdyme function *ebemul()* does an element-by-element multiplication of two Vectors and gives a Vector as its output. The floating point absolute value function, *fabs()*, as already mentioned, is a standard C++ function.

Running the Interdyme Model

With the code of MODEL.CPP ready to go, we can create the G bank with all the macrovariables of the model, write the C++ code for handling the regression equations and identities, compile this code and MODEL.CPP, link the compiled modules (whose file names end in *.obj*) into an executable program (*.exe*) and get started on forecasting the exogenous variables, all by clicking "Model" in the *G7* main menu and then "Run IdBuild and compile model".

These clicks bring up the window shown below. If there was a BUILD.CFG file in the directory where *G7* was started, then it will have been used to fill in the boxes in this form.

Run IdBuild Dialog

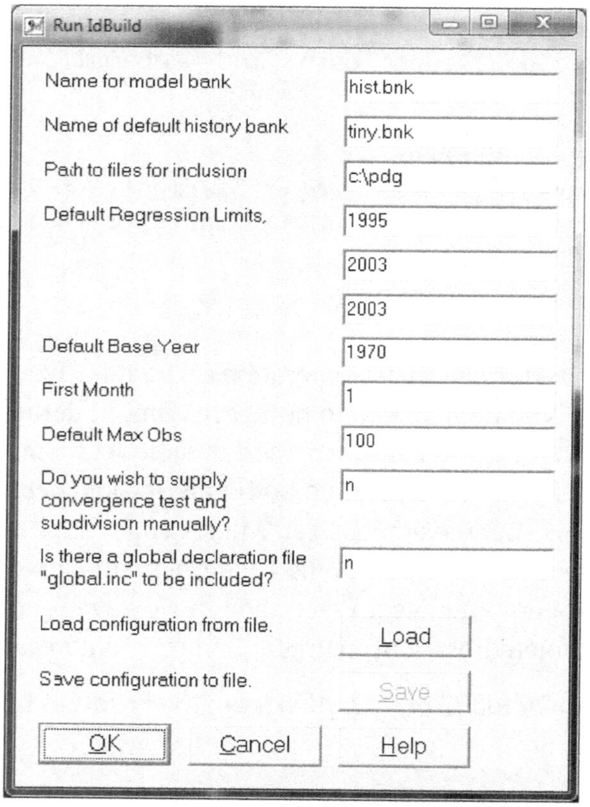

Otherwise, the user can fill them in, click OK, and the content will be written as the BUILD.CFG file. The first box, labeled "Name for model bank", contains the name of the G bank to be created having all the variables in the model, but no others. The second box, labeled "Name of default history bank", contains the name of a G bank from which to draw historical values of the variables, until a "bank" command switches to a different input bank. The first bank is created by the

IdBuild program; the second must already exist prior to running *IdBuild*. Generally, the G bank created by *IdBuild* should have the same root name as the VAM file with the historical values of the vectors and matrices.

The next three fields labeled "Default regression limits", are not actually used. They are there to keep the format of BUILD.CFG the same as that of G.CFG files; any dates will work fine. Then come the base year of the bank to be created, the first month of that year which is covered (which is always 1 for annual models), and the maximum number of observations (years) to be accommodated in the bank. The next two fields allow for advanced features we will not be using and should for our purposes just contain the letter *n* for *no*. When the form has been filled in as desired – and it will usually automatically be filled in correctly – click OK.

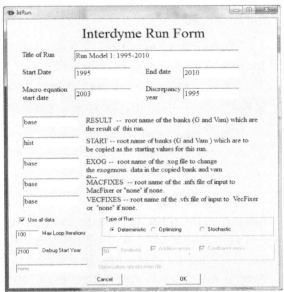

This one click runs *IdBuild*, which writes HEART.CPP. It also compiles MODEL.CPP, HEART.CPP and any other modules that need to be compiled, links them together and produces DYME.EXE, the executable file for running the model.

As described in the earlier section, running *IdBuild* also writes EXOGALL.REG and RUN.XOG. It also creates the HIST bank of macro variables in the model. You can use EXOGALL.REG to make projections of the exogenous variables, exactly as with macro models. It will put the predicted values of each exogenous variable into its own .XOG file, such as this one, GOVTOT.XOG

```
update govtot
    2003     348.1439    353.9075    360.3546    367.3013    374.6133
    2008     382.1923    389.9666    397.8835
```

As with macromodels, you can edit these .XOG files to change the forecasts. In doing so, you can make use of any function in G7.[15] When the file is edited, change the extenstion of the filename from .XOG to .XG so that your carefully edited file is not overwritten the next time *IdBuild* is run.

For the present, we are going to content use the RUN.XOG as automatically written (and shown above) and also with all the .XOG files. But we need a copy of RUN.XOG named RUN.XG. We can do that by simply opening RUN.XOG in the editor and saving it as RUN.XG. For our first example, we will also copy RUN.XG to BASE.XG, and this file will be used in the discussion below.

---

15 But the convenient device of putting a 0 for values to be linearly interpolated does not work because in *G7* it is sometimes important to give a true 0 to a variable. Instead, in the "update" command, one leaves out the value to be linearly interpolated and uses *G7*'s @lint() function. For example, if we wanted to keep the above values of *govtot* for 2003 – 2007 but set the 2010 value to 420, and interpolate 2008 and 2009 linearly between 2007 and 2010, we would put into GOVTOT.XG the following:

```
update govtot
2003 348.1439  353.9075  360.3546  367.3013
2007 374.6133
 2010 420
f govtot = @lint(govtot)
```

You can now run the Interdyme model by clicking

Model | Run Dyme Model

The form shown on the right then appears.

The "Title of Run" can be anything that fits in the space provided. It will show up on tables made with the *Compare* program.

The "Start Date" field should be a four-digit year, for example, 2008. It is the year in which the calculations begin. The "End date" field is similar; it is the last year for which calculations will be made.

The "Macro equation start date" is the first year in which the macro equations will be calculated. In forecasts, it will generally be the last year for which there is data on values of the macro variables. This data is then used to set the initial value of the rho adjustment. For historical or counter-historical simulations, the macro equation start date is some time before the last available data.

The "Discrepancy year" is used in some models as the year for calculating a discrepancy vector subsequently used in the input-output calculations. If your model does not use this device, just fill in any year.

The next five fields all use the concept of the *root name* of a file. It is the part of the filename following the directory name, but before the dot in the name. Thus, the root name of the file whose full name is C:\MALAYSIA\MODEL\BASE.BNK is just BASE. The part of the file name after the dot is called the *extension*. In the example just given, the extension is BNK. The expression *run bank* is also useful. A *run bank* is the combination of three files, the .VAM, the .BNK, and .IND files associated with a run of the model. All three of these files should have the same root name, and that root name is the root name of the run bank.

The words RESULT, START, EXOG, MACFIXES and VECFIXES will now be used as names of variables. The values of these variables are specified by the content of the edit boxes just to the left of these names on the form. The START variable should be given the root name of the run bank which the model begins its calculations. The first time the model is run, the START run bank will have been created by a *G7*-only version of the model. Once a base simulation has been established with a run named, say, BASE, this run bank can be used as the START run bank for subsequent runs of the model.

The RESULT field should be filled in with the root name of the run bank which will be created by the run of the model. Examples could be "Base" or "Boom" or "Crash". Normally, the START run bank is copied to the RESULT run bank before any calculations are done. But if START and RESULT are the same, no copy can be made – a file cannot be copied onto itself – and the model begins its calculations from the run bank specified by these two names.

The next variable to be supplied by the user is EXOG, the root name of a file having the extension .XG. This is a file of *G7 commands* which change the *exogenous* variables in the RESULT run bank. These changes can include both exogenous macro variables such as population or money supply and exogenous variables in the VAM file, such as input-output matrices.

The next variable is MACFIXES. Just as macro models need to be manipulated by fixes on their behavioral equations, so too do multisectoral models. The fixes are specified in ways that are similar to those of macromodels. The details are supplied later in this chapter. For the moment, it is enough to note that the specifications should be put in a file having the extension *.mfx*. The root name might be "Base", "Boom", "Crash" or any other descriptive word, but not *Macfixes*. That root name should be typed into the MACFIXES field, and a program called *Macfixer* is called to prepare the fixes for use by the model. If the word "none" (without the quotation marks) is typed there, *Macfixer* is not called, and no macro fixes are used.

Besides the fixes on macrovariables, there may be fixes on vectors. As with macro equation fixes, the details are specified later in this chapter. The specifications should be in a file with the extension *.vfx* and the root name of this file should be typed into the VECFIXES field It should NOT be *VecFixes*. These fixes are processed by a program called *Fixer*. If the word "none" is in the VECFIXES field, *Fixer* is not called and the simulation program does not look for vector fixes.

If the box "Use all data" is checked, all known values of endogenous macrovariables will be used. It should not be checked if it is desired to test the model inside the period of known historical values of endogenous macrovariables.

The type of run will normally be "deterministic". Optimization similar to that for macro models is available. Stochastic simulation is not presently (2011) available, but should not be especially difficult to program for macro equations.

Sometimes, when a model is not behaving correctly, it is useful to put in debugging printout. Often the problem is not visible until the model has run several years. Only then is the printout desired. The "Debug start year" field provides a way to supply the year in which such printing starts. If it is not used in the model, it may be given a value far out into the future, as has been done in the example.

When this form has been completed, just click the OK button, and the model will be run.

If all goes well, *that is all you need to know*. But if you would like to know more details about what happens when you click OK, here are the basics.

The five fields across the top of the form and the two panes at the bottom are used to create a file called DYME.CFG. The box below shows what it looks like for a base run of *Tiny* with no vector fixes.

```
Title of run              ;Demonstration of the Tiny Model
Start year                ;1995
Finish year               ;2010
Start MacEq yr            ;2003
Discrepancy yr            ;1995
Use all data?             ;yes
VecFix file               ;none
MacroFix file             ;Macfixes
Vam file                  ;base
G bank                    ;base
Debug start yr            ;2100
Max iterations            ;100
Optimization specification file; none
Number of random draws; 0
Additive random errors; no
Random coefficients; no
```

The five edit controls in the middle of the Interdyme Run Form are used to create an "add" command with arguments to the *G7* command processor. The command is:

add run.add <RESULT> <START> <EXOG> <MACFIXES> <VECFIXES>

where the values of the variables <RESULT>, <START>, etc., are taken from the form. All but the second of these names can easily be the same. For example, a base forecast might be made, starting from the historical simulation bank by the following command to *G7*:

add run.add base hist base base base

In fact, this way of working is to be recommended, for then the result of the run is a set of files which all have the same root name. In the case of the example, they would be BASE.VAM, BASE.BNK, BASE.IND, BASE.XG, and BASE.MFX. As noted, either or both of MACFIXES and VECFIXES can be "none".

The real question is now "What is the RUN.ADD file, and what does it do?" It is a simple text file that needs to be in the directory with the model. It and two helper batch files COPYTOTEMP.BAT and DYMERUNNER.BAT, also need to be in the same directory. They are shown in the boxes below.

```
                          The RUN.ADD File

# run.add - The arguments to this file are:
#   %1 <RESULT>, %2 <START>, %3 <EXOG>, %4 <MACFIXES>, %5 <VECFIXES>
dos CopyToTmp %2

# Revise macro bank and vam file with EXOG.XG
wsb tmp
vam tmp b
dvam b
add %3.xg
wsb ws
close b

# Tap Enter to run the model
pause

dos DymeRunner %1 %2 %3 %4 %5
```

```
                     The CopyToTemp.bat File

copy %1.ind tmp.ind
copy %1.bnk tmp.bnk
copy %1.vam tmp.vam
```

RUN.ADD first uses the COPYTOTEMP.BAT file to copy the <START> run bank to a temporary run bank whose components are tmp.ind, tmp.bnk and tmp.vam. Then it makes the tmp bank the G workspace bank and tmp.vam the default vam file. Then it causes *G7* to use the commands and data in EXOG.XG to update all the exogenous variables, vectors and matrices. (Remember, EXOG here is a variable which will have whatever value you gave it in the Interdyme Run Form.) With all the exogenous variables now stored in the tmp run bank, that bank is now freed by *G7* (the "wsb ws" and "close b" lines) so that it can be opened by the DYME.EXE program which runs the model.

RUN.ADD then executes the DYMERUNNER.BAT DOS batch file. If there are vector fixes, they are processed by the *Fixer* program to form the VECFIXES.FIN file. If there are macrofixes, they are processed by *MacFixer* to create the Macfixes G bank used by the Interdyme program. Note: the name of the file that specifies your macro fixes should have the extension *.mfx*, but should not be MACFIXES.MFX. Likewise, the file that specifies the vector fixes should have the extension *.vfx*, but should NOT be VECFIXES.VFX.

The DymeRunner.bat File

```
rem DymeRunner.bat
rem The arguments here have the same meaning as in run.add.
rem If there are no Vector fixes, skip to Macro fixes.
echo %1 %2 %3 %4 %5
if %5 == none goto macrofixes
rem FAILURE
rem Here when there are Vector fixes
copy %5.vfx VecFixes.vfx
zap
fixer
copy VecFixes.chk %1.vck
copy VecFixes.vfx %1.vfx
:macrofixes
if %4 == none goto runmodel
copy %4.mfx MacFixes.mfx
macfixer
copy MacFixes.chk %1.mck
copy MacFixes.mfx %1.mfx
:runmodel
dyme

echo Dyme has finished

copy tmp.* %1.*
```

With all the exogenous data and fixes read for its use, the Interdyme model is executed by the simple command "dyme". When it finishes, the tmp files are all copied to files with corresponding extensions, but with the value of the RESULT variable as their root name. Similarly, after execution of *Fixer* and *MacFixer*, their input and check files are copied to RESULT.mfx, RESULT.mck (the check file), RESULT.vfx, and RESULT.vck (the check file from *Fixer*). If EXOG is the same as RESULT, then all of the inputs and outputs of the run will have the same root name, a fact which makes it easy to keep track of what goes into and comes out of each run of the model.

If all these steps seem a bit complicated, remember that it only takes one click on the OK button to execute them all. Note also that a record of all the input files is made with the value of RESULT as their root name.

The MACFIXER.CFG file is assumed to be:

```
Input fix file      ;MacFixes.mfx
Output fixes bank ..........;MacFixes
Model G bank       ...................;tmp
Output check file ......;MacFixer.chk
```

The FIXER.CFG (for *Fixer*) is assumed to be:

Input fix file	;VecFixes.vf
x	
Fix index (.fin) output file	;vecfixes
VAM reference	........;tmp
Text check file	...;fixer.chk

While these files can be changed by the user, doing so will probably cause the Interdyme Run Form to stop working. The flexibility gained by changing these files is unlikely to be worth the confusion it will probably cause.

Here are the graphs of total investment and the output of manufacturing for this simplest version (model 1) of the *Tiny* Interdyme model.

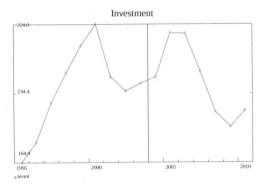

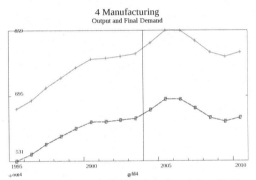

The results are clearly looking more like model results than they did with all demand exogenous.

Lest you get lost in all the details, let's review what you actually have to do to run *Tiny* Model 1. You start *G7* in the \Tiny\Model directory and follow the steps in the box on the next page.

In *G7*:

add tiny.pre (creates HIST.VAM file with historical data and project the coefficients into future periods.)

add invtot.reg (estimate regression equations)

(Here you could edit MODEL.CPP to make changes for new features)

Click **Model | Run IdBuild and compile model**

Edit EXOGALL.REG to set tdates 2003 2010 and set limits to 1995 2003 2010

In *G7*:

add exogall.reg (to generate forecasts of exogenous variables; edit the forecasts if desired)

Edit RUN.XOG to make desired changes in the exogenous forecasts; add commands to read exogenous values of matrices and vectors, and save the result as BASE.XG.

Click **Model | Run Dyme Model** and fill in the blanks as desired and click OK.

Back in *G7*, to graph the results, type

```
gdates 1995 2003 2010
vam base b
fadd graphs.fad sectors.ttl
```

To make tables, click **Model | Express Tables**

We will add a number of features to *Tiny* to illustrate things you can do with a model of a real economy. But before we go further, it is time for a few exercises.

Exercises

1.   Make alternative forecasts for some of the exogenous variables in *Tiny*, run the model with them, graph the results, and show them in tables.

2.   Estimate a regression equation for total imports as a function of GDP, put it into the model, run the model and compare graphically the results with those without your function.

More on Interdyme Programming

Before you can build a *Tiny*-like model for your own imaginary or real economy, we have to deal with one more basic question: How is the Interdyme program connected with the VAM file? How does it know, for example, that there are vectors in *Tiny*'s VAM file named *fd*, *pce*, *gov*, *inv* and so on? The answer is that the model builder has to indicate to the model the names of these vectors and matrices. The VAM file is then used to determine their dimension. This identification has to be done in two steps. First, there is a file called USER.H; the one for *Tiny* is shown in the box below.

The USER.H File for *Tiny* Model 1

```
// USER.H -- Put here any includes that refer to the user model, per se.
//   This version is for Tiny, Model 1

// These names will be read From DYME.CFG and opening screen:
GLOBAL char RunTitle[80],CfgFileName[80],VamFileName[80],GbankName[80],
   VecFixFileName[80],MacFixFileName[80];

GLOBAL char* outfix; // Determines how Seidel will determine output

// Vector declaration:
GLOBAL Vector out, pce, gov, inv, ex, im, fd,
   dep, lab, cap, ind, va, depc, labc, capc,
   indc, pcec, invc, govc, exc, imc, x, y, fix;

// Matrix declaration
GLOBAL Matrix AM;

// Integer Vector that gives the triangulation order of sectors
GLOBAL IVector triang;
```

All the variables declared in USER.H are "global", C jargon for variables which can be accessed from anywhee in the program. This fact is indicated by the word GLOBAL in front of these variables. To explain exactly what is going on here requires some explanation, which you can skip if you are familiar with C and C++, or don't want to bother with the details of exactly how this GLOBAL keyword works.

Unlike Basic and Fortran, C and C++ are strictly "typed" languages. That is, the nature of every variable must be declared before it can be used. Typical declarations are:

```
char sex;        // char is a character variable
int zip;         // int is an integer
float height, weight;   // float is a real number
char name[40];  // this is an array of characters
```

The variable *sex* is a single character, presumably 'M' or 'F'; the variable *zip* is an integer, something like 20742; *height* and *weight* are floating point numbers, that is, numbers that potentially have a fractional component like 72.5 or 217.8. The variable *name* is a string of up to 40 characters, something like "Thomas". If a variable is declared inside a function, it is local to that function. Other functions know nothing about it. But a variable declared outside of all functions, typically near the top of a file containing C code, is global and can be accessed by all functions in that file. A large program such as Interdyme usually consists of a number of files with names ending in .CPP; each of these files is called a module, and is compiled separately. If some variable, say *name*, is to be accessed in several different modules, then it must be declared globally in all the modules where it is accessed. But one and only one of the modules should actually make space for it. Which one? To answer this question, the program should mark all the declarations which are not to make space as **extern**, like this:

```
extern char name[40];
```

In one and only one module should appear the simple declaration:

```
char name[40];
```

That is the module where the space is allocated for the variable. When the compiled modules are "linked" to form one whole executable program, the references to the variable in all the modules where it was external are made to point to the space allocated by the one module where it was not external.

It could potentially be quite a nuisance to remember to mark all but one declaration as **extern**. That is where the word "GLOBAL" comes in handy. It is not a standard C keyword but is used in Interdyme, *G7,* and many other programs. The declarations of all global variables are put into "header" files like USER.H, and are marked GLOBAL. These header files are then "included" into all the modules where they are relevant by a compiler directive like

```
#include "user.h"
```

In all but one module, this directive is preceded by another:

```
#define GLOBAL extern
```

In these modules, the compiler will replace "GLOBAL" by "extern" before compiling. In that one and only one other module, namely DYME.CPP in Interdyme, the "#include" is preceded by

```
#define GLOBAL
```

which defines GLOBAL to be nothing, so that in this module the "extern" is omitted and space is made for the global variables.

When a vector or matrix is declared locally, it can be fully "constructed", that is, space allocated for its elements. But there is a problem with declaring an object like a vector globally; since the declaration is outside of any function, no computing can be done. To find out how much space to allocate for the array of numbers in the vector, the VAM file has to be read, but reading the VAM file is computing, so what needs to be done? The answer is that once computing has begun, we must *resize* all the global matrices and vectors. That is, we must read the VAM file, find out how big the matrix or vector is, grab enough memory to hold it, and stick the pointer to that memory into the space saved for the pointer by the global declaration.

That may seem complicated to understand, but it is easy to do. Look at MODEL.CPP for TINY with the *G7* or other text editor. The lines concerned with resizing are the following:

```
// Resize Vectors
out.r("out"); pce.r("pce"); gov.r("gov");
inv.r("inv"); ex.r("ex"); im.r("im"); fd.r("fd");
dep.r("dep"); lab.r("lab"); cap.r("cap"); ind.r("ind");
depc.r("depc"); labc.r("labc"); capc.r("capc"); indc.r("indc");
pcec.r("pcec"); invc.r("invc"); govc.r("govc"); exc.r("exc");
imc.r("imc"); x.r("x"); y.r("y");

// Resize Matrices
AM.r("AM");
```

The "resize" function or method is abbreviated to just .r . The argument to the resize function is the name of the vector or matrix in the VAM file. Preparing these lines for USER.H and MODEL.CPP from the VAM.CFG is a lot of rather mechanical, error-prone work. However, when you gave *G7* the command:

vamcreate vam.cfg hist

it also wrote two files, VAM.GLB and VAM.RSZ, as follows

The VAM.GLB file:

```
GLOBAL Vector out, pce, gov, inv, ex, im, fd,
   dep, lab, cap, ind, depc, labc, capc,
   indc, pcec, invc, govc, exc, imc, x,
   y;
GLOBAL Matrix FM, AM, LINV;
GLOBAL Matrix OUTlag;
```

The VAM.RSZ file

```
out.r("out"); pce.r("pce"); gov.r("gov");
inv.r("inv"); ex.r("ex"); im.r("im"); fd.r("fd");
dep.r("dep"); lab.r("lab"); cap.r("cap"); ind.r("ind");
depc.r("depc"); labc.r("labc"); capc.r("capc"); indc.r("indc");
pcec.r("pcec"); invc.r("invc"); govc.r("govc"); exc.r("exc");
imc.r("imc"); x.r("x"); y.r("y");
FM.r("FM"); AM.r("AM"); LINV.r("LINV");
OUTlag.r("out");
```

They are in the \tiny\model directory. You will notice a striking similarity to the corresponding portions of the USER.H and MODEL.CPP files. All you have to do is bring these two files written by *G7* into USER.H and MODEL.CPP , respectively, with the *G7* or other text editor. For the model, I removed the *FM* and *LINV* matrices, for they will not be used in the Interdyme model. Likewise, I removed *OUTlag* matrix, which is used to store the lagged values of the *out* vector, because the lagged values are not yet in use.

The rest of the *loop()* function should be regarded as the standard form, which the user of Interdyme should have no need to change. The *spin()* function, which we have looked at in detail, is where the changes have to be made for different models.

Exercise

3.   Build a TINY- like model for your imaginary economy or for a real economy for which you have data readily available.

17.2. Matrix Tools in Interdyme

Here is a quick overview of the actions, operators, and functions available in Interdyme. Some of them we have seen, but others were not needed in the TINY example. You need not learn the exact syntax of each of them; just make a mental note of the possibilities.

If *A* is a Matrix or Vector and *k* is a scalar (a float in C terms), then

*k*A*	multiplies each element of *A* by *k*.
A/k	divides each element of *A* by *k*.

If *A* and *B* are both Matrices or both Vectors of the same dimension, then

A + B	gives the matrix or vector sum
A - B	gives the matrix or vector difference
ebemul(*A*,*B*)	gives the element-by-element product
ebediv(*A*,*B*)	gives the element-by-element quotient, the elements of *A* being divided by the corresponding elements of *B*. If, an element of *B* is zero, the corresponding element of A is returned in that position.

If *A* has the same number of columns as *B* has rows, then

*A*B*	gives the matrix product.

If *A* and *B* have the same number of rows, then

A/B	gives the same thing as ~A*B that is, the transpose of A multiplied by B, but without actually forming the transpose of A. (Think of the / as being a ' to denote transposing the matrix.)

Interdyme understands parentheses. If all the dimensions are appropriate, the following is an acceptable statement:

A =k* (B+C+D)*(E + F + G*(H+I));

If x and y are both Vectors with the same number of elements:

    dot(x,y)   gives the inner product as a float.

If A is a Matrix and x is a Vector with the same number of elements as A has columns,

    A%x   gives the result of converting x to a diagonal matrix and then post-multiplying A by this diagonal matrix. Essentially, it multiplies each column of A by the corresponding element of x.

If A is a Matrix and x is a Vector with the same number of elements as A has rows,

    x%A   gives the result of converting x to a diagonal matrix and then premultiplying A by this diagonal matrix. Said perhaps more simply, it multiplies each row of A by the corresponding element of x.

The first of these % operations is useful in computing a flow matrix from a coefficient matrix and a vector of outputs. The second can compute a flow matrix in current prices from one in constant prices.

For a Matrix A, Vector v, float z, and int k,

v.set(z)	sets all elements of Vector v to z.
A.set(z)	sets all elements of Matrix A to z.
pulloutcol(v, A, k)	pulls column k of A into v.
putincol(v, A, k)	puts v into column k of A.
pulloutrow(v, A, k)	pulls row k of A into v.
putinrow(v, A, k)	puts v in row k of A.
v = colsum(A)	puts the column sums of A into the vector v.
v = rowsum(A)	puts the row sums of A into the vector v.
z = v.sum()	puts the sum of the elements of v into z.
v.First()	gives the number in the first row of v if v is column or in the first column if v is a row.

If A is a square, non-singular matrix,

!A	gives the inverse of A.
A.invert(i,j)	transforms A into its inverse by Gauss-Jordan pivoting. The pivot operations start in row i and stop when the pivot has been in row j. If these arguments are omitted, the pivoting starts in the first row and continues through the last, to produce the true inverse.

The difference here is that !A does not change A but creates a new matrix for the inverse while A.invert() transforms A into its inverse. Thus, if memory space is scarce, the invert action may be preferable. The algorithm in both cases is Gauss-Jordan pivoting with no niceties. Don't trust it if your matrix poses any problems for inversion.

If A a is either a Vector or Matrix object, then

365

~A	gives the transpose of *A*.
A.rows()	gives the number of rows as an integer.
A.columns()	gives the number of columns as an integer.
A.firstrow()	gives the number of the first row as an integer.
A.lastrow()	gives the number of the last row as an integer.
A.firstcolumn()	gives the number of the first column as an integer.
A.lastcolumn()	gives the number of the last column as an integer.

If A is a square Matrix and q and f are Vectors of the appropriate dimension, the equation

```
q = Aq +f;
```

can be solved by the Seidel iterative method (if it converges) by the function

```
Seidel(A, q, f, triang, toler);
```

where *triang* is an array of integers giving the order in which the rows of *A* should be selected in the Seidel process, and *toler* is a float giving the tolerance which is accepted in the iterative solution. Similarly, the equation

```
p = pA + v;
```

can be solved by

```
PSeidel(A, p, v, triang, toler);
```

If you need a temporary Matrix *A* or Vector *B* is not in the VAM file, you can declare it locally in the function where it is needed by:

```
Matrix A(n,m);
Vector B(n);
```

were *n* is the number of rows and *m* is the number of columns.

In the process of debugging a program, it is sometimes useful to display a Matrix or Vector *A* on the screen. To do so, use

```
A.Display("message", fieldwidth, decimals);
```

To write a Matrix *A* to a file use

```
writemat(A, filename,fieldwidth, decimals);
```

To write a Vector *A* to a file use

```
writevec(A, filename, fieldwidth, decimals);
```

For completeness, we mention a function which will be explained in following sections. A Matrix *A* can be balanced to have the row sums given by Vector *a* and column sums given by Vector b by the function

```
int ras(A, a, b)
```

If the sum of the elements of *a* and *b* are not equal, the user is required to pick which governs.

Finally, we should mention that all of these matrix routines are available in a matrix package called BUMP (Beginner's Understandable Matrix Package) which can be used in C++ independently of Interdyme. The code of BUMP is carefully explained so that beginners of C++ can learn how to write such functions. Understanding how it works, however, is not necessary for using the functions in Interdyme any more than it is necessary to know how Excel is programmed in order to use it.

17.3. Vector Elements in Regression Equations

This section will use *IdBuild* to develop consumption equations for personal consumption, even though the left-hand side variables are vector elements. This version of the *Tiny* model is Model 2.

So far, we have used only one behavioral, regression-estimated equation, the one for investment. In this section, we will add regression equations for all components of Personal consumption expenditures. In the process, we will introduce several new techniques. So far, we have used only macrovariables in regressions. Now we will see how to use elements of vectors in regression. To ensure that the total of the predicted values stands in a reasonable relation to disposable income, we will need to learn about static vectors and apply some vector arithmetic.

In the Tiny\Model directory, you will find the file PCE.DAT shown below.

PCE.DAT

```
# vamcr vam.cfg test
# vam test b
# dvam b
vmatdat r 1 9  1 8 5
pce 1995 1996 1997 1998 1999 2000 2001 2002 2003
#" Date" " pce1$" " pce2$" " pce3$" " pce4$" " pce5$" " pce6$" "  pce7$" pce8$
1995    14.169   1.908   76.759   283.944   288.323   109.289   443.041  0.0
1996    14.101   1.917   78.365   299.580   295.352   115.091   446.638  0.0
1997    14.127   1.934   76.941   317.095   304.522   121.077   454.966  0.0
1998    14.228   1.972   77.331   343.489   317.501   123.079   466.458  0.0
1999    14.519   2.016   77.277   375.369   334.601   126.768   478.526  0.0
2000    15.000   2.000   80.000   400.000   350.000   130.000   500.000  0.0
2001    14.947   2.001   77.527   407.622   353.149   127.153   506.602  0.0
2002    14.821   1.985   77.343   419.457   356.482   121.248   508.665  0.0
2003    14.974   1.928   75.216   435.677   364.071   115.282   507.851  0.0
```

Open *G7*, assign the HIST.VAM file as bank b, and make it the default vam file. Then introduce the data in the PCE.DAT with an "add pce.dat"statement, and check that it has been correctly read with the "show" command.

From this data, we now want to estimate simple consumption equations by regressing each component of the Personal consumption expenditure vector, *pce*, on personal disposable income (*pdisinc*) and its first difference (*dpdis*). You will also find in the \tiny\model directory the PCE.REG file shown, in abbreviated form, on the right. (The . . . . show where there are similar triplets of commands for regressions for sectors 2, 3, 4, and 5 in the full file on the disk.) You can now execute this command file in *G7* either by "add pce.reg" or by opening the file in the editor and clicking "Run". You will see that *G7* has no problem figuring out that pce1, pce2, ..., pce7 are elements of the pce vector in the default VAM bank.

The PCE.REG File

```
lim 1995 2003 2010
catch pce.cat
save  pce.sav
f dpdis = pdisinc - pdisinc[1]
ti PCE on Agriculture
r pce1 = pdisinc, dpdis
gr *

. . . .

ti PCE on Services
r pce7= pdisinc, dpdis
gr *
save off
catch off
```

IdBuild, however, is not so clever. It knows nothing about the VAM bank. In response to the command "iadd pce.sav", it will give a number of error messages such as "Cannot find pce1." The solution, however, is simple. We just need to tell *IdBuild* that pce is a vector. We do so with the command

isvector pce

in the MASTER file. Here is the complete MASTER file for the TINY model with the PCE equations. The new material is in bold type.

Master File for TINY with PCE Equations
isvector pce
iadd pce.sav
isvector clear
iadd invtot.sav
iadd account.sav
iadd pseudo.sav
end

From it, *IdBuild* will produce a HEART.CPP file with the section shown in the box below for the PCE equations. Note first that *pce* Vector must be passed to the function *pcef()*; Secondly, note that the left side of equation stores the value computed by the equation directly into the appropriate element of the *pce* vector. There is no provision here for the automatic application of fixes or rho adjustments. How fixes or adjustments may be applied we will see in a later section. Finally, back in the Master file above, note the "isvector clear" command in the third line. If it were not there, *IdBuild* would write the following *invtotf()* and *accountf()* functions so that they also had to be passed – quite unnecessarily – the *pce* vector.

368

Personal Consumption Equations in the HEART.CPP File

```
void pcef(Vector& pce)
{
dpdis[t]= pdisinc[t]- pdisinc[t-1];
/*  PCE on Agriculture */
pce[1] = coef[0][0]+coef[0][1]*pdisinc[t]+coef[0][2]*dpdis[t];
/*  PCE on Mining */
pce[2] = coef[1][0]+coef[1][1]*pdisinc[t]+coef[1][2]*dpdis[t];
/*  PCE on Gas and Electricity */
pce[3] = coef[2][0]+coef[2][1]*pdisinc[t]+coef[2][2]*dpdis[t];
/*  PCE on Manufacturing */
pce[4] = +coef[3][0]+coef[3][1]*pdisinc[t]+coef[3][2]*dpdis[t];
/*  PCE on Commerce */
pce[5] = +coef[4][0]+coef[4][1]*pdisinc[t]+coef[4][2]*dpdis[t];
/*  PCE on Transport */
pce[6] = coef[5][0]+coef[5][1]*pdisinc[t]+coef[5][2]*dpdis[t];
/*  PCE on Services */
pce[7] = coef[6][0]+coef[6][1]*pdisinc[t]+coef[6][2]*dpdis[t];
}
```

Equations for Personal consumption expenditures (PCE) need a property not required of the equations for most other variables, namely, they must add up properly. More precisely, the sum of the predicted values from the PCE equations plus Personal savings must equal Personal disposable income. We could, of course, just let savings be a residual, but it is too important for the macroeconomic properties of the model to be treated so casually. So we generally want to have an equation for Personal savings – and for any other items in the difference between total PCE and disposable income, of which there are none in *Tiny*. The best way to achieve this equality is to add up the predicted pieces, compare the sum with the desired total, and spread the difference over the components in some pre-determined shares. The shares we have used are proportional to the income coefficients of the various regression equations. The shares were chosen in this way because the discrepancy between the sum of the predicted values and the desired total can be thought of as a little more or little less income to be divided among the various goods purchased. Sometimes we have used the standard error of estimate of the different equations, on the grounds that the changes should be greatest where the uncertainty about the right value is greatest.

The mechanics of how the discrepancy is allocated is, however, independent of how the shares were determined. We create a text file, which we shall call PCESPREAD.DAT, which has the shares we want to use, however we got them. They should, of course, sum to 1.0. The box to the right shows this file for *Tiny*. In the file USER.H, we need to add at the end the line

```
GLOBAL Vector PCESpread;
```

The PCESPREAD.DAT file

0.003175
0.000236
0.000000
0.481880
0.248311
0.036523
0.229874
0.000000

to declare globally the Vector which will hold the shares for spreading.

To make use of the new equations, we need to make a few changes in MODEL.CPP. On the disk, the modified file is called MODEL2.CPP; copy it to MODEL.CPP to make the changes take effect. The code snippets below show excerpts from the new MODEL2.CPP.

The first order of new business in the *loop()* function is to resize the *PCESpread* vector which has been declared globally and then to read in its data. That job is accomplished by the lines

```
// Resize and read the vector for spreading the PCE discrepancy.
PCESpread.resize(NSEC);
PCESpread.ReadA("PCESpread.dat");
```

Note that the resizing is done by the *resize()* function of the Vector, not by the *r()* function. The *r()* function looks in the VAM file to find the dimension of the Vector, so it won't work for the *PCESpread* Vector, because it is not in the VAM file. The *resize()* function is given the size directly as its argument. In *Tiny*, NSEC has already been given the value of 8.

The predicted values of the elements of the *pce* vector are computed from the regression equations by the function call

```
pcef(pce);
```

The lines

```
// Sum up the calculated PCE elements
pcesum = pce.sum();
pcediscrep = pcetot[t] - pcesum;
// printf("\npcediscrep = %10.2f\n",pcediscrep);
// Spread discrepancy by the proportions of PCESpread vector.
pce = pce + pcediscrep*PCESpread;
```

sum up the calculated PCE elements, subtract the sum from the desired total, and spread the discrepancy among the sectors in the proportions given by the *PCESpread* vector. The line

```
// printf("\npcediscrep = %10.2f\n",pcediscrep);
```

is now just a comment without effect on the operation of the program. If the // at the beginning were removed, it would print the discrepancy at each pass through the loop. It can be used it to check that the discrepancies are indeed small. Instead, however, of totally removing it, it is left as a comment which may be a useful illustration of how to include such debugging printing.

You should now estimate the PCE equations, make the required changes in USER.H and MODEL.CPP, do Model | Run *IdBuild* and compile model, then do Model | Run dyme and graph the resulting elements of the pce vector.

To review, the two new techniques introduced in this section were the "isvector" command to *IdBuild* and the use of a static vector not in the VAM file.

The "isvector" command, by the way, also allows vector elements to be used on the right-hand side of regression equations. For example, in a more detailed model than *Tiny*, the output of the Railroad industry may be used in the equation for Railroad construction.

17.4. Systems of Detached-Coefficient Equations

In this section, we'll develop the version of *Tiny* we call Model 3, and you can copy MODEL3.CPP to MODEL.CPP. This section introduces the use of "detached-coefficient" equations.

The use of the "isvector" command in *IdBuild* is perfectly satisfactory for elements of vectors on the right-hand side of the regression equation; but for variables on the left-hand side, it has its limits. In the first place, automatic rho-adjustment is not possible. Secondly, it cannot be used to pass the whole system of import equations to the Seidel routine so that imports dependent on domestic demand can be calculated simultaneously with product outputs. Nor can it be used to pass a whole system of consumption functions, such as the PADS system (covered in chapter 20) to a function to compute predicted values as a fairly complicated function of the parameters. All of the problems are overcome in through the use of a system of "detached-coefficient" equations. Actually, this method is older than the "isvector" method and goes back to models developed in the early 1960's. The "detached-coefficient" name comes from the fact that the regression equations are "detached" from the variables names and stored in a separate file by *G7*. The added complexity of this method, however, is that program has to be written to interpret the equations. For Seidel with import equations and for PADS, however, the code is already written and part of the Interdyme system.

In this section, we will see how to use the detached-coefficient method for the PCE equations we have already estimated. We begin from the PCEEQN.REG file shown in the box to the right. It is a command file for *G7*; as usual, the four dots indicate the omission for printing here of a repetitive portion of the text of the file. There are two new commands, "punch" and "ipch". The "punch" command

punch pce.eqn 7 4 2003

opens a file to be called PCE.EQN to receive the regression coefficients. There will be 7 equations with up to 4 coefficients each. The last year of data used in estimating them will be 2003. After each equation is estimated there is an "ipch" command such as

The PCEEQN.REG File
catch pce.cat
lim 1995 2003
vam hist b
dvam b
f dpdis = pdisinc - pdisinc[1]
punch pce.eqn 7 4 2003
ti PCE on Agriculture
r pce1 = pdisinc, dpdis
ipch pce 1 L
gr *
. . . .
ti PCE on Services
r pce7= pdisinc, dpdis
ipch pce 7 L
gr *
punch off
catch off

```
        ipch pce 1 L
```

which writes to the open "punch" file the rho and the regression coefficients for the most recently estimated regression equation. In the file, it will be labeled as the equation for the pce vector, element 1. The "L" will be written to file to indicate the type of equation. It could be any one letter or number; we will write the program to interpret these letters correctly. The L in this particular case stands for "Linear". The file ends with the command

```
        punch off
```

to close the file to which *G7* has been writing the regression results. The name of the command, "punch", refers to punching the results into cards and indicates just how ancient this method is. The cards are gone, but the name works fine. The PCE.EQN file produced by *G7* from the PCEEQN.REG file shown above is shown in the box below.

```
                        The PCE.EQN File
7 4 2003
pce 1 L 3
1 2 3
    0.280107        10.1751   0.00312443   -0.00190926
pce 2 L 3
1 2 3
    0.456294        1.62189   0.000232365   0.000253049
pce 3 L 3
1 2 3
    0.150868        76.9213  -6.45766e-06    0.0127951
pce 4 L 3
1 2 3
    0.214085       -303.312    0.474066     -0.155993
pce 5 L 3
1 2 3
    0.268659       -14.8633    0.244285     -0.0810024
pce 6 L 3
1 2 3
    0.572774        66.8459    0.0359306     0.0773437
pce 7 L 3
1 2 3
   -0.0435048       164.664    0.226147     -0.179012
```

The three numbers on the first line are taken from the "punch" command that opened the file and have already been explained. For each equation there are then three lines. The first gives, somewhat redundantly, the name of the vector of the dependent variable, the number of the element in the vector, the type of equation, and the number of regression coefficients for it. The second line specifies which coefficients will be given in the next line, and the third line gives first the rho estimated for the equation and then the regression coefficients in the order specified by the second line.

In our case, the second line may seem unnecessary since it is both very simple and always the same. It can, however, add considerable flexibility. We might have had, for example, a more general form of regression in which there were five possible independent variables with a relative price term as the fourth and a time trend as the fifth variable. In that case, had the equation for element 7 used only the intercept and the time trend, the command to *G7* would have been

```
r pce7 = time
ipch pce 7 L 1 5
```

and in PCE.EQN the resulting lines would have been something like

```
pce 7 L 2
1 5
   -0.0435048        164.664        12.345
```

where 12.345 is the coefficient on time. Since the coefficient matrix is originally set to zero, this device allows one type of equation to be used for all variants of an equation that differ from a base type only by omitting one or more of the variables. Note that the numbers at the end of the "ipch" command are optional. If they are not specified, then *G7* assumes that they are the integers up to the number of variables in the equation.

Now with the equations estimated and stored away in the PCE.EQN file, we have to get them into the Interdyme program and tell Interdyme how to interpret the coefficients. To do so, we will use the C++ concept of a "class", namely, of a class called "Equation.". Generally, a class is a combination of data and ways of working with the data. We have already met the Matrix and Vector classes. Instances of a class are called "objects." For example, in USER.H we need to put the line

```
GLOBAL Equation pceeqn;
```

It will make the object *pceeqn* an instance of the class Equation. Then in MODEL.CPP, we put the lines

```
// Resize, read, and store the PCE equations; reads the pce.eqn file.
pceeqn.r("pce.eqn");
```

The second of these calls the *r()* function (sometimes called method) of the *pceeqn* object to read the file PCE.EQN, claim enough space for storing the data of the PCE equations, and read the data from the file into that space. How does the program know how to claim the space and read the data? Any object of the Equation class knows how to read the data, how to dish out the coefficients of the equations and some other data to using programs, and how to apply rho adjustments to the predicted values. It does NOT know how to use the coefficients to compute the predicted values. The user, you, must write those instructions. We will see how in a moment. First, here is an except from MODEL.CPP which shows the new code for reading the equation data in context in the *loop()* function.

```
// Resize and read the vecor for spreading the PCE discrepancy.
PCESpread.resize(NSEC);
PCESpread.ReadA("PCESpread.dat");
```

```
// Resize, read, and store the PCE equations; reads the pce.eqn file.
pceeqn.r("pce.eqn");

// pceeqn.rhostart is read as the last year used in estimating the PCE equations.
// We want it to be the year in which to start the rhoadjustment. If we are
// doing a historical simulation, that should MacEqStartDate if it is before the
// date recorded in the pce.eqn file.
if(pceeqn.rhostart > MacEqStartDate) pceeqn.rhostart = MacEqStartDate;
```

In the *spin()* function, the new equations are called to calculate the *pce* vector by the line

```
pcefunc();
```

shown in context in the lines below.

```
// Compute the estimated PCE equations with equation system
if(t>= MacEqStartDate){
    pcefunc();
    // Sum up the calculated PCE elements
    pcesum = pce.sum();
    pcediscrep = pcetot[t] - pcesum;
    // printf("\npcediscrep = %10.2f\n",pcediscrep);
    // Spread the discrepancy by the proportions of the PCESpread vector.
    pce = pce + pcediscrep*PCESpread;
    invtotf();
    }
inv = invtot[t]*invc;
....
```

As already noted, the function *pcefunc()* that calculates the predicted values must be written by the user. Consequently, it is in MODEL.CPP, and we had better have a good look at it. It is shown in full in the box below.

The first thing to be explained is the difference between the equation number, for which the program uses the variable i and the sector number, for which it uses the variable j. In the case of *Tiny*, the PCE vector has 8 elements, one for each sector, but there are only 7 equations, because one sector (sector 8) is always zero. In larger models or for other dependent variables, the difference between the number of sectors and the number of equations can be much greater. The equations are read and stored in the order estimated, which is not necessarily the order of the sector numbers. For each equation, however, the corresponding sector number is stored in the *sec* variable Thus,

```
j = pceeqn.sec(i);
```

will put into j the sector number corresponding to equation i. The single character indicating the type of equation is stored in the *type* variable. Thus

```
which = pceeqn.type(i);
```

will put into the char variable *which* the type of equation i. In our case so far, it will be the letter L. Finally, the regression coefficients of equation i are given by *pceeqn[i][1]*, *pceeqn[i][2]*, *pceeqn[i][3]*, and so on. In our case, these are the constant term, the coefficient of *pdisinc* and *dpdis*, respectively. (With this explanation, the code down to as far as the comment

```
// Apply rho-adjustment
```

Function to Calculate PCE from Detached-Coefficient Equations

```
// pcefunc() -- PCE functions for TINY
int pcefunc(){
    int n,i,j,t1;
    float cons;
    char which;

    n = pceeqn.neq; // Number of equations
    // pdisinc is personal disposable income. It is a global macro variable.
    // Compute variables used in several equations.
    dpdis[t] = pdisinc[t] - pdisinc[t-1];

    // Loop over the equations
    for(i = 1; i <= n; i++){
        j = pceeqn.sec(i); // j is the sector number of this equation.
        which = pceeqn.type(i);  // which is the equation type
        if(which == 'L'){
            cons = pceeqn[i][1] + pceeqn[i][2]*pdisinc[t] + pceeqn[i][3]*dpdis[t];
        }
        else {
            printf("Unknown equation type %c in pcefunc, category %d.\n",
                which,i);
            tap(); //Pause so that error message can be read.
            continue;
        }
        // Apply rho adjustment
        // Note the use of i and j in the following statement.
        pce[j] = pceeqn.rhoadj(cons,pce[j],i);
    }
    pce.fix(t);
    return(n);
}
```

---

should be reasonably clear.) The use of the rho-adjustment requires more explanation.

In macro models, the calculation of the initial error from which the additive rho-adjustment factor begins is simple enough. It is calculated in the first period of the run. Matters are more complicated in the multisectoral model case because not all data is equally up-to-date. We may, for example, have macroeconomic variables through 2005 but detailed PCE data only through 2003. The starting error for rho adjustments must therefore be calculated for PCE components in 2003 and used in 2004, 2005, and later years. For a macro variable, however, actual data can be used for 2004 and 2005, and the starting rho-adjustment error calculated in 2005 and used thereafter. That is why the variable *rhostart* is part of the Equation object. As read from the data file, it gives the last year of estimation, which is presumably the last year of data and therefore the last year in which the base error of the rho-adjustment process can be calculated. A further complication is that, since predicted values of one variable may depend upon calculated values of other variables, the rho-adjustment errors cannot be set until the model has converged for the period. Finally, sometimes we want to do an historical simulation and set all the rho-adjustment errors in the first period of the run. In that case, we uncheck the "Use all data" box on the screen which appears when we click Model | Run Dyme Model (see p. 53).

Bearing all that in mind, what happens when the program executes the statement

```
pce[j] = pceeqn.rhoadj(cons,pce[j],i);
```

near the end of the program shown in the box? The *rhoadj()* function of the *pceeqn* object is passed the calculated value (*cons*), the value already in the vector (*pce[j]*), and the equation number, (*i*). Simply put, the function then figures out what it is supposed to do and does it. More specifically, if we are using all data and data is still available, it returns the actual value. If we are past the end of the data, it adds on the rho-adjusted error to the value predicted by the equation and returns that. If the signal that the model has converged (*setrho*) has been set and we are in the period in which the base error should be computed, it does so, saves it, and returns the actual value. If the model has converged, but we are already past the year for calculating the error, it adds on the error for this year to the computed value and updates the error for the next year by multiplying this year's error by the appropriate rho factor.

That leaves a question. How does the *rhoadj* function know that the model has converged? Why does it need to know that? Because only then can it calculate the starting error for the rho-adjustment in the appropriate year, or in later years, multiply this year's errors by the appropriate rho to get them ready to be added to the values predicted by the equations in the next year. The signal that the model has converged is the variable *setrho*. This *setrho* can have one of two values, 'y' for yes or 'n' for no. Near the top of the MODEL.CPP file, we see the lines

```
float pcesum, pcediscrep;
setrho = 'n';
int Iteration;
```

so we know it starts off as 'n'. What happens next is shown in code snippet from MODEL.CPP in the box below. The **while** loop begun in the first line continues until convergence is reached (or the limit on iterations is hit). On reaching convergence, the program breaks out of the **while** loop, sets *setrho* to 'y', calls the two functions involving rho adjustment – namely *pcefunc()* and *invtot()* – and then puts *setrho* back to 'n'.

As with macromodels, there are other kinds of fixes besides rho adjustment. How to specify them will be explained in section 16.8. Here we just note that the statement

```
pce.fix(t);
```

at the end of the *pcefunc()* function will apply the fixes to be explained in that section.

The fact that the rho-adjustment is working is seen very clearly in the graph on the next page. For it, we made the VAM file BASE.VAM the default VAM file, copied the variable

376

pdisinc from the BASE bank into the G workspace, and then estimated the regression in test mode, the default mode. Thus, the "actual" line in the graph is history up to 2003 and model forecast thereafter, while the "predicted" line is the prediction from the equation without rho-adjustment but made with the model-predicted values of disposable income. The way the model forecast remembers the big error of the equation in 2003 indicates clearly that the rho adjustment is working.

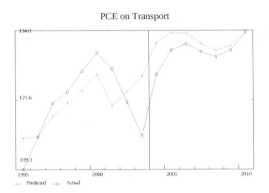

PCE on Transport

17.5. Import Equations

So far we have considered imports as exogenous. In fact, they are very dependent on domestic demand, so it makes sense to relate them to domestic demand and then calculate them from the estimated equations simultaneously with the calculation of output. In this section, we will see how to do exactly that. The new code is all in MODEL4.CPP, which you should copy to MODEL.CPP.

The IMPR.DAT file, shown to the right, will, when introduced in G7 with the "add" command, provide values for the *im* vector from 1995 to 2003. Up until now, imports have been treated as negative numbers because it is convenient to do so in the input-output table. In this file however, imports are positive numbers, as they usually are in statistical sources. We will use them henceforth as positive numbers and make the required changes in our program.

The IMPR.dat File

```
vmatdat r 1 9    1 8  5
im 1995 1996 1997 1998 1999 2000 2001 2002 2003
#Date       1        2        3       4        5 6
7         8
1995     19.753    8.118   0  108.065   0 0  14.470   0
1996     19.320    8.236   0  113.841   0 0  14.795   0
1997     18.808    8.612   0  124.300   0 0  15.561   0
1998     18.114    8.619   0  130.503   0 0  16.307   0
1999     18.732    9.068   0  145.711   0 0  17.461   0
2000     20.000   10.00    0  170.000   0 0  20.000   0
2001     19.068    9.302   0  155.832   0 0  18.902   0
2002     18.992    9.122   0  156.815   0 0  18.665   0
2003     20.105    9.763   0  166.286   0 0  19.018   0
```

It is natural to suppose that imports of product i, m_i, are a linear function of domestic

377

demand for the product, d_i, thus

$$m_i = \alpha_i + \beta_i\, d_i .$$

Conceptually, domestic demand for a product is the row total for that product in the input-output table without subtracting imports. Thus, conceptually, it does not depend on imports. Statistically, however, it is most easily calculated as domestic output, q_i, plus imports (as a positive number), thus:

$$d_i = q_i + m_i.$$

Substitution of d_i from the second of these equations into the first and solving for m_i gives imports as a linear function of domestic output:

$$m_i = a_i + b_i\, q_i$$

To estimate these regressions, we need data on domestic output, *out*; it is found in the OUT.DAT file. (In real economies, it is quite normal to have data on output in years for which the complete input-output table is not available. You may, however, wonder how we made it up for *Tiny*. In Section 16.7, we will introduce a series of input-output coefficient tables for 1995 – 2003. From the data already given for PCE and imports, and by moving the 2000 final demand vectors for investment, government, and export by the corresponding historical totals, final demand vectors for these years were calculated; with the time-varying input-output table, the implied domestic outputs shown in the OUT.DAT file were calculated.)

The G7 command file to do the regressions is shown on the left below, and the resulting IMPORT.EQN file is shown on the right. The program to compute the imports from these equations is given in the box on the following page and may be found in MODEL4.CPP.

IMPORTS.REG – Estimate Imports

```
    # Estimate the import
equations
    bank tiny
    vam hist b
    dvam b
    add impR.dat
    add out.dat
    vc out = LINV*fd

    # Regress imports on outputs
    lim 1995 2003 2003
    punch import.eqn 4 2 2003
    ti Agricultural Imports
    r im1 = out1
    gr *
    ipch im 1 L
    ti Mining Imports
    r im2 = out2
    gr *
    ipch im 2 L
    ti Manufacturing Imports
    r im4 = out4
    gr *
    ipch im 4 L
    ti Service Imports
    r im7 = out7
    gr *
    ipch im 7 L
    punch off
```

IMPORT.EQN – Equation File for Imports for *Tiny*

```
    4 2 2003
im 1 L 2
  1 2
        0.253335      18.6513    0.00365866
im 2 L 2
  1 2
       -0.104578       0.740326    0.170614
im 4 L 2
  1 2
       -0.0630504    -67.3531     0.282823
im 7 L 2
  1 2
        0.235647     -14.1671     0.049055
```

We now need a version of Seidel that will compute imports simultaneously with outputs. It is shown in the box below and may be found at the end of the MODEL4.CPP file. The prototype for it is found near the top of the MODEL4.CPP file:

```
// Prototype for Seidel used in TINY
short Seidel(Matrix& A, Vector& q, Vector& f, IVector& triang,float toler);
```

so that when a reference is made to it later, the C++ compiler will know how to set up the call to it and how to handle the return. In this same file, in the *spin()* function, right after the PCE and investment functions have be calculated, we find the lines:

```
inv = invtot[t]*invc;
gov = govtot[t]*govc;
ex  = extot[t]*exc;
fd = pce + gov + inv + ex;
Seidel(AM, out, fd, dump, triang, toler);
imtot[t] = im.sum();
```

The first three compute final demand vectors as we have done up to now. Then the *fd* vector is calculated as the sum of these components. Note that imports have not been subtracted.

The Import Function from the MODEL.CPP File

```
// Importfunc() -- Import functions for TINY
int importfunc(Vector& q){
   int n, i,j,t1;
   float imp;
   char which;

   if(t < MacEqStartDate) return(0);
   n = impeqn.neq; // Number of equations
   // pdisinc is personal disposable income. It is a global macro variable.

   // Loop over the equations
   for(i = 1; i <= n; i++){
      j = impeqn.sec(i); // j is the sector number of this equation.
      which = impeqn.type(i);
      if(which == 'L'){
         imp = impeqn[i][1] + impeqn[i][2]*q[j];
      }
      else {
         printf("Unknown equation type %c in importfunc, sector %d.\n",
            which,i);
         tap(); //Pause so that error message can be read.
         continue;
      }
      // Apply rhoadjustment
      // Note the use of i and j in the following statement.
      im[j] = impeqn.rhoadj(imp,im[j],i);
   }
   im.fix(t);
   return(n);
}
```

In the *Seidel()* function, a potentially infinite loop is started by the code of which the outline is:

```
iter = 0;
while(1){
   . . . . .
   iter++;
   if(dismax < toler || fdismax < .000001) break;
   if(iter > 25 )return(ERR);
}
return(OK);
```

The key to getting out of this loop successfully is clearly to get the *dismax* variable down to less than toler, where toler is the error tolerance for the Seidel process which was given in the call to *Seidel()* and *dismax* is the maximum discrepancy between the output of a sector calculated on the current iteration of the Seidel process and the output of the same sector calculated in the previous iteration. The exit from the while loop when the iteration count passes 25 is just a safety net to avoid a hung computer if the process fails to converge.

The first thing done under the while loop is to compute imports *im*, with a call to the import function. These imports are then subtracted from the given fd vector to get the net final demand vector, *f*, with which the rest of this iteration of the Seidel process takes as its

380

final demand. Note that the calculation of the import vector may involve not only the import equations but also rho-adjustments and perhaps other fixes. Convergence on the *q* or output vector will imply convergence on the import vector as well.

The most of the rest of the code of the *Seidel()* function just implements the process as explained above and should be fairly transparent. There is, however, one non-standard wrinkle which needs explanation. It gives the process the capability of accepting a pre-determined output for one or more products. Petroleum extraction in the United States is a good example; demand beyond some capacity level must be imported or dealt with in some way as a shortage. If *i* is a normal, non-constrained product, then in column 18 of the SECTORS.TTL file its row should have the letter 'e'. The 'e' means that the product uses the equation to determine output. Here are a few lines from *Tiny*'s SECTORS.TTL:

```
Agricul      ;1    e    "Agriculture"
Mining       ;2    e    "Mining and quarrying"
Elect        ;3    e    "Electricity and gas"
```

Whatever letter is in that column will become the value of *outfix(i)*. When our routine finds a value of 'e' in *outfix(i)*, it will set the output of product *i* equal to the demand which has been calculated. If, however, *i* is a constrained product, the routine keeps the initial, presumably exogenously set, value of *q[i]* and puts the difference between it and calculated demand into the vector called *dump*. What should be done with *dump* is then up to the model builder who is using this feature. Since *Tiny* is not using it, we will do nothing with *dump*.

At this point you may want to refresh your memory of the Seidel process, but after doing so, all the coding in the *Seidel()* function shown in the box on the next page should make sense. When it does, build and run the new model and make graphs of imports and outputs. (You will need to copy MODEL4.CPP to MODEL.CPP .)

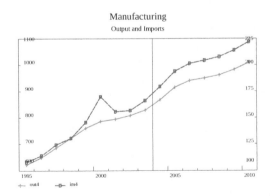

The above graph shows the similarity that we now find in the forecasted course of outputs and imports for Manufacturing. The scale for the two curves, however, is different; the scale for output is shown on the left and that of imports on the right. The imports – the blue, upper line marked with squares – are actually much less than output, but the pattern of movement is similar. (The right vertical axis for graphs drawn with the *G7* "mgr" command may be set by the "hrange" command.)

```
/* Seidel() Version 2, with imports .*****************************************

short Seidel(Matrix& A, Vector& q, Vector& fd, Vector& dump, IVector& triang,
    float toler){
    short i,j,k,first,last,n,iter,im1,imax;
    float discrep,dismax,fdismax;
    double sum;
    Vector f(fd.rows()); //scratch vector

    iter = 0; // Iteration count
    n = A.rows();
    first = A.firstcolumn();
    last =  A.lastcolumn();

    if(q.rows() < A.rows()){
        printf("In Seidel, the solution vector is not large enough.\n");
        return(ERR);
        }
    dump.set(0.);

    while(1){
        // Compute imports
        importfunc(q);
        f = fd - im;
        dismax = 0;
        for(k = triang.First(); k < triang.First()+ triang.numelm(); k++){
            i = triang[k];
            sum = f[i];
            for(j = first; j <= last; j++)
                sum += A[i][j]*q[j];
            sum -= A[i][i]*q[i]; // Take off the diagonal element of sum
            sum = sum/(1.- A[i][i]);
            if(outfix[i] != 'e'){ // Override the equation
                // Dump error into dump
                dump[i] = q[i] - sum;
                sum = q[i];
                }
            else dump[i] = 0;
            discrep = fabs(sum - q[i]);
            if(discrep > dismax){
                dismax = discrep;
                imax = i;
                if(fabs(sum)>1.0e-3) {
                    fdismax = fabs(sum);
                    fdismax = dismax/fdismax;
                    }
                }
            q[i] = sum;
            arith("in Seidel",i);
            }
        iter++;
        if(dismax < toler || fdismax < .000001) break;
        if(iter > 25 ){
            printf("No convergence in %d iterations. Discrep = %7.2f in sector %d.\n",
            iter, dismax, imax);
            return(ERR);
            }
        }
    printf("Seidel iterations: %d ",iter);
    return(OK);
    }
```

17.6. Speeding Up Solutions with Read and Write Flags

So far, we have been reading and writing the value of every vector and every matrix from the VAM file in every period. That is neither desirable nor necessary. Take the AM matrix for example. We know perfectly well that at present we do nothing to change it in the program, so writing it back to the VAM file at the end of each year's calculation is a waste of time. In the case of the *out* vector, we certainly want to write the value after it has been computed, but in the forecast period the value of *out* in the VAM file on the first run of the model will be all zero. That is not a good starting value for the Seidel process. It would be much better just to start with the previous period's value. Thus, we would want to read it only in the initial year.

Such considerations have lead to the introduction of read and write flags for the vectors and matrices which are set when they are resized in MODEL.CPP. For example, so far we have had as the first line of the resizing commands

```
out.r("out");pce.r("pce");gov.r("gov");
```

which is equivalent to

```
out.r("out",'y','y');pce.r("pce",'y','y');gov.r("gov",'y','y');
```

The second argument – the first 'y' – in one of these function calls is the read flag; the third, the write flag. Possible values for the read flag are:

'y'	yes, always read the vector or matrix
'n'	no, never read the vector or matrix
'i'	read the vector or matrix in the initial year of the run
'a'	read the vector or matrix if there is data available for it.

Possible values of the write flag are:

'y'	yes, always write the vector or matrix
'n'	no, never write the vector or matrix

The default value of both flags is 'y'; that is to say, if no flags are specified, both are assumed to be 'y'. If only one is specified, it is interpreted as the read flag. To specify a write flag, we must also specify the read flag, even if it is 'y'. For example, to set the read flag for the AM matrix to 'y' and the write flag to 'n', we would use the call

```
AM.r("am", 'y','n');
```

To set the read flag for the *out* vector to 'i' but the write flag to 'y' , it is enough to use the call

```
out.r("out", 'i');
```

The read flag 'a' can be quite convenient to read the values of a vector in years when it is known but not in later years. Its use, however, requires telling the program the last year of data for the vector or matrix in question. To do so, the first step is to remove the comment indicator (//) in front of the line

```
// lastdata(); // Use of lastdata function requires that the LastData file exist.
```

which is found just above the *resize()* commands for vectors. The call to the function *lastdata()* will read a file which must be called LASTDATA. Here is a possible LASTDATA file for *Tiny*:

```
pce 2003
im 2003
out 2000
```

It simply lists one or more of the vectors in the VAM file and the last year for which data is available for each.

Because *Tiny* is so tiny, you will not notice any acceleration of the solution by the use of these flags. For big models, however, they can make a small but measurable difference in solution time. You should experiment with them in *Tiny*, but since there is not much in the way of results to show, I will not give a more explicit application.

17.7. Changing Input-Output Coefficients and Prices

Up until now, our input-output coefficient matrix has remained constant, as have the coefficients for the value-added components: depreciation, labor income, capital income, and indirect taxes. Consequently, there has been no need to consider changes in relative prices. We must not leave *Tiny* without introducing coefficient change and relative prices, for input-output analysis has often been unjustly reproached for assuming constant coefficients. In fact, it is precisely input-output analysis which enables the specification of changing input-output coefficients. In this section, we will present Model 5, which incorporates prices and coefficient change.

I prevailed upon the *Tiny* statistical bureau to construct a coefficient matrix for 1995 and drew upon the collective wisdom of a group industry specialists to project the table to 2010. The results of these labors, together with the matrix for 2000 with which we have been working, are contained in the files AM1995.DAT, AM2000.DAT, and AM2010.DAT. For intervening years, we will have to rely upon linear interpolation. The same groups provided us with past history and projections of the labor income coefficients for the same two years. They are in the file LABC.DAT.

We need to significantly expand the VAM file so we will start from a new VAM configuration file, VAMP.CFG, which you will find on the disk. (The P in the filename stands for Prices.) We have added the vector of prices, *prices*, final demands in nominal prices, *fdN*, *pceN*, *govN*, *invN*, *exN*, and *imN*, the interindustry flow matrix in nominal terms, *FMN*, and two vectors, *fix* and *cta*, whose functions will be explained in the next section on fixes.

The TINYP.PRE File

```
# File to create VAM file for TINYP, TINY with Prices
vamcreate vamp.cfg hist
vam hist b
dvam b
# Bring in data on outputs and final demands
add out.dat
add pceR.dat
add impR.dat
# Bring in the intermediate flow matrix
add flows.dat
# Bring in the final demand vectors
add fd.dat
# Bring in the value added vectors
add va.dat
fdates 2000 2000
# The following are element-by-element vector divisions
vc depc = dep/out
vc capc = cap/out
vc indc = ind/out
# Compute share vectors of final demands
vc invc = inv/invtot{2000}
vc govc = gov/govtot{2000}
vc exc  = ex/extot{2000}
# Read I-O coefficient matrices
add AM1995.dat
add AM2000.dat
add AM2010.dat
# Interpolate matices for missing years
fdates 1995 2010
lint AM
show AM r 4
# Keep value added coefficients, except labc, constant
dfreq 1
f one = 1.
index 2000 one depc
index 2000 one capc
index 2000 one indc
#Read labc for 1995, 2000, and 2010
add labc.dat
lint labc
# Keep the structure of some final demand columns constant
index 2000 one invc
index 2000 one govc
index 2000 one exc
# Compute final demand vectors for historical years
fdates 1995 2003
vc inv = invtot*invc
vc gov = govtot*govc
vc ex  = extot*exc
store
```

Corresponding to this new configuration is a new *G7* command file, TINYP.PRE, to create the initial VAM file for the model. In some ways it is simpler than before; we do not need to compute the AM matrix but rather just read it for 1995, 2000, and 2010. The one new command following the reading of these matrices is simply

   lint AM

where "lint" stands for "linearly interpolate." This command will linearly interpolate[16] the

---

16 If this term is unfamiliar, it means to fill in missing data by drawing a straight line between two adjacent known points.

values of each and every cell between the years where non-zero values are given. The same command is applied a few lines further down to the *labc* vector. The lint command works over the range specified by the last previous "fdates" command. When you have run this file through *G7*, you will have created a new HIST.VAM file. Copy it to BASE.VAM with the following *G7* command:

    dos copy hist.* base.*

The MODEL.CPP file for the model with prices is on the disk as MODEL5.CPP; copy it to MODEL.CPP. Near the top of the file, resizing functions for the new vectors and matrix have been added. The new elements in the heart of the *spin()* function are shown in bold in the box below.

The first addition is to compute the total value added coefficient vector and then compute the *prices* vector by a call to *PSeidel()*. This routine, which may be found in SEIDEL.CPP, solves the equations

$$p = pA + v$$

where *p* and *v* are row vectors. If the sectors of an input-output matrix have been arranged in an almost triangular order for solution of the output equations by the Seidel method, the *opposite* order will most likely be good for solving for prices. Hence, *PSeidel()* uses the same *triang* vector as does *Seidel()* but takes the sectors starting from the end of the list and working towards the beginning. The remaining new commands are just to calculate the values of the nominal vectors and of the nominal flow matrix, *FMN*. This last calculation uses Interdyme's % operator. It is used between a vector and a matrix. If the vector is on the **right**, it multiplies each **column** of the matrix by the corresponding element of the vector. If the vector is on the **left**, it multiplies each **row** of the matrix by the corresponding element of the vector.

Excerpt from MODEL5.CPP File

```cpp
for (t = godate; t<= stopdate; t++) {
   . . . .
     // Start of code particular to TINY:

     // Compute total value-added coefficient vector.
     vac = depc+labc+capc+indc;
     // Compute prices
     PSeidel(AM, prices, vac, triang, 0.000001);
     // The loop for convergence on pcetot and invtot.
     while(Iteration < 20){
       . . . .
       }
     // Set error for rhoadjustment
     setrho = 'y';
     if(t >= pceeqn.rhostart)  pcefunc();
     if(t >= impeqn.rhostart)  importfunc(out);
     setrho = 'n';
     // Here when both Investment and PCE have converged
     // Compute flow matrix in current prices
     FM = AM % out;
     FMN = prices % FM;
     // Put output and final demands into nominal prices
     outN = ebemul(prices,out);
     fdN = ebemul(prices,fd);
     pceN = ebemul(prices,pce);
     invN = ebemul(prices,inv);
     exN  = ebemul(prices,ex);
     imN  = ebemul(prices,im);
     govN = ebemul(prices,gov);
     // End of code particular to TINY
   . . . .
   }
```

A final note on the economic interpretation of the prices we have calculated may be helpful. They are, in fact, relative prices and the *numeraire*[17] with price equal to 1.0 is the quantity of labor which could be bought for one dollar in the year 2000.

To obtain truly nominal prices, we need to model inflation, and to model inflation, as we already know from the *Quest* model in Part 2, we need to model employment and unemployment. Further, we need to model savings behavior more carefully and consider the role of money and interest rates in both savings and investment. All of these things can be modeled using the techniques we already have, so they make a better exercise for you than subject for me.

We can introduce optimizing in Interdyme models in exactly the same way as we did in *Quest*. All we need do is to specify the objective function and the regression coefficients to be varied in exactly the same way as in a macro model and then check the "Optimizing" radio button on the panel of window which comes up when we click Model | Run dyme. At

---

17 Unit of value on which other values are based.

present, optimization works only with respect to the coefficients of macro equations, not for the coefficients of systems of detached-coefficient equations. There are no problems of principle involved in extending the code to handle coefficients of those equations also, just writing some housekeeping code. Finally, although there is a "Stochastic simulation" radio button on that same panel, it does not work at present. Much of the necessary code has been brought over to Interdyme, but somewhat more work is needed to activate it.

It is tempting to go on elaborating the fictitious *Tiny* economy with all these features, but you surely have a real model you are eager to get to work on, so we will give *Tiny* no further features, for there are no more major new techniques that need to be explained. We do, however, need to deal with how to use fixes to discipline *Tiny* or any model if it misbehaves.

Exercise

1. Make up employment and labor force data for *Tiny*, and estimate and put into the model employment equations. Have the model compute unemployment. Modify the savings equation so that the model provides employment for roughly 96 percent of the labor force, though the exact level may vary cyclically.

17.8. Fixes in Interdyme

For smaller models, the use of the .XG files described in section 16.1 in the discussion of *IdBuild* is a quick and flexible way to input assumptions about the exogenous macro variables in the model. Analogous to the use of .XG files, one can use *G7* to write out the values of exogenous vectors and matrices in the VAM file for the forecast period. However, as the model grows in size and complexity, the need arises for more sophisticated ways to make assumptions about variables, both endogenous and exogenous variables. The use of "fixes" has evolved to satisfy this need. Fixes are assumptions about variables which are stored in a file, and read using a fixer program. A given model (including historical data, equations and code) and a given set of fixes will determine a scenario or simulation, in a way that will give reliable, repeatable results. Base and alternate scenarios can be developed by suitable modifications of the fixes files, with both sets of fixes run with the same model.

Fixes, as used here, are ways to make a model work the way we want it to, not necessarily the way that emerges from its equations. The power that fixes give over a model can certainly be abused. Nonetheless, they are extremely useful and powerful. Suppose, for example, we wish to consider the impacts of some event which the model equations were never confronted with, like a natural disaster or a massive overhaul of the health care system. Then a fix is the natural way to convey to the model that it needs to work in a way not described by its equations. Another use of fixes is to force the detailed data to agree with published aggregate data. The aggregate data is usually available up to a current quarter or month, whereas sectoral data is only published with a lag, sometimes of several years.

Control totals can be applied to the vector elements, and the projection made using the individual equations may be scaled. This is an example of a "group fix", where a defined group of elements of a vector may be fixed as a unit.

Interdyme has three types of fixes, those for macro variables, those for vectors and matrices, and a special type for industry outputs. This section will primarily serve as a useful reference to the fixes files and the commands that can be used within them. We will start with describing the fixes for macro variables.

Macro Variable Fixes

Macro variable fixes are fixes applied to variables of type Tseries, which are defined using the *Idbuild* program described above. These fixes work much like those of models built with the G-Build combination, but also have much in common with the vector fixes described in the next section. The program that handles the macro variable fixes is called *MacFixer*. The input to *MacFixer* is a file prepared by the user with a text editor. It generally has the extension .mfx . Once this file has been created, the fixes can be processed by running the program *MacFixer* The results of this program are written to a "macro fix bank", which is essentially a G bank, which can be read with *G7*. The root name (the part of the filename before the dot) of the macro fix G bank is passed to *MacFixer* through a file named MACFIXER.CFG. It must also be passed to the simulation program by the form that opens on choosing the command Model | Run Dyme .

The configuration file MACFIXER.CFG contains the name of the text input file, the root name of the G bank file used for base values for the index and growth-rate fixes (this would normally be the G bank created for use with the simulation program, such as HIST.BNK), the name of the G bank which will contain the values of the fixes, and the name of the output check file. This last file shows the values of each fix in each year, and serves as a check on the results in the binary file.

While it is up to the user to name files, it makes sense to give files for the same simulation the same root name. A simulation that involves low defense expenditures, for example, could have a G bank file called LOWDEF.BNK, and a .*mfx* file called LOWDEF.MFX.

Several varieties of macrofixes may be given. They can generally be divided into *absolute* or "hard" fixes, and *modifier* or "soft" fixes. The syntax for the hard fixes ("ovr", "ind" and "gro") is given first.

ovr   *overrides* the result of the equation with the value of the time series given. Values between given years are linearly interpolated. In the example below, the macro fix program would calculate and override a fix series that starts in 1992, ends in 2000, and moves in a straight line between the two points. For example

```
ovr uincome$
  92   154.1
  2000  182.3;
```

389

would override the value of the forecast of *uincome$* with the values shown for the years shown. Note that year can be either 2-digits or 4-digits (they are all converted to 4-digits in the program). If *uincome$* were an exogenous variable, then it *must* receive a fix. If it were endogenous, the above fix would replace the values forecasted by the equation.

ind   is a variety of the override fix that specifies the time series as an index. There must be data in the VAM file for the item being fixed up until at least the first year of the index series specified. The value for the item in that year is then moved by the index of the time series given by the fix lines. For example,

```
ind invtot
2003   1.0   1.03   1.08   1.12   1.15
2008   1.21 1.29   1.31
```

will move the value of *invtot* in 2003 forward by the index of the series given, and will replace the calculated value of *invtot* by this value when the model is run.

gro   is a type of override fix that specifies the time series by growth rates. For the growth rate fix to be legal, there must be data in the VAM file up until at least the year before the first year of the growth rate fix. Missing values of the growth rates are linearly interpolated.

```
gro wag01
1993   3.1
2000   3.4;
```

stp   is a type of override fix that specifies the growth rate in a series of steps. It is like "gro" except that a growth rate continues until a new one is provided. A value for the final period is necessary.

```
stp wag01
1993 4.1
1995 4.5
2000 5.0;
```

The next two types of fixes ("cta" and "mul") are the *modifier* or "soft" fixes

cta   does a constant term adjustment. That is, it adds or subtracts the value of the time series to the result of an equation or a previous fix. The time series is provided by the fix definition. For example,

```
cta nonagincome
1992 .0001
1995 200
2000  180;
```

is a constant term adjustment for nonagricultural income from 1992 to 2000. Intermediate values are of course linearly interpolated.

mul   multiplies the equation's forecast by a factor specified by the data series on the following line. For example:

```
mul ulfi$
1992   1.0
1995   1.05
2000   1.10;
```

multiplies the forecast results for the macrovariable *ulfi$* by the factors shown. Values of the multiplicative fix between the years shown are linearly interpolated, as usual.

Next is the "rho" fix, which plays a very important role for macrovariables.

rho is the *rho-adjustment* fix, familiar from macromodels. It may, in fact, be considered a fully legitimate part of the model. The format is:

      rho <depvar> <rho_value> [rho_set_date]

where

      depvar is the name of the dependent variable

      rho_value is the value of rho.

      rho_set_date is the year in which the rho-adjustment error is to be calculated. If none is provided, it is set in the year specified by the Macro Equation Start Date specified on the form when starting a run.

for example:

```
rho invtot .40 2003
```

tells the model to apply a rho-adjustment to the variable *invtot* using the value .40 for rho, and starting the rho-adjustment in 2003.

A rho fix with a rho_set_date works like a "skip" (see below) in years before the rho_set_date. Unlike rho fixes in macromodels, an endogenous variable can have a "rho" fix in conjunction with and a "cta" or "mul" fix. The rho-adjustment is applied before the other fix.

skip is the simplest type of fix. It simply skips the equation and uses the values in the model G bank. For example:

```
skip invn$35
```

would skip the equation for the macro variable *invn$35*, and use the value already in the model G bank.

The next several fixes ("dind", "dgro" and "dstp") are the family of *dynamic* fixes. Unlike the "ind", "gro" and "stp" fixes which establish the fix values before the model is run, and write these values to the fixes file, dynamic fixes usually begin in some future year, and base the index or growth rate on the value of the variable in that year, as it has been calculated by the model. In other words, the same fix will probably yield different results in different model runs.

dind is the "dynamic index fix". This fix can start in any year, and does not rely on historical data being present in the databank. Rather, the fix is calculated during model solution when the first year used is specifying the fix is reached. For example, if the fix is

```
dind invtot
  2005  1.0  1.03  1.08  1.12  1.15 1.20
```

and a forecast is begun in 2003, then the equation will be used for 2004 and 2005, but the value of *invtot* in 2006 will be 103 percent of whatever value was calculated for 2005.

dgro is the dynamic version of the growth rate ("gro") fix. This fix can start in any year, and does not require data to be available in the databank for the starting year of the fix. The growth rate is always applied to the value of the variable in the previous period.

dstp is the dynamic version of the "stp" fix.

The final three types of fixes ("eqn, "fol", and "shr") are very flexible. They enable the model user to play some of the roles of the model builder. Using an equation fix, a replacement equation for a variable can be specified in the fixes file, which can use any legal G7 expression of other macrovariables, vector variables and matrix variables. The body of the fix plays a special role in the fix, as shown below. Follow ("fol") and share ("shr") fixes are really special variants of the more general equation fix, but the need for them is so common that they have been made available as special types. We will now describe these fixes for macrovariables.

eqn is the *equation* fix. This type of fix lets you dynamically introduce a new equation relationship into the model at run time. The advantage of this type of fix is that users of the model who are not programmers can introduce their own assumed relationships into the model, without having to change the model program code. It is also helpful for prototyping a model, where you want to quickly try out different equation relationships to see how they work, before coding them into the model.

The equation fixes use the same expression syntax as used in the "f" command and other commands in *G7*. The format for equation fixes for macrovariables is:

```
eqn <Macroname> = <expression>
        <year> <value> [<value> <value> ...]
        <year> <value> [<value> <value> ...]
```

where: <Macroname> is a legitimate name of a macrovariable, <expression> is a legitimate expression, as described below, and the <year> <value> entries are in the same format as the data for other fixes, but indicate the years for which the equation fix is to take effect. They also represent the time series for a special variable called *fixval*, which can be used within the equation expression. This *fixval* variable can be used wherever a vector or macrovariable could be used.

Just about any expression that is legal in *G7* is legal for an equation fix, except that only a subset of functions are implemented. These functions are: @cum, @peak, @log, @exp, @sq, @sqrt, @pow, @fabs, @sin, @pct, @pos, @ifpos, @pct, @rand and @round.

Lagged values of any order can be used, with the constraint that they must not be before the starting year of the model G bank (DYME.BNK). Macrovariables are read directly from memory. Lagged values of vector variables are read from the VAM file. Therefore, you can use a lagged value of any vector as far back as the starting date of the VAM file, and you are not limited by whether or not that vector has been declared to store lagged values in memory in VAM.CFG.

Examples:

```
# Make the T bill rate equal to the average inflation plus some percent,
#   specified in "fixval".
eqn rtb = .34*gdpinf + .33*gdpinf[1] + .33*gdpinf[2] + fixval
   2016 1.0
   2030 1.5;
```

Though it is not necessary to know in order to use the function, you may be curious as to where the equation is stored and how it is calculated. To continue with the example just given, the *Macfixer* program stores a fix by the name of *rtb:e* and the values of *fixval* as the value of the fix. Then at the end of index file for this bank (MACFIXES.IND if MACFIXES is the name of the bank), where it does not interfere with *G7*'s use of the bank, it labels and stores the text of the equation. When the fix is to be applied, this text is read and the value calculated with code borrowed from *G7* for calculating *f* commands.

The equation fix was developed while Inforum was still using earlier, Fortran-based modeling software that required the model builder to estimate a regression equation with one program and then by hand write it into the model. Thus, writing an equation fix was not more trouble that putting a new equation into the model. With the present integration of G and Interdyme, it is far easier to replace an equation in the model with a newly estimated one than to write an equation fix. The equation fix may still be useful for model users who do not have access to the code of the model.

fol is the *follow* fix. The follow fix allows you to specify that a macrovariable should move like some other quantity, which may be specified as a general expression involving vector and macrovariables, just like the equation fix.

The general format for the follow fix is:

fol <Macroname> = <expression>
            <year> <value> [<value> <value> ...]
            <year> <value> [<value> <value> ...]

The variable "fixval" should not be used in the follow fix expression. Its purpose is to specify a growth rate to add to the growth of the expression.

For example, if we would like to specify that Medicaid transfer payments grow like real disposable income per capita, plus 0.1 per cent, we could write:

fol trhpmi = di09/pt
2016 0.1
2040 0.1

shr is the *share* fix. This fixed is used to specify that the macrovariable should be a certain share of another variable or expression, with the share specified by the fix value. Actually, the "share" is just a multiplier, so it can be any number.

The general format of the share fix is:

shr <Macroname> = <expression>
               <year> <value> [<value> <value> ...]
               <year> <value> [<value> <value> ...]

In the share fix, the fix value is the multiplier or share to multiply by the right hand side expression.

When the input file specifying the fixes as described above is ready, it should be saved with ".mfx" as the extension of its file name.

On the *G7* main menu, then click Model | Run Dyme Model, and the fixer programs (*MacFixer* and *Fixer*) will be run before running the model. As described previously, the macro fixes are written into a file which is structured like a G bank. For example, in the MACFIXER.CFG shown below for *Tiny*, the name of the output fixes bank is "MacFixes". Therefore, *MacFixer* will create the files MACFIXES.BNK and MACFIXES.IND, which may be assigned and viewed in *G7* just like any other G bank.

MACFIXER.CHK

```
Input fix file      ;Macfixes.mfx
Output fixes bank ;MacFixes
Model G bank        ;tmp
Output check file ;MacFixer.chk
```

The names of the series in this G bank are formed by concatenating the series name with a colon followed by a single letter indicating the type of fix to be applied to that variable. Thus, the fix

```
cta invtot
2004 10.
2010 17.
```

will put into the MACFIXES data bank a variable by the name *invtot:c* whose values will be linearly interpolated between 2004 and 2010. If you create a file by the name of MACFIXES.MFX with exactly this fix in it, save the file and click Model | Run Dyme Model to create the MACFIXES G data bank, you can then open up the bank, and give G7 the commands:

bank macfixes b

lis b

and see that the bank has a variable by the name of *invtot:c*. You can then do

type b.invtot:c

and see the interpolated add factor. Alternatively, you can look in the MACFIXES.CHK file and see

```
 Fix Number 1: cta fix on invtot
    2003        10.00       11.00       12.00       13.00       14.00
    2008        15.00       16.00       17.00
```

which should assure you that the interpolation has been done correctly. This file also serves as a record of the assumptions made for a particular run.

The correspondence between fix types and codes suffixed to the variable names are: skip ('k'), ovr ('o'), cta ('c'), ind ('i'), gro ('g'), stp ('s'), rho ('r'), and eqn ('e').

Macro fixes provide an alternative way to supply values of exogenous variables. Exogenous variables may be put into the "hist" bank in the process of running *Idbuild*. If the variable appears in no *.sav* file for a macro equation, then it is included in the PSEUDO.SAV file. The standard way of providing the values of the exogenous variables is then through "update" or other commands in *G7*. Another possibility for providing exogenous values is to have a special run of *G7* with the "hist" or other bank as the workspace bank. Finally, one can provide the exogenous values as macrofixes. For example, if we want *disinc* to be an exogenous variable, then -- however we are going to provide the values -- we need the statement

```
f disinc = disinc
```

in the PSEUDO.SAV file. To use the macrofix method of assigning values, we need in the code of the model the statements

```
depend=disinc[t];
disinc[t] = disinc.modify(depend);
```

We could then provide the values with "ovr", "ind", "gro", or "stp" commands to the macrofix program, for example, by

```
gro disinc
 1995 3.0
 2000 3.5
 2005 4.0;
```

This method has the advantage of keeping all the fixes which constitute a scenario in one place. It also allows the use of the "gro" and "stp" fixes, which may be convenient. It has the disadvantage of adding an additional series to the banks which constitute the model and an additional statement within the model.

Vector and Matrix Fixes

The vector fixes are more complicated than macro fixes because they can apply to individual elements of a vector, to the sum of a group of elements, or to the sum of all elements in the vector. However, the format of the vector fixes is similar to that of the macro variable fixes, described above. Matrix fixes at the current version are still rather simple, one fix being applicable to only one cell of a matrix. The preparation of the vector and matrix fixes is the work of the *Fixer* program.

Unlike the macro fixes, which are automatically applied when a macro regression equation is calculated, vector and matrix fixes are applied where the model builder specifies. At the point where the fixes for the vector *x* should be applied, the model builder must put into the program the line

```
x.fix(t);
```

The input to *Fixer* is a file prepared by the user in a text editor. It should have the extension *.vfx*. *Fixer* also reads the definitions of static groups of sectors and writes them into the GROUPS.BIN file which can be used both by the simulation program and by *G7*. To use the *Fixer* program, it is essential that the model's VAM.CFG file should have a vector called "fix" with enough rows to allow one for each fix. As Fixer reads the fixes from the input file, it stores the numerical values of the fixes into this "fix" vector in the vam file. It also creates a "fix index" file, which will have the extension *.fin* and tells the simulation what to do with each fix. Finally, it produces a binary file with the definitions of groups, called GROUPS.BIN. If *G7* has already produced a GROUPS.BIN file, *Fixer* reads it and may add to it.

For vectors, fixes may apply to a single element or a group of elements. The concept of a "group" is central to the working of *Fixer*. Basically, a group is simply a set of integers, usually representing sectors in the model. Defining groups is useful because we often want to impose a fix on a group of elements in a vector. For example, we may want to control the total exports of the chemical manufacturing sectors. We might then create a group named "chem" which would contain the sector numbers of all the sectors in question. The command for defining a group for *Fixer* is "grp <groupname>", where the groupname can be a number or a name. The sectors defining the group are then entered on the next line. For example:

```
grp 1
  7 10 12
```

creates a group called "1" consisting of the sectors 7, 109 and 12. The '-' sign means consecutive inclusion. Thus:

```
group zwanzig
  1-20
```

consists of the first twenty integers. Parentheses mean exclusion. Thus:

```
group duo
  :zwanzig (2 - 19)
```

makes the group "duo" consist of the integers 1 and 20.

When a group is referenced after it is defined, its name must be preceded by a colon, as shown when "zwanzig" was used in the definition of "duo" above. Names of groups are case sensitive; commands for Fixer must be lower case. Groups can be defined anywhere in the input file before the first time you used them. If you try to redefine an existing group, the program will complain, unless the new group has the same or less elements than did the old group. References to other groups can be used in new group definitions only if the groups referenced have already been defined.

Interdyme provides a number of ways for a fix to work. In all of them, a time series is specified by the fix. The forms of the fix differ in how they obtain and in how they apply this time series. The basic format of the input file for a vector fix is:

<command> <vectorname> <GroupOrSector>

followed on the next line by a year and some values of the fix. The basic format of the input file for a matrix fix is:

<command> <matrixname> <row> <col>

The fixes available for vectors and matrices are for the most part the same as those for macrovariables, with the exception that you need to provide the <GroupOrSector> for a vector fix, and the <row> and <col> for a matrix fix.

ovr   overrides the result of the equations with the value of the time series given. Again, intermediate values are linearly interpolated. In the example below, the fix program would calculate and override fix series that starts in 1992, ends in 2000, and moves in a straight line between the two points. For example,

```
ovr ex 10
 1992  154.1
 2000  182.3;
```

would override the value of the forecast of element 10 of the "ex" vector (probably exports) with the values shown for the years shown. As an example of a matrix fix,

```
ovr am 1 9
 1990 .23
 1995 .26
 2000 .28;
```

would override the value of the A-matrix in the Vam file for element (1,9), from 1990 to 2000. As before, missing values are linearly interpolated.

ind, dind

is a variety of the override fix that specifies the time series as an index. There must be data in the vam file for the item being fixed up until at least the first year of the index series specified. The value for the item in that year is then moved by the index of the time series given by the fix lines. For example,

```
ind pceio :zwanzig
 1982  1.0  1.03  1.08  1.12  1.15
 1997  1.21  1.29  1.31  1.34;
```

will calculate the sum of the elements of the pceio vector included in the group "zwanzig" in 1982, will move that sum forward by the index of the series given, and will impose that control total on the those elements when the model is run.

The "dind" version of the fix can start in any year, and indexes the series to the value of the expression in the starting year of the fix.

gro, dgro

is a type of override fix that specifies the time series by growth rates. For the growth rate fix to be legal, there must be data in the vam file up until at least the year before the first year of the growth rate fix. Missing values of the growth rates are linearly interpolated.

```
gro out 10
 1983   3.1
```

```
2000  3.4;
```
The "dgro" version of the growth rate fix can start in any year, and always calculates the series in the present period based on the value in the previous period.

stp, dstp

is a step-growth fix. It is like "gro" except that a growth rate continues until a new one is provided. A value for the final period is necessary.
```
stp out 1
83   4.1
95   4.5
2000 5.0;
```
The "dstp" version is the dynamic version, which can start in any year. It is just like "dgro", except for the method of interpolation of the fix values.

mul   multiplies the equation forecast by a factor specified by the data series on the following line. For example,
```
mul im 44
1992  1.0
1995  1.05
2000  1.10;
```
multiplies the forecast results for imports of sector 44 by the factors shown. Values of the multiplicative fix on imports between the years shown are linearly interpolated.

cta   does a constant term adjustment. That is, it adds or subtracts the value of the time series to the result of the equations. The time series is provided by the fix definition. For example,
```
cta def :Alice
1992  .0001
1995  200
2000  180;
```
is a constant term adjustment for defense expenditures of all sectors in the Alice group. Intermediate values are linearly interpolated.

eqn   The equation fix for vectors works in the same way as the version for macrovariables, with the exception that the name of the vector must be separated from the sector number by a space. For example:

```
# Make the pce deflator for category 3 grow like the aggregate PCE deflator,
#   based on the ratio in 1997, from 1998 to 2010.
eqn cprices 3 = cprices3{1997}/apc{1997} * cprices3
   1998 1
   2010 1
# Make corporate profits in sector 1 remain a constant share of total
corporate
#   profits, equal to the share in 1997:
eqn cpr 1 = cpr1{1997}/vcpr{1997} * vcpr
  1998 1
  2010 1
```

fol   The follow fix specifies that an element or group of a certain vector should follow the expression on the right, plus or minus a certain growth rate, which can be specified in the body of the fix. It is often used to make imports of a certain commodity grow like domestic demand. For example, the following follow fix makes crude petroleum imports grow like domestic demand, plus 0.2 percent per year:

```
fol im 4 = dd4
1998 0.2
2030 0.2
```

shr   The share fix takes the value of the body of the fix (fixval), and multiplies the right hand expression by it, before assigning the value to the left hand side variable or group. Like the follow fix, a typical use for this fix might be in controlling the relation between imports and domestic demand. The example below specifies the share of domestic demand for imports of Radio, television and video equipment:

```
shr im 42 = dd42
1998 .9
2000 .92
2030 1.0
```

When the input file as described above is ready and the FIXER.CFG file calls for its use, type "fixer" at the DOS prompt to invoke the *Fixer* program. *Fixer* is also run when you choose the menu option Model | Run Dyme Model in *G7*.

Output Fixes

The output fixes allow the values of output specified in the VAM file to override values computed by the input-output equations. There is then the question of what to do with the difference. Interdyme offers two possibilities: add any excess demand to imports or simply ignore the difference. The options are specified in column 18 of the SECTORS.TTL file, which is where the names of the input-output sectors are. The options for this column are:

e   use the equation
i   add the difference to imports
d   put the difference in a vam vector named "dump", where nothing is done with it, but it can be displayed.

Answers

3.2   The new outputs are
        166.14 55.21 222.30 763.57 426.48 206.41 812.58 148.00
        and the primary resources required to produce them are
        317.24 1351.84 268.34 226.58.
3.3   The net export of depreciation is -5.73.
3.4   The new price vector is (.92 .96 .89 .90 .71 .93 .96 1.00).
3.5   Net export of greenhouse gas production is -31.87.

CHAPTER 18. MATRIX BALANCING AND UPDATING

18.1. The RAS Algorithm

Making an input-output matrix from scratch for a country is a major undertaking often involving a group of ten or more people for a number of years. By the time the project is finished, the matrix refers to a year that is apt to seem part of ancient history. Hence the question arises: "Given an input-output table for a base year, is there a way to update it to a more recent year with less work than making the table from scratch?" In this updating, one usually has some data for the more recent year. One wants the matrix for this year, which we may call the target year, to conform to all those data.

Usually those data would include industry outputs, major GDP components, and value-added by industry. The value-added by each industry can then be subtracted from its output to give the total intermediate inputs by each industry. Thus, we would know the row total for each industry and the column total for each final demand column and for the intermediate use of each industry. An obvious check on the accuracy of this information is that the sum of the row totals equals the sum of the column totals. We will assume that this condition has been met, although meeting it is not always easy except by a rough scaling. Thus, we have the margins or frame for the table for the target year.

An initial guess of the inside of the table for the target year can then be made by assuming constant coefficients for the input-output coefficients and for the shares in each of the final demand vectors. More sophisticated initial estimates could also be made. One could use, for example, consumption functions to "forecast" the purchases of households. However the initial inside elements of the table are estimated, it is almost certain that they will not have the right row and column sums. Adjusting them to make them conform to these control totals is generally done by what has come to be called the RAS procedure, a name derived from notation in Richard Stone's description of the method in *A Computable Model of Economic Growth* (Chapman and Hall, London, 1962)[18].

The method is extremely simple in practice. First scale all of the rows so that each has the correct total. Then scale all the columns so that each has the correct total. The row sums are then probably no longer correct, so scale them again, and then scale the columns again, and so on until the scaling factors have converged to 1.0. The matrix at that point has the desired row and column sums. If A^t denotes the flow matrix at stage t of the operation, R^t denotes the row scaling factors at step t arrayed as the diagonal elements of an otherwise zero matrix, and S^t denotes the column scaling factors similarly arrayed, then the flow matrix at the beginning of stage t+1 is

$$A^{t+1} = R^t A^t S^t \qquad (18.1.1)$$

---

18   The idea had been mentioned by Leontief in the 1941 edition of *Structure of the American Economy*, but the idea seemed to pass unnoticed until applied by Stone.

The expression on the right gave rise to the name RAS, which may be pronounced as the three letters, or simply as "ras".

18.2. Convergence of the Algorithm

The practice is simple, but will the process converge? To answer that question, we will need some notation. Let the original matrix be A, whose elements we will denote by a_{ij}, let b be the positive vector of required row sums and c be the positive vector of required column sums. The first condition is that A be non-negative. The second is simply that there must exist at least one matrix with zeroes where A has zeroes and positive numbers where A has positive numbers. This matrix must also have row sums equal to b and column sums equal to c.

Notice that this second condition did *not* assume a solution of the form we are seeking, that is, derived from A by scaling the rows and columns. It does, however, have some important implications. The first is that the sum of the elements of b must be the same as the sum of the elements of c. A further implication is that, if it is possible rearrange the rows and columns of A so that an all-zero block appears, then the corresponding subtotals of b and c must be consistent with those blocks remaining zero while the other cells are positive. For example, if

$$A = \begin{pmatrix} 1 & 0 \\ 1 & 2 \end{pmatrix}$$

then we must also have $b_1 < c_1$ and $b_2 > c_2$. In practice, one insures that the first implied condition (the equality of the sum of row sums and column sums) is met before beginning the RAS calculations. If they fail to converge, then one looks for inconsistencies along the lines of the second implication.

The proof of the convergence of the RAS procedure under these general conditions requires a complicated notation. The essence of the proof, however, can be seen in the special case in which A is all positive, and we will limit ourselves to that case. (For the general case, see M. Bacharach, *Biproportional Matrices*. Cambridge University Press, 1970.)

We will start the process by scaling the rows, then the columns, and so on. In the first row scaling, we choose the first-round row-scaling factors by

$$r_i^{(1)} = b_i / \sum_j a_{ij} \tag{17.2.1}$$

where the superscript on the r refers to the iteration number. Then we compute the first-round column scaling factors by

$$s_j^{(1)} = c_j / \sum_i r_i^{(1)} a_{ij} \tag{17.2.2}$$

Then we come back to compute the second-round scaling factors,

$$r_i^{(2)} = b_i / \sum_j r_i^{(1)} a_{ij} s_j^{(1)}$$

$$= b_i / \sum_j \frac{b_i}{\sum_k a_{ik}} a_{ij} s_j^{(1)}$$

$$= 1 / \sum_j a_{ij} \frac{s_j^{(1)}}{\sum_k a_{ik}}$$

(17.2.3)

Thus, we can see that the second-round row factors are reciprocals of convex combinations of the first-round column factors, that is, they are reciprocals of a weighted average of those first-round column factors with positive weights which sum to 1. Thus,

$$\max_i r_i^{(2)} \le 1/\min_j s_j^{(1)} \quad \text{and} \quad \min_i r_i^{(2)} \ge 1/\max_j s_j^{(1)}$$

(18.2.4)

By similar reasoning,

$$\max_j s_j^{(2)} \le 1/\min_i r_i^{(1)} \quad \text{and} \quad \min_j s_j^{(2)} \ge 1/\max_i r_i^{(1)}$$

(18.2.5)

The inequalities in 18.2.5 imply 18.2.6

$$1/\max_j s_j^{(2)} \ge \min_i r_i^{(1)} \quad \text{and} \quad 1/\min_j s_j^{(2)} \le \max_i r_i^{(1)}$$

(18.2.6)

Then combining the first inequality of (18.2.4) with the second of (18.2.6) and the second of (18.2.4) with the first of (18.2.6) gives

$$1/\min_j s_j^{(1)} \le \max_i r_i^{(1)} \quad \text{and} \quad \min_i r_i^{(2)} \ge 1/\max_j s_j^{(1)} \ge \min_i r_i^{(1)}$$

(18.2.7)

In other words, the biggest element of r diminishes from iteration to iteration while the smallest rises. Since A is all positive, all of the inequalities in (17.2.4) through (17.2.7) will be strict inequalities unless all the elements of r are equal or all the elements of s are equal. But if they are all equal, they must be all be equal to 1, for otherwise the scaling would increase or decrease the total of all elements in the matrix, contrary to the fact that, after the first row scaling, the sum of all elements remains equal to the common sum of the vectors b and c. Since the sequences of $r^{(k)}$ and $s^{(k)}$ vectors both lie in closed, bounded sets, they have limit points. Can these limit points be anything other than the vectors that are all

1's? No, because at any such point, one more iteration of the process would bring a finite reduction of the maximum element (and a finite increase in the minimum element) of each vector. (This is where we use the all positive assumption to have strict inequalities in (18.2.7).)

Thus, for points sufficiently close to these limit points, the next iteration must also bring lower maximal and higher minimal elements than those of the limit point, contrary to the limit point being a limit point. Therefore the unique limit of each sequence of vectors is a vector of ones.

Thus the convergence is proven for the case of all positive A. The proof is similar for A with some 0 elements, but in this case, it may require several iterations to get a finite reduction in the maximal elements of r and s.

In practice, the condition that the sum of b equals the sum of c is checked and assured before the iterative process begins. The initial r and s vectors should be reported by the program because they often indicate discrepancies between b and c vectors and the initial A matrix. Once the iterations start, the largest and smallest elements of the r and s vectors should be reported every five or ten iterations. It is common to observe "wars" between a row control and a column control when one element looms large in both its row and column, but the control totals for the two are quite different. Such "wars" are symptomatic of a failure of the second assumption and an indication that the b and c vectors should be revised.

It should be noted that the RAS procedure works for rectangular matrices just as well as for square ones. It is also useful in making input-output tables and the bridge matrices used to convert investment by investor to investment by product bought or consumption by consumer categories to consumption by product categories used for productive categories.

18.3. Preliminary Adjustments Before RAS

It often happens in updating or making tables that one has better information about some cells than about others. For example, in updating the a table with a Glass row, we may have quite good information on the sales of glass products to Beer, because we have information on the production of glass beer bottles. In this case, we can simply remove the "relatively well-known flow" from both its row and column control, perform the RAS balancing on the remaining flows, and then put back in the known flow.

The problem with this procedure is that the "relatively well-known flows" tend to be big flows. If they are not quite consistent with the row or column controls, then removing them requires that all of this inconsistency should be attributed to changes in the remaining small flows. Thus, the small flows can be pushed about rather considerably. This problem can be reduced by a preliminary scaling of the relatively well-know flows before removing them from the process. To describe this adjustment, let R_i be the sum (in the base year) of the relatively well-known flows in row i ; S_i , the sum of the other flows; and B_i , the row control. Then let

$$\alpha = \frac{R_i}{R_i + S_i} \qquad (17.3.1)$$

and define z_i as the solution to

$$S_i z_i + R_i z_i^{\alpha} = B_i \qquad (17.3.2)$$

The value of z_i which satisfies (18.3.2) is readily found by Newton's method. We then scale all the relatively well-known flows by z_i^{α} and all the other flow by z_i. By (18.3.2), the row will then have the correct sum. By (18.3.1), z_i^{α} is closer to 1.0 than is z_i; that is to say, the relatively well-known flows are scaled less than the other flows. They are however, scaled somewhat. If they account for a small fraction of the total of all flows in the row, they will be scaled but little; if they account for much of the row, they will be scaled almost as much as the other flows.

After this preliminary scaling, the known flows can be removed for the rest of the RAS process. While this scaling may seem a bit arbitrary, in practice it has given plausible results in many applications. In fact, it worked so well that the first person working with it, Thomas Reimbold, felt that the z must stand for *Zauber*, "magic" in German, his native language. The procedure is therefore often referred to as the *Zauber* process.

CHAPTER 19. TRADE AND TRANSPORTATION MARGINS AND INDIRECT TAXES

19.1. Trade and Transportation Margins

A perennial problem in applied input-output analysis is the treatment of trade and transportation margins and of indirect taxes. The problem is nicely illustrated with transportation costs. If output is valued at the producer's price — the price at the factory gate, so to speak — then the cost of transporting the goods to the user must be considered to be paid separately by the purchasing industry. Thus, the cost of the rail services used in hauling the coal used by electric power plants shows up as an input of rail transportation into electric generation. The cost of hauling generation equipment to and from the utilities' repair facilities would appear in the same cell. Similarly, the cost of hauling coal to a steel mill and of hauling iron ore to the same mill will appear in the same cell.

The problems with this treatment are:

1. It puts quite diverse activities into the same cell; and

2. The table does not reflect the way the rail industry thinks about its business. It thinks in terms of products hauled — and prepares statistics on products hauled, not on industries to which it delivers.

Despite these problems, this treatment is the one most commonly followed. All of the problems apply with equal force to all the other transportation margins and to wholesale and retail trade margins.

One alternative is to change the measure of output of the industry to include the cost of delivering the product to the user. One disadvantage of this treatment is that it removes the numbers in the input-output table one step further from the numbers in terms of which people in the industry think, namely in producer prices. Another problem is that transportation margins may be very different for a dollar's worth of product delivered to different users. The transportation cost of oil delivered to an electric utility by pipeline from a marine terminal may be very different from delivering by truck or rail to a small industrial user.

A better alternative is to add another dimension to the input-output tables. Thus, corresponding to each cell of the tables we have considered so far there would be a vector. The first entry in the vector would be the transaction in producer prices; the second entry would show the rail margin; the third, the truck margin; the fourth, the air freight; and so on through the wholesale and retail trade margins. In effect, we would have a table with layers, the first layer for the producer price transaction, the second for the rail margins, and so on. In fact, the benchmark tables for the United States are prepared with all this information. It has not been commonly used because the size of the matrices involved has been, until fairly recently, large relative to the power of the computers available. That constraint has now been effectively removed, and we may ask, How would we in fact compute with such a layered table?

If A represents the coefficient matrix in producer prices and T_i represents the ith layer of transportation and trade margin coefficients, then the fundamental input-output equations become

$$q = Aq + \sum_i S_i T_i q \; + \; f = (A + \sum_i S_i T_i)q \; + \; f \tag{18.1.1}$$

where S_i is a matrix with 1's in the row which produces the service distributed by layer i and elsewhere all zero. The matrix is, in fact, the matrix in producer prices with which it has been traditional to compute. What is gained by distinguishing the layers is not a correction of the traditional computations but rather a better description of what the flows are and a better basis for studying changes in coefficients in the T_i matrices.

19.2. Indirect Taxes, Especially Value Added Taxes

Indirect taxes such as property or franchise taxes are treated as a component of value added, along with depreciation, profits, interest, and labor compensation. Excise taxes such as those on gasoline, alcohol, and tobacco are usually similarly treated, but with less justification, because some uses of these products are exempt. For example, gasoline used to power agricultural machinery or exported whiskey or cigarettes are exempt. Thus, these taxes should also be treated as a layer of the table, since they are not uniform for all cells. Retail sales taxes are usually treated as a component of value added by Retail trade. This treatment assumes that the tax is proportional to the retail margin in all products in all cells. In fact, there are different tax rates on different products, and some products are sold by retail establishments for intermediate use without retail sales tax.

The greatest problems, however, have probably been created by the value added tax (VAT) in the tables of countries which use this tax, a group that now includes all members of the European Union and numerous other countries. Producers pay VAT on the value of their sales but may deduct the VAT paid on their purchases. VAT is not charged on certain products, such as health services or exports. Many European input-output tables have been published in producer prices plus non-deductible VAT. That practice meant that the cell for paper products sold to the hotel industry did not contain VAT, because the VAT on those sales was deductible from the VAT owed by the hotels. The cell for paper products sold to hospitals, however, contained VAT, because the hospitals owed no VAT from which the VAT on the paper products could be deducted. Similarly, since households owe no VAT, they cannot deduct the VAT on the paper products they buy, so the VAT is included in the cell showing the sales of paper products to households. Thus, the cells in the paper products row of such a matrix have very diverse levels of VAT content. That means that the valuation of the product across the row is not homogeneous. It takes more wood pulp to make a dollar's worth paper towels used by a hotel than to make a dollar's worth of paper towels used by a hospital or household, because a significant portion of their dollar goes to VAT. This heterogeneity in the pricing in the row is obviously detrimental to the accuracy of the input-output calculations. The solution to the VAT problem is simply to create a VAT layer of the table.

CHAPTER 20. MAKING PRODUCT-TO-PRODUCT TABLES

20.1. The Problem

Makers of input-output tables often find data on inputs not by the *product* into which they went but by the *industry* that used them. An *industry* is a collection of establishments with a common principal or *primary* product. But besides this primary product, any one of these establishments may produce a number of *secondary* products, products primary to other industries. Establishments classified in the Cheese industry may also produce ice cream, fluid milk, or even plastic moldings. Consequently, the Cheese industry may have inputs of chocolate, strawberries, sugar, plastic resins, and other ingredients that would appall a connoisseur of cheese. The inputs, however, are designated by what the product was, not by what industry made them. Similarly, data on the final demands, such as exports and personal consumption expenditure, is by product exported or consumed, not by the industry which made it. Thus, input-output matrices usually appear in two parts. The first part, called the Use matrix, has products in its rows but industries in its columns. The entries show the use of each product (in the rows) by each industry (in the columns.) The second part, called the Make matrix, has industries in the rows and products in the columns; the entries show how much of each product was made in each industry. (Some statistical offices also publish instead of the Make matrix a Supply matrix, which is product by industry like the Use matrix, but contains the information in the Make matrix, plus information on margins and taxes on domestic production and imports. This format is now recommended by the *2008 System of National Accounts*).

How can we use these two matrices to compute the outputs of the various products necessary to meet a final demand given in product terms?

One way is to consider that each product will be produced in the various industries in the same proportion as in the base year of the table. This assumption is used, for example, in computable general equilibrium models based on social accounting matrices that explicitly show the Make and Use matrices. This assumption, however, can produce anomalous results. In the above example, an increase in the demand for cheese would automatically and immediately increase demand for chocolate, strawberries, and sugar. These are not common ingredients in most varieties of cheese! There must be a better way to handle the problem.

This highly unsatisfactory situation has led to efforts to make a product-to-product matrix. Indeed, the problem is so well recognized that the "Transmission programme of data" of the European system of accounts requires that all national statistical offices of the member states of the European Union transmit "symmetric" input output tables to Eurostat every five years. No real advice, however, is offered by Eurostat to the statistical offices on how to make these product-to-product tables. This chapter offers a valuable tool for the process. ("Symmetric" is here intended to mean that the same concepts are used in both rows and columns. Its use as applied to these matrices is both highly confusing and not descriptive. Since it is the *nature* of the rows and columns that is the same, not their measure, *symphysic* would be both a better characterization and less confusing.)

To make such a matrix, we need to employ an additional assumption. There are basically two alternatives:

1. The *product-technology assumption,* which supposes that a given product is made with the same inputs no matter which industry it is made in.

2. The *industry-technology assumption,* which supposes that all products made within an industry are made with the same mix of inputs.

The *System of National Accounts 1993* (SNA) reviews the two assumptions and finds (Section 15.146, p. 367)

> On theoretical grounds, ... the industry technology assumption performs rather poorly" and is highly implausible.

And in the following Section 15.147:

> From the same theoretical point of view, the product (commodity) technology model seems to meet the most desirable properties .... It also appeals to common sense as it is found *a priori* more plausible than the industry technology assumption. While the product technology assumption thus is favoured from a theoretical and common sense viewpoint, it may need some kind of adjustment in practice. The automatic application of this method has often shown results that are unacceptable, insofar as the input-output coefficients appear as extremely improbable or even impossible. There are numerous examples of the method leading to negative coefficients which are clearly nonsensical from an economic point of view.[19]

Since 1967, the Inforum group has used a "semi-automatic" method of making "some kind of adjustment" in calculations based on the product-technology assumption, as called for by the SNA. We have used it with satisfactory results -- and without a single negative coefficient -- on every American table since 1958. The method was published in Almon 1970 and in Almon *et al.* 1974. Despite this long and satisfactory use of the method, it seems not to have come to the attention of the general input-output community. In particular, the authors of the section quoted from the SNA seem to have been unaware of it. This chapter illustrates the method and expands the previous exposition with an example, provides a computer program in the C++ language for executing the method, and presents some of the experience of applying the method to the 1992 table for the USA.

20.2. An Example

An example will help us to visualize the problem. The Table 20.2.1 below shows the Use matrix for a 5-sector economy with a strong concentration in dairy products, especially cheese and ice cream.

We will call this matrix *U.* The use of chocolate in makings cheese and rennet in making ice cream alerts us to the fact that the columns are industries, not products. (Rennet is a substance used to make milk curdle. It is commonly used in making cheese but never in ice cream.)

---

19 The United Nations *Handbook of Input-Output Table Compilation and Analysis,* 1999 (pp. 98-103) goes into this question in further detail, and also comes out strongly in favor of using the product technology to develop product by product tables. SNA 2008 however, glosses over the topic, and falls back into the stance of arguing that since the product technology assumption will produce negatives, that it is implausible (28.56, p. 515).

Table 20.2.1. The Use Matrix

USE	Industries				
Products	Cheese	Ice cream	Chocolate	Rennet	Other
Cheese	0	0	0	0	0
Ice cream	0	0	0	0	0
Chocolate	4	36	0	0	0
Rennet	14	6	0	0	0
Other	28	72	30	5	0

The Make matrix, shown in Table 20.2.2 below, confirms that cheese is being made in the ice cream industry and ice cream in the cheese industry.

Table 20.2.2. The Make Matrix

MAKE	Products				
Industries	Cheese	Ice cream	Chocolate	Rennet	Other
Cheese	70	20	0	0	0
Ice cream	30	180	0	0	0
Chocolate	0	0	100	0	0
Rennet	0	0	0	20	0
Other	0	0	0	0	535
Total	100	200	100	20	535

This matrix shows that of the total output of 100 of cheese, 70 was made in the Cheese industry and 30 in the Ice cream industry, while of the total ice cream output of 200, 180 was in the Ice cream industry and 20 in the Cheese industry. It also shows that, of the total output of 90 by the cheese industry, 78 percent (70/90 = .77778) was cheese and 12 percent ice cream. We will need the matrix, M, derived from the Make matrix by dividing each cell by the column total. For our example, the M matrix is shown in Table 20.2.3.

Table 20.2.3. The M Matrix

M	Products				
Industries	Cheese	Ice cream	Chocolate	Rennet	Other
Cheese	0.7	0.1	0.0	0.0	0.0
Ice cream	0.3	0.9	0.0	0.0	0.0
Chocolate	0.0	0.0	1.0	0.0	0.0
Rennet	0.0	0.0	0.0	1.0	0.0
Other	0.0	0.0	0.0	0.0	1.0

Now let us suppose that, in fact, cheese is made by the same recipe wherever it is made and ice cream likewise. That is, we will make the "product-technology assumption." If it is true and the matrices made well, then there exists a "recipe" matrix, R, in which the first column shows the inputs into cheese regardless of where it is made, the second column shows the inputs into ice cream regardless of where it is made, and so on. Now the first column of U, U_1, must be $.70*R_1 + 0.10*R_2$,where R_1 and R_2 are the first and second columns of R, respectively. Why? Because the Cheese plants make 70 percent of the cheese and ten percent of the ice cream. In general,

$$U = RM '$$
(20.2.1)

Where $M '$ is the transpose of M. It is then a simple matter to compute R as

$$R = U (M ')^{-1}$$
20.2.2)

For our example, $(M ')^{-1}$ is given in table 20.2.4.

Table 20.2.4 M' Inverse

	Cheese	Ice cream	Chocolate	Rennet	Other
Cheese	1.5	-0.5	0.0	0.0	0.0
Ice cream	-0.2	1.2	0.0	0.0	0.0
Chocolate	0.0	0.0	1.0	0.0	0.0
Rennet	0.0	0.0	0.0	1.0	0.0
Other	0.0	0.0	0.0	0.0	1.0

and R works out to be

Table 20.2.5 The R or "Recipe" Matrix

R	Cheese	Ice cream	Chocolate	Rennet	Other
Cheese	0	0	0	0	0
Ice cream	0	0	0	0	0
Chocolate	0	40	0	0	0
Rennet	20	0	0	0	0
Other	30	70	30	5	0

This R is very neat. All the rennet goes into cheese and all the chocolate goes into ice cream. Unfortunately, as indicated by the quotation from the SNA, it is rare for the results to turn out so nicely.

Indeed, just a slight change in the U matrix will show us what generally happens. Suppose that the U matrix had been just slightly different, with 1 unit less of chocolate going into cheese as shown below and one less unit of rennet used in ice cream.

Table 20.2.6 An Alternative Use Matrix

Alternative USE Products	Industries Cheese	Ice cream	Chocolate	Rennet	Other
Cheese	0	0	0	0	0
Ice cream	0	0	0	0	0
Chocolate	3	37	0	0	0
Rennet	15	5	0	0	0
Other	28	72	30	5	0

Table 20.2.7 shows what the R matrix would have been:

Table 20.2.7 An Impossible R Matrix

Impossible R	Cheese	Ice cream	Chocolate	Rennet	Other
Cheese	0.0	0.0	0.0	0.0	0.0
Ice cream	0.0	0.0	0.0	0.0	0.0
Chocolate	-1.7	41.7	0.0	0.0	0.0
Rennet	21.7	-1.7	0.0	0.0	0.0
Other	30.0	70.0	30.0	5.0	0.0

Here we find the infamous small negative flows. It is not hard to see how they arise. While it is conceivable that the Cheese industry does not produce chocolate ice cream, it is also very easy for the table makers to forget to put into the Cheese industry the chocolate necessary for the ice cream it produces, or to put in too little. Wherever that happens, negatives will show up in the R matrix.

The negatives have driven at least some statistical offices to the industry-technology assumption. The so-called commodity-to-commodity matrix, C, derived from this assumption is

$$C = UN'$$

(20.2.3)

where N is the matrix derived from the Make matrix by dividing each row by the row total. For example, the Cheese column of C is $C_1 = .77778U_1 + 0.14285U_2$ because 77.778 percent of the product of the first industry is cheese and 14.285 percent of the product of the second industry is cheese. The result of applying this assumption to our example is Table 20.2.8.

Table 20.2.8 The Mess Made by the Industry Technology Assumption

C Industry Technology Products	Industries				
	Cheese	Ice cream	Chocolate	Rennet	Other
Cheese	0	0	0	0	0
Ice cream	0	0	0	0	0
Chocolate	8.254	31.746	0	0	0
Rennet	11.746	8.254	0	0	0
Other	32.063	67.936	30	5	0

This "solution" has made matters worse. The original U matrix had 4 units of chocolate going into the Cheese industry, which admittedly made some ice cream. Now this industry-technology product-to-product matrix asserts that *8.25 units of chocolate went into producing pure cheese*! Not into the Cheese industry but into the *product* cheese! And 8.25 units of rennet went into producing curdled ice cream! To call the result a product-to-product table would be little short of scandalous.

Fortunately, we do not have to choose between this sort of massive nonsense and negative flows. It is perfectly easy to rely mainly on the product-technology assumption, yet avoid the negatives, as we will now show.

20.3. The No-Negatives Product-Technology Algorithm

We wrote the basic equation relating U, M, and R as equation (20.2.1) above. It will prove convenient to rewrite equation (20.2.1) as

$$U' = MR' \tag{20.3.1}$$

Using U_i' to denote the ith column of U' and R_i' to denote the ith column of R, we can write

$$U_i' = MR_i' \tag{20.3.2}$$

Notice that this is an equation for the distribution of product i in row i of the Use matrix as a function of M and distribution of the same product in row i of the R matrix. We can simplify the notation by writing

$$u = U_i' \quad \text{and} \quad r = R_i' \tag{20.3.3}$$

Then equation (20.3.2) becomes

$$u = Mr \tag{20.3.4}$$

or

$$0 = -Mr + u \tag{20.3.5}$$

And adding r to both sides gives

$$r = (I - M)r + u \tag{20.3.6}$$

Apart from the unusual case in which less than half of the production of a product is in

413

its primary industry, the column sums of the absolute values of the elements of $(I - M)$ are less than 1, and the convergence of the Seidel iterative process for solving this equation is guaranteed a by well-known theorem. (If the share of the total production of a particular product coming from the industry to which it is primary is x, then the absolute value of the diagonal of $(I - M)$ for that product is $|1 - x|$ and the sum of all the absolute values of off-diagonal elements in the column is $|1 - x|$, so the total for the column is $2*|1 - x|$, which is less than 1 if $x > .5$.)

We start this process with

$$r^{(0)} = u \tag{20.3.7}$$

and then define successive approximations by

$$r^{(k+1)} = (I - M)r^{(k)} + u \tag{20.3.8}$$

To see the economic interpretation of this equation, let us write out the equation for the use of a product, say chocolate, in producing product j, say cheese:

$$r^{(k+1)} = u_j - \sum_{h=1; h \neq j}^{n} m_{jh} r_h^{(k)} + (1 - m_{jj}) r_j^{(k)} \tag{20.3.9}$$

The first term on the right tells us to begin with the chocolate purchases by the establishments in the cheese industry. The second term directs us to remove the amounts of chocolate needed for making the secondary products of those establishments by using our present estimate of the technology used for making those products, $r^{(k)}$. Finally, the last term causes us to add back the chocolate used in making cheese in other industries. The amount of chocolate added by the third term is exactly equal to the amount stolen, via second terms, from other industries on account of their production of product j:

$$(1 - m_{jj}) r_j^{(k)} = \sum_{h=1; h \neq j}^{n} m_{hj} r_j^{(k)} \tag{20.3.10}$$

because

$$\sum_{h=1}^{n} m_{hj} = 1 \tag{20.3.11}$$

It is now clear how to keep the negative elements out of r. When the "removal" term, the second on the right of (20.3.9), is larger than the entry in the Use matrix from which it is being removed, we just scale down all components of the removal term to leave a zero balance. Then instead of adding back the "total-stolen-from-other-industries" term, $(1 - m_{jj}) r_j$, all at once, we add it back bit-by-bit as it is captured. If a plundered industry, say Cheese, runs out of chocolate with only half of the total chocolate claims on it satisfied, we simply add only half of each plundering product's claim into that product's chocolate cell in the R matrix. We will call the situation where the plundered industry runs out of the product being removed before all claims are satisfied a "stop".

To express this process in equations, we introduce scale factors, $s_j^{(k)}$, defined by

$$s_j^{(k)} = 1 \quad \text{if} \quad u_j \geq \sum_{h=1;\, j \neq j}^{n} m_{hj} r_j^{(k)} \tag{20.3.12}$$

and

$$s_j^{(k)} = \frac{u_j}{\displaystyle\sum_{h=1;\, h \neq j}^{n} m_{hj} r_j^{(k)}} \quad \text{otherwise} \tag{20.3.13}$$

Equation (20.3.9), which expresses the Seidel process without the no-negatives condition, is then replaced by

$$r^{(k+1)} = u_j - s_j^{(k)} \sum_{h=1;\, h \neq j}^{n} m_{jh} r_h^{(k)} + \sum_{h=1;\, h \neq j}^{n} s_h^{(k)} m_{hj} r_j^{(k)} \tag{20.3.14}$$

By the choice of the scale factors, **s**, we are sure that $r_j^{(k+1)}$ is not negative. By summing both sides of (20.3.14) over j, it is easy to see that

$$\sum_{j=1}^{n} r_j^{(k+1)} = \sum_{j=1}^{n} u_j \tag{20.3.15}$$

That is to say, the row sum is unchanged by the iterative process. In the computer program, it should be pointed out, there is no need for a vector, **s**, of scale factors. Instead, a vector combining the second and third terms is built up as each scale factor is calculated. In this way, the multiplications do not have to be done twice.

The process can also be applied to the rows of the value added part of the matrix. It is not certain, however, that the column sums of the resulting value-added table will match the value added as calculated from product output minus intermediate input. An option of the program provides for the automatic RAS balancing at the end of the no-negatives algorithm to ensure that the resulting matrix has matching row and column totals.

20.4. When Is It Appropriate to Use This Algorithm?

This algorithm is appropriate where the product-technology assumption itself is at least approximately true. Essentially, it allows there to have been slightly different technologies in industries where assuming strictly the average product technology would produce negatives. It is appropriate where the negatives arise because of inexactness in making the tables or because of slight differences in technologies in different industries. Applied to the Use matrix of either Table 1 or Table 6, this method gives the "neat" Recipe matrix of Table 5 with no rennet in ice cream and no chocolate in cheese. It never produces negative entries nor positive entries where Use has a zero. The row totals are unaffected by the process. It is, moreover, equivalent to deriving Recipe from equation (20.2.1) if no negatives would arise, so that if the product-technology assumption is strictly consistent with the Use and Make tables, the method produces the true matrix. It may even produce a correct Recipe matrix from a faulty Use matrix — as it has perhaps done in our example — so that equation (20.2.1) could be used to revise the estimate of the Use matrix.

Certain accounting practices, however, may produce situations which appear to be incompatible with the product-technology assumption, even though the underlying reality is quite compatible. For example, local electric utilities generally buy electricity and distribute it. In the U.S. tables, they are shown as buying electricity (not coal), adding a few intermediate inputs and labor, and producing only a secondary product, electricity, which is transferred, via the Make matrix, back to electricity. Looked at mechanically, this method of making electricity is radically different from that used in the Electricity industry, which uses coal, oil, and gas to make electricity, not electricity itself. If our algorithm is applied thoughtlessly to this situation, it cannot be expected to give very sensible results.

Fortunately, it is easy to generate signs of this sort of problem. One can compute the "NewUse" matrix implied by equation (20.2.1) with the Recipe matrix found by the algorithm and the given Make matrix. This "NewUse" matrix can then be compared with the original Use matrix and the causes of the differences investigated. We will follow this procedure in section 20.6 on the experience of using the method on the 1992 tables for the USA.

To fix the problem in the above example about electricity, we have only to consider the output of the State and local utilities as production of their own primary product, which is then sold, via the Use matrix — not transferred via the Make matrix — to the Electricity industry. In essence, we use the industry technology assumption for the local electric utilities — and for all other industries where all of the output is secondary. The industry technology assumption may also be preferable for transfers to some catch-all sectors such as "Miscellaneous food preparations" (SIC2099), which includes such disparate products as vinegar, yeast, Chinese noodles, and peanut butter. It is probably just as reasonable to suppose that a product transferred into this industry is made with the average technology of the industry where it is made as with the average technology of this catchall sector. Indeed, this sort of industry can produce the reverse of the negatives problem. For example, because of the importance of peanut butter in this industry, it has significant inputs of oil seeds. Now the no-negatives algorithm will not pull oil seeds out of the "Macaroni, spaghetti, vermicelli, and noodles" industry, (SIC2098), (which used no oil seeds) just because it transferred some Chinese noodles to 2099. But neither will it take out an adequate amount of flour for those noodles, because flour is quite unimportant in the 2099 input mix. This problem shows up only indirectly by substantial oil-seed inputs to many food industries in the NewUse matrix which transferred products to 2099 but, in fact, used no oil seeds. That is a signal to switch to the industry technology for these transfers by converting them to sales in the Use matrix.

Thus, in the use of this method, a number of iterations may be necessary. Changes in concepts, in treatments of some transactions, and occasionally in underlying data may be necessary. Although the calculation of the non-negative Recipe matrix is totally automatic, it may be necessary to make several runs to get acceptable results.

In this process, it must be recognized that a nice, clean accounting system may not be operational, that is, it may not provide by itself a simple, automatic way to go from final demand vectors specified by products to total outputs of those products. We may have to change slightly some of the concepts in the accounting system to make it operational. In making the change required for the Electricity example, we have messed up the neat accounting concept of the Electricity column of the Use matrix as a picture of what came into a particular group of establishments. We have, however, taken a step toward creating what might be called an operational Use matrix. I do not say, therefore, that statistical offices should not produce pure accounting Use matrices. But I do feel that they should also prepare the operational use matrix and the final product-to-product matrix, for in the process, they will learn about and deal with the problems which the users of the matrix will certainly encounter. They may even discover and correct errors in their work before they are discovered by their users.

This process is totally inappropriate for handling by-products such as hides produced in the meat packing industry or metal scrap produced in machinery industries. Their treatment is a different subject.

20.5. A Brief History of the Negatives Problem

The idea to compute R from equation (20.2.1) seems to have been first put in print by Van Rijckeghem (1967). He realized that there could be negatives but did not think they would be a serious problem. The idea of using equation (20.2.1) in this way, however, must have been in the air, for by early 1967, I had used it, without thinking that it was original, found negatives, and started work on the algorithm presented here.

The problem was encountered by ten Raa, Chakraborty and Small [1984] in the course of work which was primarily concerned with identifying by statistical means true by-products. They note the existence of the method presented here but write:

> [Almon] iterates truncated Neumann series in which matrix multiplications are carried out only to a limited extent to avoid negatives. This arithmetic manipulation goes without justification, is arbitrary and depends on the choice of [make matrix]-decomposition as well as the iteration scheme.

I do not believe that any of this comment is correct. The Neumann series is the expansion $(I-A)^{(-1)} = I + A + A^2 + A^3 + ...$. The algorithm used here makes no use of this series; rather it uses the Seidel procedure. There are no matrix multiplications, nor is there is any equivalence between a "limited" number of terms in the Neuman series and the Seidel solution. The procedure is carried to convergence. We have seen that the procedure has a perfectly reasonable economic interpretation; indeed, it arose from the economic interpretation of the Seidel procedure. The only thing perhaps "arbitrary" is that 0 is considered a reasonable input flow while negatives are considered unreasonable. I do not know what the "[make matrix]-decomposition" refers to, but I can assure the reader that the solution does not depend on the "iteration scheme." While I could not see how it could, given that it is carried to convergence, I changed the program and ran the "robberies" in the opposite order. The answers were identical.

The ingenious attempt of ten Raa [1988] to modify elements of the matrices in such a way as to find a most probable U matrix consistent with a non-negative R should be mentioned even though it ended, in the author's view, in frustration.

Rainer and Richter [1992] have documented a number of steps which they took towards making what I have called here the operational Use and Make matrices. Such steps should certainly be considered and applied if need. These authors still ended up with hundreds of negative flows in the R matrix because they were using just equation (1). At that point, the process described here could have been applied.

Steenge and Konijn [1992] point out that if the R matrix computed from equation (20.2.1) has any negatives in it, then it is possible to change the levels of output of the various industries in such a way that more of all products is produced without using more of all inputs. They feel that it is implausible that such a rearrangement is possible and observe that perhaps the negatives "should not be regarded as rejecting the commodity technology assumption, but as indicators of flaws in the make and use tables." (p. 130). I feel that there is much merit in that comment. It seems to me that the right time and place to use the algorithm presented here is in the process of making the tables. If there are not good statistical grounds for preferring the original Use matrix, the recomputed NewUse might well be argued – following the reasoning of Steenge and Konijn – to be a better estimate.

The caveat here is that there may well be cases where it really would be possible to increase the outputs of all products while using less of some product. For example, if there are shoes made in the Plastics products industry without any use of leather, while the Footwear industry uses leather, then by moving shoe production from Footwear to Plastic products it may be possible to produce more of all products while using less leather. Where such cases arise, a different solution is necessary, for example, moving the shoes made in the Plastics products industry together with their inputs into the Footwear industry or insisting that the two kinds of shoes are separate if substitutible products.

20.6. Application to the U.S.A Tables for 1992

The method described here has been applied to all of the USA tables since 1958 with experiences broadly similar to those described here for the 1992 table. This table has 534 sectors, counting some construction sectors which have no intermediate sales. Of these 534, 425 have secondary production. Of the 283,156 possible cells in a 534 X 534 matrix, the Use matrix has 44,900 non-zero cells, and the Make matrix has 5,885. The matrix was produced in two versions. In one, certain activities, such as restaurant services of hotels, were removed from the industry where they were produced (Hotels) and put into the sector where these activities were primary (Restaurants). In the other, these activities were left in the industry where they were conducted. The first version was designed to make the product-technology assumption more valid, and it has been used here. The matrix also puts true by-products (such as hides from meat packing) in a separate row, not one of the 534 considered here.

To try to convey a feeling of what it is like to work with the algorithm, we will look at the process midway along, rather than at the very beginning or the somewhat polished end. That is, some adjustments in the Use and Make matrix from which the algorithm starts will have already been made. As a result of this application, further adjustments will be suggested before the next application.

Before this application of the algorithm, the output of industries which had only secondary production had been changed, for reasons explained above, to be primary and the flows moved from the Make to the Use matrix.

In the following rather detailed descriptions, necessary to give a picture of what the process is really like, I will, to avoid confusion, capitalize the first letter of the first word in industry names but not in product names.

The industry Water and sewer systems failed to satisfy the requirement that at least half of the output of a product should be in the industry where it is primary. Indeed, some 85 percent of this product's output comes from Other state and local enterprises, and the iterative procedure failed to converge for a few rows until this secondary transfer was converted into a primary sale. Production of secondary advertising services, which occurred in many sectors, was also converted to a primary product of the producing industry and "sold" via the Use matrix to the Advertising industry. Secondary production of recreational services in agricultural industries was similarly converted. Much of the output of the several knitting industries had been treated originally as secondary production, and these had been changed to primary sales before the calculations shown here. Finally, the diagonals of many columns of the Use matrix are large, in part because intra-firm services, such as those of the central offices, often appear there. Thus the same sort of service that is on the diagonal of industry i is also on the diagonal of industry j. In this case, the product-technology assumption does not apply, not because it is untrue, but because of the way the table was made. Until we are able to obtain tables without this problem, we have just removed half of the diagonals from the Use table before calculating Recipe, and have then put back this amount in both of these matrices and in the NewUse matrix.

The data in both Use and Make tables were given to the nearest 1 million dollars, and all dollar figures cited here are in millions. The convergence test in the iterative process was set at one tenth of that amount, .1 million dollars. The iterative process converged for most rows of the R matrix in less than five iterations. The most iterations required for any row was 15.

The resulting Recipe matrix looks very similar in most cells to the original Use table. The Recipe matrix contains, of course, only non-negative entries and can have strictly positive entries only where *U* has positive entries. It may, however, as a result of the "robbing" process, have a zero where *U* has a positive entry. In all, there were only 95 cells in which Recipe had a zero where Use had a positive entry.

Although it is the Recipe matrix that we need from this process, it is also interesting, as noted above, to compare the original Use matrix with what we may call NewUse, computed by the equation (20.2.1) by NewUse = Recipe*Make'. The difference between Use and NewUse shows the changes in the Use matrix necessary to make it strictly compatible with product-technology assumption, the given Make matrix, and the calculated Recipe matrix. If there was no "stop" in a row, the two matrices will be identical in that row. There were 118 such identical rows, 109 of them having no secondary output.

In the other rows, these differences turn out to be mostly small but very numerous. The first and most striking difference is that NewUse has almost twice as many non-zero cells as does Use. Nearly all of these extra non-zeros are very small, exactly the sort of thing to be reasonably ignored in the process of making a table. But it is precisely this "reasonable ignoring" that leads to the problem of many small negatives in the product-to-product tables calculated without the no-negatives algorithm.

To get a closer look at how Use and NewUse compare, we may first divide each column by the corresponding industry output and then look at the column sums of the absolute values of the differences of individual coefficients in the column. This comparison is shown in Table 20.6.1. Clearly the vast majority of industries show only small differences compatible with "reasonable ignoring" of small flows in the Use matrix. They, therefore, cast no serious doubt on the product-technology assumption or the usability of the Recipe matrix obtained by the no-negatives algorithm. If what we are interested in is the *R* matrix, we can ignore the small differences between Use and NewUse.

Table 20.6.1 Comparison of Use and NewUse

Sum of Absolute Differences	Count
.050 - .250	17
.030 - .050	24
.020 - .030	54
.010 - .020	117
.000 - .010	312

There are, however, a few cases that should be looked at more closely. Table 20.6.2 shows a list of all of industries which had a sum of absolute differences greater than .050. We will look at the top five.

Table 20.6.2 Largest Differences Between Use and NewUse

Sum	Column	Column			Largest single difference	
|dif|	Number	Name	Row	|dif|	Row Name
0.250	272	Asbestos products	31	0.023	Misc. nonmetallic minerals
0.232	88	Sausages	3	0.151	Meat animals
0.167	125	Vegetable oil mills, nec	15	0.074	Oil bearing crops ind s
0.118	493	Auto rental & leasing	232	0.025	Petroleum refining
0.088	128	Edible fats and oils, nec	15	0.043	Oil bearing crops ind s
0.088	126	Animal & marine fats	126	0.038	Animal & marine fats &
0.086	87	Meat packing plants	3	0.057	Meat animals
0.079	285	Primary metals, nec	22	0.006	Iron & ferroalloy ore m
0.079	225	Manmade organic fibers	212	0.036	Indl chem: inorg & org
0.074	450	Transportation services	232	0.019	Petroleum refining
0.068	123	Cottonseed oil mills	5	0.048	Cotton
0.065	357	Carburetors, pistons,	391	0.011	Electronic components
0.060	99	Pickles, sauces	1	0.011	Dairy farm products
0.060	95	Canned & cured sea food	19	0.039	Commercial fishing
0.059	139	Yarn mills & textile fini	212	0.035	Indl chem: inorg & org
0.055	459	Sanitary services, steam	413	0.018	Mechanical measuring devices
0.051	248	Leather gloves	244	0.012	Leather tanning

There are, however, a few cases that should be looked at more closely. Table 20.6.2 shows a list of all of industries which had a sum of absolute differences greater than .050. We will look at the top five.

For Asbestos products, the cause of the difference is quickly found. The fundamental raw material for these products comes from industry 31 Misc. non-metallic minerals. Over forty percent of the output of Asbestos products, however, is produced in industry 400 Motor vehicle parts and accessories, but this industry buys neither miscellaneous non-metallic minerals nor asbestos products. In other words, it seems to be making almost half of the asbestos products without any visible source of asbestos. This anomaly seems to me to be an oversight in making the Use matrix which should be simply corrected. If our only interest is the Recipe matrix, the algorithm seems to have computed pretty nearly the right result from the wrong data. On the other hand, if we want to correct the Use table, NewUse, gets us started with the right entry for Misc. non-metallic minerals into both Motor vehicle parts and Asbestos products. To keep the right totals in these two columns of Use will require manual adjustments.

The second largest difference between Use and NewUse shown in Table 20.6.2 is in the input of meat animals into Sausage. The Sausage industry is shown in the Use matrix to buy both animals ($655) and slaughtered meat ($9688). It had a primary output of $13458 and a secondary output of $2612 of products primary to Meat packing. Meat packing had a secondary output of $4349 of sausage. Now in Meat packing, the cost of the animals is over eighty percent of the value of the finished product, so the purchases of animals in the Sausage industry is insufficient to cover even the secondary meat output of this industry, not to mention making any sausage. In making Recipe, the input of animals directly into sausage is driven to zero and cut off there rather than being allowed to become negative. Then when NewUse is made, the direct animal input for all the secondary production of meat packing products is put in, thus making a flow some six times as large as the purchase of meat animals by the Sausage industry in the original Use matrix.

What I believe to be really happening here is that Sausage plants are mostly buying halves of slaughtered animals from meat packers, selling off the best cuts as a secondary product, and using the rest to make sausage. Over in the Meat packing plants, the same thing is happening. Fundamentally, there is only one process of sausage making. The question is how to represent it in the input-output framework. The simplest representation of it in the Use matrix would be to have packing houses sell to sausage plants only the meat that would be directly used in sausage. The rest, the choice cuts sold off as meat by Sausage mills, would simply be considered sold by the packers without ever passing through the Sausage mills. The industry output of Sausage mills is reduced but cost of materials (namely, meat) is reduced by exactly the same amount, so there is no need to adjust other flows. Product output of meat is reduced, but not the industry output. Thus, a slight adjustment in the accounting makes it broadly compatible with the product-technology assumption. The seventh item in Table 20.6.2, by the way, is just the other side of this problem.

The third largest of the discrepancies lies in row 16, oil-bearing crops, of industry 125 Vegetable oil mills n.e.c (not elsewhere classified). The differences in the underlying flows is not large, $298 in Use and $251 in NewUse, but it turns up in Table 20.6.2 because the cost of these oil crops is such a large fraction of the output of the Vegetable oil mills. A comparison of the oil-bearing crops row of Use and NewUse shows that NewUse has a number of small positive entries for industries where, as for Cheese, Use has a zero and where, moreover, it is highly implausible that there was any use of oil seeds. On the other hand, most of the large users of oil seeds, like Vegetable oil mills have had their usage trimmed back. The key to what is going on is found in industry 132 Food preparations n.e.c.. In Use, this industry bought $558 from oil bearing crops, nearly twice the consumption of the vegetable oil mills themselves. Peanut butter, as noted above, is in this catchall industry. That fact, by itself, is not a problem. The problem is that about a quarter of the production of products primary to this industry are made in other industries. In fact, most of the food manufacturing industries have some secondary production of the miscellaneous food preparations. Probably "preparations" made in the Cheese industry are quite different from those made in the Pickles industry. And it certainly makes no sense to spread oil seed inputs all over the food industries. Here we have a clear case of the inapplicability of the product-technology assumption if all these secondary products are considered to be truly the same product. On the other hand, as argued above, the very heterogeneity of the products makes it appropriate to consider each as a primary product of the industry which produces it and then "sell" it, via the Use matrix, to Food preparations for distribution. In the next pass at making Recipe, this change is to be made.

The vegetable oil industries also present another interesting case of apparent but perhaps not real violation of the product-technology assumption, which shows up in the fifth item in Table 20.6.2. Industry 125 Vegetable oil mills n.e.c. has inputs of oil-bearing crops, cotton, and tree nuts totaling $437. It uses these oil sources to produce a primary output of $572. Industry 128 "Edible fats and oils" produces $92 of products primary to 125 without a penny of any of these inputs! Surely this is flat violation of the product-technology assumption. But is it really? "Edible fats and oils" buys lots of the products primary to Vegetable oil mills. Thus, it is entirely possible to have two bottles of chemically identical oil made of identical raw materials by identical refining processes but with one bottle made entirely in Vegetable oil mills while the oil in the other bottle was pressed in those mills and then sold to Edible fats and oils for finishing. We might call this situation "trans-market product technology." Our algorithm gave the right answer for the Vegetable oil mills column of Recipe, that is, it combined output of products primary to the oil mills with the inputs of oil sources which this industry had.

The fourth largest discrepancy in Table 20.6.2 is for the gasoline input into Automobile renting and leasing. Use shows $1131; Recipe ups that to $1197.2; but NewUse cuts it back to $565.5. What happened? The problem is that slightly more than half of the output Auto renting is produced in Credit agencies, with a minuscule input of gasoline. When NewUse is made, more than half of the gasoline in Recipe is allocated over to Credit agencies. Here we are confronted with a failure of the product-technology assumption not because of different processes for producing the same product but because two quite different products have been called one and the same in the accounting system. The output of the Credit agencies, long-term leasing, is quite distinct from the short-term renting, which is were the gasoline was used. The best solution would be to recognize the difference of the two products. Short of that, the worst of the problem can be fixed by turning the secondary transfer from Credit agencies to Automobile rental into a primary flow. The present Recipe matrix, incidentally, is about right in the gasoline row but makes no connection between a final demand for automobile renting and leasing and the output of credit agencies.

From these five or six cases, we see that our algorithm cannot be expected to give usable results on the first try. The problems are likely to lie, however, neither in the fundamental economic reality nor in the algorithm, but in an accounting system which needs a few modifications in Use and Make to make it operational in our sense. Most importantly, the algorithm gives us the means to identify the places that need attention and a way of progressing systematically through the problems. It also provides a way of producing a final, non-negative Recipe matrix that implies a NewUse matrix close enough to the modified Use matrix that the differences can be safely ignored.

Making an input-output table requires fussing over details, and making a good Recipe matrix with the algorithm presented here is no different in this respect from any other part of the process. Use of the algorithm reveals and pinpoints problems. Moreover, the important problems are likely to be small in number. We have covered all of those causing a difference of as much as .100 between columns of Use and NewUse. To get to a Recipe table we would be ready to accept might require another week's work. But in the total effort which went into making this table, that is minuscule. Most importantly, the use of the algorithm gives us a way to work on the problems rather than just wring our hands over negatives.

In this sense, this algorithm has performed satisfactorily over many years on every U.S. table since 1958. The use of the method seems to me to deserve to become a standard part of making input-output tables and, in particular, for making product-to-product tables.

20.7. The Computer Program

The C++ code for this algorithm, using functions from *BUMP*, the Beginner's Understandable Matrix Package, for handling matrices and vectors, is given below. It is reproduced here because the code shows more clearly than the verbal or formulaic description exactly what is done. The program and the supporting *BUMP* code made be downloaded from the Inforum Internet site: www.inforum.umd.edu. The main program here reads in the matrices that were used in the examples. The main program for the actual calculations of the full-scale American matrices is significantly larger and has various diagnostic output, such as that shown in Table 20.6.2. It is available on request.

In using the algorithm, it is important for documenting what has been done to have a method of input of the original Use and Make matrices that preserves the original version at the top of the input file and introduces the modifications as over-rides later in the file. It is also important to have software, such as *ViewMat*, which will show corresponding columns of several large matrices side-by-side in a scrolling grid. *ViewMat* is also available on the Inforum Internet site.

```c
#include <stdio.h>      // for printf();
#include <math.h>     // for abs()
#include "bump.h"
int purify(Matrix& R, Matrix& U, Matrix& M, float toler);

void main(){
    Matrix Use(5,5), Make(5,5), R(5,5), NewUse(5,5);
    Use.ReadA("Use.dat");
    Make.ReadA("Make.dat");
    purify(R,Use,Make,.000001);
    R.Display("This is R");
    writemat(R,"Recipe");
    NewUse = R*(~NewUse);
    writemat(NewUse,"NewUse");
    tap();
    printf("\nEnd of calculations.\n");
    }

/* Purification produces a product-to-product (or Recipe) matrix R from a Use matrix U and a Make
    matrix M. M(i,j) shows the fraction of product j made in industry i. U(i,j) shows the amount of
    product i used in industry j. The product-technology assumption leads us to expect that there
    exits a matrix R such that U = RM'. If, however, we compute R = U*Inv(M') we often find many small
negative elements in  R. This routine avoids those small negatives in an iterative process.
*/

int purify(Matrix& R, Matrix& U, Matrix& M, float toler){
    int row, i, j, m, n, iter, imax;
    const maxiter = 20;
    float sum,rob,scale,dismax,dis;
    n = U.rows();   // n = number of rows in U
    m = U.columns(); // m = number of columns in U
    Vector C(m), P(m), Flow(m), Discrep(m);
```

424

```
// Flow is row of U matrix and remains unchanged.
// P becomes the row of the purified matrix.
// C is the change vector at each iteration.
// At the end of each iteration we set P = Flow + C, to start // the next iteration.

// Purify one row at a time
for(row = 1; row <= n; row++){
   C.set(0.); // C, which will receive the changes, is
   // initialized to zero.
   // P = Flow + C will be the new P.
   pulloutrow(Flow,U,row);
   P = Flow;
   iter = 0;
   start: iter++;
   for(j = 1; j<=m; j++){
      // Calculate total claims from other industries on
      // the inputs into industry j.
      sum = 0;
      for(i = 1; i <= m; i++){
         if(i == j) continue;
         rob = P[i]*M(j,i);
         sum += rob;
         C[i] += rob;
         }
      // Did we steal more from j than j had?
      if (sum > Flow[j] && sum > 0){
         // scale down robbery
         scale = 1. - Flow[j]/sum;
         for(i = 1; i <= m; i++){
            if(i == j) continue;
            C[i] -= scale*P[i]*M(j,i);
            }
         sum = Flow[j];
         }
      C[j] -= sum;
      }
   // Check for convergence
   imax = 0;
   dismax = 0;
   for(i = 1; i <= m; i++){
      dis = fabs(P[i] - Flow[i] - C[i]);
      Discrep[i] = dis;
      if(dis >= dismax){
         imax = i;
         dismax = dis;
         }
      }
   }
P = Flow + C;
C.set(0);
if(dismax > toler){
   if(iter < maxiter) goto start;
   printf("Purify did not converge for row %d. Dismax = %7.2f. Imax = %d.\n",
      row,dismax,imax);
   }
putinrow(P,R,row);
   }
return(OK);
}
```

References

Almon, C. (1970) "Investment in input-output models and the treatment of secondary products," *Input-Output Techniques, vol. 2, Applications of Input-Output Analysis*, pp.103-116 (Amsterdam, North Holland Publishing Co.)

Almon, C., Buckler, M., Horwitz, L., and Reimbold, T.,(1974) *1985, Interindustry Forecasts of the American Economy* (Lexington, Lexington Books) pp.151-154.

European system of accounts: ESA 1995, Transmission programme of data. Eurostat.

Rainer, N. and Richter, J. (1992) "Some Aspects of the Analytical Use of Descriptive Make and Absorption Tables," *Economic Systems Research*, 4(2), pp.159 - 172

Steenge, A.E. and Konijin, P.J.A. (1992) "A new Approach to Irreducibility in Multisectoral Models with Joint Production," *Economic Systems Research*, 4(2), pp 125-132

The *System of National Accounts 1993* (published by the United Nations, the World Bank, the IMF, the OECD, and the European Union)

ten Raa, Thijs, D. Chakraborty, and J.A. Small (1984) "An Alternative Treatment of Secondary Products in Input-Output Analysis," *Review of Economics and Statistics*, 66, pp. 88-97.

ten Raa, Thijs (1988) "An Alternative Treatment of Secondary Products in Input-Output Analysis: Frustration," *Review of Economics and Statistics*, pp. 535-538.

Van Rijckeghem (1967) "An Exact Method for Determining the Technology Matrix in a Situation with Secondary Products," *Review of Economics and Statistics*, 49, pp. 607-608.

CHAPTER 21. A PERHAPS ADEQUATE DEMAND SYSTEM

Long-term, multisectoral modeling requires calculation of consumer expenditures in some detail by product. Finding a functional form to represent the market demand functions of consumers for this work has proven a surprisingly thorny problem. Clearly, the form must deal with significant growth in real income, the effects of demographic and other trends, and changes in relative prices. Both complementarity and substitution should be possible among the different goods. Increasing income should certainly not necessarily, by the form of the function, force the demand for some good to go negative. Prices should affect the marginal propensity to consume with respect to income, and the extent of that influence should be an empirical question, not one decided by the form of the function.

This chapter will present a form which meets these requirements and extends a form I suggested many years ago (Almon [1979]). Applications of the form to forty-product demand systems for France, Italy, Spain and the United States are reported and the results compared.

Before presenting this form, however, it may be well to see just how tricky it can be to find a form with these simple requirements by looking at another form, the "Almost Ideal Demand System" (AIDS) suggested by Deaton and Muellbauer [1980]. Its name, the eminence of its authors and its place of publication have led to wide usage. It has, however, a most peculiar property which is likely to utterly vitiate any growth model in which it is used. Like many others, it is derived from utility maximization; its problems will therefore emphasize the important fact that such derivation does not automatically imply reasonable properties. One of the properties it does imply, however, is Slutsky symmetry in the market demand functions. This property was not mentioned above. Should it have been? What role should this symmetry play in market demand functions? His questions also needs to be examined before presenting the new form, for it plays a key role its formulation.

21.1. Problems and Lessons of the AIDS Form

The AIDS form can be written as an equation for the budget share of good i:

$$s_i = a_i + \sum_{j=1}^{n} d_{ij} \log(p_j) + b_i \log(y/P) \tag{21.1.1}$$

where s_i is the budget share of product i, p_j is the price of product j, y is nominal income and P is an overall price index, the matrix of d's is symmetric and has zero row and column sums, the sum of all the a_i is one, and the b_i sum to zero. Consequently, if any b_i is positive, then one or more others must be negative. Thus, *increasing real income must ultimately drive the consumption of one or more goods negative,* unless, of course, it has no effect at all on budget shares. This property seems rather less than "ideal". Moreover, the partial derivative of the share with respect to real income is independent of the relative prices, whereas common sense suggests that it should depend on them. Because of these properties, the AIDS form, while possible "almost ideal" from some point of view, is surely absolutely inadequate for use in any growth model. Since it is derived from utility maximization, it also serves as a clear warning that the mere fact of such ancestry is no assurance whatsoever of the adequacy of the form, a lesson which has been heeded in the PADS form proposed here.

A number of other forms derived from utility maximization were reviewed in the article cited and found wanting relative to the simple properties set out above. The only study which to my knowledge has estimated these forms, AIDS, and the Almon form all on the same data and compared the results is Gauyacq [1985]. Using French data for 1959-1979, he estimated "the linear expenditure system of Stone; the model with real prices and income of Fourgeaud and Nataf; the additive quadratic model of Houthakker and Taylor; the logarithmically additive model of Houthakker, ... the Rotterdam model of Theil and Barten, the Translog model based on a logarithmic transformation of the utility function; the AIDS model of Deaton and Muellbauer; ....[and] the model proposed by Clopper Almon." The conclusion was not surprising to anyone who had compared the properties of the forms to the simple requirements stated above: "De l'étude que nous avons effectué, il apparaît en définitive que seul le modèle de C. Almon constitue un système que satisfasse approximativement aux attendus théoriques et présente un réel intérêt pour l'étude économétrique de fonctions de demande détaillées." (p. 119). (From the study which we have done, it appears that definitely only the model of C. Almon offers a system which satisfies approximately theoretical expectations and is of real interest for the econometric study of detailed demand functions.) Elegant theoretical derivations, apparently, are of little help in finding adequate forms. Despite this relative success, there is a problem with the Almon suggestion, as we will see in section 21.3, where we will also see a way to fix it.

21.2. Slutsky Symmetry and Market Demand Functions

Just about the only useful non-obvious implication of the theory of the single consumer who maximizes utility subject to a budget constraint is the Slutsky symmetry shown in equation (21.2.1).

$$\frac{\partial x_i^k}{\partial p_j} + \frac{\partial x_i^k}{\partial y^k} x_j^k = \frac{\partial x_j^k}{\partial p_i} + \frac{\partial x_j^k}{\partial y^k} x_i^k \qquad (21.2.1)$$

Here x_i^k is the consumption of product i by individual k, y^k is the nominal income of individual k, and p_j is the price of product j. A comparable relation, however, need not hold for the market demand functions, the sum over all k of individuals' demand functions. Summing the above equation over the individuals gives equation (21.2.2).

$$\frac{\partial \sum_k x_i^k}{\partial p_j} + \frac{\sum_k \partial x_i^k}{\partial y^k} x_j^k = \frac{\partial \sum_k x_j^k}{p_i} + \frac{\sum_k \partial x_j^k}{\partial y^k} x_i^k \qquad (21.2.2)$$

which is in general not the same as – and does not imply – equation 21.2.3

$$\frac{\partial \sum_k x_i^k}{\partial p_j} + \frac{\partial \sum_k x_i^k}{\partial \sum_k y^k} \sum_k x_j^k = \frac{\partial \sum_k x_j^k}{\partial p_i} + \frac{\partial \sum_k x_j^k}{\partial \sum_k y^k} \sum_k x_i^k \qquad (21.2.3)$$

which is what Slutsky symmetry of the market demand functions would imply. Thus, strict micro theory does not imply Slutsky symmetry of market demand functions. Consequently, there is in general no "representative consumer." To suppose that market demand functions derived by maximizing the utility of this non-existent entity have "micro foundations" not enjoyed by functions not so derived is hardly respectful of micro theory. Rather, any market demand functions so derived are on exactly the same theoretical footing as market demand functions made up without any reference to utility maximization. Both kinds of functions must meet the same "adequacy" criteria. With that point clearly established, we may, however, ask: Are there restrictive conditions under which equation (21.2.2) would imply equation (21.2.3)? One condition is, of course, that all individuals should have not only the same utility function but also the same income, and that the increase in aggregate income is accomplished by giving each the same increase. That condition is hardly interesting for empirical studies. A less restrictive condition is that the marginal propensity to consume a given product with respect to income should be the same for all individuals, or in effect, that the Engel curves for all products should be straight lines. If, for example,

$$\frac{\partial x_i^k}{\partial y^k} = a_i \qquad (21.2.4)$$

Then the second term on each side of equation 21.2.1 can be factored to yield

$$\frac{\partial \sum_k x_i^k}{\partial p_j} + a_i \sum_k x_j^k = \frac{\partial \sum_k x_j^k}{\partial p_i} + a_j \sum_k x_i^k \qquad (21.2.5)$$

This is exactly what equation (21.2.3) states, for in this case it makes no difference to whom the "infinitesimal" increase in income is given and

$$\frac{\partial \sum_k x_i^k}{\partial \sum_k y^k} = a_i \qquad (21.2.6)$$

Now the assumption that all Engel curves are straight lines is generally contradicted by cross-section budget studies, even when one uses total expenditure in place of income in the Engel curves. (See, for example, Chao [1991] where Figure 2.2 shows Engel curves for 62 products). On the other hand, many products have virtually straight Engel curves over a considerable middle range of total expenditure where most households find themselves. Thus, one gets the impression that while Slutsky symmetry is certainly not a necessary property of market demand curves, *it probably does no great violence to reality to impose symmetry to reduce the number of parameters to be estimated.*

21.3. A Perhaps Adequate Form

The 1979 Almon article introduced a form with a multiplicative relation between the income terms and the price terms. Its general form is:

$$x_i(t) = (a_i(t) + b_i(y/P)) \prod_{k=1}^{n} p_k^{c_{ik}} \qquad (21.3.1)$$

where the left side is the consumption per capita of product i in period t and $a_i(t)$ is a function of time. The b_i are positive constants. The y is nominal income per capita; p_k is the price index of product k; and P is an overall price index defined by

$$P = \prod_{k=1}^{n} p_k^{s_k} \qquad (21.3.2)$$

where s_k is the budget share of product k in the period in which the price indexes are all 1, and the c_{ik} are constants satisfying the constraint

$$\sum_{k=1}^{n} c_{ik} = 0 \qquad (21.3.3)$$

Any function of this form is homogeneous of degree 0 in all prices and income and satisfies all of the properties set out in the first paragraph. It has three problems:

1. It is not certain that expenditures will add up to income.

2. There is no way to choose the parameters to guarantee Slutsky symmetry at all prices if we want to. We can, however, arrange to have symmetry in some particular base period. As long as the shares of various products in total expenditure do not change very much from those of that base period, we will continue to have approximate symmetry.

3. There are a lot of c's to be estimated.

Problem 1 can be easily fixed by adding on a "spreader," that is, by summing all expenditures, comparing them with y, and allocating the difference in proportion to the marginal propensities to consume with respect to y at the current prices. The amount to be spread is usually small and the form with spreader has essentially the same properties as the form without, plus the adding up property. We need not complicate the mathematics here by adding the spreader, but in practice it should be added when the equations are used in forecasting.

Problem 2, in view of section 2, is more a cautionary note than a real problem. Symmetry in a base year is probably quite adequate.

Problem 3 – which occurs in all forms which provide for varying degrees of substitution and complementarity – can be quite severe. If we have 80 categories of expenditures, we have 6,400 c's less the 80 determined by equation (10). If we have 20 years of annual data, we have 1,600 data points from which to determine these 5,600 parameters, or 3.5 parameters per data point! Clearly, we have to have employ some restrictions. Even if we had only one parameter per data point, we would probably want restrictions to insure reasonableness of the parameters. Indeed, the principal theoretical problem in consumption analysis is find ways to specify what is "reasonable."

Part of the solution of problem 3 can be found, if we wish, in the point noted in problem 2, namely that we can impose Slutsky symmetry at some prices. The Slutsky condition may be derived either from equation (21.2.1) or, more simply, by assuming that the compensating change in income is that which keeps y/P constant. Either approach gives as the symmetry condition equation (21.3.4):

$$\frac{c_{ij}\, x_i}{p_j} = \frac{c_{ji}\, x_j}{p_i} \tag{21.3.4}$$

Multiplying both sides by $\dfrac{p_i\, p_j}{y}$ gives equation 21.3.5.

$$\frac{c_{ij}}{s_j} = \frac{c_{ji}}{s_i} \tag{21.3.5}$$

If we then define

$$\lambda_{ij} = \frac{c_{ij}}{s_j} \tag{21.3.6}$$

then the form can be written as

$$x_i(t) = \left(a_i(t) + b_i(y/P)\right) \prod_{k=1}^{n} p_k^{\lambda_{ik} s_k} \tag{21.3.7}$$

where

$$\lambda_{ij} = \lambda_{ji} \tag{21.3.8}$$

This restriction cuts the number of parameters by a half. That reduction is a big help but is clearly insufficient. Further help with this problem can be found through the idea of groups and subgroups of commodities. The accompanying box shows an example with fifteen basic commodity categories. These are subdivided into three groups and several categories which are not in any group. The first group is divided into two subgroups; the second,

Illustration of Groups and Subgroups

	Product	Group	Subgroup
Food	1. Meat	I	A
	2. Fish	I	A
	3. Dairy products	I	A
	4. Cereal products	I	B
	5. Fruits and vegetables	I	B
	6. Other food products	I	B
Transportation	7. Automobiles	II	C
	8. Gasoline and oil	II	C
	9. Tires, batteries, repair	II	C
	10. Public transportation	II	
Clothing and Shoes	11. Clothing	III	
	12. Shoes	III	
No Group	13. Other durables		
	14. Other non-durables		
	15. Other services		

into one subgroup and a category not in the subgroup; the third group has no subgroup.

The idea of the Almon [1979] article was to assume that $\lambda_{ij} = \lambda_0$ if i and j are not members of the same group or subgroup, while if they are in the same group, G, $\lambda_{ij} = \lambda_o + \mu'_G$, and if they are in the same subgroup, g, of the group G, $\lambda_{ij} = \lambda_o + \mu'_G + v'_g$. Thus, there were as many parameters to estimate as there were groups + subgroups + 1. Estimation was fairly simple because, given a value of λ_0, estimation of the other parameters had to involve only products within the same group or subgroup. Several values of λ_0 were chosen, all equations estimated, and the value of λ_0 chosen which gave the best over-all fit.

The problem with this form was that products which had no natural partners with which to form a group all ended up either in very strange groups or, if they were given no group at all, all with nearly the same own price elasticity, namely $-\lambda_0$. It is often difficult to find groups for such goods as Telephone service, Medical service, Education, or Religious services. A specification which forces them all to have, for that reason, nearly the same own price elasticity is certainly inadequately flexible. An adequate form, it now seems, should allow every product to have its own own-price elasticity. We will then have as many price exponent parameters as there are products plus groups plus subgroups. A simple way to achieve this generalization is to introduce n parameters, $\lambda_1, ..., \lambda_n$, and use them to define the λ_{ij} as follows. If i and j are not members of the same group or subgroup, then

$$\lambda_{ij} = \lambda_i + \lambda_j \tag{21.3.9}$$

while if they are in the same group, G, $\lambda_{ij} = \lambda_i + \lambda_j + \mu'_G$, and if they are in the same subgroup, g, of the group G, $\lambda_{ij} = \lambda_i + \lambda_j + \mu'_G + v'_g$. The definitions apply only for i not equal to j. The λ_{ii} are each determined by equation (21.3.3), the homogeneity requirement.

Using these definitions, for product i, a member of group G and subgroup g, the equation becomes

$$x_i(t) = (a_i(t) + b_i(y/P)) \prod_{k=1, k \neq i}^{n} p_k^{(\lambda_i + \lambda_k)s_k} \prod_{k \in G, k \neq i}^{n} p_k^{\mu_G' s_k} \prod_{k \in g, k \neq i}^{n} p_k^{v_g' s_k} p_i^{c_{ii}} \tag{21.3.10}$$

Equation (21.3.3) requires

$$\sum_{k \neq i} \lambda_k s_k + \lambda_i \sum_{k \neq i} s_k + \mu_G' \sum_{k \in G, k \neq i} s_k + v_g' \sum_{k \in g, k \neq i} s_k + c_{ii} = 0 \tag{21.3.11}$$

If we solve this equation for c_{ii} and substitute in equation (21.3.10), we obtain, after a bit of simplification,

432

$$x_i(t) = (a_i(t) + b_i(y/P))(\frac{p_i}{P})^{-\lambda_i} \prod_{k=1}^{n} (\frac{p_k}{p_i})^{\lambda_k s_k} \left(\prod_{k \in G} (\frac{p_k}{p_i})^{s_k} \right)^{\mu' G} \left(\prod_{k \in g} (\frac{p_k}{p_i})^{s_k} \right)^{\nu' g} \qquad (21.3.12)$$

where we have inserted the terms involving p_i/p_i into all of the products, because this term is always 1.0 no matter to what power it is raised. We can make the form even simpler by introducing price indexes for the group G and subgroup g defined by:

$$P_G = \left(\prod_{k \in G} p_k^{s_k} \right)^{1/\sum_{k \in G} s_k} \quad \text{and} \quad P_g = \left(\prod_{k \in g} p_k^{s_k} \right)^{1/\sum_{k \in g} s_k} \qquad (21.3.13)$$

We then obtain equation (21.3.14)

$$x_i(t) = (a_i(t) + b_i(y/P)) \cdot (\frac{p_i}{P})^{-\lambda_i} \prod_{k=1}^{n} (\frac{p_i}{p_k})^{-\lambda_k s_k} \cdot \left(\frac{p_i}{P_G} \right)^{-\mu_G} \left(\frac{p_i}{P_g} \right)^{-\nu_g} \qquad (21.3.14)$$

where

$$\mu = \mu' \sum_{k \in G} s_k \quad \text{and} \quad \nu = \nu' \sum_{k \in g} s_k \qquad (21.3.15)$$

This is the form for estimation. Note that it has one parameter, a λ, for each good, plus one parameter, a μ, for each group, plus one parameter, a ν, for each subgroup. Thus, it appears to have an adequate number of parameters. The Slutsky symmetry of (21.3.14) at the initial prices and income may be verified directly by taking partial derivatives of (21.3.14).

A special case of some interest arises when all the λ_i are the same and equal to $\lambda_0/2$, for in that case equation (21.3.14) simplifies to

$$x_i(t) = (a_i(t) + b_i(y/P)) \left(\frac{p_i}{P} \right)^{-\lambda_i} \left(\frac{p_i}{P_G} \right)^{-\mu_G} \left(\frac{p_i}{P_g} \right)^{-\nu_g} \qquad (21.3.16)$$

which is exactly the form suggested in the Almon [1979] article. Thus, the present suggestion is a simple generalization of the earlier one. In practice, there are apt to be a few commodities, such as Tobacco, Sugar, or Medical care which show so little price sensitivity that they cannot be fit well by this system. For them, we will assume that all the λ_{ij} in their rows and columns are 0. Note that this assumption is perfectly consistent with the symmetry of the lambda's. When there are such "insensitive" commodities in the system, equation (21.3.14) is modified in two ways. For these items, there are no price terms at all, while for other items the product term which in (21.3.14) is shown with k running from 1 to n is modified so that k runs only over the "sensitive" and not the "insensitive" commodities.

It is useful in judging the reasonableness of regression results to be able to calculate the compensated own and the cross price elasticities. ("Compensated" here means that y has been increased so as to keep y/P constant.) Their derivation is straight-forward but complicated enough to make the results worth recording. In addition to the notation already introduced, we need

u_{ij} = the share in the base year of product j in the group which contains product i, or 0 if i is not in a group with j.

w_{ij} = the share in the base year of product j in the subgroup which contains product i or 0 if i is not in a subgroup with j.

μ_i = the μ for the group which contains product i, or 0 if i is not in a group. Note that μ_i is the same for all i in the same group.)

v_i = the v for the subgroup which contains product i, or 0 if i is not in a subgroup. (Similarly, note that v_i is the same for all i in the same subgroup.)

L = The share-weighted average of the λ_i :

$$L = \sum_{k=1}^{n} \lambda_k s_k \qquad (21.3.17)$$

The compensated own-price elasticity of product i is then:

$$\eta_{ii} = -\lambda_i(1-s_i) - L + \lambda_i s_i - \mu_i(1-u_{ii}) - v_i(1-w_{ii}) \qquad (21.3.18)$$

While the cross-price elasticity, the elasticity of the demand for good i with respect to the price of good j, is

$$\eta_{ij} = \lambda_i s_j + \lambda_j s_j - u_{ij}\mu_i + w_{ij}v_i \qquad (21.3.19)$$

Two tables are produced by the estimation program. One shows, for each product, its share in total expenditure in the base year, the group and subgroup of which it is a member and its share in them, its λ and the μ and v of its subgroups, its own price elasticity, and various information on the income parameters. Thus, it contains all the data necessary for calculating any of the cross elasticities. It is small enough to be reasonably reproduced. The other table shows the complete matrix of own- and cross-price elasticities. It is generally too large to be printed except in extract.

It should be noted that the complexity in estimating equation (21.3.14) comes from the term indicated by the product sign. Without this term, the equation could be estimated separately for each product or group of products. On the other hand, it is this term which gives Slutsky symmetry at the base point. If one did not care about this symmetry, then this term could omitted from the equation, with a great reduction in complexity in estimation. Once the programming has been done to estimate with this term, however, it is little trouble to use the program.

So far, we have said little about the "income" term, the term within the first parenthesis of equation (21.3.14). In the equations reported below we have used just a constant, real income per capita, the first difference of real income per capita, and a linear time trend. Furthermore, we have used the same population measure, total population, for computing consumption per capita for all items. The estimation program, however, allows much greater diversity. By use of adult-equivalency weights, different weighted populations can be used for computing the per capita consumption of different items. Further, if the size distribution of income is known, it can be used to compute income-based indicators of consumption more appropriate to each item than just average income. Thus, the program allows a different income variable to be used for each consumer category. Finally, instead of just a linear time trend, one can use a "trend" variable appropriate to a particular category. For example, the percentage of the population which smokes could be used in explaining spending on tobacco. The estimation program allows for all these possibilities. On the other hand, in view of this diversity, it seemed pointless to try to place constraints on the parameters of the income terms to make the income terms add up to total income. Instead, in applying the estimated functions, one should calculate the difference between the assumed total expenditure and that implied by the equations and allocate it to the various items.

21.4. The Mathematics of Estimation

The function in equation (21.3.14) is nonlinear in all its parameters. In a system with 80 consumption categories there will be over 400 parameters involved in the simultaneous non-linear estimation. This size makes it worthwhile to note in this section some simplifying structure in the problem. All non-linear estimation procedures take some guess of the parameters, evaluate the functions with these values to obtain vectors of predicted values, $\hat{x}_i$, and subtract these from the vectors of observed values, x_i , to obtain vectors of residuals, r_i , thus:

$$r_i = x_i - \hat{x}_i \tag{21.4.1}$$

They then, in some way, pick changes in the parameters, and re-evaluate the function with the new values. The only difference in the various methods is how the changes in the parameters are picked. The Marquardt algorithm, which we use, is very nearly the same as regressing the residuals on the partial derivatives of the predicted values with respect to the parameters. It requires, in particular, these derivatives. For equation (21.3.14), they are reasonably easy to calculate if one remembers (or works out) the formula:

$$\frac{d\,a^x}{dx} = a^x \ln a \tag{21.4.2}$$

where *ln* denotes the natural logarithm. Then the derivative of the demand for the ith good with respect to its own λ is

$$\frac{\partial \hat{x}_i}{\partial \lambda_i} = \hat{x}_i \left(\ln \left(\frac{\prod p_k^{s_k}}{p_i} \right) \right) = \hat{x}_i \left(\sum s_k \ln p_k - \ln p_i \right) \tag{21.4.3}$$

and for *j* not equal to *i*

$$\frac{\partial \hat{x}_i}{\partial \lambda_j} = \hat{x}_i \ln\left(\frac{p_j}{p_i}\right) s_j = \hat{x}_i (\ln p_j - \ln p_i) s_j \tag{21.4.4}$$

And if i is a member of the group G

$$\frac{\partial \hat{x}_i}{\partial \mu_G} = \hat{x}_i \ln\left(\frac{P_G}{p_i}\right) = \hat{x}_i (\ln P_G - \ln p_i) \tag{21.4.5}$$

and if i is a member of the subgroup g

$$\frac{\partial \hat{x}_i}{\partial v_g} = \hat{x}_i \ln\left(\frac{P_g}{p_i}\right) = \hat{x}_i (\ln P_g - \ln p_i) \tag{21.4.6}$$

To explain the estimation process, we shall denote the vector of parameters of the "income-and-time term," the term preceding the first dot in equation (21.3.14), for product i by $\mathbf{a}_i$ and the vector of parameters of the "price term", the rest of the formula, by $\mathbf{h}$. Thus, $\mathbf{h}$ consists of all values of λ, μ, and v. Note that $\mathbf{h}$ is the same for all products, though a particular μ or v may not enter the equation for a given commodity. If we let $\mathbf{A}_i$ be the matrix of partial derivatives of the predicted values for product i with respect to the $\mathbf{a}_i$ and similarly let $\mathbf{B}_i$ be the matrix of partial derivatives of the predicted values of product i with respect to $\mathbf{h}$, and finally let $\mathbf{r}_i$ be the residuals, all evaluated at the current value of the parameters, then the regression data matrix, $(\mathbf{X},\mathbf{y})$ in the usual notation, for three commodities is:

$$(X, y) = \begin{bmatrix} A_1 & 0 & 0 & B_1 & r_1 \\ 0 & A_2 & 0 & B_2 & r_2 \\ 0 & 0 & A_3 & B_3 & r_3 \end{bmatrix} \tag{21.4.7}$$

If we now form the normal equations $\mathbf{X'Xb} = \mathbf{X'y}$ in the usual notation, we find

$$\begin{bmatrix} A_1' A_1 & 0 & 0 & A_1' B_1 \\ 0 & A_2' A_2 & 0 & A_2' B_2 \\ 0 & 0 & A_3' A_3 & A_3' B_3 \\ B_1' A_1 & B_2' A_2 & B_3' A_3 & \sum_{i=1}^{3} B_i' B_i \end{bmatrix} \begin{bmatrix} da_1 \\ da_2 \\ da_3 \\ dh \end{bmatrix} = \begin{bmatrix} A_1' r_1 \\ A_2' r_2 \\ A_3' r_3 \\ \sum_{i=1}^{3} B_i' r_i \end{bmatrix} \tag{21.4.8}$$

After initial values of the parameters have been chosen and the functions evaluated with these values and the sum of squared residuals (SSR) calculated, the Marquardt procedure consists of picking a scalar, which we may call M, and following these steps:

1. Compute the matrices of equation (21.4.8), multiply the diagonal elements in the

matrix on the left by $1 + M$ and solve for the changes in the $\mathbf{a}_i$ and $\mathbf{h}$ vectors. Make these changes and evaluate the functions at the new values.

2. If the SSR has decreased, divide M by 10 and repeat step 1.

3. If the SSR has increased, multiply M by 10, go back to the values of the parameters before the last change, evaluate the functions again at these values, and repeat step 1.

The process is stopped when very little reduction in the SSR is being achieved and the changes in the parameters are small. (As M rises, the method turns into the steepest descent method, which can usually find a small improvement if one exists, while as M diminishes, the method turns into Newton's method, which gives rapid convergence when close enough to a solution that the quadratic approximation is good.)

To economize on space in the computer and to speed the calculations, we can take advantage of the structure of the matrix on the left side of equation (21.4.8). To do so, let $\mathbf{Z}_i$ be the inverse of $\mathbf{A}_i'\mathbf{A}_i$. Then by Gaussian reduction (21.4.8) can be transformed into

$$
\begin{bmatrix}
I & 0 & 0 & Z_1 A_1' B_1 \\
0 & I & 0 & Z_2 A_2' B_2 \\
0 & 0 & I & Z_3 A_3' B_3 \\
0 & 0 & 0 & \sum_{i=1}^{3} B_i' B_i - B_i' A_i Z_i A_i' B_i
\end{bmatrix}
\begin{bmatrix}
da_1 \\
da_2 \\
da_3 \\
dh
\end{bmatrix}
=
\begin{bmatrix}
Z_1 A_1' r_1 \\
Z_2 A_2' r_2 \\
Z_3 A_3' r_3 \\
\sum_{i=1}^{3} B_i' r_i - B_i' A_i Z_i A_i' r_i
\end{bmatrix}
\tag{21.4.9}
$$

The columns of the matrix on the left which are just columns of the identity matrix do not need to be stored in the computer. Instead, the program computes the terms in the last column of this matrix and in the vector on the right, stores only them, and at the same time builds up the sums in the lower right corner of the matrix and in the bottom row of the vector on the right. Once the matrix and vector of equation (21.4.9) are ready, the program solves the equations in the last row for $\mathbf{dh}$ and then substitutes back into the other equations to solve them for the $\mathbf{da}_i$.

The estimation program initializes the income parameters by regressing the dependent variables on the just the constant, income, and trend terms. Then all lambda's are started at .25 and all mu and nu at 0. The program was written in Borland C++ with a double-precision version of the BUMP library of matrix and vector objects and operators. The time required to do the estimation seems to be roughly proportional to the fourth power of the number of sectors. The work of evaluating the $\mathbf{B}$ matrices and taking $\mathbf{B'B}$ grows roughly with the cube of the number of sectors, so the time required for a single iteration grows with the cube of the number of sectors. The number of iterations, however, seems to grow at least linearly with the number of sectors, so the total time required should grow with the fourth power of the number of sectors. Thus, a 90-sector study can be expected to take about 16 times as long to estimate as a 45-sector study. This is roughly what we have experienced, with the 93-sector USA system requiring about 100 minutes and the 42-sector Spanish study five or six minutes on a 133 MHz pentium. The USA study required about 120 iterations. The big drops in the objective function started to appear after about 80 iterations.

21.5. Comparative Estimation for France, Italy, Spain, and the USA

To test how adequate this system is for representing the consumer behavior in a variety of countries, it has been estimated for France, Italy, Spain, and the USA. At the same time, so that the results would tell us something about the similarities and differences among these countries, the categories have been a been made as similar as possible. The categories, the groups, and the sub-groups are shown in the box to the right.

In using the word "test", I should make clear that I do not mean any sort of test of statistical "significance", which I regard as essentially meaningless here. The test is rather to see whether the system is flexible enough to fit the historical data with plausible values of the parameters. Moreover, it is not a test to see whether the program can find those reasonable values from the data alone. Whether or not that is possible depends upon what range of experience history has given us. It is often necessary to tell the program what values are plausible by soft constraints. The details of how that has been done are described in Appendix A on using the program. The Italian and Spanish data were for forty categories of consumer expenditures, most of them being exactly comparable. The French data were more detailed but were clearly based on the same statistical concepts and could be aggregated to match the Spanish and Italian. The three European datasets showed that the statisticians who had prepared them had been talking to one another and had achieved some degree of comparability. No such fundamental comparability infected the U.S. data. It was, however, available in much more detail than was the European, and in most cases, it was possible to match the European concept – as I understand it from the words in the definition – fairly closely. There were a few exceptions among foods. The Europeans had the following sectors:

6 Fruits and vegetables, except potatoes

Groups and Subgroups for International Comparison

I. Food group
  1 Cereal and bakery products
  A. Protein source subgroup
    2 Meat
    3 Fish & seafood
  4 Dairy products
  5 Fats & oils
  6 Fresh fruit
  7 Fresh vegetables
  8 Sugar & sweets
  9 Processed fruit and vegetables
  10 Other prepared food, Pet food
  11 Nonalcoholic beverages
  12 Alcoholic beverages
II. Clothing group
  14 Clothing and its cleaning and repair
  15 Footwear and repair
III. House furnishing and operation group
  18 Furniture
  19 Floor coverings and textile products
  20 Kitchen & hh appliances
  21 China & glaswr, tablwr & utensils
  22 Other non-durables and services
  23 Domestic services
  32 TV, radio, audio, musical instruments, computers
IV. Medical group
  24 Drug preparations and sundries
  25 Ophthalmic & orthopedic eqpt
  26 Physicians, dentists, other
  27 Hospitals, nursing homes
V. Transportation group
  A. Private transportation
    28 Vehicles
    29 Operation of motor vehicles
  30 Public transportation
Ungrouped products
  13 Tobacco
  16 Tenant-occupied nonfarm space
  17 Electricity, oil, gas, coal, water
  31 Communication
  33 Books & maps, Magazines and newspapers
  34 Education
  35 Recreational services
  36 Personal care
  37 Hotels & motels, restaurants
  38 Other goods
  39 Financial services and insurance
  40 Other services
Extra American sectors not in European accounts
  41 Food furnished to employees and food consumed on farm
  42 Owner-occupied housing
  43 Foreign travel
  44 Imputed financial services

7 Potatoes
9 Coffee, tea, and cocoa

I could not match these in the U.S. data but made up three sectors which at least keep the numbering the same for the other sectors. These were:

6 Fresh fruit
7 Fresh vegetables
9 Processed fruits and vegetables

Other known noncomparabilities included the Italians having no sector for Education but only one for text books, while the Spanish did not attempt to divide "all-included" vacation packages between Transportation and Hotels and restaurants though the others did. Finally, the U.S. has four categories which have no corresponding component in the European accounts. First, and largest, is the imputed space-rental value of owner-occupied housing, which is seemingly not in the System of National Accounts (SNA) used by the Europeans. Second is Services rendered without payment by financial intermediaries (e.g. free checking accounts). The existence of these services is recognized by the SNA, but the European statistical offices (incorrectly) consider that all of these services are rendered to businesses, and thus appear in the intermediate part of the input-output table and do not enter GDP. Foreign travel shows up elsewhere in the European accounts and was not among the data series I had. Finally, Food furnished to employees or eaten on farms seems not to be part of the European system or appears directly in the various food categories. These extra sectors account for about 15 percent of American consumption. Within the forty more or less comparable sectors, the share of the American sectors in total consumption will average about 15 percent below the European.

The regressions were run from 1971 to 1994 (1993 for France.) It quickly became apparent that nearly all of the histories could be fit well, but often one or more of the parameters would have nonsense values. The income elasticity might turn out negative while there was a strong positive time trend. The own price elasticities, which should be negative, frequently turned out positive, perhaps at the same time that the income elasticity was negative. In short, the data were insufficiently varied to identify the parameters. Fortunately, the program used for the estimation (our creation) allowed for imposing "soft" constraints, which are essentially extra, artificial observations designed to tell the computer, before the estimation, what would be sensible regression coefficients. By using soft constraints, it is often possible to find equations with sensible coefficients which fit almost as well as the unconstrained equation. Except in Spain, where there was a drop in income in the mid 1980's before entry into the Common Market, time and income were very collinear, and it was necessary to softly constrain the time variable to be close to zero, though not exactly zero. In Spain, there was also a very soft constraint suggesting that the time trend coefficient should be small, but it was softer than in the other countries and consequently stronger time trends appear in the Spanish equations than in the others. In cases of products which evidently had strong time trends in tastes, such as fats and oils or tobacco, the soft constraint on the time trend was removed. Of course, the fact that soft constraints were used which were not identical in the different countries may reduce the comparability of the results. But it also shows that the system can be adapted to the situation in different countries.

Before commenting on the individual products, let us look at the results for the group parameters, as shown below.

Table 21.5.1 Comparison of Group and Subgroup Parameters for Four Countries

| | $\mu's$ across countries | | | | | $v's$ | |
	Food	Clothing	Housing	Medical	Transport	Protein	PvtTrans
USA	0.25	0.96	-0.23	-0.26	0.06	-0.05	-0.54
Italy	-0.02	1.83	0.70	0.33	0.02	0.09	0.48
Spain	0.12	-0.34	0.21	0.00	0.07	0.20	-0.28
France	0.61	0.15	0.77	-1.36	0.07	0.57	-0.51

The components of the Food group did indeed turn out to be substitutes in the USA, Spain, and, especially, France. The protein sources were especially strong substitutes with one another in France and less so in Spain and Italy. In the USA, their special interaction was in the direction of complementarity. Buying cars and operating them were decidedly complements in the USA, Spain, and France, but were rather strongly substitutes in Italy. The Italians may not, however, be totally crazy; automobile repair and new cars may indeed be substitutes. Shoes and Clothing turn out to be strongly substitutes in the USA and Italy, weak substitutes in France, and complements in Spain. he household furnishing and operating sectors showed considerable interaction, but were complements in America and substitutes in Europe. The medical sectors were complements in America and France and weakly substitutes in Italy. There is little interaction between public and private transportation in any of the countries.

Examining the individual sectors shows many interesting differences as well as some basic similarities among the countries. For each product, we will show the results of estimation for all four countries. The order of lines in these mini tables is USA, Italy, Spain, France. The sector titles have been left in the original language both to indicate the country and to describe as exactly as possible the content. On each line in the minitables for each product, you will find:

nsec   The sector number

title   The title of the product group in the language of the country

G   The number of the group in which the product is included. A 0 indicates that it was not in a group.

S   The number of the product's subgroup. A 0 means that it was not in a subgroup.

I   Inclusion code: 1 if the product was included in the estimation of the system, otherwise 0.

440

lamb	The value of lambda, λ, for this product.	

lamb The value of lambda, λ, for this product.

Share The share of this product in total consumption in the base year, the year when all the prices were equal to 1. Unfortunately for purposes of comparison of these shares, the base years were different: 1992 for the USA, 1988 for Italy, 1986 for Spain, and 1980 for France. These differences should have little effect on comparability except on these shares.

IncEl The income elasticity, the percentage by which purchases of this item increase when income increases one percent.

Dinc The ratio of the coefficient on the change in income to the coefficient on income.

Time% The change in demand for the product due to the passage of one year (without change in income or price) expressed as a percentage of the average purchase.

PrEl The elasticity of demand for the product with respect to its own price.

Err% Standard error of estimate expressed as a percentage of the average value.

Rho Autocorrelation coefficient of the residuals.

The commentary on each group also reflects looking at the graph of the fit in each country for each product. These graphs are, unfortunately, too space-intensive to print.

1. Bread and bakery products

nsec title	G	S	I	lamb	share	IncEl	DInc	time%	PrEl	Err%	rho
1 Cereal and bakery produ	1	0	1	0.18	0.013	0.18	-0.60	0.01	-0.55	4.33	0.80
1 Pane e cereali	1	0	1	0.06	0.024	0.13	-1.59	0.00	-0.12	1.56	0.74
1 Pan y cereales	1	0	1	-0.12	0.026	0.18	-0.17	-0.26	-0.02	2.53	0.61
1 Pain et cereales	1	0	1	0.05	0.024	0.45	-0.03	0.00	-0.69	1.44	0.49

The Food group holds some striking similarities among the countries as well as big differences. *Bread and bakery products* (1) have seen virtually no growth in per capita consumption over the years covered here. Note, however, that the share is nearly twice as high in Europe as in America. The income elasticities, however, do not come out at zero but have been offset in the US and France by significant price elasticities. Italy shows both smaller income elasticities and small price elasticity, while in Spain the income elasticity comes out the same as that in the US but is offset by a negative trend of half a percent per year. The higher income elasticity in France may reflect the attractiveness of real croissants, brioche, and the like.

2. Meat

nsec title	G	S	I	lamb	share	IncEl	DInc	time%	PrEl	Err%	rho
2 Meat	1	1	1	-0.16	0.018	0.03	0.47	-0.20	-0.19	3.98	0.74
2 Carne	1	1	1	0.05	0.056	0.23	2.00	0.00	-0.15	2.78	0.81
2 Carne	1	1	1	0.01	0.066	0.49	-1.00	-0.13	-0.21	2.94	0.50

441

```
       2 Viandes                   1 1 1 -0.80 0.062 0.54  0.00  0.00 -0.04 1.89 0.81
```

Only Spain has seen any noticeable growth in *Meat* (2) demand since 1980. It showed an income elasticity of .5 as did France, but Spain has had greater income growth. Both the US and Italy have very low income elasticities, though Italy has a positive "taste" term, while the US and Spain both show negative "taste" trends.

3. Fish and seafood

```
nsec title                   G S I  lamb share IncEl DInc  time% PrEl Err% rho
3 Fish & seafood             1 1 1  1.78 0.002 1.17 -0.07 -0.20 -2.12 8.90 0.52
3 Pesce                      1 1 1  0.01 0.013 0.89  0.20  0.00 -0.15 4.17 0.83
3 Pescado                    1 1 1 -0.02 0.024 0.35 -0.13 -0.34 -0.27 4.45 0.80
3 Poissons                   1 1 1  0.00 0.008 1.58  0.11  0.00 -1.22 5.19 0.65
```

In striking contrast to Bread and Meat, *Fish and seafood* (3) shows strong income elasticities, above 1.0 in the USA, Italy, and especially France. Fish is definitely the food of the affluent in these countries, while it definitely is not in Spain, where consumption has declined steadily as income rose. Note, however, that the share of fish in the budget of Pedro was twice that of Pietro, three times that of Pierre, and twelve times that of Peter.

4. Milk and dairy products

```
nsec title                   G S I  lamb share IncEl DInc  time% PrEl Err% rho
4 Dairy products             1 1 1 -0.01 0.008 0.11 -0.13 -2.35 -0.34 6.53 0.70
4 Latte, formaggi            1 1 1  0.07 0.029 0.48  0.64  0.00 -0.20 1.97 0.69
4 Leche, queso y huevos      1 1 1 -0.10 0.033 0.07 -0.33  0.86 -0.18 3.68 0.79
4 Lait fromages et oeufs     1 1 1  0.04 0.025 0.83  0.04  0.00 -1.11 3.86 0.82
```

When it comes to *Milk and dairy products* (4), the US is the outlier. The European countries, where consumption runs from 2.5 to 3.3 percent of the total budget, have been increasing consumption steadily, while the USA is cutting back sharply from its already low share of .8 percent. The equation for France attributes the growth to income, the Spanish and Italian equations, more to taste trends. One may say that the American concern about cholesterol has not penetrated the European mind, or one may say that the American cheese industry has never approached the European in placing temptation in front of the consumer.

5. Fats and oils

```
nsec title                   G S I  lamb share IncEl DInc  time% PrEl Err% rho
5 Fats & oils                1 0 1 -0.08 0.002 0.06 -0.14 -0.37 -0.32 6.84 0.66
5 Oli e grassi               1 0 1 -0.04 0.008 0.07  2.43 -0.04 -0.03 2.85 0.73
5 Aceites y grasas           1 0 1 -0.08 0.011 0.06 -1.05 -0.54 -0.06 2.77 0.72
5 Huiles et graisses         1 0 1 -0.17 0.009 0.10 -0.62 -1.36 -0.53 2.42 0.34
```

6. Fruit and vegetables

```
nsec title                   G S I  lamb share IncEl DInc  time% PrEl Err% rho
6 Fresh fruit                1 0 1  0.15 0.003 0.86 -0.21 -2.48 -0.55 6.35 0.67
6 Frutta                     1 0 1  0.05 0.043 0.26 -0.73  0.00 -0.11 1.64 0.04
```

nsec title		G	S	I	lamb	share	IncEl	DInc	time%	PrEl	Err%	rho
6	Frutas y verduras	1	0	1	0.01	0.033	0.44	0.23	-1.04	-0.14	3.38	0.62
6	Fruits et legumes sauf	1	0	1	-0.45	0.025	0.20	0.52	0.00	-0.22	2.70	0.74

7. Fresh vegetables

nsec title		G	S	I	lamb	share	IncEl	DInc	time%	PrEl	Err%	rho
7	Fresh vegetables	1	0	1	0.12	0.004	0.93	-0.20	-1.82	-0.52	8.96	0.77
7	Patate	1	0	1	-0.05	0.002	0.18	0.62	-0.01	-0.01	3.45	0.23
7	Patatas y tubérculos	1	0	1	-0.05	0.005	0.03	-1.07	-2.35	-0.10	6.60	0.70
7	Pommes de terre et autr	1	0	1	-0.63	0.002	-0.04	-6.46	-1.48	-0.09	7.63	0.67

Fats and oils (5) have uniformly low income elasticities and negative taste trends. Fruit has been declining in the US, while *Fruit and vegetables* (6), including canned and frozen, have been rising in Italy and stable in Spain and France. Recall that the sectoral definitions are not comparable here. The rest of the story for the US is found in *Fresh vegetables* (7), also in gentle decline, and in Processed fruits and vegetables (9), which also fails to show any growth. The total share for the US is 1.3 percent of the budget,only a half or a third of that of the European countries. That low share does not necessarily mean that we consume less than they do of these products. There are at least two other factors: larger total consumption and lower prices on agricultural products. The graphs for Potatoes show that the French are rapidly losing their appetite for French fries, as are the Spanish, while the Italians are not.

8. Sugar

nsec title		G	S	I	lamb	share	IncEl	DInc	time%	PrEl	Err%	rho
8	Sugar & sweets	1	0	1	0.02	0.006	-0.01	2.83	-0.52	-0.41	5.92	0.47
8	Zucchero	0	0	0	0.00	0.003	0.10	7.14	-0.01	0.00	3.32	0.48
8	Azúcar	0	0	0	0.00	0.002	0.09	-0.65	-0.50	0.00	4.32	0.87
8	Sucre	1	0	1	-0.30	0.002	0.09	0.97	-2.83	-0.42	5.11	0.34

9. Coffee, tea & chocolate

nsec title		G	S	I	lamb	share	IncEl	DInc	time%	PrEl	Err%	rho
9	Processed fruit and veg	1	0	1	-0.09	0.006	0.02	-0.27	-0.07	-0.30	6.16	0.86
9	Caffe, te, cacao	1	0	1	-0.03	0.005	0.43	-0.31	0.00	-0.03	2.73	0.67
9	Café, té y cacao	1	0	1	-0.01	0.006	0.03	-1.12	-0.44	-0.14	3.65	0.77
9	Cafe, thé	1	0	1	-0.44	0.006	0.24	-0.43	0.00	-0.27	6.84	0.90

Sugar (8) proved to be a problem in both Italy and Spain and was removed from the system in these two countries. The problem arose from substantial fluctuations in the price which had little effect on consumption. In the US and France, the system had no problem handling the product, and virtually identical price elasticities, -.4, were found. In France, however, there has been a strong trend away from sugar not seen in the US.

10. Other prepared foods

nsec title		G	S	I	lamb	share	IncEl	DInc	time%	PrEl	Err%	rho
10	Other prepared food, Pe	1	0	1	-0.05	0.017	1.63	-0.72	0.00	-0.31	4.52	0.79
10	Altri generi alimentari	1	0	1	-0.03	0.006	0.64	-0.85	-0.01	-0.03	5.02	0.79
10	Otros alimentos	1	0	1	-0.02	0.007	0.34	-0.21	0.88	-0.13	2.08	0.71
10	Autres produits aliment	1	0	1	0.06	0.014	1.83	0.08	0.00	-0.74	3.25	0.49

The *Other prepared foods* (10) category , which includes the sauces, mixes, and just-run-it-in-the-microwave products have shown strong growth. For the USA, Italy, and France the equations attribute this growth to income, because of the aversion to time trends expressed in the soft constraints. In Spain, however, there were greater fluctuations in income and it was easier for the regression to distinguish time from income. It found that the income elasticity was actually fairly low, .34, and used a strong time trend, .9 percent per year, to account for the growth.

11. Soft drinks

nsec	title	G	S	I	lamb	share	IncEl	DInc	time%	PrEl	Err%	rho
11	Nonalcoholic beverages	1	0	1	0.11	0.009	0.77	1.35	-0.01	-0.50	4.83	0.60
11	Bevande analcoliche	1	0	1	-0.01	0.004	1.58	-1.37	-0.04	-0.05	7.68	0.83
11	Bebidas no alcohólicas	1	0	1	-0.12	0.005	1.12	-0.60	-0.66	-0.03	3.50	0.57
11	Boissons non alcoolisee	1	0	1	0.12	0.004	1.82	0.18	0.01	-0.83	10.11	0.77

The *Soft drink* industry (11), stagnant in the U.S. despite an income elasticity of .8 because of sharp price increases, has boomed in Italy and France, with income elasticity estimates of 1.6 and 1.8, respectively. The Spaniards have not been so easily seduced; they show an income elasticity of 1.1 and a negative time trend of .7 percent per year.

12. Alcoholic beverages

nsec	title	G	S	I	lamb	share	IncEl	DInc	time%	PrEl	Err%	rho
12	Alcoholic beverages	1	0	1	0.38	0.018	0.03	-0.02	-0.05	-0.73	3.55	0.84
12	Bevande alcoliche	1	0	1	-0.04	0.012	0.01	23.43	-0.90	-0.02	2.80	0.52
12	Bebidas alcohólicas	1	0	1	-0.07	0.014	0.09	4.24	-1.17	-0.08	5.70	0.72
12	Boissons alcoolisees	1	0	1	-0.01	0.024	0.17	-0.07	0.00	-0.64	2.36	0.75

Alcoholic beverage (12) sales have been static in the USA country and France, but declining in Italy and Spain. All countries showed very low income elasticities.

13. Tobacco

nsec	title	G	S	I	lamb	share	IncEl	DInc	time%	PrEl	Err%	rho
13	Tobacco	0	0	1	0.33	0.012	0.11	-0.02	-1.20	-0.48	3.16	0.21
13	Tabacco	0	0	0	0.00	0.016	0.03	37.79	1.03	0.00	7.10	0.86
13	Tabacos	0	0	1	0.06	0.016	0.34	-0.65	0.16	-0.09	3.00	0.53
13	Tabac	0	0	1	0.06	0.011	0.93	0.02	0.00	-0.17	2.82	0.76

The sharp decline in the use of *Tobacco* (13) in the USA has no parallel in Europe. In France, it was even rising up until 1992, showing an income elasticity of .93.

14. Clothing

nsec	title	G	S	I	lamb	share	IncEl	DInc	time%	PrEl	Err%	rho
14	Clothing and its cleani	2	0	1	0.00	0.044	1.36	-0.72	0.00	-0.30	1.31	0.46
14	Vestiario incl.riparazi	2	0	1	0.09	0.083	0.88	1.14	0.00	-0.53	2.57	0.64
14	Vestido	2	0	1	0.07	0.064	0.78	0.00	-0.74	0.00	2.97	0.46
14	Habillement sf chaus.	2	0	1	0.22	0.059	0.15	-0.13	0.00	-0.33	2.16	0.66

One of the surprises for me was the sad story of France in the consumption of *Clothing* (14). I had thought of the French as fashion conscious. Not at all, according to these equations. Clothing accounts for a smaller share in France than in any of the other European countries. The French income elasticity is only .15, against .8 for Spain, 1.4 for the U.S., and .9 for Italy, which has also the highest share of the budget going to clothes. Clearly it is the Italians who are the sartorially conscious nation.

15. Footwear

nsec	title	G	S	I	lamb	share	IncEl	DInc	time%	PrEl	Err%	rho
15	Footwear and repair	2	0	1	0.04	0.008	1.23	-0.03	0.02	-1.00	4.48	0.62
15	Calzature incl riparazi	2	0	1	-0.13	0.022	1.20	1.71	0.00	-1.40	6.28	0.86
15	Calzado	2	0	1	0.14	0.024	1.23	-0.21	-2.96	0.09	2.94	0.35
15	Chaussures y.c.reparat.	2	0	1	0.05	0.014	0.17	-0.32	0.00	-0.28	2.40	0.70

The same story holds for *Footwear* (15). The U.S., Spain, and Italy all came out with an income elasticity of 1.2, while in France it was only .2.

16. Rent

nsec	title	G	S	I	lamb	share	IncEl	DInc	time%	PrEl	Err%	rho
16	Tenant occupied nonfrm	0	0	1	0.05	0.046	0.98	-0.39	0.00	-0.21	2.20	0.71
16	Affitti per abitazioni	0	0	1	0.00	0.107	1.00	-0.42	0.00	-0.08	1.84	0.77
16	Alquileres y agua	0	0	1	0.03	0.111	0.53	-0.26	0.48	-0.05	6.98	0.96
16	Logement et l'eau	0	0	1	0.02	0.123	1.69	0.05	0.00	-0.12	2.55	0.69

Rent (16) on living quarters has risen steadily in all four countries; the income elasticities are 1.0 in the U.S. and Italy; 1.7 in France; but only .5 in Spain. Rental payments did not fall during the Spanish slump of the early 1980's, so the equation attributes most of the growth to the time trend rather than to income.

17. Energy

nsec	title	G	S	I	lamb	share	IncEl	DInc	time%	PrEl	Err%	rho
17	Electricity, oil, gas,	0	0	1	-0.11	0.027	0.15	-0.08	0.00	-0.05	2.90	0.56
17	Combust.&energia elettr	0	0	1	-0.01	0.033	0.87	-0.07	0.00	-0.06	3.74	0.70
17	Calefacción y alumbrado	0	0	1	0.01	0.025	0.84	-0.28	2.08	-0.04	1.99	0.56
17	Electricité et combusti	0	0	1	0.00	0.052	0.53	-0.10	0.00	-0.11	3.95	0.45

Energy consumption (17) has been virtually constant in the U.S.; the equation found low income and price elasticities. All three European countries, but especially Spain, have seen significant growth. It is interesting that in Spain, where the equation was given less indication to avoid trend terms than in Italy and France, it used that extra freedom to get virtually the same income elasticity as was found in Italy, attributing the extra growth in Spain to the time trend.

18. Furniture

nsec	title	G	S	I	lamb	share	IncEl	DInc	time%	PrEl	Err%	rho
18	Furniture	3	0	1	-0.03	0.009	1.06	-0.03	-0.01	0.06	4.36	0.49
18	Mobili	3	0	1	0.04	0.028	1.57	0.26	0.00	-0.67	2.79	0.49
18	Muebles	3	0	1	0.08	0.021	1.38	-0.37	-1.95	-0.27	2.85	0.38

```
18 Meubles, tapis, y.c. re3 0 1  0.57 0.031 0.43 -0.44  0.00 -1.23 4.67 0.66
```

The French are again the outlier in demand for *Furniture* (18). Spanish and Italian income elasticities are high and similar, 1.6 and 1.4 respectively; the US is a respectable 1.1; but France is only .4. Clearly the French have other priorities.

19. Carpets, curtains and household linens

```
nsec title              G S I  lamb share IncEl DInc  time% PrEl  Err% rho
19 Floor coverings and tex3 0 1  0.06 0.004 1.64 -0.02 -0.17 -0.01 8.43 0.73
19 Biancheria e altri arti3 0 1 -0.04 0.011 1.42 -0.30  0.00 -0.68 6.98 0.87
19 Artículos textiles     3 0 1  0.00 0.009 1.19  0.38 -1.08 -0.22 5.69 0.80
19 Art. de ménage en texti3 0 1  0.00 0.007 0.00 -59.48 -0.03 -0.84 3.59 0.54
```

The story is the same for *Carpets, curtains, and household linens* (19). The French Income elasticity is exactly 0, while it is 1.2 to 1.6 for the other three countries.

20. Kitchen and household appliances

```
nsec title              G S I  lamb share IncEl DInc time%  PrEl Err% rho
20 Kitchen & hh appliances 3 0 1  0.10 0.005 0.53 -0.06 -0.04 -0.05 5.31 0.65
20 Elettrodomestici       3 0 1 -0.37 0.012 1.14  0.64  0.00 -0.35 2.55 0.44
20 Electrodomésticos      3 0 1 -0.10 0.010 1.64  0.71 -1.27 -0.12 5.30 0.69
20 Ap. de cuis., de chauf. 3 0 1 -0.02 0.016 0.44 -0.31  0.00 -0.76 4.10 0.59
```

Kitchen and household appliances (20) show a similar pattern, except that both the U.S. and France have income elasticities close to .5, while in Italy and Spain, they are 1.1 and 1.6 respectively.

21. China, glassware and tableware

```
nsec title              G S I  lamb share IncEl DInc time%  PrEl Err% rho
21 China & glaswr, tablwr 3 0 1  0.32 0.005 0.74 -0.03  0.08 -0.27 3.47 0.64
21 Cristallerie,vasellame 3 0 1 -0.66 0.006 1.02  0.21 -0.03 -0.10 3.28 0.61
21 Utensilios domésticos  3 0 1  0.04 0.005 0.17 -0.38 -1.65 -0.27 9.62 0.82
21 Verrerie, vaisselle et 3 0 1 -0.01 0.015 0.41 -0.17  0.00 -0.78 2.41 0.47
```

It is Italians and Americans who care about *China, glassware, and tableware* (21). The French have been particularly sensitive to the rising relative price of these products.

22. Other non-durables

```
nsec title              G S I  lamb share IncEl DInc  time% PrEl Err% rho
22 Other non-durables and 3 0 1  0.59 0.019 0.52 -0.01  0.00 -0.57 2.05 0.45
22 Art.non dur. e servizi 3 0 1 -0.24 0.011 1.32 -1.92  0.01 -0.49 7.99 0.72
22 Mantenimiento          3 0 1 -0.10 0.015 0.95  0.12 -1.07 -0.11 3.82 0.70
22 Art. de ménage non-dur 3 0 1  0.01 0.018 1.15  0.02  0.00 -0.78 2.08 0.72
```

23. Domestic service

```
nsec title              G S I  lamb share IncEl DInc time%  PrEl Err%  rho
```

```
23 Domestic services      3 0 1  1.14 0.003 0.84 -0.02 -5.13 -1.08 10.45 0.80
23 Servizi domestici      3 0 1  0.03 0.025 1.44  0.33  0.00 -0.68  6.83 0.89
23 Servicio doméstico     3 0 1 -0.06 0.007 1.10 -1.06 -2.24 -0.17  7.91 0.79
23 Services domestiques   3 0 1  0.01 0.010 0.56 -0.04  0.00 -0.82  5.56 0.75
```

Domestic service (23) fell steadily in the U.S. from 1950 up to 1981, whereupon it suddenly stabilized and began a slow rise. Strikingly similar patterns appear in Spain and France, with low points in 1986 or 1987. Italy, by contrast, has shown strong growth all along, with an income elasticity of 1.4. All equations except the Spanish showed strong price elasticities.

24. Medicines

```
nsec title               G S I lamb share IncEl DInc  time% PrEl  Err% rho
24 Drug preparations and s 4 0 1 0.08 0.018 1.42 -0.02  0.04  0.00  3.48 0.62
24 Medicinali e prod. farm 0 0 0 0.00 0.022 2.58 -1.01 -0.04  0.00  6.66 0.82
24 Medicamentos            4 0 0 0.00 0.016 3.03 -0.96 -1.42  0.00 15.31 0.84
24 Medicaments et autres p 0 0 1 1.06 0.021 1.50  0.21  0.00 -1.13  7.62 0.70
```

Medicines (24) have shown explosive growth in Europe. Note that all three European graphs ran off the standard scale. In Italy and France, this sector had to be thrown out of the system. The prices were rising and demand was soaring. Clearly, the problem was that the medicines were being paid for by third parties. The budget constraint had little relevance for the European buying medicine.

25. Ophthalmic and orthopedic devices

```
nsec title               G S I lamb share IncEl DInc time% PrEl Err% rho
25 Opthalmic & orthopedic  4 0 1 0.07 0.003 2.35 -0.02 -0.34 0.02 9.62 0.73
25 Apparecchi e mater. ter 0 0 0 0.00 0.003 1.67 -0.70 -0.06 0.00 4.85 0.82
25 Aparatos terapéuticos   4 0 0 0.00 0.003 1.31 -1.28  0.20 0.00 9.59 0.82
25 Ap. et mat. therapeutiq 0 0 0 0.10 0.002 2.35  0.09  1.94 0.00 8.81 0.75
```

Similarly, *Ophthalmic and orthopedic devices* (25) could not be accommodated in the system in Italy and France. No price sensitivity but enormous income sensitivity is found in all countries.

26. Services of physicians, dentists and other medical professionals

```
nsec title               G S I lamb share IncEl DInc  time% PrEl Err% rho
26 Physicians, dentists, o 4 0 1 0.00 0.066 1.60 -0.02  0.00 -0.01 4.16 0.76
26 Serv. medici, infermier 4 0 1 0.26 0.024 1.29 -0.09  0.00 -0.44 4.85 0.79
26 Servicios médicos       4 0 0 0.00 0.010 1.80 -0.91 -0.70  0.00 8.58 0.81
26 Serv. des medecins infi 4 0 1 1.73 0.033 1.00  0.07  2.82 -1.25 5.02 0.66
```

Services of physicians, dentists, and other medical professionals (26) could be handled by the system in all countries. Only France, however, showed strong price sensitivity -- the U.S. showed none.

27. Hospitals

```
nsec title                    G S I lamb share IncEl DInc  time% PrEl Err% rho
27 Hospitals, nursing home 4 0 1 0.07 0.063 1.40 -0.57  0.00 -0.07 3.54 0.86
27 Cure in ospedali&clinic 4 0 1 0.09 0.013 0.58 -2.59  0.00 -0.38 3.25 0.41
27 Atención hospitalaria y 4 0 0 0.00 0.006 0.89 -1.70 -0.83  0.00 5.07 0.63
27 Soins des hopitaux et a 4 0 1 0.91 0.018 0.32 -0.18  0.00 -0.11 2.93 0.53
```

The demand for Hospitals (27) has been decidedly more moderate than for the other members of the health care group. Only the U.S. shows an income elasticity greater than 1.0, and the French is down to .3.

28. Automobiles

```
nsec title                    G S I lamb share IncEl DInc time%  PrEl Err% rho
28 Vehicles                5 2 1 0.16 0.043 1.32 -0.35 -0.01 -0.03 8.65 0.64
28 Acquisto di mezzi trasp 5 2 1 0.90 0.044 1.27  2.55  0.00 -1.17 5.98 0.46
28 Compra de vehículos     5 2 1 0.16 0.036 1.85  1.04  0.99 -0.04 8.06 0.42
28 Automobiles, caravanes, 5 2 1 0.17 0.041 1.36 -0.04  0.00  0.03 8.87 0.56
```

The income elasticity for *Automobiles* (28) is strong in all countries: 1.3 in the U.S., Italy, and France, and 1.8 in Spain -- and the Spanish equation has a 1 percent per year time trend on top of that income elasticity. The Spanish are plainly making up for lost time in equipping themselves to congest their streets and highways. Price sensitivity was slight, except in Italy.

29. Motor vehicle operation

```
nsec title                    G S I  lamb share IncEl DInc  time% PrEl Err% rho
29 Operation of motor vehi 5 2 1  0.27 0.060 0.67 -0.03 0.00 -0.20 2.20 0.42
29 Spese es. dei mezzi tra 5 2 1 -0.04 0.052 0.87 -1.26 0.00 -0.28 2.67 0.52
29 Gasto de uso de vehícul 5 2 1  0.10 0.075 1.10 -0.07 0.48 -0.06 2.15 0.54
29 Utilisation des véhicul 5 2 1  0.19 0.089 0.76 -0.13 0.00 -0.14 2.07 0.44
```

Motor vehicle operation (29), however, has an income elasticity of only .7 to .9 in three countries and 1.1 in Spain, where there is also a noticeable positive time trend.

30. Public transportation

```
nsec title                    G S I lamb share IncEl DInc  time%  PrEl Err% rho
30 Public transportation   5 0 1 0.17 0.008 0.43 -0.04 -0.05 -0.38 5.04 0.74
30 Acquisto serv. di trasp 5 0 1 0.00 0.016 0.90 -0.89  0.00 -0.09 2.43 0.39
30 Servicios de transporte 5 0 1 0.04 0.018 0.45  0.42  0.97 -0.13 1.95 0.16
30 Services de transport   5 0 1 0.07 0.022 0.89 -0.06  0.00 -0.24 2.76 0.74
```

Public transportation (30) claims a share of the consumer budget in Europe that is twice as large as the American share. Moreover, the income elasticities in Italy and France are twice what they are in the U.S. The U.S., however, is the most price sensitive, though the elasticity is only -.4.

31. Communications

```
nsec title                     G S I  lamb share IncEl  DInc time% PrEl Err% rho
31 Communication               0 0 1  0.20 0.019 1.52  -0.92 0.00 -0.35 2.71 0.80
31 Comunicazioni               0 0 1  1.16 0.011 1.55  -1.10 0.08 -1.22 5.84 0.58
31 Comunicaciones              0 0 1 -0.01 0.008 1.28  -0.33 2.76 -0.02 3.85 0.41
31 Telecommunications et p     0 0 1  0.04 0.015 3.75   0.08 0.01 -0.15 6.73 0.63
```

Communications (31) ran off the standard scale in all the European graphs. In Spain, where the equation was freer to use a time trend, the income elasticity came in at 1.3 with a strong positive trend of 2.8 percent per year added on to the income effect. In France, the equation attributed all the growth to income with a elasticity of 3.7! Since in both countries, much of the growth is attributable to the modernization of a once stodgy telephone monopoly, I suspect the Spanish equation is more appropriate.

32. TV, radio, audio, musical instruments and computers

```
nsec title                     G S I  lamb share IncEl  DInc time% PrEl Err% rho
32 TV, radio, audio, music     3 0 1  1.13 0.014 1.52  -0.01 0.00 -1.08 4.07 0.61
32 Apparecchi radio, tv, e     3 0 1 -0.46 0.040 1.87  -0.04 0.00 -0.14 2.17 0.44
32 Artículos de esparcimie     3 0 1  0.02 0.024 1.57  -0.04 0.00 -0.21 4.52 0.66
32 Radios, televiseurs, ar     3 0 1  0.02 0.036 1.52  -0.02 0.00 -0.69 4.13 0.57
```

The one and only runaway sector in the U.S. is *TV, radio, audio, musical instruments, and computers* (32). The enormous growth is, of course, in the computer component. We have not used the official "computer deflator" which would have made it grow even faster, but have left computers undeflated. It is not clear to me whether or not computers are in this category in Europe. They probably are, because the category's share in total spending is considerably smaller here than in Europe. Even so, the income elasticity in the U.S. 1.5, the same as in Spain and France, and below Italy's 1.9. The key to the super fast growth is the relatively strong price elasticity, -1.1, coupled with the rapid decline of the relative price of these products.

33. Books, magazines and newspapers

```
nsec title                     G S I lamb share IncEl  DInc time% PrEl Err% rho
33 Books & maps, Magazines     0 0 1 0.01 0.009 0.56  -0.05 0.01 -0.17 4.24 0.59
33 Libri, giornali e perio     0 0 1 0.01 0.017 0.73   0.61 0.00 -0.09 3.51 0.64
33 Libros, periódicos y re     0 0 1 0.06 0.017 0.60  -0.15 0.39 -0.08 2.56 0.64
33 Livres quotidiens et pe     0 0 1 0.04 0.015 0.54   0.13 0.00 -0.15 2.92 0.70
```

Despite the onslaught of electronic information and entertainment, *Books, magazines, and newspapers* (33) have hung on to their absolute level of sales, though they have been losing share in the consumer's dollar, as appears from the modest income elasticities of .6 or .7, the highest being in Italy, which, with Spain, has the highest share of the consumer's budget, almost twice that in the USA.

34. Education

```
nsec title                     G S I  lamb share IncEl  DInc time% PrEl  Err% rho
34 Education                   0 0 1  0.04 0.022 0.92  -0.02 0.00 -0.20  2.86 0.84
```

```
34 Libri per l'istruzione 0 0 1 -0.03 0.008 1.49  0.05  0.01 -0.05  6.22 0.85
34 Enseñanza             0 0 1  0.01 0.008 0.67 -1.68 -0.72 -0.04  4.82 0.66
34 Enseignement          0 0 1 -0.01 0.004 0.37  1.17  2.16 -0.10 16.51 0.77
```

Lest that dismal comparison leaves you a bit embarrassed to be American, take heart from *Education* (34), for which the American budget share is nearly three times that of the European. Alas, however, the difference is much affected by accounting conventions. In the U.S., all of the endowment income of schools and colleges counts as consumption expenditures on education. The income elasticity in the USA is .9, .7 in Spain, and a paltry . 4 in France, where the budget share is less than a fifth of that here. The French expect the state to cover all the costs of education.

35. Recreational services

```
nsec title                G S I  lamb share IncEl DInc  time% PrEl Err% rho
35 Recreational services  0 0 1  0.07 0.031 1.84 -0.64  0.00 -0.22 2.49 0.71
35 Spettacoli, serv. ricre 0 0 1 -0.02 0.023 1.05 -0.88  0.00 -0.06 3.13 0.73
35 Servicios de esparcimie 0 0 1 -0.03 0.019 0.67 -0.43 -1.01  0.00 2.36 0.66
35 Serv. de loisir, specta 0 0 1  0.08 0.019 1.08  0.03  0.00 -0.18 2.46 0.77
```

Recreational services (35), which includes spectator sports, have been a growth industry everywhere except in Spain. The U.S. leads with an income elasticity of 1.8, and a budget share of 3.1 percent. Italy and France also have elasticities above 1 and budget shares of 2.3 and 1.9 percent respectively. In Spain, however, the income elasticity was only .7 and there was a negative time trend of a percent per year. My suspicion is that the great national spectator sport of bull fighting is to some extent losing its hold on the imagination of young, urban Spaniards.

36. Personal care articles and services

```
nsec title                G S I  lamb share IncEl DInc time% PrEl Err% rho
36 Personal care          0 0 1  0.28 0.015 0.72 -0.04 0.00 -0.43 3.93 0.82
36 Beni e servizi igiene p 0 0 1  0.04 0.030 1.21 -0.59 0.00 -0.11 6.07 0.91
36 Cuidados y efectos pers 0 0 1  0.00 0.014 0.76 -0.98 0.88 -0.03 2.80 0.37
36 Soins personnels, art.  0 0 1 -0.01 0.015 1.38  0.05 0.00 -0.10 4.30 0.83
```

Personal care articles and services (36), which includes everything from tooth paste to hair salons, has been a growth industry in Europe, with income elasticities of 1.4 in France and 1.2 in Italy, in contrast to .7 in America. The Spanish equation used its greater freedom to use a trend term to find almost exactly the American income elasticity but add to it a time trend of .9 percent per year.

37. Hotels and restaurants

```
nsec title                G S I lamb share IncEl DInc time% PrEl Err% rho
37 Hotels & motels, restau 0 0 1 0.07 0.053 0.90 -0.03 0.00 -0.22 2.53 0.63
37 Spese alberghi e pubbl. 0 0 1 0.09 0.095 1.03 -0.25 0.00 -0.15 1.47 0.37
37 Restaurantes cafés y ho 0 0 1 0.08 0.013 0.88 -1.14 0.59 -0.11 3.32 0.43
37 Hotels, cafés, restaur. 0 0 1 0.10 0.065 0.82  0.00 0.00 -0.20 1.95 0.51
```

The *Hotels and restaurant* (37) business enjoys fairly good income elasticities (.8 to 1.0) in all four countries.

38. Other goods

```
nsec title                    G S I lamb share IncEl DInc time% PrEl Err% rho
38 Other goods                0 0 1 0.08 0.031 1.54 -0.02 0.00 -0.23 3.43 0.54
38 Altri beni                 0 0 1 0.72 0.031 1.83 -0.25 0.00 -0.75 3.94 0.62
38 Otros artículos n.c.o.p    0 0 1 0.04 0.153 1.34 -0.30 0.19 -0.05 8.11 0.92
38 Autres articles            0 0 1 0.34 0.016 0.11 -2.44 0.00 -0.43 9.51 0.63
```

The *Other goods* category (38) seems to be totally non-comparable across countries. Just the fact that it accounts for 15 percent of the Spanish budget and 1.6 percent of the French budget indicates that the contents of the sector must be quite different.

39. Financial services and insurance

```
nsec title                    G S I lamb share IncEl DInc  time% PrEl  Err% rho
39 Financial services and     0 0 1 0.05 0.039 1.60 -0.53  0.00 -0.20  2.57 0.67
39 Serv. finanz. e assicur    0 0 1 1.04 0.005 1.76 -0.69  0.18 -1.10 11.54 0.87
39 Servicios financieros n    0 0 1 0.12 0.002 1.72 -0.82 -4.83 -0.15 19.92 0.85
39 Services financiers n.d    0 0 1 0.10 0.007 3.67  0.06  0.09 -0.21  9.28 0.54
```

Financial services and insurance (39) has been a major growth industry in France and Italy, where it found income elasticities of 3.7 and 1.8, respectively. What looks like a change of definition has dominated the Spanish series. In America, this is a much more mature industry with roughly ten times the budget share it carries in Europe. (The services rendered without payment by financial intermediaries are not included here.)

40. Other services

```
nsec title                    G S I  lamb share IncEl DInc time% PrEl Err% rho
40 Other services            0 0 1  0.07 0.064 1.27 -0.03 0.00 -0.22 2.87 0.61
40 Altri servizi             0 0 1 -0.07 0.008 1.16 -1.06 0.02 -0.01 7.90 0.88
40 Otros servicios n.c.o.p   0 0 1  0.10 0.033 0.55 -0.07 2.23 -0.12 3.61 0.76
40 Autres services n.d.a     0 0 1  0.07 0.022 0.88 -0.06 0.00 -0.18 2.86 0.75
```

Other services (40) are also much more important in the US than in Europe, but continue to have a higher elasticity here (1.3) than in France (.9) or Spain (.5). The Italian elasticity is high (1.2) but on a very small base, only 0.8 percent of the budget.

It would be safe and politic to conclude that this comparison has shown that the new functional form is capable of representing a variety of behavior, including significant substitution and complementarity. While that is, from a technical point of view, the most important conclusion, I cannot pass up the temptation to try to picture the national characters as they appear from these estimates. This venture is especially dangerous since citizens of all the four countries may be readers. Please take no personal offense.

The American has enough if not too much to eat, has become diet conscious and is cutting down on cholesterol but is, sad to say, bothering less and less to prepare fresh fruits and vegetables. He would like to eat more fish but is very sensitive to its price. He has no particular interest in more alcohol; soft drinks are sort of a necessity, not a special treat, and smoking is just a way to make yourself into a social outcast. Ms. America is very concerned about how she and her family are dressed. Housing and furnishing and equipment for the house are important, but using more energy for running the home is a matter of no interest. More domestic help for the working woman is becoming important again. The nation has gone bonkers over home computers. Every child of any age must have one. Books? Well, of course, a few books. But sports, concerts, plays, skiing, sailing, any kind of recreation, that's what America is all about. Relative to the Europeans, the American is not starved for medical care, and growth in this area has been less here than there. Automobiles are important but not much of a class symbol; operating them is just a necessity. Private education and tuition at public universities is a serious matter. Use of communication has grown because of the declines in its price. Public transport is to be avoided.

The Italian is outstanding among Europeans for dressing well. He is proud of his country's cucina, and would gladly eat more cheese, fish, and, above all, soft drinks; but he is losing interest in vino. Of pasta, he has, thank you, enough. Eating out at a good trattoria, ah, that's worth the price. He continues to puff away on his cigarette just to show his defiance of statistics. In an energy-poor country, he wants more electricity and fuel. Signora is concerned not only with dressing the family well but is especially concerned to have a well-furnished house, refined furniture, attractive carpets and linens, and a bit of style and elegance in china and crystal. She wants appliances to help her with the house work. But most of all she wants domestic help. Dispensing with domestic servants was a modern idea that never crossed her sensible mind. The family has been upgrading its car, especially because prices have been coming down relative to other goods. The modest motor scooter is giving way to the even noisier motorcycle. But public transport is still a respectable way to get around. Especially if you have a portable telephone -- and who doesn't? Yes, computers and audio equipment have caught on fast, just not to the mania level of the Americans. Reading the newspaper is very important, and books still hold more allure than in any of the other three countries. One might suppose that just watching Italian politics would provide spettacoli enough, but no, recreation is high on the list of priorities. Socialized medicine led to explosive growth of spending on medicine but not on doctors, and certainly not on hospitals.

The Spanish are the newly rich of Europe. And the riches come after a period of declining income in the early 1980's. They have increased meat consumption in the last five years. Eating out is great, but please, no more fish! And less potatoes and wine. But an extra cigarette, por favor. Clothing is a good thing to economize on, as are shoes, though, of course, as income goes up you should look just a little better. Pretty much the same goes for furniture, rugs, and linens. China and glassware are an especially good place to economize when your income rises. One good place to put some of the savings on these goods is into more and better appliances along with the electricity to run them. Indeed, electricity is showing such a growth that one becomes suspicious that air conditioning might be catching on. But top priority for these savings is the car. No other of our countries is close to the Spanish income elasticity for cars. And if you have bought the car, then you have to drive it. But the new high-speed rail lines are making public transportation competitive again. Right behind the car in priority comes "recreational equipment" which seems to correspond to home electronics, including possibly the computer. Never mind, however, about those recreational services that everybody else is so crazy about. Just living in Spain is recreation enough. As in all three European countries, medical expenditures have skyrocketed: medicines, therapeutic devices, and services of doctors. Even hospital services have seen some rise.

Now the French seem utterly indifferent to improving, when income rises, how they are dressed or to how their house is furnished or to what sort of china or glassware they use, but not to what they eat and drink. Increase the French family's income by one percent, and it will spend .8 percent more on dining out, .5 percent more on meat, 1.6 percent more on fish and those delicious shellfish, .8 percent more on cheese, 1.8 percent more on candy and "other" prepared foods, 1.8 percent more on soft drinks, including, of course, mineral water, and even a bit more, .2 percent, on wine. If the French don't uphold their reputation as the fashion center of Europe, they are certainly les gourmands of the continent. It must be added that they are cutting back sharply on sugar and potatoes. Alone among the four countries, they are increasing their use of tobacco. They attach less priority to buying household appliances than to increasing meat consumption. A pleasant effect of that indifference is that energy consumption has remained stable. They have relatively little interest in new cars, relative, that is, to their neighbors in Spain and Italy, and expenditures on operating the cars are correspondingly stable. Public transport is more income elastic than is operation of cars. Besides their interest in food, they spend added income on personal care, on home electronics and recreational equipment, on cultural and sporting events, on financial services, and on communications. As in the other European countries, the large shares of increased income have gone to -- or come in the form of -- medicines, therapeutic devices, and services of doctors.

Well, it seems we are not all the same. There do appear to be national differences that go beyond language. For the present purposes, however, the important point is that this new functional form seems to be able to work well in what turns out to be a surprising variety of situations. Perhaps it is adequate.

References

Almon, C. (1979) "A system of consumption functions and its estimation for Belgium," *Southern Economic Journal*, vol. 46, No. 1, July, pp. 85-106.

Chao, Chang-yu I. (1991) *A Cross-sectional and Time-series Analysis of Household Consumption and a Forecast of Personal Consumption Expenditures.* Ph.D. Thesis, University of Maryland.

Deaton, A. and Muellbauer, J. (1980) "An almost ideal demand system," *American Economic Review*, vol. 70, No. 3, June, pp. 312-326.

Gauyacq, Daniel (1985) *Les systemes interdependants de fonctions de consommation, Prevision et Analyse Economique*, Cahiers du Gamma, vol. 6, No. 2, June 1985 (entire issue).

Appendix A. Use of the Estimation Program

The Interdyme system has a module, PADS.CPP, for calculation of simulations with the PADS system. Several versions of PADS are offered, and the user should look at the comments in the program to see which is the appropriate version. The estimation program, known as *Symcon*, produces output compatible with input requirements of this module. *Symcon* has two control input files, GROUPS.TTL and SOFTCON.DAT, and several data matrices, CONSUM.DAT, PRICES.DAT, CSTAR.DAT, POPUL.DAT, and TIME.DAT.

The GROUPS.TTL file, as the name suggests, defines the groups. It also specifies which categories are sensitive and which insensitive to price, which weighted population, which income variable, and which trend variable is to be used by each category. This file for the Spanish study is shown in the box below. Its first column consist of simply the integers from 1 to n, the number of categories of consumption. The second column carries the number of the group in which the category falls, or a zero if it is not assigned to a group, and the third column carries the number of the subgroup to which the category belongs or a zero if it belongs to none. The fourth is the number of the weighted population to be used for the item, the fifth is the number of the "income" (or Cstar) series to be used, the sixth is the number of the "trend" series to be used, and the seventh is a 1 if the category is a regular, price-sensitive commodity or a 0 if it is not. Although conceptually we have thought of neatly defined groups and subgroups strictly within the groups, the computer program makes no effort to enforce this tidy structure. It is possible to form "subgroups" with categories drawn from more than one group.

The second major control file is SOFTCON.DAT, which gives soft constraints for the various equations. It is, in fact, hardly to be expected that all parameters would come out with reasonable values when so many of the variables have similar trends. Thus the use of soft constraints on the coefficients is an integral part of the estimation process. The estimation program allows the user to specify the desired value of any parameter except the constant term and to specify a "trade-off parameter" to express the user's trade-off between closeness of fit and conformity with desired values of the parameters. In these studies, I began with constraints saying that I wanted the time trends to be close to zero. I then worked on the income elasticities to get them all positive; for some products, that meant relaxing the soft constraint on the time trend. Then I added soft constraints to make the own price elasticities all negative. Finally, some of the coefficients on the change in income had to be constrained to keep them from being more negative that the income term is positive.

The SOFTCON.DAT file for Spain is shown in a box below. For each product, there can be specified desired values of the income elasticity, the change in income in elasticity units, the time trend as a percent of the base year (1988) value, *lambda*, and the *mu* and *nu* of the group and subgroup. The table shows for each of these a pair of numbers, the desired value and the trade-off parameter. If the trade-off parameter is 0, the desired value has no effect on the estimation. The higher the parameter, the stronger the constraint relative to the data. A value of 1.0 for the trade-off parameter gives about equal weight to the constraint and to the data. Constraints on *mu* and *nu* values can be specified on the line for any member of the group or subgroup, but I have always placed them on the line of the first item in the group or subgroup. This table is, in fact, precisely the way the constraints are entered into the program; the table shows the contents of the file SOFTCON.DAT, which is read by the estimation program.

The GROUPS.TTL File for Spain

éúóíñ

```
# Groups.ttl. Columns are
# 1 The consumption category number
#     2 The group number
#         3 The subgroup number
#             4  Which weighted population number to be used with this category
#                 5 Which Income (Cstar) variable
#                     6 Which Trend variable
#                         7 Use price terms ( 1 = yes, 0 = no)
#                             8 The title of the category
  1  1  0  1  1  1 1 Pan y cereales
  2  1  1  1  1  1 1 Carne
  3  1  1  1  1  1 1 Pescado
  4  1  1  1  1  1 1 Leche, queso y huevos
  5  1  0  1  1  1 1 Aceites y grasas
  6  1  0  1  1  1 1 Frutas y verduras
  7  1  0  1  1  1 1 Patatas y tubérculos
  8  0  0  1  1  1 0 Azúcar
  9  1  0  1  1  1 1 Café té y cacao
 10  1  0  1  1  1 1 Otros alimentos
 11  1  0  1  1  1 1 Bebidas no alcohólicas
 12  1  0  1  1  1 1 Bebidas alcohólicas
 13  0  0  1  1  1 1 Tabacos
 14  2  0  1  1  1 1 Vestido
 15  2  0  1  1  1 1 Calzado
 16  0  0  1  1  1 1 Alquileres y agua
 17  0  0  1  1  1 1 Calefacción y alumbrado
 18  3  0  1  1  1 1 Muebles
 19  3  0  1  1  1 1 Artículos textiles
 20  3  0  1  1  1 1 Electrodomésticos
 21  3  0  1  1  1 1 Utensilios domésticos
 22  3  0  1  1  1 1 Mantenimiento
 23  3  0  1  1  1 1 Servicio doméstico
 24  4  0  1  1  1 0 Medicamentos
 25  4  0  1  1  1 0 Aparatos terapéuticos
 26  4  0  1  1  1 0 Servicios médicos
 27  4  0  1  1  1 0 Atención hospitalaria y seguro médico privado
 28  5  2  1  1  1 1 Compra de vehículos
 29  5  2  1  1  1 1 Gasto de uso de vehículos
 30  5  0  1  1  1 1 Servicios de transporte
 31  0  0  1  1  1 1 Comunicaciones
 32  3  0  1  1  1 1 Artículos de esparcimiento
 33  0  0  1  1  1 1 Libros, periódicos y revistas
 34  0  0  1  1  1 1 Enseñanza
 35  0  0  1  1  1 1 Servicios de esparcimiento
 36  0  0  1  1  1 1 Cuidados y efectos personales
 37  0  0  1  1  1 1 Restaurantes cafés y hoteles
 38  0  0  1  1  1 1 Otros artículos n.c.o.p.
 39  0  0  1  1  1 1 Servicios financieros n.c.o.p.
 40  0  0  1  1  1 1 Otros servicios n.c.o.p
 41  0  0  1  1  1 1 Viajes turísticos todo incluido
```

The SOFTCON.DAT File for Spain

sec	Title	Income		DIncome		Time		lambda		mu		nu
1	Pan y cereales	0	0	0	1	0	.5	.2	5.	.1	1.	
2	Carne	0	0	0	0	0	.5	.2	5.	0	0	.2
3	Pescado	0	0	0	0	0	.5	.2	5.			
4	Leche, queso y huevos	.1	1.	0	1.	0	1.0	.2	5.			
5	Aceites y grasas	.1	1.	-.04	1.	0	.0	.2	10.			
6	Frutas y verduras	0	0	0	0	0	.5	.2	5.			
7	Patatas y otros tubérculos	.0	1.	-.02	1.	0	.5	.2	10.			
8	Azúcar	.1	1.	-.06	1.	0	.5					
9	Café, té y cacao	.05	1.	-.03	1	0	.5	.2	10.			
10	Otros alimentos	0	0	0	0	0	.5	.2	10.			
11	Bebidas no alcohólicas	0	0	0	0	0	.5	.2	5.			
12	Bebidas alcohólicas	.05	1.	0	0	0	.5	.2	10.			
13	Tabacos	0	0	-.2	1.	0	.5	.2	20.			
14	Vestido	0	0	0	0	0	.5	.2	5.			
15	Calzado	0	0	0	0	0	.5	.2	5.			
16	Alquileres y gasto de agua	0	0	-.05	1.	0	1.					
17	Calefacción y alumbrado	0	0	0	0	0	.5	.2	5.			
18	Muebles	0	0	0	0	0	1.	.2	5.	.1	1.	
19	Art. textiles para el hogar	0	0	0	0	0	.5	.2	10.			
20	Electrodomésticos	0	0	0	0	0	.5	.2	10.			
21	Utensilios domésticos	.1	1.	-.06	1.	0	.5	.2	5.			
22	Mantenimiento	0	0	0	0	0	.5	.2	5.			
23	Servicio doméstico	0	0	-1.2	1	0	.1	.2	5.			
24	Medicamentos	0	0	0	0	0	1.					
25	Aparatos terapéuticos	0	0	0	0	0	1.					
26	Servicios médicos	0	0	0	0	0	.5					
27	Atención hospitalaria y smp	0	0	0	0	0	.5					
28	Compra de vehículos	0	0	0	0	0	.5	.2	20.	.1	5.	-.3 1.
29	Gasto de uso de vehículos	0	0	0	0	0	.5	.2	5.			
30	Servicios de transporte	0	0	0	0	0	.5	.2	10.			
31	Comunicaciones	0	0	0	0	0	.5	.2	10.			
32	Artículos de esparcimiento	0	0	0	0	0	.5	.2	10.			
33	Libros, periódicos y revist	0	0	-.1	1.	0	.5	.2	5.			
34	Enseñanza	0	0	0	0	0	.5	.2	10.			
35	Servicios de esparcimiento	0	0	-.30	1.	0	.5	.2	5.			
36	Cuidados y efectos personal	0	0	0	0	0	.5	.2	10.			
37	Restaurantes cafés y hotele	0	0	0	0	0	.5	.2	10.			
38	Otros artículos n.c.o.p.	0	0	-.40	1.	0	2.	.2	10.			
39	Serv. financieros n.c.o.p.	0	0	-1.4	1.	0	2.0	.2	5.			
40	Otros servicios n.c.o.p	0	0	0	0	0	.5	.2	5.			
41	Viajes turís. todo incluido	1.0	1.	0	0	0	.5	.2	5.			

1.

The CONSUM.DAT file begins with some dimensions and dates and then contains the data on consumption in almost exactly the form in which it would be written by the *G7* command "matty". The layout is shown in the above box for the Spanish case; the "..." show where material has been cut out of the file to make it fit on the page. Notice the four numbers with which it begins. Each should be on its own line. Then come the data, with 20 series at a time across the "page". Comments may be introduced in the data by beginning the line with a #.

The CONSUM.DAT File for Spain

```
42 Sectors
24 years of data
1971 First year
1986 Base year
# Consumption, constant 1986 prices, total (not percapita)
# Date kcpi1 kcpi2 kcpi3 kcpi4 ... kcpi20
# 70.000 499.340 1021.118 549.566 467.982 ... 164.161
71.000 490.641 1022.712 571.055 466.638 ... 175.657
72.000 506.050 1017.367 574.642 472.211 ... 201.513
73.000 548.905 1182.404 582.436 498.514 ... 210.624
74.000 554.821 1338.080 536.756 562.671 ... 202.528

... ... ... ... ... ...
94.000 599.644 1666.945 606.117 735.611 ... 289.384
# Date kcpi21 kcpi22 kcpi23 kcpi24 ... kcpi40
# 70.000 109.692 286.789 184.407 272.749 ... 68.330
71.000 117.373 299.460 188.615 313.366 ... 74.745
72.000 134.650 342.775 189.809 337.034 ... 79.912
73.000 140.738 351.768 187.654 340.828 ... 85.539
74.000 135.328 350.958 180.607 370.052 ... 86.795

... ... ... ... ... ...
94.000 121.689 412.728 183.031 780.092 ... 165.796
# Date kcpi41 kcpi42
70.000 34.073 298.342
71.000 38.251 334.738
72.000 45.404 395.237
73.000 48.923 425.776
74.000 55.430 479.674

... ... ...
94.000 48.288 934.576
The ... indicate where data have been removed to fit the into this
box.
```

Exactly the same format is followed for the PRICES.DAT file, which give the price indexes, except that the four numbers at the top are omitted. The CSTAR.DAT file, which gives the income series, begins with the number of such series. It then has these series arranged in columns. It has one extra year of data at the beginning so that the first difference of income can be calculated. The POPUL.DAT file is very similar; it begins with an integer giving the number of populations, followed by data in the same format. It also has the extra year at the beginning. Finally the TEMPI.DAT file gives various series which may be used as the time trend. Like the POPUL.DAT file, it has the number of series at the beginning but does not have the extra year of data at the beginning.

Once the files GROUPS.TTL, CONSUM.DAT, PRICES.DAT, CSTAR.DAT, TEMPI.DAT, and SOFTCON.DAT are ready, the program is run by the command "symcon [n]" from the DOS prompt. The optional parameter, n, is the number of iterations to be run before turning over control to the user. Thus *Symcon* will run only 1 iteration and then give the user the option of quitting (by tapping 'y') or continuing the Marquardt process another iteration. If the command given is "symcon 40", then 40 iterations are automatically run without pausing for user input. To check that data have been read correctly, use "symcon d". (The d is for "debug".)

35930068R00256

Made in the USA
Middletown, DE
09 February 2019